PENGUIN REFERENCE BOOKS

THE PENGUIN DICTIONARY
OF ECONOMICS

Graham Bannock is a graduate of the London School of Economics and author of several books on finance and business. He has worked in market research for Ford and Rover, and in economic research at the O.F.C.D. and The Economist Intelligence Unit, of which he was managing director. He is now with Graham Bannock and Partners, an economic research and computer software company in London. He is co-author of *The Penguin International Dictionary of Finance*, and two of his other books, *The Juggernauts: The Age of the Giant Corporation* and *How to Survive the Slump*, are also published by Penguin.

Ron Baxter graduated from the London School of Economics with a degree in economics. He worked first with the International Nickel Company and Hoover and, subsequently, at the Electricity Council, London. He was the Director of Economics and Statistics at the National Ports Council for many years, where he was engaged on port planning, forecasting international trade and the appraisal of investments, as well as the development of port statistics. Ron Baxter is now a director in the firm of economic consultants Baxter Eadie Ltd, and is closely involved with advising clients on a wide range of practical economic problems.

Evan Davis graduated from St John's College, Oxford, in 1984 with a degree in economics and philosophy. He then joined the research team at the Institute for Fiscal Studies in London, where he was involved in applied microeconomic policy analysis. In 1986 he moved to Harvard University to continue his studies, and since 1988 has been a Research Fellow at the Centre for Business Strategy at London Business School. He also acts as a general consultant to clients in both Britain and the United States.

THE PENGUIN DICTIONARY OF

ECONOMICS

GRAHAM BANNOCK, R. E. BAXTER AND EVAN DAVIS

Fourth Edition

PENGUIN BOOKS

PENGUIN BOOKS

Published by the Penguin Group
Penguin Books Ltd, 27 Wrights Lane, London W8 5TZ, England
Viking Penguin, a division of Penguin Books USA Inc.
375 Hudson Street, New York, New York 10014, USA
Penguin Books Australia Ltd, Ringwood, Victoria, Australia
Penguin Books Canada Ltd, 2801 John Street, Markham, Ontario, Canada L3R 1B4
Penguin Books (NZ) Ltd, 182–190 Wairau Road, Auckland 10, New Zealand

Penguin Books Ltd, Registered Offices: Harmondsworth, Middlesex, England

First published 1972
Second edition 1978
Third edition 1984
Fourth edition 1987
5 7 9 10 8 6 4

Printed in England by Clays Ltd, St Ives plc
Filmset in Monophoto Times

Foreword to the Fourth Edition

'. . . no dictionary of a living tongue can ever be perfect, since while it is hastening to publication, some words are budding, and some falling away'

– SAMUEL JOHNSON, *The Dictionary of English* (1755)

'In the case of economics there are no important propositions that cannot, in fact, be stated in plain language'

– J. K. GALBRAITH, *Annals of an Abiding Liberal* (1979)

For this fourth edition the dictionary has been comprehensively revised, extended and reset. The extent of these changes is much greater than in earlier editions. All the entries on economic theory and most of those on applied economics and statistics have been completely rewritten and few of the other entries have escaped change. Many new entries have been added and some deleted.

Both the intended readership and the scope and method of the book are unaltered. The dictionary is planned as a companion to two kinds of users of economics. First, for the general reader who wants to follow economic discussion in the press or elsewhere and for the increasing number of people who need some knowledge of economics in their daily work, in teaching, business, the civil service, representative bodies and the professions. Secondly, it is aimed at students, especially those up to the second-year university courses in the subject, but also others, for example those at business schools for whom economics is part of the curriculum.

Our distinctive approach remains unique. This approach consists of a micro-encyclopedic treatment with extensive cross-referencing, up-to-date institutional material and a level of exposition that attempts to combine a reasonable degree of academic rigour with brevity and practical relevance.

Our subject is large and growing continuously and we have had to be highly selective. Words in common usage are not normally included unless they have a specialized meaning in economics. Economic theory, including international, monetary and welfare economics, has been treated fairly comprehensively. We have also given considerable emphasis to the history of economics in keeping with our view of the subject as a developing one. Individual economists are included only where they have made an important and definable contribution to the body of economic thought as it exists today. We have been particularly sparing in our inclusion of contemporary economists, so that many distinguished living members of the profession are left out. We have tried to include all the key terms used by econometricians and statisticians that are in general use. Our treatment of financial and business economics, public finance, international trade and development and payments has been more selective still but, institutions apart, we hope that nothing important has been omitted.

We have been helped and encouraged by the response we have recieved from our readers. We hope that they will continue to point out to us any errors or omissions.

June 1987

G.B.
R.E.B.
E.D.

List of Abbreviations

A.C.C.	Agricultural Credit Corporation
A.C.T.	Advance corporation tax
A.D.B.	African Development Bank; Asian Development Bank
A.I.B.D.	Association of International Bond Dealers
A.M.C.	Agricultural Mortgage Corporation
A.P.C.	Average propensity to consume
A.P.S.	Average propensity to save
A.S.E.A.N.	Association of South East Asian Nations
A.S.P.	American selling price
B.I.S.	Bank for International Settlements
B.O.T.B.	British Overseas Trade Board
B.S.O.	Business Statistics Office
C.A.P.	Common agricultural policy
C.C.A.	Current-cost accounting
C.C.C.	Competition and credit control
C.D.	Certificate of deposit
C.D.B.	Caribbean Development Bank
C.D.C.	Commonwealth Development Corporation
C.I.C.	Capital Issues Committee
c.i.f.	Cost, insurance, freight
C.S.D.	Civil Service Department
C.S.O.	Central Statistical Office
C.T.T.	Capital transfer tax
D.C.E.	Domestic credit expansion
d.c.f.	Discounted cash flow
D.N.S.	Department for National Savings
E.C.A.	Economic Cooperation Administration
E.C.G.D.	Export Credits Guarantee Department
E.C.I.	Equity Capital for Industry
E.C.O.W.A.S.	Economic Community of West African States
E.C.S.C.	European Coal and Steel Community
E.D.C.	Economic Development Committee
E.D.F.	European Development Fund
E.E.C.	European Economic Community
E.F.T.A.	European Free Trade Association
E.I.B.	European Investment Bank
E.M.A.	European Monetary Agreement
E.P.U.	European Payments Union
E.R.D.F.	European Regional Development Fund

9

E.U.A.	European Units of Account
F.A.O.	Food and Agriculture Organization
F.C.I.	Finance Corporation for Industry
FED	Federal Reserve System
F.F.I	Finance for Industry
F.H.A.	Finance Houses Association
F.I.F.O.	First in, first out
f.o.b.	Free on board
G.A.T.T.	General Agreement on Tariffs and Trade
G.D.P.	Gross domestic product
G.F.C.F.	Gross fixed capital formation
G.N.I.	Gross national income
G.N.P.	Gross national product
H.H.F.A.	Housing and Home Finance Agency
H.P.	Hire purchase
I.B.A.	Industrial Bankers Association
I.B.R.D.	International Bank for Reconstruction and Development
I.C.F.C.	Industrial and Commercial Finance Corporation
I.C.O.R.	Incremental capital output ratio
I.D.A.	International Development Association
I.D.B.	Inter-American Development Bank
I.F.C.	International Finance Corporation
I.H.A.	Issuing Houses Association
I.L.O.	International Labour Organization
I.M.F.	International Monetary Fund
I.R.C.	Industrial Reorganization Corporation
I.R.R.	Internal rate of return
I.S.I.C.	International Standard Industrial Classification
I.T.O.	International Trade Organization
L.A.F.T.A.	Latin American Free Trade Association
L.I.F.O.	Last in, first out
M.C.A.	Monetary compensatory amounts
M.N.C.	Multinational corporation
M.N.E.	Multinational enterprise
M.P.C.	Marginal propensity to consume
M.P.S.	Marginal propensity to save
M.R.S.	Marginal rate of substitution
N.E.B.	National Enterprise Board
N.E.D.C.	National Economic Development Council
N.E.D.O.	National Economic Development Office
N.N.I.	Net national income
N.N.P.	Net national product
N.R.D.C.	National Research Development Corporation

N.S.B.	National Savings Bank
O.D.E.C.A.	Central American Common Market
O.E.C.D.	Organization for Economic Cooperation and Development
P.A.Y.E.	Pay-as-you-earn
P.O.S.B.	Post Office Savings Bank
P.P.B.S.	Programme, planning, budgeting system
P.S.B.R.	Public-sector borrowing requirement
R.&D.	Research and development
R.P.M.	Resale price maintenance
S.A.Y.E.	Save-as-you-earn
S.D.R.	Special drawing rights
S.E.A.Q.	Stock Exchange Automated Quotation
S.I.C.	Standard Industrial Classification
T.D.R.	Treasury deposit receipt
T.P.I.	Tax and Prices Index
T.S.B.	Trustee Savings Bank
U.N.C.T.A.D.	United Nations Conference on Trade and Development
V.A.T.	Value-added tax

Terms that are commonly abbreviated, e.g. O.E.C.D., are listed in the dictionary under the full term, i.e. Organization for Economic Cooperation and Development. The use of single and double arrows (◇ ◇◇) in the text indicates, respectively, *see* and *see also* where a point is either amplified or complemented in another entry.

Where a cross-reference is given in parentheses, it refers only to the phrase or sentence immediately preceding it, and not to the whole entry.

THE DICTIONARY

A

'A' shares. ◊ SHARE.

Above the line. ◊ BELOW THE LINE.

Absolute cost advantage. ◊ BARRIERS TO ENTRY.

Abstinence theory of interest. ◊ INTEREST, ABSTINENCE THEORY OF.

Accelerated depreciation. ◊ CAPITAL ALLOWANCES.

Acceleration principle. The principle states that INVESTMENT (other than autonomous investment such as government expenditure on roads, hospitals, etc.) is related to output and that each level of output requires a particular amount of CAPITAL stock to produce it (◊ FACTORS OF PRODUCTION). If output increases, the capital stock must increase. A change in output, therefore, induces investment in order to maintain the stock of capital at the required level. In essence, therefore, the principle states that in order for investment to take place, there must be an increase in output and it plays down the role of the RATE OF INTEREST in determining the level of investment. (◊ ACCELERATOR CO-EFFICIENT; ACCELERATOR–MULTIPLIER MODEL; CLARK, J. M.; ECONOMIC GROWTH; HARROD–DOMAR MODEL.)

Accelerator coefficient. The factor which determines how much INVESTMENT is induced by a change in output (◊ ACCELERATION PRINCIPLE). Its value is influenced by the availability of spare capacity, the productivity of capital, the rate of INTEREST, the price of labour, etc. (◊ CAPITAL–OUTPUT RATIO; PRODUCTIVITY.)

Accelerator–multiplier model. A model of economic growth, incorporating the effects of the ACCELERATION PRINCIPLE and the MULTIPLIER. An increase in government expenditure, say, raises consumers' incomes which through the multiplier leads to an increase in output which in turn, through the accelerator, raises investment. The increase in expenditure, in the latter, itself raises incomes and the process is repeated. The model reveals that the multiplier and the accelerator interrelate in a way that produces a cyclical pattern to economic growth. (◊ HARROD–DOMAR MODEL; SAMUELSON, P. A.)

Accelerator theory of investment. ◊ ACCELERATION PRINCIPLE; TRADE CYCLE.

Accepting house. An institution specializing in accepting or guaranteeing BILLS OF EXCHANGE. All accepting houses have taken on other functions as the use of bills of exchange has declined, returning to their original, wider, function of merchant banking (◊ MERCHANT BANKS). There are sixteen accepting houses in the City of London (all British) represented on the Accepting Houses Committee, a body that ensures policy coordination between them, the TREASURY and the BANK OF ENGLAND. Members of this committee are eligible for finer DIS-COUNTS on bills bought by the Bank of England, though this privilege has recently been extended to other banks, including foreign banks, and the term accepting house is now an indication of status rather than function.

Account. 1. A record of financial transactions in the form of STOCKS or flows. ⇨ BALANCE OF PAYMENTS; BALANCE SHEET; CURRENT AC-COUNT; SOCIAL ACCOUNTING. **2.** An arrangement between a seller and a buyer under which a period of CREDIT is allowed before payment; for example the period in which STOCK EXCHANGE transactions take place and after the end of which settlement must be made. Up to the end of an account, transactions are made without payment and account dates are thus of vital importance to speculators. There are twenty-four account periods in a year.

Account day. The day on which all transactions made during the previous ACCOUNT at the STOCK EXCHANGE must be settled. It is normally a Monday, ten days after the last day of dealings of the account, and is also known as *settlement day*, and more rarely as *pay day*.

Accounting equation, basic. ⇨ BALANCE SHEET.

Accruals. ⇨ ACCRUED EXPENSES.

Accrued expenses. The cost of services utilized in advance of payment and written into a company's accounts as LIABILITIES.

Activity analysis. ⇨ LINEAR PROGRAMMING.

Activity rate. ⇨ PARTICIPATION RATE.

Actuary. Someone trained in the calculation of RISK and PREMIUMS for ASSURANCE purposes.

Ad valorem tax. ⇨ TAX, AD VALOREM.

Adaptive expectations. The formulation of beliefs about the future value of variables based on their past value and direction of movement. If economic agents wanted to predict inflation next year, using adaptive expectations they would take last year's rate and adjust it. The adjustment would depend on how wrong they had been last year when predicting inflation this year – if they had underestimated inflation, they would upwardly revise their prediction for next year. Adaptive expectation will respectively always under- or overestimate a variable which is consistently rising or falling. ⇨ EXPECTATIONS; RATIONAL EXPECTATIONS.

Administered prices. Strictly, prices which are set by management decision rather than by negotiation between buyer and seller. True MARKET prices are to be found only in the STOCK EXCHANGE and other places where prices change constantly. Most retail and industrial prices are set by management, though they will be altered in response to competition.

The term administered prices is often used to refer to price-fixing by a MONOPOLY firm, a CARTEL or a government body. Some economists have argued that inflexible administered prices have been an important contributory cause of INFLATION.

Advance corporation tax (A.C.T.). ♦ CORPORATION TAX.

Advanced countries. States with the highest levels of NATIONAL INCOME per head, such as most of the member countries of the ORGANIZATION FOR ECONOMIC COOPERATION AND DEVELOPMENT (O.E.C.D.). Unlike the DEVELOPING COUNTRIES they have become industrially advanced.

Advances. Loans (♦ BANK LOAN).

Adverse selection. The problem that, in certain markets, the inability of one trader to assess the quality of the other makes it likely that poor-quality traders will predominate. Noted by Akerlof in 1970, adverse selection is sometimes referred to as *the lemon problem*. A popular example of the phenomenon is in the second-hand-car market, where *sellers* know whether or not their car is a lemon (i.e. performs badly), but where *buyers* cannot make that judgement without running the car. Given that buyers can't tell the quality of any car, all cars of the same type will sell at the same price, regardless of whether they are lemons or not. The risk of purchasing a lemon will lower the price buyers are prepared to pay for a car, and because second-hand prices are low, people with non-lemon cars will be little inclined to put them on the market. There are three ingredients in this problem. Firstly, a random variation in product quality in the market; secondly, an asymmetry of information about product quality between traders in the market; and thirdly, a greater willingness for poor-quality traders to trade at low prices than for high-quality ones to. (Lemon car owners will still put their cars on the market when the prices drop; other car owners will not.) There are many important markets where adverse selection is held to be significant – notably insurance and the market for credit. (♦ MARKET FAILURE.)

Advertising. Paid announcements to persuade or inform members of the public. Outside the theoretical world of PERFECT COMPETITION, advertising of goods and services is necessary to ensure that potential buyers are informed and helps to make markets function efficiently. However, advertising can create or increase BARRIERS TO ENTRY into an industry and enhance PRODUCT DIFFERENTIATION and, it has been argued, promote CONCENTRATION. Proponents of heavy advertising expenditure argue that it helps to achieve ECONOMIES OF SCALE and thus reduces costs, while others point out that consumers may have little choice in a concentrated industry but to bear the cost of unnecessary advertising which serves only to keep out new entrants. Although 'own brand' products in supermarkets (which are not advertised) have not replaced advertised brands, this could be explained by the power of advertisers to manipulate consumer psychology. The full effects of advertising are not easily measured, but many economists believe that expenditure on advertising is excessive in some oligopolistic markets (◊ OLIGOPOLY) such as household detergents and cigarettes. ◊ SUNK COSTS.

African Development Bank. A regional international bank (◊ BANKING) established in 1964 for assisting in the economic growth of the independent African states. In 1972 an affiliated organization, the African Development Fund, was set up with a membership open, unlike that of the Bank, to non-African states. It is through this Fund that loans are made to African member states at low RATES OF INTEREST (◊ SOFT LOAN). Affiliation to the Fund has enabled the Bank to broaden its sources of funds for investment. In 1982, the African members of the Bank agreed to open its membership to non-African states. In 1985 the Bank and the Fund together made available a total of over $1 billion in grants and loans for development aid. ◊ ASIAN DEVELOPMENT BANK; CARIBBEAN DEVELOPMENT BANK; COLOMBO PLAN; FOREIGN AID; INTER-AMERICAN DEVELOPMENT BANK.

African Development Fund. ◊ AFRICAN DEVELOPMENT BANK.

Aggregate concentration. ◊ CONCENTRATION.

Aggregate demand. The sum of all DEMAND within an economy, making up NATIONAL INCOME and expenditure. The main categories are consumers' expenditure on goods and services, INVESTMENT in capital goods and stocks (◊ INVENTORIES), EXPORTS of goods and services, less expenditure on IMPORTS of goods and services. Since KEYNES, it has been believed that the level of and changes in aggregate demand are important influences in the determination of economic output and growth. More recently, however, attention has been paid to the factors affecting the supply of goods and services in the economy ◊ SUPPLY-SIDE ECONOMICS (◊ SOCIAL ACCOUNTING). ◊ IS–LM MODEL; NATIONAL INCOME, DETERMINATION OF.

Aggregate supply. The total of all goods and services produced in an economy, less EXPORTS, plus IMPORTS. Prior to KEYNES, it was believed that NATIONAL INCOME was determined by aggregate supply. Keynes shifted the emphasis on to AGGREGATE DEMAND, with supply meeting whatever demand existed up to a point. More recently, supply factors have gained prominence as determinants of total output. (◊ SUPPLY-SIDE ECONOMICS.)

Aggregated rebate. ◊ DEFERRED REBATE.

Aggregation problem. ◊ CAMBRIDGE SCHOOL.

Agricultural Credit Corporation Ltd (A.C.C.). Established in 1964 with government support to extend the availability of medium-term bank credit for buildings, equipment, livestock and working capital to farmers, growers and their cooperatives. After a satisfactory appraisal the

A.C.C. offers a guarantee to the farmer's bank and negotiates the required credit facilities. The A.C.C. guarantees to repay the bank borrowing if the farmer fails to do so. An initiation fee and an annual percentage charge on the amount guaranteed is made. ⟡ CREDIT GUARANTEE.

Agricultural Mortgage Corporation (A.M.C.). Set up to make LOANS to farmers against MORTGAGES on their land by the Agricultural Credits Act 1928. The A.M.C. operates in England and Wales only, and offers loans for periods of five to thirty years. The capital of the corporation was originally supplied by the BANK OF ENGLAND and the joint-stock banks (⟡ COMMERCIAL BANKS), but the corporation also issues state-guaranteed DEBENTURES. The corporation's loans are irrevocable except in cases of default, and are usually made through the local branches of the commercial banking system.

Aid. ⟡ DEVELOPING COUNTRY; FOREIGN INVESTMENT; INTERNATIONAL MONETARY FUND; INTERNATIONAL BANK FOR RECONSTRUCTION AND DEVELOPMENT; UNITED NATIONS CONFERENCE ON TRADE AND DEVELOPMENT.

Allen, Sir Roy George Douglas (b.1906). Educated at Sidney Sussex College, Cambridge, England. Sir R. G. D. Allen began lecturing at the London School of Economics in 1928. During the Second World War he moved from the U.K. TREASURY to Washington as Director of Records and Statistics of the British Supply Council and of the combined Production and Resources Board. In 1944 he was appointed Professor of Statistics at London University, a position he held until 1973. His publications include *Mathematical Analysis for Economists* (1938), *Statistics for Economists* (1949), *Mathematical Economics* (1956) and *Macro-Economic Theory – A Mathematical Treatment* (1967). In 1934 he published an article in *Economica* with Sir J. R. HICKS which demonstrated the use of the INDIFFERENCE CURVE based on ORDINAL UTILITY as an analytical tool in the theory of consumer behaviour. ⟡ ALLEN REPORT; SLUTSKY, E.

Allen Report. The Report of the Committee of Inquiry into the Impact of Rates on Households (1965), under the chairmanship of Professor R. G. D. ALLEN. This committee found that the impact of rates was regressive. Although only 2·9 per cent of total disposable HOUSEHOLD income (⟡ DISPOSABLE INCOME) was taken by rate taxation, the burden was as much as 8·2 per cent of the income of households earning less than £6 per week, and 6·2 per cent of the income of those earning between £6 and £10 per week. (⟡ RATES.)

Allotment letter. A letter addressed to a subscriber to an issue of SHARES informing him of the number of shares that he has been allotted and – where payment was not made with the application – the amount due.

American Depository Receipt (A.D.R.). A document issued by a U.S. bank against SHARES deposited with it or a bank overseas. The A.D.R. circulates as a bearer document, in effect giving title to the underlying shares.

American loan. ◊ WASHINGTON AGREEMENT.

American selling price. ◊ GENERAL AGREEMENT ON TARIFFS AND TRADE.

Amortization. Provision for the repayment of DEBT by means of accumulating a 'sinking fund' through regular payments which, with accumulated INTEREST, may be used to settle the debt in instalments over time, or in a lump sum. The term is also used as a synonym for DEPRECIATION.

Andean Pact. A CUSTOMS UNION established by the Cartagena Agreement in 1969 between Chile, Peru, Colombia, Bolivia and Ecuador. Venezuela joined the Pact in 1973, but Chile terminated her agreements in 1976. The aims of the group include the setting up of a common external TARIFF, the freeing of trade between member countries and a policy of development and rationalization for specific industries on a regional basis. Tariffs on manufactured goods have been virtually eliminated between all member countries save Ecuador and Bolivia, which have been given a further ten years to adjust. ◊ CENTRAL AMERICAN COMMON MARKET; LATIN AMERICAN FREE TRADE ASSOCIATION.

Annual allowances. ◊ CAPITAL ALLOWANCES.

Annuity. 1. A constant annual payment. **2.** A guaranteed series of payments in the future purchased immediately for a lump sum. Annuities are described as 'certain' where payment is specified for a fixed number of years. A 'life' annuity payment continues until the death of the person for whom it was purchased. Annuities may be 'immediate', where payment commences on purchase, or 'deferred', where payment starts at a future specified date. The British government sold annuities until 1962, but they are now only available from INSURANCE companies, whose pension schemes (◊ PENSION FUNDS) are often annuities purchased with accumulated contributions and INTEREST. The price of an annuity is based on the PRESENT VALUE of the stream of income payments it provides, and it varies with RATES OF INTEREST and, in the case of life annuities, the age and sex of the person who will draw the annuity.

Anti-trust (U.S.). Legislation to control MONOPOLY and restrictive practices in favour of COMPETITION. It applies not only to amalgamations of firms (◊ TRUST) but also to single companies. The *Sherman Act* (1890) made monopoly or the restraint of trade illegal. The *Clayton Act* (1914) clarified earlier legislation and prohibited specific activities, notably PRICE DISCRIMINATION, EXCLUSIVE DEALING, and

INTERLOCKING DIRECTORATES and shareholdings among competitors. The *Celler–Kefauver Act* (1950) amended the Clayton Act by prohibiting mergers which might lessen competition. The *Robinson–Patman Act* (1936) strengthened the provisions in the Clayton Act against price discrimination and made it illegal to sell goods to retailers or wholesalers at different prices unless justified by differences in the cost of supply. Anti-trust policy is overseen by the *Federal Trade Commission* (*F.T.C.*), a federal government agency created in 1914 which cooperates with, but is independent of, the Anti-Trust Division of the Department of Justice. U.S. anti-trust law is intended to be non-discretionary, in contrast to the U.K. approach which is more pragmatic. (⟡ COMPETITION POLICY; MONOPOLIES COMMISSION; RESTRICTIVE TRADE PRACTICES ACTS.)

Appreciation. Increase in the value of an ASSET; the antonym of DEPRECIATION. Appreciation may occur through rising PRICES as a result of INFLATION, increased scarcity or increases in earning power. ⟡ CURRENCY APPRECIATION.

Appropriation account. A business account showing how net PROFIT is distributed between DIVIDENDS, reserves, PENSION FUNDS, etc.

Appropriation accounts. ⟡ PUBLIC EXPENDITURE.

Arbitrage. The exploitation of differences between the prices of financial ASSETS or CURRENCY or a COMMODITY within or between markets by buying where prices are low and selling where they are higher. If wheat is cheaper in Chicago than in London, after allowing for transport and dealing costs, it will pay to buy in Chicago and sell in London. If interest rates are higher on a Deutschmark deposit in London than in Frankfurt, a higher return will be obtained by switching funds from one centre to the other. It will also pay to switch funds from a Deutschmark deposit in Frankfurt to a sterling deposit in London if the interest rate differential is greater than the cost of covering against the risk of a fall in the exchange rate of the pound against the Deutschmark (⟡ FORWARD EXCHANGE MARKET). Unlike SPECULATION, arbitrage does not normally involve significant risks, since the buying and selling operations are carried out more or less simultaneously and the profit made does not depend upon taking a view on future price changes. By eliminating price differentials, arbitrage contributes to the achievement of EQUILIBRIUM PRICE DISCRIMINATION between markets is difficult or impossible where possibilities for arbitrage exist. ⟡ EFFICIENT MARKETS HYPOTHESIS.

Arithmetic progression. A sequence of numbers in which the differences between all adjacent numbers in the sequence are the same, e.g. 2, 4, 6, 8, 10 ... (⟡ GEOMETRIC PROGRESSION).

Arrow, Kenneth Joseph (b. 1921). After graduation at Columbia University and a period at the Cowles Commission, Professor Arrow went to

Stanford University in 1949, where he became a professor in 1953. In 1968, he accepted a Chair at Harvard University, but returned to Stanford University in 1979. He was awarded the NOBEL PRIZE for economics in 1972 (with J. R. HICKS). His publications include *Social Choice and Individual Values* (1951), *Existence of an Equilibrium for a Competitive Economy* (1954) with G. DEBREU, *Studies in Mathematical Theory of Inventory and Production* (1958), *Public Investment, the Rate of Return and Optimal Fiscal Policy* (1970), *Essays in the Theory of Risk-Bearing* (1971) and *General Competitive Analysis* (1971).

Professor Arrow showed that it was logically impossible for a community to make a choice between a number of options by any method of voting which did not result in some part in contradicting the preferences between options expressed by individuals (◊ IMPOSSIBILITY THEOREM). He made important contributions to GENERAL EQUILIBRIUM ANALYSIS which placed the theory on a firmer basis after the work of M. E. L. WALRAS. He has also made contributions to the theory of decision-making under uncertainty (◊ RISK) and to GROWTH THEORY.

Articles of association. ◊ MEMORANDUM OF ASSOCIATION.

Arusha Agreement. ◊ LOMÉ CONVENTION.

Asian Development Bank (A.D.B.). The Bank, which is based in Manila, was set up in November 1966 following the recommendations of the United Nations Economic Commission for Asia and the Pacific. It was formed 'to foster economic growth and cooperation in the region of Asia and the Pacific and to contribute to the acceleration of economic development of the DEVELOPING COUNTRIES of the region'. It encourages economic and financial cooperation among the regional members. Membership carries the right to contract for projects supported by bank loans. About 60 per cent of the total subscribed CAPITAL of $1,100 million was contributed by the nineteen countries within the United Nations commission region, which include the three developed countries of Japan, Australia and New Zealand. The remaining nonregional members include the U.S.A., which subscribed $200 million (as did Japan), West Germany, Canada, the U.K. and Switzerland. The bank operates as a viable BANKING institution, charging realistic RATES OF INTEREST and encouraging a flow of capital to the region from outside sources. The Bank's affiliate, the Asian Development Fund, gives SOFT LOANS to the poorest nations in the region. In 1986, the People's Republic of China became a member and the authorized capital stock of the Bank was increased to S.D.R. 15,900 million (◊ SPECIAL DRAWING RIGHTS). The Bank has a membership of thirty-three countries in Asia and the Pacific and fourteen countries outside the region. ◊ AFRICAN DEVELOPMENT BANK; CARIBBEAN

DEVELOPMENT BANK; COLOMBO PLAN; FOREIGN AID; INTER-AMERICAN DEVELOPMENT BANK.

Assessable profits. The taxable PROFIT of a business, normally after the deduction of CAPITAL ALLOWANCES, interest and other business expenses. It differs, however, from accounting profit not only because of different treatment of DEPRECIATION, but because some business expenses, e.g. some forms of entertaining, are not allowable in computing taxable profit.

Assets. 1. A business accounting term. On the BALANCE SHEET of a company, everything that the company owns and which has a money value is classified as an asset, total assets being equal to total liabilities. Assets fall into the following categories, roughly in order of the extent to which realizing their money value would disrupt the company's business: (a) *Current assets:* CASH, bank deposits and other items that can readily be turned into cash, e.g. bills receivable, STOCK and work in progress, marketable SECURITIES. (b) *Trade investments:* INVESTMENT in subsidiary or associated companies. (c) *Fixed assets:* LAND, buildings, plant and machinery, vehicles and furniture, usually at cost less DEPRECIATION written off. (d) *Intangible assets:* goodwill, patents, etc. The assets of an individual are those possessions or the liabilities of others to him, which have a positive money value. **2.** *Financial assets* are titles to cash, such as a bank DEPOSIT or income and/or CAPITAL GAINS. Financial assets may be classified according to their LIQUIDITY, the protection they offer against INFLATION (⟡ INDEXATION) or changes in EXCHANGE RATES and the risk of default. Some financial assets are income-certain (for example GILT-EDGED SECURITIES) while some are not (for example ORDINARY SHARES). Some assets are capital-certain, for example a fixed-interest security which is redeemable at PAR (⟡ REDEEMABLE SECURITIES) but ordinary shares are subject to a price risk.

Assisted area. ⟡ DEVELOPMENT AREAS.

Association of South East Asian Nations (A.S.E.A.N). An association set up in 1967 of five DEVELOPING COUNTRIES in South-East Asia, comprising Indonesia, Malaysia, the Philippines, Singapore and Thailand. In 1976, the Association agreed to a list of industrial projects covering petrochemicals, fertilizers, steel, soda ash, newsprint and rubber, on which the group would cooperate in the construction of major plants. The Association also agreed to set up a permanent secretariat. Some TARIFF concessions have been agreed for intra-A.S.E.A.N. trade in a number of basic commodities. Progress in developing joint projects has been slow, but in 1980 it was agreed to relax the rule that all five member countries must participate in each project. The Association has an emergency oil-sharing scheme to assist any member country whose supplies fall significantly short of requirements.

Assurance. That branch of INSURANCE under which a contract is made to pay a CAPITAL sum on a specified date or on the death of the person assured. The former contract or policy is called term or endowment assurance, and the latter whole-of-life. Both types of policy may be with or without PROFITS. By paying a higher PREMIUM, the policy-holder can receive a share of the PROFITS earned by the life fund. Policies may also be linked in some way to EQUITIES so that the final payment is determined by the stock market prices current at the time (◊ UNIT TRUST). Life assurance is an important source of private SAVINGS.

Austrian school. A tradition of economic thought originating in the work of CARL MENGER (1840–1921), who was Professor of Economics at Vienna until 1903. He was succeeded in the Chair by VON WIESER (1851–1926) and BÖHM-BAWERK (1851–1914). Menger's principal achievement was the construction of a marginal utility theory of value (◊ VALUE, THEORIES OF). His work was developed by Von Wieser, who, in addition, clearly formulated the important concept of OPPORTUNITY COST. Böhm-Bawerk's main contributions were in the fields of CAPITAL and interest rate theory (◊ RATE OF INTEREST). The Austrian tradition was followed in the work of VON MISES and F. A. VON HAYEK, and, later, in work by J. R. HICKS. ◊◊ JEVONS, W. S.; LONGFIELD, S. M.

Autarky. National economic self-sufficiency (i.e. exclusion from international trade) pursued as a policy by means of TARIFFS, EXCHANGE CONTROLS and other devices of the PLANNED ECONOMY as in Fascist Germany and Italy in the 1930s. ◊ CLOSED ECONOMY. Sometimes confused with *autarchy* (absolute sovereignty).

Authorized capital. The amount of share CAPITAL fixed in the MEMORANDUM OF ASSOCIATION and the articles of association of a company as required by the Companies Acts (◊ COMPANY LAW). Also known as *nominal capital* or *registered capital*.

Auto-correlation. The theory of ordinary LEAST-SQUARES REGRESSION assumes that the error terms in the regression are not correlated. CORRELATION in these error terms, called auto-correlation or serial correlation, requires other analytical methods to be adopted.

Autonomous investment. Investment expenditure which is not induced by changes in output (◊ ACCELERATION PRINCIPLE). Examples of such investment are government expenditure on infrastructure and firms' expenditure on new plant to exploit an invention.

Average. A single number calculated to summarize and represent the values of a number of items in a set (◊◊ FREQUENCY DISTRIBUTION). The most common such measure is the *arithmetic mean*. This is derived by adding together the values of the items in the set and dividing the total by the number of items. For example, suppose a firm's payroll showed that five employees earned £100 per week, £120 p.w., £180 p.w., £200 p.w. and £250 p.w. respectively. The arithmetic mean is £100 + £120 + £180 + £200 + £250 = £850/5 = £170 and, therefore, the average weekly wage of these five employees is said to be £170 p.w.

There is an implied assumption in the arithmetic mean that the values from which the mean is calculated are more or less of the same order of magnitude. For instance, if another employee were included who earned £1,000 p.w. the arithmetic mean would show an average wage of the six employees to be over £300 p.w., which would be clearly misleading as all but one earned less than this. (◊ STANDARD DEVIATION).

The *median* avoids this problem of extremes by taking that value for which there are an equal number of items with values below it as above it. For instance, in the above example of five employees, the median is £180 as there are two employees with wages higher and two with wages below this. If we include the sixth employee, the median is the average of the two middle values (as there is an even number of items), that is (£180 + £200)/2 = £190. The median, therefore, is less affected by extreme values and will be less than the arithmetic mean where the items include an extreme high value and will be higher than the arithmetic mean where there is an extreme low value.

The third important measure of average is the *mode*. This is simply the 'most popular' value in a set of numbers. For instance, if there were not five employees sampled in the above payroll but fifty, we may have: 5 earned £100 p.w., 10 earned £120 p.w., 25 earned £180 p.w., 5 earned £200 p.w. and 5 earned £250 p.w. The mode would be £180 p.w. because more employees earned that sum than any other of the sums specified. It is to be noted that unlike the other two measures the mode is totally uninfluenced by other items in the set. Further weekly wage examples could be added to the set without affecting the mode, provided each was earned by fewer than twenty-five employees (◊ WEIGHTED AVERAGE).

Average cost. Total production costs per unit of output. Calculated by adding total FIXED COSTS to total VARIABLE COSTS and dividing by the number of units produced. The effect of indivisibilities (◊ ECONOMIES OF SCALE) will be for average fixed costs to fall as output expands in the short run, spreading the fixed cost over more units, and bringing down average costs. After a time, however, average variable costs may increase as, for example, workers are paid overtime to operate machinery nearer to its full capacity and more has to be spent on maintenance. This is said to give short-run average cost curves a characteristic U-shape. In the LONG RUN all costs are variable because more fixed ASSETS can be acquired or surplus capacity scrapped. The shape and slope of the long-run average cost curve, when all costs are variable, will be determined by the extent of long-run economies of scale (if any).

Average cost pricing. Where PRICE is set to equal AVERAGE COST, then total revenue will equal total costs, since price multiplied by quantity will be the same as average cost times quantity. ▷▷ MARGINAL COST PRICING.

Average productivity. ▷ PRODUCTIVITY.

Average propensity to consume. The proportion of income, whether of individuals, households or countries, spent on goods and services, other than for INVESTMENT (▷ CONSUMPTION FUNCTION; MARGINAL PROPENSITY TO CONSUME).

Average propensity to save. The proportion of income, whether of individuals, households or countries, which is not spent on consumption (▷ AVERAGE PROPENSITY TO CONSUME). Also known as the SAVINGS RATIO.

Average revenue. Total sales value divided by the number of units sold and equal, therefore, to average PRICE.

Avoidable costs. ▷ PRIME COSTS.

B

'Back door.' When the DISCOUNT HOUSES are short of funds they can, as a last resort (◊ LENDER OF LAST RESORT), go to the BANK OF ENGLAND and sell their holdings of TREASURY BILLS at the discount or BANK RATE. This is a 'front door' operation. However, when bank rate is very high and the discount houses are in temporary difficulties, the government BROKER may buy bills from them at the market rate to ease the pressure on their LIQUIDITY. This operation is called 'back door'.

Backwardation. 1. In a COMMODITY market, the amount by which the spot PRICE (including the cost of stocking over time) exceeds the forward price. ◊ SPOT MARKET and FORWARD EXCHANGE MARKET. **2.** On the STOCK EXCHANGE, a sum of MONEY paid by a BEAR to a BULL for the right to delay delivery of SECURITIES sold forward at a fixed price. A bear will have sold securities to a bull for delivery on a certain date in the expectation that, by that date, the market price will have fallen. If it does not, in fact, fall, he may consider it worth while to pay a backwardation so as to defer delivery of the shares until the next account period.

'Bad money drives out good.' Before paper MONEY (◊ BANKNOTE) became universally accepted as a means for settling DEBTS precious metals were the most common forms of money. Gold and silver coins were struck bearing a FACE VALUE equivalent to the value of their metal content. Debasement of the coinage occurred when the face value was kept above the value of the metal content of the coinage. The holders of the correctly valued coinage became unwilling to exchange for the debased coinage because they would obtain less metal in exchange than if they bought direct. The result was that the 'good', undebased coinage did not circulate. The process is referred to as GRESHAM'S LAW.

Bagehot, Walter (1826–77). Bagehot graduated in mathematics at University College, London, and qualified as a lawyer in 1852. After a spell as a banker in his father's business he succeeded his father-in-law as editor of the *Economist* newspaper in 1860, a post he held until 1877. He was an influential commentator on current economic affairs and a prolific writer who is often quoted today. His publications include *Universal Money* (1869), *Physics and Politics* (1872), *Lombard Street. A Description of the Money Market* (1873) and *Postulates of English Political Economy* (1876).

Balance of payments. A tabulation of the CREDIT and debit transactions of a country with foreign countries and international institutions, drawn up and published in a similar form to the INCOME and expenditure ACCOUNTS of companies. These transactions are divided into two broad groups: CURRENT ACCOUNT and capital account. The *current account* is made up of visible trade (i.e. merchandise EXPORTS and IMPORTS) and invisible trade (i.e. income and expenditure for SERVICES such as BANKING, INSURANCE, tourism and shipping, together with profits earned overseas and interest payments). The balance on current account is the difference between the NATIONAL INCOME and national expenditure in the period.

U.K. Balance of Payments – 1985

Current Account	£m
Exports	78,051
Imports	80,162
Visible balance	−2,111
Interest, profits, dividends (net balance)	+4,353
Transport (net balance)	−804
Government (net balance)	−5,600
Other* (net balance)	+7,764
Invisible balance	+5,713
Balance on current account	+3,602
Capital Account	
Overseas investment in the U.K.	+10,435
U.K. private investment overseas	−25,527
Other capital transactions	+7,796

* Includes travel, banking, insurance, royalties, etc.
Source: *U.K. Balance of Payments, 1986*, H.M.S.O., London.

The *capital account* is made up of such items as the inward and outward flow of money for INVESTMENT and international grants and loans. The U.K. traditionally had a DEFICIT ON VISIBLE TRADE – that is, she imported more goods than she exported. However, in the past this has been more than compensated for by the surplus which she earned on invisible account. Indeed, from the middle of the nineteenth century up until 1931, the U.K.'s balance on current account was always in surplus (except for the period during the First World War and perhaps to a minor extent in 1926). Even after 1931, up until the Second World War, the deficits were relatively small. In the 1940s the U.K. was forced to liquidate many of its overseas assets and to borrow substantial sums to pay for the war, with the result that, although on average the current balance continued in surplus, the immediate post-war years saw considerable changes. After 1958, the current balance tended downwards into deficit until 1968. It recovered, however, to a surplus in the following years until in 1973 the increase in the price of oil by O.P.E.C. put the U.K., as it did many other developed countries, into the largest ever deficit in VISIBLE trade. The visible imbalance reached over £5,000 million in 1974. The visible balance remained in deficit until, with the development of the U.K.'s own oil resources, the visible balance recorded in 1980 a substantial surplus for the first time. The deficit in visible trade returned in 1983. The table shows the composition of the balance of payments in the U.K. in 1985.

The overall deficits or surpluses are brought into balance by movements in the GOLD AND FOREIGN EXCHANGE RESERVES or sterling liabilities. The transactions between foreigners and residents are carried out through the EXCHANGE EQUALIZATION ACCOUNT which operates to keep the EXCHANGE RATE for sterling within agreed limits. A balance-of-payments surplus means that there is a net demand for sterling greater than the supply during the period, and conversely for a deficit. Since sterling was floated the demand and supply may be brought into balance by means of an alteration in the exchange rate (i.e. the price of sterling relative to other currencies or gold). With fixed exchange rates, the central authority must achieve balance either by (if in surplus) buying foreign currency or gold in exchange for sterling or by (if in deficit) selling gold or foreign exchange for sterling. The success of this policy depends on the size of the gold and dollar reserves (▷ RESERVE CURRENCY) and whether the deficit/surplus is persistent or temporary. A deficit in the balance of payments is not necessarily a bad thing, any more than a surplus need be a good thing. It is a form of borrowing which could be used to enhance domestic savings to boost investment to the benefit of future growth. On the other hand if the deficit is occasioned by, for instance, an excess of AGGREGATE DEMAND over supply in the domestic market, it will persist until the home market has reached EQUILIBRIUM and, if the overseas borrowing is used to finance immediate consumption rather than investment, will yield little benefit in the form of higher rates of growth in the future.

There are many measures which can be taken in an attempt to correct a DISEQUILIBRIUM in the balance of payments. If the imbalance is expected to be temporary, borrowing (or lending) from other countries or international institutions, either through direct arrangements or through adjustments in the level of interest rates, may be possible (▷

INTERNATIONAL MONETARY FUND). Import, TARIFFS, import QUOTAS, IMPORT DEPOSITS and EXPORT INCENTIVES could be applied in order to affect the visible trade balance quickly, but such measures are subject to the GENERAL AGREEMENT ON TARIFFS AND TRADE. Other measures include EXCHANGE CONTROL and operations designed to ease the strain on the balance of payments by adjusting the level of aggregate demand in the home economy (◊ STOP–GO). ◊ INVISIBLE; J-CURVE.

Balance sheet. A statement of the WEALTH of a business, other organization or individual on a given date, usually the last day of the FINANCIAL YEAR; not to be confused with the profit-and-loss account (◊

At 31 March	*Group*	
	1986	*1985*
	(£000)	*(£000)*
Fixed assets		
Tangible assets	6,230	5,948
Investments	1,236	278
	7,466	6,226
Current assets		
Stocks	1,163	1,336
Debtors	8,661	7,996
Investments	10,511	9,099
Cash and deposits	6,246	3,915
	26,581	22,346
Creditors: due within one year	(18,357)	(15,529)
Net current assets	8,224	6,817
Total assets less current liabilities	15,690	13,043
Provisions for liabilities and charges	(967)	(1,014)
	14,723	12,029
Capital and reserves		
Called-up share capital	1,260	1,260
Revaluation reserve	2,241	2,245
Profit-and-loss account	11,222	8,524
	14,723	12,029

Source: The Economist Newspaper Ltd and subsidiary companies, *Report and Accounts, 1986.*

DOUBLE-ENTRY BOOKKEEPING), which records changes in the company's wealth over one year. A balance sheet is in two parts: (a) on the left-hand side or at the top, ASSETS, and (b) on the right-hand side or at the bottom, LIABILITIES. The assets of the company – DEBTORS, cash, investments and property – are set out against the claims or liabilities of the persons or organizations owning them – the CREDITORS, lenders and shareholders – so that the two parts of the balance sheet are equal. This is the principle of double-entry bookkeeping. The fact that the assets and liabilities are equal does not mean that the EQUITY shareholders owe as much as they own; they are included among the claimants.

According to the *basic accounting equation*, Assets = Liabilities + Equity; therefore, Assets − Liabilities = Equity. Equity, shareholders' interest or *net worth* (which are all the same thing) calculated from the balance sheet in this way may not reflect its true market value, since assets are normally written into the balance sheet at historical cost ($\Diamond$ BOOK VALUE) without any adjustment for APPRECIATION ($\Diamond$ INFLATION ACCOUNTING).

Until the 1981 Companies Act the law did not, in Britain, lay out requirements for financial reporting of companies in detail or to any particular format, so that the layout and content of balance sheets varied considerably. The example above sets out a balance sheet in the optional vertical format in conformity with the E.E.C. Fourth Directive ($\Diamond$ COMPANY LAW). Notes to the accounts provide breakdowns of some of the elements of the balance sheet, for example tangible assets, as well as other information required by statute, for example details of directors' and employees' remuneration.

Balanced budget. Planned expenditure equals expected income. In public finance it refers to a situation where current income from TAXATION and other receipts of central government are sufficient to meet payments for goods and services, TRANSFER PAYMENTS and debt interest. In fact, the U.K. BUDGET is normally in deficit (does not balance) on both CURRENT ACCOUNT and CAPITAL ACCOUNT and these deficits are financed by net borrowing and changes in the MONEY SUPPLY ($\Diamond$ PUBLIC-SECTOR BORROWING REQUIREMENT (P.S.B.R.)). The importance of the budget balance and the means by which it is financed is that it may affect the levels of demand and prices in the economy ($\Diamond$ FISCAL POLICY; KEYNES). Excluding asset sales ($\Diamond$ PRIVATIZATION) the U.K. general ($\Diamond$ PUBLIC SECTOR) balance (deficit) varied between −2·3 and −4·2 per cent of GROSS DOMESTIC PRODUCT between 1978 and 1986. $\Diamond$ PUBLIC-SECTOR FINANCIAL DEFICIT.

Balanced budget multiplier. The effect upon the NATIONAL INCOME of equal changes in government expenditure and revenues. If government expenditure is increased by £100m. and income-tax rates are increased to raise an additional £100m. in revenue, AGGREGATE DEMAND may not, as might be expected, remain the same since, although personal DISPOSABLE INCOME has been reduced by £100m. some of that income would have been saved, whereas all the increase in government expenditure results in increased demand. If the SAVINGS RATIO were 10 per cent then the additional demand would be £10m., which would have a MULTIPLIER effect upon the national income.

Balanced growth. The state of an economy in which there is a constant relationship between the components of aggregate NATIONAL INCOME. Consumption expenditure, INVESTMENT and employment grow at the same rate as national income. The model is applied to the study of equilibrium conditions in GROWTH THEORY. ⟡ STEADY-STATE GROWTH.

Balancing allowance. ⟡ CAPITAL ALLOWANCES.

Bancor. An international currency proposed by J. M. KEYNES to be issued by an international bank for use in the settlement of international debts. His proposals were rejected at the BRETTON WOODS Conference in 1944. However, the INTERNATIONAL MONETARY FUND then established did introduce SPECIAL DRAWING RIGHTS in 1970 which were similar in concept.

Bank, clearing. ⟡ CLEARING BANKS.

Bank, commercial. ⟡ COMMERCIAL BANKS.

Bank, industrial. ⟡ INDUSTRIAL BANK.

Bank, joint-stock. ⟡ COMMERCIAL BANKS.

Bank, overseas. ⟡ OVERSEAS BANKS.

Bank, secondary. ⟡ SECONDARY BANK.

Bank advances. ⟡ BANK LOAN.

Bank bill. ⟡ BILL OF EXCHANGE.

Bank clearings. ⟡ CLEARING HOUSE.

Bank credit. ⟡ CREDIT.

Bank deposits. The amount of money standing to the CREDIT of a customer of a bank. Bank deposits are ASSETS of its customers and LIABILITIES of the bank. Deposits may arise from the payments of CASH or a CHEQUE to a bank for credit to a customer, or by transfer into an account from another account, including a LOAN from a bank to its customer. Bank deposits are simply I.O.U.s written in the books of the bank. They do not necessarily reflect actual holdings of cash by the bank. Since bank deposits are used in the settlement of debts, they are MONEY in the economic sense, so that by creating deposits banks create money (⟡ BANKING). A deposit may be on CURRENT ACCOUNT or DEPOSIT ACCOUNT. These two types of account are known as DEMAND DEPOSITS and TIME DEPOSITS in the U.S. Bankers' deposits are deposits by a COMMERCIAL BANK at the CENTRAL BANK.

Bank for International Settlements (B.I.S.). An institution, with head offices in Basle, set up on the basis of a proposal by the Young Committee in 1930. The original purpose was to enable the various national CENTRAL BANKS to coordinate through their own central bank the receipts and payments arising mainly from German war reparations. It was hoped, however, that it would develop beyond this, but many of the functions which it might have performed were in fact taken over by the INTERNATIONAL MONETARY FUND after the Second World War. Since then the B.I.S. has acted like a bank for the central banks by accepting deposits and making short-term loans. It has, however, in recent years played a more active part in attempting to mitigate the effects of international financial SPECULATION and acts as a trustee for international government loans. In addition the bank has carried out financial transactions for the ORGANIZATION FOR EUROPEAN ECONOMIC COOPERATION, ORGANIZATION FOR ECONOMIC CO-OPERATION AND DEVELOPMENT, EUROPEAN PAYMENTS UNION, EUROPEAN MONETARY AGREEMENT, EUROPEAN COAL AND STEEL COMMUNITY and the I.M.F. Although the major functions of a central bank for central banks are performed by the I.M.F., the monthly meetings of the directors of the B.I.S. held in Basle have been a useful means of central-bank cooperation, especially in the field of offsetting short-term monetary movements of a speculative kind. The board is made up of the representatives of the central banks of the U.K., France, West Germany, Belgium, Italy, Switzerland, the Netherlands and Sweden. Other countries' representatives, e.g. from the U.S., Canada and Japan, attend meetings regularly. In 1986, the B.I.S. agreed to act as a clearing-house for inter-bank transactions in EUROPEAN CURRENCY UNITS. ⟡ BRUSSELS CONFERENCE; EUROPEAN MONETARY SYSTEM.

Bank loan. A LOAN by a bank, normally for a fixed period of two to three years or more for a specific purpose, usually to a commercial concern. The phrase 'bank loan' is also loosely used to include OVERDRAFTS and PERSONAL LOANS. In this broader sense bank loans are more commonly known as *bank advances*. In Britain about 7·5 per cent of bank advances by value are for business purposes, although the COMMERCIAL BANKS have recently begun making MORTGAGE loans for house purchase on a large scale. Bank loans are normally secured (⟡ COLLATERAL SECURITY), repaid in regular instalments and with interest charged at rates which vary with the bank's BASE RATE. British banks have been compared unfavourably with banks in other countries in the extent to which they provide long-term loans to industry. It is true that until about twenty years ago the bulk of bank advances were in the form of overdrafts, which are repayable on demand. This was partly because the banks in Britain have not in general been able to attract long-term deposits, and it is regarded as bad banking practice 'to borrow short and lend long'. However, commercial customers of the banks in Britain have also preferred overdraft finance, which is cheaper and more flexible than other types of borrowing, provided the banks were willing to renew overdraft facilities and allow, as they have done, much overdraft borrowing to become 'hard core'. In recent years the British banks have greatly increased contractual medium-term lending (TERM LOANS), and this type of advance now accounts for about half the bank advances to non-personal customers. Most medium-term lending is for periods of five to seven years, and lending for longer periods than this is still less common in Britain than in some continental countries. ⟡⟩ BUSINESS FINANCE; WILSON COMMITTEE.

Bank of England. The CENTRAL BANK of the U.K. Set up in 1694 as a JOINT-STOCK COMPANY by Act of Parliament, the bank was a private company formed by a group of London merchants to lend MONEY to the state and deal with the NATIONAL DEBT. The Bank of England Act of 1946 brought the bank into public ownership. The Bank of England is the government's banker, to which it lends through WAYS AND MEANS ADVANCES and for which it arranges borrowing through the issue of GILT-EDGED SECURITIES. The bank is also the principal organ for implementing the state's financial and MONETARY POLICY (⟡ BANKING). It is managed by a governor, a deputy governor and a court (board) of sixteen directors (four full-time executive directors) appointed by the Crown for periods of five and four years. The bank is obliged by law to accept directives from the TREASURY, although the governor has a statutory right to be consulted and in fact acts as a channel of communication between the Treasury and the private financial institutions. In its turn the bank has wide statutory powers to supervise and direct the banking system, including the COMMERCIAL BANKS to which, through the DISCOUNT MARKET, it acts as LENDER OF LAST RESORT. Under the Bank Charter Act of 1844 (⟡ BANKING AND CURRENCY SCHOOLS) the Bank of England is divided into an issue department and a banking department. The issue department is responsible for the issue of BANKNOTES and coins, which it buys from the ROYAL MINT, against its holdings of government SECURITIES and a relatively small amount of gold, coin and other securities. The banking department's liabilities consist of: bankers' DEPOSITS, i.e. deposits of the commercial banks including SPECIAL DEPOSITS; deposits of government departments, including the EXCHEQUER, which receives the proceeds of TAXATION; the Post Office Savings Bank (⟡ SAVINGS BANK), etc.; and the bank's own CAPITAL, held by the Treasury since nationalization. The Bank of England also holds deposits from a small number of private customers. The principal assets of the banking department are government securities, discounts and advances, notes and coin. The ASSETS and LIABILITIES of the

Balance Sheet of Bank of England, 20 August 1986

Liabilities	£m	Assets	£m
Issue Department			
Notes in circulation	12,764	Government securities	2,573
Notes in Banking		Other securities	10,197
Department	6		
	12,770		12,770
Banking Department			
Public deposits	79	Notes and coin	7
Special deposits	–	Premises, equipment and	
		other securities	1,050
Bankers' deposits	963	Advances and other	
		accounts	762
Reserves and other		Government securities	611
accounts	1,373		
	2,430		2,430

Source: *Bank of England Quarterly Bulletin.*

Bank of England are set out in the bank return issued every Wednesday. An example of the Balance Sheet is printed above.

The bank also publishes an annual report and a *Quarterly Bulletin*. In addition to the operation of monetary policy the bank supervises the activities of the commercial banks and other financial institutions and, when necessary, supports them, to prevent the failure of any institution which might endanger public confidence and the viability of the financial system as a whole. The slump in property values in 1975, for example, created difficulties for a number of fringe BANKS and property companies, and the bank intervened in several instances to provide financial assistance. Besides its management of the national debt, the operation of monetary policy and the other domestic activities mentioned above, the bank manages the EXCHANGE EQUALIZATION ACCOUNT and conducts transactions between Britain and the rest of the world, including other central banks and international financial institutions such as the INTERNATIONAL MONETARY FUND. The bank also acts as the agent of government in administering EXCHANGE CONTROL regulations in force and as a registrar for government securities. ⟫ BANK RATE; CREDIT CONTROL; LIQUIDITY RATIO.

Bank overdraft. ⟫ OVERDRAFT.

Bank rate. A now obsolete term for the RATE OF INTEREST at which the CENTRAL BANK lends to the banking system, which in practice meant the rate at which it would rediscount 'ELIGIBLE PAPER' presented by the DISCOUNT HOUSES or make LOANS to them ($\Diamond$ LENDER OF LAST RESORT). Changes in bank rate, which were normally announced on Thursdays, were intended to have two types of effect. The first was upon the level of short-term interest rates in the MONEY MARKET and hence, through the related effects upon the whole pattern of interest rates and investment through the MULTIPLIER, upon the level of economic activity. There was some controversy about the strength of these effects even where the BANK OF ENGLAND succeeded in making bank rate effective by open market operations ($\Diamond$ BANKING). The second effect of bank-rate changes was upon international capital movements. If interest rates in London, as a result of an increase in bank rate, became higher than in other financial sectors, money for investment in London would be attracted from abroad and vice versa. In some instances, however, the level of domestic activity might be low (requiring reduction in bank rate) and the balance of payments might be in deficit (requiring an increase), so that monetary authorities were faced with conflicting objectives.

Although probably of 'psychological' importance as an indicator of government intentions, it is doubtful whether in themselves changes in bank rate were of great importance in affecting the pattern of interest rates. For some time the clearing and other banks had set their base interest rates independently of bank rate and in October 1971 the penal rate for assistance to the DISCOUNT MARKET became the MINIMUM LENDING RATE (M.L.R.) and the term 'bank rate' has not been used since.

Banker's draft. A CHEQUE drawn by a bank as opposed to a bank's customer. Banker's drafts are drawn at the request of a customer, and that customer's account is debited when it is drawn. They are regarded as CASH since they cannot be returned unpaid and are used when a creditor is not willing to accept a personal cheque in payment.

Banking. The business of accepting DEPOSITS and lending MONEY. Banking defined in this way, however, is carried out by some other FINANCIAL INTERMEDIARIES that perform the functions of safeguarding deposits and making LOANS. BUILDING SOCIETIES and FINANCE HOUSES, for example, are not normally referred to as banks and are not regarded as being part of the banking system in the narrow, traditional sense. The key to this confusing distinction between *banking* and *the banking system* is that the latter is the principal mechanism through which the money supply of the country is created and controlled. Since 1971 the role of banks (in the widest sense) in the determination of the money supply has been recognized, however ($\Diamond$ CREDIT CONTROL). The banking system is still normally understood to include the COMMERCIAL BANKS (joint-stock banks), the secondary banks, the CENTRAL BANK, the MERCHANT BANKS or ACCEPTING HOUSES and the DISCOUNT HOUSES (which are not banks as such), but to exclude the SAVINGS BANKS and INVESTMENT BANKS and other intermediaries. The deposits of some types of bank, e.g. the Post Office Savings Bank, cannot be used in the settlement of debts until they are withdrawn, but a deposit in a commercial bank can be used to settle debts by the use of CHEQUES or CREDIT TRANSFER. When the manager of a branch of one of the CLEARING BANKS opens an OVERDRAFT account for a customer, the loan creates a deposit; that is to say, a book debt has been incurred to the customer in return for a promise to repay it. Whether or not the overdraft is secured by COLLATERAL SECURITY, such as an INSURANCE policy, or some other ASSET, when the customer draws upon the loan the bank has added to the total MONEY SUPPLY. In BALANCE SHEET terms, the deposit is a claim on the bank – that is, a LIABILITY – while the customer's promise to repay it (or the collateral security) is an asset to the bank. In the absence of government control on lending the limitation on the bank's ability to create deposits is their obligation, if they are to remain in business, to pay out CURRENT ACCOUNT deposits in cash on demand. Since the bank's customers meet most of their needs for money by writing cheques on their deposits, the cash holdings the banks need are only a small fraction of their total deposits. (The settlement of debts between the clearing banks is also made by cheque. ◊ CLEARING HOUSE.) This ratio between their deposit liabilities and their cash holdings is called the CASH RATIO (sometimes called the primary ratio). Banks also hold other LIQUID assets (BILLS OF EXCHANGE, loans at call and other loans to the money market) (◊ LIQUIDITY RATIO (secondary ratio)). The object of the banker is, of course, to keep his reserves as near as possible to the minimum, since no return at all is earned on holdings of cash and a relatively low return in the money market. The banking system is based on confidence in the system's ability to meet its obligations. In the short run, no bank is able to meet all its obligations in cash, and if demands upon it exhausted its cash reserves, the bank would be obliged to close its doors.

The table (p. 39) shows the aggregate balance sheet of the RETAIL BANKS as reported to the Bank of England. 'Notes issued' refers to the banknotes issued by the Scottish and Northern Ireland banks. Foreign currency business has grown as a proportion of the total and non-sterling deposits are now approaching 40 per cent of sterling deposits. The private sector, personal and business, accounts for the bulk of sterling deposits. 'U.K. monetary sector' is the banking sector, as defined by the BANK OF ENGLAND. CERTIFICATES OF DEPOSIT are included under both liabilities and assets since banks both issue and

Balance Sheet of Retail Banks, 20 August 1986 (rounded figures)

Liabilities	£m	£m	Assets	£m
Notes issued		1,066	Notes and coin	2,308
U.K. monetary sector	9,553		Balances with the Bank of England	626
U.K. public sector	3,363		Market loans	28,275
U.K. private sector	91,186		Bills	3,954
Overseas	10,972		Advances	85,495
Certificates of deposit, etc.	6,989		Bank of England net lending to central government	599
Sterling deposits		122,064	Investments	9,330
U.K. monetary sector	6,383		Other currency assets	56,658
Other U.K.	5,538		Miscellaneous	16,354
Overseas	29,870			
Certificates of deposit, etc.	6,001			
Other currency deposits	47,791			
Items in transition, capital, etc.	32,736			
TOTAL LIABILITIES		203,597	TOTAL ASSETS	203,597
			Eligible liabilities	94,726

Source: *Bank of England Quarterly Bulletin.*

hold these securities. The large 'items in transition, capital, etc.' includes unclaimed deposits, shareholders' capital and funds in transmission. It will be noticed that under assets, notes and coin amount to over 11 per cent of the balance sheet total ($\diamond$ CASH RATIO). 'Balances with the Bank of England' includes the mandatory cash-ratio deposits ($\diamond$ LIQUIDITY RATIO), while the Banking Department of the Bank of England, which is included with the Retail Banks, in this period had net deposits from the government (for part of the year it is normally a net lender to the government). 'Market loans' include secured money with the discount houses and certificates of deposit. 'Bills' includes TREASURY BILLS and local authority bills, but is mainly eligible bank bills. 'Advances', 95 per cent of which are to the U.K. private sector, are the largest item on the asset side of the balance sheet, though there is substantial overseas lending (included under 'Other currency assets'). 'Eligible liabilities' ($\diamond$ CREDIT CONTROL) are a subset of the liabilities shown in the upper half of the balance sheet.

The prevention of bank failure and the protection of bank customers against fraud and loss is one objective of the control and regulation of the banking system which is the responsibility of the Bank of England. Since the money supply is a basic tool of economic policy, the government also wishes to exert control over the creation of credit by the banking system through its finance ministry. In Britain this function is performed by the TREASURY and the Bank of England. Under the 1979 Banking Act, virtually all deposit-takers must be licensed by the bank, which monitors their activities through regular statistical returns and attempts to control their exposure to risk by indicative controls on capital ratios and uncovered foreign-currency positions. The Act also set up a fund to cover losses of small depositors. Direct controls on bank lending in the interests of controlling the MONEY SUPPLY were removed in 1971 in an attempt to introduce more competition into the banking system, but the system of credit control has been subjected to many changes since then and is still evolving ($\diamond$ COMPETITION AND CREDIT CONTROL). Recent years have seen substantial growth and change in the banking system. The main features have been an increase in the importance of OVERSEAS BANKS operating in the U.K. and other non-clearing banks, the increasing use of new parallel markets as a source of funds for the banks and a decline in the number of merchant banks. At the same time, traditional distinctions between the various types of bank are breaking down as most FINANCIAL INTER-MEDIARIES diversify their activities. Building societies and merchant banks are offering high-interest cheque accounts. The clearing banks have become major providers of MORTGAGE lending for house purchase and are increasingly providing non-banking financial services such as insurance broking, EQUITY purchases, traveller's cheques and, of course, credit cards (◊ CREDIT ACCOUNT). ◊◊ BANKNOTE (for the origin of banking).

Banking, retail. ◊ COMMERCIAL BANKS.

Banking, wholesale. ◊ WHOLESALE BANKING.

Banking Act 1979. ◊ BANKING.

Banking and currency schools. The representatives of the two sides of opinion in a controversy which centred on Sir Robert Peel's Bank Charter Act of 1844. This Act effectively limited the creation of BANKNOTES to the BANK OF ENGLAND and regulated their issue. The *banking school* argued that, given that banknotes were convertible into gold, there was no need to regulate the note issue because the fact of convertibility would prevent any serious over-issue. Moreover, it was pointless to try to regulate the issue of banknotes because the demand for currency would be met by an expansion of BANK DEPOSITS, which would have the same effect as an expansion of the note issue. The *currency school*, on the other hand, argued that the check offered by convertibility would not operate in time to prevent serious commercial disruption. Banknotes should be regarded as though they were the gold specie they in fact represent, and consequently the quantity at issue should fluctuate in sympathy with the BALANCE OF PAYMENTS. ◊◊ BANKING; FIDUCIARY ISSUE; GOLD STANDARD; MONEY SUPPLY.

Banknote. A note issued by a bank undertaking to pay the bearer the FACE VALUE of the note on demand. Banknotes in England had their origin in the receipts issued by London goldsmiths in the seventeenth century for gold deposited with them for safe keeping. The whole practice of BANKING had its origin in the activities of these goldsmiths, who began lending money and whose deposit receipts came to be used as money. Later the goldsmiths issued banknotes, and so did the banks that developed later still. Today only the BANK OF ENGLAND and the Scottish and Irish banks in the U.K. are allowed to issue banknotes. Since 1931, when banknotes became inconvertible to gold, the promise on a banknote to 'pay the bearer on demand' has simply been an undertaking that the note is legal tender. Thus, the Currency and Bank Notes Act of 1954, which regulates the issue of banknotes in Britain, refers to the FIDUCIARY ISSUE. Only four denominations of notes are now issued to the general public, the largest being the £50 note. Most other developed countries issue notes of much larger denominations than this, probably because the use of CHEQUES is less developed elsewhere than in Britain. (The 10s. note was replaced by the 50p coin in 1969 and a £1 coin was introduced in 1983, entirely replacing the £1 note in 1986.) ◊◊ BANKING AND CURRENCY SCHOOLS.

Bankruptcy. A declaration by a court of law that an individual or company is insolvent, that is, cannot meet its DEBTS on the due dates (◊ IN-SOLVENCY). A bankruptcy petition may be filed either by the debtor or by his creditors requesting a receiving order. An inquiry into the debtor's affairs is then conducted by, in Britain, the Official Receiver, an official of the Department of Trade and Industry, who retains temporary control of the debtor's financial affairs. If he thinks fit, the receiver may call a meeting of the debtor's creditors and, if they wish it, declare the debtor bankrupt. The debtor's assets are then realized and distributed among his creditors either by the receiver or by a trustee appointed by the creditors and approved by the Department of Trade. In the case of a company it goes into LIQUIDATION. Until he is discharged, i.e. has paid off his debts and has been declared a discharged bankrupt in law, a bankrupt may not incur CREDIT in excess of £10 without making it known that he is an undischarged bankrupt, nor may he serve as a director in a limited company without permission from the court.

Bargaining theory of wages. A theory of wage determination based on negotiations between employers and unions. The theory has been set within a number of different assumptions. For instance, as a GAME THEORY problem in which both sides wish to divide the firm's profits but also to maximize them: an exercise in COST–BENEFIT ANALYSIS where each is aware of the costs of a strike and the risks of participating in one. These theories are complementary to those based on SUPPLY and DEMAND analysis (⟡ PRICE THEORY) in the sense that the bargaining is seen to be carried out within the framework of the conditions existing at the time in the LABOUR market (⟡ WAGE-FUND THEORY).

Barriers to entry. Economic or technical factors which prevent or make it difficult for firms to enter a market and compete with existing suppliers. An established firm may enjoy an *absolute cost advantage* which might arise from the possession of patent rights to certain production processes or a long-term contract for the supply of energy or the ownership of sources of raw materials. In the same way, existence of ECONOMIES OF SCALE might mean that a new entrant would have to invest large sums and produce on a large scale in order to compete on price. If the market were small in relation to the OPTIMUM scale of production, new entrants might calculate that the risk of entry would be unacceptably high because any new supplier would reduce the output of all suppliers below the optimum, so that either the new or an existing supplier would fail. PRODUCT DIFFERENTIATION can also raise the cost of entry by necessitating heavy expenditure on advertising and the support of dealer outlets to overcome significant buyer preferences. Finally, COLLUSION on pricing and restrictive practices, such as FULL-LINE FORCING and EXCLUSIVE DEALING, may exclude newcomers as may legislation, such as a requirement for licensing. Barriers to entry may allow established firms to charge prices above the level that would obtain in the absence of these barriers. ⟡ COMPETITION POLICY; CONTEST-ABILITY; MONOPOLY; SUNK COSTS.

Barter. Acquiring goods or services by means of exchange with other goods or services, rather than with MONEY ($\Diamond$ COUNTER TRADE).

Base period. The reference date from which an INDEX NUMBER of a TIME SERIES is calculated. For instance, the price index of commodities produced in the U.K. has a base period of 1980. The base year may be changed to reflect any changes over time in the composition of items making up the index. ($\Diamond$ LASPEYRES INDEX; WEIGHTED AVERAGE.)

Base rate. The RATE OF INTEREST which forms the basis for the charges for BANK LOANS and OVERDRAFTS or deposit rates of the COMMERCIAL BANKS. Following the changes heralded in 1971 by COMPETITION AND CREDIT CONTROL the banks fix their base rates independently of one another, though obviously they cannot differ very much for long periods. Prior to 1971 the banks agreed on their deposit and overdraft rates, but this CARTEL arrangement has been abandoned. Very large first-class risk companies may borrow at one percentage point above base rate or even less, but small firms and individuals will have to pay several percentage points more than this. When, as sometimes happens, rates on the INTER-BANK MARKET rise much above base rate, large companies have taken advantage of the interest-rate differential, borrowing on overdraft and lending in that market.

Basing point price system. A system of price fixing by an industry whose product has a low value-to-weight ratio and therefore relatively high transport costs. A limited number of plants are designated base plants and sale prices (including delivery costs), from whatever plant actual delivery is made, are quoted at the agreed base price (including a transport-cost element). All firms in the industry, therefore, will quote the same price to a buyer at a particular location. Apart from high transport costs, industries carrying out such a price system have: (a) few firms ($\Diamond$ OLIGOPOLY); (b) large FIXED COSTS; (c) fluctuating product demand. Examples of such industries are steel and cement, which have used such a price system ($\Diamond$ MONOPOLY).

Bear. A STOCK EXCHANGE speculator who sells STOCKS or SHARES that he may or may not possess because he expects a fall in prices and, therefore, that he will be able to buy them (back) later on at a PROFIT; the antonym of BULL. A bear who sells SECURITIES that he does not possess is described as having 'sold short'. If he does possess the securities he sells, he is described as a 'covered' or 'protected' bear. A 'bear market' is one in which prices are falling.

Bearer bonds. BONDS the legal ownership of which is vested in the holder, no TRANSFER DEED being required. An endorsed CHEQUE, or a cheque made payable to a bearer, or a BANKNOTE are similar in nature to bearer SECURITIES. Bearer securities normally have dated interest COUPONS attached to them which can be presented to the issuer of the security for payment.

Bearer securities. ◊ BEARER BONDS.

'Beggar-my-neighbour' policy. ◊ RECIPROCITY.

Behavioural assumption. The pattern of human motivation built into any economic theory. For example, the *theory of the firm* (◊ FIRM, THEORY OF THE) assumes that entrepreneurs are profit-maximizers; the *cobweb theory* (◊ COBWEB MODEL) assumes that market suppliers are motivated by price in the period preceding that in which they sell their supply. (◊ MODEL.)

Behavioural theory of the firm. An approach to the study of firms which analyses how decisions are reached within them, rather than, as is more traditional, assuming that their behaviour conforms to the pursuit of some single goal. It was primarily developed by R. Cyert, J. G. March and H. A. Simon. The main tenets of the behavioural theory are: (a) that firms attempt to SATISFICE rather than adopt maximizing behaviour; (b) that the firm is a set of individuals and groups each of which has its own aspirations; these groups, sometimes in coalitions, continuously bargain over the decisions the firm makes, leading to the pursuit of many complex goals. The theory has not displaced the traditional approach, for a number of reasons, most notably that it fails to generate any specific predictions about what firms would actually do in any particular circumstances. Its primary influence has been in reminding economists of the fact that, in practice, maximizing profits may be expensive for a firm (acquiring full and unbiased information from all departments is no easy task) and institutional factors may impede the single-minded pursuit of any one goal. (◊ FIRM, THEORY OF THE.)

Below the line. Items in an account which are underneath the line at which a total is made. If *above the line* an item is included in the total. In the BALANCE OF PAYMENTS, for example, the basic balance includes the net flow of long-term capital above the line together with the current balance, i.e. the basic balance equals the current balance plus net long-term capital flows. In reported results for QUOTED COMPANIES, *extraordinary items* that arise from transactions which are outside the ordinary activities of a business (for example, the sale of an office building) may be taken below the line for the purposes of calculating EARNINGS per share, whereas *exceptional items* that do derive from the ordinary activities may be taken above the line for that purpose.

Benelux. The CUSTOMS UNION between Belgium and Luxembourg on the one hand and the Netherlands on the other, agreed in principle before the end of the Second World War and set up in 1948. The union abolished internal TARIFFS, reduced import QUOTAS between the three countries and adopted a common external tariff. The aim of the union is the eventual merging of the fiscal and monetary systems of the member countries. There is free movement of LABOUR and CAPITAL within the union and a common policy with other countries. In 1958 Benelux joined the EUROPEAN ECONOMIC COMMUNITY.

Bentham, Jeremy (1748–1832). The leading philosopher of UTILITAR-IANISM. Self-interest was deemed the sole stimulus to human endeavour and the pursuit of happiness an individual's prime concern. The purpose of government should be to maximize the sum of the happiness of the greatest number of individuals.

Bernoulli, Daniel (1700–82). ◊ BERNOULLI'S HYPOTHESIS.

Bernoulli's hypothesis. A proposition by Daniel Bernoulli (1700–82) that a decision as to whether or not to accept a RISK depended not just on money but also on UTILITY. For instance, a bet would appear to be worth accepting, if, at the toss of a coin, you won £10 for every head and lost only £5 for every tail. Given the coin is unbiased, there is an equal chance of a head or a tail turning up. However, if £5 was all you had in the world, the bet would not seem so attractive. The £5 would have a high utility attached to it and Bernoulli suggested that this is what counted in such decisions. (◊ MARGINAL UTILITY OF MONEY; RISK AVERSION.)

Beveridge, William Henry (Lord Beveridge) (1879–1963). Director of the London School of Economics from 1919 to 1937, Lord Beveridge's work in economics arose from a continuous interest through his life in the problem of UNEMPLOYMENT. His major contribution to the subject was published in *Unemployment* (1931). He was a major influence in the setting up of labour exchanges, and his 1942 report, *Social Insurance and Allied Services*, which became known as the Beveridge Report, led to the extension of the welfare services. His definition of full employment, which he gave in *Full Employment in a Free Society* (1944) as being reached at a level of 3 per cent unemployed, became a reference point for subsequent government policy. ◊ SISMONDI, J. C. L. S. DE.

Big Bang. Term used to encapsulate the changes occurring on the London STOCK EXCHANGE before and after 27 October 1986 when the strict segregation between JOBBERS and BROKERS and fixed commissions on securities, purchases and sales were abolished, thus bringing the U.K. more into line with major stock exchanges overseas. In July 1983, the government agreed to exempt the stock exchange from the provisions of the RESTRICTIVE TRADE PRACTICES ACTS in return for lifting a number of restrictions on competition, including fixed commissions. In 1982, the Stock Exchange Council had raised the limit on any one outside shareholder in a stock-exchange member firm from 10 per cent to 29.9 per cent and on 1 March 1986 this limitation on outside shareholdings was removed completely. Average commission rates fell by about 40 per cent to 0.26 per cent immediately following Big Bang, but many bargains (transactions) are now carried out at net prices i.e. the market maker ($\Diamond$ JOBBER) quotes a price direct to the purchaser (who may be a large INSTITUTIONAL INVESTOR) which includes his profit margin. Many banks and other financial institutions, both domestic and foreign, have acquired interests in, or control of, stock-exchange companies since March 1986. Other changes associated with Big Bang have been a major extension in off-the-floor electronic dealing and a major expansion in dealings in international EQUITIES.

'Big Four.' The four largest COMMERCIAL BANKS in Britain: Barclays, Lloyds, Midland and National Westminster. Coutts & Co. is a subsidiary of National Westminster and Clydesdale Bank a subsidiary of Midland Bank.

Bilateral monopoly. A market in which a single seller (a MONOPOLY) is confronted with a single buyer (a MONOPSONY). Under these circumstances, the theoretical determination of output and price will be uncertain and will be affected by the interdependence of the two parties.

Bilateralism. The agreement between two countries to extend to each other specific privileges in their INTERNATIONAL TRADE which are not extended to others. These privileges may, for instance, take the form of generous import QUOTAS or favourable import duties ($\Diamond$ TARIFFS). In so far as such agreements tend to proliferate, and in that they impose artificial restraints on the free movements of goods between countries, in the long run they could have an unfavourable effect on international trade compared with MULTILATERALISM, under which there is no discrimination by origin or destination. Bilateralism became widespread in the 1930s as countries tried to protect themselves from the fall in international trade during the depression. After 1945, there was a fear that a restrictionist policy would be followed by the Commonwealth and Western European countries in order to protect themselves from the influence of the U.S.A., which had emerged from the war in a relatively strong position. However, the GENERAL AGREEMENT ON TARIFFS AND TRADE was established in 1947 on multilateral principles, and has since been pursuing a policy designed to eliminate bilateralism and other restrictions on international trade. The success of this policy has been somewhat constrained by the setting up of a number of trading areas ($\Diamond$ EUROPEAN ECONOMIC COMMUNITY; FREE-TRADE AREA). The communist countries of the U.S.S.R. and Eastern Europe conduct their international trade predominantly in terms of bilateral agreements in which quotas are set on both sides. Exchange agreements of this kind enable these countries to set their international trade requirements into their national plan objectives ($\Diamond$ COUNTER TRADE; PLANNED ECONOMY).

Bill. A document giving evidence of indebtedness of one party to another. A bill may simply be a written order for goods which can be used as security for a loan to the supplier from a bank, or it may be a security such as a TREASURY BILL or BILL OF EXCHANGE.

Bill broker. A firm or individual that deals in TREASURY BILLS and BILLS OF EXCHANGE on the London MONEY MARKET. Normally a bill broker is a DISCOUNT HOUSE. ⟡ BROKER.

Bill of exchange. An I.O.U. used in INTERNATIONAL TRADE by which the drawer makes an unconditional undertaking to pay to the drawee a sum of MONEY at a given date, usually three months ahead. In principle a bill of exchange is similar to a post-dated CHEQUE, and like a cheque it can be endorsed for payment to the bearer or any named person other than the drawee. A bill of exchange has to be 'accepted' (endorsed) by the drawee before it becomes negotiable. This function is normally performed by an ACCEPTING HOUSE, but bills may also be accepted by a bank (it is then known as a *bank bill*) or by a trader (*trade bill*). Once accepted, the drawee does not have to wait for the bill to mature before getting his money; he can sell it on the MONEY MARKET for a small discount (⟡ DISCOUNT HOUSE; ELIGIBLE PAPER). Bills of exchange, also referred to as *commercial bills*, were first developed in inland trade by merchants who wished to resell goods before making payment for them (⟡ INLAND BILL OF EXCHANGE). They later became of great importance in international trade, but with the development of other means of CREDIT, their use declined, although in recent years there has been some revival of interest in their use by commercial corporations.

Bill of lading. A document giving details of goods shipped, the ship on which the goods are consigned and the names of the consignor and consignee. Bills of lading are normally sent ahead of the ship and give proof of title to the consignor. Copies of the documents are held on the ship and by the exporter.

Bill of sale. A document that gives evidence of transfer of ownership but not of possession of goods. It is not often used nowadays, but was once a common method of raising a LOAN on the security of personal possessions, the borrower retaining possession of goods until the DEBT is repaid. ⟡ MORTGAGE.

Birth rate. The crude birth rate is the average number of live births occurring in a year for every 1,000 population. The birth rate of the U.K. fell steadily from about thirty-five per 1,000 population in the 1870s to about twenty in the 1920s. It fell dramatically to about sixteen in the 1930s and rose equally dramatically in 1947 to nearly twenty-one. After falling back from this exceptionally high figure, it was on an upward trend from the early 1950s until the mid-1960s. From 1964 it fell every year until it reached 11·8 in 1977, the lowest ever recorded. Since then, however, it has recovered to 12·9 in 1984, after a peak of 13·4 in 1980. Other statistical measurements which are computed for the study of population trends include (a) the *fertility rate*, which measures the average number of live births per 1,000 for all women between the ages of fifteen and forty-four, a statistic which has in fact exhibited trends in the U.K. similar to the crude birth rate (it reached a low level of 59·4 in 1977 and rose to 63·6 in 1980, to fall to 58·4 in 1984), and (b) the rate specific for age of mother in which the number of live births per 1,000 is given for different age groups of mother. There has been growing anxiety about the social and economic consequences of the rapidly expanding size of the world population. At the present rate of growth the current world population of 5,290 million people will double in less than forty years. The DEVELOPING COUNTRIES will account for about 85 per cent of the total by 2025 compared with 75 per cent today. A major factor in this growth has been the extension of life expectancy achieved by modern medicine, but high birth rates have also played an important part. Measures of family control are being taken, particularly in critical developing countries such as India, in order to try to achieve a growth in population more in line with available economic and social resources (◊ MALTHUS, T. R.). It has been suggested that the recent decline of the birth rate in the ADVANCED COUNTRIES is associated with the growth in *per capita* REAL INCOME, combined with the ability of parents to control family size. In developing countries children are looked upon as PRODUCER GOODS in that they are required to augment HOUSEHOLD incomes and support the old; as countries develop their wealth, children come to be regarded as CONSUMPTION GOODS and this is reflected in the smaller size of families. If this interpretation is correct, the birth rate in the advanced countries is unlikely to return to a high level, although it will fluctuate more in accordance with the cyclical changes in real incomes and expectations. The inference for the world population problem is that the route to a solution is through permanent increases in the *per capita* real wealth of the developing countries.

Black economy. 'Underground' economic activity which is not declared for TAXATION purposes. By definition not included in official statistics and impossible to measure accurately, the black economy is probably heavily concentrated in personal services and repair work carried out by the SELF-EMPLOYED, including those 'moonlighting' from paid employment. Although estimates of the tax revenue lost through the black economy range from 3 to 5 per cent or more of the GROSS DOMESTIC PRODUCT, it cannot be assumed that these activities would be viable and would all continue if captured by the tax net. Not to be confused with a *black market*, which is illicit trade in goods in most cases produced legitimately.

Black market. ◊ BLACK ECONOMY.

Blue book. A digest of statistics published annually by the Central

Statistical Office containing the U.K. national income and expenditure statistics. ($\Diamond$ NATIONAL INCOME; SOCIAL ACCOUNTING.)

Blue chip. A first-class EQUITY share, the purchase of which (the hope is) entails little RISK, even of sharp declines in EARNINGS, in economic recessions ($\Diamond$ DEPRESSION). The term is, of course, applied as a matter of subjective judgement. In the U.K., I.C.I., Unilever and Shell equities, for example, are commonly regarded as blue chip.

Böhm-Bawerk, Eugen von (1851–1914). A member of the AUSTRIAN SCHOOL who took over the Chair of Economics at Vienna from VON WIESER. His analyses of the rate of INTEREST and CAPITAL have had an important influence on the development of these aspects of economic theory. His major publications include *Capital and Interest* (1884) and the *Positive Theory of Capital* (1889). The nature of the rate of interest could be found, he argued, in the three propositions, (a) that people expect to be better off in the future, (b) that people put a lower valuation on future goods than on present goods – 'jam today is better than jam tomorrow' – these two 'psychological' factors making people willing to pay to borrow against their future income to spend on consumption goods now ($\Diamond$ TIME PREFERENCE), and (c) the proposition that goods in existence today are technically superior to goods coming into existence at some future date because today's goods could be capable of producing more goods during the interval. ($\Diamond$ FISHER, I.; INTEREST, PRODUCTIVITY THEORIES OF). Capital is associated with roundabout methods of production. In order to reap a harvest you could send workers into the fields to pluck the ears of corn. A more efficient method is to spend capital on making scythes and then use these to cut the corn. An even more efficient method is to spend even more capital manufacturing reaping machinery and use this to harvest your corn. Progress is achieved through the use of LABOUR in more roundabout methods of production; a widening of the gap between INPUTS and outputs ($\Diamond$ INPUT–OUTPUT ANALYSIS). Capital supplies the necessary subsistence to labour during the 'waiting time' before new consumer goods are produced ($\Diamond$ WAGE-FUND THEORY). This waiting time is extended to yield increased productivity until, in equilibrium, productivity is equated with the RATE OF INTEREST. This theory was later developed into a theory of the TRADE CYCLE by members of the Austrian school ($\Diamond$ HAYEK, F. A. VON; HICKS, J. R.; MISES, L. VON; WICKSELL, K.).

Bolton Committee. A committee of inquiry set up by the President of the (then) Board of Trade in 1968 under the chairmanship of John Bolton to report on the role of small firms in the British economy. The committee reported in November 1971 that there were one and a quarter million small firms in the U.K. economy contributing some 24 per cent of the net output of the private sector, or 19 per cent of the GROSS

NATIONAL PRODUCT. The small-firm sector was in secular decline, both in number and in its share of economic activity. Quite apart from the social and political value of small firms, the committee distinguished a number of important economic functions performed by them (while recognizing their organic role and the difficulty of distinguishing single functions). Two of these functions – 'as a breeding ground of new industries and the source of dynamic competition' – were regarded as of crucial importance, and it could not be assumed that the ordinary working of market forces would necessarily preserve a small-firm sector large enough to perform them. The report found that the small-firm sector in the U.K. was significantly smaller than in other advanced countries, but the committee judged that the decline 'has not yet reached a stage at which deliberate discrimination in favour of small firms on the part of the government would be justified'. The committee re-commended, and this was subsequently accepted by the government, that a small-firms division should be established in the Department of Trade and Industry to monitor the health of the small-firm sector. The committee made a number of recommendations for improving the availability of statistical information on small firms, including a census of ENTERPRISES and many other matters including TAXATION, indus-trial training, form filling, competition policy, disclosure (◇ PRIVATE COMPANY), industrial development and planning controls. The committee concluded that the MACMILLAN GAP had been filled, al-though it was 'important to remember that the role of (financial) ... institutions, however adaptable and sensitive to market needs ... is necessarily limited ... (and) can never take the place of personal wealth and ploughed-back profits'. The causes of the decline in the small-firm sector were identified as increasing taxation, increased importance of MARKETING economies, the increasing role of the state, the emergence of the giant corporation, improved transport and communication and other technological factors. ◇ SMALL BUSINESS; WILSON COMMITTEE.

Bond. 1. A form of fixed-interest SECURITY issued by central or local governments, companies, banks or other institutions, e.g. National Savings Income Bonds. Bonds are usually a form of long-term security but do not always carry fixed interest and may be irredeemable and may be secured or unsecured. Economists frequently make use of the term bond in theoretical analysis, for example of choices between holding cash and other financial assets, in which a bond is a proxy for a whole range of securities. *Eurobonds* have been defined by Morgan Guaranty, the investment bankers, as a 'bond underwritten by an international syndicate and sold in countries other than the country of the currency in which the issue is denominated'. There is no specific STOCK EXCHANGE for these bonds, new issues of which exceeded $135 billion in 1985 (◇ EUROCURRENCY). The term bond has also been given to types of non-fixed-interest security, such as property bonds, which provide the holder with a yield on funds invested in property, or 'managed bonds', in which the funds are placed in a variety of investments. ⬦ PREMIUM SAVINGS BONDS. In the U.S.A. the term bond includes DEBENTURES. 2. A term used to describe goods in a warehouse on which customs duty (⬦ TARIFFS) has not yet been paid.

Bonus issue, or scrip issue, capitalization issue (U.S. stock dividend, stock split). Virtually synonymous terms describing SHARES given without charge to existing shareholders in proportion to the shares already owned. A *scrip issue* does not add to the CAPITAL EMPLOYED by the firm, but is made where the capital employed has been increased by withholding profits, and is therefore, out of line with the ISSUED CAPITAL. Consequently, it is a purely bookkeeping transation. DIVIDENDS, for example, will, after a scrip issue, be divided among a larger number of shares, so that the dividend per share will fall in proportion to the number of bonus shares issued. ⬦ NEW-ISSUE MARKET.

Book value. The value of ASSETS in the BALANCE SHEET of a firm. This is often the purchase price, and may be less than the market value. ⬦ INFLATION ACCOUNTING.

Branch banking. A BANKING system, most highly developed in the U.K., where the small number of COMMERCIAL BANKS have a large number of branches (over 10,000). Many other ADVANCED COUNTRIES have a much larger number of banks with fewer branches. A banking system in which each bank is a separate enterprise without affiliations with other banks or branches is called *unit banking*. In the U.S.A. it was believed that branch banking led to CONCENTRATION of the banking system and lack of competition. Many states prohibit branch banking in the U.S.A.

Brassage, mintage. A charge made by a mint for converting metals into coin. The Royal Mint no longer makes such a charge.

Bretton Woods. An international conference was held at Bretton Woods, New Hampshire, U.S.A., in July 1944 to discuss alternative proposals relating to post-war international payments problems put forward by the U.S., Canadian and U.K. governments. The agreement resulting from this conference led to the establishment of the INTERNATIONAL MONETARY FUND and the INTERNATIONAL BANK FOR RECONSTRUCTION AND DEVELOPMENT. ⬦ KEYNES PLAN; SMITHSONIAN AGREEMENT.

British funds. ⬦ STOCK EXCHANGE.

British Overseas Trade Board (B.O.T.B.). Export promotion agency of the Department of Trade and Industry. It was set up in 1972 to replace the British Export Board, which in turn was the successor to the British National Export Council. The board includes representatives of business, the trade unions and government departments such as the EXPORT CREDITS GUARANTEE DEPARTMENT. Its main function is to ensure the best use of the government's export promotion services and to advise on education, training and other matters. Through its regional offices throughout the U.K., the board provides information, assists in the organization of overseas missions and exhibitions and provides help to exporters needing overseas representation and market research.

British Technology Group. ◊ NATIONAL ENTERPRISE BOARD; NATIONAL RESEARCH DEVELOPMENT CORPORATION.

Broker. An intermediary between a buyer and a seller in a highly organized market, e.g. a STOCKBROKER, INSURANCE BROKER, commodity broker or a market operator working on his own account, e.g. a PAWNBROKER, BILL BROKER. On the STOCK EXCHANGE, a broker is the intermediary between a MARKET MAKER and the public.

Brokerage. Commission or fee charged by a BROKER. It is characteristic of the broking profession that they operate only in highly organized markets where margins are relatively small.

Brussels Conference (1920). An international conference at Brussels which with that at Genoa in 1922 obtained agreement that every country should have a CENTRAL BANK through which to control its financial affairs. This was a necessary preliminary to the establishment of the BANK FOR INTERNATIONAL SETTLEMENTS at Basle.

Buchanan, James McGill (b. 1919). Professor Buchanan studied at the University of Tennessee prior to obtaining his Ph.D. at the University of Chicago in 1948. He became Professor of Economics at the University of Virginia in 1956 and was appointed, in 1969, Director of the Center for Study of Public Choice, and is currently Professor at George Mason University, Virginia. Professor Buchanan was awarded the NOBEL PRIZE in Economics in 1986. His published work includes: *The Calculus of Consent: Logical Foundations of Constitutional Democracy* (1962); *Public Finance in a Democratic Process* (1966); *The Demand and Supply of Public Goods* (1968); *Cost and Choice. An Enquiry in Economic Theory* (1969); *Theory of Public Choice. Political Applications of Economics* (1972); *The Limits of Liberty. Between Anarchy and the Leviathan* (1975); *Freedom in Constitutional Contracts. Perspectives of a Political Economist* (1977); *Democracy in Deficit. The Political Consequences of Lord Keynes* (1977); *The Power of Tax* (1980).

Professor Buchanan established, and inspired study in, the *theory of public choice*. As 'economic man' acted in his own self-interest so government officials behaved also. Government actions, therefore, will be pursued according to the self-interest of politicians and lobbyists rather than for the public good. Unpopular, but inevitably required, corrective actions will be delayed by governments to force others into the responsibility, and political costs, of taking action. Individuals yield up their freedom of decision-making to representative government, subject to constitutional constraints. The growth and complexity of government, however, renders these constraints ineffective unless they are continually reconstituted. Professor Buchanan is anti-Keynesian (◊ KEYNES, J. M.) and is an advocate of the BALANCED BUDGET for the control it imposes on governments.

Budget. An estimate of INCOME and expenditure for a future period as opposed to an account which records financial transactions. Budgets are an essential element in the planning and control of the financial affairs of a nation or business, and are made necessary essentially because income and expenditure do not occur simultaneously.

In modern large-scale business the annual budget, which is normally broken down into monthly and weekly periods, is a complex document that may take several months to prepare. The starting-point will be an estimate of sales and income for the period, balanced by budgets for purchasing, administration, production, distribution and research costs. There will also be detailed budgets of CASH FLOWS and CAPITAL expenditure. These are often also made for periods of further than one year ahead, so that borrowing requirements and capacity requirements can be assessed (◊ CAPITAL BUDGETING). A *flexible budget* is one based on different assumed levels of plant activity.

The national budget sets out estimates of central government expenditure and revenue for the financial year, and is normally presented by the Chancellor of the EXCHEQUER to the British Parliament early in April. The budget is concerned mainly with CONSOLIDATED FUND revenue and not with NATIONAL INSURANCE or local government finance. In his statement, the chancellor reviews economic conditions and government expenditure for the past year, makes forecasts for the coming year and announces proposed changes in TAXATION. These changes normally become effective immediately, but are subject to parliamentary debate and approval in the Finance Bill and Act. With the increasing importance of government expenditure in the economy, the annual budget is an important instrument in government economic policy. Fiscal changes may have more to do with decisions to modify the budget surplus (or more rarely deficit) in the interest of demand management (◊ BALANCED BUDGET) than with planned expenditure which, in any case, is essentially discussed and presented earlier in the year, though the supply estimates (◊ SUPPLY SERVICES) are, in fact, presented to Parliament at the same time as the budget (◊ PUBLIC EXPENDITURE). Economic conditions sometimes require interim budgets, although the government normally has sufficient discretionary powers to make the necessary changes in fiscal or monetary policy.

Budget deficit. ◊ BALANCED BUDGET.

Budget line. A set of combinations of different commodities which, given a consumer's income, can just be afforded. If there were only two commodities – cornflakes and milk – the budget line could be drawn on a graph which had cornflakes on one axis and milk on the other. Given the price of each and the consumer's income, it would be a straight downward-sloping line cutting each axis at the quantity of that commodity which could be purchased if all income were devoted to it. The budget line represents the constraint facing the consumer when consumption decisions are made and is used in INDIFFERENCE-CURVE ANALYSIS.

Budget surplus. ♢ BALANCED BUDGET.

Budgetary control. A system of budgetary control checks actual INCOME and expenditure against a BUDGET so that progress towards set objectives may be measured and remedial action taken if necessary. Budget control statements comparing actual and estimated expenditure are issued weekly or monthly. These statements will be issued in considerable detail to department heads, and in less detail to higher management. Budget control statements must, if any necessary remedial action is to be taken in time, be issued as soon as possible after the close of the period to which they relate, and for this reason need not be of the same accuracy as accounting statements and may be based on estimated data. The development of computerized accounting procedures has greatly facilitated budgetary control.

Building society. An institution that accepts DEPOSITS, upon which it pays INTEREST and makes LOANS for house purchase secured by MORTGAGES. Building societies, which are unique to Britain, grew out of the Friendly Society movement in the late seventeenth century and are non-PROFIT-making. Their activities were initially regulated by the Building Societies Act of 1874, which set up a Registrar of Building Societies. Subsequent Acts have tightened controls over the societies' financial management and the 1986 Building Societies Act (see below) promises to initiate fundamental changes to the whole movement. The societies accept deposits which can be withdrawn on demand up to a limited amount or at one month's notice, or 'shares' which may be subject to a longer notice of withdrawal. Interest on building-society deposits is paid by special concession net of ordinary INCOME TAX, the society paying the tax to the Inland Revenue. Traditionally, the societies' deposits are fed by regular small savings and the average holdings are about £5,000. Loans are made to persons wishing to purchase their homes, or more rarely to builders, and administrative costs are financed by the difference between the borrowing and lending rates. The loans are usually repaid on regular monthly instalments of CAPITAL and interest over a period of years, usually on a REDUCING BALANCE basis. Sometimes loans can be repaid with an ASSURANCE policy and

53

remain outstanding until the policy matures; in these instances only interest (and the premiums on the policy) are paid during the period of the loans. Building societies' RATES OF INTEREST must bear a close relationship to rates charged or obtained elsewhere since they compete with other institutions for funds, but their rates are relatively stable and are only altered when a sustained imbalance occurs between the rates at which deposits come in and loans are made. Investors in building societies may put their money into shares or into deposit. The former have no relation to EQUITY shares, but are simply a form of deposit for which slightly more restrictive withdrawal terms are rewarded by a higher interest rate. Special interest-rate incentives are provided for regular savers. Originally highly localized in their operations, the building societies are now increasingly operating on a national scale, their numbers in Great Britain having fallen from over 500 in the late 1960s to 167 in 1985, mainly as a result of MERGERS. In recent years the building societies have begun to compete with the COMMERCIAL BANKS, which in turn have rapidly expanded their share of the market for housing finance. The 1986 Act allows the societies to widen their services from their traditional property-mortgage business to include loans to individuals for other purposes, money transmission and foreign-exchange services, personal financial planning services (acquisition and disposal of shares, insurance, pension schemes), estate agency, valuation and conveyancing services. The Act also provides for a regulatory agency, the Building Societies Commission, and an Investor Protection Scheme. ⟡ FINANCIAL INTERMEDIARIES.

Built-in stabilizers. Institutional features of the economy which without explicit government intervention automatically act to dampen down fluctuations in EMPLOYMENT and NATIONAL INCOME. Examples of these are (a) unemployment benefits and welfare payments, which automatically increase in total when unemployment increases and fall in total when unemployment falls, so that this part of government expenditure adjusts automatically in the desired directions to offset in part changes in other components of AGGREGATE DEMAND, and (b) government taxation, which falls in total as national income falls and rises as national income rises, both because the incidence of INCOME TAXES changes and because, with changes in CONSUMPTION expenditures, sales taxes also change. Since an increase in taxation tends to restrain expenditure, while a fall in taxation stimulates it, we again have 'automatic' factors counteracting inflationary and deflationary pressures in the economy (⟡ INFLATION; DEFLATION). The effectiveness of these built-in stabilizers must not be exaggerated, however. They rarely have sufficient force to render positive corrective policies unnecessary.

Bull. A STOCK EXCHANGE speculator who purchases STOCKS and SHARES in the belief that prices will rise and that he will be able to sell them again later at a profit ($\Diamond$ SPECULATION); the opposite of BEAR. The market is said to be *bullish* when it is generally anticipated that prices will rise.

Bullion. Gold, silver, or other precious metal in bulk, i.e. in the form of ingots or bars rather than in coin. Gold bullion is used in international monetary transactions between CENTRAL BANKS and forms partial backing for many CURRENCIES ($\Diamond$ GOLD STANDARD). A *bullion market* is a GOLD MARKET.

Bureaucracy. An administrative system characterized by rigid rules of procedure and hierarchical authority in large-scale organizations with centralized decision-taking, both public and private. The problems of coordination which arise in bureaucracies require the use of committees and extensive paperwork, while the necessary rules of procedure may result in inflexibility, hence the pejorative connotations of the term in everyday language. In economics, these characteristics of bureaucracy are an element in the DISECONOMIES OF SCALE, but it is also recognized that the nature of reward systems in a bureaucracy (for example, failure can be identified with individual action but responsibility for success is widely diffused) can affect responsiveness to market forces and this has important implications for the theory of the firm. ($\Diamond$ BE-HAVIOURAL THEORY OF THE FIRM; x-EFFICIENCY).

Business Expansion Scheme (B.E.S.). A scheme to encourage INVEST-MENT in SMALL BUSINESS introduced under the 1981 Finance Act under the title Business Start-up Scheme and subsequently renamed and modified under the 1983 Finance Act. The scheme provides INCOME TAX relief on investments of up to £20,000 in unlisted companies ($\Diamond$ UNLISTED SECURITIES MARKETS) which have not been trading for more than five years. Neither paid employees nor directors nor persons owning more than 30 per cent of the capital of the company are eligible. Companies in some trades are also excluded.

Business finance. The provision of MONEY for commercial use. The CAPI-TAL requirements of business may be divided into short and medium term, or long term. Short-term capital consists of the current LIA-BILITIES of a business plus medium-term capital. The main sources of short- and medium-term capital (for a company) can be further subdivided into internal and external:

Internal: RETAINED EARNINGS, including ACCRUED EXPENSES and tax reserves. $\Diamond$ CASH FLOW; CORPORATION TAX; SELF-FINANCING.

External: Temporary LOANS from sister companies, directors and others; FACTORING; BILLS OF EXCHANGE; trade creditors and expense creditors; and short-term TRADE INVESTMENTS.

Short-term capital should in theory only be used for investment in relatively liquid ASSETS ($\Diamond$ LIQUID) so that it is readily available to discharge the liability if necessary. Thus, these sources of short-term capital may be used for finished goods in stock and work in progress, trade debtors, prepaid expenses, cash in hand and at the bank.

Correspondingly, the main sources of long-term liabilities or capital can be subdivided in the same way.

Internal: Reserves, retained earnings and DEPRECIATION provisions.

External: Share capital, i.e. ORDINARY SHARES, PREFERENCE SHARES, long-term loans including MORTGAGES, LEASEBACK arrangements and DEBENTURES.

Long-term capital may be used for long-term investment in fixed assets (land, buildings, plant, equipment and machinery, etc.), in goodwill, patents and trademarks and long-term trade investments.

There are important differences in the sources of capital open to large and small firms. The latter do not have access to the STOCK EXCHANGE and rely more heavily upon family and friends for equity capital, as well as upon the COMMERCIAL BANKS. The main institutional sources of business finance are the COMMERCIAL BANKS, the MERCHANT BANKS, the FINANCE HOUSES, the DISCOUNT HOUSES, factoring companies and the institutions concerned with new issues (⟡ NEW-ISSUE MARKET). INSURANCE companies and PENSION FUNDS hold a large proportion of all quoted securities (⟡ QUOTATION). A number of other institutions specialize in providing TERM LOANS and RISK CAPITAL, especially for innovation and smaller businesses, e.g. the NATIONAL RESEARCH DEVELOPMENT CORPORATION, INDUSTRIAL AND COMMERCIAL FINANCE CORPORATION, ESTATE DUTIES INVESTMENT TRUST and TECHNICAL DEVELOPMENT CAPITAL LTD.

Business saving. That part of the net revenue of a firm which is not paid out as interest, DIVIDENDS or TAXATION, but rather is kept in the business as reserves and DEPRECIATION allowances or to finance new INVESTMENT. Sometimes called *retentions*. ⟡ SELF-FINANCING.

Business taxation. ⟡ CORPORATION TAX.

Buyer's market. A MARKET in which prices are falling, owing, for instance, to an excess of SUPPLY of the goods or services traded compared with DEMAND. (⟡ PRICE SYSTEM.)

By-product. The output from a process designed for the production of some other product. It is a necessary outcome of the production process and cannot be avoided. Its opportunity cost is zero (⟡ COST). ⟡ ECONOMIES OF SCOPE.

C

Calculus. The area of mathematics concerned with expressing the gradient of curves. Basic calculus consists of a set of rules which allow any FUNCTION to be taken and, for any point on the x-axis, the slope of the curve of the function to be derived. Thus, if $y = x^2$, calculus reveals that when $x = 3$, the slope of the curve depicting this function is 6. The value of the function is 9 at this point.

The importance of calculus is that the slope of a function effectively says how much the DEPENDENT VARIABLE changes for a very small unit change in the INDEPENDENT VARIABLE. Thus, working out the slope of a function gives us valuable information as to the responsiveness of one variable to changes in another. More specifically, the slope of a function gives the marginal value of that function. In the example above, if y is 'utility' and, x is 'number of chocolate bars eaten', we know from calculus that when 3 bars are eaten, the number of 'utils' gained from very small increments of chocolate bar is 6; this is MARGINAL UTILITY. ⪧ MARGINAL ANALYSIS.

Call. An unpaid portion of the price of a SHARE. This may arise when an applicant for a new share issue pays only part of the price of the share on application and the remainder on allotment or when the issued shares of a company are not fully paid up (⪧ PAID-UP CAPITAL).

Call option. A contract giving a right to buy SHARES from the dealer making the contract at the price ruling at the time within a specified future period, usually three months. Call options carry a COMMISSION to the dealer on the price of the shares traded. The opposite of *put option* (⪧ OPTION).

Cambridge school. A system of economic thought influenced by economists at the University of Cambridge, England. ALFRED MARSHALL (1842–1924) held the Chair of Political Economy until 1908 and A.C. PIGOU (1877–1959) until 1944, and during this period the school was characterized by the theory of late CLASSICAL ECONOMICS. After the end of the Second World War, the school refuted what became known as NEO-CLASSICAL ECONOMICS and developed ideas based on those of J. M. KEYNES (1883–1946), although linked also with the early CLASSICAL period. The leading figures in the post-war debate were J. V. ROBINSON (1903–83) and N. KALDOR (1908–86). The Cambridge school emphasized a MACROECONOMIC approach compared with the MICROECONOMIC approach of the neo-classical school. The Cambridge school denied that there was a direct functional relationship between the rate of PROFIT and the capital intensity of an economy. They have demonstrated the possibility of CAPITAL RE-SWITCHING (◊ WICKSELL EFFECT, PRICE) and have criticized the neo-classical school for leaping to conclusions about the aggregates derived from micro-analysis. For instance, they argue that the aggregate PRODUCTION FUNCTION of the COBB–DOUGLAS type is not compatible in practice with the micro-functions from which it is derived. The neo-classical theory of DISTRIBUTION which relates relative FACTOR PRICES to relative MARGINAL REVENUE PRODUCTIVITIES is deficient in throwing light on aggregate factor distributed shares of product (◊ EULER, L.). *Per contra*, they themselves are criticized for neglecting MICROECONOMIC THEORY. The Cambridge school has attempted to develop GROWTH THEORY, following J. M. KEYNES but assuming FULL EMPLOYMENT, from which the distributed shares of profits and wages may be determined. Generally, however, the Keynesian approach assumes under-employment of resources, with investment as the motive force. This is in contrast to the neo-classical economists who focus on full-employment equilibrium so that savings rather than investment determines growth.

Cantillon, Richard (1680–1734). An Irish international banker who wrote *Essai sur la nature du commerce en général*, which was not published until 1755 but had circulated from about 1730. This work was one of the first synoptic descriptions and analyses of the economic process. His views on the importance of agriculture, based on its receipt of pure RENT, and his analysis of the circulation of wealth foreshadowed the PHYSIOCRATS and the 'TABLEAU ÉCONOMIQUE'.

Capacity utilization rate. The output of a plant, firm or a whole economy divided by its output at full capacity. ◊ EXCESS CAPACITY.

Capital. 1. Assets which are capable of generating income and which have themselves been produced. Capital is one of the four FACTORS OF PRODUCTION, and consists of the machines, plant and buildings that make production possible, but excludes raw materials, LAND and LABOUR. All capital is itself, however, the product of labour and raw materials and can be seen as holding the stored value of them. If a Stone Age man spent one day producing a tool (a capital good) he gained no utility from doing so at the time. He did however save labour by using the tool thereafter. By building the tool he had in effect put some labour away for use at a later date. The essence of capital, therefore, is that it represents deferred consumption. **2.** In more general usage, any asset or stock of assets – financial or physical – capable of generating income. (◊ WEALTH.)

Capital, authorized. ◊ AUTHORIZED CAPITAL.

Capital, circulating. ◊ CIRCULATING CAPITAL.

Capital, cost of. 1. The RATE OF INTEREST paid on the CAPITAL EMPLOYED in a business. Since capital will be usually drawn from a variety of sources it will be an average cost derived from weighting the cost of each source, including EQUITY capital, by its proportion of the total. **2.** The cost of raising additional capital, i.e. the marginal cost. The marginal cost of capital on a DISCOUNTED CASH FLOW basis may be used as the minimum level of return in assessing investment projects. ⟡ MODIGLIANI–MILLER THEOREM.

Capital, issued. ⟡ ISSUED CAPITAL.

Capital, marginal efficiency of. ⟡ INTERNAL RATE OF RETURN.

Capital, marginal productivity of. ⟡ INTERNAL RATE OF RETURN.

Capital, nominal. ⟡ AUTHORIZED CAPITAL.

Capital, registered. ⟡ AUTHORIZED CAPITAL.

Capital, sources of. ⟡ BUSINESS FINANCE.

Capital, working. ⟡ WORKING CAPITAL.

Capital account. ⟡ BALANCE OF PAYMENTS.

Capital allowances. Reductions in tax (⟡ TAXATION) liability which are related to a firm's CAPITAL expenditure. In most countries expenditure on new capital assets is encouraged by various kinds of allowances, and annual DEPRECIATION is recognized as an expense of the business in calculating tax liability. The taxation authorities' methods of depreciating an ASSET are not necessarily the same as those used by the company in the published ACCOUNTS. Where a company may claim depreciation for tax purposes at will, e.g. to write off the whole of the cost of an asset against tax in a single year, or to spread it over twenty years as it chooses, this is known as *free depreciation* or *depreciation at choice*.

In Britain from 1972 until 1983/4 a business could obtain a first-year allowance of 100 per cent of the cost of plant and machinery. This allowance was subsequently reduced and eliminated altogether in 1986/7. The business now qualifies instead for the *writing-down allowance* or annual depreciation allowance of 25 per cent which previously applied to motor vehicles and certain other capital goods. Industrial buildings qualify for a writing-down allowance of 4 per cent of the construction cost (excluding the cost of land). *Balancing allowance* and *charges* are made where assets are sold, to ensure that tax relief is ultimately given which is equivalent to the net cost of the asset over its life, and no more. The rules have varied between incorporated and unincorporated enterprises and between assisted and non-ASSISTED AREAS, and the system of capital allowances as a whole has been subjected to many changes and modifications. Before October 1970 there was no first-year allowance but instead the authorities paid an initial allowance at rates of up to 30 per cent and *investment grants* in cash for certain capital expenditures.

In November 1974 measures were introduced to give relief on the taxation of STOCK APPRECIATION but this relief was abolished from 1985/6 onwards. ⟡ INVESTMENT INCENTIVES.

Capital asset pricing model. A model of the market for different financial assets which suggests that asset prices will adjust to ensure that the return an asset makes precisely compensates investors for the risk of that asset when held with a perfectly diversified *portfolio*. The model has dominated economists' understanding of the financial sector. Under simplifying assumptions, the following propositions hold:

(a) Everybody will hold a portfolio of assets which is as diversified as possible (⬦ DIVERSIFICATION).

(b) This means the risk of each individual asset will be unimportant because the ups and downs of assets' performances will cancel out (⬦ PORTFOLIO THEORY).

(c) There will nevertheless be some remaining market risk – the risk of factors that affect all the assets together.

(d) This risk depends on how closely the assets' performances coincide.

(e) The risk any particular asset adds to a portfolio will thus depend only on how closely its performance tracks that of the rest of the portfolio.

(f) The price of assets which closely track other assets will be low because they are unattractive – when other assets do well, they do well and vice versa.

(g) The price of assets which hardly move at all with the market will be high, because they pay out good returns when they are needed most.

The capital asset pricing model is a development of this chain of reasoning.

Capital budgeting. The process of budgeting CAPITAL expenditure by means of an annual or longer-period capital BUDGET. Planned and actual CASH FLOWS and capital expenditures can be compared. In recent years, the methods of selecting INVESTMENT projects for inclusion in the capital budget have been extensively refined (⬦ INVESTMENT APPRAISAL).

Capital charges. Charges in the ACCOUNTS of a company or individual for interest paid on CAPITAL, DEPRECIATION or repayment of LOANS.

Capital consumption. ⬦ CAPITAL STOCK.

Capital deepening. ⬦ CAPITAL WIDENING.

Capital employed. The CAPITAL in use in a business. There is no universally agreed definition of the term. It is sometimes taken to mean NET ASSETS (i.e. fixed plus current assets minus current LIABILITIES), but more usually BANK LOANS and OVERDRAFTS are included and other adjustments made for purposes of calculating the return on *net capital employed* (⬦ RATE OF RETURN), such as the exclusion of intangible assets and the revaluation of TRADE INVESTMENTS at market prices. ⬦ INVESTMENT APPRAISAL.

Capital expenditure. The purchase of fixed ASSETS (e.g. plant and equipment), expenditure on TRADE INVESTMENTS or acquisitions of other businesses and expenditure on current assets (e.g. stocks); to be distinguished from CAPITAL FORMATION.

Capital formation. NET INVESTMENT in fixed ASSETS, i.e. additions to the stock of real CAPITAL. *Gross fixed capital formation* includes DEPRECIATION; *net capital formation* excludes it.

Capital gains. A realized increase in the value of a capital ASSET, as when a share is sold for more than the price at which it was purchased. Strictly speaking, the term refers to CAPITAL appreciation outside the normal course of business. The 1962 Finance Act imposed INCOME TAX on such capital gains for assets sold within six months of purchase (*'short-term gains'*). In the 1965 Act the time limit was extended to twelve months and a separate long-term gains tax was introduced; there is now a single tax rate for all capital gains. The tax does not cover gains arising from the sale of personal belongings, including cars or principal dwelling houses, but it does cover gains from the sale of STOCK EXCHANGE securities, with the exception of GILT-EDGED SECURITIES, after one year. The tax for individuals is 30 per cent of the gain. CAPITAL LOSSES may be set against tax liability and the first £6,300 is exempt from tax (1986/7). Capital gains arise from changes in the supply and demand for capital assets, but also from INFLATION, and for assets disposed of after the beginning of the 1982 tax year the original cost may be increased by INDEXATION, i.e. the expenditure scaled up in proportion to the increase in the retail price index between, in most cases, a year after the acquisition and the date of sale. Capital gains are taxed in a similar way in other countries, including the U.S.A., and companies as well as individuals are liable (⟐ CORPORATION TAX; INDEX NUMBER).

Capital gearing. ⟐ GEARING.

Capital goods. ⟐ CAPITAL.

Capital-intensive. The production of a commodity in which a higher proportion of CAPITAL is used in the mix of inputs compared with other factor inputs, such as labour. ⟐ FACTORS OF PRODUCTION.

Capital Issues Committee (C.I.C.). A non-statutory body that advised the TREASURY on applications from overseas borrowers to make issues on the British CAPITAL MARKET. After the Second World War and until 1959 the C.I.C. also effectively controlled larger domestic issues in the interests of general economic policy. The C.I.C. grew out of the Foreign Transactions Advisory Committee set up in the 1930s to control the export of CAPITAL. The C.I.C. was disbanded in November 1967. Sterling fixed-interest issues are now subject to permission from the BANK OF ENGLAND, a procedure known as 'The Queue'. The object of this procedure is to control the timing of issues, however, rather than the volume.

Capital loss. A reduction in the MONEY value of an ASSET; opposite of CAPITAL GAIN.

Capital market. The market for longer-term loanable funds as distinct from the MONEY MARKET, which deals in short-term funds. There is no clear-cut distinction between the two MARKETS, although in principle capital market LOANS are used by industry and commerce mainly for fixed INVESTMENT. The capital market is an increasingly international one and in any country is not one institution but all those institutions that canalize the SUPPLY and DEMAND for long-term capital and claims on capital, e.g. the STOCK EXCHANGE, banks and INSURANCE companies. The capital market, of course, is not concerned solely with the issue of new claims on capital (the *primary* or NEW-ISSUE MARKET), but also with dealings in existing claims (the SECONDARY MARKET). The marketability of SECURITIES is an important element in the efficient working of the capital market, since investors would be much more reluctant to make loans to industry if their claims could not easily be disposed of. All advanced countries have highly developed capital markets, but in DEVELOPING COUNTRIES the absence of a capital market is often as much of an obstacle to the growth of investment as a shortage of savings, and governments and industrialists in these countries are obliged to raise capital in the international capital market, i.e. that composed of the national capital markets in the advanced countries. ▷ BUSINESS FINANCE; PUBLIC FINANCE.

Capital movements. ▷ FOREIGN INVESTMENT.

Capital–output ratio, incremental. The capital–output ratio is derived by dividing the level of output into the stock of CAPITAL required to produce it. The incremental capital–output ratio is, therefore, the change in output divided into a change in capital stock (i.e. INVESTMENT). The relationship between incremental capital (investment) and output is described by the ACCELERATION PRINCIPLE and the incremental capital–output ratio is the ACCELERATOR COEFFICIENT. The interdependence of capital and output play an important role in GROWTH THEORY, in which various assumptions about the ratio are explored. For example:

(a) The ratio may be assumed to be a fixed constant, in contrast, for instance, to Marxian economics (▷ MARX, K.) which implies that the capital–output ratio increases, corresponding to the argument of a falling rate of profit (▷ PROFIT, FALLING RATE OF).

(b) Labour and capital may be substitutable depending on wages and the rate of interest.

(c) Capital-embodied technical progress may occur, meaning that new investment is more efficient than old, so that the ratio falls as old capital is replaced ($\diamond$ TECHNOLOGY).

Capital reserves. $\diamond$ COMPANY RESERVES.

Capital re-switching. A phenomenon which played an important part in the controversy over CAPITAL THEORY between a group of economists led by Professor J. V. ROBINSON at Cambridge, England, and a group at Cambridge, Mass., U.S.A., led by Professors P. A. SAMUELSON and R. Solow. Specifically, it can be shown that the proposition that INVESTMENT increases as the required RATE OF RETURN ($\diamond$ INTERNAL RATE OF RETURN) falls may not in fact be valid. We could imagine that, as the required rate of return falls, firms would switch from less to more CAPITAL-INTENSIVE methods of production, thus increasing the rate of investment. However, it is possible to show that under quite plausible circumstances the rate of return could reach a level at which firms would switch back, i.e. re-switch, from more to less capital-intensive production methods, thus causing investment to fall as the required rate of return falls. This possibility then undermines the NEO-CLASSICAL model on which the Cambridge, Mass., argument was based ($\diamond$ WICKSELL EFFECT, PRICE).

Capital stock. The total amount of physical CAPITAL in the economy or, less commonly, in a firm or industry. In theory, the only correct valuation of the stock is the PRESENT VALUE of the INCOME stream it will generate in the future and changes in the capital stock should provide a guide to changes in the productive potential of the economy. Since the different parts of the capital stock, roads, machinery and buildings, cannot be added together, in practice they have to be valued to produce an estimate of the capital stock at the prices of a given year. In the BLUE BOOK the U.K. gross capital stock at 1980 replacement values (including dwellings) was estimated at £1,215 billion and the net capital stock at current replacement cost, i.e. after capital consumption, at £998.3 billion for 1985. *Capital consumption* is the replacement value of capital used up in the process of production, an identical concept to the DEPRECIATION provisions in company accounts, though not necessarily measured in the same way.

Capital structure. The sources of long-term CAPITAL of a company. A company's capital structure is determined by the numbers and types of SHARES it issues and its reliance on fixed-interest debt ($\diamond$ GEARING). A company's choice between different sources of finance will be determined by their cost, the type of business it is, its past and expected future earnings, TAXATION and other considerations. $\diamond$ BUSINESS FINANCE; CAPITAL, COST OF.

Capital theory. That part of economic theory concerned with analysis of the consequences of the fact that production generally involves INPUTS which have themselves been produced. The existence of these 'produced means of production', or CAPITAL, has profound implications for the nature of the economic system. A central element is the role of time and intertemporal planning. The production of capital requires the sacrifice of current consumption in exchange for future, possibly uncertain, consumption, and the mechanisms by which this process is organized influence the growth and stability of the economy in important ways. The existence of capital is also central to the analysis of the INCOME DISTRIBUTION. A major and controversial question has been: what determines the income derived by the owners of capital relative to that of the suppliers of labour power, and can their share be justified in terms of their contribution to the production of output? An understanding of the nature and implications of capital is fundamental to an understanding of our economic system, and indeed, as one leading contributor to the subject has remarked, the problem in attempting to define capital theory is to do it in such a way 'as to embrace something less than the whole of economics' (C. J. Bliss, in *Capital Theory and the Distribution of Income*). ⇨ BÖHM-BAWERK, E. VON.

Capital transfer tax (C.T.T.). A tax on the transmission of wealth by gift, both during a person's lifetime and on his or her death. C.T.T. was introduced in 1975 to replace ESTATE DUTY and to prevent the avoidance of that tax, by cumulating gifts made during the lifetime of the donor and adding them to the estate at death. C.T.T. was charged at progressive rates on the cumulative totals of chargeable gifts made. Limited gifts could be made each year free of tax and there were a number of exemptions and reliefs affecting, for example, transfers between spouses and transfers of ownership of woodlands, agricultural or business property. Many changes were made to the provisions of C.T.T. and with effect from 18 March 1986 it was replaced by inheritance tax. This tax is similar to C.T.T. in that chargeable lifetime transfers are added to the total with a final addition made on death, but the total does not include transfers made earlier than seven years before death; these are free of tax, and those during the seven-year period are taxed on a sliding scale. The new inheritance tax, therefore, has some resemblance to the original estate duty. In previous general usage, the term inheritance tax applied to a tax upon beneficiaries in proportion to the size of their inheritance, so that the total tax paid would be smaller the greater the dispersion of the estate.

Capital widening. Increasing the quantity of capital without altering the proportions of the other FACTORS OF PRODUCTION. This will occur where the CAPITAL STOCK and employment are both increasing. Where the capital stock is increased and the numbers employed remain constant or fall then production has become more capital-intensive and *capital deepening* has occurred.

Capitalism. A social and economic system in which individuals are free to own the means of production and maximize PROFITS and in which resource allocation is determined by the PRICE SYSTEM. KARL MARX argued that capitalism would be overthrown because it inevitably led to the exploitation of labour.

Capitalization. 1. The amount and structure of the CAPITAL of a company. **2.** The conversion of accumulated PROFITS and reserves into ISSUED CAPITAL. **3.** *Market capitalization* is the market value of a company's issued SHARE capital, i.e. the quoted price of its shares multiplied by the number of shares outstanding.

Capitalization issue. ◊ BONUS ISSUE.

Capitalized ratios. Ratios which describe the CAPITAL STRUCTURE of a company, by indicating the proportion of each type of SECURITY issued.

Capitalized value. The CAPITAL sum at current RATES OF INTEREST required to yield the current earnings of an ASSET. For example, if the earnings of an asset were £5 per annum and the appropriate rate of interest were 5 per cent, its capitalized value would be £100. Capitalized value does not represent a satisfactory means for the VALUATION of most capital assets, since the capitalized value of an asset would not necessarily compensate an owner for the loss of the asset.

Caribbean Common Market. Formed in 1973, the Caribbean Common Market has twelve member states: Belize and Guyana on the American mainland and Antigua, Barbados, Dominica, Grenada, Jamaica, Montserrat, St Kitts/Nevis/Anguilla, St Lucia, St Vincent and Trinidad/Tobago in the Caribbean. The community has a secretariat in Georgetown, Guyana. The common market has an agreed common external import TARIFF. The member states also have policies for cooperation in health and education, agriculture and transport.

Caribbean Development Bank. A regional development bank which channels SOFT LOANS and grants for the financing of agricultural and industrial projects in the Caribbean. In 1979 the Bank's loans and grants to the region amounted to $32 billion. ◊ AFRICAN DEVELOPMENT BANK; ASIAN DEVELOPMENT BANK; INTER-AMERICAN DEVELOPMENT BANK; INTERNATIONAL BANK FOR RECONSTRUCTION AND DEVELOPMENT.

Carry-over. Postponement of settlement of ACCOUNT on the STOCK EXCHANGE until the following period involving payment of a RATE OF INTEREST on the account. Also called *Contango* (◊ BACKWARDATION).

Cartel. An association of producers to regulate PRICES by restricting output and competition. Illegal in the United States but cartels have been promoted by governments to achieve 'rationalization', as in Germany in the 1930s. Cartels tend to be unstable because a single member can profit by undercutting the others, while price-fixing stimulates the development of substitutes. The most prominent example of an international cartel is the ORGANIZATION OF PETROLEUM EXPORTING COUNTRIES (O.P.E.C.). ⟡ OLIGOPOLY; PRISONER'S DILEMMA.

Cascade tax. ⟡ TURNOVER TAX.

Cash. 1. Coins and BANKNOTES. **2.** LEGAL TENDER in the settlement of DEBT.

Cash flow. The flow of MONEY payments to or from a firm. Expenditure is sometimes referred to as a 'negative' cash flow. The *gross cash flow* of a business is the gross PROFIT (after payment of a fixed RATE OF INTEREST) plus DEPRECIATION provisions in any trading period, i.e. that sum of money which is available for INVESTMENT, DIVIDENDS or payment of taxes. The *net cash flow* is retained EARNINGS and depreciation provisions before or after tax (⟡ TAXATION). Net cash flows of a particular project are usually defined as those arising after taxes have been paid, expenditure on repairs and maintenance carried out, any necessary adjustments made to WORKING CAPITAL, and account is taken of any residual value of ASSETS at the end of a particular project's life or other miscellaneous income accruing to the project or business. This term is important in INVESTMENT APPRAISAL. 'Cash-flow statement' is often used synonymously with 'statement of SOURCES AND USES'. ⟡ BUDGET.

Cash-flow accounting. ⟡ INFLATION ACCOUNTING.

Cash limits. System for the control of PUBLIC EXPENDITURE under which plans are expressed in CURRENT PRICES. This system was introduced in 1976 in partial form and 1982 in complete form. Under the previous system, government future expenditure plans were in volume terms, i.e. REAL TERMS, so that the high rates of INFLATION in the mid-1970s led to unexpectedly large increases in public expenditure.

Cash ratio. 1. The ratio of a bank's CASH holdings to its total deposit LIABILITIES. ⟡ LIQUIDITY RATIO; BANKING. **2.** For an individual firm, the proportion of its current liabilities that are accounted for by cash in hand, including BANK DEPOSITS, and sometimes payments due from customers.

Cash-ratio deposit. ⟡ LIQUIDITY RATIO.

Cassel, Gustav (1866–1945). ⟡ PURCHASING-POWER PARITY THEORY.

Celler–Kefauver Act. ⟡ ANTI-TRUST (U.S.).

Census. A statistical survey covering every member of a POPULATION. ⟡ SAMPLE.

Central American Common Market (O.D.E.C.A.). A common market of four Central American states – Guatemala, El Salvador, Honduras and Nicaragua – agreed at Managua in the General Treaty of Central American Economic Integration signed in December 1960. This treaty came into operation in June 1961, and a headquarters was established in San Salvador. Costa Rica acceded in 1962. There is also an economic secretariat, an economic council and an executive council. FREE TRADE between the member countries was expected to be established by June 1966. In the event, although duties have been eliminated on about 95 per cent of products, duties on many of the remaining products, particularly agricultural, are likely to continue. An agreement on the Equalization of Import Duties and Charges was made in September 1959, and subsequent agreements have established a common external TARIFF on all but a small number of products. The member countries agreed to harmonize fiscal incentives granted to industries if they effectively contributed to the growth of the region. In 1961 the Central American Bank for Economic Integration was formed to finance industrial projects, housing and hotels in the region. In 1964 the five CENTRAL BANKS agreed to establish, in the long term, a common CURRENCY. However, ODECA suffered a set-back on the imposition of import duties on a number of commodities by Costa Rica in 1971 and Nicaragua in 1978. ◊ CUSTOMS UNION; INTER-AMERICAN DEVELOPMENT BANK.

Central bank. A bankers' bank and LENDER OF LAST RESORT (◊ BANK OF ENGLAND). All developed and most DEVELOPING COUNTRIES have a central bank that is the instrument of the government's function of controlling the CREDIT system. Central banks, such as the Bank of France, the Federal Reserve Bank and the Bank of Canada, control the note issue (◊ BANKNOTE), act as the government's bank, accept DEPOSITS from and make LOANS to the COMMERCIAL BANKS and the MONEYMARKET, lead the interest-rate structure (◊ RATE OF INTEREST) through establishing the rate at which loans of last resort will be made, and conduct transfers of MONEY and BULLION with central banks in other countries. ◊ BANK FOR INTERNATIONAL SETTLEMENTS; BRUSSELS CONFERENCE; FEDERAL RESERVE SYSTEM.

Central bank of central banks. ◊ BANK FOR INTERNATIONAL SETTLEMENTS; INTERNATIONAL MONETARY FUND; KEYNES PLAN.

Central government. ◊ PUBLIC SECTOR.

Central government borrowing requirement. ◊ PUBLIC-SECTOR BORROWING REQUIREMENT.

Certificate of deposit (C.D.). A negotiable claim issued by a bank in return for a term DEPOSIT. C.D.s are SECURITIES which are purchased for less than their face value, which is the bank's promise to repay the deposit and thus offer a YIELD to maturity. The SECONDARY MARKET in C.D.s is made up by the DISCOUNT HOUSES and the banks in the INTER-BANK MARKET. Where a depositor knows that he can, if necessary, sell his C.D. he will be willing to place his funds with a bank for long periods. C.D.s were first issued in New York in the 1960s and

thus denominated in dollars. Sterling C.D.s followed in 1968. ▷ PARAL-
LEL MONEY MARKETS

Certificate of incorporation. A document issued by the Registrar of
Companies certifying the legal existence of a company after certain
legal requirements for registration have been met. ▷ COMPANY LAW.

Certificate of origin. A certificate required by a customs authority to
accompany imported goods which can claim preferential TARIFF rates
by virtue of their country of origin. Such certificates are required in the
U.K., as a member of the EUROPEAN ECONOMIC COMMUNITY. The
certificates are prepared for exporters and issued by associations, such
as the local chambers of commerce, approved by the Department of
Trade and Industry. ▷ EUROPEAN FREE TRADE ASSOCIATION.

Chamberlin, Edward Hastings (b. 1899). After a period at the University of
Michigan, Professor Chamberlin joined Harvard as a tutor in 1922 and
became a Professor of Economics there in 1937. His publications include
Theory of Monopolistic Competition (1933), *Towards a More General
Theory of Value* (1957) and *The Economic Analysis of Labour Union
Power* (1958). In *Theory of Monopolistic Competition* he proposed a
new emphasis for economic theory which broke away from the old concepts of pure or PERFECT COMPETITION or pure MONOPOLY. These
two cases he saw as special limiting ones. In between was 'monopolistic
competition', which was the condition under which most industries,
in fact, operated. Each firm pursued a policy of product DIFFEREN-
TIATION by special packaging or advertising so that it created a 'penum-
bra' of monopoly around its product. He also analysed the problem
of selling costs, e.g. advertising. ▷ MONOPOLISTIC (IMPERFECT)
COMPETITION; ROBINSON, J. V.

Charge account (U.S.). ▷ CREDIT ACCOUNT.

Chartist. A stock-market analyst who predicts share-price movements
solely from a study of graphs on which individual SHARE prices, price
indices and sometimes trading volumes are plotted. This technique is
called *technical analysis*. Unlike *fundamental analysis*, which requires
the study of financial accounts of companies, technical analysis is based
upon the belief that all the necessary information is in the share price.
In contrast to both chartists and fundamentalists the adherents of the
EFFICIENT MARKETS HYPOTHESIS believe that stock-market prices
adjust rapidly and fully to all information as soon as it becomes available
and that neither existing nor past price levels are of any help in predicting
the future.

Cheap money. A deliberate MONETARY POLICY of keeping RATES OF
INTEREST low, either, as from 1932 onwards in Britain, to stimulate
borrowing and economic recovery, or, as during the Second World
War, to reduce the cost of government borrowing. In most of the 1930s
and 1940s, BANK RATE was 2 per cent, and that rate could not, there-

fore, be used as a flexible instrument of monetary policy during that period. The cheap money era came to an end in 1951.

Check trading. The practice whereby a company, generally a FINANCE HOUSE, sells a voucher or check on CREDIT. The purchaser repays the DEBT by agreed regular instalments and with INTEREST. The purchaser exchanges the check for goods at certain shops. The finance house reimburses the retailer at the face value of the check, less a discount. It is a very old-established method of CONSUMER CREDIT financing, especially in the north of England. It came into prominence as a method of avoiding HIRE PURCHASE regulations. The latter do not apply to check trading because (a) the finance house does not sell goods, it only extends credit; and (b) the retailer does not sell goods by instalments. ⟡ CONSUMER CREDIT ACT.

Cheque. An order written by the drawer to a COMMERCIAL BANK or CENTRAL BANK to pay on demand a specified sum to a bearer, a named person or corporation.

Chicago school. ⟡ FRIEDMAN, M.; QUANTITY THEORY OF MONEY.

C.i.f. Cost, insurance and freight, or charged in full. The U.K. Overseas Trade Accounts records IMPORTS in terms of their value c.i.f. (charged in full) and exports F.O.B. (free on board) or f.a.s. (free alongside ship). In order to determine the VISIBLE TRADE balance for the BALANCE OF PAYMENTS accounts, the import figures are adjusted to an f.o.b. basis. The insurance and freight element, which accounts for about 10 per cent of the total import bill, is included in the balance of payments as INVISIBLES.

Circular flow of income. A simple model of the workings of an economy depicting the movement of resources between producers and consumers. A number of flows comprise the circular flow of income. First, there are the wages and salaries paid by firms to HOUSEHOLDS. Secondly, there is the money spent by households and received by firms. Corresponding to each of these flows of cash is a flow of some resource in return – labour is provided by households to firms; goods and services are provided by firms for households. There is then a total of four flows in this highly stylized account of how economies function, and there is complete symmetry between the two sectors: households and firms. Each provides the other with some real resource and each receives cash in return; and each spends that cash on the supplies of the other. The same cash is spent by one sector and then the other continuously.

NATIONAL INCOME can be measured by either of the two cash flows; total wages and salaries comprise the *income measure*, while total household spending comprises the *expenditure measure*. These two are different sides of the same coin and, in an economy where all income is spent domestically, will necessarily be equal to each other. In reality, there are leakages from the circular flow: SAVINGS (when money is received by households but not spent); IMPORTS (where money flows to foreign firms); and TAXATION (when money flows to the government). Each of these 'withdrawals', however, gives rise to a corresponding 'injection': INVESTMENT, EXPORTS and government spending – and, if all markets are in equilibrium, each pair will balance exactly. (Other complications include transactions on the INVISIBLE account such as dividend income received from abroad.)

MACROECONOMICS can be seen as the study of and extension to the circular-flow model, removing the unrealistic assumptions underlying it and allowing for deviations from the equilibrium. (◊ MULTIPLIER; 'TABLEAU ÉCONOMIQUE'.)

Circulating capital. *Funds embodied in* STOCKS and work in progress or other current as opposed to fixed ASSETS. A now little-used synonym for WORKING CAPITAL.

Clark, John Bates (1847–1938). Educated at Amherst College, and Heidelberg and Zürich Universities, Clark taught at Amherst until, in 1895, he was appointed Professor of Economics at Columbia University. He held this post until his retirement in 1923. His major publications include *Philosophy of Wealth* (1885), *Distribution of Wealth* (1899), *Essentials of Economic Theory* (1907), *The Control of Trusts* (1901) and *The Problem of Monopoly* (1904). He is regarded as the founder of the marginal productivity theory of distribution in the U.S. (◊ DISTRIBUTION, THEORY OF).

Clark, John Maurice (1884–1963). The son of JOHN BATES CLARK. He succeeded his father to the Chair of Economics at Columbia University in 1926. His publications include *Economics of Overhead Costs* (1923) and *Essays in Preface to Social Economics* (1963). In an article, 'Business Acceleration and the Law of Demand', in the *Journal of Political Economy* in 1917, he formulated the ACCELERATION PRINCIPLE, one of the basic theories upon which has been constructed modern dynamic macroeconomic theory (◊ MACROECONOMICS).

Classical economics. The classical period of economics ranges from ADAM SMITH's *Wealth of Nations*, which was published in 1776, to JOHN STUARTMILL's *Principles of Political Economy* of 1848, and was dominated by the work of DAVID RICARDO. The French PHYSIOCRATS had laid stress on the position of agriculture in the economy, claiming that this sector was the source of all economic wealth. Smith rejected this view and drew attention to the development of manufacturing and the importance of labour PRODUCTIVITY. Ultimately LABOUR was the true measure of VALUE. Ricardo took up this idea and propounded a theory of relative prices based on costs of production in which labour cost played the dominant role, although he accepted that CAPITAL costs were an additional element. Capital played an important role, not only by improving labour productivity, but also by enabling labour to be sustained over the period of waiting before work bore fruit in consumable output. This was the idea of the wages fund (◇ WAGE-FUND THEORY). Wages were dependent on two forces: (a) the demand for labour, derived from the availability of capital, or savings, to finance the wage bill; and (b) the supply of labour, which was fixed in the short run, but in the long run was dependent on the standard of living. The latter was related to the level of subsistence. This was not regarded as merely the basic necessities required to keep the workers alive and to reproduce themselves. It was determined by custom, and was accepted to be increasing as real living standards improved. T. R. MALTHUS, in his theory of population, pointed to the need for restraint because of the presumption that there was a natural tendency for the growth of population to outstrip agricultural output. Ricardo analysed the implications of the productivity of land at the margin of cultivation. The Physiocrats and Adam Smith had attributed agricultural RENT to the natural fertility of the soil, but Ricardo refuted this. Rent existed because of the poor fertility of the final increment of land taken under cultivation. Because of competition, PROFITS and labour costs must be the same everywhere and therefore a surplus must accrue to all land that was more fertile than that on the margin. This surplus was rent. The presumption of competition was the foundation of classical thought. The classical economists believed that, although individuals were each motivated by self-love and personal ambition, free competition ensured that the community as a whole benefited. As Adam Smith put it, 'It is not from the benevolence of the butcher that we expect our dinner, but from [his] regard to [his] own interest.' As a consequence, they concluded government interference should be kept to a minimum. The classical economists gave little attention to macroeconomic problems (◇ MACROECONOMICS), such as the TRADE CYCLE. Most of the classicists accepted J.-B. SAY's 'law of markets', the gist of which purported to maintain the impossibility of any severe economic recession (◇ DEPRESSION) arising from an overall deficiency in AGGREGATE DEMAND. Malthus disputed this. He argued that increased savings would not only lower consumption but would also increase output, through increased investment. However, his view was not accepted. The classical economists, including Malthus, held a theory in which savings were equated with investment through changes in the RATE OF INTEREST (◇ TURGOT, A.). Classical economists continue to influence economists both in the U.K. and in other countries to this day. J. S. Mill's book was used as a school text until the end of the nineteenth century. ALFRED MARSHALL in his *Principles of Economics* of 1890 assimilated the old classical economics with the new marginalism of JEVONS, MENGER and WALRAS. The great controversy which raged in the years of the Great Depression of the 1930s between the late classical

71

economists and the advocates of deficit spending on public works was resolved at the time when the classical macroeconomic theory gave way to the new economic revolution set in train by J. M. KEYNES. Classical economics continues to influence economists, however (◊ NEO-CLASSICAL ECONOMICS).

Classical school. The tradition of economic thought that originated in ADAM SMITH and developed through the work of D. RICARDO, T. R. MALTHUS and J. S. MILL down to A. MARSHALL and A. C. PIGOU (◊ CLASSICAL ECONOMICS; NEO-CLASSICAL ECONOMICS).

Classical unemployment. A situation in which the number of people able and willing to work at prevailing wages exceeds the number of jobs available. In short, the real wage (the price of labour) is higher than that at which the market clears. Classical unemployment is explained by imperfections in the labour market that prevent the unemployed bidding down wages until it is profitable for firms to find jobs for everyone. It contrasts with STRUCTURAL UNEMPLOYMENT or FRICTIONAL UNEMPLOYMENT which occurs when the prevailing wage is too low to attract some people into employment. Classical unemployment also contrasts with KEYNESIAN UNEMPLOYMENT, although both represent different regimes of QUANTITY RATIONING. Under classical unemployment, firms are not rationed at all – they can get all the labour they want and can sell all the goods they produce. Households, however, can neither sell all the labour they wish nor obtain all the goods they would like to buy with their excessively high wages.

Clearing banks. Members of the London Bankers' CLEARING HOUSE. Often used as a synonym for COMMERCIAL BANKS or joint-stock banks.

Clearing-house. 1. Any institution that settles mutual indebtedness between a number of organizations. **2.** More specifically, the London Bankers' Clearing House until 1984 set all claims among its members (i.e. CHEQUES and orders paid into banks other than those upon which they were drawn) against one another, and each day struck a balance; the differences in total indebtedness were paid by cheque drawn on the BANK OF ENGLAND. From 1968 this system was progressively automated, with the Bankers' Automated Clearing Service (B.A.C.S.) clearing standardized payment instructions (standing orders) and, from 1984, for large cheques, the Clearing House Automated Payments System (C.H.A.P.S.). Similar institutions exist in other countries, for example, the Clearing House Interbank Payments System (C.H.I.P.S.) in New York. Similar arrangements exist to clear transactions between members of COMMODITY EXCHANGES and other markets, for example, the International Commodities Clearing House.

Close company (U.S. **closed company**). A company that is effectively controlled by five or fewer shareholders. The purpose of close-company tax legislation, introduced in Britain with CORPORATION TAX under the 1965 Finance Act, was to prevent the avoidance of INCOME TAX, which cannot be levied on shareholders who choose to retain PROFITS in their business. The Inland Revenue was able for tax purposes to treat certain income of close companies as distributed, but these powers were subsequently relaxed following changes to the corporation-tax system. A company in which the public hold 35 per cent or more of the EQUITY is not treated as a close company.

Closed economy. An economic system with little or no external trade, as opposed to an *open economy*, in which a high proportion of output is absorbed by exports and similarly domestic expenditure by imports. ⟡ INTERNATIONAL TRADE.

Closed-end trust (U.S.). An INVESTMENT TRUST.

Closing prices. Price of a COMMODITY, e.g. SECURITIES on the STOCK EXCHANGE, at the end of a day's trading in a MARKET.

Cobb–Douglas function. A PRODUCTION FUNCTION or UTILITY function with special characteristics, proposed by K. WICKSELL and tested against statistical evidence by C. W. Cobb and P. H. Douglas in 1928. For production, the function is $Y = A \cdot L^{\alpha} \cdot C^{\beta}$, where Y = output, L = Labour input, and C = Capital input. A, α and β are constants determined by TECHNOLOGY. If α and $\beta = 1$, the production function has constant returns to scale (⟡ ECONOMIES OF SCALE) (i.e. if L and C are increased by 10 per cent, Y increases by 10 per cent). If $\alpha + \beta$ is less than 1, returns to scale are decreasing; if greater than 1, increasing. Assuming perfect competition in markets, α and β can be shown to be labour's and capital's share, respectively, of the value of output. Cobb and Douglas were influenced by statistical evidence at the time that appeared to show that labour and capital shares of total output (i.e. NATIONAL INCOME) were constant over time in developed countries. They sought explanations for this by statistical fitting (⟡ LEAST-SQUARES REGRESSION) of their production function. There is doubt now whether, in fact, such constancy of shares is true. The Cobb–Douglas form can also be applied to utility. Consumer satisfaction or utility is represented by $U = A X_1^{\alpha} X_2^{\beta}$, where X_1 and X_2 are quantities of commodities or services consumed (⟡ EULER, L.).

Cobweb model. This is a simple dynamic MODEL of cyclical DEMAND and SUPPLY in which there is a time lag between the responses of producers to a change in price. Farming, because of the gap between seed-time and harvest, is illustrative of such a model. Consider the diagram (overleaf). EQUILIBRIUM is represented at the point of intersection of the demand and supply curves at which Q satisfies demand and supply at price P. Suppose in the following period (1), there is a very poor harvest and supply falls to Q_1. At Q_1, prices will rise to P_2 corresponding to (2) on the demand curve. Producers then initiate a new production phase

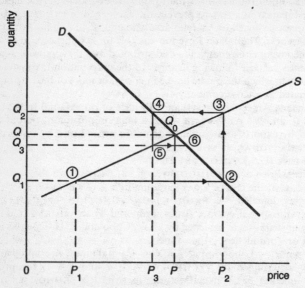

influenced by this high price and in the next period supply Q_2 (point (3) on the supply curve). But prices must now fall to P_3 (point (4) on the demand curve) for all the output to be sold. The process then repeats itself. It can be seen in the diagram that the path converges to the equilibrium point Q_0, so that the system is stable. However, if the demand and supply curves were drawn such that the latter was steeper than the former (to the P axis), the fluctuations in price and quantity would get wider and wider. If the slopes were equal the cycle would simply oscillate around the equilibrium point (◊ ELASTICITY; RATIONAL EXPECTATIONS).

Coefficient of determination. ◊ MULTIPLE CORRELATION COEFFICIENT.

Collateral security. A second security (in addition to the personal surety of the borrower) for a LOAN. BANK LOANS, other than PERSONAL LOANS, are normally made against the security of STOCKS and SHARES, property or INSURANCE policies.

Collusion. Cooperation between independent firms so as to modify competition. Collusion may be tacit or explicit and may involve fixing prices. In *collusive oligopoly* (◊ OLIGOPOLY), where two or more firms produce identical or near identical products, levels of price and output may be similar to those obtaining under MONOPOLY. ◊ CARTEL.

Collusive oligopoly. ◊ COLLUSION.

Colombo Plan for Cooperative Economic and Social Development in Asia and the Pacific. A plan for economic assistance for the DEVELOPING COUNTRIES of Asia and the Pacific agreed in 1950, originally with special concern for the re-establishment of economic activity on a sound basis in the aftermath of the Second World War. The member countries include the U.S.A., the U.K., Australia, Canada, New Zealand and Japan as well as developing Asian and Pacific countries. The consultative committee publishes an annual report describing the economic progress and aims of the developing countries in the plan and the nature and level of assistance received. Grants and loans from the six developed countries to the developing countries in the plan amounted to $3·8 billion in 1984. The secretariat is in Colombo, Sri Lanka. ⟡ ASIAN DEVELOPMENT BANK.

Comecon. ⟡ COUNCIL FOR MUTUAL ECONOMIC AID.

Commercial banks. Privately owned banks operating cheque CURRENT ACCOUNTS, receiving DEPOSITS, taking in and paying out notes and coin and making LOANS, in the U.K. through a large number of branches (⟡ BANKING; BANK LOAN; BRANCH BANKING). Sometimes referred to as *retail* (⟡ RETAIL BANKING) *or deposit banks.* Formerly and still sometimes called *joint-stock banks* and also incorrectly CLEARING BANKS, since not all the commercial banks in the U.K. are members of the London Bankers' CLEARING HOUSE. In the U.S.A. these banks are sometimes referred to as *member banks* (⟡ FEDERAL RESERVE SYSTEM) and in Western Europe as *credit banks* to distinguish them from INVESTMENT BANKS. In most countries the commercial banks are concerned mainly with making and receiving payments, receiving DEPOSITS and making short-term LOANS to private individuals, companies and other organizations. The banks increasingly provide a number of other services to their customers: trustee and executor facilities, the supply of foreign currency, the purchase and sale of SECURITIES, INSURANCE, CREDIT TRANSFER, PERSONAL LOAN and credit-card facilities (⟡ CREDIT ACCOUNT). The banks have also over the years diversified into other financial services in competition with the FINANCE HOUSES and the MERCHANT BANKS, e.g. venture or RISK CAPITAL and the management of UNIT TRUSTS. In Britain the number of commercial banks has been greatly reduced in recent years. Apart from the 'BIG FOUR' and their subsidiaries, the major commercial banks are the Royal Bank of Scotland, the Bank of Scotland, the Ulster Bank and the TRUSTEE SAVINGS BANK. There are 427 foreign banks in London, more than in any other financial centre, some of them with branches outside London, and their number has greatly increased in recent years. The U.K. clearing banks have had to face growing competition from these foreign banks, other British banks and the BUILDING SOCIETIES in recent years and their share of sterling bank deposits has fallen to little more than one-third from 85 per cent in the early 1960s.

The TREASURY, through the BANK OF ENGLAND, has wide powers to control the activities of the commercial banks in the interest of national monetary policy. Until recently, competition between the commercial banks was mainly restricted to the services they offer, since OVERDRAFT and deposit rates were identical and bank charges very similar. The abandonment of ceilings on bank advances in favour of the new system of CREDIT CONTROL in 1971, however, was carried out on the understanding that the banks would end their agreement not to compete in RATES OF INTEREST. The banks no longer base their deposit and overdraft rates on BANK RATE, but publish their own BASE RATES.

Commercial bills. ◊ BILL OF EXCHANGE.

Commercial paper. ◊ PROMISSORY NOTE.

Commission. A percentage of the VALUE of a transaction taken by an intermediary as payment for his services, e.g. BROKER's commission, estate agency's commission.

Commodity. 1. In economic theory, a commodity is a tangible good or service resulting from the process of production. Differences between commodities, real or imagined, will determine whether or not they are close SUBSTITUTES for one another. **2.** In general usage, a primary product, such as coffee, copper, cotton, wool, rubber and tin. ◊ COMMODITY EXCHANGE.

Commodity agreements. ◊ INTERNATIONAL COMMODITY AGREEMENTS.

Commodity control schemes. ◊ INTERNATIONAL COMMODITY AGREEMENTS.

Commodity exchange. A MARKET in which COMMODITIES are bought and sold. It is not necessary for the commodities to be physically exchanged; only rights to ownership need be. The old practice of auctioning commodities from warehouses in which samples could be inspected beforehand has become less important. An efficient system of grading and modern systems of communication have enabled the practice of 'C.I.F. trading' to develop. A buyer can buy a commodity in the country of origin for delivery c.i.f. to a specific port at which he can off-load for direct delivery to his own premises. This method saves warehousing costs and auction charges. The market not only enables commodities to be sold 'spot' or for delivery at some specified time and place (◊ SPOT MARKET), but it also includes a market in 'FUTURES'. This latter enables merchants to avoid the effect of price fluctuations by buying for forward delivery at an agreed price; which will not be affected by intervening changes in the 'spot' rate (◊ CLEARING HOUSE).

Commodity stabilization agreements. ◊ INTERNATIONAL COMMODITY AGREEMENTS.

Commodity tax. ◊ A levy on the price of a good or service. ◊ DIRECT TAXATION.

Common agricultural policy (C.A.P.). The system of agricultural support adopted by the EUROPEAN ECONOMIC COMMUNITY. The C.A.P. covers about 90 per cent of E.E.C. farm output. The central feature of the policy is that it raises the income of farmers by keeping agricultural prices to the consumer at a high level. 'Target' prices are fixed by the E.E.C. Commission for specified commodities. Import prices are kept above the target prices by the imposition of levies. 'Intervention' prices for domestic supplies are set somewhat below the 'target' prices. If sales can only be made on the market below the 'intervention' price, the community buys into store in order to drive the price up. The 'intervention' price may vary from place to place in the community in order to induce 'surplus' areas to transport to 'deficit' areas and the community may also subsidize exports in order to keep prices above the intervention level. For some commodities there is no intervention system and the E.E.C. relies on high import TARIFFS to keep prices high. The accumulation of large surpluses in some commodities has led to the use of direct payments to farmers. Criticism has been made of the high cost of C.A.P. About 75 per cent of the community budget is absorbed by agriculture which is channelled through the European Agricultural Guidance and Guarantee Fund. The fund also allocates improvement grants to farmers. ◊ GREEN CURRENCY.

Common Market. ◊ ANDEAN PACT; BENELUX; CENTRAL AMERICAN COMMON MARKET; CUSTOMS UNION; EUROPEAN ECONOMIC COMMUNITY.

Commonwealth Development Corporation (C.D.C.). A statutory body established by the U.K. government originally to channel overseas aid to the DEVELOPING COUNTRIES of the Commonwealth. Under the Overseas Resources Development Act of 1969, the C.D.C. was enabled to extend its overseas assistance to developing countries outside the Commonwealth. Finance is allocated to the corporation by the U.K. government from the Overseas Aid BUDGET. It may invest indirectly through EQUITIES or DEBENTURES or directly in projects administered by its own staff. The corporation has regional directors in the Caribbean, Africa, Asia and the Pacific.

Company law. The law governing the establishment and conduct of incorporated business enterprise. It originally developed from the PARTNERSHIP, and has its origins in common law and, from the eighteenth century onwards, in a series of company and other Acts. The first companies were created by Royal Charter, and the whole basis of company law is that certain benefits are conferred (in many of these first instances, that of a MONOPOLY) in return for certain obligations. The Act of 1720 created the Statutory Company with LIMITED LIA-BILITY, making possible, for example, the establishment of the early British railway companies. By 1825 the expansion of business had made the creation of companies by separate Acts of Parliament too cumbersome, and in that year a new Act made it possible to form JOINT-STOCK COMPANIES by registration with a Registrar of Companies. It was not until 1862, however, that limited liability was extended to certain private as well as public companies. Company law has continued to evolve under successive Acts as the needs of business have developed and altered. The 1907 Act introduced the distinction between the PRIVATE COMPANY and the PUBLIC COMPANY. Other laws such as the Prevention of Fraud Act also apply to companies. Under present law (deriving principally from the 1948, 1967, 1976, 1980 and 1981 Companies Acts which were repealed and consolidated in the Companies Act 1985) there are three classes of company: (a) limited and (b) unlimited private companies; and (c) public limited companies (plc). Compared with the two other forms of business unit, the SOLE PROPRIETOR and the partnership, INCORPORATION confers advantages for financing and in certain circumstances TAXATION, in addition to limited liability where appropriate. (An unlimited private company does not have limited liability, i.e. its owners are responsible for company debt to the full extent of their fortune.) However, companies, unlike individuals or partnerships, are obliged to make public certain information about their business. Both private and public limited companies are obliged to file certain information for public inspection and to circulate accounts to their shareholders. Until 1967 certain PRIVATE COMPANIES, 'exempt private companies', were not obliged to comply with all of the accounting and disclosure requirements and under present legislation there are exemptions for small and medium-sized companies which are not public companies. A small company is presently defined as one with a turnover not exceeding £2m., assets not exceeding £975,000 and with 50 or fewer employees. A medium-sized company is defined as one with a turnover not exceeding £8m., assets of not more than £3,900,000 and with 250 or fewer employees.

The amount of information which larger companies are required to publish has increased in successive Companies Acts, and the directors' report must now cover such matters as employment, exports, employee aggregate remuneration and donations to political causes or charities. The 1976 Companies Act contained provisions to speed up the publication of accounts and covered the appointment and removal of auditors and other matters. The 1981 Companies Act allowed companies to acquire their own shares under certain circumstances and required them to publish details of such transactions. That Act also, in a major departure, laid down detailed schedules for the form and content of the BALANCE SHEET and profit-and-loss account (◊ DOUBLE-ENTRY BOOKKEEPING) to give effect to the E.E.C. Fourth Directive harmonizing company law in the community. All these provisions remain essentially the same in the 1985 Act.

A public company may have an unlimited number of shareholders and may offer SHARES for public subscription. The nominal value of the allocated share capital may not be less than £50,000. Quoted companies are public limited companies whose shares are listed on a recognized STOCK EXCHANGE. Private companies may place certain restrictions on the transfer of shares, but not offer shares to the public. Company law sets out other provisions dealing with the powers, appointment and terms of directors, the protection of investors, including minorities, ownership and control, the regulation of shares, the disclosure of interest in shares, the group accounts prepared by a holding company, winding up and other matters.

Company reserves. PROFITS retained in the business and set aside for specified purposes. The various Companies Acts have drawn distinctions between capital and revenue reserves and undistributable and distributable reserves. Capital reserves are created when new shares are issued at a PREMIUM over par or when the book value of existing assets is revalued to bring it into line with replacement costs or when CAPITAL GAINS are made. These capital reserves may later be transformed into issued capital (◊ CAPITALIZATION). Revenue, or distributable reserves, are created by transfers of undistributed profits into special accounts, out of which a dividend may be paid in a later year in which the company makes a loss. Reserves of either type may be converted into capital by a BONUS ISSUE. *Provisions* are not the same as reserves but arise out of DEPRECIATION or allowances made for LIABILITIES, for example provisions for doubtful debts.

Company taxation. ◊ CORPORATION TAX.

Comparative advantage. The idea that economic agents are most efficiently employed in activities in which they perform relatively better than in others. The importance of comparative advantage is that it suggests that, even if someone is very bad at some activity, perhaps even worse than anyone else at it, it could still be efficient for him to pursue it if he is even more inept at other activities. The idea is particularly important in international trade, where it is suggested that countries should specialize in areas in which they have a comparative advantage. ◊◊ DIVISION OF LABOUR; INTERNATIONAL TRADE; RICARDO, D.

Comparative cost. ◊ INTERNATIONAL TRADE; RICARDO, D.

Comparative static equilibrium analysis. The analysis of markets or economies in terms of their different EQUILIBRIUM positions, without reference to the process by which adjustment between equilibria is achieved. Most non-mathematical economics is static in this sense. It consists of comparing diagrams which represent snapshots of the state of a market at a single point in time, and it aims to assess the characteristics of the equilibrium state and discover the position of a new equilibrium when some variable is changed. For example, most DEMAND and SUPPLY analysis is of this sort. An equilibrium is noted; then, the effect of a shift in demand or supply is analysed; its impact on price and quantity sold is determined, and the effect of demand or supply curves with different slopes can be assessed.

What is missing from such analysis is any trace of the path or speed of adjustment between different equilibria. In PERFECT COMPETITION, for example, firms are assumed to have no influence on price and be unable to deviate from the going market rate at all – yet, by what process can the market price change? As there is no auctioneer telling everybody what price to set, the price-takers themselves must also be the price-setters, even though this contradicts the basic assumption of the model. (◊ TATONNEMENT PROCESS.) Comparative statics simply ignores problems such as these. ◊ DYNAMICS.

Comparative statics. ◊ COMPARATIVE STATIC EQUILIBRIUM ANALYSIS.

Compensation principle. An unambiguous increase in total economic welfare is achieved if, after a change, a number of individuals are better off and nobody is made worse off (◊ PARETO, V. F. D.). If, however, some individuals are made worse off, the compensation principle states that total welfare will be increased by the change if those who gain from the change could compensate the losers to their mutual satisfaction. It is not necessary for money transfers actually to take place. However, the principle has been criticized in this respect because, without actual transfers, inter-personal comparisons of UTILITY of money are implied. Actual transfers are required if individuals are to reveal the total worth they place on their gains and losses (◊ ECONOMIC EFFICIENCY). ◊ SOCIAL-WELFARE FUNCTION; WELFARE ECONOMICS.

Compensatory finance. ◊ UNITED NATIONS CONFERENCE ON TRADE AND DEVELOPMENT.

Competition. ◊ PERFECT COMPETITION.

Competition Act 1980. Extended the powers of the Office of Fair Trading (◊ FAIR TRADING ACT), subject to the approval of the Secretary of State, to undertake preliminary investigations into anti-competitive practices (not defined in the Act) in any commercial firm and certain public-sector bodies, including public corporations. The O.F.T. could therefore investigate the efficiency of nationalized industries and could be ordered by the Secretary of State to investigate prices (both these powers had hitherto been restricted to the PRICE COMMISSION which was abolished in the Act). On completion of the investigation the O.F.T. may obtain undertakings from firms to cease any anti-competitive practices identified or, with the approval of the Secretary of State, it may make a reference to the MONOPOLIES COMMISSION. Competition in the U.K. is also covered by articles 85 and 86 of the Treaty of Rome. ⬦ EUROPEAN ECONOMIC COMMUNITY. ⬦ COMPETITION POLICY.

Competition and credit control (C.C.C.). The title of a paper issued by the BANK OF ENGLAND in 1971 which announced a number of important changes affecting the banking system. These changes, which were put into operation in October 1971, included a new system of reserve requirements (⬦ CREDIT CONTROL), the abandonment of agreements between banks on interest rates and changes in the Bank of England's operations in the GILT-EDGED SECURITIES market. The changes were part of a general shift in policy towards the control of the total MONEY SUPPLY, and were intended to stimulate more active competition between the banks, as well as a move towards greater reliance upon interest rates as a means of controlling credit. A number of modifications were introduced to the new system subsequently and major changes in 1981 included the abolition of the MINIMUM LENDING RATE and the reserve asset ratio (⬦ LIQUIDITY RATIO).

Competition policy. The name given to any set of government measures aiming to stimulate competition and protect consumers against MONOPOLY. The areas of such policy include (a) control of dominant firms by REGULATION, such as British Telecom through the Office of Telecommunications, (b) control of mergers to prevent industries becoming monopolized, and (c) control of anti-competitive acts, such as FULL-LINE FORCING and *predatory pricing*.

Complementary demand. Pairs of goods for which consumption is interdependent, for example cars and petrol or cups and saucers, are known as *complements* or complementary goods and changes in the demand for one will have a complementary effect upon the demand for the other. Complements have a negative CROSS-PRICE ELASTICITY OF DEMAND: if the price of one rises the demand for both may fall. Complementary demand creates difficulties in the application of the theory of MARGINAL UTILITY since it cannot be said that the level of utility yielded by a complementary good is yielded directly by that good and in isolation. ⬦ SUBSTITUTES.

Compliance cost. Expenditure of time or money in conforming with government requirements. The compliance COSTS of INCOME TAX will include the cost of record-keeping, payments to an accountant, etc. Compliance costs are additional to the costs of collection, which are borne by the government and may be lesser or greater than compliance costs. The compliance costs of REGULATION include the payment of licence fees for permission to trade and, for example, the cost of fire-proof doors installed to comply with fire regulations.

Compound interest. The calculation of total interest due by applying the rate to the sum of the capital invested plus the interest previously earned and reinvested. In contrast, *simple interest* is calculated only on the capital invested.

Concealed discount. ◊ TRADE DISCOUNT.

Concentration. The extent to which a small number of firms account for a high proportion of sales or another dimension of economic importance in an industry. Concentration is said to be high, for example, if 90 per cent of industry sales or employment is accounted for by three firms – this is the three-firm concentration ratio. *Industry concentration* is the key element in MARKET STRUCTURE and an important determinant of conduct and performance and hence of the nature of competition. The two extremes are: PERFECT COMPETITION, in which products are homogeneous and firms small in relation to the size of the total market so that they cannot individually influence price (concentration is low), and MONOPOLY, in which there is a single seller (concentration is absolute). Most markets in the ADVANCED COUNTRIES have high (OLIGOPOLY) to intermediate levels of concentration and operate under conditions of MONOPOLISTIC COMPETITION in which prices tend to exceed marginal cost in theory and even if there is no COLLUSION, BARRIERS TO ENTRY may keep concentration high.

Industry concentration, measured by the CONCENTRATION RATIO, generally increased in the U.K. from 1950 to the early 1970s, though there are a number of practical and conceptual difficulties in measuring concentration and in generalizing about trends over time. According to the census of production (◊ PRODUCTION, CENSUS OF), the largest five firms accounted for an average of 65 per cent of sales at the four-digit STANDARD INDUSTRIAL CLASSIFICATION level in some 250 U.K. manufacturing industries in 1975. Attitudes to concentration among economists vary according to their assessment of the relative importance of competition and the ECONOMIES OF SCALE. Where the OPTIMUM scale of output is high relative to the size of the total market, more competitors might lead to higher costs through lower scale economies. In general, however, ENTERPRISE concentration in a given market is much higher than ESTABLISHMENT (or plant-) concentration, indicating that leading firms have a larger share of markets than would be necessary for them to operate at optimum scales of output (though there may be economies in distribution or other aspects of multi-plant operation). Larger firms also operate in more than one product market ($\diamond$ DIVERSIFICATION) and this can result in high levels of *aggregate concentration* in which a small number of firms have a significant share in economic output as a whole. In fact, the share of the 100 largest manufacturing enterprises was about 41 per cent of total manufacturing net output in the U.K. in 1968 compared with some 27 per cent in 1953 and only 16 per cent in 1909, though there appears to have been little change in recent years. Although concentration appears to be relatively high in the U.K. compared with other, comparable, E.E.C. countries and the United States, there is some controversy about how important national concentration is, at least in manufacturing, given the extent of actual and potential competition from imports.

Concentration ratio. A ratio calculated to show the degree to which an industry is dominated by a small number of large firms or made up of many small firms. There are many ratios that may be calculated, based on turnover, capital employed, employment, etc, for instance, the ratio of the total capital employed of the top five firms as a percentage of the industries' capital employed. However, a comprehensive ratio is the Herfindahl index. This index is given by the sum of the squares of the market shares of each firm in the industry: $H = \Sigma_n f_n^2$, where f_n = the market share of firm n (e.g. the sales of firm n divided by industry sales). A pure MONOPOLY would take the value of 1. At the other extreme, if all the firms in the industry had equal market shares the value would be $1/n$. $\diamond$ CONCENTRATION.

Confirming house. An agency in Britain which purchases and arranges the export of goods on behalf of overseas buyers.

Conglomerate (U.S.). A business organization generally consisting of a HOLDING COMPANY and a group of subsidiary companies engaged in dissimilar activities. $\diamond\!\!\diamond$ INTEGRATION.

Consolidated fund. Sums standing to a particular account of the EX-CHEQUER (for which it is often used synonymously) into which the proceeds of TAXATION are paid and from which government expenditures ($\diamond$ BUDGET) are made. Prior to 1787, different funds were maintained for various purposes and taxation receipts divided among them, but after that date the various funds were consolidated, leaving, of major significance, only the *National Insurance Fund*, which receives NATIONAL INSURANCE contributions and a grant from the Consolidated fund to meet social-security payments. *Consolidated fund standing services* is an item in the British budget which includes expenditure authorized by specific legislation. This expenditure, such as the salaries of judges and payments to the NATIONAL LOANS FUND for service of the NATIONAL DEBT, is paid out of the consolidated fund but, unlike SUPPLY SERVICES, does not have to be voted annually in Parliament.

Consolidated stock. ⟡ CONSOLS.

Consols. Abbreviation for *consolidated stock*: unredeemable government stock first issued in the eighteenth century as a consolidation of the NATIONAL DEBT. Consols bear an interest of $2\frac{1}{2}$ per cent and have a total nominal value of £267 million.

Conspicuous consumption. A term used by Thorstein Veblen (1857–1929) in his book *The Theory of the Leisure Class* (1899) to identify that ostentatious personal expenditure which satisfies no physical need but rather a psychological need for the esteem of others. Goods may be purchased not for their practical use but as 'status symbols' and to 'keep up with the Joneses'. ⟡ GIFFEN GOOD.

Constant prices. ⟡ REAL TERMS.

Constant returns to scale. ⟡ RETURNS TO SCALE.

Consumer behaviour. ⟡ DEMAND, THEORY OF; INDIFFERENCE-CURVE ANALYSIS; INDIFFERENCE CURVE; MARGINAL UTILITY; MARSHALL, A.

Consumer credit. Short-term LOANS to the public for the purchase of specific goods. Consumer credit takes the form of CREDIT by shopkeepers and other suppliers, CREDIT ACCOUNTS, PERSONAL LOANS and HIRE PURCHASE. OVERDRAFTS, money-lenders and other private sources of borrowing are not referred to as consumer credit, either because they are not tied to the purchase of specific goods or because they are long-term loans, e.g. MORTGAGES. ⟡ BANKING; CHECK TRADING; FINANCE; FINANCE HOUSE.

Consumer Credit Act. The Consumer Credit Act was passed in 1974, following closely the recommendations of the CROWTHER COMMITTEE. The Act tidied up and consolidated legislation in the field of CONSUMER CREDIT, some of which had existed on the statute books since Victorian times. The Act introduced a licensing system which not only applied to credit and hire firms such as FINANCE HOUSES and banks, but to all agencies connected with consumer credit such as credit brokers and debt collectors. Licences are issued by the Office of Fair Trading if it is satisfied that the applicant has in no way infringed any of the consumer protection laws. Group licensing may be granted to cover the individual members of a professional body which has the authority and standing to discipline its members; such a licence has, for example, been issued to solicitors. Regulations may be made under the Act with respect to the content and style of advertising material or other documents relating to consumer credit, and also to the way the effective annual RATE OF INTEREST is calculated and explained to the consumer (⟡ FAIR TRADING ACT).

Consumer durables. Products purchased by HOUSEHOLDS which are designed to yield benefits spread over a number of years. Examples are vehicles, furniture, refrigerators and washing-machines. New demand for such products will be affected by the age and level of the existing stock owned by households, as well as DISPOSABLE INCOMES and PRICES (⟡ DEMAND, THEORY OF).

Consumer good. An ECONOMIC GOOD or COMMODITY purchased by HOUSEHOLDS for final consumption. Consumer goods include e.g. chocolate or draught beer consumed immediately as well as DURABLE GOODS which yield a flow of services over a period of time, for example a washing-machine. It is the use to which it is put which determines whether a good is a consumer good (sometimes referred to as a *consumption good* or final goods), not the characteristics of the good itself. Electricity, or a computer, bought for the home is a consumer good, but the same thing bought for a factory is a PRODUCER GOOD.

Consumer Protection Advisory Committee. ⟡ FAIR TRADING ACT.

Consumer surplus. Before the phrase was coined by Alfred MARSHALL, the idea of a surplus of UTILITY over the price paid for a good or service was explored by A. J. E. J. DUPUIT in his study of the benefits arising from the construction of public facilities such as roads and bridges. Marshall explained consumer surplus: 'The price which a person pays for a thing can never exceed and seldom comes up to that which he would be willing to pay rather than go without it: so that the satisfaction which he gets from its purchase generally exceeds that which he gives up in paying away its price: and he thus derives from the purchase a surplus of satisfaction. The excess of the price which he would be willing to pay rather than go without the thing, over that which he actually does pay, is the economic measure of this surplus satisfaction.' Marshall's surplus is illustrated in the following diagram (*overleaf*) of a DEMAND curve.

The consumer buys on the market quantity Q_n at a price P_n. However, following his demand schedule, if only Q_1 were available he would be willing to pay P_1, if Q_2 to pay P_2 and so on. If the supplier had a MONOPOLY and could practise PRICE DISCRIMINATION, he could extract as revenue the whole of the area under the demand curve, that is $XY0Q_n$. However, there is a market price P_n, so that the supplier only obtains P_nY0Q_n and leaves the difference XP_nY as a benefit to the consumer. A difficulty is that as the price falls along Marshall's demand curve, the real income of the consumer increases. To get a more accurate measure of the benefit of the surplus, therefore, an adjustment must be made to offset the effect of the difference in real income at the higher price (P_1) and the lower price (P_n). (⟡ COMPENSATED DEMAND CURVE; INCOME EFFECT.) Consumer surplus plays an important role in WELFARE ECONOMICS. (⟡ PRODUCER'S SURPLUS.)

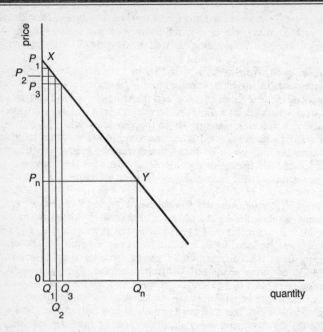

Consumers' expenditure. Consumers' expenditure amounts to about 60 per cent of the U.K.'s GROSS DOMESTIC PRODUCT. It comprises expenditure by HOUSEHOLDS (including certain non-profit-making organizations). It excludes house purchase (including charges for services on the transfer of ownership) and major house improvements, which are regarded as capital expenditure. It includes, however, an imputed rent for owner-occupied houses and expenditure on durables such as motor vehicles.

Consumers' preference. Attitudes which determine consumer choice between alternative COMMODITIES or groups of commodities. When good X is preferred to good Y it will have greater UTILITY to the buyer, so that the allocation of expenditure between these alternatives will, in a FREE-MARKET ECONOMY, be determined by consumer preference and their relative PRICES. These preferences will, in conjunction with the PRODUCTION FUNCTION and the prices of the FACTORS OF PRODUCTION, therefore, determine the allocation of scarce resources to the production of various goods. Consumer preferences may change independently with, say, fashion or may be influenced by ADVERTISING and other forms of sales promotion as well as by the availability of new goods arising from technological progress (◊

TECHNOLOGY). Although preferences are something the economist takes as given, and makes no VALUE JUDGEMENT about, at the same time preferences are assumed to be consistent and rational in certain ways (◊ INDIFFERENCE-CURVE ANALYSIS; REVEALED PREFERENCE; TRANSITIVITY).

Consumers' sovereignty. RESOURCE ALLOCATION determined by CONSUMERS' PREFERENCE rather than by STATE PLANNING. In a FREE-MARKET ECONOMY consumers vote with their purses for the pattern of production and consumption they want; the outcome, however, will be affected by the INCOME DISTRIBUTION.

Consumption. The use of resources to satisfy current needs and wants. It may be measured statistically by the sum of consumers' and government's current expenditure (including defence expenditure), the remainder of NATIONAL INCOME being made up by INVESTMENT. However, such statistics may be inappropriate in some cases. For instance, expenditure on consumer durables, such as washing-machines, in a given period may exaggerate consumption in that period, because consumer durables have a life of, say, seven years over which they are consumed and, therefore, are not entirely consumed in the current period (quarter or year) as implied in the statistics (◊ CONSUMPTION FUNCTION).

Consumption function. With stable preferences, CONSUMPTION depends on INCOME: consumption is a function of income. As income increases, other things being equal, consumption will increase, though not at the same rate as income. As income rises, consumers will save proportionately more and spend proportionately less and the reverse happens when income falls. This relationship between income and consumption assumes that a number of possible influences remain neutral. For instance: (a) Purchases of consumer durables are related to income in the stated way, e.g. they are replaced at a rate related to income and not to other factors. (b) There are no expectations of price changes which might delay or bring forward consumption. (c) No change takes place in the availability or the cost of credit. (d) There is a constant level of SAVINGS in real terms at any level of income, e.g. INFLATION could decrease the real value of savings such that consumers react by increasing their contributions to their savings stock from current income until their real value has been restored; they then revert back to the previous rate of saving (◊ PERMANENT-INCOME HYPOTHESIS). The consumption function was introduced by J. M. KEYNES and applied to his analysis of INCOME DETERMINATION. (◊ AVERAGE PROPENSITY TO CONSUME; MARGINAL PROPENSITY TO CONSUME; MULTIPLIER.)

Consumption good. ◊ CONSUMER GOOD.

Contango. Synonym for CARRY-OVER.

Contestability. The degree of ease with which firms can enter or leave an industry. A *perfectly contestable* industry is one in which, as in PERFECT COMPETITION, there are no barriers to entry at all. Unlike perfect competition, however, perfect contestability implies nothing about how many firms currently exist in the industry – it is possible for an efficient monopolist to exist while no barrier to entry prevents other firms from competing. Contestability theory was stimulated by W. J. Baumol in the early 1980s. He showed that the attractive features of perfect competition could be achieved merely by the threat to incumbent firms that entry would occur should large profits be made.

The threat of entry should induce MARGINAL-COST PRICING and efficient production. In practice, entry barriers *do* exist, and because incumbent firms can often scare potential entrants away from entering, the discipline that potential competition provides is considered less effective than that of actual competitors. (◇ BARRIERS TO ENTRY; COMPETITION POLICY; SUNK COSTS.)

Continuation. Synonymous with CARRY-OVER.

Contract curve. The curve of exchange between two parties along which their MARGINAL RATES OF SUBSTITUTION are the same in relation to the commodities traded. Any bargain concluded at a rate of exchange other than one on the contract curve could be improved (that is, by making at least one party better off without making the other worse off) by moving to the contract curve. A term introduced by F. Y. EDGE-WORTH. (◇ PARETO, V. F. D.) ◇ ECONOMIC EFFICIENCY.

Contracting out. The practice by governments or firms of employing an outside agent to perform some specific task rather than perform it themselves. Contracting out is one type of PRIVATIZATION, with local or national authorities transferring activities from themselves to the private sector. The practice is defended on the grounds that it stimulates competition between companies for contracts to provide services which might otherwise be run by complacent in-house staff who feel little pressure to cut costs and offer a good service. ◇ FRAN-CHISING.

Control. ◇ SEPARATION OF OWNERSHIP FROM CONTROL.

Conversion. Issue of a new STOCK to replace another. This may arise where a DEBENTURE or WARRANT is convertible into EQUITY shares or where holders of GOVERNMENT STOCK at or near redemption are offered a new stock in exchange for existing stock.

Convertibility. A CURRENCY is said to be convertible when it may be freely exchanged for another currency or gold. During the Second World War sterling was inconvertible, and it was made a condition of the WASHINGTON AGREEMENT of 1945 that it should be made fully convertible by July 1947. In fact, the sterling area's GOLD AND FOREIGN EXCHANGE RESERVES were not able to support the demand for conversion, and convertibility lasted little more than five weeks. It was not until 1958 that sterling was fully convertible for non-residents. All foreign EXCHANGE CONTROLS were completely removed by the U.K. in 1979. ⬦ FOREIGN-EXCHANGE MARKET.

Convertible debenture stock. ⬦ DEBENTURES.

Corporate income tax (U.S.). ⬦ CORPORATION TAX.

Corporate planning. A business function concerned with the formulation of long-term objectives and the development of plans to achieve them. Corporate planning has become more and more formalized as business units have grown larger and more diversified. J. K. GALBRAITH argued in the *New Industrial Estate* that the enormously large CAPITAL requirements of modern technology require that the consumer and the MARKET become subservient to the planning needs of the large corporations which have come increasingly to characterize the modern economy.

Corporation tax. A tax (⬦ TAXATION), at present (1986/7) at the rate of 35 per cent, levied on the assessable PROFITS of companies and unincorporated associations. It is calculated after INTEREST and all Inland Revenue allowances (⬦ CAPITAL ALLOWANCES; STOCK APPRECIATION), but before DIVIDEND distribution. A company with assessed profits of £100 would have a corporation tax liability of £35. However, because U.K. corporation tax is now an imputation system, companies are obliged to 'impute' to the shareholders a tax of twenty-nine seventy-firsts of their dividends. This amount is remitted to the Inland Revenue as advance corporation tax (A.C.T.) and is deductible from liability for mainstream corporation tax. The shareholder receives his dividend without tax deductions and with a credit for the amount of tax 'imputed' to him. If he pays tax at the standard rate then he is considered to have prepaid his income tax on the dividend. The purpose of this complex arrangement is to ensure that shareholders paying at the standard rate will be in the same position after tax whether their company retains its profits or distributes them. This result comes about because the company's corporation tax liability is reduced by the A.C.T. paid on distributed dividends; shareholders (who own the profits of the company), therefore, are no better off if dividends are distributed or remain undistributed. From 1973/4 a progressive element was introduced into corporation tax to assist small companies. In 1986/7 the corporation tax rate for companies with taxable profits of less than £100,000 is 29 per cent, with tapering relief up to the full tax rate of 35 per cent for companies with profits in excess of £500,000. In the U.S. companies are liable for *corporate income tax*, which also has a progressive element.

The imputation system was introduced in the U.K. in April 1973. Corporation tax as such had been introduced earlier in 1966–7, but at that time, although the rate was lower than it was to be under the new system, companies were obliged to pay corporation tax *and* to deduct income tax from dividends. This tax was regarded as being paid by the shareholder and could not be offset against corporation tax. Where the shareholder was a company, tax deducted in this way might be set off against income-tax deductions from its own dividends, for which it had to account to the tax authorities. (Under the imputation system the tax credits on FRANKED INVESTMENT INCOME of companies on which tax has been deducted can be deducted from liability for A.C.T.) Prior to 1966/7 a profits tax of 15 per cent plus income tax at the standard rate was levied on trading profits, and shareholders were also taxed in the ordinary way on dividend INCOME.

Corporation tax was originally introduced to encourage the retention of earnings by companies, in the hope that this would stimulate INVEST-MENT. The imputation system was introduced to facilitate tax harmonization with the EUROPEAN ECONOMIC COMMUNITY. It is not, in fact, clear whether or not corporation tax has encouraged retention and there is some controversy among economists as to whether or not it is desirable to do so. Some economists argue that the allocation of capital RESOURCES is best determined by the CAPITAL MARKET, and would prefer to see a higher proportion of dividends distributed and then rechannelled back to investment via the capital market; this, it appears, is the object of the present system. Moreover, the possibility of TAX AVOIDANCE by individual investors liable to high rates of tax in CLOSE COMPANIES has in the past led to the application of special rules to enforce distributions by these companies, so-called *shortfall assessments*. Close-company tax law is somewhat complex, and there are also special provisions regarding LOANS to participators, INTEREST and salaries or fees paid to directors as well as special reliefs for small trading companies.

Companies are also liable to corporation tax on CAPITAL GAINS, effectively at the rate of 30 per cent. *Stock relief* was available to companies or individuals between 1974/5 and 1983/4 to offset the effects of inflationary increases in the value of stocks upon assessable profits for tax purposes. Special provisions allow capital gains taxation on the sale of productive ASSETS to be deferred (*roll-over*) where the proceeds are used to purchase new assets of the same type. There is also a special relief for persons of retirement age.

Individuals in business on their own (operating on own account) and members of PARTNERSHIPS pay income tax on their individual share of total profits (broadly defined in the same way as for companies). For an established business, tax is payable in any year on the profits earned in the accounting period that ended in the previous fiscal year (▷ FINANCIAL YEAR).

Correlation. A statistical measure of the closeness of the variations in the values of one VARIABLE to the variations in the values of another. The 'correlation coefficient' (r) is calculated by the following formula,

$$r = \frac{\Sigma(x_i - \bar{x})\,(y_i - \bar{y})}{\sqrt{[\Sigma_i(x_i - \bar{x})^2]}\sqrt{\Sigma[_i(y_i - \bar{y})^2]}}$$

in which x_i and y_i are the values of the two variables, $\bar{x}$ and $\bar{y}$ are their means ($\diamondsuit$ AVERAGE); r can take any value between $+1$ and -1, at which extremes there is perfect correspondence between the variations of the variables. At the value zero, there is no correspondence. It should be noted that a value of r close to unity does not imply a causative connection between the two variables. $\diamondsuit$ MULTIPLE CORRELATION COEFFICIENT; PARTIAL CORRELATION; REGRESSION ANALYSIS: SLUTSKY, E.

Corset. Term for the system of supplementary SPECIAL DEPOSITS.

Cost. The value of that which must be given up to acquire or achieve something. Economists attempt to take a comprehensive view of the cost of an activity. If a firm invests undistributed PROFITS to spend £1,000 on new machinery which requires less electricity to run than the equipment it replaces, the cost of that machinery is not the *outlay* of £1,000 alone: what could be earned from the best alternative use of the money also has to be taken into account. If, for example, the firm is paying 12 per cent interest on an overdraft and the saving in electricity is less than £120 a year, the cost of the investment will be greater than the return; to disregard the full cost of what is being given up to acquire the machinery would be to reach a wrong decision. If a self-employed person makes a PROFIT of £8,000 a year but pays himself no wage, he needs to consider the alternative use to which his time could be put. He might, for example, be able to earn £10,000 a year working for someone else: this is the *opportunity cost* of his time. Accounting costs, as in these examples, normally allow only for outlays, but cash outlays will only approximate to opportunity costs where competition ensures that the prices of all FACTORS OF PRODUCTION are equal to those for their best alternative use ($\diamondsuit$ WIESER, F. VON). Under the assumptions of PERFECT COMPETITION, the self-employed person would be aware that he could earn more in employment and since we assume profit maximization he would do so (if we ignore, for simplicity, the intangible benefits of self-employment). Economists also distinguish between private costs and SOCIAL COSTS and costs in REAL TERMS and money terms. $\diamondsuit$ AVERAGE COST; IMPUTED COST; PRIME COSTS.

Cost, average. $\diamondsuit$ AVERAGE COST.

Cost, avoidable. $\diamondsuit$ AVOIDABLE COSTS.

Cost, opportunity. ◊ COST.

Cost, overhead. ◊ FIXED COSTS.

Cost accounting, costing and cost control. Procedures by which the expenditure of a firm is related to units of output. Cost accounts, while they can be directly related to financial accounts, are concerned with the detailed elements of COST in identifiable output for purposes of pricing, departmental budgeting and the control of manufacturing methods, material and LABOUR usage for these products rather than the overall financial results of the firm's operations.

Cost–benefit analysis. The appraisal of an investment project which includes all social and financial costs and benefits accruing to the project. The techniques adopted in order to evaluate and decide whether a proposed project should proceed, whether, that is, its benefits would exceed its costs, are the same as adopted in INVESTMENT APPRAISAL (◊ DISCOUNTED CASH FLOW; PRESENT VALUE). However, the valuation in money terms of the social or welfare costs and benefits (◊ WELFARE ECONOMICS) presents special problems; for instance, the costing of the loss of an area of outstanding natural beauty or the valuation of the benefits arising from the reduction in road accidents due to the construction of a motorway. In other cases, the market prices prevailing may not be appropriate. For instance, the real cost of labour may be much lower than the going wage rate, because of very high unemployment. The opportunity COST (which is the cost that matters in cost–benefit appraisals) is lower and, therefore, a SHADOW PRICE is used to represent this low opportunity cost in place of the wage rate. Similarly, the rate of interest at which the future time streams of costs and benefits are discounted has to be chosen with care. The current money rate of interest may not be realistic for investments with a long economic life. (◊ INTEREST, TIME PREFERENCE RATE OF.)

Cost control. ◊ COST ACCOUNTING.

Cost curves. The graphical representation of cost schedules, AVERAGE COSTS or MARGINAL COSTS, dependent on various levels of output or production.

Cost of capital. ◊ CAPITAL, COST OF.

Cost-of-living index. A synonym for the retail price index (◊ INDEX NUMBER).

Cost-plus. A method of PRICE-fixing in which the contractor charges the actual cost of the goods he supplies or the work he carries out plus either a percentage or an agreed absolute amount for his services. Used both during the Second World War for some government contracts, the cost-plus formula provides no incentive for the contractor to keep his costs to the minimum, and where the percentage service charge is applied, he actually has an incentive to inflate them. The justification for the cost-plus system is that for certain kinds of work, e.g. development contracts in advanced techniques, it is not possible to estimate costs in advance.

Cost-plus is also often used in competitive business as a method for calculating prices, for example in retailing, by adding a GROSS MARGIN or mark-up to the bought-in cost of goods and where there may be no simple alternative. Competitive forces, however, are always tending to equate MARGINAL COST to MARGINAL REVENUE. If one retailer charges more than another he may lose custom and be obliged to reduce his margins or go out of business. In this way PRICE THEORY (⟡ FIRM, THEORY OF THE) is not invalidated by the widespread use of the cost-plus method.

Cost-push inflation. INFLATION induced by a rise in the costs of production of goods and services. Such cost increases may arise abroad and be transmitted through higher prices of imported raw materials. The rapid escalation in oil prices in the 1970s (⟡ ORGANIZATION OF PETROLEUM EXPORTING COUNTRIES) accelerated price inflation in the period, although the rate of inflation had begun to rise before this. Cost increases may also arise within the domestic economy from firms attempting to increase profits and/or employees to increase their earnings. Success in achieving increases depends on their degree of market dominance (⟡ MONOPOLY) and, therefore, bargaining power. Any money gains greater than PRODUCTIVITY will result in price increases. The cost-push argument for inflation is traditionally held to contrast with DEMAND-PULL INFLATION and has been associated with the different policy prescriptions. (⟡ PRICES AND INCOMES POLICY.) However, cost push cannot lead to inflation, in the long run, without monetary demand being sufficient to support it. (⟡ MONETARISM.)

Cost schedule. A table showing the total costs of production at different level of output and from which MARGINAL COSTS and AVERAGE COSTS can be calculated and cost curves drawn. A *price schedule*, in a similar way, would give information about prices at different levels of sales or output. Cost and price schedules are basic tools in economic theory, though in practice they are not easily constructed, especially over wide ranges of output where the PRODUCTION FUNCTION may not be linear.

Costing. ⟡ COST ACCOUNTING.

Costs, fixed. ⟡ FIXED COSTS.

Costs, historical or historic. Actual costs at the time incurred. An ASSET in the BALANCE SHEET at historical cost is shown at the price actually paid for it, even though it might be worth more or cost more to replace. ⟡ DEPRECIATION.

Costs, prime. ⟡ PRIME COSTS.

Costs, selling. The expenses incurred in creating or maintaining the MARKET for a product. Distribution costs are normally excluded, but ADVERTISING, sales staff, sales campaign costs and sales office expenses are included.

Costs, supplementary. ◊ SUPPLEMENTARY COSTS.

Council for Mutual Economic Aid (Comecon). A council set up in 1949 consisting of six East European countries, namely Bulgaria, Czechoslovakia, Hungary, Poland, Romania and the U.S.S.R., followed later by the German Democratic Republic (1950), Cuba (1972) and Vietnam (1978). A number of developing countries attend as observers. Its aim is, by means of central planning, to develop the member countries' economies on a complementary basis for the purpose of achieving self-sufficiency. Comecon has established international cooperation agreements with Finland, Iraq, Mexico and Nicaragua.

Counter trade. A form of BARTER in INTERNATIONAL TRADE in which the buyer requires the seller to accept goods (of the buyer's choosing) in lieu of currency. The seller has the task of marketing the goods. Another form of counter trade is the agreement by a seller of plant and machinery to 'buy back' the products produced by the plant and machinery in settlement of the debt.

Counter trade has developed rapidly in recent years as a favoured trading method by Communist Bloc and DEVELOPING COUNTRIES, when there is a shortage of foreign exchange in those countries. Counter trade may take the form of the exchange of one commodity for another or the exchange of a mixed selection of commodities. Multinational firms and banks have specialist divisions to advise on counter trade and firms have been established specializing in the giving of advice on conducting counter trade.

Countervailing duty. A special additional import duty (◊ TARIFFS) imposed on a COMMODITY to offset a reduction of its price as a result of an export subsidy in the country of origin. ◊ DUMPING; EXPORT INCENTIVES.

Countervailing power. The balancing of the market power of one economic group by another. Advanced by J. K. GALBRAITH in the first of his books on the domination of the modern economic system by large firms (*American Capitalism*), along with ECONOMIES OF SCALE and technological development (◊ TECHNOLOGY) and the need for planning, to meet the criticism that this system of MONOPOLISTIC COMPETITION is inferior to PERFECT COMPETITION. The power of large manufacturers was, he suggested, balanced by that of large retailing groups; the power of large employers by that of the trade unions.

Coupon. A piece of paper entitling the owner to MONEY payment (as in BEARER BONDS), cut-price or free goods (gift coupons) or rations.

Cournot, Antoine Augustin (1801–77). Cournot was made Professor of

Analysis and Mechanics at Lyons in 1834, and Rector of Grenoble University in 1835 and of Dijon University in 1854. His main economic work, *Recherches sur les principes mathématiques de la théorie des richesses*, was published in 1838. Other economic works were *Principes de la théorie des richesses* (1863) and *Revue sommaire des doctrines économiques* (1877). In *Recherches*, Cournot set out in mathematical form the basic apparatus of the theory of the firm ($\diamond$ FIRM, THEORY OF) which, after being refined by A. MARSHALL, appears in elementary economic textbooks today. He was the first to set out the VARIABLES and functions facing a firm; DEMAND as a diminishing function of PRICE; COST CURVES and revenue curves. By the use of calculus he demonstrated that a monopolist will maximize his profit at the output at which his MARGINAL COST is equal to his MARGINAL REVENUE. Cournot traced a direct logical line from the single seller (MONOPOLY) through two (DUOPOLY) or many (OLIGOPOLY) sellers to 'unlimited competition'. He showed how, in the latter case, 'the marginal cost equals the marginal revenue relationship of the monopolist' becomes 'the price equals the marginal cost relationship of the firm in PERFECT COMPETITION'. In doing so, he analysed the situation of duopoly and showed that, given that each seller assumed the other's output was unaffected by his own, they would each adjust prices and output until a position of EQUILIBRIUM was reached, somewhere between that reflected by the equations for monopoly and that for unrestricted competition. In spite of the undoubted significance of Cournot's work, he had no influence on the mainstream of economic thought until his ideas were taken up and developed by Marshall.

Cover. The ratio of total to distributed PROFIT of a limited company. A DIVIDEND is said to be twice covered if it represents half the earnings of the company.

Covered bear. $\diamond$ BEAR.

Crawling peg. $\diamond$ EXCHANGE RATE.

Credit. Granting the use or possession of goods and services without immediate payment. There are three types of credit: (a) *consumer credit:* credit extended formally and informally by shopkeepers, FINANCE HOUSES and others to the ordinary public for the purchase of consumer goods ($\diamond$ CONSUMER CREDIT), (b) *trade credit:* credit extended, for example, by material suppliers to manufacturers, or by manufacturers to wholesalers or retailers ($\diamond$ TRADE CREDIT) – virtually all exchange in manufacturing industry, services and commerce is conducted on credit, and firms may provide small discounts on accounts settled within, say, one month – and (c) *bank credit:* credit consisting of LOANS and OVERDRAFTS to a bank's customers ($\diamond$ BANKING).

Credit enables a producer to bridge the gap between the production and sale of goods, and a consumer to purchase goods out of future INCOME.

Bank and other kinds of credit form part of the MONEY supply and have considerable economic importance. Hence the use of credit restrictions, or CREDIT SQUEEZES, by governments to restrain the growth of total demand in time of rising prices. Credit restrictions can take the form of a limitation on the level of bank overdrafts or on the repayment periods and deposit requirements for HIRE PURCHASE agreements. In a credit squeeze, restrictions on the availability of credit are normally accompanied by higher RATES OF INTEREST. ⟡ DEAR MONEY; QUANTITY THEORY OF MONEY.

Credit account. 1. An account against which purchases may be made and paid monthly (U.S. = *charge account*). 2. A form of revolving INSTALMENT CREDIT offered by some retail stores in which the consumer makes fixed regular monthly payments into an account and receives in return credit to purchase goods up to the limit of a certain multiple of the monthly payments, normally eight or twelve. A service charge, which is in effect an INTEREST charge, is normally made as a percentage of the value of each purchase. 3. Bank and agency credit cards in which the consumer pays his account monthly are also a form of credit account.

Credit banks. ⟡ COMMERCIAL BANKS.

Credit cards. ⟡ CREDIT ACCOUNT.

Credit control. An arrangement for the control of all bank CREDIT in Britain, announced in September 1971 to replace 'credit ceilings'. Prior to the Second World War the BANK OF ENGLAND controlled the volume of bank credit and hence the MONEY SUPPLY through the cash base, as well as the ratio of cash to deposits of the COMMERCIAL BANKS. After the war it controlled bank credit through the LIQUIDITY RATIO and SPECIAL DEPOSITS. In 1968 ceilings on bank advances were introduced, but these also appeared to be ineffective in restraining the growth in the money supply and were, moreover, undesirable on the grounds that they inhibited competition between the banks. From 16 September 1971 the new system of credit control was introduced (⟡ COMPETITION AND CREDIT CONTROL), which unlike the previous system of ratio control applied to all banks. Banks were required to work on a day-to-day ratio of '*reserve assets*' to 'eligible assets' of not less than $12\frac{1}{2}$ per cent. *Eligible liabilities* consisted of sterling deposits and CERTIFICATES OF DEPOSIT and overseas net liabilities. Banks were required to maintain $1\frac{1}{2}$ per cent of eligible liabilities in the form of balances with the head office of the Bank of England, which no longer fixed the BANK RATE. Eligible liabilities were defined as all sterling deposits made for a period of less than two years, plus funds obtained by switching overseas currencies into sterling. The new definition of reserve assets included TREASURY BILLS and certain other government securities and money at call on the MONEY MARKET, but excluded CASH and SPECIAL DEPOSITS and was different in other, more technical ways from the 'liquid assets' employed in the previous system of ratio control. All deposit-taking FINANCE HOUSES not classed as banks were subjected to similar controls as banks, except that their minimum reserve asset ratio was 10 per cent. Overseas banks were also included in the new system. The DISCOUNT HOUSES were treated differently from the rest of the banking system in that they were not subject to the reserve ratio on their deposits, although they entered into a commitment to keep not less than 50 per cent of their assets in certain kinds of government securities. The reserve asset ratio was abolished in August 1981, leaving only a cash-ratio deposit of 0·5 per cent (◊ LIQUIDITY RATIO). Other substantial changes to this new system have been made since 1971 and are continuing; examples are the introduction of supplementary special deposits (◊ SPECIAL DEPOSITS) in 1973 and the cessation of regular announcements of changes in bank rate (now called MINIMUM LENDING RATE). The monetary authorities have retained their powers to impose direct controls on credit by means of instructions to the banks and now have three other methods for controlling the money supply: influence over interest rates, special deposits and public borrowing and debt management. ◊ BANKING.

Credit guarantee. A type of insurance against default provided by a credit guarantee association or other institution to a lending institution. Credit guarantees enable otherwise 'sound' borrowers who lack COLLATERAL SECURITY, or are unable to obtain loans for other reasons, to obtain the credit they require through banks in the normal way. A government loan guarantee scheme insuring loans to small firms by the COMMERCIAL BANKS was introduced in the U.K. in 1980. Under this scheme at present (January 1987) the government guarantees repayment to the bank of 70 per cent of the loan in return for an annual premium of 2·5 per cent on the guaranteed portion. ◊ AGRICULTURAL CREDIT CORPORATION; EXPORT CREDITS GUARANTEE DEPARTMENT.

Credit restrictions. ◊ CREDIT SQUEEZE.

Credit sale. ◊ CONSUMER CREDIT.

Credit squeeze. Government restriction on the expansion of bank CREDIT and FINANCE HOUSE credit as part of a policy to reduce the growth of AGGREGATE DEMAND. Until 1971 the principal instruments employed to squeeze credit were changes in BANK RATE to make borrowing more expensive, the imposition of more stringent HIRE PURCHASE terms and control of bank lending through calls for SPECIAL DEPOSITS and limitations on bank advances. In 1971 credit squeeze was replaced by CREDIT CONTROL, reflecting greater emphasis upon control of the quantity of MONEY. Under the new system credit ceilings have been abandoned and in 1982 restrictions on hire-purchase terms were also abolished, though the use of special deposits and administered changes in interest rates remain. ⟡ COMPETITION AND CREDIT CONTROL; QUANTITY THEORY OF MONEY; RADCLIFFE REPORT.

Credit transfer, or Giro. A system in which a bank or post office will transfer MONEY from one account to another on receipt of written instructions. Several accounts, e.g. HOUSEHOLD or trade bills, may be included in a list which must state the location or account numbers of the payee. Standing orders for giro transfer of regular payments may be made. Credit transfers, which have been used by post offices in Europe for many years, were first introduced into Britain by the COMMERCIAL BANKS in 1961 and the Post Office in 1968. Benefits to the customer include the saving on stamp duty payable on CHEQUES (since abolished in Britain) and economies in accounting procedures, though banks may make a charge for each item transferred.

Credit union (U.S.). A non-profit organization accepting deposits and making loans, operated as a cooperative. Credit unions exist in the U.S.A. and some European countries. A mutual SAVINGS BANK.

Creditor. One to whom an amount of money is due. A firm's creditors are other firms, individuals and perhaps the government to which it owes money in return for goods supplied, services rendered and taxes for which it is liable. Antonym of DEBTOR.

Creditor nation. A country with a BALANCE OF PAYMENTS surplus. The KEYNES PLAN recognized that DISEQUILIBRIUM in international payments was as much the responsibility of creditor as of *debtor nations*. Under that plan, the International Clearing Union or international CENTRAL BANK would have given OVERDRAFTS to debtor countries and by so doing would have created deposits for the creditor countries in terms of its special CURRENCY called BANCOR, in a similar way to normal BANKING operations. However, INTEREST would be charged not only on the debtors' overdrafts, but also on the creditors' deposits. Although the Keynes Plan was not accepted at the BRETTON WOODS Conference, the principle that a surplus country had 'obligations' was accepted and a scarce-currency clause written into the INTERNATIONAL MONETARY FUND agreement. ⟡ INTERNATIONAL LIQUIDITY.

Critical-path analysis. Between the start of a project and its finish there are a number of separate tasks which have to be done before others. For instance, in the construction of a house, the foundations are laid before its walls are built and the walls are built before the roof is put in place. Each separate task requires a length of time for it to be accomplished. Some tasks may be carried out simultaneously, such as the fitting of window frames as the roof is being tiled. There is, therefore, a mix of separate pieces of work some of which can be done simultaneously and some of which must be done in sequence. Each piece requires a certain time. Setting out the pattern of work showing time required and their sequence will reveal a set of tasks which *must* be done in sequence: at which points time is required to await the completion of tasks and which tasks are such that they do not require the completion of others. There then emerges a critical path showing the sequence of tasks which minimize the time to completion for the whole project. Any reduction in the time required to bring the project on stream must be looked for along this critical path as any of the other tasks is not critical and cannot affect the completion of the whole project.

Cross-price elasticity of demand. The proportionate change in the quantity demanded of one good divided by the proportionate change in the price of another good. If the two goods are SUBSTITUTES (e.g. butter and margarine), this ELASTICITY is positive. For instance, if the price of margarine increases, the demand for butter will increase. If the goods are complementary (◊ COMPLEMENTARY DEMAND) (e.g. pot plants and flower pots), this elasticity is negative. If the price of pot plants rises, the demand for flower pots will fall.

Cross-section analysis. Statistical analysis of the members of a POPULATION at one point in time. It contrasts with TIME-SERIES ANALYSIS, in which the population is drawn from a number of time periods (generally months, quarters or years).

Cross-subsidy. ◊ SUBSIDY.

Crowding out. The process by which an increase in government borrowing displaces private spending. If a government borrows money from the private sector, it will probably have an effect on NATIONAL INCOME; however, the size of this effect will depend on the volume of crowding out. If an increase in government borrowing has a large effect on interest rates, private spending will fall as investors slim down their plans. Therefore, overall, spending will not increase much. If the government borrowing has no effect on interest rates, however, then there will be no reduction in private spending and aggregate demand will rise by the full amount of the increase in government spending. ◊ IS–LM MODEL; KEYNES, J. M.; MONETARISM.

Cum dividend. With DIVIDEND; the purchaser of a security quoted 'cum dividend' is entitled to receive the next dividend when due. The term 'cum', meaning 'with', is also used in a similar sense in relation to BONUS ISSUES, RIGHTS ISSUES, or INTEREST attached to SECURITIES, etc.

Cumulative preference shares. ◊ PREFERENCE SHARES.

Currency. Notes and coin that are the 'current' medium of exchange in a country (◊ MONEY SUPPLY). Gold and, to a lesser extent, national currencies that act as RESERVE CURRENCIES, such as the dollar, are referred to as *international currency* because they are regarded as acceptable for the settlement of international DEBTS. BALANCE OF PAYMENTS problems have forced many countries to impose restrictions on the amount of currency which may be taken in and out of the country. ⟡ BANKNOTE; DECIMAL COINAGE; EXCHANGE CONTROL; EXCHANGE RATE; SOFT CURRENCY.

Currency, trading. ⟡ TRADING CURRENCY.

Currency appreciation. The increase in the EXCHANGE RATE of one CURRENCY in terms of other currencies. The term is usually applied to a currency with a floating rate of exchange; upward changes in fixed rates of exchange are called *revaluations*. For example, sterling appreciated from $3·50 to $5 during 1933, from $1·70 in 1977 to $2·40 in 1980; and from $1·16 at the end of 1984 to $1·45 at the end of 1985. ⟡ CURRENCY DEPRECIATION; DEVALUATION; EXCHANGE RATE.

Currency depreciation. The fall in the EXCHANGE RATE of one CURRENCY in terms of other currencies. Usually applied to floating exchange rates. Downward changes in fixed rates of exchange are called DEVALUATIONS. When the U.K. came off the GOLD STANDARD in September 1931 sterling depreciated immediately from $4·86 to $3·97. It continued to depreciate until November 1932, by which time it had fallen by 30 per cent. In June 1972 sterling floated. By 1977 it had depreciated to about $1·70, compared with the rate of $2·6057 fixed at the SMITHSONIAN AGREEMENT in 1971. After recovering to $2·40 in 1980 it subsequently depreciated again to $1.16 in 1984. ⟡ CURRENCY APPRECIATION.

Currency notes. ⟡ TREASURY NOTES.

Currency school. ⟡ BANKING AND CURRENCY SCHOOLS.

Currency snake. ⟡ EUROPEAN CURRENCY SNAKE.

Current account. 1. The most common type of bank account, on which DEPOSITS do not earn INTEREST, but can be withdrawn by CHEQUE at any time (U.S. = *demand deposit*). The bank charges according to the number of cheques cleared through the account and the credit balance. If the average balance is high, the customer may pay no bank charges 2. That part of the BALANCE OF PAYMENTS accounts recording current, i.e. non-capital, transactions.

Current assets. ⟡ ASSETS.

Current balance. The net position on the current account of the BALANCE OF PAYMENTS.

Current-cost accounting. ⟡ INFLATION ACCOUNTING.

Current expenditure. Expenditure on recurrent, i.e. non-CAPITAL, items in business or private accounts.

Current liabilities. ⟡ LIABILITIES.

Current prices. PRICES unadjusted for changes in the purchasing power of money. Whether prices are in current or constant terms in historical series of economic statistics is of great importance at times of INFLA-TION or DEFLATION. ⟡ REAL TERMS.

Current purchasing-power accounting. ⟡ INFLATION ACCOUNTING.

Current ratio. The ratio of the current LIABILITIES to the current ASSETS of a business. Current assets normally exceed current liabilities. The difference between the two is WORKING CAPITAL, which is normally financed from long-term sources. The amount of working capital required varies with the type of business and its commercial practices – e.g. on the proportions of its output sold for cash and on three months' CREDIT – so that the current ratio is not a universally useful guide to the solvency of a business. ⟡ LIQUIDITY RATIO.

Current yield. ⟡ YIELD.

Customs drawback. The repayment of customs duties (⟡ TARIFFS) paid on imported goods which have been re-exported or used in the manufacture of exported goods.

Customs duties. ⟡ TARIFFS.

Customs union. A customs union is established within two or more countries if all barriers (such as TARIFFS or QUOTAS) to the free exchange of each other's goods and services are removed and, at the same time, a common external tariff is established against non-members. This contrasts with a FREE-TRADE AREA in which each member country retains its own tariffs *vis-à-vis* non-members (⟡ BENELUX; CENTRAL AMERICAN COMMON MARKET; EUROPEAN ECONOMIC COMMUNITY; EUROPEAN FREE TRADE ASSOCIATION; LATIN AMERICAN FREE TRADE ASSOCIATION). At one time it was generally accepted that customs unions unambiguously yielded economic benefits. Without the distortions imposed by tariffs, trade was directed in favour of the producer with advantageous costs (⟡ RICARDO, D.). It was believed that as FREE TRADE was itself beneficial in that it led to the optimal allocation of world resources, so a customs union, which was a step in that direction, must also be beneficial. However, Jacob Viner in *The Customs Union Issue*, published in 1950, pointed out that the creation of a customs union could have two effects: (a) a trade-creating effect and (b) a trade-diversion effect. Although the former might be a gain, greater losses might be incurred by the latter. Take the example of two countries *A* and *B* and the rest of the world *C* producing a particular commodity for £50, £40 and £30 respectively. The home market of *A* is protected by a 75 per cent *ad valorem* import duty, so that *A* has no trade. Country *A* is devoting £50 of resources to the production of the commodity. Country *A* then forms a customs union with *B* and trade is *created* because it is cheaper for *A* to obtain the commodity from *B* than to produce it itself. There is a gain in so far as *A* is £10 better off. On the other hand, if Country *A*'s original import duty had been 50 per cent *ad* valorem, trade would then have taken place and with the rest of the world C as this would be the least-cost source to A. In this example, if A forms a customs union with B it will *switch* its trade because it can obtain the commodity for £40 from B compared with £30 + 50% = £45 from C. This trade diversion represents a move away from the optimum of RESOURCE ALLOCATION, because B is a higher real-cost source than C ($\Diamond$ SECOND BEST, THEORY OF). Whether, therefore, a customs union will yield overall gains from shifts in the location of production will depend on the superiority of trade creation to trade diversion. However, this type of analysis covers only a part of the problem; many other factors must be taken into account in assessing whether a customs union is beneficial. In particular, the removal of tariff barriers between countries will change the TERMS OF TRADE and therefore the relative volumes of the different commodities demanded, because of the price changes. It will shift the commodity pattern of trade as well as the geographical origins of the commodities traded. Whether a community will finish up better off therefore depends on the price and income elasticities of demand for the commodities traded ($\Diamond$ ELASTICITY). An added benefit may accrue because the increase in the size of markets may enable ECONOMIES OF SCALE to be made. Finally, a protective tariff is initially imposed because home costs are high; but home costs may remain high because a protective tariff is imposed. Removal of the tariff may induce more efficient operation and lower costs.

Cycle, trade. $\Diamond$ TRADE CYCLE.

Cyclical unemployment. Temporary UNEMPLOYMENT resulting from lack of aggregate demand in a downswing in the business cycle ($\Diamond$ TRADE CYCLE).

D

Dated securities. BONDS, BILLS OF EXCHANGE or other SECURITIES which have a stated date for redemption (repayment) of their nominal value. *Short-dated securities* are those for which the REDEMPTION DATE is near; *long-dated securities* are those for which it is a long time ahead.

Deadweight debt. A DEBT incurred to meet CURRENT EXPENDITURE, or which for any other reason is not covered by a real ASSET. Most of the NATIONAL DEBT is deadweight debt since it was incurred to finance war and other current PUBLIC EXPENDITURE.

Dear money. A period when interest rates are exceptionally high. A 'dear money policy' involves keeping interest rates up to restrict the MONEY SUPPLY. ⟡ MONETARY POLICY.

Death rate. The number of deaths occurring in any year for every 1,000 of the population is referred to as the crude death rate. It may be quoted for each sex and each age group. The rapid growth in U.K. population in the early nineteenth century is attributed more to the decline in the death rate than to an increase in BIRTH RATE. A similar effect is to be observed in the highly populated DEVELOPING COUNTRIES. The U.K. death rate of male children under five years of age was 57 in 1900, compared to 2·6 at the present time.

Debentures, debenture stock. Fixed-interest SECURITIES issued by limited companies in return for long-term LOANS. The former term is sometimes also used to refer to any title on a secured interest-bearing loan. Debentures are dated for redemption (i.e. repayment of their nominal value by the borrower to the holder) between ten to forty years ahead (⟡ REDEMPTION DATE) but occasionally may be irredeemable. Debentures are usually secured. There are two main types of secured debenture: (a) *mortgage debentures*, which are secured by a MORTGAGE on specific ASSETS of the company; and (b) *floating-charge debentures*, where its assets are not suitable for a fixed charge (⟡ FLOATING DEBENTURES). Debenture interest must be paid whether the company makes a PROFIT or not. In the event of non-payment, debenture holders can force LIQUIDATION and rank ahead of all shareholders in their claims on the company's assets. The interest which debentures bear depends partly on long-term RATES OF INTEREST prevailing at the time and partly on the type of debenture, but will in any case, because of the lower risk involved, be less than borne by PREFERENCE SHARES. Debenture shares are most appropriate for financing companies whose profits are stable and which have substantial fixed assets, such as property companies.

Convertible debentures carry an option at a fixed future date to convert the STOCK into ordinary SHARES at a fixed price. This option is compensated for by a lower rate of interest than an ordinary debenture, but convertible debentures are attractive since they offer the investor, without sacrificing his security, the prospect of purchasing EQUITY shares cheaply in the future. For this reason, convertible debentures are issued at times when it is difficult to raise CAPITAL either by equity or fixed-interest securities. ◊ NEW-ISSUE MARKET.

Debreu, Gérard (b. 1921). A graduate in mathematics at the University of Paris, Debreu joined the Cowles Commission in 1950. In 1960 he was appointed to the Chair of Economics and Mathematics at the University of California. His published works include *Existence of an Equilibrium for a Competitive Economy* (1954) with K. J. ARROW and *Theory of Value, an Axiomatic Analysis of Economic Equilibrium* (1959). Professor Debreu, who was awarded the NOBEL PRIZE in Economics in 1983, has applied the mathematical theory of sets and topology to economic analysis and advanced the study of the conditions under which markets attain EQUILIBRIUM.

Debt. A sum of MONEY or other property owed by one person or organization to another. Debt comes into being through the granting of CREDIT or through raising LOAN CAPITAL. *Debt servicing* consists of paying interest on a debt. Debt is an essential part of all modern, capitalist economies (◊ CAPITALISM). ◊ NATIONAL DEBT.

Debt conversion. ◊ CONVERSION.

Debt management. The process of administering debt, for example the NATIONAL DEBT, i.e. providing for the payment of INTEREST, and arranging the refinancing of maturing BONDS.

Debt ratio. ◊ GEARING.

Debtor. One who owes money to another. A firm's debtors, for example, are those to whom invoices have been sent for goods or services supplied and which remain unpaid. Antonym of CREDITOR.

Decentralized decision-taking. ◊ FREE-MARKET ECONOMY.

Decile. ◊ PERCENTILE.

Decimal coinage. A CURRENCY system in which the basic unit is divided into multiples of ten. The U.K. government set up a Committee of Inquiry on Decimal Currency (the Halesbury Committee) in 1961, to advise on the introduction of a decimal currency to replace the existing pounds, shillings and pence duodecimal system. The U.K. switched to a decimal currency based on the pound on 15 February 1971. The 5p and 10p coins were introduced in April 1968, the 50p in October 1969 and the rest in February 1971. The halfpenny was demonetized in August 1969, and the half-crown in January 1970. Other coins were demonetized within eighteen months of February 1971, with the exception of the old 6d. The latter remained legal tender at a value of 2½p until 1980. The new ½p was abolished in 1984.

Decreasing returns. ⟡ DISECONOMIES OF SCALE; RETURNS TO SCALE.

Deemed disposal. The assumed realization of an ASSET in the calculation of liability for CAPITAL GAINS taxation or ESTATE DUTY. Shares in a company, for example, might be valued and tax charged on the difference between that value and the price originally paid for them, even where the shares did not change hands.

Deep discounted bonds. BONDS which are issued at a price much lower than that at which they can be redeemed (⟡ REDEEMABLE SECURITIES) at the specified date. The intention is to provide large CAPITAL GAINS for the holders and the interest rate is correspondingly low. For higher-rate taxpayers less tax is payable on a gain than upon interest income; however, the 'capital gain' on deep discounted bonds is liable to be treated as income by the tax authorities.

Deferred rebate. A rebate or discount on a purchase which is accumulated for a specified period to encourage customers to remain with a particular supplier. Also called *aggregated rebate*. ⟡ MONOPOLIES COMMISSION.

Deferred shares. A SHARE issued where ORDINARY SHARES have a fixed DIVIDEND and which entitle the holders to all PROFITS after prior charges have been met. Now virtually unknown.

Deficit. An excess of LIABILITIES over ASSETS, or of an expenditure flow over an income flow, e.g. BUDGET deficit, BALANCE OF PAYMENTS deficit.

Deficit financing. A planned excess of expenditure over INCOME. Most governments now often spend more than they raise in taxation, the difference being financed by borrowing. The term is normally used in economics to refer to a planned budget deficit (⟡ BALANCED BUDGET) incurred in the interests of expanding AGGREGATE DEMAND by relaxing FISCAL POLICY and thus injecting purchasing power into the economy, a policy advocated by J. M. KEYNES to increase employment in the 1930s. ⟡ PUBLIC-SECTOR BORROWING REQUIREMENT; REFLATION.

Deflation. 1. A sustained reduction in the general level of prices. Deflation is often, though not inevitably, accompanied by declines in output and employment and is distinct from 'disinflation' which means a reduction in the rate of inflation. Deflation can be brought about by either internal or external forces in an OPEN ECONOMY. **2.** A deliberate policy of reducing AGGREGATE DEMAND and output so as to reduce prices and imports and lower the EXCHANGE RATE, thus improving export performance and the BALANCE OF PAYMENTS. Aggregate demand may be reduced by FISCAL POLICY (increasing taxes or reducing government expenditure) or MONETARY POLICY (increases in the RATE OF INTEREST and slower growth or contraction in the MONEY SUPPLY). **3.** In economic statistics, the adjustment of index numbers or economic aggregates to eliminate the effects of price changes, as in dividing an index of the GROSS DOMESTIC PRODUCT (G.D.P.) at CURRENT PRICES by a price index (⟡ INDEX NUMBER) to give an index of G.D.P. in REAL TERMS. In estimating changes in net output in real terms there are two alternative methods. One is to deflate the series of the value of net output at CURRENT PRICES by a single index of output prices, the other is to deflate separately the inputs by appropriate indices of the prices of materials, fuels etc., and to subtract the sum of these from the value of gross output deflated in the same way by indices of output prices. The second method is called *double deflation* which has the advantage of capturing changes in the ratio of net to gross outputs in real terms. This may be important where, for example, profit margins are being squeezed by faster increases in input than in output prices. To deflate net output directly by output prices in these circumstances would lead to an overstatement of the real rise in net output.

De-industrialization. A decline in the share of manufacturing in the NATIONAL INCOME. In the U.K. the contribution of manufacturing to the GROSS DOMESTIC PRODUCT fell from 29 per cent in 1975 to 25 per cent in 1985 and the real value of manufacturing output also actually declined over this period. Although a decline in the manufacturing ratio is common to most of the ADVANCED COUNTRIES, reflecting the growth of SERVICES, fears have been expressed that since manufactures constitute the bulk of exports, the process of decline could continue to the point where a large imbalance on VISIBLE TRADE could not be offset by the growth of INVISIBLE exports without a decline in REAL INCOME. However, it has been argued that the exceptional weakness in British manufacturing exports over the last decade reflects the strength of sterling buoyed up by the effects of North Sea oil and that now that oil production has peaked, the growth of manufacturing output since 1981 can be expected to continue.

Demand. The desire for a particular good or SERVICE supported by the possession of the necessary means of exchange to effect ownership. ⟡ DEMAND, THEORY OF; DEMAND CURVE; MARSHALL, A.; MONEY.

Demand, theory of. The area of economics concerned with the allocation of limited resources to different commodities in the purchasing decisions of rational consumers. Together with the THEORY OF THE FIRM (which is really a theory of supply), it forms the basis of MICROECONOMICS. There are several different approaches to consumer behaviour: the first is the cardinal UTILITY approach associated with ALFRED MARSHALL and other economists of the last century. This was superseded by INDIF-FERENCE-CURVE ANALYSIS (⟡ ORDINAL UTILITY), which dispensed with the need for an absolute measure of utility. A third approach, REVEALED PREFERENCE is largely a re-expression of indifference-curve analysis, in which no explicit notion of utility is used at all. All these approaches give rise to the same qualitative analysis of consumer behaviour and support the laws of demand and supply, such as that price rises lead to cuts in demand. (◊ DEMAND FUNCTION.)

Demand curve. The graphical representation of a schedule listing the quantities of a commodity a consumer would be willing to buy at various prices. The schedule is drawn up on   assumption that other economic factors remain the same between the consideration of one price and another. Such factors are income, prices of SUBSTITUTES or COMPLEMENTARY goods, consumer preferences or EXPECTATIONS. In most cases, the curve would slope downwards from eft to right, reflecting the fact that the higher the price of a commodity the lower the demand for it. However, the response of demand to a change in price (◊ ELASTICITY) will influence the slope and shape of the demand curve in specific cases. ◊ DEMAND, THEORY OF; EXCESS DEMAND; INCOME EFFECT; INDIFFERENCE-CURVE ANALYSIS; SUBSTITUTION EFFECT; SUPPLY CURVE.

Demand deposit (U.S.). Money on CURRENT ACCOUNT, i.e. a BANK DEPOSIT that can be withdrawn without notice.

Demand for labour. ◊ LABOUR, DEMAND FOR.

Demand function. A relationship which shows mathematically how the quantity demanded of a good or service responds to changes in a number of economic factors such as its own price, the prices of SUBSTITUTES and COMPLEMENTARY goods, income, credit terms, etc. The quantity demanded is the *dependent variable* and the other factors are *independent variables*. The effect of each *independent variable* on the *dependent variable* may be estimated statistically by TIME-SERIES ANALYSIS or CROSS-SECTION ANALYSIS of HOUSEHOLD expenditure data. ◊ DEMAND, THEORY OF; DEMAND CURVE; ELASTICITY.

Demand management. ◊ FISCAL POLICY.

Demand price. The price a consumer would be willing to pay for a specified quantity of a good or service (◊ DEMAND CURVE).

Demand-pull inflation. INFLATION induced by a persistence of an excess of aggregate DEMAND in the economy over aggregate SUPPLY. The balace of aggregate supply and demand does not reach EQUILIBRIUM because supply reaches a capacity limit at the FULL EMPLOYMENT level (◊ MARSHALL, A.; PRICE SYSTEM). The excess demand persists because there is a growth in the quantity of MONEY either through the creation of money by government to finance the budgetary gap between its expenditure and income or because the quantity of money is allowed to expand to accommodate the rise in prices. (◊ FRIEDMAN, M.; KEYNES, J. M.; QUANTITY THEORY OF MONEY.)

Demand schedule. A list showing the quantities of a good or service a consumer would be willing to buy at various prices. ⟡ DEMAND CURVE.

Demography. ⟡ POPULATION.

Dependent variable. A VARIABLE whose value is conditional on the value of another variable. For instance, if the amount of butter a person buys falls or rises as the price of butter rises or falls, the quantity of butter is a variable depending on the movements in the variable price. ⟡⟡ ECONOMETRICS; ENDOGENOUS VARIABLE; INDEPENDENT VARIABLE.

Depletion theory. The branch of economics concerned with the rate at which natural resources are consumed over time. For example, what determines the speed at which the world does (or ought to) use up its stock of oil? In general, economists view abstinence from using up a resource as a form of investment: by *not* using oil up now, we forgo some current consumption, and leave ourselves more to consume in the future, just as if we invest in machines today that will produce consumer goods tomorrow. People who own resources and keep them in the ground earn a return worth the increase in the price of the asset. If an oil company believes the price of oil will rise by 10 per cent over the next year, and the market rate of interest is 5 per cent, it will keep its oil in the ground. If the oil price is expected to rise by 5 per cent and the interest rate is 10 per cent, the oil company will do better by selling the oil now and investing the proceeds, earning 10 per cent. If all oil companies behave like this, they will push the oil price down by supplying so much that it will quickly become expected that the price *will* rise by 10 per cent over the next year.

Thus the fundamental principle of depletion theory is that consumption should occur at a rate which ensures that profits to be made from not depleting stocks of the resource are equal to those on other forms of investment. In reality, extraction costs and many other factors throw into question whether the principle explains either how quickly stocks of resources do get depleted, or how quickly they ought to.

Deposit. Money placed in an account at a bank and constituting a claim on the bank. The term 'bank deposit' includes deposits on all types of account, including CURRENT ACCOUNTS. ⟡⟡ BANKING.

Deposit account. A bank account in which DEPOSITS earn INTEREST, and withdrawals from which require notice. In the U.K. the COMMERCIAL BANKS formally require seven days' notice of withdrawal, although this is often waived. Until 1971, interest was paid by the bank at a rate fixed by agreement between the clearing banks and normally 2 per cent below BANK RATE. Since that date, banks have been obliged to fix their rates individually. Deposit accounts are called *time deposits* in the U.S. and *savings accounts* in France and other European countries. ⟡⟡ BANKING.

Deposit bank. ⟡ COMMERCIAL BANK.

Depreciation. 1. The reduction in VALUE of an ASSET through wear and tear. An allowance for the depreciation on a company's assets is always made before the calculation of PROFIT, on the grounds that the consumption of CAPITAL assets is one of the costs of earning the revenues of the business and is allowed as such, according to special rules, by the tax authorities. Since depreciation can only be accurately measured at the end of the life of an asset (i.e. EX POST), depreciation provisions in company accounts require an estimate of both the total amount of depreciation and the asset life. Annual depreciation provisions are normally calculated according to two methods: (a) the 'straight-line method', where the estimated residual (e.g. scrap) value of an asset is deducted from its original cost and the balance divided by the number of years of estimated life to arrive at an annual depreciation expense to set against revenue; and (b) the 'reducing-balance method'. In this case the actual depreciation expense is set at a constant proportion of the cost of the asset, i.e. a diminishing annual absolute amount. There are other methods of calculating depreciation and also of dealing with the fact that, in periods of rising prices, the replacement cost of an asset may be very much greater than its original cost. This latter problem is dealt with by revaluing assets at intervals, or even annually, using special capital cost indices and adjusting depreciation charges accordingly. This is called *replacement-cost depreciation* as opposed to *historic-cost depreciation* (⟡ INFLATION ACCOUNTING; COSTS, HISTORICAL) when the original cost of purchase is retained throughout the period. It should be noted that OBSOLESCENCE is distinct from depreciation, in that the former is an unforeseen change in the value of an asset for technological or economic reasons. If an asset becomes obsolescent its undepreciated value is usually written off (depreciated) completely in the year of replacement. In some cases the life of an asset may be very difficult to determine because it is specific to the production of a product the demand for which is subject to rapid changes in taste or fashion, i.e. there is a high risk of product obsolescence. In these cases the life of the asset is written off over a very short period. The purpose of depreciation provisions in accounting is to ensure that the cost of the flow of services provided by capital assets is met in the price of the company's products; it is not to build up funds for the replacement of these assets to be available at a certain date. In practice, depreciation provisions are treated as part of the net CASH FLOW of a business and are used to repay LOANS, to purchase other fixed assets or to invest in other businesses; that is, they are put to the use that will give the highest possible return. Much confusion is caused by this point, since what happens to depreciation provisions – which are, in effect, transfers of funds from fixed assets to current assets and sometimes back again – is not often clear from the BALANCE SHEET. ⟡ AMORTIZATION.

Depreciation is accepted for tax purposes as a charge against profits, but this depreciation has to be calculated according to certain rules and does not necessarily bear any relation to the depreciation actually charged by the business in its accounts. ⟨⟩ CAPITAL ALLOWANCES.
2. A reduction in the value of a CURRENCY in terms of gold or other currencies under FREE MARKET conditions and coming about through a decline in the DEMAND for that currency in relation to the SUPPLY. Corresponds to DEVALUATION under a fixed-parity system. ⟨⟩ CURRENCY DEPRECIATION.

Depreciation at choice. ⟨⟩ CAPITAL ALLOWANCES.

Depressed areas. ⟨⟩ DEVELOPMENT AREAS.

Depression. A business cycle (⟨⟩ TRADE CYCLE) in which there is UNEMPLOYMENT. Only the period 1929–33 in the United Kingdom is usually referred to as a depression. ⟨⟩ RECESSION.

Deregulation. ⟨⟩ REGULATION.

Derived demand. The demand for a FACTOR OF PRODUCTION where the demand for the factor is derived indirectly from the demand for the finished product to which the factor has contributed in production. (⟨⟩ LABOUR, DEMAND FOR.)

Devaluation. The reduction of the official rate at which one CURRENCY is exchanged for another (⟨⟩ DEPRECIATION). Under the original articles of the INTERNATIONAL MONETARY FUND, its member countries agreed to the stabilization of their EXCHANGE RATES in terms of the dollar and gold. Fluctuations about the agreed par rate of ± 1 per cent (widened to ± 2·25 per cent in December 1971) were permissible, but changes in the par rate itself had to be agreed by the I.M.F. and made only in the face of serious BALANCE OF PAYMENTS problems. The system of fixed parities was abandoned in the U.K. in June 1972 (⟨⟩ EUROPEAN MONETARY SYSTEM). Governments regarded devaluation as a means of correcting a balance-of-payments deficit only as a measure of last resort. They predominantly relied on DEFLATION of the home market and international borrowing. Devaluation or depreciation of the exchange rate can correct a balance-of-payments deficit because it lowers the price of EXPORTS in terms of foreign currencies and raises the price of IMPORTS on the home market. This does not necessarily succeed in its purpose. The immediate effect is similar to an unfavourable change in the TERMS OF TRADE (⟨⟩ J-CURVE). For the same resources devoted to the production of exports, less foreign exchange is earned with which to pay for imports. If the level of imports remained the same, more output would have to be diverted to exports and away from home consumption and INVESTMENT simply to maintain the status quo. Devaluation or depreciation could lead to a loss of REAL INCOME without any benefit to the balance of payments. The implicit expectation in a controlled devaluation therefore is that the price ELAS-

TICITIES of demand and supply are such that the 'terms of trade' effect is more than offset by shifts of both foreign and domestic demand in favour of home production (◊ MARSHALL–LERNER CRITERION). If, therefore, the home economy is at the time of devaluation in a position of FULL EMPLOYMENT, additional governmental action is required to create the spare capacity needed to meet the increased demand on home production. Unless this is carried out the excess demand will generate INFLATION and possibly renewed deficits in the balance of payments.

Developing country. A country that has not yet reached the stage of ECONOMIC DEVELOPMENT characterized by the growth of industrialization, nor a level of NATIONAL INCOME sufficient to yield the domestic SAVINGS required to finance the INVESTMENT necessary for further growth (◊ ROSTOW, W. W.). The attempt by developing countries to obtain significant increases in their REAL INCOMES has been frustrated by the deterioration in their TERMS OF TRADE and the rapid expansion of their populations. Their trend growth of exports has been only about one half that of world trade as a whole, and this has been further reduced in real terms by the fall in their terms of trade. Developing countries are primary producers, so their economies are vulnerable to movements in commodity prices. Since 1980 the average price of foodstuffs has fallen by 15 per cent per year. Many ideas have been put forward to assist these countries bridge the gap between themselves and the developed countries (◊ UNITED NATIONS CONFERENCE ON TRADE AND DEVELOPMENT). Agreement was reached in 1979 to set up a common fund through U.N.C.T.A.D. to finance INTERNATIONAL COMMODITY AGREEMENTS for the stabilization of the markets in primary products. ◊ ASIAN DEVELOPMENT BANK; ASSOCIATION OF SOUTH EAST ASIAN NATIONS; COLOMBO PLAN FOR COOPERATIVE ECONOMIC AND SOCIAL DEVELOPMENT IN ASIA AND THE PACIFIC; GENERAL AGREEMENT ON TARIFFS AND TRADE; LEAST-DEVELOPED COUNTRY; WORLD BANK.

Development areas. Regions in Great Britain which attract government assistance because of their persistent high levels of unemployment relative to the rest of the country (Northern Ireland has its own forms of financial aid). First introduced in the 1930s, they were substantially extended following the recommendations made by the Hunt Committee in 1969. There are three categories: Special Development Area, Development Area and Intermediate Area. The forms of assistance include cash grants for investment, favourable tax allowances, training allowances, removal expenses and factories constructed by the government and leased on favourable terms (◊ INVESTMENT INCENTIVES). The INDUSTRY ACT of 1972 introduced regional development grants which are made not only to firms establishing themselves in the region and directly generating new employment, as was the case previously under the Local Employment Acts, but also to existing firms investing in new plant and equipment for modernization. The Act also enables the government to give assistance to selected firms in the forms of loans or subsidies for interest payments. The government can also use the negative instrument of the Industrial Development Certificate (I.D.C.). Since 1948 such certificates have been required for any new factory building over a certain maximum square footage in any region except Special Development Areas and Development Areas. Since the accession of the U.K. to the EUROPEAN ECONOMIC COMMUNITY in 1973, projects which stimulate employment in the assisted areas attract a grant of up to 30 per cent of the capital cost from the European Regional Development Fund. Development Areas covered about 40 per cent of Britain's working population up to 1982, although revisions of their coverage announced in that year aimed to reduce this to below 30 per cent. ⟡ ENTERPRISE ZONES; FREE-TRADE ZONES.

Differentiation, product. Distinguishing essentially the same products from one another by real or illusory means, as in petrol, washing-powder, cigarettes. The significance of product differentiation in economic theory is that by relaxing the assumption of product homogeneity under PERFECT COMPETITION, each supplier may create an opportunity to depart from the market price, charge a premium for his product and make greater PROFITS. Under perfect competition this supplier would sell nothing if he raised the price above market levels (he faces a horizontal DEMAND CURVE); with product differentiation he may be able to build up some loyalty from his customers (and introduce a downward slope to the demand curve, which is a characteristic of MONOPOLISTIC COMPETITION). The means by which suppliers differentiate their products may involve improved product performance and INNOVATION, for example, radial-ply tyres which though more expensive initially than conventional tyres have a longer life, or they may be restricted to ADVERTISING and packaging. In the latter case, the contribution of product differentiation to consumer satisfaction is more doubtful, though it has been argued that it may allow the exploitation of ECONOMIES OF SCALE (or the opposite) through creating a proliferation of brands. Under OLIGOPOLY product differentiation through real innovation may be avoided if it involves excessive risk of non-acceptance by consumers, especially in industries with long product lead-times, for example the motor industry.

Diminishing marginal product. ⟡ DIMINISHING RETURNS, LAW OF.

Diminishing marginal utility. The psychological law that as extra units of a commodity are consumed by an individual, the satisfaction gained from each unit will fall. For example, although for every extra Mars bar someone eats they derive extra pleasure, the more Mars that are eaten, the less the pleasure gained from each incremental one. Eventually, as sickness strikes, subsequently consumed Mars bars will yield disutility.

The approach to consumer theory which uses the notion of diminishing marginal utility is flawed, as there is no single unit or scale by which the utility derived from a wide range of items can be measured (⟡ ORDINAL UTILITY). Nevertheless, the concept remains relevant to many issues, especially when applied to consumption in general. For example, it provides a case against a POLL TAX which, it shows, cuts the utility of the poor (who treasure their every possession) more than the rich (who hardly notice small losses). It also explains why people may like to avoid risk: the utility lost from a £100 cut in income is greater than the utility gained by a £100 increase in income and, consequently, most consumers would reject a fair bet in which they were faced with a 50 per cent chance of either, despite the fact that on average they would lose nothing in cash terms. (⟡ MARGINAL UTILITY; RISK AVERSION.)

Diminishing returns, law of. A law that states that as extra units of one FACTOR OF PRODUCTION are employed, with all others held constant, the output generated by each additional unit will eventually fall. In effect, that the MARGINAL PRODUCT of factors declines when they are employed in increasing quantities. For example, a farm owner with one field might find that one man could produce two tons of grain; two men five tons of grain – more than twice as much; but three men only seven tons of grain. The extra production gained from adding a worker started at two, rose to three, then fell back to two.

Diminishing returns should not be confused with negative returns – successively adding workers to a factory can increase its total output but at a falling rate; only when the factory becomes very overcrowded would the presence of an extra worker actually cause production to fall. (⟡ DISECONOMIES OF SCALE; RETURNS TO SCALE; SHORT-RUN COST CURVES; TURGOT, A. R. J.)

Direct costs. ⟡ VARIABLE COSTS.

Direct investment. INVESTMENT in the foreign operations of a company. Direct investment implies control and managerial and perhaps technical input and is generally preferred by the host country to PORTFOLIO investment. ⟡ FOREIGN INVESTMENT; MULTINATIONAL CORPORATION (M.N.C., M.N.E.).

Direct taxation. TAXATION on the income and resources of individuals or organizations. In general, direct taxation (INCOME TAX, CORPORATION TAX, CAPITAL TRANSFER TAX, NATIONAL INSURANCE contributions) is levied on WEALTH or INCOME and is in contrast to *indirect taxation* (VALUE-ADDED TAX, EXCISE DUTIES, betting duties, vehicle-licence duties, STAMP DUTY) which is levied on expenditure. Taxes on income, capital and social-security contributions accounted for almost 58 per cent of U.K. general government (⟡ PUBLIC SECTOR) taxation in 1985 compared with 63·5 per cent a decade earlier. It has been argued that this shift in favour of indirect taxation will improve incentives for higher earnings and capital accumulation; however, an indirect tax may be a REGRESSIVE TAX and may distort RESOURCE ALLOCATION. The categorization of direct and indirect taxation is not as precise as it may appear because it tells us nothing about the INCIDENCE OF TAXATION. ◊ EXPENDITURE TAX; FISCAL NEU-TRALITY; MARGINAL TAX RATE.

Dirty float. ◊ MANAGED CURRENCY.

Disclosure requirements. ◊ PRIVATE COMPANY.

Discount. Generally meaning a deduction from FACE VALUE, i.e. the opposite of PREMIUM. Discount has a number of specific applications in economics and commerce: (a) A *discount for cash* is a percentage deductible from an invoice as an incentive for the debtor to pay within a defined period. (b) A deduction from the retail price of a GOOD allowed to a wholesaler, retailer or other agent. (c) A charge made for cashing a BILL OF EXCHANGE or other promissory note before its maturity date (◊ DISCOUNT HOUSE; FACTOR). (d) The difference, where negative, between the present price of a SECURITY and its issue price. ◊◊ DIS-COUNTED CASH FLOW.

Discount house. 1. An institution in the London DISCOUNT MARKET that purchases promissory notes and resells them or holds them until maturity. Essentially a BILL BROKER. The discount houses finance their purchases of securities mainly by borrowing at short term from banks and other financial institutions. These borrowings are secured against their holdings of securities. There are nine members of the London Discount Market Association, all independent public companies, and a number of smaller, more specialized firms engaged in the same business. **2.** A 'cut-price' retail store selling goods at a DIS-COUNT.

Discount market. The market dealing in TREASURY BILLS, BILLS OF EXCHANGE and short-dated BONDS and consisting of the BANK-ING system, the ACCEPTING HOUSES and the DISCOUNT HOUSES. Although the existence of discount houses as such is unique to the City of London, a MONEY MARKET of some kind is a feature of all financial centres. The discount houses originally dealt mainly in bills of exchange accepted by the MERCHANT BANKS, but over half of their assets now consist of government (including local government) securities, and they also hold negotiable CERTIFICATES OF DEPOSIT. The discount houses purchase these securities from the government and the PRIVATE SECTOR with MONEY borrowed from the banking system, including overseas banks in London, and to a lesser extent from industrial and commercial companies, supplemented by their own CAPITAL. Their profit is made by borrowing at very short-term (normally twenty-four-hour call-loans) and lending by DISCOUNTING securities at slightly higher RATES OF INTEREST. In this way the discount houses take up the surplus LIQUIDITY of the banking system and lend it to the government and those isssuing bills of exchange. The discount houses retain some bills to maturity; others are sold to the banking system as they near maturity. The discount houses perform a useful function in providing a flexible and smooth MARKET in short-term securities, and also play an important part in the mechanism by which the authorities exert control over the monetary system. The ability of the discount houses to borrow short and lend long depends on their knowledge that they can borrow from the BANK OF ENGLAND at any time (◊ LENDER OF LAST RESORT). This borrowing, which arises when the COM-MERCIAL BANKS and overseas banks call in their loans, comes about through the bank discounting ELIGIBLE PAPER for the discount houses, in which circumstances the market is said to be 'in the bank'. There is an understanding that the discount houses will always take up the treasury bill weekly tender, although since the new policy of CREDIT CONTROL they no longer do so by a 'syndicated bid' at a uniform price. The rate at which their bids are made naturally reflects and influences the level of all short-term interest rates, which, therefore, the TREASURY authorities push up or down by varying the amount of the tender.

Discount rate. ◊ BANK RATE; DISCOUNTING.

Discounted cash flow (d.c.f.). A method of appraising INVESTMENTS based on the idea that the VALUE to an individual or firm of a specific sum of MONEY depends on precisely when it is to be received. Given the existence of INTEREST rates and the possibilities of borrowing and lending, it is always better to receive money earlier rather than later and to pay money later rather than earlier. For example, if the current annual interest rate is 10 per cent and I have £100 today, that could be worth £110 in one year's time, £121 in two years' time, £133·10 in three years' time, and so on. It follows that if I am to receive £110 in one year's time, that is worth only £100 held today, since that is the amount which would grow to £110 in one year's time if I invested it at 10 per cent today. Since the value of a sum of money depends on when it is received, it follows that, in appraising investments, which typically yield PROFITS over future time, we cannot simply add up the profits accruing at different points in time. It is necessary first to correct for the 'time-value' of money, and this is done by DISCOUNTING, i.e. dividing by a suitable factor to find what the present worth or PRESENT VALUE of a future sum really is. The result of this procedure will then be a dis-counted CASH FLOW on the basis of which the true profitability of the investment can be assessed. There are several specific procedures based on the idea of discounted cash flow (◊ INTERNAL RATE OF RETURN).

Discounting. 1. The application of a discount or RATE OF INTEREST to a CAPITAL sum or title to such a sum. Calculations of PRESENT VALUE or the price of a bill before maturity are made by discounting at the current appropriate rate of interest. **2.** The future effects of an anticipated decline or increase in PROFITS or some other event on SECURITY prices, commodity prices, or EXCHANGE RATES, is said to be discounted if buying or selling leads to an adjustment of present prices in line with expected future changes in these prices. **3.** (U.S.) The pledging of accounts receivable, i.e. sums owed by debtors, as COLLATERAL SECURITY against a LOAN. ⟡ DISCOUNT.

Discriminating duty. An import duty (⟡ TARIFFS) imposed at a level different from other comparable import duties such as to favour (or discourage) the importation of a particular commodity or imports from a particular country of origin. ⟡ CUSTOMS UNION; GENERAL AGREEMENT ON TARIFFS AND TRADE; MOST-FAVOURED NATION CLAUSE.

Diseconomies of scale. Increase in long-run AVERAGE COSTS which may set in as the scale of production increases. Although the unit cost of production may fall as plant size increases (⟡ ECONOMIES OF SCALE), there are several reasons why this process is eventually reversed:

(a) The different processes within a plant will probably not have the same OPTIMUM scale. For example, a car-body press might be at its most efficient at 150,000 units a year, while an engine transfer machining line may be optimal at 100,000 units a year. When 150,000 cars are produced it will be necessary either to have a sub-optimal engine line with a capacity of 50,000 in addition or to run a second line at 50 per cent capacity.

(b) As firm size increases, problems of administration and coordination increase and there is a growth of BUREAUCRACY.

(c) If output for a national or international market is concentrated at one large plant in a single location, transport costs of raw materials and finished goods to and from distant markets may offset scale economies of production at the large plant.

These are *internal diseconomies. External diseconomies* may arise through traffic congestion or pollution, for example (⟡ EXTERNALITIES). Diseconomies of scale are not to be confused with diminishing returns. ⟡ DIMINISHING RETURNS, LAW OF.

Disequilibrium. A state in which the forces influencing a SYSTEM are not in balance and there is a tendency for one or more VARIABLES in the system to change. The operation of some mechanism or process is central to the concept of disequilibrium, as it is this that drives the system variables to move. The direction of movement caused by a process in most applications is towards a state of equilibrium, but this need not be the case. The COBWEB MODEL provides an example of a mechanism that can take either form. ($\Diamond$ DYNAMICS; EQUILIBRIUM; STABILITY ANALYSIS.)

Disguised unemployment. A situation where more people are available for work than is shown in the UNEMPLOYMENT statistics. Married women, some students or prematurely retired persons may register for work only if they believe opportunities are available to them. Also referred to as *concealed unemployment* and the 'discouraged worker effect'. Disguised unemployment will be revealed in an unusually low PARTICI-PATION RATE. In some countries, for example the U.S.A., unemployment is measured by surveys rather than numbers registered as available for work (unemployed) as in the U.K. and this term is less relevant.

Dishoarding. The reduction of stocks of goods or money previously accumulated by HOARDING.

Disinflation. The reduction or elimination of INFLATION. $\Diamond$ DEFLATION.

Disintermediation. Flows of funds between borrowers and lenders avoiding the direct use of FINANCIAL INTERMEDIARIES. Companies, for example, may lend surplus funds to each other without the use of the banking system or may issue bills guaranteed (accepted) by the banks but sold to non-banks. Disintermediation may make it more difficult to measure and control the MONEY SUPPLY since the authorities' measures to do so are focused upon financial intermediaries which can avoid controls based upon deposits by lending through PARALLEL MONEY MARKETS ($\Diamond$ SPECIAL DEPOSITS). The use of financial intermediaries for lending and borrowing activities previously carried out outside them, i.e. the opposite of disintermediation, is called *re-intermediation*.

Disinvestment. Negative investment which occurs where part of the capital stock is destroyed or where gross INVESTMENT is less than CAPITAL CONSUMPTION, i.e. capital equipment is not replaced as it wears out. Antonym for investment. $\Diamond$ DIVESTMENT.

Disposable income. Total INCOME of HOUSEHOLDS less INCOME TAX and employee NATIONAL INSURANCE contributions.

Dissaving. Negative SAVING, i.e. CONSUMPTION in excess of INCOME. Dissaving is financed either by the running down of ASSETS or by borrowing, and results in a reduction in *net worth* ($\Diamond$ BALANCE SHEET; $\Diamond$ PUBLIC-SECTOR FINANCIAL DEFICIT).

Distribution, theory of. Explanation of the determination of the INCOMES of the FACTORS OF PRODUCTION. The theory of distribution is actually part of the more comprehensive theory of production and distribution ($\Diamond$ PRODUCTION, THEORY OF), since in their determination output and factor prices are interdependent. It is one of the oldest branches of economic theory ($\Diamond$ MARX, K.; RICARDO, D.) and is still dominated by the basic theoretical structure of NEO-CLASSICAL

ECONOMICS. Under this theory, the incomes of LAND, LABOUR and CAPITAL are determined by the SUPPLY and DEMAND for them, which in turn is a DERIVED DEMAND for COMMODITIES. In the market for the factors of production, the owners of the factors will seek to maximize their incomes and the purchasers (firms) will seek to maximize their PROFIT from the use of the factors in the production process. Firms will adjust their output and their employment of each factor to the point where the MARGINAL COST and MARGINAL REVENUE of each additional unit of the factor are equal. This EQUILIBRIUM QUANTITY and EQUILIBRIUM PRICE will be determined by supply and demand. For instance, shortages of computer programmers will tend to push up their incomes. On the other hand, if there are more programmers than jobs, their wages will fall. The theory does not state, it should be noted, that a computer programmer will receive his marginal product (the amount he personally adds to his employer's revenue) but the increase in output that would arise from the employment of one additional programmer if inputs of all other factors of production were held constant. Profit maximization and competition between them should, in theory, ensure that factor incomes equate to their marginal products. ◊ MARGINAL PRODUCTIVITY THEORY OF WAGES. This is how the first part of the theory explains the reward to the factors of production.

The second part of the theory describes the share of total output accruing to different groups, for example the amount going to workers equals the wage rate multiplied by the number of workers employed. When the number of workers increases, the MARGINAL PRODUC-TIVITY of labour is assumed to fall and the wage level will fall, but as the total number of workers has risen, the share of output going to labour may *not* fall.

The third part of the theory holds that with total output divided up in this way between the different groups, there will be nothing short and nothing over. This is, in fact, true in conditions of perfect competition with constant returns to scale or zero profits. ◊ BARGAINING THEORY OF WAGES; EULER, L.

For these reasons, alternative theories to replace each part of the traditional account have been developed. On the first part, wage bargaining is viewed as occurring outside perfectly competitive markets with collective bargaining by trade unions. On the second part, shares of national income have been explained in terms of the distribution necessary to maintain BALANCED GROWTH in a macroeconomic approach associated with N. KALDOR. On the third part, the existence of monopoly profits suggests that some portion of total output does not accrue to workers, investors or property owners, but to those fortunate enough to be in monopoly industries. ◊◊ COBB–DOUGLAS FUNCTION.

Disutility. Negative UTILITY. An economic good may generate disadvantages as well as advantages. For instance, a new motorway may cause distress to adjacent householders because of noise and pollution. ($\diamondsuit$ EX-TERNALITIES.)

Diversification. 1. Extending the range of goods and services in a firm or geographic region. The motives for diversification will include declining profitability or growth in traditional markets, surplus capital or management resources and a desire to spread risks and reduce dependence upon cyclical activities. Diversification appears to be growing among U.K. enterprises and accounts for a significant proportion of the growth of MULTINATIONAL CORPORATIONS. The means of diversification are either internal growth or MERGER. By definition a CONGLOMER-ATE is a diversified firm. **2.** The holding of shares in a range of firms in a PORTFOLIO in order to spread the risk. $\diamondsuit$ CAPITAL ASSET PRICING MODEL; PORTFOLIO THEORY; RISK.

Divestment. The liquidation or sale of parts of a firm. Divestment is, in effect, the opposite of acquisition or MERGER.

Dividend. The amount of a company's PROFITS that the board of directors decides to distribute to ordinary shareholders. It is usually expressed either as a percentage of the NOMINAL VALUE of the ORDINARY SHARE capital, or as an absolute amount per SHARE. For example, if a company has an issued CAPITAL of £100,000 in 400,000 25p ordinary shares and the directors decide to distribute £10,000, then they would declare a dividend of 10 per cent or 2½p per share. A dividend is only the same as a YIELD if the shares stand at their nominal value. Some shareholders may not have bought their shares at PAR VALUE and might have paid, say, 50p each for them, in which case the yield would not be 10 but 5 per cent.

Dividends are declared at general meetings of the shareholders. Interim dividends are part payments of the annual dividend made during the year. Dividends are paid out of profits for the current year, or if profits are inadequate but the directors consider that a dividend is justified, out of reserves from profits of previous years. The profits after tax from which dividends are paid are those after payments to holders of PREFER-ENCE SHARES and DEBENTURES have been allowed for, the balance being split between dividends and reserves. Dividends are paid to shareholders after deduction of INCOME TAX at the standard rate, COR-PORATION TAX where applicable having already been paid out by the company.

Cooperative Society dividends are distributed in proportion to the value of purchases of its members, e.g. a credit is paid for every pound's worth of purchases by each member. $\diamondsuit$ CUM DIVIDEND; EX-DIVIDEND.

Dividend cover. The number of times the net PROFITS available for distribution exceed the DIVIDEND actually paid or declared. For example, if a company's net profits are £100,000 and the dividend was £5,000, then the dividend cover would be 20.

Dividend limitation. During the incomes policy in Britain (◊ PRICES AND INCOMES POLICY), and at other times when wages have been 'frozen' in the interests of controlling INFLATION, the government also imposed a DIVIDEND limitation. In 1969, total ordinary dividends in respect of company account years were limited to not more than $3\frac{1}{2}$ per cent above the amount declared for the previous year.

Dividend warrant. The CHEQUE by which companies pay DIVIDENDS to shareholders.

Dividend yield. ◊ YIELD.

Division of labour. The allocation of labour such that each worker specializes in one or a few functions in the production process. A. SMITH illustrated the principle in the different stages of pin-making: drawing the wire, cutting, head-fitting, sharpening. The division improved labour productivity (a) by the more efficient acquiring of specialist skills and (b) through the saving of time because workers did not have to move from one operation to another. Through the division of labour ECONOMIES OF SCALE could be achieved. The exchange economy was essential to its operation. Each worker could so specialize as long as he was assured that he could exchange his product for others to satisfy his needs. The principle applies to firms and countries also: similar benefits may be achieved by the specialization in those activities in which the firm or country has a COMPARATIVE ADVANTAGE (◊◊ RICARDO, D.).

Dollar certificate of deposit. ◊ EUROCURRENCY.

Domar, Evsey David (b. 1914). ◊ HARROD–DOMAR MODEL.

Domestic bill of exchange. ◊ INLAND BILL OF EXCHANGE.

Domestic credit expansion (D.C.E.). A measure of monetary growth that allows for changes in the BALANCE OF PAYMENTS. It is equal to the PUBLIC-SECTOR BORROWING REQUIREMENT minus public-sector borrowing from the domestic non-bank private sector plus the increase in bank lending to the private sector in domestic currency at home and overseas. The significance of the D.C.E., a measure favoured by the INTERNATIONAL MONETARY FUND, is that it nets out changes in the MONEY SUPPLY created by overseas capital flows on capital and current account of the balance of payments. ◊ MONETARY POLICY.

Double deflation. ◊ DEFLATION.

Double-entry bookkeeping. The accounting system in which every business transaction, whether a receipt or a payment of MONEY, sale or purchase of GOODS or SERVICES, gives rise to two entries, a DEBIT and a corresponding credit, traditionally on opposite pages of a ledger. The credit entries record the sources of finance, e.g. shareholders' CAPITAL, funds acquired from third parties or generated through current operations; the debit entries record the use to which that finance is put, e.g. acquisition of fixed ASSETS, STOCKS, financing of debtors and current operating expenses, etc. Since every debit entry has an equal and corresponding credit entry, it follows that if the debit and credit entries are added up they will (or should) come to the same figure, i.e. balance (◊ BALANCE SHEET). Confusion is caused by identifying credits and debits with gains or losses. While this is basically true in the very long run, the profit or loss over a short period of time is measured by selecting from ledger balances items of income and expenditure which are then used to produce a *profit-and-loss account* (U.S. *income and earned surplus statement*). ◊ BUSINESS FINANCE.

Double option. ◊ OPTION.

Double taxation. The situation in which the same TAX BASE is taxed more than once. Double-taxation agreements between two countries are designed to avoid, for example, INCOMES of non-residents being taxed both in the country they are living in and in their country of origin.

Dow–Jones industrial average. A daily index (◊ INDEX NUMBER) of prices on the principal STOCK EXCHANGE in New York. It is an AVERAGE of the prices of thirty industrial stocks accounting for about 25 per cent of the market CAPITALIZATION of the shares quoted on the New York Stock Exchange and is calculated and published every day the exchange is open. In its present form the index dates from 1928. The Dow–Jones index stood at the record level of 2,002·25 on 8 January 1987.

Drawback. ◊ CUSTOMS DRAWBACK.

Dumping. Strictly, the sale of a COMMODITY on a foreign MARKET at a PRICE below MARGINAL COST. An exporting country may support the short-run losses of this policy in order to eliminate competition and thereby gain a MONOPOLY in the foreign market. Alternatively, it may dump in order to dispose of temporary surpluses in order to avoid a reduction in home prices and therefore producers' INCOMES. The GENERAL AGREEMENT ON TARIFFS AND TRADE approves the imposition of special import duties (◊ TARIFFS) to counteract such a policy if it can be established that dumping is taking place. The practice of dumping is prohibited under the terms of the EUROPEAN ECONOMIC COMMUNITY Treaty of Rome. Note that export prices which are lower than home market prices are not conclusive evidence of the existence of dumping. Rules to be followed by governments were agreed as part of the KENNEDY ROUND OF TRADE NEGOTIATIONS by the E.E.C., North America and the EUROPEAN FREE TRADE ASSOCIATION. Market economies are more open to the making of comparisons of the prices and input costs of products in different markets in order to judge whether dumping is taking place. In regard to exports from the COMECON countries, the E.E.C. compares the price of the product exported with that produced in a free-market non-E.E.C. country in order to decide whether the product is being dumped. If such a free-market price cannot be found, the E.E.C. judges a fair price on the basis of its own calculations of the costs of production. ◊ FREE TRADE; PROTECTION; RECIPROCITY.

Duopoly. Two sellers only of a good or service in a market. A feature of this situation is that any decision by one seller, such as the raising or lowering of his price, will stimulate a response from the other which, in turn, will affect the market response to the first seller's initial decision. Depending on assumptions made about the market and each seller's responses, price EQUILIBRIUM may exist at any point between that of a MONOPOLIST and that of PERFECT COMPETITION (◊ COURNOT, A. A.).

Duopsony. Two buyers only of a good or service in a market.

Dupuit, Arsène Jules Étienne Juvénal (1804–66). A French civil engineer, whose main works relating to economics were *De la mesure de l'utilité des travaux publics* (1844) and *De l'influence des péages sur l'utilité des voies de communication* (1849). His studies of the pricing policy for public SERVICES such as roads and bridges led him to the ideas of CONSUMER SURPLUS and PRODUCER'S SURPLUS. These terms were, in fact, invented by MARSHALL, but the ideas were clearly brought out by Dupuit. He realized that the prices were not the maximum users would be willing to pay for services, except those users at the very margin who found it just worth while to pay. Consumers, therefore, benefited by the difference. Similarly, the producer selling the service obtains a surplus in so far as his fixed charge is related to his cost at the margin (◊ MARGINAL COST) and this is greater than his AVERAGE COST. These concepts were refined by Marshall.

Durable goods. Consumer goods like washing-machines, motor-cars and TV sets, which yield SERVICES or UTILITY over time rather than being completely used up at the moment of CONSUMPTION. Most consumer goods are in fact durable to some degree, and the term is often used in a more restricted sense to denote relatively expensive, technologically sophisticated goods – 'consumer durables' – such as the examples given above. The significance of the durability of these goods is that the conventional apparatus of demand analysis must be supplemented by the modes of analysis developed in CAPITAL THEORY. ◊ DEMAND, THEORY OF.

Dynamic peg. ◊ EXCHANGE RATE.

Dynamics. Analysis which aims to trace and study the behaviour of variables through time, and determine whether these variables tend to move towards EQUILIBRIUM. Although the word 'dynamic' is used rather loosely, it safely describes any analysis which gives an account of the process by which equilibrium is achieved, or disequilibrium sustained. An example of dynamic analysis is the COBWEB MODEL, which traces the path of demand and supply in a market where lags in the response of supply to price occur. This contrasts with static analysis of markets where snapshots of the equilibrium positions are held to describe all that needs to be understood about the workings of such markets. (⟡ COMPARATIVE STATIC EQUILIBRIUM ANALYSIS.)

E

Earned income. EARNINGS such as salary or wages, income of working partners or proprietors and certain pensions and social-security benefits which are treated as earned income for tax purposes. Earned income used to be taxed on a more favourable basis than 'unearned income', which includes dividends, interest and other investment income. ⋄ INCOME TAX.

Earnings. 1. The return for human effort, as in the earnings of LABOUR and the earnings of management. In labour economics, wage earnings are distinguished from wage rates; the former include overtime, the latter relate only to earnings per hour or standard working week. Earnings may be quoted as pre- or post-tax (gross or net) and other deductions and in REAL TERMS or money terms. **2.** The INCOME of a business, part of which may be retained in the business and part distributed to the shareholders (⋄ RETAINED EARNINGS). Earnings per SHARE (post-tax), which is a measure of the total return earned by a company on its ORDINARY SHARE capital, are calculated by taking gross income after DEPRECIATION, INTEREST, PREFERENCE SHARES and minority interests, deducting tax and dividing the resulting figure by the number of ordinary shares. Note that earnings per share are normally higher than the DIVIDEND per share. For example, a firm may earn 10p per share but may only pay a 5p or 20 per cent dividend on its 25p ordinary shares.

Earnings yield. ⋄ YIELD.

East African Community. ⋄ LOMÉ CONVENTION.

East and Southern Africa, preferential trade area for. ⋄ PREFERENTIAL TRADE AREA FOR EAST AND SOUTHERN AFRICA.

Econometrics. The setting up of mathematical models describing economic relationships (such as that the quantity demanded of a good is dependent positively on income and negatively on price), testing the validity of such hypotheses (⋄ STATISTICAL INFERENCE) and estimating the PARAMETERS in order to obtain a measure of the strengths of the influences of the different independent VARIABLES. (⋄ CORRELATION; CROSS-SECTION ANALYSIS; REGRESSION ANALYSIS; TIME-SERIES ANALYSIS.) Sets of such models are used to make MACROECONOMIC forecasts (e.g. by the U.K. TREASURY). ⋄ FRISCH, R. A. K.

Economic Community of West African States (E.C.O.W.A.S.). The sixteen members of E.C.O.W.A.S. agreed on the basis of the Treaty of Lagos in 1975 to develop a CUSTOMS UNION, and in 1981, at Freetown,

Sierra Leone, concluded a plan for the elimination of trade restrictions within the community by 1989. ◊ LOMÉCONVENTION; PREFERENTIAL TRADE AREA FOR EAST AND SOUTHERN AFRICA.

Economic development. The growth of NATIONAL INCOME per capita of DEVELOPING COUNTRIES. Such countries need to generate sufficient savings (◊ SAVING) and INVESTMENT to be able to diversify their economies, shifting the emphasis from agriculture to industry, with the necessary supporting infrastructure such as roads and seaports (◊ ECONOMIC GROWTH, STAGES OF). In recent years their growth rates have been reduced because of a fall in export demand and export prices resulting from the slow-down in the growth of the industrialized countries. As a result their BALANCE OF PAYMENTS has run into substantial deficit on current account and a high burden of debt financing has been incurred. Loans and grants are channelled to developing countries through such institutions as the INTERNATIONAL BANK FOR RECONSTRUCTION AND DEVELOPMENT, the INTERNATIONAL DEVELOPMENT ASSOCIATION and the INTERNATIONAL FINANCE CORPORATION.

Economic Development Committee. ◊ NATIONAL ECONOMIC DEVELOPMENT COUNCIL.

Economic doctrines. Sets of beliefs about how economies function and their corresponding policy implications. Since Keynes, several doctrines have enjoyed the support of a significant number of academic economists. These can be listed in terms of the role they leave for government intervention in the economy: (a) Keynesian disequilibrium economics (◊ KEYNESIAN ECONOMICS; QUANTITY RATIONING); (b) neo-Keynesian/NEO-CLASSICAL ECONOMICS; (c) monetarist economics (◊ MONETARISM; QUANTITY THEORY OF MONEY); (d) NEW CLASSICAL ECONOMICS. (◊ IS–LM MODEL.)

Economic efficiency. The state of an economy in which no one can be made better off without someone being made worse off. For this to be the case, three types of efficiency must hold. The first is *productive efficiency*, in which the output of the economy is being produced at the lowest cost. The second is *allocative efficiency*, in which resources are being allocated to the production of the goods and services the society requires. The third is *distributional efficiency*, in which output is distributed in such a way that consumers would not wish, given their DISPOSABLE INCOME and market PRICES, to spend these incomes in any different way.

In a two-person, two-product economy with two factors of production, these three types of efficiency are achieved when three conditions hold: productive efficiency demands that the MARGINAL RATE OF TRANSFORMATION for the two products must be equal, to ensure a unit of one factor of production is worth the same amount in terms of the other factor whichever product it is used in. Otherwise, factors could be swapped between products and extra output gained. Second, that the MARGINAL RATE OF SUBSTITUTION must be equal for both consumers; otherwise, the consumers could swap commodities to their mutual benefit. Third, allocative efficiency requires that the marginal rate of transformation must equal the marginal rate of substitution: if consumers feel one banana is worth two apples, and producers can make one extra banana at the sacrifice of only one apple, it will pay society for them to produce one apple less and one extra banana, and to go on making that switch, until eventually consumers tire of bananas and value apples more highly than they did; and land suitable for banana production will be so marginal that for every bit of land removed from apples, hardly any bananas will be produced. At this stage, the two rates of substitution will be equal.

Economic efficiency will exist in an economy in which perfect competition characterizes every sector. (↔ MARGINAL-COST PRICING; PARETO, V. F. D.; PERFECT COMPETITION; PRICE SYSTEM; RICARDO, D.; WELFARE ECONOMICS.)

Economic good. Any physical object, natural or man-made, or service rendered, which could command a price in a market.

Economic growth. The increase in a country's per capita NATIONAL INCOME. There are problems in the measurement of national income because some activities may not take place in a MARKET (or not in a market for which statistics are collected): for instance, do-it-yourself car maintenance rather than buying the services of a garage mechanic, or transactions in the BLACK ECONOMY. Moreover, growth in national income should not be equated necessarily with growth in welfare (↔ WELFARE ECONOMICS). The processes of growth, such as industrialization, the expansion of the motorway network, the construction of airports, yield disbenefits such as pollution, noise and the destruction of countryside amenity, all of which are costs that are not subtracted from the statistical measures of the national income. (↔ ECONOMIC DEVELOPMENT; ECONOMIC GROWTH, STAGES OF; ↔ GROWTH THEORY.)

Economic growth, stages of. The five stages of economic growth which all economies are considered as going through in their development from fairly poor agricultural societies to highly industrialized mass-consumption economies. These five stages were defined and analysed by W. W. ROSTOW in his book *The Stages of Economic Growth*, namely:
(a) The traditional society, in which adherence to long-lived economic and social systems and customs means that output per head is low and tends not to rise.
(b) The stage of the establishment of the pre-conditions for 'take-off' (see (c)). This stage is a period of transition, in which the tradi-

tional systems are overcome, and the economy is made capable of exploiting the fruits of modern science and technology.

(c) The take-off stage. 'Take-off' represents the point at which the 'old blocks and the resistances to steady growth are finally overcome', and growth becomes the normal condition of the economy. The economy begins to generate its own INVESTMENT and technological improvement at sufficiently high rates so as to make growth virtually self-sustaining.

(d) The 'drive to maturity', which is the stage of increasing sophistication of the economy. Against the background of steady growth, new industries are developed, there is less reliance on IMPORTS and more exporting activity, and the economy 'demonstrates' its capacity to move beyond the original industries which powered its take-off, and to absorb and to apply efficiently the most advanced fruits of modern technology.

(e) The fourth stage ends in the attainment of the fifth stage, which is the age of high mass consumption, where there is an affluent population and durable and sophisticated consumer goods (⟡ ECONOMIC GOOD) and SERVICES are the leading sectors of production.

As a broad and imaginative description of the process of economic growth, this characterization of the stages of growth is interesting and possibly useful, having much the same flavour as KARL MARX's famous theory of the evolution of society from feudalism to bourgeois CAPITALISM and finally to communism. It also leads directly to a policy conclusion which was already favoured by many: aid should be given to the economies at the pre-take-off stages, in an attempt to get them to the take-off stage. Once this is achieved, these economies will have their own dynamic and momentum, and hence aid becomes much less necessary. The theory has had only limited impact among professional economists concerned with the problem of ECONOMIC DEVELOPMENT. Partly this is because Rostow's analysis of exactly what factors were responsible for take-off and subsequent self-generating growth tended to be vague, ambiguous and incomplete. Also the theory is framed in such general terms that it can be made consistent with virtually any past growth situation. Partly also perhaps, the broad sweep of the historian's vision, with the implication of the inexorability of the historical processes, is not of very much help in trying to solve the particular development problems of particular economies.

Economic imperialism. The exploitation of the DEVELOPING COUNTRIES by the ADVANCED COUNTRIES. MARX held that the capitalist classes were inexorably driven to overseas economic expansion by falling profit opportunities at home. The export of high VALUE ADDED goods and the import of raw materials developed with exported capital

buttressed by TARIFFS and other restrictions on imports of cheap manufactured goods, such as textiles, are the continuing essential features of
economic imperialism even after the granting of political independence,
according to critics of the advanced countries.

Economic rent. The difference between the return made by a factor of
production and the return necessary to keep the factor in its current
occupation. Examples of economic rent: (a) For a brain surgeon earning
£60,000 whose only other possible occupation is nursing on £6,000, the
economic rent is £54,000. The surgeon would remain in his current job
even if it paid only £6,100. (b) A firm making excess profits (⟡ PROFITS)
is earning economic rent.

In PERFECT COMPETITION, no rents are made by any factor, because
changes in supply bid prices of inputs and labour down to the level just
necessary to keep them employed. In general, economic rents accrue
where changes in supply of this sort are not possible: to a brain surgeon
with rare skills, difficult to emulate; or to a monopoly protected by
barriers to entry. Economic rents are among the few returns that can be
taxed (⟡ TAXATION) without distorting production decisions.

Economic sanction. A measure, taken in respect of some economic activity,
which has the effect of damaging another country's economy. Examples
would be a complete embargo on trade between countries, or refusal to
permit BANK DEPOSITS held in the country imposing the sanction to
be drawn upon by the government and residents of another. Examples
are the banning by the U.S.A. of exports of grain to the U.S.S.R.
following the Afghan crisis, the embargo on trade with Argentina
imposed by the E.E.C. at the time of the U.K. conflict with Argentina,
and the ban placed by the U.S.A. on exports of supplies and equipment
to the U.S.S.R. for the construction of a pipeline into Western Europe.

Economics. The study of the production, distribution and consumption of
wealth in human society. Economists have never been wholly satisfied
with any definition of their subject. This one is as good as any. It should
not be interpreted to restrict the subject-matter of economics to the
positive aspects of material welfare alone. L. ROBBINS criticized this
limitation by pointing out, for example, that the economy of war, which
may destroy material welfare, is an aspect of choice in the use of resources and therefore a proper subject for economic inquiry. His definition was: 'Economics is the science which studies human behaviour
as a relationship between ends and scarce means which have alternative
uses.' In fact, no short definition can convey to the beginner the scope
and flavour of the whole subject as it has evolved. The reader will gain a
good notion of the scope of economics by examining the coverage of
this dictionary, but the borderlines between such other disciplines as
psychology, sociology, accounting and geography are not easily defined
and it is, perhaps, not particularly productive to attempt to do so.

Political economy, an early title for the subject, now has an old-fashioned ring to it but usefully emphasizes the importance of choice between alternatives in economics which remains, despite continuing scientific progress, as much of an art as a science.

Economies of scale. Factors which cause the average cost of producing a commodity to fall as output of the commodity rises. For instance, a firm or industry which would less than double its costs, if it doubled its output, enjoys economies of scale.

There are two types of such economies. The first – called *internal* – accrue to the individual firm regardless of the size of its industry. They generally result from technological factors which ensure the optimal size of production is large: (a) With high fixed costs in plant and machinery, the larger its production, the lower the cost per unit of the fixed inputs. For example, producing steel without a blast furnace is possible but very expensive; once a blast furnace is built, it is inefficient only to make small quantities of steel with it: hence, steel companies tend to be large. (b) Large firms can also arrange for the specialization of labour and machines – as in the techniques of the production line – which can increase productivity. (◊ SMITH, A.) (c) Only large firms can afford the high costs of research and development. Non-technological factors are important, too, however. For example, by buying inputs in bulk, large firms can get discounts from their suppliers (who are prepared to grant them because of economies of scale in distributing the supplies).

The second type – *external* economies – arise because the development of an industry can lead to the development of ancillary services of benefit to all firms: a labour force skilled in the crafts of the industry; a components industry equipped to supply precisely the right parts; or a trade magazine in which all firms can advertise cheaply.

The existence of economies of scale in most industries is used to explain the predominance of large firms in the world economy. (◊ DIS-ECONOMIES OF SCALE; ECONOMIES OF SCOPE; RETURNS TO SCALE.)

Economies of scope. Factors which make it cheaper to produce a range of related products than to produce any of the individual products on their own. In the absence of state controls of these activities, companies producing the one would thus be in a good position to dominate the market for the other. Economies of scope can provide a base for corporate DIVERSIFICATION. (◊ ECONOMIES OF SCALE.)

Économistes, les. ◊ PHYSIOCRATS.

Edgeworth, Francis Ysidro (1845–1926). Edgeworth held the Chair of Political Economy at Oxford University from 1891 to 1922 and edited the *Economic Journal* from 1891 to 1926. His published work includes *Mathematical Physics* (1881), *Theory of Monopoly* (1897), *Theory of*

Distribution (1904) and *Papers Relating to Political Economy* (1925). The latter includes the two reports of 1887 and 1889 of the committee on the study of INDEX NUMBERS set up by the British Association for the Advancement of Science, for which Edgeworth acted as secretary. Apart from economics, Edgeworth made valuable contributions to statistics, and statistical method. In showing the inadequacy of the VALUE theory of W. S. JEVONS, Edgeworth invented the analytical tools of INDIFFERENCE CURVES and CONTRACT CURVES. ⟨⟩ PARETO, V. F. D.

Efficient markets hypothesis. The idea that the prices prevailing in a market make it impossible to earn abnormal economic profits by trading in that market on some specified amount of information. The hypothesis is invariably applied to financial markets. Here, it says that if the price of an asset is expected to rise tomorrow, traders, anticipating this, will buy the asset today. This will drive the price of the asset up until it is no longer expected that it will rise further tomorrow. Thus no quick capital gain could be expected to be made. If the market were not efficient, the possibility of making ARBITRAGE profits would exist, and a clever trader could make speculative gains. ⟨⟩ CHARTIST; RATIONAL EX-PECTATIONS

Elasticity. The elasticity of a function is the proportionate change in the DEPENDENT VARIABLE divided by the proportionate change in the INDEPENDENT VARIABLE at a given value of the independent variable. Elasticity, being the product of ratios, is independent of the units in which the variables are measured. For example, suppose $q = -ap + k$ is the function relating quantity demanded (q) of a good to the price (p) of the good, a and k are constants. (⟨⟩ DEMAND FUNCTION.) The elasticity is given by $(dq/q) \div (dp/p) = (dq/dp) \cdot (p/q)$, where dq and dp are small marginal changes in the variables. It can be shown (by differential calculus) that $dq/dp = -a$, so that the elasticity is equal to $-a(p/q)$. The equation above traces a straight line sloping downwards on a graph, reflecting the fact that demand falls as price rises. The elasticity, $-a(p/q)$, of price p is negative. It will, however, vary in value along the demand curve, because the higher the price (and lower the demand), the larger is p/q and, therefore, the bigger the numerical value (ignoring the sign) of the elasticity. Similarly, the lower the price, the smaller the elasticity. If elasticity is numerically less than unity, the quantity demanded is price inelastic; that means that if the price is increased (marginally) the quantity demanded will not fall proportionately as much and, therefore, the total expenditure on the good will increase. If the good is price elastic, that is, elasticity is numerically greater than unity, demand will be reduced more than price, and therefore, less will be spent on the good than before the price was increased. Elasticity is a general expression applicable to any relationship, or function, between variables (⟨⟩ CROSS-PRICE ELASTICITY OF DEMAND;

ELASTICITY OF SUBSTITUTION; INCOME ELASTICITY OF DEMAND). The term elasticity was invented by A. MARSHALL.

Elasticity of substitution. Given a PRODUCTION FUNCTION with two INPUTS, say labour and capital, the marginal rate of substitution or RATE OF TECHNICAL SUBSTITUTION is defined as the increase in the input of one factor (say labour) required to keep output constant when the other factor (capital) is reduced marginally. This rate will change as the ratio of the factor inputs used changes. For instance, more and more labour would, generally speaking, be required to keep the same level of output, the more the capital input is reduced. The elasticity of substitution shows how the marginal rate of substitution varies as the ratio of units varies. It is defined as the percentage change in the ratio of inputs (labour divided by capital) divided by the percentage change in the MARGINAL RATE OF SUBSTITUTION. It is defined in terms of percentages in this way so that it is independent of the units of measurement in which labour and capital inputs are calculated. If this elasticity is zero, it means that the inputs have to be used in fixed proportions. If the value is infinity, the two factors are perfect substitutes.

Eligible liabilities. ◊ CREDIT CONTROL.

Eligible paper. A first-class SECURITY. 'Eligible paper' is a TREASURY BILL, short-dated government BOND or BILL OF EXCHANGE, accepted by an ACCEPTING HOUSE or a British bank and which the BANK OF ENGLAND will rediscount or accept as COLLATERAL security for LOANS to the DISCOUNT HOUSES. Since the discount office of the Bank of England is the LENDER OF LAST RESORT for the MONEY MARKET, what it classifies as eligible paper has an important influence on the PORTFOLIOS held by the discount houses which do not wish to have too great a proportion of their ASSETS in a form that could not be turned into CASH in this way.

Empirical testing. Checking theories against facts. In contrast to the physical sciences, it is rarely possible to conduct controlled experiments in economics, for example to see what would happen to exports if the EXCHANGE RATE were reduced and all other variables in the international economy remained unchanged. It is possible, however, to test HYPOTHESES with facts, for example to verify historically the extent to which changes in the exchange rate have been associated with changes in exports. ◊ ECONOMETRICS. In fact, experiments can be and are carried out in economics, for example laboratory simulations of market behaviour, and there is a growing interest in *experimental economics* as an adjunct to historical empiricism and theoretical work.

Employment, full. A situation in which everyone in the LABOUR FORCE who is willing to work at the market rate for his type of labour has a job, except for those who are switching from one job to another, i.e. it excludes FRICTIONAL UNEMPLOYMENT. Under full employment there is no STRUCTURAL UNEMPLOYMENT nor any unemployment arising from a deficiency in AGGREGATE DEMAND. It does not imply anything about the rate of INFLATION ($\Diamond$ UNEMPLOYMENT; UNEMPLOYMENT NATURAL RATE OF) but the term does normally apply to a situation in which the CAPITAL STOCK and the labour force are in balance, i.e. the full employment level of GROSS DOMESTIC PRODUCT is one in which capacity is fully utilized.

Endogenous variable. A VARIABLE whose value is determined within a set of equations, or MODELS, established to make predictions or test an hypothesis. ($\Diamond$ EXOGENOUS VARIABLE; PARAMETER.)

Engel, Ernst (1821–96). $\Diamond$ ENGEL'S LAW.

Engel's law. A law of economics stating that, with given tastes or preferences, the proportion of INCOME spent on food diminishes as incomes increase. The law was formulated by Ernst Engel, the director of the Bureau of Statistics in Prussia, in a paper published by him in 1857.

Enterprise. One or more firms under common ownership or control. A term used in the CENSUS of production to distinguish the reporting unit (ESTABLISHMENT) from the firm or unit of control.

Enterprise zones. A designated zone in a depressed, generally inner-urban area, in which firms located in the zone are given favourable TAXATION concessions and freedom from a number of planning constraints. Eleven zones (with a maximum size of about 200 hectares) were adopted when such zones were introduced in Great Britain in 1981. Firms were granted a ten-year exemption from RATES and a 100 per cent taxation allowance on new building. By 1986, a further twelve zones had been established. In the same year the United States government introduced a similar policy covering twenty-six zones in the United States. In 1982 Belgium also announced plans for the setting up of seven enterprise zones of 50 hectares each. $\Diamond$ ASSISTED AREA; FREE-TRADE ZONE.

Entrepôt. A centre at which goods are received for subsequent distribution. An *entrepôt* port has facilities for the trans-shipment of imported goods or their storage prior to their re-export, without the need to pass through customs control. The port of Rotterdam is an example of an *entrepôt*. ($\Diamond$ FREE PORT.)

Entrepreneur. An economic agent who perceives market opportunities and assembles the FACTORS OF PRODUCTION to exploit them in a firm. As the prime mover in economic activity the entrepreneur has received attention from the beginnings of economics (for example, by CANTILLON and SAY) but, as Mark Casson has recently pointed out, he has never been fully integrated into modern economic theory. In the static NEO-CLASSICAL ECONOMICS of PERFECT COMPETITION there is no place for the entrepreneur since it is assumed that there is perfect information and perfect freedom of entry. After FRANK KNIGHT the pure function of the entrepreneur is to deal with uncertainty in the dynamic, imperfect, real world in which PROFIT is a return to uncertainty and entrepreneurship is inseparable from control of the firm in which he operates. The essence of the entrepreneur, therefore, is that he is alert to gaps in the market which others do not see and is able to raise the finance and other resources required by a firm to exploit the market that he initiates. If successful he will make a super-normal PROFIT that will later reduce to a normal profit as new competitors are attracted into the market. In this conception, the pure function of the entrepreneur is as a fourth factor of production. Other functions than risk-taking have been attributed by economists to the entrepreneur: invention; the provision of RISK CAPITAL and management, for example. Though not part of the pure entrepreneurial function which is remunerated by profit, all these functions may be embodied in the owner-manager of a SMALL BUSINESS. His remuneration may be made up of RENT as an owner of LAND, INTEREST as a return on CAPITAL, a wage or salary for his management function and therefore as a return for his LABOUR, and profit as a return for his entrepreneurship. In the large firm the entrepreneur is a theoretical abstraction whose functions are divided between the management (the board of directors and senior executives) and the shareholders. Many economists have argued that the SEPARA-TION OF OWNERSHIP FROM CONTROL has important implications for the behaviour of managers and market performance.

Entry. ◇ BARRIERS TO ENTRY; FREEDOM OF ENTRY.

Equalization grant. Funds paid by central government to regional government out of general tax revenue so as to reduce disparities in income or tax rates that would otherwise arise from differences in taxable capacity among subordinate government, for example the U.K. RATES support grant.

Equation of international demand. The law of comparative cost (◇ RICARDO, D.) sets out the limits of the TERMS OF TRADE within which one country will exchange commodities with another. JOHN STUART MILL realized that the point at which exchange actually took place within these limits set by costs would depend on the reciprocal DEMAND of each country for the other's commodities. This 'equation of international demand' will determine the EQUILIBRIUM terms of trade. It will depend, *inter alia*, on the ELASTICITIES of demand and SUPPLY of the goods traded (◇ MARSHALL−LERNER CRITERION).

Equilibrium. A situation in which the forces that determine the behaviour of some variable are in balance and thus exert no pressure on that variable to change. It is a situation in which the actions of all economic agents are mutually consistent. It is a concept meaningfully applied to any variable whose level is determined by the outcome of the operation of at least one mechanism or process acting on countervailing forces. For example, equilibrium price is affected by a process which drives suppliers to increase prices when demand is in excess and to undercut each other when supply is in excess – the mechanism thus regulates the forces of supply and demand.

It is possible for a short-run equilibrium to exist, when some quickly adjusting processes are in balance, while other longer-term forces are still causing change to occur. For example, in PERFECT COMPETITION, in the short run firms' profit-maximizing behaviour can lead to a market equilibrium with price equal to marginal cost; yet if abnormal PROFITS exist at that price new firms might enter the industry – a process quite separate from the price-setting behaviour of those already in it – that will change the long-term equilibrium price.

A distinction can be drawn between a static equilibrium, when the value of the relevant variable is unchanging, and a dynamic equilibrium, when the value of the variable is changing but in a regular way. Equilibrium growth, for example, might manifest itself in a steady 3 per cent rise in GDP.

Finally, equilibrium should not be confused with efficiency. Although the efficient level of a variable is likely to be an equilibrium, there is no guarantee that equilibria are efficient.

Equilibrium price. The PRICE at which a MARKET is in EQUILIBRIUM. ▷ MARKET ANALYSIS; PRICE SYSTEM.

Equilibrium quantity. The quantity of a good which is bought and sold when a MARKET is in EQUILIBRIUM.

Equities. ▷ EQUITY.

Equity. The residual VALUE of a company's ASSETS after all outside LIABILITIES (other than to shareholders) have been allowed for. In a MORTGAGE, or HIRE PURCHASE contract, equity is the amount left for the borrower if the asset concerned is sold and the lender repaid. The equity in a company under LIQUIDATION is the property of holders of ORDINARY SHARES, hence these shares are popularly called *equities*. Because equity yields and prices, although fluctuating, have risen as the value of MONEY has fallen, they have proved better long-term INVESTMENTS than fixed-interest STOCKS in the period since the Second World War.

Equity Capital for Industry (E.C.I.). A financial institution created to supply EQUITY funds for U.K. industry. E.C.I. was set up in May 1976 by a number of City institutions under the sponsorship of the BANK OF ENGLAND. The initiative was a reaction to criticism of the functioning of the CAPITAL MARKET as it affected the supply of capital for manufacturing industry. There was considerable controversy about the need for a new institution, however, and some large City institutions did not support the venture. Subscribers of the initial capital of £42 million were INSURANCE, UNIT TRUST and INVESTMENT TRUST companies and FINANCE FOR INDUSTRY.

Equity/efficiency trade-off. The conflict that is traditionally held to arise between maximizing average consumption and making that consumption equal across the population. Under certain conditions, a FREE MARKET economy is generally recognized as exhibiting ECONOMIC EFFICIENCY, but would have no tendency to result in equality of earnings. To achieve an alternative income distribution, a PROGRESSIVE TAX system is required. However, it is possible that high taxes have a negative effect on the incentives people have to work, or create other distortions, and thus depress output. In so far as there is a trade-off, however, a SOCIAL-WELFARE FUNCTION must be defined to derive the optimal combination. ⟡ WELFARE ECONOMICS.

Equity gearing. ⟡ GEARING.

Equity-linked assurance. ⟡ ASSURANCE.

Escalator clause. ⟡ INDEXATION.

Establishment. An operating unit of a business, to be distinguished from a firm or ENTERPRISE which is a controlling unit. In British censuses an establishment is a reporting unit; thus a large firm may have several factories, each of which will complete a census form but all of which will be owned or controlled by the firm itself.

Estate Duties Investment Trust (Edith) PLC. An INVESTMENT TRUST formed in 1953 to acquire holdings in small companies. The trust, which is operated by Investors in Industry (⟡ FINANCE FOR INDUSTRY), does not interfere in the management of the companies and its facilities are designed to be of service to executors and trustees of family companies who need to realize SHARES in companies in order to pay ESTATE DUTY, but do not wish to relinquish control.

Estate duty. A TAX payable on a person's property at his death and before it passes into the hands of others. Thus *estate duty* differs from an *inheritance tax*, which is payable by the recipient and which may vary according to the financial circumstances of the inheritor. Estate duty was phased out when CAPITAL TRANSFER TAX was introduced, and stopped applying to deaths occurring after March 1974. The duty was introduced in 1894, and has been described as a 'voluntary tax', because of the ease with which it could be avoided.

Estimates. An Estimate is the document which the U.K. government presents to Parliament by way of asking for a given sum for a particular service. It also shows in some detail how it is proposed to spend that sum. As such, it forms an important part of the control of government expenditure. ⟡ BUDGET; SELECT COMMITTEE ON ESTIMATES.

Euler, Leonhard (1707–83). Economists have found that certain propositions in pure mathematics developed by Leonhard Euler, a Swiss mathematician, can be usefully applied to problems in economic theory. The most notable application concerns a theory of distribution based on MARGINAL PRODUCTIVITY. This theory states that FACTORS OF PRODUCTION (i.e. LAND, LABOUR and CAPITAL) will each earn an INCOME corresponding to the VALUE of OUTPUT produced by the last unit of the factor employed. For instance, if a firm employs nineteen workers at an average wage of £20 per week, it will be willing to employ an additional worker as long as his output is worth more than £20. Moreover, if the twentieth worker yields, say, £21 per week it will be worth while to pay him more than £20 to attract him. The firm cannot, however, pay its workers different wages if they have the same skill, and therefore must pay all of them more than £20 per week. The earnings of each worker are therefore made equal to that at which it is just worth while to the firm to employ one more worker. A similar argument is applied to other factors of production and for the total national output as well as for a single firm. However, total output must, by definition, equal total income (◊ NATIONAL INCOME). National output is distributed among the three basic factors of production: land, labour and capital. No arithmetical reasons, however, could be thought of as to how the different factor incomes, derived from marginal productivities, could necessarily add up to the same as total output. Euler's theorem resolved the problem by showing what assumptions about the nature of the PRODUCTION FUNCTION (which describes how the factors of production are combined to produce outputs) had to be made in order for the equality between the sum of incomes and the sum of outputs to be achieved. ◊ CAMBRIDGE SCHOOL; DISTRIBUTION, THEORY OF; NEO-CLASSICAL ECONOMICS.

Euler's theorem. ◊ EULER, L.

Eurobond. ◊ BOND; EUROCURRENCY.

Eurocurrency. CURRENCY held by individuals and institutions outside the country of issue. In its annual report in 1966 the BANK FOR INTERNATIONAL SETTLEMENTS described Eurodollars as the dollars acquired 'by banks located outside the United States, mostly through the taking of DEPOSITS, but also to some extent through swapping other currencies into dollars, and the relending of these dollars, often after redepositing with other banks, to non-bank borrowers anywhere in the world'. It should be noted, therefore, that the market for Eurocurrencies is not confined to Europe. In terms of a simple example, what happens is as follows. A London bank, as a result of a commercial transaction of one of its customers has, say, a CREDIT balance with an American bank in New York. A Belgian businessman asks his bank for dollars to finance imports from the United States. In order to meet this request the Brussels bank accepts the dollar deposit transferred by the London bank from its account in New York. The essential point about this operation is that it creates credit. The London bank still has a claim, on Brussels instead of New York, whereas the Brussels bank now has a claim on New York which its customer can use to finance his trade. The questions are naturally raised as to why London should be willing to transfer its deposit and why Brussels should finance its requirements in this way. The former can be answered broadly by the U.S. BALANCE OF PAYMENTS deficits and *dollar certificates of deposit* issued by overseas branches of U.S. banks supplying the means and interest-rate ARBITRAGE (New York *versus* Brussels) supplying the PROFIT. On the second question, again relative RATES OF INTEREST are a factor, but in addition the existence of national EXCHANGE CONTROLS and credit controls encourages the practice. The Brussels bank avoids the need to exchange francs for dollars. In practice, of course, there can be many relending transactions between banks in response to differentials in interest rates. London has obtained the major share (about 30 per cent) of the transactions in this business, acting as a BROKER by borrowing a currency from a country with a surplus in that currency and lending it out to foreign banks or directly at favourable interest rates. The size of the Euromarkets has increased substantially in recent years, from about $59 billion in 1970 to about $500 billion in 1975 and $1,800 billion in 1982. The setting up of international banking facilities in the United States, which gives banks freedom from domestic regulations, may cause a shift in this market in favour of New York as a centre rather than London. ◊ FREE-TRADE ZONE.

Eurodollars. ◊ EUROCURRENCY.

European Coal and Steel Community (E.C.S.C.). The Schuman Plan (named after the then French foreign minister) for the establishment of a common market in coal and steel was embodied in a treaty and ratified by the member countries – Germany, France, Italy, and BENELUX – in 1952. All import duties and QUOTA restrictions on coal, iron ore, steel and scrap were eliminated on intra-community trade. The treaty also provided for the control of restrictive practices and MERGERS considered contrary to the maintenance of free competition. Overall executive responsibility is vested in the High Authority, which has power to raise finance by means of a TAX on producers. This INCOME finances a readaption fund that gives assistance to redundant or deployed workers. The authority may make LOANS for capital INVESTMENT. It may also, at the request of the Council of Ministers, fix price levels and production and trade quotas. In addition, the treaty established a parliamentary common assembly and a court of justice, both of which were merged with the corresponding institutions of the EUROPEAN ECONOMIC COMMUNITY. Denmark, the Republic of Ireland and the United Kingdom became members in 1973, Greece in 1979, and Spain and Portugal in 1986. ◊ CUSTOMS UNION.

European Cooperation Administration (E.C.A.). ◊ EUROPEAN RECOVERY PROGRAMME.

European currency snake. The countries of the EUROPEAN ECONOMIC COMMUNITY agreed in 1972 to manage their currencies so that their EXCHANGE RATES moved in relation to one another, and, within certain narrow bands, in relation to the dollar, It was considered that the management of the currencies of the community in this way was the necessary first step to monetary union and, eventually, to the ideal of a common currency. The fluctuations in the rates of each currency were confined within a margin of $\pm 2 \cdot 25$ per cent. In addition, the group as a whole was also managed in respect to the dollar, with fluctuations confined within a range of $\pm 4 \cdot 45$ per cent. Initially the arrangement was referred to as the 'snake in the tunnel'. After 1973, however, the 'snake' was left to float against the dollar, and the 'tunnel' has vanished. The countries in the 'snake' were, for varying periods of time, Belgium, Denmark, the Netherlands, West Germany, the United Kingdom, Italy, France and, outside the E.E.C. itself, Sweden and Norway. This method of managing European currencies was replaced in 1979 by the EURO-PEAN MONETARY SYSTEM.

European Currency Unit (E.C.U.). The E.C.U. was introduced as a unit of account (◇ MONEY) of the EUROPEAN ECONOMIC COMMUNITY on the formation of the EUROPEAN MONETARY SYSTEM in 1979. By 1981, the E.C.U. had replaced all other units of account that had been used in the E.E.C. for accounting purposes, e.g. for the COMMON AGRICULTURAL POLICY, European Development Fund (◇ LOMÉ CONVENTION) and budgeting. As with previous units of account the E.C.U. is a WEIGHTED AVERAGE of the currencies of the member countries of the E.E.C. (excluding Portugal and Spain). The weight given to each currency is proportional to that country's share of the E.E.C.'s total GROSS DOMESTIC PRODUCT (◇ SPECIAL DRAWING RIGHTS). The E.C.U. is now a currency adopted by all the E.E.C. institutions as a means of intergovernmental settlement of debts and in the operations of the E.M.S. The *international reserves* of the E.E.C. countries are partially held in E.C.U.s. The E.C.U. has also in recent years developed as a 'currency' used by firms and organizations in the private sector, because of its inherent EXCHANGE RATE stability, for borrowing and lending in the MONEY MARKETS and also for costing and pricing goods in INTERNATIONAL TRADE. In 1986, the BANK FOR INTERNATIONAL SETTLEMENTS agreed to act as a clearing-house for inter-bank settlements in E.C.U.s.

European Development Fund. ◇ LOMÉ CONVENTION.

European Economic Community (E.E.C.). Six countries of Western Europe – France, West Germany, Italy, Belgium, the Netherlands and Luxembourg – signed the Treaty of Rome in 1957 for the creation between them of a CUSTOMS UNION or common market. By this treaty the E.E.C. came into force on 1 January 1958. The primary aims of the treaty were the elimination of all obstacles to the free movement of goods, SERVICES, CAPITAL and LABOUR between the member countries and the setting up of a common external commercial policy, a common agricultural policy and a common transport policy. The treaty foresaw the prohibition of most industrial SUBSIDIES and DUMPING and the supranational control of public MONOPOLIES and the vetting of MERGERS. The executive management of the E.E.C. is vested in a commission whose members are appointed for periods of four years. Problems of policy are the concern of the Council of Ministers, to which the commission's proposals are submitted. Each member country is represented by one minister in the council. The treaty also established a parliamentary assembly and a court of justice. Decisions of the E.E.C. are transmitted through the member countries' governments by means of directives (if advisory) or regulations (if mandatory). Consultative institutions include an economic and social committee and a monetary committee. The EUROPEAN INVESTMENT BANK has been formed and a European Regional Development Fund established with powers to lend and grant money for the development of backward regions of the community. In addition, a European Social Fund has been set up to assist the redeployment of workers thrown out of work, particularly if caused by the creation of the community, and a European Development Fund established to provide aid to countries of the LOMÉ CONVENTION. All internal import duties were abolished and the common external tariff established by 1 July 1968. For agricultural products, all protectionist measures such as QUOTAS and import duties have been replaced by a levy that is determined by the difference between the world price and the internal (guaranteed) price. ◊ COMMON AGRICULTURAL POLICY. Workers and their families can move from one country to another without a permit, and foreign workers from within the community have the same rights to social security and are subject to the same taxation as nationals. Under a 'Treaty of Fusion' the E.E.C. institutions have been merged with those of the EUROPEAN COAL AND STEEL COMMUNITY and Euratom. As from 1 January 1973 the Republic of Ireland and two members of the EUROPEAN FREE TRADE ASSOCIATION – the United Kingdom and Denmark – became full members of the community. The elimination of tariffs between the original six and the new members and the adoption by them of the common external tariff was completed on 1 January 1977. At the same time, industrial FREE TRADE agreements have been concluded with the remaining members of the European Free Trade Association. Greece became a member of the community in 1981, and in 1986 Portugal and Spain. The commission has an association agreement with Turkey, which is also expected to become a full member at some future date. In 1985 about 80 per cent of the community's budget income was derived from IMPORT duties and VALUE-ADDED TAX and about 75 per cent was spent on agriculture. ◊ DEVELOPMENT AREAS; EUROPEAN MONETARY SYSTEM; GENERAL

AGREEMENT ON TARIFFS AND TRADE; TOKYO ROUND OF TRADE NEGOTIATIONS.

European Free Trade Area. Pressure for the formation of a FREE-TRADE AREA between the seventeen countries of the ORGANIZATION FOR EUROPEAN ECONOMIC COOPERATION gathered strength in the early 1950s. Impetus was given to this idea by the conferences in 1955 and 1956, which led to the signing of the Treaty of Rome in 1957 between the six countries which were to establish the EUROPEAN ECONOMIC COMMUNITY. The O.E.E.C. opened negotiations which, it was hoped, would lead to the formation of a free-trade area between the E.E.C. and the other member countries of the O.E.E.C. These negotiations proved abortive, the E.E.C. fearing that the integrity of its own association might be prejudiced. In the event, a free-trade area was established in the EUROPEAN FREE TRADE ASSOCIATION, but was restricted to the three countries of Scandinavia, the U.K., Austria, Portugal and Switzerland, with the later additions of Finland and Iceland.

European Free Trade Association (E.F.T.A.). The text of the convention setting up the European Free Trade Association was approved at Stockholm in November 1959 by the United Kingdom, Norway, Sweden, Denmark, Austria, Portugal and Switzerland. In April 1961 these seven concluded a trade agreement with Finland, which in effect brought Finland within the association. In March 1970 Iceland was also admitted as a full member, but Denmark and the United Kingdom left the association on becoming members of the EUROPEAN ECONOMIC COMMUNITY in 1973 and Portugal in 1986. The Stockholm Agreement established a FREE-TRADE AREA between the member countries. While retaining their own individual tariffs on imports from non-members, they agreed to eliminate import duties on goods originating in any member country. As the group is a free-trade area rather than a CUSTOMS UNION, rules are necessary to prevent products from non-members from being sold in a high-tariff member country via a low-tariff member. These rules were amended in 1973 following the conclusion of a number of free-trade agreements with the European Economic Community. The E.F.T.A. accepted the proposal of the E.E.C. that goods subject to those agreements should be granted certificates of origin if they were 'wholly produced' or sufficiently 'processed' within the member countries. The principal test for 'sufficient processing' is that the goods should be given a tariff classification different from that of the components entering into their production. ⟡ GENERAL AGREEMENT ON TARIFFS AND TRADE.

European Fund. The EUROPEAN MONETARY AGREEMENT which came into force at the end of 1958 established a European Fund with a capital of $600 million, partly from the transfer of the CAPITAL residue of the defunct EUROPEAN PAYMENTS UNION and partly from fresh contributions. The fund was empowered to extend two-year loans to countries to finance short-run BALANCE OF PAYMENTS deficits. The fund was closed down in 1973.

European Investment Bank (E.I.B.). A bank established in 1958 by the EUROPEAN ECONOMIC COMMUNITY whose board of governors is made up of the ministers of finance of the community. It is a non-profit-making institution whose function is to make loans and give guarantees with respect to (a) projects in the underdeveloped areas of the community and associated countries (◊ LOMÉ CONVENTION), (b) projects of modernization, conversion or development that are regarded as necessary for the establishment of the Common Market and (c) projects in which member countries of the community have a common interest. The loans, which are generally not more than 50 per cent of the capital cost of the project, are for terms of from seven to twelve years and are made in a mix of foreign currencies. They have to be repaid in the currencies in which they were granted. Under the E.I.B.'s charter, loans and outstanding guarantees cannot exceed two and a half times its subscribed capital. The latter was raised to 14·4 billion E.C.U.s (◊ EUROPEAN MONETARY SYSTEM) in 1981. About 85 per cent of the E.I.B.'s funds have been for projects within the E.E.C. and the rest for DEVELOPING COUNTRIES overseas.

European Monetary Agreement (E.M.A.). After the post-war recovery had been completed in Europe, the countries of Western Europe were able to restore the CONVERTIBILITY of their CURRENCIES. During the recovery period, a clearing system had been established for their international payments under the EUROPEAN PAYMENTS UNION. With the restoration of convertibility the E.P.U. was replaced by the E.M.A., which came into operation in December 1958. It continued the BANKING function of the E.P.U. in relation to the clearing of balances between members, the main difference being that all settlements had to be made in gold or convertible currencies and the granting of automatic credits was terminated. The agreement also established a EUROPEAN FUND for the finance of temporary BALANCE OF PAYMENTS deficits. ◊ INTERNATIONAL LIQUIDITY; INTERNATIONAL MONETARY FUND.

European Monetary Cooperation Fund. ◊ EUROPEAN MONETARY SYSTEM.

European Monetary Fund. ◊ EUROPEAN MONETARY SYSTEM.

European Monetary System (E.M.S.). The EUROPEAN ECONOMIC COMMUNITY agreed in 1978 to the setting up of the European Monetary System to replace the existing EUROPEAN CURRENCY SNAKE procedure for the control of EXCHANGE RATES. The E.M.S. was introduced in 1979 for an initial phase of two years with the intention to proceed to a more comprehensive system in 1981. The second phase has, however, been postponed. The system is similar to that of the European currency snake in that it is designed to keep the member countries' exchange rates within specified bands in relation to each other. Each currency in the system may fluctuate only between ±2·25 per cent against any other currency. This applies to the West German Deutschmark, the French franc, the Belgian franc, the Danish krone and the Irish punt. The Italian lira, although within the E.M.S., is exceptionally allowed to fluctuate within a margin of ±6 per cent. The U.K. is not a member of the system. In addition to the limits set, within which currency rates may move one with another, each currency is allowed to diverge from its European Currency Unit central rate by only a given percentage. This percentage differs between currencies according to the weight of the currency which is used in calculating the E.C.U. The E.C.U. is defined by a weighted AVERAGE of all E.E.C. currencies (including sterling), the weights used being the share of each country's output in the E.E.C. total. The E.C.U. is, therefore, a 'basket' of currencies, similar in principle to S.D.R.s (◊ SPECIAL DRAWING RIGHTS; EUROPEAN UNITS OF ACCOUNT). The previous European currency snake system did not include the requirement to contain movements in rates in relation to the E.C.U. There have been several realignments (◊ DEVALUATION; REVALUATION) of the intervention rates in the E.M.S. since it was established. For instance, in 1986, the Deutschmark and the Dutch guilder were revalued by 3 per cent, the Belgian franc and the Danish krone by 1 per cent, whilst the French franc was devalued by 3 per cent. The CENTRAL BANKS of the member countries in the E.M.S. (and the U.K., although not a member) deposit 20 per cent of their GOLD AND FOREIGN EXCHANGE RESERVES on a short-term basis in exchange for E.C.U.s with the European Monetary Cooperation Fund. The fund is the CLEARING-HOUSE for the central banks in the E.M.S. operations, although in practice the actual day-to-day running of the system is carried out by the BANK FOR INTERNATIONAL SETTLEMENTS. In the intended second phase of the development of the E.M.S., the European Monetary Cooperation Fund would be replaced by a European Monetary Fund which would take over the ownership of the Cooperation Fund's deposits and act more like a central bank for the E.E.C.

European Payments Union (E.P.U.). The seventeen member countries of the ORGANIZATION OF EUROPEAN ECONOMIC COOPERATION established the European Payments Union between themselves in 1950. The E.P.U. replaced the INTRA-EUROPEAN PAYMENTS AGREEMENT set up under the EUROPEAN RECOVERY PROGRAMME. The E.P.U. was a clearing system for the multilateral international debits and credits which arose between the member countries. In addition, however, it afforded a mechanism for the extension of automatic lines of credit to any member with a BALANCE OF PAYMENT deficit with fellow members. The union was replaced in 1958 by the EUROPEAN MONETARY AGREEMENT when the Western European countries restored currency CONVERTIBILITY. The union was an important stimulus to European unification and prevented the growth of BILATERALISM in Europe.

European Recovery Programme. In June 1947 the U.S. secretary of state, General G. C. Marshall, made clear in a speech at Harvard the willingness of the United States to extend economic assistance to countries whose productive ASSETS had been destroyed in the Second World War. This offer did not exclude the U.S.S.R. and the Eastern European countries but was never accepted by them. The resultant European Recovery Programme became known as MARSHALL AID. Sixteen West European countries attended a conference in Paris in 1947, which led to the establishment of the ORGANIZATION FOR EUROPEAN ECONOMIC COOPERATION in 1948, to coordinate the recovery programme in conjunction with the U.S. Economic Cooperation Administration. It was established on the basis of a four-year commitment to provide Western Europe with between $15,000 million and $17,000 million.

European Regional Development Fund (E.R.D.F.). ◊ EUROPEAN ECONOMIC COMMUNITY.

European Social Fund. ◊ EUROPEAN ECONOMIC COMMUNITY.

European Units of Account. Because of the variety of national currencies the EUROPEAN ECONOMIC COMMUNITY found it necessary to invent a common unit of account for bookkeeping purposes (◊ MONEY). Units of account have been invented for the BUDGET, the EUROPEAN COAL AND STEEL COMMUNITY, agriculture, the EUROPEAN INVESTMENT BANK, customs tariff and the European Development Fund (◊ LOMÉ CONVENTION). Initially, all these units were defined as having the value of 0·88867088 g. of fine gold and were converted into member countries' currencies at their par rates of exchange. After the international policy of fixed exchange rates was abandoned in 1972, the gap between the conversion rate of units of account and actual market rates made the system impractical. The revised unit of account was defined as the sum of amounts of each member country's currencies. These amounts were fixed at a level relating to the size of each member country's economy. The value of a unit of account in terms of any currency was calculated, daily, by translating each amount of currency in the 'basket' into, say, dollars according to the going rates of exchange for that currency and adding up the resultant sums. In 1979 the EUROPEAN MONETARY SYSTEM was formed and by 1981 the EUROPEAN CURRENCY UNIT had replaced the European Units of Account.

Ex ante. Expected or intended before the event as distinct from *ex post* which is the result after the event. Since the future is largely unpredictable, expectations and outcomes will often be different. The concepts of ex ante and ex post are particularly useful in economics because the nature of expectations may help either to realize or to falsify expectations in the process of moving towards EQUILIBRIUM. For example, if investors expect security prices to rise today ex ante, this will increase demand for them and their price now, so that ex post and ex ante prices may be similar. If intended aggregate SAVINGS (ex ante) are larger than intended INVESTMENT, this will set in train forces, via lower incomes, to reduce savings so that ex post savings and investment will be equal (◊ INCOME DETERMINATION, THEORY OF). ◊◊ MYRDAL, G. K.

Ex-dividend. Without DIVIDEND. The purchaser of a SECURITY quoted ex-dividend does not have the right to the next dividend when due. The term 'ex-', meaning excluding, is also used in a similar sense in relation to RIGHTS ISSUE, capitalization issue (◊ BONUS ISSUE), etc.

Ex post. ◊ EX ANTE.

Exceptional items. ◊ BELOW THE LINE.

Excess capacity. 1. The difference between the amount produced by a firm or group of firms and the higher amount that could most efficiently be produced. If a firm produces 1,000 cars at a cost of £5,000 each, but the lowest cost output would be 1,300 cars at £4,000 each, there is said to be excess capacity of 300 cars. It will exist at any point on an AVERAGE COST curve to the left of the lowest point. Sustained excess capacity is a feature of firms in MONOPOLISTIC COMPETITION. In PERFECT COMPETITION, it will only exist in the short term. **2.** The difference between actual output and maximum possible output in a firm, industry or economy. Excess capacity exists when there are unemployed resources; for a national economy it implies the existence of a *deflationary gap*.

Excess demand. The state of a market for a commodity in which consumers would choose to buy more of the commodity than is available at the prevailing price. Excess demand will be equal to zero at the EQUILIBRIUM price; it will be negative (i.e. EXCESS SUPPLY will exist) when the price is higher and will be positive when the price is lower. If price does not ration the available supply, something else must; usually it will be state-organized rationing or a queueing system coupled with a first-come first-served distribution. The situation can result from price control in which suppliers are legally prevented from raising their prices in response to high consumer demand.

Excess profit. ◊ PROFIT.

Excess supply. The state of the market for a commodity in which more of the commodity is available for purchase than consumers choose to buy at the prevailing price. Usually, such a situation leads to a price fall and excess supply disappears. In a market in which minimum price control is applied it can, however, persist; if, for example, trade unions prevent wages from falling enough, some argue that there can be an excess supply of labour (or unemployment) at the prevailing wage. (✧ EXCESS DEMAND.)

Exchange control. The control by the state through the BANKING system of dealings in gold and foreign CURRENCIES. Exchange control is concerned with controlling the purchase and sale of currencies by residents alone, since governments do not have complete powers to control the activities of non-residents. This must be done through the MARKET and is a matter of exchange management (✧ EXCHANGE EQUALIZATION ACCOUNT). Exchange control is only required where a country wishes to influence the international value of its currency. It is not willing to leave the value of its currency in terms of other currencies or gold to be determined in the FREE MARKET, as it would be under a system of floating EXCHANGE RATES, or to allow the fixed external value of its currency to be the determinant of the domestic price level. In its most extreme form, a country facing a balance-of-payments deficit may use exchange control to restrict imports to the amount earned in FOREIGN EXCHANGE by its nationals. All forms of exchange control are discouraged by the ORGANIZATION FOR ECONOMIC COOPERATION AND DEVELOPMENT and other international organizations concerned with encouraging INTERNATIONAL TRADE. It should be noted that a currency is not fully convertible (✧ CONVERTIBILITY) when exchange control is operated.

Exchange controls were introduced in the U.K. at the beginning of the Second World War and embodied in the Exchange Control Act of 1947. These controls were abolished in 1979, although the powers set out in the 1947 Act have not been repealed.

In 1986, the West German government made it a condition of allowing German residents to transact business in EUROPEAN CURRENCY UNITS that other countries in the EUROPEAN ECONOMIC COMMUNITY should abolish exchange controls (✧ COUNTER TRADE).

Exchange economy. An economy which has progressed beyond the point at which each household produces goods solely for its own consumption. Exchange, whether by BARTER or by the use of MONEY, enables the benefits of the specialization (✧ DIVISION OF LABOUR) and the ECONOMIES OF SCALE to be realized. (✧ ECONOMIC GROWTH.)

Exchange equalization account. An account controlled by the TREASURY and managed by the BANK OF ENGLAND which buys and sells sterling for gold and foreign CURRENCIES with the object of offsetting major fluctuations in the exchange value of the pound and keeping the SPOT MARKET price for the pound around some required rate. The account was set up by the 1932 Finance Act after the abandonment of the GOLD

STANDARD in the previous year. The ASSETS of the account include the GOLD AND FOREIGN EXCHANGE RESERVES and sterling, provided by the EXCHEQUER, invested in TREASURY BILLS. Similar funds or stabilization accounts are operated by other countries. ⟡ EXCHANGE RATE; INTERNATIONAL MONETARY FUND.

Exchange equation. ⟡ FISHER, I.

Exchange of shares. A means of business combination which can take two forms. In form (a) the companies retain their separate identities, but exchange a quantity of SHARES so that each company holds shares in the other and normally some directors will sit on both boards (⟡ INTERLOCKING DIRECTORATES). In form (b) two companies will merge, shares of one company being exchanged with or without a cash adjustment, for the whole of the issued share CAPITAL of the other. ⟡ MERGER; REVERSE TAKE-OVER.

Exchange rate. The price (rate) at which one CURRENCY is exchanged for another currency, for gold, SPECIAL DRAWING RIGHTS or EUROPEAN CURRENCY UNITS. These transactions are carried out spot or forward (⟡ SPOT MARKET and FORWARD MARKET) in the FOREIGN-EXCHANGE MARKETS. The actual rate at any one time is determined by SUPPLY and DEMAND conditions for the relevant currencies in the market. These in turn would depend on the BALANCE OF PAYMENTS deficits or surpluses of the relevant economies and the demand for the currencies to meet obligations and expectations about the future movements in the rate. If there were no government control over the exchange market (such as the U.K. exercises through the EXCHANGE EQUALIZATION ACCOUNT), there would be an entirely *free* or *floating exchange rate* in operation. With a freely floating system, no GOLD AND FOREIGN EXCHANGE RESERVES would be required as the exchange rate would adjust itself until the supply and demand for the currencies were brought into balance (⟡ PURCHASING-POWER PARITY THEORY). Under the rules of the INTERNATIONAL MONETARY FUND, established at the BRETTON WOODS Conference towards the end of the Second World War, exchange rates were fixed at a par value in relation to the dollar and fluctuations around this value were confined within a ±1 per cent band. The dollar itself was not subject to this restriction, because the U.S. government was committed to buying gold on demand at a fixed rate of \$35·0875 per ounce. However, in August 1971 the United States suspended the CONVERTIBILITY of the dollar into gold and other currencies, imposed a 10 per cent surcharge on IMPORTS and took other measures aimed at eliminating its balance-of-payments deficit. There followed a period during which some major currencies were allowed to float but subject to exchange-control regulations to keep the exchange-rate movements within limits (a '*dirty float*'). In December 1971, the 'Group of Ten' in the I.M.F. meeting at the Smithsonian Institute, Washington, agreed to a realignment of exchange rates which left the dollar devalued by about 5 per cent against an average of all other currencies, in exchange for a rise in the dollar price of gold to $38 per ounce and the removal of the import surcharge. In addition, it was agreed that the margin of permitted fluctuations should be ±2·25 per cent.

There has been much discussion in the past of the relative merits of floating compared with fixed exchange rates, and indeed of many hybrid systems which lie between these extremes. The floating rate has apparent attractions comparable to the advantages obtained, in terms of efficient resource allocation (⟡ RESOURCES), by a freely operating price mechanism (⟡ PRICE SYSTEM). This comparison, however, is superficial, because exchange rates are not just a PRICE; changes in exchange rates are likely to alter substantially the INCOME levels of communities. Fluctuations in the rate may be inconvenient for trading, and these fluctuations could be volatile if left to move freely. Moreover, because of the pressure of short-term CAPITAL movements or SPECULATION, the exchange rate could move in a direction different from what might be required by the domestic economy as reflected in its basic balance of payments. The system of fixed rates has been criticized on the grounds of its inflexibility and the fact that it places too much of the adjustment burden on the domestic economy. A middle course has been proposed in the 'moving parity', 'sliding parity', 'dynamic' or 'crawling peg' idea. In the *moving parity*, the par rate is automatically adjusted according to a moving average of past rates taken over a number of months. Professor J. E. MEADE has put forward a refined version of this called the *sliding parity* or *crawling peg*. In this, instead of the whole amount of a revaluation or devaluation taking place at once, it is spread in small percentages over a number of months, e.g. a 10 per cent devaluation may be achieved by a monthly ½ per cent reduction for fifty months. This system has the advantage that it is known and certain, while the monthly adjustment is too small to cause excessive speculative flows. Hendrick Houthakker, in his capacity as a member of the U.S. President's Council of Economic Advisers, has put forward proposals for a crawling peg which are similar to Professor Meade's. He has suggested that gradual adjustments in the exchange rate should be allowed up to 2 to 3 per cent per annum. These adjustments should be linked to the level of a country's reserves rather than past exchange rates. The Smithsonian system of flexible but fixed parities did not, in the event, last long. The floating of sterling in June 1972, described by the U.K. Chancellor of the Exchequer as 'temporary', marked the end of the fixed-parity system and by the following year all the currencies were subject to a 'managed' float. A survey, financed by the Rockefeller Foundation, among bankers and multinational corporations, was carried out in 1980 to obtain their views on their experience of the 'managed' float. The research showed that these institutions were generally in favour of it. Even the multinationals preferred floating to fixed exchange rates, though they admitted that foreign exchange now took up more management time. ⟡ CURRENCY APPRECIATION; EUROPEAN MONETARY SYSTEM; INTERNATIONAL LIQUIDITY.

Exchequer. The account of the central government kept at the BANK OF ENGLAND. ⟡ CONSOLIDATION FUND.

Excise duties. Taxes levied upon goods (e.g. beer) produced for home consumption as distinct from customs duties (⟡ TARIFFS, IMPORT), which are levied on goods entering or leaving the country. ⟡ TAXATION. Both excise duties and tariffs in the U.K. are administered by H.M. Customs and Excise.

Exclusive dealing. A 'tie' under which a retailer or wholesaler contracts to purchase from a supplier on the understanding that no other distributor will be appointed or receive supplies in a given area. Examples are tied petrol-filling stations and public houses. Where the sales outlets are owned by the supplier, as is frequently the case with public houses, exclusive dealing is an instance of VERTICAL INTEGRATION, but where the outlets are independently owned it is, in principle, illegal under the RESTRICTIVE TRADE PRACTICES ACT, though if registered and approved it is allowed. Exclusive dealing may be a BARRIER TO ENTRY but it can be defended on grounds of benefits to the consumer, such as after-sales service. ⟡ COMPETITION POLICY; FAIR TRADING ACT.

Exempt company. ⟡ PRIVATE COMPANY.

Exogenous variable. A VARIABLE whose value is not determined within the set of equations, or MODELS, established to make predictions or test a hypothesis. (⟡ ENDOGENOUS VARIABLE.)

Expectations. The views held by economic agents as to the future behaviour of relevant economic variables. Although expectations have some role in the theory of MICROECONOMICS (in particular, the COBWEB MODEL and in pricing behaviour in OLIGOPOLY) their primary importance is in MACROECONOMICS. In almost all models of the economy, in-built assumptions are made as to what views individuals hold about the future: when future rates of return in asset markets are uncertain, for example, the expectations of investors will determine the prevailing rate of interest more than the actual return made on any asset; when wage bargainers target a REAL WAGE, they must have a view of expected inflation to know what money wage to seek; under the ACCELERATION PRINCIPLE of investment, it is the expectations of firms about future demand that determines their investment behaviour. In any model where uncertainty is prevalent, the expectation-forming process of individuals will be important.

There are various different assumptions that can be made about expectations. First, they could be an EXOGENOUS VARIABLE; in this case they are not influenced by any events in the model, but are just imposed from outside. Secondly, they could be *backward looking*, made by economic agents on the basis of past values of the variables in question (◊ ADAPTIVE EXPECTATIONS). Thirdly, they can be RATIONAL EXPECTATIONS, in which case agents are assumed not to make systematic errors in their forecasting of variables. In certain economic models, by assuming rational expectations, very strong conclusions can be reached about how the economy should be controlled.

Expected utility. A measure of the welfare accruing to a consumer from an asset which yields an uncertain flow of benefits. Suppose, for example, a consumer takes part in a lottery, in which there is a 50 per cent chance of winning £10 and a 50 per cent chance of winning nothing. The consumer's expected UTILITY will be 50 per cent of the utility of winning £10 and 50 per cent of the utility of winning nothing. An important distinction should be made between the expected utility of a lottery and the utility of the expected outcome. In the example above, the expected utility of £5 may not be the same as the average of the utility of £10 and the utility of zero pounds. (◊ DIMINISHING MARGINAL UTILITY; RISK; RISK AVERSION.)

Expenditure tax. A form of DIRECT TAXATION on spending. Advocated by Nicholas KALDOR and more recently by James MEADE and others on the grounds that it would eliminate the necessity to define INCOME, which is a source of complexity and, many would argue, inequity in the common form of INCOME TAX. In practice expenditure would be defined as receipts in cash and kind (such as FRINGE BENEFITS) that would include receipts from disposals of financial assets minus admissible expenses connected with work and all saving (net acquisition of financial assets). The taxation of receipts minus saving and business expense in this way could be at progressive rates in the same way as income tax. Among the advantages claimed for an expenditure tax are that it would encourage saving and would not discriminate between alternative savings media (eliminating one set of distortions in CAPITAL MARKETS) and would close loopholes in the present system which allow the avoidance of income tax by converting income into CAPITAL. It should be understood that indirect taxes such as VALUE-ADDED TAX, although taxes on expenditure, are quite different from the proposed expenditure tax both in the method of collection and in their inability to take the individual financial circumstances of the spender into account.

Experimental economics. ◊ EMPIRICAL TESTING.

Export credits. ◊ EXPORT CREDITS GUARANTEE DEPARTMENT.

Export Credits Guarantee Department (E.C.G.D.). A U.K. government department (set up in 1930 as an independent department, although it had operated in another form from 1919), responsible to the Secretary of State for Trade and Industry, that has the authority, under TREAS-URY control, to issue INSURANCE policies to cover risks met by exporters. The risks are, broadly, insolvency or default of debtor, refusal of goods on delivery and risks of a political nature such as the imposition of import licensing and EXCHANGE CONTROLS. The policies may be either 'comprehensive' or 'specific', the former being in respect of short-term cover up to six months and the latter of longer-term cover up to ten years or more. The E.C.G.D. also covers losses incurred on the forward exchange market on the default of a buyer. The E.C.G.D. may also give an interest-rate subsidy to other financial institutions, such as the COMMERCIAL BANKS, by offering export credits. The department has been induced to grant better terms in the past to bring its rates into line with those of similar institutions in other countries that have used this type of insurance as a vehicle for concealed export subsidies ($\Diamond$ EXPORT INCENTIVES). There has been increasing international concern about the use of export-credit subsidies to capture export markets in the developing countries. As a consequence, twenty-two developed countries within the O.E.C.D. ($\Diamond$ ORGANIZATION FOR ECONOMIC CO-OPERATION AND DEVELOPMENT) concluded an 'Arrangement on Guidelines for Officially Supported Export Credits' which fixes minimum interest rates and maximum repayment periods for specified categories of borrower. These guidelines are revised as market conditions change.

Export-Import Bank. A U.S. government agency, established in 1934 for the purpose of encouraging U.S. trade by supplying CREDIT at subsidized rates of interest and financial guarantees to customers of U.S. exporters. It also gives U.S. exporters INSURANCE cover ($\Diamond$ EXPORT CREDITS GUARANTEE DEPARTMENT).

Export incentives. Preferential treatment for firms that sell their products abroad, compared with firms that sell to the home market. They may take the form of direct SUBSIDIES, special CREDIT facilities, grants, concessions in the field of DIRECT TAXATION, benefits arising from the administration of indirect taxation, and export credit INSURANCE on exceptionally favourable terms ($\Diamond\!\!\Diamond$ EXPORT CREDITS GUARANTEE DEPARTMENT). Various international associations discourage the practice of artificially stimulating exports by any of these methods. The GENERAL AGREEMENT ON TARIFFS AND TRADE lays down special provisions relating to export subsidies, direct or indirect, in an attempt to limit them. The Stockholm Convention setting up the EUROPEAN FREE TRADE ASSOCIATION lists various forms of aid to exporters which member countries are required to avoid. The Treaty of Rome, which established the EUROPEAN ECONOMIC COMMUNITY, although less specific than the Stockholm Convention, nevertheless discourages the granting of privileged aid to any economic sectors. In the field of '*tied aid*' (◊ FOREIGN AID) the O.E.C.D. rules insist that at least 25 per cent of the finance must be aid where the grant is conditional on the donor country receiving the contract for the project being financed.

Export multiplier. The ratio of the total increase in a country's NATIONAL INCOME to the increment in export revenue generating the increase. The size of the multiplier depends on the propensities to save (◊ AVERAGE PROPENSITY TO SAVE; MARGINAL PROPENSITY TO SAVE) of the recipients of the increases in INCOMES derived from the increase in export revenue and the country's PROPENSITY TO IMPORT. The export multiplier can be regarded as a special case of the general MULTIPLIER.

Export rebates. ◊ CUSTOMS DRAWBACK; EXPORT INCENTIVES.

Export surplus. ◊ BALANCE OF PAYMENTS.

Exports. The goods and SERVICES produced by one country which are sold to another in exchange for the second country's own goods and services for gold and FOREIGN EXCHANGE or in settlement of DEBT. Countries tend to specialize in the production of those goods and services in which they can be relatively most efficient, because of their indigenous factor endowments (◊ FACTORS OF PRODUCTION).

Countries devote home resources to exports because they can obtain more goods and services by international exchange than they would from the same resources devoted to direct home production. The U.K. exports about 22 per cent of its domestic output compared with about 6 per cent in the U.S.A. and 13 per cent in Japan. ◊◊ BALANCE OF PAYMENTS; INTERNATIONAL TRADE; MERCANTILISM.

Exports unrequited. ◊ UNREQUITED EXPORTS.

External deficit. A synonym for BALANCE OF PAYMENTS deficit.

External diseconomies. ◊ DISECONOMIES OF SCALE.

External effects. ◊ EXTERNALITIES.

Externalities. Consequences for welfare or COSTS not fully accounted for in the PRICE and MARKET system. *External diseconomies* of production include traffic congestion and pollution created by a manufacturing plant. These cause reductions in the welfare of people living near the factory and perhaps increased costs to adjacent factories which might need to purify water taken from a river bordering both plants. Because the third parties receive no compensation (do not charge) for these external diseconomies there are costs of production not accounted for in the price system. External diseconomies also arise in CONSUMPTION, for example, where people eating ice-cream leave paper on the pavement or cigarette smokers pollute the air in a public building. Both production and consumption externalities can occur simultaneously where, for example, a restaurant creates noise, congestion and smell.

External economies of production may arise where the existence of several factories stimulates the availability of skilled labour, shopping facilities or component supplies. External economies of consumption include a garden at the front of a house which gives pleasure to passers-by as well as to the occupants and increases the value of adjoining property. Defence or other public expenditure on research and development is sometimes justified on the additional grounds that it stimulates the development of new TECHNOLOGY which may become freely available to all. This is usually called a *spillover effect*, an alternative term for externality.

Externalities are important in determining the efficient allocation of resources. In a FREE-MARKET ECONOMY individuals only attempt to maximize their own private utility or profit, and external costs and benefits will not be reflected in the prices of things. A firm may make perfumes very cheaply, but nevertheless be polluting the atmosphere in the process, to the detriment of non-perfume buyers. Unless the cost of this pollution is reflected in the price of the perfume, people will buy more of it than they would choose to if they had to pay for the entire cost to society of its production. In short it is full *social* costs which are important in determining an efficient resource allocation, and *private* costs which determine prices.

There are two means of dealing with externalities. First, a structure of taxes and subsidies can be designed to *internalize* the externalities and ensure that the full costs or benefits of production are reflected in the prices charged. In this case, even if a factory causes pollution, it can carry on producing as long as it properly compensates society for the damage caused. A second approach is to put restrictions on certain unsocial activities and make other beneficial activities compulsory. This will, however, usually not be as efficient as the optimal taxes or subsidies could be, because you may restrict activity that, despite its negative external effects, still benefits the performer more than its restriction helps society. ◊ SOCIAL WELFARE.

Extraordinary items. ◊ BELOW THE LINE.

F

Face value. Nominal as distinct from MARKET value. The face value of a SECURITY is the price at which it will be redeemed; of an ORDINARY SHARE its PAR VALUE or issued price; of a coin the amount stamped on it, which might for a silver or gold coin be less than its market value.

Factor. 1. ⟡ FACTORS OF PRODUCTION. **2.** ⟡ FACTORING. **3.** An agent who buys and sells goods on behalf of others for a COMMISSION called *factorage*.

Factor cost. A term used in the national accounts (⟡ SOCIAL AC-COUNTING) to describe the valuation of output at market prices less taxes on expenditure plus subsidies.

Factor endowment. The relative availability of the different FACTORS OF PRODUCTION in a country. An important determinant of the pattern of international trade ⟡ HECKSCHER–OHLIN principle. ⟡ COM-PARATIVE ADVANTAGE.

Factor markets. The LABOUR market, the CAPITAL market and other MARKETS in which the FACTORS OF PRODUCTION are bought and sold. The theory of distribution (⟡ DISTRIBUTION, THEORY OF) attempts to explain how the PRICES of factors are determined and how they are allocated between alternative uses.

Factor payments. Payments made to the owners of the FACTORS OF PRODUCTION in return for their use in the production process.

Factor price equalization theorem. ⟡ SAMUELSON, P. A.

Factorage. ⟡ FACTORING.

Factoring. The business activity in which a company takes over the responsibility for the collecting of the DEBTS of another. It is a service primarily intended to meet the needs of small and medium-size firms. It developed comparatively slowly in the U.K. compared with the U.S.A., in spite of the fact that the banks took important interests in the leading factoring companies. Typically, the client debits all his sales to the factor and receives immediate payment from him less a charge of about 2–3 per cent and interest for the period of TRADE CREDIT given to the customer, thus improving the client's cash flow considerably. The factor takes over the entire responsibility for retrieving the debts due from the client's customers and protects the client from bad debts. The factor, however, has some control over sales either by imposing a maximum CREDIT limit which he is willing to meet or by vetting specific prospective clients. Through international factoring companies, the factor can offer a service to exporters by protecting his customers from bad debts overseas and by giving, for instance, expert advice on FOREIGN EXCHANGE transactions (⟡ EXPORT CREDITS GUARANTEE DEPARTMENT).

Factors of production. The INPUTS or resources used in the process of production. LAND, LABOUR and CAPITAL are the three main headings used in analysis of the factors, with entrepreneurship (⟡ ENTRE-PRENEUR) often counted as a fourth. ⟡ FACTOR ENDOWMENT; NATURAL RESOURCES; SAY, J.-B.

Fair trade policy. ⟡ RECIPROCITY.

Fair Trading Act. The Fair Trading Act of 1973 replaced the Monopolies and Restrictive Practices (Inquiry and Control) Act of 1948 and the Monopolies and Mergers Act of 1965, but generally consolidated this previous legislation. The Act established a new office in the Director-General of Fair Trading and gave him wide powers, enabling him to monitor and investigate trading activities and to refer monopoly situations to the Monopolies and Mergers Commission, a power previously confined to the appropriate minister. The director-general cannot refer a merger but may be called upon to act as adviser to the minister. (The powers of the Office of Fair Trading were extended by the COMPETITION ACT of 1980.) The Act also changed the guidelines of the previous Acts with regard to restrictive practices. A monopoly is now deemed to exist when the market share is one-quarter, compared with one-third in the 1948 Act; although, as before, a monopoly need not necessarily be considered to be against the public interest. Further, the monopoly may now be in relation to a local market, whereas previously the U.K. or a large part of it was deemed to be the market in question. Finally, the Fair Trading Act extended the monopoly legislation to nationalized industries and other statutory undertakings, which had previously been exempted. Ministers can also refer restrictive labour agreements to the commission, although in these cases the minister is not empowered to make Orders on the outcome of the investigations. As for collective restrictive agreements which were placed under the jurisdiction of the Restrictive Practices Court by the RESTRICTIVE TRADE PRACTICES ACT of 1956, the Director-General of Fair Trading has taken over the responsibilities of the Registrar of Restrictive Practices. The relevant Acts have not been repealed, e.g. the Restrictive Trade Practices Act of 1956 and 1968 and the Resale Prices Act of 1964. However, the Fair Trading Act extended the coverage of the restrictive practices legislation to include restrictive agreements and information agreements affecting the supply of commercial services. The registration of most commercial services with restrictive agreements was required from March 1976. These cover almost all commercial services such as hairdressers, travel agencies, hotels, passenger transport organizations, etc. The director-general has a duty to keep under review and identify any commercial practices which might be against consumers' interest, that, for instance, might mislead or confuse, and on the basis of his investigations can recommend a course of action to the Secretary of State for Trade and Industry (◊ COMPETITION ACT). He may also seek an undertaking from individuals or firms that any unfair trading practices they have committed will be discontinued. The Office of Fair Trading publishes such undertakings in *Trade and Industry*, naming the individuals and firms and describing the nature of their offence. The director-general's responsibilities cover not only the consumer's economic welfare but also his health and safety. The Act enables the secretary of state to act moderately quickly against new forms of unwelcome trade practices by issuing Statutory Orders which obviate the need for the cumbersome procedure of progressing bills through Parliament. The Office of Fair Trading also has the duty to supervise and grant licences under the CONSUMER CREDIT ACT. (◊ MONOPOLIES COMMISSION; RESALE PRICE MAINTENANCE).

Farm subsidies. ◊ COMMON AGRICULTURAL POLICY.

F.a.s. (free alongside ship). ◊ C.I.F.

Federal reserve bank. ◊ FEDERAL RESERVE SYSTEM.

Federal reserve board. ◊ FEDERAL RESERVE SYSTEM.

Federal Reserve System (FED). The central banking system of the United States. It differs from that of most other countries' CENTRAL BANKS in that it consists not of one bank but of twelve regional banks, twenty-five branches and eleven offices under the control of the Federal Reserve Board in Washington. The capital of the reserve banks (total ASSETS $238 billion) is owned by the 5,978 member banks, i.e. COMMERCIAL BANKS, who receive a fixed DIVIDEND. The considerable surpluses that the reserve system earns go to the U.S. internal revenue. The regional reserve banks act as central banks for their members, act as LENDERS OF LAST RESORT by rediscounting bills (◊ DISCOUNTING), hold their CASH requirements and provide clearing facilities. The commercial banks are required to hold reserves in the Federal Reserve, which were $32·9 billion in September 1986. The U.S. commercial BANKING system is a unit rather than a BRANCH BANKING system; three-quarters of the 14,285 banks in the U.S. have no branches. In many states branches are not allowed by law, although through the development of amalgamations and holding companies the U.S. commercial banking system is not as fragmented as it appears. Considerably less than half the commercial banks are members of the Federal Reserve System, but these members hold about 85 per cent of the total DEPOSITS of all commercial banks. Some of the commercial banks, the 'national banks', are required to join the reserve system by law, and others may apply for membership if they wish to do so. The Federal Reserve Board consists of governors appointed for a term of fourteen years by the President of the United States with Senate approval. The Chairman of the FED has a term of only four years, allowing each President to appoint his own chairman. The Board acts in effect as the central bank and approves the discount and other RATES OF INTEREST of the system, sets CASH RATIO requirements, supervises foreign business and generally regulates the operation of the banking system including the review of applications for mergers. The Federal Open Market Committee, a subcommittee of the board, through controlling the purchases of government SECURITIES by the reserve banks, effectively gives the board power to conduct open-market operations. The FED was created in 1913 by the Federal Reserve Act in response to the widespread and severe problems of 1907 during which many banks failed.

Federal Trade Commission. ◊ ANTI-TRUST.

Fertility rate. ◊ BIRTH RATE.

Fiduciary issue. Paper MONEY (◊ BANKNOTE) not backed by gold or silver. The term has its origins in the Bank Charter Act of 1844, which fixed the fiduciary issue limit at £14 million. Any notes issued in excess of this amount had to be fully backed by gold. The fiduciary limit has been successively raised and the monetary authorities are now free to alter the note issue as they wish; effectively the note issue is now entirely fiduciary. ◊◊ BANKING AND CURRENCY SCHOOLS.

Final consumption. ◊ FINAL GOODS.

Final expenditure. ◊ FINAL GOODS.

Final goods. Something which is produced for CONSUMPTION rather than as an INTERMEDIATE PRODUCT used in the process of production. *Final consumption*, i.e. consumption of final goods alone, is included in the totals of national output in SOCIAL ACCOUNTING; if intermediate goods were also included there would be double counting of output. Only government final consumption (which excludes TRANSFER PAYMENTS), consumers' expenditure (all of which, by definition, is final) and investment goods enter into *final expenditure* and thus into the GROSS DOMESTIC PRODUCT.

Finance. The provision of MONEY when and where required. Finance may be short-term (usually up to one year), medium-term (usually over one year and up to five to seven years) and long-term. Finance may be required for CONSUMPTION or for INVESTMENT. For the latter when provided it becomes CAPITAL. ◊◊ BUSINESS FINANCE; CONSUMER CREDIT; PUBLIC FINANCE.

Finance company. An imprecise term covering a wide range of FINANCIAL INTERMEDIARIES, most commonly a synonym for FINANCE HOUSE.

Finance Corporation for Industry (F.C.I.). ◊ FINANCE FOR INDUSTRY.

Finance for Industry (F.F.I.). *Investors in Industry* (3i). A holding company for the Industrial and Commercial Finance Corporation

(I.C.F.C.) and the Finance Corporation for Industry (F.C.I.). Both these organizations were formed in 1945 with the support of the BANK OF ENGLAND and other financial institutions. I.C.F.C. provides long-term finance for small- and medium-sized companies unable to raise funds from the banks or the stock market (⟡ MACMILLAN COMMITTEE). It has since regularly supplemented its resources by raising LOAN CAPITAL and has steadily expanded. It now has eighteen branches throughout Britain. F.C.I. performs a similar function for larger companies. The grouping of the I.C.F.C. and the F.C.I. under F.F.I. in 1975 and the increased resources made available to them at that period represented a response to increasing criticism over the facilities available for the provision of long-term capital for industry. The controversy surrounding this issue also resulted in the launching of the Equity Bank in 1976 (⟡ EQUITY CAPITAL FOR INDUSTRY). F.F.I. was renamed *Investors in Industry* in 1984. ⟡ TECHNICAL DEVELOPMENT CAPITAL LTD.

Finance house. A financial institution engaged in the provision of HIRE PURCHASE and other forms of instalment credit. Also called finance companies, hire-purchase finance companies and INDUSTRIAL BANKS. There are several hundred finance houses in the U.K., which account for the bulk of INSTALMENT CREDIT debt, the remainder being owed to retailers. Some of the hire-purchase debt of retailers is purchased by the finance houses under what are known as 'block discounts'. The bulk of hire-purchase business is accounted for by the members of the FINANCE HOUSES ASSOCIATION. About half the funds of the finance houses comes from interest-bearing deposits, not only from the general public, but from industrial and commercial companies and other financial institutions including the COMMERCIAL BANKS (the interest paid is generally higher than that offered by the commercial banks); other sources of funds are capital reserves, BILLS discounted and bank overdrafts. The largest source of the finance houses' funds is in fact the commercial banks, and most of the larger finance houses are subsidiaries of the banks. Similarly, several finance houses are subsidiaries of manufacturing companies and advance instalment credit only for their parent company's products, e.g. Ford Motor Credit Co. Although advances for cars and other consumer durables represent a major proportion of their business, the CROWTHER COMMITTEE found that 59 per cent of the outstanding balances of the finance houses were for business purposes and only 41 per cent for end consumers. This is the result of the controls which have been imposed by the government on hire-purchase lending in the past. These controls were relaxed under the system of CREDIT CONTROL which places similar restraints on hire-purchase lending as upon other types of credit. Hire purchase is not the sole, although it is the main, activity of the finance houses; they also make loans for other purposes, including bridging finance, leasing and FACTORING, stocking loans for motor dealers and second mortgages.

Finance Houses Association (F.H.A.). An association of FINANCE HOUSES in the U.K. mainly concerned with HIRE PURCHASE. The association represents the industry to the government, especially on MONETARY POLICY, maintains a code of practice and a creditworthiness register of clients. It has absorbed the INDUSTRIAL BANKERS ASSOCIATION, which represented the smaller INDUSTRIAL BANKS.

Financial assets. ◇ ASSETS.

Financial intermediaries. Institutions which hold MONEY balances of, or which borrow from, individuals and other institutions, in order to make loans or other INVESTMENTS. Hence, they serve the purpose of channelling funds from lenders to borrowers. In standing between lenders and borrowers, intermediaries provide services to each, often at little or no cost compared with direct investment. By virtue of their size and expertise, financial intermediaries are able to reduce risks for lenders by enabling them to spread their investments widely, for example through ASSURANCE or INVESTMENT TRUSTS. They also provide *maturity transformation.* BUILDING SOCIETIES, for example, allow depositors to withdraw their money on demand but provide long-term funds for MORTGAGE lending. It is usual to distinguish between banks in the banking sector and so-called non-bank financial intermediaries. The importance of this distinction arises from the fact that the LIAB-ILITIES of banks are part of the MONEY SUPPLY, and this may not be true of the non-bank financial intermediaries. (◇ BANKING.) The most important of the non-bank financial intermediaries are the building societies, HIRE PURCHASE companies, INSURANCE companies, SAVINGS BANKS, PENSION FUNDS and investment trusts.

Financial ratios. 1. Specifically, measures of creditworthiness. The principal measures are the CURRENT RATIO, the DEBT or NET WORTH ratio (long-term debt to net worth), DIVIDEND COVER, INTEREST COVER and the net tangible ASSETS ratio (total tangible assets less current LIABILITIES and minority interests to long-term debt). All these ratios are measures of the asset or income cover available to the suppliers of CAPITAL to the business. **2.** Generally calculations based on company accounts and other sources, such as STOCK EXCHANGE share prices, designed to indicate the profitability or other financial aspects of a business, e.g. return on net assets, PRICE–EARNINGS RATIO and stock–sales ratio (◇ INVENTORIES). ◇ RATE OF RETURN.

Financial Services Act 1986. ◇ SECURITIES AND INVESTMENTS BOARD.

Financial Times Actuaries Share Indices. A detailed series of price indices, EARNINGS and YIELD averages for British SECURITIES on the London STOCK EXCHANGE published daily, with some history, in the *Financial Times* newspaper. The indices are produced in cooperation with the

London and Edinburgh Actuary Institutes, and are of particular value to PENSION FUND managers and others who wish to follow movements in the values of share PORTFOLIOS. Unlike the FINANCIAL TIMES STOCK INDICES, the actuaries' share indices are base-weighted chain-link indices, 10 April 1962 = 100. Over fifty price indices and averages are published in the series, based on approximately 730 shares and a sample of individual fixed-interest STOCKS. In addition to price indices, average earnings, dividend yields and PRICE–EARNINGS RATIOS are provided for equities, while for fixed-interest securities prices and yields are given. The 500 Share Index consists of equities broken down into CAPITAL goods, CONSUMER goods, and further into industry, e.g. chemicals, household goods; the financial group of equities is broken down into sectors, e.g. banks, property. The 500 Share Index stood at 916·38 and the All-Share Index at 836·29 on 2 January 1987. This broadly based index provides the best representation of movements in the prices of securities on the London Stock Exchange, but it is supplemented by other, more narrowly based, indices. ◊ FINANCIAL TIMES STOCK INDICES; F.T./S.E. 100 SHARE INDEX. ◊ INDEX NUMBER; SHARE INDICES.

Financial Times Industrial Ordinary Share Index. ◊ FINANCIAL TIMES STOCK INDICES.

Financial Times Stock Indices. A series of price indices published daily in the *Financial Times* newspaper for GOVERNMENT SECURITIES (1926 = 100), fixed-interest SECURITIES (1928 = 100), gold-mine shares (1955 = 100) and industrial ORDINARY SHARES (1935 = 100). For ordinary shares, EARNINGS, YIELD and PRICE–EARNINGS RATIO averages are also given. There are also indicators of STOCK EXCHANGE activity, for example the number of bargains (transactions) recorded on S.E.A.Q. The Financial Times Industrial Ordinary Index is probably the best-known barometer for the stock MARKET: like the time or cricket scores, it is available to telephone subscribers by dialling a number. The index is a geometric average calculated hourly for thirty BLUE CHIPS and stood at 1,320·2 on 2 January 1987. ◊ INDEX NUMBER; SHARE INDICES.

Financial trusts. ◊ TRUST.

Financial year. Years of account for financial purposes often do not coincide with calendar years, and are hence referred to as financial years. A financial year 1978/9, for example, might run from 31 August 1978 to 1 September 1979, or from 31 May 1978 to 1 June 1979. The British government fiscal or tax year runs from 6 April of one year to 5 April in the following year. In the United States, the fiscal year runs from 1 July to 30 June.

Firm, theory of the. The study of the behaviour of firms with respect to: the inputs they buy; the production techniques they adopt; the quantity they produce; and the price at which they sell their output. Two basic approaches to the theory can be identified: (a) The traditional approach assumes that producers aim to maximize profits; whether they are monopolists or perfect competitors, they produce at a point where MARGINAL COST equals MARGINAL REVENUE and employ inputs to a point at which their MARGINAL REVENUE PRODUCT is equal to the cost of employing them (◊ LABOUR, DEMAND FOR; PERFECT COMPETITION). (b) More modern theories attempt to represent the complications of the large institutions which characterize society today, especially the SEPARATION OF OWNERSHIP FROM CONTROL of firms, which, it is suggested, may lead to objectives other than profit maximization. These alternative theories postulate the aim as being: the maximization of sales; growth; or management utility – with profit merely held to some minimum level (SATISFICING). The BEHAVIOURAL THEORY OF THE FIRM postulates the existence of a multiplicity of conflicting objectives. It is not clear whether the alternative theories actually contradict the claim of the traditional approach that firms maximize profits because in the long run the maximization of, for example, sales growth might merely amount to the maximization of profit. Moreover, as a single goal, profit maximization perhaps better and more simply approximates to the behaviour of firms than any other single objective. It is thus usually accepted that the insights of traditional theory are useful despite their dependence on apparently unrealistic assumptions. ◊ COURNOT, A. A.; GALBRAITH, J. K.; SIMON, H. A.

First in, first out (F.I.F.O.). An accounting term referring to the principle on which stocks are valued. Under F.I.F.O., raw materials are assumed to be withdrawn from stock in the order in which they were put in, the oldest items being 'drawn first'. This traditional convention results in valuation at original rather than current prices. In a period of INFLATION this may mean that material costs are understated, and current stock values and profits overstated. Last in, first out is an alternative procedure, which has the opposite effect. A second alternative is to average the opening and closing stock. ◊ STOCK APPRECIATION.

Fiscal drag. The effect of INFLATION upon effective tax rates. Under progressive INCOME TAX systems, increases in earnings may push taxpayers into higher tax brackets, even though their REAL INCOME might be declining. This could result in an unintended shift in FISCAL POLICY with a depressing effect upon the growth of demand and output. A similar process can work in reverse and under conditions of DEFLATION; for example, if prices fall tax rates will also fall even though real incomes have increased. Fiscal drag therefore can have the effect of a BUILT-IN STABILIZER.

Fiscal neutrality. The idea that the tax system should be designed so that as few distortions are caused to economic behaviour as possible. It is not fiscally neutral, for example, to apply VALUE-ADDED TAX to some items but not others, for this causes consumers to switch spending from taxed items to untaxed ones. This distortion of behaviour is economically inefficient. Despite the ECONOMIC EFFICIENCY of applying the principle of fiscal neutrality, it is often argued that distributional or other objectives are served by manipulating different taxes. For this reason, LUMP-SUM TAXES, which are the most neutral, are rarely applied in practice and fiscal neutrality is seen as only one of a number of desirable features of a tax system.

Fiscal policy. The budgetary stance of central government. Decisions to lower taxation or increase PUBLIC EXPENDITURE in the interests of stimulating AGGREGATE DEMAND are referred to as loosening fiscal policy. Higher tax rates or reductions in public expenditure will tighten fiscal policy. There is often considerable controversy about the appropriate stance of fiscal policy and the balance between fiscal and MONETARY POLICIES, the two main tools of government for influencing the general level of economic activity. ⟡ BALANCED BUDGET; FRIEDMAN, M.; KEYNES, J. M.; KEYNESIAN ECONOMICS; PUBLIC-SECTOR BORROWING REQUIREMENT; QUANTITY THEORY OF MONEY; REFLATION.

Fiscal year. ⟡ FINANCIAL YEAR.

Fisher equation. ⟡ FISHER, IRVING; QUANTITY THEORY OF MONEY.

Fisher, Irving (1867–1947). A mathematician by professional training, Fisher was Professor of Political Economy at Yale University from 1898 to 1935. His main works on economics were *Mathematical Investigations in the Theory of Value and Prices* (1892), *Nature of Capital and Income* (1906), *Rate of Interest* (1907), *Purchasing Power of Money* (1911), *The Making of Index Numbers* (1922) and *Theory of Interest* (1930). *The Rate of Interest*, which was substantially revised in 1930, progressed the theory of INTEREST onwards from BÖHM-BAWERK towards the modern theory of INVESTMENT APPRAISAL. The RATE OF INTEREST is governed by the interaction of two forces: (a) the 'willingness or impatience' of individuals with respect to the giving up of INCOME now compared with income in the future (Fisher invented the term TIME PREFERENCE); and (b) the 'investment opportunity principle', the technological ability to convert income now into income in the future. He called the latter the 'rate of return over cost', which KEYNES said was the same as his 'marginal efficiency of capital' (⟡ INTERNAL RATE OF RETURN). He defined this 'rate of return over cost' as that discount rate (⟡ DISCOUNTING) which equalized the PRESENT VALUE of the possible alternative investment choices open. He showed how the ranking of investment choices depended on the rate of interest used. He clarified economists' ideas on the nature of CAPITAL, distinguishing between a stock and a flow of WEALTH. A house is capital stock, but its use is a flow of income. He was the author of the 'quantity of money' (exchange) equation $MV = PT$, in which $M =$ the stock of money, $V =$ the VELOCITY OF CIRCULATION, $P =$ the PRICE level and $T =$ the output of goods and SERVICES ($\lozenge$ QUANTITY THEORY OF MONEY).

Fisher developed the theory of INDEX NUMBERS and established a set of conditions which an ideal index should satisfy.

Fixed asset. $\lozenge$ ASSETS.

Fixed capital. $\lozenge$ BUSINESS FINANCE; CAPITAL.

Fixed charge. $\lozenge$ FLOATING CHARGE.

Fixed costs. COSTS which do not vary with output, for example, the RENT on a factory LEASE. Also called *overhead*, although in accounting terminology all costs except direct labour and materials are usually regarded as overheads and some of these overhead costs, for example, electricity, postage, may vary with output. In the LONG RUN all costs are variable and the SHORT RUN is defined as the period of time in which all the FACTORS OF PRODUCTION cannot be varied. $\lozenge$ AVERAGE COST; SUNK COSTS.

Fixed debenture. $\lozenge$ FLOATING DEBENTURES.

Fixed exchange rate. $\lozenge$ EXCHANGE RATE.

Fixed trust. A form of UNIT TRUST in which the investment PORTFOLIO is fixed in the trust deed and the proportions of different SECURITIES in which the trust funds are invested is not varied during the life of the trust. The unit share certificates in the trust represent a specific number of each of the SHARES in the trust portfolio. The advantage of the fixed trust as opposed to other types of unit trust are that the small investor can buy into a known and wide cross-section of shares and that there is no risk of loss through inefficient management. On the other hand, fixed trusts are clearly less satisfactory than a well-managed FLEXIBLE TRUST, which can weed out poor INVESTMENTS and switch funds into better securities. For these reasons, new fixed trusts are now relatively less common than they were in the early days of the unit trust movement.

Flags of convenience. An expression relating to the practice of many shipowners of registering their vessels with countries other than those of their own home ports in order to avoid taxes, or stringent safety or crewing regulations. The extent of the movement can be seen from the growth of the merchant fleets of such small countries as Panama and Liberia.

Flat yield. A YIELD on a fixed-interest SECURITY calculated by expressing the annual INTEREST payable as a proportion of the purchase price of the security. It omits any allowance for the difference between the purchase price and the redemption price. $\lozenge$ REDEEMABLE SECURITIES.

Flexible budget. $\lozenge$ BUDGET.

Flexible exchange rate. $\lozenge$ EXCHANGE RATE.

Flexible trust. The most common form of UNIT TRUST, in which the PORTFOLIO of SECURITIES purchased by the trust can be varied at the discretion of the managers. Also called a 'managed' trust. Flexible trusts were developed in the 1930s to overcome the problems raised by the inflexibility of FIXED TRUSTS.

Floating asset. ◊ FLOATING CAPITAL.

Floating capital. CAPITAL which is not invested in fixed ASSETS, such as machinery, but in work in progress, wages paid, etc. Synonymous with WORKING CAPITAL. ◊◊ CURRENT RATIO.

Floating charge. An assignment of the total ASSETS of a company or individual as COLLATERAL SECURITY for a DEBT, as opposed to particular assets, when such an assignment is called a *fixed charge*.

Floating debentures. A type of DEBENTURE where the LOAN is secured by a charge on the assets of a firm generally. Where specific assets secure a debenture LOAN, it is known as a *fixed debenture*.

Floating debt. 1. Generally, any short-term DEBT as opposed to FUNDED DEBT. **2.** Specifically, that part of the NATIONAL DEBT that consists of short-term borrowing, i.e. TREASURY BILLS, TREASURY DEPOSIT RECEIPTS, and to a minor extent, WAYS AND MEANS ADVANCES from the BANK OF ENGLAND. Treasury bills form an important part of the LIQUID assets of the money market, so that the size of the floating debt has considerable influence over the total MONEY SUPPLY.

Floating exchange rate. ◊ EXCHANGE RATE.

Floating pound. ◊ EXCHANGE RATE.

Flotation. Raising new CAPITAL by public subscription. A private company issuing SHARES to the public for the first time is said to be 'going public'. ◊◊ STOCK EXCHANGE; UNLISTED SECURITIES MARKET.

F.o.b. (free on board). A term applied to the valuation of goods up to the point of embarkation. It compares with C.I.F. (charged in full or cost-insurance-freight), which is the valuation including all transport costs and INSURANCE to destination. U.K. imports are entered by Customs in the overseas trade accounts as c.i.f., and exports as f.o.b. For the BALANCE OF PAYMENTS accounts, the IMPORT figures are adjusted to an f.o.b. basis to make them comparable with exports, the revenues or costs represented by the difference between c.i.f. and f.o.b. being included in INVISIBLES.

Food and Agriculture Organization (F.A.O.). An organization set up in 1945, within the framework of the United Nations, which has its headquarters in Rome. It conducts research and offers technical assistance with the aim of improving the standards of living of agricultural areas. It is concerned with the improvement of PRODUCTIVITY and distribution networks for the agricultural, forestry and fishing industries. It conducts surveys, issues statistics, produces forecasts of the world food situation and sets minimum nutritional standards.

163

Forced saving. A situation in which expenditure falls short of DISPOSABLE INCOME because goods are not available for CONSUMPTION, rather than because consumers have voluntarily decided to accumulate SAVING. Under these circumstances, PRICES of goods would rise and supply would increase in a FREE-MARKET ECONOMY so that forced saving would be a temporary symptom or DISEQUILIBRIUM. If for any reason there were LONG RUN constraints on the increase in output the increase in prices would reduce demand and stimulate the development of SUBSTITUTES. Forced saving does occur in PLANNED ECONOMIES and, at a MACROECONOMIC level democratic governments can enforce saving by increasing TAXATION while holding PUBLIC EXPENDITURE constant. ◊〉 QUANTITY RATIONING; REPRESSED INFLATION.

Forces of the market. ◊ MARKET FORCES.

Foreign aid. The administered transfer of resources from the ADVANCED COUNTRIES for the purpose of encouraging economic growth in the DEVELOPING COUNTRIES (◊ ECONOMIC GROWTH, STAGES OF). Funds transferred to the developing countries from governments and international institutions (◊〉 INTERNATIONAL BANK FOR RECONSTRUCTION AND DEVELOPMENT) in the form of official aid account for about one-third of the total transfer of funds to the developing countries (the remainder being accounted for by loans through the COMMERCIAL BANKS and DIRECT INVESTMENT). For the least-developed countries, however, official aid accounts for over 80 per cent of such transfers. In 1984 the U.K. committed a total of £1·3 billion to all forms of foreign aid. U.K. aid is administered by the Overseas Development Administration. ◊〉 EUROPEAN ECONOMIC COMMUNITY; EXPORT INCENTIVES; ORGANIZATION OF PETROLEUM EXPORTING COUNTRIES.

Foreign balance. ◊ BALANCE OF PAYMENTS.

Foreign bill of exchange. ◊ FOREIGN-EXCHANGE MARKET.

Foreign exchange. Claims on another country held in the form of the currency of that country or interest-bearing BONDS. ◊〉 GOLD AND FOREIGN EXCHANGE RESERVES.

Foreign-exchange market. The MARKET in which transactions are conducted to effect the transfer of the CURRENCY of one country into that of another. The market is not located at a single centre, but is international, with transactions conducted electronically. The need to settle accounts with foreigners gave rise to the *foreign bill of exchange*, which was accepted by banks or other institutions of international standing (◊ ACCEPTING HOUSE). These bills were traded at discount, and in this way the foreign-exchange market was established, the bills reflecting actual international trade flows. However, the market has developed in modern times and is now dominated by financial institutions which buy and sell foreign currencies, making their PROFIT from the divergences between the EXCHANGE RATES and RATES OF INTEREST in the various financial centres. ⬦ CONVERTIBILITY; FORWARD EXCHANGE MARKET.

Foreign investment. The acquisition by governments, institutions or individuals in one country of ASSETS in another. Foreign investment is defined to cover both DIRECT INVESTMENT and PORTFOLIO investment and includes both public authorities and private firms and individuals. For a country in which SAVINGS are insufficient relative to the potential demand for INVESTMENT, foreign capital can be a fruitful means of stimulating rapid growth. In addition, direct investment may be a means of easing the strain on the BALANCE OF PAYMENTS which might otherwise occur in response to an increase of home demand. Direct investment often involves the setting up of subsidiary companies for the domestic production of goods which previously were imported from the parent company (⬦ INDUSTRY ACTS). There have been in recent years some major shifts in the U.K. balance of foreign investment overseas. In 1975 the investment account of the BALANCE OF PAYMENTS was in *surplus* by an unprecedented £1·6 billion, largely due to the increase in net investment by the oil companies in the development of the U.K. offshore oil industry. However, from 1977 the net flow of foreign investment was reversed. In 1985 there was a *deficit* of about £7 billion. In 1979 EXCHANGE CONTROLS were removed and this stimulated a substantial increase in U.K. portfolio investment overseas. In addition there has been an expansion by the U.K. of net direct foreign investment in recent years.

Foreign Operations Administration. ⬦ EUROPEAN RECOVERY PROGRAMME.

Forward exchange market. A MARKET in which contracts are made to supply CURRENCIES at fixed dates in the future at fixed PRICES. Currencies may be bought and sold in the FOREIGN-EXCHANGE MARKET either 'spot' or 'forward' (⬦ SPOT MARKET and FORWARD MARKET). In the former case the transaction takes place immediately, and it is in this market that EXCHANGE RATES are kept at their managed levels by government intervention. In the forward exchange market, currencies are bought and sold for transacting at some future date, i.e. in three months' or six months' time. The difference between the 'spot' rate of exchange and the 'forward' rate is determined by the RATE OF INTEREST and the exchange risk; that is, the possibility of APPRECIATION or DEPRECIATION of the currencies transacted. Therefore, the size of the PREMIUM or DISCOUNT of, for instance, forward sterling compared with spot sterling indicates the strength of the market's expectation of an appreciation or depreciation of sterling and its extent.

Forward market. Any MARKET in FUTURES; that is to say, a market in which promises to buy or to sell SECURITIES or COMMODITIES at some future date at fixed PRICES are bought and sold. An example of a forward market is the FORWARD EXCHANGE MARKET.

Franchising. A contractual arrangement under which an independent franchisee produces or sells a product or service under the brand name of the franchisor and to his specifications and with marketing and other support. The franchisee pays a royalty to the franchisor and may purchase supplies from him. The franchisee provides his own CAPITAL and is legally an independent ENTERPRISE which is none the less highly dependent upon the franchisor, though, as Curran and Stanworth have pointed out, many SMALL BUSINESSES, say with a high proportion of sales to a single customer, may enjoy no greater degree of independence than many franchised enterprises. There are, according to one estimate, 80,000 businesses running on a franchised basis in Britain; examples are filling-stations and various fast-food outlets.

Franked investment income. INCOME, normally of a company, on which TAXATION has already been paid at source, i.e. income received as a DIVIDEND by one company from another (◊ CORPORATION TAX).

Free depreciation. ◊ CAPITAL ALLOWANCES.

Free-enterprise economy. ◊ FREE-MARKET ECONOMY.

Free exchange rate. ◊ EXCHANGE RATE.

Free goods. COMMODITIES that have no PRICE because they are not scarce and do not require the use of scarce FACTORS OF PRODUCTION to create them, for example, fresh air and sunshine (in certain parts of the world). Things that are given away without charge, for example book matches or government services, are not free goods, because they have OPPORTUNITY COSTS.

Free market. A MARKET in which SUPPLY and DEMAND are not subject to REGULATION.

Free-market economy. Strictly, an economic system in which the allocation of RESOURCES is determined solely by SUPPLY and DEMAND in FREE MARKETS, though in practice there are some limitations on market freedoms in all countries. Usually used as synonymous with CAPITAL-ISM.

Free port. A port which will accept cargo without the imposition of any import TARIFF or certain TAXES. In addition, they may be granted special dispensation regarding legislation affecting businesses in the domestic market outside the port, such as employment conditions, health and safety and development planning. There are several hundred such ports throughout the world, the largest being Hong Kong and Singapore. In 1984 the U.K. set up six such free ports, in which imports are free of customs tariffs, EXCISE DUTIES and VALUE-ADDED TAX.

Goods become liable to these taxes on passing from the free-port zone into the domestic market.

Free reserves. ◊ COMPANY RESERVES; NET WORTH.

Free trade. The condition in which the free flow of goods (◊ ECONOMIC GOOD) and SERVICES in international exchange is neither restricted nor encouraged by direct government intervention. Now virtually an archaism, since all governments are heavily involved in regulating overseas trade. The most common means of affecting the distribution and levels of international trade are import TARIFFS, import QUOTAS and export subsidies (◊ EXPORT INCENTIVES). It has been broadly accepted among economists that an international free-trade policy is desirable to optimize world output and INCOME levels in the long run. The ORGANIZATION FOR EUROPEAN COOPERATION AND DE-VELOPMENT and the United Nations are both committed to freeing world trade, but most economists would agree that under present conditions complete freedom of trade would not be desirable. In any case, it is clear that individual countries could gain from protectionism (◊ CUSTOMS UNION; INFANT-INDUSTRY ARGUMENT; PROTECTION). Towards the end of the eighteenth century there was a reaction against MERCANTILISM, which had advocated government intervention to obtain surpluses on VISIBLE TRADE. This reaction was consolidated in a new economic liberalism and the doctrine of LAISSEZ-FAIRE. The CLASSICAL ECONOMISTS' support of a free-trade policy was not so much based on specific economic analyses of international trade as simply part of their general belief in what ADAM SMITH called the 'hidden hand': the greatest good is achieved if each individual is left to seek his own PROFIT. The free-trade era lasted in England for almost a century. After the First World War economic nationalism reached its peak and free trade was abandoned for protectionism. However, since the end of the Second World War there has been a general acceptance internationally of the dangers of protectionism and some reduction in INTERNATIONAL TRADE barriers, especially for manufactured goods. Progress has been slow, and has paradoxically been associated with the growth of regional CUSTOMS UNIONS. ◊◊ EUROPEAN ECONOMIC COMMUNITY; EUROPEAN FREE TRADE ASSOCIATION; GENERAL AGREEMENT ON TARIFFS AND TRADE.

Free-trade area. An association of a number of countries between whom all import TARIFFS and QUOTAS and export subsidies and other similar government measures to influence trade (◊ EXPORT INCENTIVES) have been removed. Each country, however, continues to retain its own inter-national trade measures *vis-à-vis* countries outside the association. ◊◊ CUSTOMS UNION; ECONOMIC COMMUNITY OF WEST AFRICAN STATES; EUROPEAN FREE TRADE ASSOCIATION; PREFERENTIAL TRADE AREA FOR EAST AND SOUTHERN AFRICA.

Free-trade zone. A customs-defined area in which goods or services may be processed or transacted without attracting taxes or duties or being subjected to certain government regulations. A special case is the FREE PORT, into which goods are imported free of customs TARIFFS or taxes. Free-trade zones have been approved at fifty-six locations in the United States. In these, customs duties are not paid until, and if, the goods are sold in the United States outside the zone. A plan was approved by the Federal Reserve Bank in 1980 for the setting up of free-trade zones for banks dealing in international finance. This enables the banks to service the accounts of multinational firms without attracting city and state taxes and also to be free from the normal banking regulations such as the FED's reserve requirements and RATE OF INTEREST ceilings (◊ ENTERPRISE ZONES; EUROCURRENCY).

Freedom of entry. Absence of BARRIERS TO ENTRY preventing new suppliers entering a MARKET. One of the assumptions of PERFECT COMPETITION. ◊ CONTESTABILITY.

Frequency distribution. A tabulation showing a statistical population allocated numerically into subcategories of a specified classification. For instance, the following frequency distribution shows how the population of a total of 22 million U.K. taxpayers divided into different categories of income before tax in 1982/3.

Income	Thousands
Less than £5,000	8,154
£5,000 to £10,000	9,080
£10,000 to £20,000	4,103
Over £20,000	633
Total	21,970

Source: *Annual Abstract of Statistics*, 1986 (H.M.S.O.).

Frictional unemployment. Minimum level of UNEMPLOYMENT, even under so-called full-employment conditions (◊ EMPLOYMENT, FULL). Frictional unemployment arises from people being in between jobs, from SEASONAL UNEMPLOYMENT and from the need for retraining when economic growth creates a mismatch between local unfilled vacancies and people suited for them. Frictional unemployment arises because of time lags in the functioning of LABOUR markets which are inevitable in a FREE-MARKET ECONOMY; there are search delays involved, for example in moving from one job to another. Frictional unemployment is conceptually distinct from STRUCTURAL UNEMPLOYMENT, which results in heavy local concentrations of unemployment and, of course, from unemployment arising from a deficiency of demand. ◊ CLASSICAL UNEMPLOYMENT; LABOUR, MOBILITY OF.

Friedman, Milton (b. 1912). Professor of Economics at the University of Chicago and leading member of the Chicago school. After a short period with the Natural Resources Commission in Washington, Professor Friedman joined the research staff of the National Bureau of Economic Research in 1937 and, apart from a short period, has maintained a close association with this important research organization. During the Second World War he served in the Tax Research Division of the U.S. Treasury. In 1946 he was appointed Associate Professor of Economics and Statistics at the University of Chicago, becoming Professor of Economics there from 1948 until he retired in 1979. In 1976 he was awarded the Alfred Nobel Memorial Prize (✧ NOBEL PRIZE) in Economics by the Royal Swedish Academy of Science. His main published works in economics include *Taxing to Prevent Inflation* (1943), *Essays in Positive Economics* (1953), *A Theory of the Consumption Function* (1957), *A Program for Monetary Stability* (1960), *Price Theory* (1962), *A Monetary History of the United States 1867–1960* (1963), *Inflation: Causes and Consequences* (1963), *The Great Contraction* (1965), *The Optimum Quantity of Money* (1969), *A Theoretical Framework for Monetary Analysis* (1971), *An Economist's Protest: Columns in Political Economy* (1975), *Free to Choose. A Personal Statement* (1980) and *Monetary Trends in the United States and the United Kingdom* (1982). Friedman has made contributions to the THEORY OF DISTRIBUTION, arguing for an approach in which high incomes are regarded as a reward for taking risks. He has also been a leading defender of the Marshallian tradition in MICROECONOMICS (✧ MARSHALL, A.) and made a methodological defence of classical economics that stimulated controversy for a decade. His PERMANENT-INCOME HYPOTHESIS was also an important contribution to the theory of the CONSUMPTION FUNCTION. His main work, however, has been on the development of the QUANTITY THEORY OF MONEY and its empirical testing. He has extended the Fisher equation (✧ FISHER, IRVING) to include other VARIABLES such as WEALTH and RATES OF INTEREST, and has made statistical tests to attempt to measure the factors determining the demand for money to hold. Friedman has advocated strict control of the MONEY SUPPLY as a means for cutting INFLATION. ✧ LIQUIDITY PREFERENCE; UNEMPLOYMENT, NATURAL RATE OF.

Friendly society. A mutual INSURANCE association. There are several thousand friendly societies in Britain set up voluntarily to provide benefits and assistance during sickness, unemployment, retirement or death. The tax advantages enjoyed by the friendly societies have been reduced in recent years.

Fringe benefits. Non-wage or salary rewards provided for employees, for example pensions and company cars. Some fringe benefits, within certain limits, such as pension arrangements, luncheon vouchers or subsidized canteens are not assessed for INCOME TAX while others, such as low-interest loans, are. Holidays (in excess of any legal minimum requirement), private health insurance, 'free' coal or other products and discounts on goods purchased through the employer are other examples of fringe benefits. In England, a series of laws from 1749 onwards culminating in the Truck Acts in the nineteenth century made it illegal to pay workers wholly in kind, because of abuse by employers of rights given, for example, in 'company stores'.

Frisch, Ragnar A. K. (1895–1973). Born in Norway, Professor Frisch graduated in economics at the University of Oslo. He was appointed to the Chair of Economics at that university in 1931, a post he held until he retired in 1965. His published works include *Statistical Confluence Analysis by Means of Complete Regression Systems* (1943), *Planning for India* (1960), *Theory of Production* (1965), *Maxima and Minima* (1966) and *Economic Planning Studies: A Collection of Essays* (1976). He won the NOBEL PRIZE in Economics (jointly with J. Tinbergen) in 1969. Professor Frisch pioneered work in the application of mathematics and statistics in the testing of hypotheses in economics. He invented the word ECONOMETRICS and founded the Econometric Society. He contributed to the analysis of the dynamics of TRADE CYCLES and the application of econometrics to economic planning.

'Front door.' ⟡ 'BACK DOOR.'

F.T./S.E. 100 Share Index (Footsie). A weighted (⟡ WEIGHTED AVERAGE) arithmetic index of the EQUITY shares of the 100 largest companies quoted on the London STOCK EXCHANGE. The components of the index are weighted by the issued share capital of the companies included in it. Started in January 1984 (30 December 1983 = 1,000) to provide a more representative index than the Financial Times Industrial Ordinary Share Index (⟡ FINANCIAL TIMES STOCK INDICES) and one which could be calculated minute by minute from prices taken from S.E.A.Q. On 2 January 1987, the Footsie index stood at 1,681·1.

Full employment. ⟡ EMPLOYMENT, FULL.

Full-line forcing. The exercise of market power to oblige a buyer to take a whole range of products rather than only one of them.

Function. A description of the relationship which governs the behaviour of two or more related variables. Functions can be expressed in different ways. If consumption (C) is $0·9 \times$ income (Y), we can represent this information as: an equation ($C = 0·9Y$); a graph (C on one axis, Y on the other); or a tabulation (with certain values of C in one column and the corresponding values of Y in the other). The function is an important feature of many different areas of economics: the UTILITY *function* maps the quantities of different goods consumed on to levels of consumer utility. A DEMAND FUNCTION maps different price levels on to the corresponding quantities demanded. (⟡ PRODUCTION FUNCTION.)

Fundamental analysis. ◊ CHARTIST.

Funded. ◊ PERSONAL PENSION.

Funded debt. Generally, short-term DEBT that has been converted into long-term debt (◊ FUNDING). Specifically, the funded debt was orginally that consisting of CONSOLS, the INTEREST on which was paid out of the CONSOLIDATED FUND. Then it came to mean all government perpetual LOANS where there is no obligation on the part of the government to repay, such as consols 3½ per cent war loan, but it is sometimes taken to include all government SECURITIES quoted on the STOCK EXCHANGE.

Funding. The process of converting short-term to long-term DEBT by the sale of long-term SECURITIES and using the funds raised to pay off short-term debt. Funding may be carried out by a company because its CAPITAL STRUCTURE is inappropriate, i.e. to take advantage of the fact that long-term CAPITAL is normally cheaper and less likely to be withdrawn than short-term capital. Companies or governments may also take advantage of a period of low RATES OF INTEREST to repay long-term STOCKS at the earliest possible date and replace them with new stocks at lower rates of interest. Funding has also been used as an instrument of MONETARY POLICY by the government as well as for NATIONAL DEBT management. By selling long-dated securities and purchasing TREASURY BILLS (which are treated as part of the CASH reserves of the COMMERCIAL BANKS), the LIQUIDITY of the BANK-ING system is reduced. ◊ PENSION FUNDS.

Funding operations. The conversion of short-term fixed-interest DEBT (FLOATING DEBT) to long-term fixed-interest debt (FUNDED DEBT). It is normally used in relation to the work of the NATIONAL DEBT commissioners, but the BANK OF ENGLAND's operations in TREAS-URY BILLS and government BONDS approaching maturity are also covered by the term. Private companies with bank OVERDRAFTS or other short-term sources of CAPITAL may also decide to convert them to long-term debt by funding operations.

Futures. Contracts made in a 'future MARKET' for the purchase or sale of COMMODITIES or financial ASSETS, on a specified future date. Many commodity exchanges, e.g. wool, cotton and wheat, have established futures markets which permit manufacturers and traders to HEDGE against changes in PRICE of the raw materials they use or deal in. ◊ FORWARD EXCHANGE MARKET; LONDON INTERNATIONAL FINANCIAL FUTURES EXCHANGE; SPECULATION.

G

Galbraith, John Kenneth (b. 1908). A leading American political economist, he was born in Canada and, after graduating at Toronto in agriculture, took a Ph.D. at the University of California. In 1949 he became Professor of Economics at Harvard University and was, from 1961 to 1963, U.S. ambassador to India. His major books include *A Theory of Price Control* (1952), *American Capitalism* (1952), *The Great Crash 1929* (1955), *The Affluent Society* (1958), *The Economic Discipline* (1967), *The New Industrial State* (1967), *Economics, Peace and Laughter* (1971), *Economics and the Public Purpose* (1974) and *The Nature of Mass Poverty* (1979). He has been a sharp critic of current economic theory because of its preoccupation with growth (◊ GROWTH THEORY). He has accused advanced societies of producing waste simply to satisfy the need for growth for its own sake. He has argued that in modern advanced economies the problems of the distribution of the total product to the different sectors of society should be given more attention. At the same time, he believes that academic theoretical economics is too bound by its old tradition of the efficacy of competition to the extent of losing touch with the real world. In *American Capitalism* he showed how modern society breeds monopolistic power systems. MONOPOLY in industry induces a countervailing monopoly or MONOPSONY in distribution, in LABOUR and even in government purchasing agencies.

In *The New Industrial State* he argued that the 'technostructure' (managers) of the largest corporations in modern industrial society is motivated primarily by a desire to remain secure and to expand its corporation rather than to maximize PROFITS. The highly capitalized nature of the industrial system has required a considerable extension of planning and control, notably of the CAPITAL supply, through SELF-FINANCING, and of demand, through advertising and distribution techniques. Under these conditions the assumption of CONSUMERS' SOVEREIGNTY that underlies modern microeconomic theory (◊ MICROECONOMICS) is invalid and the theory no longer relevant to much of the economic system. Galbraith's views have been challenged by many economists as an overstatement of monopolistic power but are none the less sometimes accepted as an accurate statement of tendency in the modern economy. He has been critical of the advocates of the strict control of the supply of MONEY as a means of reducing INFLATION. ◊ CONSUMPTION; FIRM, THEORY OF; KEYNES, J. M.; MILL, J. S.; OLIGOPOLY; QUANTITY THEORY OF MONEY.

Galiani, Ferdinando (1728–87). A Neapolitan priest who wrote a number of treaties on economic subjects, in particular *Della moneta* (1751) on MONEY and exchange, and *Dialogues sur le commerce des blés* (1770) on FREE TRADE in cereals. He resolved the so-called *paradox of value*, e.g. water is useful but cheap, whereas diamonds are useless but expensive, by analysing the PRICE of a COMMODITY in terms of its SCARCITY on the one hand and its UTILITY on the other; utility being not only a reflection of a commodity's usefulness, but also its pleasure-giving potential. He explained how price both influences and is influenced by DEMAND. Much of his work in VALUE theory was original, though part of a long tradition of ecclesiastical thought. However, he was not familiar to English economists of the early nineteenth century, and much of the ground covered by Galiani was gone over again by them. ⟡ MARGINAL UTILITY.

Galloping inflation. ⟡ HYPERINFLATION.

Game theory. Much of economic theory is concerned with the processes and conditions under which individuals or firms maximize their own benefits or minimize their own costs in markets in which their individual actions do not materially influence others (⟡ PERFECT COMPETITION). There are, however, many cases in which economic decisions are made in situations of conflict, where one party's action induces a reaction from others. An example is wage bargaining between employers and unions. A more simple case is that of DUOPOLY, in which the price set by one seller will be based on his view of that set by the other in reply. The mathematical theory of games has been applied to economics to help elucidate problems of this kind. In order to illustrate the principle of game theory, consider the case of two 'players', *X* and *Y*. *X*, when considering his choice of action, knows that *Y* will respond. *X*, therefore, plans his best action (his *maximum* strategy) on the basis of his judgement of the worst (the *minimum* strategy) that *Y* could do against him. *Y* will plan and decide on his own strategy in a similar way. The theory of games is concerned with the study of the optimal strategies to maximize pay-offs, given the risks involved in judging the responses of adversaries, and also the conditions under which there is a unique solution (i.e. that the optimum strategy for *X* and that of *Y* are both possible and not inconsistent). Games may be classified into *zero-sum games*, in which one player's gain is another player's loss; *non-zero-sum games*, in which one player's decision may benefit all players; *cooperative games*, in which collusion is possible; and *non-cooperative games*, when it is not. The application of the theory of games to economics was first introduced by J. von Neumann and O. Morgenstern in *Theory of Games and Economic Behaviour* (1944). ⟡ NASH EQUILIBRIUM; PRISONER'S DILEMMA.

Gearing. The relative importance of LOANS in the CAPITAL STRUCTURE of a firm. Also called the *debt ratio* and, in the U.S.A., *leverage*. There are several ways of measuring gearing. The usual way is the ratio of fixed-interest DEBT to shareholder's interest plus the debt (◇ NET WORTH). *Equity gearing* is the ratio of borrowings to EQUITY or risk capital. *Capital gearing* may be defined as bank borrowings and other debt as a percentage of *net tangible assets* (◇ ASSETS; FINANCIAL RATIOS). A corporation may borrow CAPITAL at fixed interest, and if it can earn more on that capital than it has to pay for it in interest, then the additional earnings accrue to the EQUITY shareholders. A firm with high gearing will be able to pay higher DIVIDENDS per SHARE than a firm with lower gearing earning exactly the same return on its total capital, provided that return is higher than the rate it pays for LOAN CAPITAL. However, the contrary is also true, so that the higher the gearing, the greater the risk to the equity shareholder. Roughly speaking, if a firm's initial capital consists of £7,000 subscribed by ordinary shareholders and £3,000 borrowed at fixed interest, for example through DEBENTURES, it would be said to have a gearing of 30 per cent.

General Agreement on Tariffs and Trade (G.A.T.T.). An international organization with a secretariat in Geneva which came into operation in January 1948 as a result of an agreement made at an international conference the previous year, which also included plans for an INTERNATIONAL TRADE ORGANIZATION. Nothing came of the latter, but G.A.T.T. has proved a useful body for international TARIFF bargaining. Its Articles of Agreement pledge its member countries, which now number ninety-two, to the expansion of multilateral trade (◇ MULTILATERALISM) with the minimum of barriers to trade, reduction in import tariffs and QUOTAS and the abolition of preferential trade agreements. There have been successive negotiations between the contracting parties, aimed at reducing the levels of tariffs, from the first meeting in Geneva in 1947, up to the seventh, the so-called TOKYO ROUND OF TRADE NEGOTIATIONS, which began in 1974 and was concluded in 1979. The first major revision of G.A.T.T. was ratified in March 1955. The provisions regarding the treatment of SUBSIDIES designed to reduce IMPORTS or increase exports were strengthened (◇ EXPORT INCENTIVES). Members are required to give details of any subsidies, and if these are liable to prejudice the interests of any other member they are required to discuss the possibility of reduction or elimination. On export subsidies, in particular, member governments 'should seek to avoid' the use of subsidies on the export of primary products. For exports of other products, subsidies, whether direct or indirect, should cease 'as soon as practicable' if they result in export prices lower than the home prices of the product. In 1965 a revision came into force of the section of the agreement dealing with trade and development which laid emphasis on the special problems of the DE-VELOPING NATIONS and a committee on trade and development was given the responsibility for progress on the elimination of barriers on the trade in products of particular interest to the developing nations. This new approach enables the MOST-FAVOURED NATION principle to be waived in relation to agreements entered into with developing countries (generalized system of preferences). There has been a growing tendency for countries to become more protectionist (◊ PROTECTION) through the imposition of non-tariff barriers and for economic blocs to make preferential trade agreements with other countries. Examples of the latter are the EUROPEAN ECONOMIC COMMUNITY in respect of countries in the Mediterranean and the U.S.A. in respect of Latin America.

Since the Tokyo Round the recession in world trade and the growth in unemployment have led to renewed demands for protectionist measures to safeguard domestic economies. Accordingly, a ministerial meeting of G.A.T.T. was held in 1982 to reaffirm the free-trade principles upon which G.A.T.T. was founded. However, no further liberalization measures were agreed at the meeting of the kind that had been concluded at the previous rounds. The ministers, however, affirmed that they would 'make determined efforts to resist protectionist measures and refrain from taking or maintaining any measures inconsistent with G.A.T.T.'. Studies were initiated to examine farm export subsidies, financial support for domestic industries, a formula by which a country may impose import restrictions to protect its domestic industry, textiles, tropical products and trade in SERVICES. Agreement was eventually reached, at a meeting of delegates at Punta del Este, Uruguay, in 1986 on an agenda for a new round of negotiations. This round will consider aspects such as agricultural export subsidies, restrictions on trade in services (e.g. banking, insurance, transport, etc.) and restrictions on direct FOREIGN INVESTMENT.

General agreement to borrow. ◊ INTERNATIONAL MONETARY FUND.

General equilibrium. The state of a set of interrelated markets when there is no EXCESS DEMAND or supply in any market. In a world of two commodities, an increase in the demand for one must lead to a decrease in demand for the other if all consumers spend what they have and no more. Given this interrelation, it is not as obvious that equilibrium can prevail in all markets simultaneously as it is that it can prevail in one market at a time. (◊◊ GENERAL EQUILIBRIUM ANALYSIS.)

General equilibrium analysis. 1. The study of the behaviour of economic variables taking full account of the interaction between those variables and the rest of the economy. For example, a general equilibrium approach to the study of advertising would concentrate both on demand

and supply in the market for advertising space *and* the effects of advertising on demand more generally. In this it contrasts with PARTIAL EQUILIBRIUM ANALYSIS. **2.** The study of simultaneous equilibria in a group of related markets. The prime focus is whether there is a set of prices that would ensure that equilibrium exists in each market. If so, is such an equilibrium stable – if disruptions occurred, would there be a tendency to return to equilibrium? And is such an equilibrium unique, or are there many sets of prices at which all markets clear? The analysis is attributable to WALRAS, who limited his consideration to a theoretical economic system in which all consumers were utility-maximizers and firms perfectly competitive. A unique, stable equilibrium can exist in such an economy. (⟡ LEONTIEF, W. W.)

General government. ⟡ PUBLIC SECTOR.

Geneva Conference (1947). ⟡ GENERAL AGREEMENT ON TARIFFS AND TRADE (G.A.T.T.).

Genoa Conference (1922). ⟡ BRUSSELS CONFERENCE (1920).

Geometric progression. A sequence of numbers in which the ratio of each number to the preceding one is a constant, e.g. 2, 4, 8, 16 ... (⟡ ARITHMETIC PROGRESSION).

George, Henry (1839–97). An American economist and politician who stood for election as Mayor of New York for the 'single tax' party. His major publication was *Progress and Poverty* (1879). He was considerably influenced by the English classical economists, ADAM SMITH, DAVID RICARDO and J. S. MILL (⟡ CLASSICAL ECONOMICS). Ricardo's analysis had drawn attention to the way in which agricultural production could yield an INCOME to landowners in the form of RENT which was surplus to all costs, including normal PROFIT. J. S. Mill had suggested that all future additions to rental income should be taxed away. This would have the merit, George claimed, of enabling the exchequer to be financed by one TAX only and of avoiding the distortions caused by multiple taxation of different economic activities. This idea has some affinity with the '*impôt unique*' of the PHYSIOCRATS. Some similarity with these ideas appears in the Central Land Board, set up in Britain by the Town and Country Planning Act 1947, which taxed development rental profits by 100 per cent, and also with the Land Commission of 1967–71.

Giffen good. A commodity for which demand increases at higher prices and falls at lower prices. This odd feature – that price rises cause demand to increase – was observed by Sir Robert Giffen (1837–1910) of basic commodities in the budgets of the nineteenth-century poor. As the price of bread rose, the poor, who always relied on it as their staple diet, could simply no longer afford to buy other relatively more luxurious food items, which they had to replace with increased purchases of bread.

Similarly, because bread constituted the bulk of their spending, when its price fell, they enjoyed such a large increase in their REAL INCOME that they could then afford to substitute for bread in their diet other more palatable food.

The 'giffen paradox' is explained within the normal framework of demand and supply analysis. When the price of any good rises, it has two effects: it changes the relative attractiveness of other goods, increasing the desire of consumers to buy more of items whose price has not risen – the SUBSTITUTION EFFECT. It also has an effect on the spending power of consumers, who can do less with their money than they could before prices rose, as though their income had fallen and no prices had changed. This is called the INCOME EFFECT. Two features explain the characteristics of a giffen good. First, demand for it rises as the income of consumers falls (it is always INFERIOR). But secondly, what essentially accounts for its perverse behaviour is the fact that this income effect on the demand for the giffen good outweighs the substitution effect which for all commodities causes consumers to switch purchases from items whose prices rise.

The giffen good, usually considered too much of a freak to be of anything except theoretical interest, should not be confused with items that enjoy 'snob value'. These too can enjoy simultaneously rising prices and demand, accounted for by the fact that some consumers delight in paying for the knowledge that certain of their possessions are expensive. The usual way of viewing this 'snob effect' is to treat a change in price of an item to which it applies as a change in the fundamental characteristics of the product sold, making it wholly incomparable to the same physical object sold at a different price and not therefore an item for which a single demand curve can be constructed.

Gift tax (U.S.). A levy on the VALUE of certain property given away to others and paid by the donor. In Britain, prior to the introduction of CAPITAL TRANSFER TAX there was no tax on gifts as such, although they were added back into the estate of the donor for duty purposes if made within seven years of the donor's death. In certain instances, a gift is counted as a realization of an asset by the donor, who is liable to CAPITAL GAINS tax on any increase in its value since it was originally acquired by him. ⟡ ESTATE DUTY.

Gilt-edged securities. Fixed-interest British GOVERNMENT SECURITIES traded on the STOCK EXCHANGE. They are called gilt-edged because it is certain that INTEREST will be paid and that they will be redeemed (where appropriate) on the due date. Some gilt-edged securities are DATED SECURITIES, some are UNDATED SECURITIES and some are index-linked (⟡ INDEXATION). Gilt-edged securities are not, of course, a risk-free investment, because of fluctuations in their market value. Gilt-edged securities do not include TREASURY BILLS. ⟡ YIELD.

Gini coefficient. A coefficient based on the LORENZ CURVE showing the degree of inequality in a FREQUENCY DISTRIBUTION such as personal incomes. It is measured as:

$$G = \frac{\text{area between Lorenz curve and } 45° \text{ line}}{\text{area above the } 45° \text{ line}}$$

If the frequency distribution is equal, the Lorenz curve coincides with the 45° line, and $G = 0$. ($\diamond$ CONCENTRATION RATIO.)

Giro system. $\diamond$ CREDIT TRANSFER.

Gold and foreign exchange reserves. The stock of gold and foreign CUR- RENCIES held by a country to finance any calls that may be made from its creditors for the settlement of DEBT. The extent of these requests for settlement are dependent, firstly, on the size of the out- standing LIABILITIES, which, in turn, is related to the BALANCE OF PAYMENTS surplus or DEFICIT, and secondly, on the willingness of creditors to hold the debt (currency) in question. Pressure on the reserves, therefore, may be a reflection either of the underlying trading problems of the country or of the expectation of a fall in the EX- CHANGE RATE of the country's currency. The official published figures of reserves, however, do not necessarily reflect the total amount of gold and foreign currency which could be used to meet obligations, any more than an individual's CURRENT ACCOUNT at the bank does. The reserves exclude, for instance, the CREDIT facili- ties available through the INTERNATIONAL MONETARY FUND and PORTFOLIO foreign investments.

Gold exchange standard. A special form of the GOLD STANDARD. In this system the CENTRAL BANK will not exchange its CURRENCY for gold on demand (as is the case under the gold standard), but will exchange it for a currency which is itself on the gold standard. The central bank holds the parent country's currency in its reserves along with gold itself. The Scandinavian countries adopted this system in respect of sterling up until 1931, when the U.K. came off the gold standard.

Gold market. There are five member firms in the gold MARKET in London, in which dealings in gold BULLION take place. Each day the members meet to fix the price of gold for that day in relation to the pressure of demand ($\diamond$ INTERNATIONAL LIQUIDITY).

Gold points. $\diamond$ SPECIE POINTS.

Gold standard. A country is said to be on the gold standard when its CENTRAL BANK is obliged to give gold in exchange for any of its CURRENCY presented to it. When the U.K. was on the gold standard before 1919, anybody could go to the BANK OF ENGLAND and demand gold in exchange for BANKNOTES. The gold standard was central to the CLASSICAL ECONOMIC view of the equilibrating processes in INTERNATIONAL TRADE. The fact that each currency was freely convertible into gold fixed the EXCHANGE RATES between currencies (◊ SPECIE POINTS), and all international debts were settled in gold. A BALANCE OF PAYMENTS surplus caused an inflow of gold into the central bank's reserves. This enabled the central bank to expand the money supply without fear of having insufficient gold to meet its LIABILITIES. The increase in the quantity of money (◊ MONEY SUPPLY) raised prices, resulting in a fall in the demand for EXPORTS and therefore a reduction in the balance-of-payments surplus. The reverse happened in the event of a DEFICIT. The U.K. came off the gold standard in 1914, partly returned to it in 1925, but was forced to abandon gold finally in 1931. The U.S. dollar was convertible into gold at $35 per ounce, a rate fixed by the BRETTON WOODS agreement. This was subsequently raised until in 1973 it was fixed at $42 per ounce. In 1976 this system was finally abandoned and gold was removed from the articles of the INTERNATIONAL MONETARY FUND. ◊ BANKING AND CURRENCY SCHOOLS; GOLD EXCHANGE STANDARD.

Gossen, Hermann Heinrich (1810–58). Born in Düren, near Aachen, in Germany, Gossen studied law and went into government service in deference to his father's wishes. It was not until after his father's death in 1847 that he dedicated himself to the study of economics. His major economic work is *Entwicklung der Gesetze des menschlichen Verkehrs und der daraus fliessenden Regeln für menschliches Handeln* (1854). In this book, Gossen set out a theory of consumer behaviour based on theories which were subsequently to be independently rediscovered and enshrined in the theory of MARGINAL UTILITY by JEVONS, MENGER and WALRAS. The first edition of his book was completely ignored, and Gossen's recognition had to wait until after his death. It was Jevons who, in the preface to his own *Theory of Political Economy* (1871), drew attention to the significance of Gossen's achievement, admitting that Gossen had 'completely anticipated him as regards the general principles and methods of economics'. Gossen's first law states that the pleasure obtained from each additional amount consumed of the same COMMODITY diminishes until satiety is reached. Gossen's second law states that once a person had spent his entire INCOME, he would have maximized his total pleasure from it only if the satisfaction gained from the last item of each commodity bought was the same for each commodity. Gossen's third law, derived from the first two, states that a commodity has a subjective VALUE, and the subjective value of each additional unit owned diminishes and eventually reaches zero. ◊ BERNOULLI'S HYPOTHESIS.

Government expenditure. ◊ BUDGET.

Government securities. All government fixed-interest paper, including FUNDED DEBT and TREASURY BILLS. The government does not, of course, issue EQUITY capital. ◊ GILT-EDGED SECURITIES.

Government stocks. Fixed-interest SECURITIES issued by the government, often known as 'GILT-EDGED'. ⟡ FUNDED DEBT.

Graduated Pension Scheme. ⟡ NATIONAL INSURANCE.

Green currency. The EUROPEAN ECONOMIC COMMUNITY fixes farm prices according to the COMMON AGRICULTURAL POLICY. The prices of agricultural products subject to the C.A.P. are set in terms of EURO-PEAN CURRENCY UNITS, so that in principle the price of each product is the same throughout the community. Within each country, however, these E.C.U. prices have, of course, to be translated into national currencies according to some EXCHANGE RATE. Now that exchange rates are normally left to float, it would mean that farm prices would alter more or less continuously if values of these exchange rates were used. The E.E.C. decided, therefore, to use a fixed rate of exchange specifically for the C.A.P. agricultural prices. This exchange rate is called the 'green' rate and is fixed unless and until the relevant national government wishes to change its rate and its request to the E.E.C. to do so is not vetoed by any of the member countries. There can be a different rate for different agricultural products.

However, because this 'green' currency rate of exchange differs from that prevailing on the market, prices in terms of national currencies in the various E.E.C. countries may fall out of line. For instance, suppose that the E.C.U. price of wheat on conversion by 'green' rates of exchange gives a price of £100 per tonne in the U.K. and 1,000 fr. in France. If the rate of exchange for sterling rises from 10 fr. to 12 fr., it would pay a trader to buy a tonne of wheat in France for 1,000 fr. and sell it in the U.K. for the fixed price of £100, because this revenue of £100 may be converted on the exchanges into 1,200 fr., so giving a profit of 200 fr. This process can then, of course, be repeated by the trader ad infinitum to make a profit of 200 fr. on each completion of the cycle, the reason being that the price of wheat is fixed by the C.A.P. and will not adjust to market forces, which would otherwise have caused the U.K. price of wheat to fall.

In order to prevent such a trade practice, Monetary Compensatory Amounts are calculated by the E.E.C. on a continuing basis in line with the movements of the various intra-E.E.C. exchange rates. These amounts are taxes and subsidies which are imposed on trade within the E.E.C. of C.A.P. products to offset the gap between the fixed 'green' currency rate and the floating exchange rates of the national currencies. In the above example, the M.C.A. would have taken the form of a tax on the export of wheat from France to the U.K., equivalent in effect of the profit of 200 fr. per tonne.

Green pound. ⟡ GREEN CURRENCY.

Gresham's law. If two coins are in circulation whose relative FACE VALUES differ from their relative BULLION content, the 'dearer' coin will be extracted from circulation for melting down. 'BAD MONEY DRIVES OUT GOOD.' The law is named after Sir Thomas Gresham (1519–79), a leading Elizabethan businessman and financial adviser to Queen Elizabeth I.

Gross cash flow. ◊ CASH FLOW.

Gross domestic product (G.D.P.). A measure of the total flow of goods and SERVICES produced by the economy over a specified time period, normally a year or a quarter. It is obtained by valuing outputs of goods and services at MARKET prices, and then aggregating. Note that all INTERMEDIATE PRODUCTS are excluded, and only goods used for final CONSUMPTION or investment goods (◊ CAPITAL) or changes in STOCKS are included. This is because the VALUES of intermediate goods are implicitly included in the PRICES of the final goods. The word 'gross' means that no deduction for the value of expenditure on capital goods for replacement purposes is made. Because the INCOME arising from INVESTMENTS and possessions owned abroad is not included, only the value of the flow of goods and services produced in the country is estimated; hence the word 'domestic' to distinguish it from the GROSS NATIONAL PRODUCT. Since no adjustment is made for indirect taxes (◊ DIRECT TAXATION) and SUBSIDIES, the measure here defined is often referred to as 'Gross domestic product at market prices'. ◊ GROSS DOMESTIC PRODUCT AT FACTOR COST.

Gross domestic product at factor cost. In measuring GROSS DOMESTIC PRODUCT, MARKET prices are used to value outputs so that they can be aggregated. This implies that, to the extent that market prices include indirect taxes, i.e. PURCHASE TAX, and SUBSIDIES, the VALUE of output will not equal the value of INCOMES paid out to FACTORS OF PRODUCTION. This is because it is the revenue received by firms after indirect taxes (◊ DIRECT TAXATION) which is distributed as factor incomes. Thus, by subtracting the total of indirect taxes (and, since subsidies have the opposite effect of taxes, by adding in subsidies) from the G.D.P. we arrive at the estimate of the G.D.P. at factor cost, which is consistent with the value of incomes paid to factors of production.

Gross fixed capital formation (G.F.C.F.). ◊ CAPITAL FORMATION.

Gross investment. INVESTMENT expenditure inclusive of replacement of worn-out and obsolescent equipment, i.e. inclusive of DEPRECIATION. ◊ NET INVESTMENT.

Gross margin. In a retail business, the margin on a sale which is the difference between the purchase PRICE of a GOOD and the price paid by the retailer, i.e. it makes no allowance for OVERHEADS, STOCK APPRECIATION or TAX. The gross margin is sometimes loosely referred to as *gross profit*, but this term has a different, strictly defined, meaning in accounting (◊ PROFIT).

Gross national expenditure. ◊ NATIONAL INCOME.

Gross national product (G.N.P.). GROSS DOMESTIC PRODUCT plus the INCOME accruing to domestic residents arising from INVESTMENT abroad less income earned in the domestic market accruing to foreigners abroad.

Gross national product at factor cost. GROSS NATIONAL PRODUCT at MARKET prices minus all indirect taxes (◊ DIRECT TAXATION) and SUBSIDIES. ◊◊ GROSS DOMESTIC PRODUCT AT FACTOR COST.

Gross national product at market prices. GROSS NATIONAL PRODUCT with all flows valued at MARKET prices. Since market prices include indirect taxes (◊ DIRECT TAXATION) and SUBSIDIES, and since taxes and subsidies are regarded simply as TRANSFER PAYMENTS, it is often preferable to measure national output excluding these. This gives the measure of national output, net of TAXATION and subsidies, known as GROSS NATIONAL PRODUCT AT FACTOR COST.

Gross national product deflator. An index of prices (◊ INDEX NUMBER) applied to the value estimates of the gross national product (◊◊ NATIONAL INCOME) over a time period in order to remove the effects of changes in the general level of prices. The resultant revised estimates give a more accurate picture of movements during the period in the physical or *real* output of goods and services.

Gross profit. ◊ PROFIT.

Gross trading profit. Gross PROFIT before allowing for DEPRECIATION, INTEREST and stock APPRECIATION.

Group of Ten. ◊ INTERNATIONAL MONETARY FUND.

Growth theory. The area of economics concerned with the development of models which explain the rate of ECONOMIC GROWTH in an economy. The most important questions in growth theory are about (a) the optimal level of growth (◊◊ OPTIMAL GROWTH THEORY), and (b) whether the economic system has a natural tendency to achieve BALANCED GROWTH, a position in which all variables grow at the same rate. If growth in the economy is balanced, it can be shown that $n = s/v$ where n is the rate of growth of the labour force, s the AVERAGE PROPENSITY TO SAVE and v the ratio of capital in the economy to output produced (◊ CAPITAL–OUTPUT RATIO, INCREMENTAL). For balanced growth to be sustained with INVESTMENT equal to savings and with constant full employment, some mechanism has to exist to cause one of these three factors to change when one of the other two moves out of balance. In the neo-classical (◊ NEO-CLASSICAL ECONOMICS) approach to growth, it is the capital–output ratio, v, which alters. If, for example, the labour force was growing too fast to maintain full employment with the given level of savings and stock of capital, the capital–output ratio would fall as entrepreneurs switched from employing capital to labour in response to the lower wages that the excess supply of labour caused. The fixed relationship between the three factors would thus still hold.

In the HARROD–DOMAR MODEL, none of the three variables is endogenous (◇ ENDOGENOUS VARIABLE) and thus there is no tendency for balanced growth to occur at all. The capital–output ratio is assumed to be fixed by technological factors or by sticky interest rates (◇ LIQUIDITY TRAP). In models associated with the CAMBRIDGE SCHOOL, it is the propensity to save which is the endogenous variable; in particular, if there is a difference between the inclination for profit-earners and wage-earners to save, growth can lead to redistributions from one group to the other in such a way as to alter the savings necessary to maintain a full employment steady-state growth path.

H

Halesbury Committee. ◊ DECIMAL COINAGE.

Hammered, hammering. Terms used in the situation of a member of the STOCK EXCHANGE who cannot meet his obligations, when a formal announcement to that effect is made by the council.

Hard currency. A CURRENCY traded in a FOREIGN-EXCHANGE MARKET for which DEMAND is persistently high relative to the SUPPLY. ◊◊ SOFT CURRENCY.

Harrod, Sir Roy Forbes (1900–78). Educated at New College, Oxford, he began his career in 1922 as lecturer at Christ Church, Oxford, and continued teaching there until 1952. From 1940 until 1942, Professor Harrod served under Lord Cherwell and in the prime minister's office and then held the post of Statistical Adviser to the Admiralty until 1945. In 1952 he was appointed Nuffield Reader of International Economics. His publications include *The Trade Cycle, an Essay* (1936), *Towards a Dynamic Economics* (1948), *The Life of John Maynard Keynes* (1951), *Policy Against Inflation* (1958), *The British Economy* (1963), *Reforming the World's Money* (1965), *Towards a New Economic Policy* (1967), *Dollar–Sterling Collaboration* (1968), *Money* (1969) and *Economic Dynamics* (1973).

His *Essay in Dynamic Theory* (1939) brought together in a mathematical framework the accelerator and the MULTIPLIER (◊◊ ACCELERATOR–MULTIPLIER MODEL). Professor Harrod shifted economic theory away from its preoccupation with the conditions of stationary EQUILIBRIUM towards the analysis of the problems of growth (◊ GROWTH THEORY). Harrod investigated the implications for growth of the interactions of the ACCELERATION PRINCIPLE and the multiplier (◊ HARROD–DOMAR MODEL).

Harrod–Domar model. A theory of economic growth (◊ GROWTH THEORY) which suggests that there is no natural tendency for an economy to enjoy BALANCED GROWTH. In the model, developed by R. F. HARROD in 1939 and independently by E. D. DOMAR, shortly afterwards, there are three concepts of growth. The first is *warranted* growth: the rate of output growth at which firms believe they have the right amount of capital and don't feel it necessary to increase or decrease investment, given their expectations of future demand (◊ CAPITAL–OUTPUT RATIO). The second is the *natural rate of growth*, which corresponds to the increase in the labour force: if the labour force rises, growth must rise to maintain full EMPLOYMENT.

The third is *actual* growth: the change in aggregate output that finally materializes.

In the model, two problems are seen to arise in the growth pattern of an economy. The first concerns the relationship between actual and natural growth; the second concerns the relationship between actual and warranted growth. The first is that the factors determining actual growth are quite independent of the factors determining natural growth, and so there is no reason that an economy will achieve a level of growth necessary to maintain full employment. The natural rate of growth is determined by factors such as attitudes to birth control, and the tastes of the population with respect to family size. Actual growth, however, is affected by the propensity to save (the more SAVING, the more INVEST-MENT, and the more growth) and the increase in output caused by each pound's worth of investment. Neither the capital–output ratio nor the propensity to save will adjust to meet the requirements of the labour market, however.

The second problem is that, in the model, if entrepreneurs expect output to grow they will increase their investment to meet the anticipated demand. If the increase in demand is forthcoming, the aspirations of firms will be met and warranted growth will be equal to actual growth and no problem arises. If, however, actual growth exceeds expectations, then entrepreneurs will discover they have not invested as much as they would have wanted to if they had known what was coming. In response, they will increase their investment to the level warranted by actual growth; *but this increase in investment will cause actual growth to rise even more.* A reverse story can be told when actual growth falls short of warranted growth: entrepreneurs, in the model, set up a vicious circle, by which any discrepancy between their expected growth and actual growth magnifies as they attempt to change the level of their investment to the level warranted. The result is instability. (⟡ COBWEB MODEL.)

The conclusion of the Harrod–Domar model – that the economy does not naturally find a full-employment, stable-growth rate – is analogous to the Keynesian (⟡ KEYNES, J. M.) belief that it need not find a full-employment equilibrium level of output. However, the model's results can be criticized because of the severity of the assumptions built into it. The first problem suggested by the model – that there is no reason for growth to equal the level necessary to maintain full employment – is largely because it assumes that the relative price of labour and capital is fixed, and that they are always employed in equal proportions. It is quite possible, however, that increases in labour supply might drive down wages and lead to an increase in the amount of labour used relative to capital. Secondly, the model naïvely assumes that investors are only influenced by one thing: the level of output. This is the ACCEL-ERATION PRINCIPLE. This explains the way in which discrepancies between warranted and actual growth may lead to spiralling increases or decreases in growth. (◊ ECONOMIC GROWTH; OPTIMAL-GROWTH THEORY; STEADY-STATE GROWTH.)

Hawtrey, Sir Ralph George (1879–1975). After a long career in the TREASURY, which lasted from 1904 to 1945, Sir Ralph Hawtrey was appointed Professor at the Royal Institute of International Affairs. He held his post until his retirement in 1952. Hawtrey's publications include *Currency and Credit* (1919), *The Gold Standard in Theory and Practice* (1927), *The Art of Central Banking* (1937), *Capital and Employment* (1937), *A Century of Bank Rate* (1938), *The Balance of Payments and the Standard of Living* (1950), *Cross-Purposes in Wages Policy* (1955), *The Pound at Home and Abroad* (1961), and *Incomes and Money* (1967). His theory of the TRADE CYCLE emphasizes monetary factors. The amount which consumers and investors were willing to save or spend depended on the level of RATES OF INTEREST. Fluctuations in economic activity arose through variations in the quantity of money (◊ MONEY SUPPLY), especially bank CREDIT, because these variations alter the level of the rate of interest (◊ MISES, L. E. VON). He criticized the Radcliffe Committee (◊ RADCLIFFE REPORT) because he felt that it had not given sufficient attention to the possibility that the rate of interest had a significant influence on a firm's willingness to hold stocks of commodities (◊ INVENTORIES).

Hayek, Friedrich August von (b. 1899). Born in Vienna, Hayek was director of the Austrian Institute for Economic Research from 1927 to 1931 and lectured at Vienna University. In 1931 he was appointed Tooke Professor of Economic Science and Statistics at the London School of Economics, a post he held until 1950. From 1950 until 1962 he was Professor of Social and Moral Science at Chicago University. He was Professor of Economics at the University of Freiburg until 1969, when he was appointed Visiting Professor of Economics at the University of Salzburg. In 1974 he received the Alfred Nobel Memorial Prize (◊ NOBEL PRIZE) in Economics jointly with G. K. MYRDAL. His published works include *Monetary Theory and the Trade Cycle* (1929), *Prices and Production* (1931), *Profits, Interest, Investment* (1939), *The Pure Theory of Capital* (1941), *Road to Serfdom* (1944), *Individualism and Economic Order* (1948), *The Constitution of Liberty* (1961), *Studies in Philosophy, Politics and Economics* (1967), *Law, Legislation and Liberty* (3 volumes, 1973–9), *Denationalization of Money* (1976) and *New Studies in Philosophy, Politics, Economics and the History of Ideas* (1978).

A member of the AUSTRIAN SCHOOL, Hayek elaborated the TRADE CYCLE theory of L. E. VON MISES by integrating it with E. VON BÖHM-BAWERK's theory of CAPITAL. In a boom REAL WAGES fall because of the rise in prices, and firms therefore switch to less 'roundabout' (CAPITAL-INTENSIVE) methods of production. In conse quence, INVESTMENT in total is reduced. In RECESSION the reverse situation induces 'roundabout' production methods, and investment is stimulated. Professor Hayek believes that a very severe restriction on the growth of the MONEY SUPPLY is necessary in order to control the growth of INFLATION, even if such a policy leads to very high levels of UNEMPLOYMENT. ◊ ACCELERATION PRINCIPLE; KEYNES, J. M.; RICARDO EFFECT.

Heckscher–Ohlin principle. The law of comparative advantage (◊ RICARDO, D.) had been established by economists as an explanation for the existence and pattern of international trade based on the relative COST advantages between different countries of producing different commodities. The law says nothing about why or how a comparative advantage exists. The Heckscher–Ohlin principle states that advantage arises from the different relative factor endowments of the countries trading. A country will export those commodities that are intensive (◊ CAPITAL-INTENSIVE; LABOUR-INTENSIVE) in the factor in which it is most well endowed. The principle was first put forward by Eli F. Heckscher (1879–1952) in an article published in 1919 and reprinted in *Readings in the Theory of International Trade* (1949). It was refined by BERTIL OHLIN in his *Interregional and International Trade* (1933). The principle has been developed further by Professor P. A. SAMUELSON in his factor price equalization theorem.

Hedge. Action taken by a buyer or seller to protect his business or assets against a change in PRICES. A flour miller who has a contract to supply flour at a fixed price in two months' time can hedge against the possibility of a rise in the price of wheat in two months' time by buying the necessary wheat now and selling a two months FUTURE in wheat for the same quantity. If the price of wheat should fall, then the loss he will have sustained by buying it now will be offset by the gain he can make by buying in the wheat at the future price and supplying the futures contract at higher than this price, and vice versa. In practice, perfect hedging may not be possible because spot (◊ SPOT MARKETS) and future prices will not balance one another out after the event, but a significant reduction in risk is normally possible. Hedging in this form is, in effect, shifting risk on to specialized futures operators. The purchase of EQUITIES, or other things for which prices are expected to move at least in line with the general price level, is often referred to as a 'hedge' against INFLATION.

Hedonism. The theory that all human action is motivated by pleasure and the avoidance of pain or the ethic that it should be so motivated.

Herfindahl Index. ◊ CONCENTRATION RATIO.

Hicks, Sir John Richard (b. 1904). Educated at Balliol College, Oxford, Hicks lectured at the London School of Economics from 1926 until 1935, when he became a Fellow of Gonville and Caius College,

Cambridge. In 1938 he was appointed to the Chair of Political Economy at the University of Manchester. In 1946 he was made Official Fellow of Nuffield College, Oxford, and in 1952 Drummond Professor of Political Economy at Oxford, a post he held until 1965; In 1972, he was awarded the Alfred Nobel Memorial Prize (◊ NOBEL PRIZE) in Economics jointly with Professor K. J. ARROW. His major published works include *The Theory of Wages* (1932), *Value and Capital* (1939), *The Social Framework* (1942), *A Contribution to the Theory of the Trade Cycle* (1950), *A Revision of Demand Theory* (1956), *Capital and Growth* (1965), *Critical Essays in Monetary Theory* (1967), *A Theory of Economic History* (1969), *The Crises of Keynesian Economics* (1974), *Capital and Time: A Neo-Austrian Theory* (1976), *Economic Perspectives: Further Essays on Money and Growth* (1977) and *Causality in Economics* (1979). In an article in *Economica* in 1934, Hicks and Professor R. G. D. ALLEN showed how the INDIFFERENCE CURVE could be used to analyse consumer behaviour on the basis of ORDINAL UTILITY. Their exposition gave an important impetus to the development of this tool of analysis in economic theory. ◊ SLUTSKY, E. In his work on the TRADE CYCLE, Hicks demonstrated by means of mathematical MODELS how the *accelerator* could induce several types of fluctuation in total output. In an article in *Econometrica* in 1937, 'Mr Keynes and the Classics', he expounded the analytical tool of the IS–LM MODEL, which he had invented in order to explore the assumptions relating to the equilibrium between the supply and demand for MONEY, SAVINGS and INVESTMENT, the rate of INTEREST and INCOME ◊ KEYNES, J. M.; ◊ HARROD, R. F.

Hidden economy. ◊ BLACK ECONOMY.

Hidden hand. ◊ 'INVISIBLE HAND'; SMITH, ADAM.

Hire purchase (H.P.). A form of CONSUMER CREDIT in which the purchaser pays a DEPOSIT on an article and pays the balance of the purchase price plus INTEREST in regular instalments over periods of six months to two years or more; hence the U.S. name 'INSTALMENT CREDIT'. The credit is usually arranged by the vendor, at least for consumer purchases such as motor-cars. In a hire-purchase contract, unlike a credit sale, ownership of the goods does not pass from the seller to the buyer until the final payment is made, i.e. the goods are SECURITY for the LOAN. Until that time the seller is entitled to repossess the goods under law. Abuse of the right, extortionate RATES OF INTEREST and the practices of certain salesmen, who persuaded customers to buy more than they could afford, led to a series of Hire Purchase Acts from 1938 onwards to give protection to the buyer. Because interest charges are calculated on the total loan and not the amount outstanding, hire purchase is a more expensive form of CREDIT than it often seems to be. Private purchases now account for less than one-third of H.P. sales, and it is an important source of credit for certain types of machinery and equipment (◊ FINANCE HOUSE). Hire purchase originated with retailers in the U.S. during the nineteenth century but is now giving way, for consumers, to forms of non-vendor credit such as PERSONAL LOANS and credit-card loans (◊ CREDIT ACCOUNT), although some vendors, for example department stores, have their own credit-card accounts.

The control of the volume of hire-purchase activity was an important object of monetary policy in the 1960s, and for this reason H.P. credit grew little during the second half of that decade. Initial attempts at control were directed at limiting the supply of bank credit for H.P. companies and restricting CAPITAL issues by the finance houses. These measures were unsuccessful and H.P. terms, i.e. the percentage minimum deposit and maximum repayment periods, were controlled directly. These restrictions were abolished in 1982 and credit creation by the finance houses is now controlled by the same means as those by which bank credit is controlled. ◊ CREDIT CONTROL.

Historical costs. ◊ COSTS, HISTORICAL.

Hoarding. The accumulation of idle MONEY balances, ◊ INACTIVE MONEY.

Holding company. A company that controls one or more other companies, normally by holding a majority of the SHARES of these SUBSIDIARIES. A holding company is concerned with control, and not with INVESTMENT, and may be economically justifiable where one holding company can perform financial, managerial or marketing functions for a number of subsidiaries; I.C.I. is a very good example of this, and, indeed, most large companies in Britain are holding companies exercising a greater or lesser degree of control over their subsidiaries. The holding-company form of organization also has a number of practical advantages, e.g. it is a simpler and less expensive way of acquiring control of another company than by purchasing its ASSETS, and the original company can retain its name and goodwill. It is possible for a holding company to control a large number of companies with a combined CAPITAL very much greater than its own, since it needs to hold only half or even less of the shares of its subsidiaries. Abuse of this possibility of 'pyramiding', as it is sometimes called, is now limited by company legislation (◊ COMPANY LAW).

Homogeneous products. Goods and services purchased by consumers which the latter consider to be perfect substitutes (◊ PERFECT COMPETITION).

Horizontal integration. ◊ MERGER.

Hot money. Funds which flow into a country to take advantage of favourable RATES OF INTEREST in that country. They improve the BALANCE OF PAYMENTS and strengthen the EXCHANGE RATE of the recipient country. However, these funds are highly volatile and will be shifted to another FOREIGN-EXCHANGE MARKET when relative interest rates favour the move. ◊ ARBITRAGE; BANK FOR INTERNATIONAL SETTLEMENTS.

Hotelling, Harold (1895–1973). Associate Professor of Mathematics at Stanford University from 1927, Hotelling became Professor of Economics at Columbia University in 1931. He held this post until 1946, when he was appointed Professor of Mathematical Statistics of the University of North Carolina. In an article in the *Economic Journal* in 1929, 'Stability in Competition', he showed how profit maximization can lead retail outlets or competing companies to locate close to each other. ◊ HOTELLING'S LAW. His article 'The General Welfare in Relation to Problems of Taxation and of Railway and Utility Rates', published in *Econometrica* in 1938, put forward the case for MARGINAL-COST PRICING by public utilities. He argued that even if by so doing such industries ran at a loss which had to be financed by lump-sum payments by the state, total economic welfare would be increased by such a pricing policy (◊ WELFARE ECONOMICS).

Hotelling's law. The observation by H. HOTELLING that in many markets it is rational for all the producers to make their products as close as possible to that demanded by the consumer. Suppose, for example, there are two newsagents in a street, each wanting to maximize its share of local business by locating its shop so that it is the nearest newsagent for as much of the trade visiting the street as possible. In this situation, both newsagents will position themselves in the middle of the street guaranteeing themselves half the market. It would be socially more desirable for them to separate themselves, and sit a third of the way along the street from different ends. Unfortunately, if one newsagent did this, the other could position himself so as to capture more than half the total market. Too little variety results from the process. Hotelling's law manifests itself in numerous markets – competing bus operators scheduling their buses to run at the same times for example. ◊ NASH EQUILIBRIUM.

Household. An economic unit which is defined for the purpose of the CENSUS of population as a single person living alone or a family or group voluntarily living together, having meals prepared together and benefiting from housekeeping shared in common. Because of the fact of shared use, which is a household's characteristic, it is an important economic statistic when considering the MARKET potential for certain consumer products. The percentage of households owning certain consumer durables such as washing-machines, television sets, refrigerators and video recorders is critical to the growth of the future sales of these products. In the initial introductory period sales grow fast as households buy for the first time, but they slow down rapidly when a high proportion of the households own the product (◊ LOGISTIC

CURVE). Thereafter, sales can only be for replacement. The number of households in the U.K. in 1981 was about 21 million.

Human capital. The skills and knowledge embodied in the LABOUR FORCE. A metallurgist can expect to earn more than a laboratory assistant because he has invested more in education and training and these higher earnings are a return on the investment he (or his parents, or the state) have made in school fees and forgone earnings. Investment in human CAPITAL should increase labour PRODUCTIVITY in the same way as investment in machinery.

Hume, David (1711–76). Scottish philosopher whose systematic treatment of economics is contained in several chapters of his *Political Discourses* (1752). He exposed as unwarranted the mercantilist fear (◇ MER-CANTILISM) of a chronic imbalance of trade and loss of gold. He argued that the international movement in BULLION responded to the rise and fall of prices and in so doing kept national price differences within limits and prevented permanent BALANCE OF PAYMENTS surpluses or deficits. He also foresaw how this mechanism could be distorted by the growth of domestic BANKING and of paper money. He accepted a QUANTITY THEORY OF MONEY but distinguished between SHORT RUN and LONG RUN effects. By tracing the course of the effects of a rise in the quantity of MONEY, he came to the conclusion that MONEY was not neutral but could affect employment, although only in the short run. His belief that the level of the RATE OF INTEREST depended on the rate of business profits became the basis of ADAM SMITH's interest-rate theory. ◇ INTEREST, CLASSICAL THEORY OF.

Hutcheson, Francis (1694–1746). The teacher of ADAM SMITH at Glasgow University. Smith succeeded him to the Chair of Moral Philosophy.

Hyperinflation. Very rapid growth in the rate of INFLATION in which MONEY loses its value to the point where BARTER is a preferred system of exchange. An earlier term for the same phenomenon is *galloping inflation*.

Hypothesis. A theoretical explanation of the behaviour of phenomena which can be tested against the facts. A hypothesis can be refuted, unlike a tautology which is true by definition, but it may not be possible to prove that it is correct. An example of a hypothesis is that SAVING is a function of DISPOSABLE INCOME such that when disposable income doubles, savings will also double (the SAVINGS RATIO is a constant). The statement that saving equals income minus expenditure, however, is a tautology. ◇ EMPIRICAL TESTING.

I

Idle money. ◊ INACTIVE MONEY.

Illiquidity. A situation in which ASSETS cannot easily and quickly be turned into MONEY. Antonym of LIQUIDITY.

Impact effect. The first effect of a change in a variable, before any secondary responses can be made to the change. It amounts to the very short-run effect. For example, when demand in a market increases, because output is fixed in the short period involved, price rises by more than it does once producers have had time to respond to the increases in demand.

Imperfect Competition. ◊ MONOPOLISTIC COMPETITION.

Imperfect market. A market in which the forces that tend to ensure productive and allocative efficiency are thwarted (◊ ECONOMIC EFFICIENCY). In a perfect market, three characteristics predominate: price equals MARGINAL COST (or MARGINAL REVENUE equals marginal cost); there are no abnormal PROFITS (i.e. AVERAGE COST equals AVERAGE REVENUE); and production takes place at the minimum cost (that is at the bottom of the average cost curve, where average cost equals marginal cost). Although price acceptance by consumers and firms, and free entry and exit of firms, are the important features to ensure these hold, underlying them are a number of other conditions. These include: rational consumers; profit-maximizing firms; HOMOGENEOUS PRODUCTS made without ECONOMIES OF SCALE; a smooth pattern of DEMAND without peaks; a smooth pattern of SUPPLY where the quantity of output is easily adjusted; no collusion between producers; and the existence of complete and costless market information. In the absence of any of these, imperfect markets exist and fail to act efficiently. (◊ PARETO, V. F. D. ◊ PERFECT COMPETITION.)

Import deposits. A system of IMPORT RESTRICTION under which importers are required to deposit with a government institution a percentage of the value of their IMPORTS. This DEPOSIT is held by the government for a period of time, after which it is then repaid to the importer. The system restricts imports because it reduces the LIQUIDITY of importers and also imposes an extra charge on them, in as much as they are, in effect, forced to give an interest-free loan to the government. However, the impact of import deposits may be weakened if there is sufficient liquidity generally in the economy to enable importers to obtain loans at favourable RATES OF INTEREST against the COLLATERAL SECURITY of their import deposit receipts. Again, foreign exporting companies may be willing to finance the deposits themselves rather than lose their market position, especially if it is expected that the scheme is only a temporary one. (◊ GENERAL AGREEMENT ON TARIFFS AND TRADE.)

Import duties. ◊ TARIFFS.

Import Duties Act 1932. An Act which marked the final abandonment of the FREE TRADE policy which dominated the U.K.'s foreign trade in the nineteenth century and to which she had clung with increasing difficulty after the First World War. The Act imposed a 10 per cent duty on all IMPORTS, except foodstuffs and raw materials and some other items, originating from non-Commonwealth countries

Import licence. A document which gives the importer authority to import the commodity to which the licence applies. It is a device to enable the government to regulate and supervise the flow of IMPORTS, for instance under its import QUOTA regulations.

Import quota. ◊ QUOTAS.

Import restrictions. Restrictions on the importation of products into a country may be effected by means of TARIFFS, QUOTAS or IMPORT DEPOSITS, and are generally imposed to correct a BALANCE OF PAYMENTS deficit. Their purpose, as with DEVALUATION, is to divert expenditure away from foreign-produced goods in favour of goods produced at home. The magnitude of this diversionary effect will depend on the ELASTICITY of demand for the IMPORTS in question; that is to say, the degree to which acceptable SUBSTITUTES are available on the home market. In addition, import restrictions could be used to increase a country's economic welfare (◊ WELFARE ECONOMICS) at the expense of foreign countries to the extent that it has power to exploit its foreign suppliers, e.g. as a monopolist (◊ MONOPOLY), without fear of retaliation. Finally, import duties may be applied to protect the market of domestic industry while it is being established (◊ FREE TRADE; INFANT-INDUSTRY ARGUMENT; PROTECTION). Non-tariff barriers to trade include revenue duties, such as value-added tax, which, being imposed as a percentage on landed, i.e. duty-paid, VALUE, increase the cost of imported goods more than locally produced goods and thus discriminate in favour of the latter. Other examples are domestic taxes applied according to the technical characteristics of goods, e.g. on engine capacity, which may subtly discriminate against imports. ◊ GENERAL AGREEMENT ON TARIFFS AND TRADE.

Import surcharge. A temporary increase in import tariffs (◊ TARIFFS, IMPORT) designed to correct a short-term BALANCE OF PAYMENTS deficit and to stabilize the EXCHANGE RATE.

Import tariffs. ◊ TARIFFS, IMPORT.

Imports. The flow of goods and SERVICES which enter for consumption into one country and which are the products of another country. In the

U.K., goods currently account for about 80 per cent of the total, compared with about 75 per cent in 1970. The U.K. has relatively few indigenous natural resources apart from oil and coal and must therefore obtain its requirements from overseas in exchange for EXPORTS. About 28 per cent of total domestic expenditure in the U.K. is spent on imports compared with, for instance, the U.S.A., where the proportion is about 10 per cent. One of the features of U.K. trade in recent years has been the acceleration in imports of goods which compete with domestic production. In 1975, about 23 per cent of U.K. demand for manufactures was met by imports, compared with a current level of over 30 per cent. This is partly a reflection of a change in world trade generally. With the growth of DEVELOPING COUNTRIES, the traditional raw materials, such as cotton, are no longer coming to the industrialized countries in that form, but as semi-manufactured goods. At the same time, the growth in technology and the advantage of specialization (◊ DIVISION OF LABOUR) have stimulated trade in manufactures between the advanced nations. However, there is no doubt that the growth in the share of manufactures in U.K. imports is also a reflection of the loss of competitive edge in world MARKETS arising from the relatively fast rise in U.K. PRICES. ◊◊ BALANCE OF PAYMENTS; INTERNATIONAL TRADE.

Impossibility theorem. A proof that it is impossible to devise a constitution or voting system, complying with certain reasonable conditions, which can guarantee to produce a consistent set of preferences for a group from the preferences of the individuals making up the group. Suppose, for example, that a society wants to vote on whether to spend the proceeds of a national lottery on a tax cut, an increase in defence spending or an increase in spending on health care. If resources are to be efficiently allocated, it would be desirable that individual rankings of the three options could be aggregated by some voting system to produce a ranking to determine which option was the choice of the society as a whole. K. J. ARROW showed in the impossibility theorem that no system could be found that was both rational and egalitarian. For example, a simple majority voting system, although giving equal weight to everybody's opinion, gives rise to the PARADOX OF VOTING, allowing the possibility of an inconsistent ordering of preferences. A system that may be consistent would be to allow one individual – a dictator – always to determine what choice to make, but this lacks the feature of equality. It has since been shown that a democratic system can at least meet a weaker rationality condition, but only by abandoning a third desirable property of a voting system – decisiveness. Such a system would allow every individual a personal veto over any decision so that society would simply be unable to do anything unless there was no one opposed to it. ◊ SOCIAL-WELFARE FUNCTION.

Imputation system. ◊ CORPORATION TAX.

Imputed cost. The cost attributed to using an asset which is owned by the user. The OPPORTUNITY COST of not putting an asset to its best alternative use. For instance, a shopkeeper who owns his own shop forgoes rent which he could earn if he did not use the shop for his own business. This loss of income is an imputed cost, which he would compare against the revenue from his business when considering whether it were truly profitable. Similarly an imputed income is the amount an owner would pay not to put his asset to an alternative use. If the shopkeeper had to pay £10 a day to rent an alternative to his own shop, he would willingly forgo £10 to keep it, and he thus enjoys an imputed income of £10 from his shop. (◊ INCOME.)

Imputed income. ◊ IMPUTED COST.

'In the bank.' When DISCOUNT HOUSES need to borrow MONEY from the BANK OF ENGLAND, the MONEY MARKET is said to be 'in the bank'. ◊ LENDER OF LAST RESORT.

Inactive money. MONEY which is not in circulation, i.e. not on DEPOSIT or invested in other financial ASSETS or being used for transactions. Inactive money is also referred to as *idle money* or idle balances. According to KEYNES's theory of LIQUIDITY PREFERENCE the amount of idle balances will depend, among other things, upon the RATE OF INTEREST. ◊ VELOCITY OF CIRCULATION.

Incidence of taxation. ◊ TAXATION, INCIDENCE OF.

Income. A flow of money, goods or services to any economic agent or unit. Such flows can take a variety of forms. At the level of individuals, income is usually a return to a FACTOR OF PRODUCTION. LABOUR yields wages; CAPITAL yields INTEREST; land yields RENT; and entrepreneurship yields PROFIT. Otherwise, income can be a TRANSFER PAYMENT in the form of a state benefit or receipt from a private-sector source such as alimony payments. At the level of the firm, income can be seen as either total sales receipts (turnover) or receipts minus costs. For a country, NATIONAL INCOME is taken as the sum of all incomes.

Economists do not view income in conventional ways. First, their concept of income extends more widely than a cash receipt: the person who lives in his own house effectively derives an income in the form of housing consumption worth the rental values of his property. Secondly, great importance is attached to the concept of 'permanent income': the flow of resources that is sustainable in the long term. For example, North Sea oil provides Britain with sale receipts but these will expire when the oil runs out. The permanent income deriving from the oil is therefore the money that would be earned from investing these receipts and making a return on them that lasts for ever. This would be lower than the actual flow of receipts while the oil is still being tapped, but it would provide a flow of income after the oil had gone. (✧ PERMAN-ENT-INCOME HYPOTHESIS.)

Income, circular flow of. ✧ CIRCULAR FLOW OF INCOME.

Income, distribution of. A FREQUENCY DISTRIBUTION showing numbers of persons, taxpayers or households classified by levels of annual income. A feature of this distribution is that it is skewed: a greater number appear in the low-income classifications than in the high-income classifications. (✧ LORENZ CURVE; PARETO, V. F. D.) ✧✧ POVERTY.

Income and earned surplus statement (U.S.). ✧ DOUBLE-ENTRY BOOK-KEEPING.

Income determination, theory of. The body of theory which describes the factors affecting NATIONAL INCOME. The term is usually used to describe specifically Keynesian models of the economy, in which AGGRE-GATE DEMAND is the primary factor explaining output and employment. ✧✧ KEYNESIAN ECONOMICS.

Income effect. The change in demand for a product caused by the impact of a change in its price on the spending power of consumers. The change in price of a product leads to a change in the REAL INCOME of individuals, who either can no longer afford the 'basket' of goods that they previously bought or who can afford the old basket with cash over to spend on extra items. The *income effect* is the impact of this change in spending power on the demand for the product whose price has changed. It is equivalent to some change in income with all prices remaining constant. It can be added to the SUBSTITUTION EFFECT to derive the total effect of the price change on the demand for the product.

The main factor in determining the size of the income effect of a product is the proportion of total spending that item comprises. The effect on total spending of a change in the price of matches, for example, is trivial, but it is large for a change in the price of food. Unlike the substitution effect, the income effect can move in either direction. If a product is demanded more as incomes fall, for example second-hand clothes, it is called an INFERIOR GOOD. If, as is more usual, it is demanded more as income rises, it is called *normal*. (✧✧ GIFFEN GOOD; INCOME ELASTICITY OF DEMAND.)

Income elasticity of demand. The proportionate change in the quantity of a commodity demanded after a unit proportionate change in the income of consumers with prices held constant. For example, a product which has an income ELASTICITY of 2 will enjoy demand growth of 2 per cent for every 1 per cent growth in consumer income. Commodities can be grouped by their income elasticities. First, luxury items which comprise a high proportion of the spending of the rich have income elasticities in excess of 1 and enjoy growth in demand above that of average incomes. Secondly, basic items such as food enjoy some increased demand when the economy grows, but proportionately not as much as the growth in average incomes. Thirdly, INFERIOR GOODS have negative income elasticities: as soon as people can afford to stop buying them they do – examples are second-hand clothes and certain cheap but unsavoury foods.

Income elasticities can be measured at the level of individual consumers or the economy as a whole, and can be assessed for individual commodities or groups of commodities taken together. In the most general case, the income elasticity of all spending in the long term must be equal to 1, that is, spending must rise in the same proportion as income, otherwise savings would have to be unsustainably growing or contracting. The income elasticity is of practical importance to business and policy-makers because any product which has an income elasticity below 1 in a growing economy will have a falling share of total spending and countries which export commodities with low income elasticities will suffer balance-of-payments problems in the long term if world economic growth occurs.

The income elasticity is equal to the negative of the sum of the elasticity of demand of a commodity with respect to its own price and all other prices.

Income tax. A tax on INCOME. In the U.K. individuals are taxed on the full amount of their income from employment or INVESTMENT in the FISCAL YEAR. (Not including gifts: ◊ CAPITAL TRANSFER TAX; CAPITAL GAINS are taxed separately.) Deductions, such as personal allowances, dependant's allowance, certain life-assurance premiums on policies taken out prior to March 1984 and mortgage interest paid, are allowed by the Tax Act in arriving at taxable income. Child relief was also available until 1979/80. Income tax is progressive in its effect. Before 6 April 1973 there was a 'standard rate' of tax with a system of allowances and earned income reliefs coupled with SURTAX on higher incomes. After that date the 'unified system' of personal taxation became applicable. Surtax was abolished and successive slices of total EARNED INCOME (after allowances) are now (1987/8) taxed at 27 per cent (the 'basic rate'), 40 per cent and so on up to 60 per cent. The average rate of income tax (after allowing for married and single personal reliefs only) for total earnings of £10,000 per annum is 22·2 per cent for a single person under 65, and 18·4 per cent for a married couple. Persons in employment are normally taxed under the PAY-AS-YOU-EARN system under the so-called Schedule E. The self-employed, including those in PARTNERSHIPS, are taxed under the so-called Schedule D, Cases I and II. Under this schedule, the assessment is made on the PROFITS of a continuing trade or profession for the year preceding the year of assessment, which is called the *basis year*. Other schedules deal with investment income (where tax is not deducted at source), income from abroad and other sources of income. Company income is taxed under a different system (◊ CORPORATION TAX; LAYFIELD COMMITTEE). There is some disagreement amongst economists on the effects of income tax on incentives to work and save and these effects are difficult to verify empirically. On equity grounds a progressive income tax places a higher burden on those with the means to bear it, but this may discourage effort through the SUBSTITUTION EFFECT or encourage people to work harder (and encourage sophisticated tax avoidance) to make up their income (INCOME EFFECT). The system of income-tax reliefs for particular types of saving (for example, pension contributions) distorts savings decisions and this is one of the reasons why many economists advocate an EXPENDITURE TAX in place of income tax. (◊ SUPPLY-SIDE ECONOMIC; TAXATION.)

Income velocity of circulation. ◊ VELOCITY OF CIRCULATION.

Incomes policy. ◊ PRICES AND INCOMES POLICY.

Incorporation. The action of forming a company by carrying out the necessary legal formalities. ◊ COMPANY LAW.

Increasing returns, law of. ◊ ECONOMIES OF SCALE.

Independent commodity. ◊ COMPLEMENTARY DEMAND.

Independent variable. A VARIABLE from which the values of other variables are derived. ◊ DEPENDENT VARIABLE.

Index-linked. ◊ INDEXATION.

Index number. A WEIGHTED AVERAGE of a number of statistical observations of some economic attribute, as a percentage of a similar weighted average calculated for the attribute at an earlier, or base, period. Typical economic attributes for which index numbers are calculated are prices and production, the most familiar being the retail-price index, or cost-of-living index. In principle, the method of indexation is the same for all indices and, therefore, can be explained by reference to this price index. The price of each commodity or service included in the index is recorded in the current period (say 1988) and divided by its price in the base period (say 1985), to obtain a *price relative* for each item. Each price relative is then multiplied by a weight and all the items summed and averaged. The weights used may be either the amount spent on each item in the current period (1988) – a *current-weighted* index or PAASCHE INDEX or the amount spent on each item in the base period (1985) – a *base-weighted* index or LASPEYRES INDEX. (◊ INDEX-NUMBER PROBLEM.)

Index-number problem. This problem arises from the use of INDEX NUMBERS, which are summary single numbers encapsulating a range of values and used to describe succinctly changes in the range of values over time. The retail-price index, for instance, could equally rationally, for the above purpose, be calculated as a *base-weighted* or a *current-weighted* index, but the two types of index do not necessarily give the same answer. For instance, consider a simple example of two goods X and Y which have the following prices and quantities purchased in the base year 1 and the current year 2:

		Year 1		Year 2
	Price	Quantity	Price	Quantity
X	10p	5	8p	6
Y	20p	5	25p	1

The current-weighted index is given by:

$$\text{Year 2} = \frac{(8p \times 6) + (25p \times 1)}{(10p \times 6) + (20p \times 1)} = \frac{73}{80} = 0.91. \quad \text{Year 1} = 100)$$

The base-weighted index is given by:

$$\text{Year 2} = \frac{(8p \times 5) + (25p \times 5)}{(10p \times 5) + (20p \times 5)} = \frac{165}{150} = 1.10. \quad (\text{Year 1} = 100)$$

According to the base-weighted index, the general level of prices rose in year 2 compared with year 1 (by 10 per cent), but according to the current-weighted index, prices fell in year 2 (by 9 per cent). The problem of choice is that if base weights are not updated, items will continue to be included that are no longer relevant in household expenditure. On the other hand, changing weights in order to keep them current could lead to the index being influenced by changes in quantities and therefore not be properly representative of price movements only.

Indexation. The introduction of automatic linkage between monetary obligations and the price level. In practice this would mean, for example, that the money value of a long-term loan would be increased in line with the RETAIL-PRICE INDEX so that the borrower would have to repay the loan in REAL TERMS. In the absence of indexation, rapid INFLATION, by eroding the real value of loans, shifts resources from lenders to borrowers and therefore disrupts the credit mechanism and the CAPITAL MARKET. Some economists consider that indexation helps to reduce inflationary expectations and thus contributes to the control of inflation. General indexation has been used in some countries, for example Brazil, to help control inflation in the past. The U.K. government introduced an index-linked security in 1981 for financial institutions and has subsequently issued others for private investors as well as institutions, for example, $2\frac{1}{2}$ per cent Index-linked Treasury Stock 2011. Some NATIONAL SAVINGS CERTIFICATES are also *index-linked*.

Indexed. ◊ INDEXATION.

Indifference curve. A graphical representation of sets of different combinations of commodities which each yield to the consumer the same level of satisfaction. Indifference curves can be plotted on graphs called indifference maps, on each axis of which is represented the quantity of some commodity. To produce such a curve, any point can be taken to start with, representing a basket of two goods (though the analysis can be extended to more than two very easily). One unit of the first commodity, books say, could be removed from the basket and units of the second commodity, cassettes for example, added until a point was found at which the consumer felt that the new cassettes exactly compensated for the loss of the book. This new basket, with perhaps two more cassettes in it but one less book, is the second point on the same indifference curve as the first. The exercise can be repeated with steadily fewer books and increasing numbers of cassettes and then again with increasing numbers of books and correspondingly falling numbers of cassettes. A new indifference curve altogether could be derived by taking a starting-point with both more cassettes and books than the previous basket and repeating the whole process again.

Indifference curves can never intersect. If a point A lies on two intersecting indifference curves then all the points on each curve must have the same utility as Point A, and the two curves must both represent bundles of goods of equal utility. It is then logically impossible for them to be separate indifference curves. As a result of this, every point on the indifference map lies on one and only one indifference curve. Normally, various assumptions are made about consumers and their tastes, with the result that indifference curves have the following properties. Firstly, they slope downwards. As the consumer loses some of one commodity, he must receive more of another if he is to remain as satisfied as he was. Similarly, a consumer should always prefer a basket with more of both commodities than another.

Secondly, they are convex to (that is, bulge towards) the origin. This is because, as units of the first commodity are removed from the basket, increasing amounts of the second commodity will be required to compensate. A consumer may start off valuing cassettes and books equally, but after he has piled up a basket of books with only a tiny selection of cassettes remaining, he will want a large number of extra books in return for one cassette.

Various extreme forms of indifference curve can be drawn without the usual properties described above. Perfect SUBSTITUTES (two identical brands of washing powder for example) have indifference curves which are straight downward-sloping lines. At no stage will the consumer change the rate at which he swaps one item for the other. Perfect complements (◊ COMPLEMENTARY DEMAND) on the other hand, have L-shaped indifference curves; increasing quantities of a left shoe will derive for a consumer no extra utility at all unless extra right shoes are found to match. If a consumer actively hates one commodity, his indifference curves will slope upwards. Indifference maps are used extensively in theoretical economics. By plotting money against any commodity, the individual's demand curve for that commodity can be derived. If leisure is compared to money on an indifference map, analysis of the decision of individuals on how much to work (and earn) and how much to relax can be analysed. (⟢ DEMAND, THEORY OF; INDIFFERENCE-CURVE ANALYSIS; MARGINAL RATE OF SUBSTITUTION; ORDINAL UTILITY.)

Indifference-curve analysis. The study of consumer demand in terms of ranked combinations of commodities consumed subject to the constraints of price and income. Under this approach, there is no need for an absolute measure of utility or satisfaction; consumers merely need to be able to choose between different bundles of goods (⟢ ORDINAL UTILITY). One can view the basic task of the consumer as ranking all the combinations of items that can be bought with the income available and choosing the bundle at the top of the resulting list. The tools for this analysis are the *indifference map* (built of INDIFFERENCE CURVES), which expresses the consumers' tastes; and the BUDGET LINE, which shows the combinations of items that can be bought for a given income and set of prices.

Indifference analysis suggests that people should consume items such that the rate at which they are prepared to swap them with complete indifference equals the ratio of the prices of the two items. For example, if two glasses of milk cost the same as one glass of wine and a milk consumer values one glass of each equally, he can enhance his utility by reducing his wine consumption by a glass and increasing his milk consumption by two glasses, without an extra cost. This process can go on until the consumer has so much milk and so little wine that he would actually enjoy a single glass of the one rather than two glasses of the other. On the indifference map, this corresponds to the point at which the budget line is tangential to the indifference curve. (⟢ MARGINAL RATE OF SUBSTITUTION.)

Indirect taxation. ⟢ DIRECT TAXATION.

Induced investment. That part of INVESTMENT which is determined by changes in output, as opposed to *autonomous investment* such as government expenditure on infrastructure capital (⟢ ACCELERATION PRINCIPLE).

Industrial and Commercial Finance Corporation (I.C.F.C.). ⟢ FINANCE FOR INDUSTRY; MACMILLAN COMMITTEE; RISK CAPITAL.

Industrial bank. Another name for a FINANCE HOUSE, i.e. an institution providing HIRE PURCHASE credit; mainly applied to the smaller institutions, of which there are large numbers outside London. Although receiving DEPOSITS and making LOANS and other financial activities ancillary to their hire-purchase business for consumer and capital goods, the industrial banks do not offer a full range of BANKING services like the COMMERCIAL BANKS.

Industrial Bankers Association (I.B.A.). ◊ FINANCE HOUSES ASSOCIATION.

Industrial democracy. The participation of employees in decision-taking in industrial organizations. There are several ways in which workers' participation can be organized. In Yugoslavia employees elect their management and determine both their own and the managers' remuneration by free vote. In West Germany larger companies are obliged to have a two-tier board system consisting of a supervisory board and a management board. Employees in works councils elect the same number of representatives to the supervisory board as shareholders and these two groups together co-opt the remaining board members. The 1974–9 Labour government was committed to introducing legislation to facilitate industrial democracy and the Bullock Committee, which was set up to examine how this might be done, recommended in its report of February 1977 that a single-tier board system be set up with equal representation of workers and shareholders. The committee's report was not unanimous, however, and has not been implemented. There is considerable controversy about the effects of the extension of worker participation (as distinct from employee shareholdings) upon economic efficiency.

Industrial organization. Branch of applied MICROECONOMICS dealing with the performance of business enterprises and especially with the effects of MARKET STRUCTURES on market conduct (pricing policy, restrictive practices, INNOVATION, for example) and how firms are organized, owned and managed. ◊ CONCENTRATION; FIRM, THEORY OF THE.

Industry Acts. The Industry Act of 1972 reorganized the structure by which the development of the economic planning regions is administered by the U.K. Department of Industry. An Industrial Development Executive was set up within the department, supported by an Industrial Development Unit staffed by recruits from the City, industry and the government. This executive is responsible for giving advice on the allocation of financial assistance to industry which the Act enabled the government to do in special cases. This assistance might be in the form of loans or subsidies for the repayment of interest. It is not confined to the ASSISTED AREAS. The financial limit of £550 million fixed in the 1972 Act was subsequently raised to £1,600 million in 1976 and again to £2,700 million in 1982. The Act also established an 'Industrial Development Advisory Board', made up of experts in banking, international finance and industry, whose duty it is to advise the Regional Industrial Development Boards which the Act also created. These boards may make decisions at the local level without reference to the department, provided the sums involved do not exceed £1 million. The

Industry Act of 1975 set up the National Enterprise Board with a capital of £700 million and authority to increase this to £1,000 million by statutory order. The board is a state HOLDING COMPANY, which took over existing government shareholdings in private industry and has the remit to increase its interests in profitable enterprises in the private sector. It has no powers of compulsory purchase and a shareholding in excess of 30 per cent or a total investment exceeding £10 million in any one company must have the approval of the Secretary of State for Industry. The N.E.B. must forewarn the government of its intention to take more than a 10 per cent shareholding in a company if it does not have the agreement of the directors of the company to do so, and, if any project exceeds £10 million, the Secretary of State must have prior notice of the board's intentions. The N.E.B. may make loans, give guarantees or engage in joint ventures. The board is expected to be run commercially and any of its projects to accord with certain financial constraints laid upon it by the government. In 1981, the N.E.B. revenue was £11·4 million. The board may also finance selected assistance determined under the Industry Act of 1972. The 1975 Act also introduced the idea of voluntary planning agreements which could be made between the government and the major private-sector companies or the nationalized industries. The Act also gave the Secretary of State for Industry the power to require companies to disclose information about their affairs and their plans and gave the government powers to prevent the take-over of U.K. firms by non-residents (◊ ASSISTED AREA; FOREIGN INVESTMENT).

Industry concentration. ◊ CONCENTRATION.

Infant-industry argument. An argument in support of the retention of a protective import TARIFF. An industry does not operate at an optimum least-cost output until it has reached a sufficient size to obtain significant ECONOMIES OF SCALE. A new industry, therefore, in, say, a DEVELOPING COUNTRY, will always be in a competitively vulnerable position *vis-à-vis* an established industry in an advanced country. It follows that the stage of growth at which the industry (or country) can 'take off' (◊ ROSTOW, W. W.) industrially will be postponed indefinitely. The argument concludes that protection is necessary until the industry has reached its optimum size.

Inferior good. A good the demand for which falls as income rises; that is, its INCOME ELASTICITY OF DEMAND is negative. An example would be the demand of married couples for small apartments. A good which is not inferior is called a *normal good*. ◊ GIFFEN GOOD; INCOME EFFECT.

Inflation. Persistent increases in the general level of prices. It can be seen as a devaluing of the worth of money. Inflation is a recurring but only intermittent historical phenomenon. Its most serious recent appearance occurred during the 1970s in the wake of the quadrupling of oil prices in 1973, when annual inflation rates in the developed world rose as high as 25 per cent, but for the rest of the post-war period it has not been unusual for the inflation rate to be exceeded by the real growth rate. A crucial feature of inflation is that price rises are sustained. A once-only increase in the rate of VALUE-ADDED TAX will immediately put up prices, but this does not represent inflation, unless the indirect effects of the V.A.T. rise have repercussions on prices in periods after the direct effects.

Accounts of the causes of inflation are numerous. The most popular arguments are that it is caused by EXCESS DEMAND in the economy (DEMAND-PULL INFLATION), that it is caused by high costs (COST-PUSH INFLATION) and that it results from excessive increases in the money supply (◊ MONETARISM). These causes often amount to the same thing. The mechanism by which the increase in money supply causes inflation is by creating excess demand, making monetarism compatible with the demand-pull argument. The demand-pull and cost-push theories are also linked. An excess of demand causes producers to raise their prices – but this leads workers to demand higher wages to maintain their living standard; this causes higher demand and the process begins again. Similarly, if under the cost-push argument the cost increases stimulating price rises are wage costs (which represents most of the total net costs of the economy), firms can still only raise their prices if the demand is there for their goods to sell – if not, high costs merely bankrupt them. All three of these causes amount to an attempt by a nation to live beyond its means, or to enjoy a living standard higher than that allowed by its output and borrowing. This implies that inflation can rarely be cured by a measure which does not suppress attempts at maintaining high living standards and explains why the reduction of inflation is associated with austerity measures. When oil prices rose in the 1970s, countries without oil suffered a loss of their REAL INCOME and should have accepted a cut in living standards; unable to impose a cut, however, governments attempted to maintain higher levels of income than were merited by the products to be bought by that income. Too much money chasing too few goods inevitably caused inflation. Controlling inflation by restricting demand (either through tight control of the money supply or through cuts in government spending) has costs, however. If wages are growing rapidly, and the government squeezes demand in the economy, unemployment may result because employers will not be able to afford to pay their staff if they cannot raise their sales prices because of low demand. In other words, if wages are high, but aggregate demand is restricted, firms will have high costs but will not be able to pass these on in higher prices because sales will be too low, and many will go out of business or sack some of their employees. By allowing higher demand, inflation occurs, but unemployment can be lower than otherwise.

The inverse relationship between money wages and unemployment was described by the *Phillips curve* (◊ PHILLIPS, A. W. H.) However, the Phillips relationship did not hold through the 1960s and the role of EXPECTATIONS in pre-empting rises in prices was stressed, mainly on account of the work of M. FRIEDMAN. Inflation could not act as a break on real wages, it was asserted, unless it outstripped the expectations of wage bargainers. If, in the longer term, inflation rates could be anticipated, inflation would have no effect on unemployment (◊ UN-EMPLOYMENT, NATURAL RATE OF). Inflation disrupts investment, by causing interest rates to rise, shortening pay-back periods, and affecting company cash flow. It arbitrarily distributes wealth away from those whose incomes are fixed in money terms or rise more slowly than inflation. To allow inflation to develop carries the risk of incurring rates high enough to disrupt economic life (◊◊ HYPERINFLATION; INDEXA-TION; PRICES AND INCOMES POLICY; SUPERNEUTRALITY OF MONEY.)

Inflation accounting. Methods of keeping a record of financial transactions and analysing them in a way which allows for changes in the purchasing power of money over time. Until recently, solely *historic-cost accounting* methods have been used, that is to say, accounts were derived more or less directly from bookkeeping records of actual expenditures and receipts. Fixed ASSETS, for example, such as buildings, were recorded in the balance sheet at their actual (depreciated) cost (◊ DEPRECIATION). In a period of rapidly rising prices the replacement cost of these assets is likely to be much higher than their recorded cost, and historic-cost accounting, therefore, may understate depreciation and costs in REAL TERMS and overstate profits. Over a period of time this may lead to a situation where CAPITAL is not being maintained in real terms at all but distributed as 'illusory' money profit in dividends and tax payments.

The problem of the effects of INFLATION on accounts has been under discussion since the 1930s. In the 1960s firms increasingly revalued their assets in a partial attempt to avoid overstating profits and more recently tax relief has been given on profits arising from STOCK AP-PRECIATION. Various approaches to a more complete solution to the problem have been put forward. The *current purchasing-power* method (C.P.P.; U.S. *general purchasing power* (G.P.P.)), which retains historic-cost accounting conventions but expresses accounts in terms of 'purchasing units' using a RETAIL-PRICE INDEX rather than money data, has received the support of professional accounting bodies in the U.S.A. and Britain but was rejected by the SANDILANDS COMMITTEE. Another alternative, *cash-flow accounting*, in which accounts are prepared on a 'cash' rather than on a conventional 'accruals' basis (◊ ACCRUED EXPENSES), was regarded as having useful features but also rejected. The committee recommended a change to *value accounting* in which 'net assets are measured by reference to their value rather than their cost'. Among the different approaches to asset valuation (which include PRESENT VALUE), the committee adopted a form of *replacement-cost accounting* which involves revaluing assets from historic costs to current costs. The main features of the system which is called *current-cost accounting* (C.C.A.) are that money is retained as the unit of measurement, that both 'assets and liabilities are shown in the balance sheet at a valuation' and that OPERATING PROFIT 'is struck after charging the "value to the business" of assets consumed during the period thus excluding holding gains from profit and showing them separately'. The committee recommended that the new system should be introduced as soon as possible and that a steering group should be set up to oversee its introduction. The group published a series of exposure drafts of the new standards and finally current-cost accounting standard S.S.A.P. 16 in 1980 for a three-year experimental period. S.S.A.P. 16 has now been adopted as a voluntary standard, but relatively few firms have used it in their published accounts.

Inflation tax. A form of incomes policy (◊ PRICES AND INCOMES POLICY) under which firms granting pay rises above a set level are taxed on those pay rises.

Inflationary gap. A situation in which aggregate demand is at an equilibrium level in excess of the full-employment level of output. If it exists, all resources in the economy are fully utilized and prices have to rise to eliminate the excess demand. Based on Keynesian models of the economy, the inflationary gap leads to a DEMAND-PULL INFLATION which can be removed by DEFLATION. However, persistent inflation has been combined with high unemployment (something that should not occur in the inflationary gap) and in recent years in DEVELOPED COUNTRIES other theories of inflation have been developed. (◊ INFLATION; STAGFLATION.)

Infrastructure. Roads, airports, sewage and water systems, railways, the telephone and other public utilities. Also called *social overhead capital*, infrastructure is basic to economic development and improvements in it can be used to help attract industry to a disadvantaged area.

Inheritance tax. ◊ CAPITAL TRANSFER TAX.

Initial allowances. ◊ CAPITAL ALLOWANCES.

Inland bill of exchange. A BILL OF EXCHANGE drawn and payable in one country. Sometimes called *domestic bill of exchange*.

Innovation. Putting new products and services on to the market or new means for producing them. Innovation is preceded by research that may lead to an invention which is then developed for the market (◊

RESEARCH AND DEVELOPMENT). Innovation is an important source of economic expansion and PRODUCTIVITY to which SCHUMPETER gave a central role in his theory of economic growth. For this reason and because technological innovation can create UNEMPLOYMENT in the short and medium term, the factors affecting the rate of innovation and the diffusion of technology, for example MARKET STRUCTURE and, in particular, the role of public policy and firm size, have received a great deal of attention from economists.

Input. ◊ FACTOR OF PRODUCTION.

Input–output analysis. The output of a good or service in an economy is either used in the production of goods and services (including itself) or it goes into final consumption (e.g. households, exports, government). Each output in an economy can be represented by an equation, with output equal to its final consumption plus the sum of its inputs used in all production activity throughout the economy. The amounts used in production will depend on the PRODUCTION FUNCTIONS for each. Consider the simplified MODEL of two commodities, Y_1 and Y_2:

$$Y_1 = C_1 + a_{11}Y_1 + a_{12}Y_2$$
$$Y_2 = C_2 + a_{21}Y_1 + a_{22}Y_2$$

Y_1 and Y_2 are total outputs, C_1 and C_2 are the final consumptions for each and a_{11}, a_{12}, a_{21} and a_{22} are the input–output coefficients representing the amounts of Y_1 and Y_2 required to produce one unit of Y_1 and Y_2. These equations may be put in MATRIX form:

$$Y = C + AY \quad \text{or} \quad Y = (I - A)^{-1}C$$

where Y is the VECTOR Y_1Y_2, C the vector C_1C_2 and A the matrix

$$\begin{matrix} a_{11} & a_{12} \\ a_{21} & a_{22} \end{matrix}$$

AY is the total of intermediate demands and A is the matrix of input–output coefficients or *technology matrix*. By structuring the production functions of an economy in this way, it is possible to trace the effects of a change in final demand, or change in output, of one good or service, throughout its inter-industry linked relationships, so that the knock-on effects on other industries may be measured. ◊ LEONTIEF, W. W.

Input–output matrix. ◊ INPUT–OUTPUT ANALYSIS; LEONTIEF, W. W.; MATRIX.

Insolvency. A firm is insolvent if its LIABILITIES, excluding EQUITY capital, exceed its total ASSETS.

Instalment credit (U.S.). Term for HIRE PURCHASE, though sometimes used generally to refer to a credit sale when payment is made in instalments (◊ CONSUMER CREDIT).

Institutional economics. A school of economic thought which flourished in the 1920s in the U.S.A. Economists holding institutional views criticize orthodox economists for relying on theoretical and mathematical models which not only distort and oversimplify even strictly economic phenomena, but, more important, ignore their non-economic, institutional environment. The political and social structure of a country may block or distort the normal economic processes. Institutionalists believe that there is a need for economists to recognize the relevance of other disciplines, e.g. sociology, politics, law, to the solution of economic problems. T. B. VEBLEN (1857–1929), W. C. Mitchell (1874–1948) and G. K. MYRDAL (1898–1987) have been the leading economists sympathetic to institutionalism.

Institutional investor. An organization, as opposed to an individual, which invests funds arising from its receipts from the sale of SECURITIES, from DEPOSITS and other sources, i.e. INSURANCE companies, INVESTMENT TRUSTS, UNIT TRUSTS, PENSION FUNDS and trustees. Institutional investors probably own 70 per cent of all quoted securities and insurance companies and pension funds alone invested £17,300 million in securities, mortgages and property in 1985. (▷ INSURANCE for details of investments by insurance companies.)

Insurance. A contract to pay a PREMIUM in return for which the insurer will pay compensation in certain eventualities, e.g. fire, theft, motor accident. The premiums are so calculated that, on average in total, they are sufficient to pay compensation for the policy-holders who will make a claim together with a margin to cover administration costs and profit (▷ ACTUARY; UNDERWRITING). In effect insurance spreads risk, so that loss by an individual is compensated for at the expense of all those who insure against it, and as such it has an important economic function.

The traditional forms of insurance are *general insurance*, i.e. marine and other property insurance against theft, fire and accident, and *life insurance*, the last named strictly being ASSURANCE, because the cover is given against the occurrence of an event which is inevitable. There are also many other kinds of insurance, including public or professional liability, sickness and unemployment insurance, some of which, like NATIONAL INSURANCE and the B.U.P.A. insurance for private medical treatment, are not carried out by the traditional insurance companies. Traditional insurance is carried out in Britain by some 800 companies, of which 500 operate in the U.K. The U.K. is an important centre for the world insurance industry and nearly half of the premium income of British insurance companies is derived from their overseas operations. The bulk of their ASSETS consist of INVESTMENTS made out of premium income against their LIABILITIES to 'pay out' on life policies; only about 10 per cent of their assets are in respect of general funds. Of the combined funds in 1985 of £154,000 million, 3 per cent were MORTGAGES on houses, factories and other buildings, 23 per cent were U.K. GOVERNMENT SECURITIES, 40 per cent in ORDINARY SHARES and other U.K. company securities, 14 per cent in property, 12 per cent in overseas securities and most of the remainder in cash and short-term SECURITIES. The flow of life funds for new investment was about £10,000 million in 1985, i.e. about one-sixth of total fixed CAPITAL FORMATION in that year (◊ INSTITUTIONAL INVESTOR). Life insurance is a popular way of providing for old age and purchasing a house or even EQUITY shares, as well as protecting the financial position of dependants. ◊ LLOYD'S; PENSION FUNDS; UNIT TRUST.

Insurance broker. An intermediary who brings together persons or organizations requiring INSURANCE with insurance companies who provide it. He obtains a COMMISSION from the insurance companies, but, being independent from them, he is in a position to advise his clients on which companies offer the most favourable terms. Insurance brokers handle claims, queries and loans against insurance policies as well as arranging insurance in the first instance.

Intangible assets. ◊ ASSETS.

Integration. ◊ MERGER; VERTICAL INTEGRATION.

Inter-American Development Bank (I.D.B.). The bank was established in 1959 to give financial assistance to the developing countries of Latin America and the Caribbean. Until 1974 membership was limited to the United States and twenty-two Latin American and Caribbean countries. However, membership now covers twenty-five countries in Latin America and the Caribbean and fifteen countries in Europe, the United States, Canada, Israel and Japan. The bank's total cumulative lending reached $17,800 million by 1980, with energy projects absorbing about 25 per cent of the total. The United States holds 34·8 per cent of the voting shares of the bank. The bank provides finance on both strictly commercial terms and as soft loans for projects within the region. It also provides expert technical assistance as required. ◊ ASIAN DEVELOPMENT BANK.

Inter-bank market. The MONEY MARKET in which banks (◊ BANKING) borrow or lend among themselves for fixed periods either to accommodate short-term LIQUIDITY problems or for lending on. The interest rate at which funds on loan are offered to first-class banks is called the *inter-bank offered rate* (I.B.O.R.) or, in London, the *London inter-bank offered rate* (L.I.B.O.R.). The corresponding rate for deposits is known as the *inter-bank market bid rate* (I.B.M.B.R.).

Inter-company loans market. Loans made between larger commercial and industrial companies. The market originated in 1969 as a result of quantitative restrictions on bank credit (◊ CREDIT SQUEEZE) which companies were able to avoid by borrowing and lending directly among themselves or through a BROKER. ◊◊ DISINTERMEDIATION.

Interest, abstinence theory of. An explanation of F . ES OF INTEREST in terms of a reward for choosing to abstain from consumption. ⟡ INTEREST, CLASSICAL THEORY OF; SENIOR, N. W.; TIME PREFERENCE.

Interest, classical theory of. In the early tradition of classical theory, e.g. that of ADAM SMITH and DAVID RICARDO, the RATE OF INTEREST was regarded as simply the RATE OF RETURN on CAPITAL invested. It was considered to be an INCOME to capital rather like RENT to land. With the subsequent development of the classical system, the nature and the determinants of the rate of interest came to be regarded in terms of a more complex pattern. The rate was arrived at by the interaction of two forces operating on the supply of, and the demand for, funds. On the other hand, the strength of demand was related to businessmen's expectations regarding PROFITS. This was connected with the marginal productivity of INVESTMENT. On the other hand, the supply was dependent upon the willingness to save. This willingness was in turn related to the marginal rate of TIME PREFERENCE. People judge how much a pound is worth to them today compared with a pound in the future. They make their decision whether to save by comparing this 'rate of exchange' between now and the future with the current rate of interest. In the classical system, therefore, it was the rate of interest which brought SAVINGS into balance with investment. J. M. KEYNES attacked this assumption in his *General Theory of Employment, Interest and Money*. The balance was brought about, he argued, by means of changes in INCOME and output. The rate of interest was itself more closely confined to monetary factors. ⟡ HUME, D.; LIQUIDITY PREFERENCE; LOANABLE FUNDS.

Interest, natural rate of. One of the conditions put forward by K. WICKSELL for monetary EQUILIBRIUM – i.e. a situation in which there are no forces tending to make PRICES in general go on rising – was that the money RATE OF INTEREST should be equal to the 'natural rate'. The owner of a forest has a choice between two alternatives in any one year. He can either cut down his trees and lend out the money obtained from them, or let the trees grow another year. The RATE OF RETURN he gets from lending is the 'money rate'; the return he gets from growing his trees heavier is the 'natural rate'. Wicksell thought of the natural rate, therefore, in terms of a physical investment. However, MYRDAL in developing this theme pointed out that the natural rate should also take into account the price at which the timber was expected to sell. ⟡ FISHER, I.; KEYNES, J. M.

Interest, productivity theories of. Theories which place the emphasis of the explanation for the existence of a RATE OF INTEREST on the YIELD from INVESTMENT. BÖHM-BAWERK, in particular, developed this theory as one of his reasons for the existence of a positive interest rate. It was built upon his theory of 'roundabout' production methods. A direct method of obtaining drinking water, for example, is to go to a stream and drink. A more roundabout method is to manufacture a bucket and use it to fetch water. An even more roundabout method is to build a water-pipe, pump and tap. Each stage involves more CAPITAL, and also more time, but nevertheless yields increased product. Goods available today, therefore, have more value than goods available tomorrow, for two reasons. First, goods today can be used in a time-consuming roundabout process to yield benefits tomorrow which are greater than could be obtained by the same goods applied to direct production tomorrow. Secondly, they also yield greater benefits over the same goods applied to roundabout production tomorrow. This is because there are DIMINISHING RETURNS to the extension of round-about methods. Present goods are, therefore, always technically superior to future goods, and it follows that there must exist a positive rate of interest by which future goods are equated to present goods. ⟡ INTEREST, CLASSICAL THEORY OF; INTEREST, NATURAL RATE OF; KEYNES, J. M.

Interest, time preference theory of. A psychological theory of the existence of RATES OF INTEREST. An individual prefers consumption now to consumption in the future for two reasons. First, he is aware of the possibility that he may be dead before he can derive the benefits from postponing consumption. Second, and less rationally, there exists a tendency for people to undervalue future benefits – a 'deficiency of the telescopic faculty'. ⟡ BÖHM-BAWERK, E. VON; FISHER, I.; INTEREST, CLASSICAL THEORY OF; INTEREST, NATURAL RATE OF; INTEREST, PRODUCTIVITY THEORIES OF; TIME PREFERENCE.

Interest cover. The number of times the fixed-interest payments made by a company to service its LOAN CAPITAL are exceeded by EARNINGS. This ratio shows the decline in earnings that could take place before interest payments could not be met out of current income and is therefore a useful guide for the prospective fixed-interest investor.

Interest rate. ⟡ RATE OF INTEREST.

Interim dividend. ⟡ DIVIDEND.

Interlocking directorate. The holding by an individual of directorships in two or more separate companies.

Intermediate goods, intermediate products. Something which is used in the production of other goods; for example sheet steel used in the production of car bodies. Also called producer goods.

Intermediate products. ⟡ INTERMEDIATE GOODS.

Internal rate of return. That RATE OF INTEREST which discounts the flow over time of net revenue generated by an investment (⟡ DISCOUNTED CASH FLOW) such that the PRESENT VALUE of the net revenue flows is equal to the capital sum invested. The internal rate of return, therefore, is the discount rate at which the net present value is zero. It may be used in INVESTMENT APPRAISAL to determine whether a prospective investment is viable. For instance, if the internal rate of return is higher than the rate of interest at which a firm can borrow, the investment would be worth pursuing. However, the internal rate of return has two disadvantages. First, if the period (e.g. annual, quarterly) costs and revenues of the project being considered change sign more than once (costs exceeding revenues give negative flows and revenues exceeding costs give positive flows) during the life of the project, a solution cannot be found giving a unique internal rate of return. Secondly, in ranking alternative investment proposals in priority order, the internal rate of return procedure could give a different ranking from that of net present value. For instance, consider the following two investment projects:

	(1)	(2)
Capital cost	£100	£300
Net revenue per year	£40	£40
Project life (years)	3	12
Net present value at 5 per cent	£8·9	£54·5
Internal rate of return (per cent)	9·7	8

According to the ranking by net present value, (2) is preferable to (1), whereas by ranking according to the internal rates of return (1) is preferred to (2). The net present value calculation always gives the correct answer because it shows the absolute amount of profit to be made on the investment. The internal rate of return is also the *marginal efficiency of capital* and *investor's yield*.

International Bank for Reconstruction and Development (I.B.R.D.). Also known as the World Bank, the establishment of the I.B.R.D., like the INTERNATIONAL MONETARY FUND, was agreed by the representatives of forty-four countries at the U.N. Monetary and Financial Conference at BRETTON WOODS in July 1944. It began operations in June 1946. The purpose of the bank is to encourage CAPITAL investment for the reconstruction and development of its member countries, either by channelling the necessary private funds or by making LOANS from its own resources. Two per cent of each member's subscription is paid into the bank's funds in gold or dollars, 18 per cent in the country's own CURRENCY, and the remainder is retained but available for call to meet any of the bank's LIABILITIES if required. The bank also raises money by selling BONDS on the world market. Generally speaking, the bank makes loans either direct to governments or with governments as the guarantor. Contributions of member countries to the capital of the bank are made in proportion to that member's share of world trade. Members' voting rights are allocated in the same way. In 1981 the capitalization of the bank was increased to $80 billion. China became a member of the bank in 1980. In 1986 there were 148 member countries.

In 1980 the bank introduced a new policy under its structural adjustment programme by which it makes loans to ease the BALANCE OF PAYMENTS problems of the DEVELOPING COUNTRIES. These loans, however, are conditional upon the recipient country's adopting economic policies specified by the bank. Loans to the developing countries totalled $21·4 billion in the year ending June 1985. The bank operates through its affiliates, the INTERNATIONAL FINANCE CORPORATION and the INTERNATIONAL DEVELOPMENT ASSOCIATION.

International Clearing Union. ⇨ KEYNES PLAN.

International commodity agreements. A number of international commodity agreements have been signed in the past. They include coffee, olive oil, sultanas, sugar, wheat and tin. It has been a feature of the MARKETS in primary commodities that imbalance between SUPPLY and DEMAND gives rise to wide fluctuations in PRICES. Primary commodities often have long production cycles which are difficult to adjust to bring into EQUILIBRIUM with relatively short-run fluctuations in demand. At the same time, the development of the economies of the primary producing countries depends heavily on the export earnings of these commodities, with the result that, in response to a fall in demand, there is a tendency to increase supply to maintain total earnings in the face of intensified competition, thereby forcing prices down even further. There are two features, therefore, of commodity agreements. They may be concluded (a) for the stabilization of prices, or (b) for the raising or maintenance of prices. The first Coffee Agreement signed in 1962, covering the five years to 1968, was designed to halt the long decline in prices by fixing export QUOTAS for each producing country. The agreement has since been regularly renewed. The current agreement expires in 1989. The International Tin Agreement is an example of a 'price stabilization' agreement. The first operated for five years from July 1956. A 'buffer' stock of tin was created and a manager appointed who had the responsibility of buying and selling tin such as to keep the PRICE within a 'ceiling' at which point he sold, and a 'floor' when he bought, tin. However, the sixth agreement failed in 1985 when the resources of the International Tin Council were insufficient to halt the fall in prices. In 1973 an International Cocoa Agreement was concluded which was renewed in 1980. This agreement also failed, in 1982, when the International Cocoa Organization had to suspend support buying. However, agreement was reached between sixty producing and consuming countries, establishing a new buffer stock and support-price regime for a period of three years. At the end of 1976 an agreement was concluded between Indonesia, Malaysia, Singapore, Sri Lanka and Thailand for the stabilization of the prices of natural rubber by means of a buffer stock and controls on production. An International Natural Rubber Council was set up. The current agreement expires in 1987. The

Multi-Fibre Arrangement regulates world trade in textiles and clothing. The first M.F.A. was signed in 1974, renewed in 1978 and the second in 1982. ⬦ DEVELOPING COUNTRIES; ORGANIZATION OF PETROLEUM EXPORTING COUNTRIES; UNITED NATIONS CONFERENCE ON TRADE AND DEVELOPMENT.

International company. ⬦ MULTINATIONAL CORPORATION.

International Cooperation Administration. ⬦ ECONOMIC COOPERATION ADMINISTRATION.

International corporation. ⬦ MULTINATIONAL CORPORATION.

International Development Association (I.D.A.). An institution affiliated to the INTERNATIONAL BANK FOR RECONSTRUCTION AND DEVELOPMENT and established in 1960. It gives long-term LOANS to governments at little or no interest for projects in the poorer of the DEVELOPING COUNTRIES. It is intended for INVESTMENTS for which finance cannot be obtained through other channels without bearing uneconomically high interest charges and is mainly for items of infrastructure, e.g. roads or power supply. The repayment period for the loan may be up to fifty years with repayments being delayed by up to ten years. In 1984–7 the I.D.A. lent about $9 billion to developing countries.

International Energy Agency (I.E.A.). An organization established in 1974 by the member countries of the O.E.C.D. (except Finland, France and Iceland). Its aims are to (a) reduce the member countries' dependence on oil supplies, (b) maintain an information system relating to the international oil markets, (c) develop a stable international energy trade and (d) through cooperative sharing, prepare and protect member countries against a disruption of oil supplies. Member countries agree to hold a particular level of oil stocks. ⬦ ORGANIZATION OF PETROLEUM EXPORTING COUNTRIES.

International Finance Corporation (I.F.C.). An affiliate of the INTERNATIONAL BANK FOR RECONSTRUCTION AND DEVELOPMENT. In the early 1950s it was recognized that the requirement that I.B.R.D. loans should have a government guarantee was a significant handicap to the attraction of private INVESTMENT to DEVELOPING COUNTRIES. The I.F.C. was created in 1956 so that greater advantage could be taken of private initiative in the launching of new CAPITAL projects. Until 1961, when its charter was amended, its activities were restricted because it had few resources and could not participate itself in EQUITY holdings. Since that time its activities have been able to develop rapidly. The corporation can invest directly and give LOANS and guarantees for private investors. It can hold equity interests in private companies, although its interest in any one company is generally restricted to below 25 per cent. The I.F.C. is empowered to borrow from the I.B.R.D. to relend to private investors without government guarantee. It is financed by subscriptions from the 128 countries that make up its membership. At the end of 1984/5 the I.F.C. had approval to borrow up to $3·2 billion from the I.B.R.D. to finance its lending.

International investment. ◊ FOREIGN INVESTMENT.

International Investment Bank. ◊ COMECON.

International Labour Organization (I.L.O.). An organization established in 1919 under the Treaty of Versailles that became affiliated to the United Nations in 1946. Its aims are the improvement of working conditions throughout the world, the spread of social security and the maintenance of standards of social justice. It has drawn up a labour code based on these aims. The I.L.O. offers technical assistance to DEVELOPING COUNTRIES, especially in the field of training. Its budget is financed by contributions from its 151 member countries. The organization was awarded the Nobel peace prize in 1969.

International liquidity. The amount of gold, RESERVE CURRENCIES and SPECIAL DRAWING RIGHTS available for the finance of international trade. In 1958, when sterling became convertible (◊ CONVERTIBILITY), the leading reserve currencies were the dollar and sterling. Therefore, apart from *ad hoc* LOANS made by the INTERNATIONAL MONETARY FUND, the growth in LIQUIDITY needed to finance the expansion of world trade for the following almost fifteen years had to be found in the expansion of the output of gold and the supply of dollars and sterling. The physical supply of gold is virtually limited to the output of the mines in South Africa and the U.S.S.R. The official price of gold in terms of dollars had been fixed until the end of 1971 at its 1934 level of $35 an ounce. With the decline in the United Kingdom's position in world trade, sterling's acceptability as a reserve currency declined. The needed growth of liquidity was therefore met by the outflow of dollars from the United States arising from the persistent U.S. BALANCE OF PAYMENTS deficit. Pressures eventually built up for the elimination of this deficit, and consequently concern developed as to whether there would be adequate liquidity in the future to finance trade. Broadly, if sufficient reserves are not available, a fall in prices and world trade could follow (◊ QUANTITY THEORY OF MONEY). A crisis of confidence finally led in November 1967 to sterling being devalued (◊ DEVALUATION), and early in 1968 control over the gold market broke down. The old fixed price survived but only for gold in international finance. In August 1971, the U.S. government imposed a 10 per cent import surcharge, suspended the convertibility of the dollar and introduced other measures to correct the the balance-of-payments deficit. In December 1971 the 'Group of Ten' countries in the I.M.F., at the Smithsonian Institute, Washington, agreed to revalue their currencies to give the U.S. dollar an effective devaluation of 10 per cent, and the import surcharge was lifted. Having taken measures to reverse the U.S.

deficit, it was agreed to hold discussions to consider the reform of the international monetary system over the long term. There are two types of solution to the problem: (a) a system of flexible EXCHANGE RATES that would at the theoretical extreme make international liquidity held in the form of gold and FOREIGN EXCHANGE reserves unnecessary, and (b) an increase in liquidity by raising the price of gold or by inventing a new CURRENCY. The Smithsonian Agreement in December 1971 reaffirmed that discussions take place against the need for stable exchange rates. In the event this policy did not hold, for in June of the following year sterling was floated, and this heralded an era in which all major currencies came off fixed parities and floated, albeit the float was 'managed'. In the late 1960s a new source of international liquidity began to develop, partly as a result of the U.S. deficit, in the form of EUROCURRENCY. J. M. KEYNES had already put forward a scheme for a CENTRAL BANK for central banks, at the BRETTON WOODS Conference, which would issue its own currency called BANCOR. Keynes argued: 'We need a quantum of international currency, which is neither determined in an unpredictable and irrelevant manner as, for example, by the technical progress of the gold industry, nor subject to large variations depending on the gold reserve policies of individual countries, but is governed by the actual current requirements of world commerce.' In 1969 the I.M.F.'s articles of agreement were revised so that it could set up and distribute to member countries special drawing rights, which have a strong affinity with Keynes's bancor. The first distribution of S.D.R.s, valued at $3,500 million, was made at the beginning of 1970. Another important new source of liquidity emerged with the introduction of the EUROPEAN CURRENCY UNIT, used by the members of the EUROPEAN COMMON MARKET for their internal trading. A dramatic change in the balance of world liquidity was caused by the increase in oil prices by O.P.E.C. (◊ ORGANIZATION OF PETROLEUM EXPORTING COUNTRIES) in 1972–3. As a result, the foreign DEBT of less developed countries rose from $75 billion in 1970 to $400 billion in 1980. The balance-of-payments deficits of the non-oil L.D.C.s in 1980 was about $75 billion; the developed countries together had a deficit of about $60 billion in contrast to a surplus of $103 billion earned by O.P.E.C. In 1981, however, the O.P.E.C. surplus dropped to $45 billion and in 1982 the O.P.E.C. balance of payments went into deficit. The balance-of-payments deficits of the developing countries led to an acute financing need which was met by the international institutions. However, this has left a heavy burden of interest payments, totalling $58 billion in 1985 (22 per cent of their export earnings). ◊ CREDITOR NATION; UNITED NATIONS CONFERENCE ON TRADE AND DEVELOPMENT.

International Monetary Fund (I.M.F.). The I.M.F. was set up by the

BRETTON WOODS Agreement of 1944 and came into operation in March 1947. The fund was established to encourage international co-operation in the monetary field and the removal of FOREIGN EXCHANGE restrictions, to stabilize exchange rates and to facilitate a multilateral (◊MULTILATERALISM) payments system between member countries. In 1985 the fund had 148 members. Under the I.M.F.'s articles of agreement, member countries were required to observe an EXCHANGE RATE, fluctuations in which should be confined to ±1 per cent around its PAR VALUE. This par value was quoted in terms of the U.S. dollar, which was in turn linked to gold. In December 1971 the 'Group of Ten' (see below), meeting at the Smithsonian Institute, Washington, agreed on new 'central values' of currencies in order to achieve a dollar devaluation of 10 per cent with a permissible margin of ±2·25 per cent. Each member country of the I.M.F. was required to subscribe to the fund a quota paid 25 per cent in gold and 75 per cent in the member's own currency. In 1985, quotas totalled S.D.R. $89·3 billion. This fund is used to tide members over temporary BALANCE OF PAYMENTS difficulties and thus to help stabilize exchange rates. Borrowing ability and voting rights are determined by this quota. Under the present system, the United States holds about 22 per cent of the voting strength and the EUROPEAN ECONOMIC COMMUNITY about 27 per cent; and so, since an 85 per cent majority is required to make a major change in I.M.F. procedure, both the United States and the E.E.C. have the power to veto. A member in temporary balance-of-payments deficit obtains foreign exchange from the fund in exchange for its own currency, which it is required to repurchase within three to five years. Members in deficit with the fund are obliged by the terms of the agreement to consult with the I.M.F. on the procedures being taken to improve their balance of payments.

During the early 1960s it became evident that there was a strong case for increasing the size of the fund, and in 1962 the General Agreement to Borrow was signed by ten countries, namely the United States, the United Kingdom, West Germany, France, Belgium, the Netherlands, Italy, Sweden, Canada and Japan – called the 'Group of Ten' or the 'Paris Club' – under which S.D.R. $6,500 million credit was made available to the I.M.F. should it be required. In addition, Switzerland, which is not a member of the I.M.F., made available $200 million. This agreement has been regularly renewed and in 1985 the credit limit was S.D.R. $17,000 million. Countries in difficulty can also negotiate standby credit on which they can draw as necessary. The I.M.F. cannot, however, make use of any of the currency in this scheme without the prior consent of the lending country. In September 1967, at the I.M.F. meeting in Rio de Janeiro, the creation of an international unit of account was agreed in principle, and ratified in July 1969. The system proposed was that annual increases in international credit would be distributed to I.M.F. members by means of SPECIAL DRAWING RIGHTS (S.D.R.s). These credits are distributed among member countries in proportion to their quotas and may be included in their official reserves; the first, $3,500 million, was distributed in this way on 1 January 1970. Total S.D.R.s are now about $21,400 million. There is a limit on the acceptability for payment in S.D.R.s, in that no country need hold more than twice its S.D.R. quota. In 1976 an agreement reached in Jamaica led to a major revision of the fund's articles. First, it is no longer required for member countries to subscribe 25 per cent of their quotas in gold, and gold is no longer the unit of account of the S.D.R. The I.M.F. was authorized to sell its gold holding. The revenue from its gold sales is used to finance aid to the DEVELOPING COUNTRIES. Second, the commitment to fixed par values contained in the original articles was abolished.

The increase in the price of oil in 1973 placed a severe balance-of-payments strain on the consuming countries, and the I.M.F. set up an oil-facility loan scheme by means of which the surpluses earned by O.P.E.C. were recycled. In 1974–5 a total of S.D.R. $6,900 million was allocated for the facility, mostly financed by borrowings from O.P.E.C. The scheme was wound up in 1976. ♢ GOLD STANDARD.

International Securities Regulatory Organization (I.S.R.O.). ♢ STOCK EXCHANGE.

International Settlements, Bank for (B.I.S.). ♢ BANK FOR INTERNATIONAL SETTLEMENTS.

International Standard Industrial Classification (I.S.I.C.). ♢ STANDARD INDUSTRIAL CLASSIFICATION.

International trade. The exchange of goods and services between one country and another. This exchange takes place because of differences in costs of production between countries, and because it increases the economic welfare of each country by widening the range of goods and services available for CONSUMPTION. DAVID RICARDO showed by the law of comparative advantage that it was not necessary for one country to have an absolute cost advantage in the production of a commodity for it to find a partner willing to trade. Even if a country produced all commodities more expensively than any other, trade to the benefit of all could take place provided only that the relative costs of production of the different commodities were favourable. Differences in costs of production exist because countries are differently endowed with the resources required. Countries differ as to the type and quantity of raw materials within their borders, their climate, the skill and size of their labour force and their stock of physical CAPITAL. Countries will tend to export (♢ EXPORTS) those commodities whose production requires relatively more than other commodities of those resources (♢

FACTORS OF PRODUCTION) of which it has most (◊ HECKSCHER–OHLIN PRINCIPLE). By increasing the scope for the specialization of labour (◊ DIVISION OF LABOUR) and for achieving ECONOMIES OF SCALE by the enlargement of MARKETS, there is a presumption that international trade should be free from restrictions (◊ FREE TRADE). The classical economists (◊ CLASSICAL ECONOMICS) condemned MERCANTILISM for its advocacy of government control over trade in order to achieve export surpluses, and from the nineteenth to the early twentieth century there was free trade. This philosophy gave place to the economic protectionism (◊ PROTECTION) of the inter-war years but it was revived again in the GENERAL AGREEMENT ON TARIFFS AND TRADE in 1948. The latter has had some success in reducing tariffs (◊ TARIFFS, IMPORT) on IMPORTS, culminating in the TOKYO ROUND OF TRADE NEGOTIATIONS in 1974 and the initiation of the Uruguay Round in 1986. However, many trade restrictions still remain (◊ PROTECTION). At the same time there has been an increase in the number of CUSTOMS UNIONS and FREE-TRADE AREAS such as the EUROPEAN ECONOMIC COMMUNITY, the EUROPEAN FREE TRADE ASSOCIATION, the LATIN AMERICAN FREE TRADE ASSOCIATION and the CENTRAL AMERICAN COMMON MARKET. While these unions do establish free trade between member countries, they discriminate against outsiders. International trade since the end of the Second World War has grown rapidly, and many changes in the pattern of goods and services traded have taken and are taking place. The DEVELOPING COUNTRIES, in their attempt to achieve faster ECONOMIC GROWTH, are changing from being simply raw-material exporters to exporters of finished or semi-finished goods. At the same time the developed nations are taking advantage of technological specialization, so that trade in high-value finished manufactures is increasing between them.

International Trade Organization (I.T.O.). At the U.N. conference held at Geneva in 1947 at which the GENERAL AGREEMENT ON TARIFFS AND TRADE was signed, a charter was put forward for the setting up, within the U.N. Organization, of a new agency to be called the International Trade Organization. Fifty nations signed the charter in Havana the following year, but it was never subsequently ratified by the required number of countries. The aim of the proposed organization was to work out principles for the general conduct of international trade and to draw up proposals for the implementation of policies based on these principles. Its terms of reference covered TARIFFS, QUOTAS, taxes, INTERNATIONAL COMMODITY AGREEMENTS and whatever was considered to have a bearing on the development of international trade and was based on policies of non-discrimination and tariff reductions. In practice, G.A.T.T. and the UNITED NATIONS CONFERENCE ON

TRADE AND DEVELOPMENT (U.N.C.T.A.D.) have carried out most of the functions envisaged for the I.T.O.

Intervention. Any form of government interference with MARKET FORCES to achieve economic ends. The EXCHANGE EQUALIZATION ACCOUNT, for example, buys or sells sterling or foreign CURRENCIES in order to influence the EXCHANGE RATE of the pound.

Intra-European Payments Agreement. A payments system established between the member countries of the ORGANIZATION FOR EUROPEAN ECONOMIC COOPERATION in 1948 to facilitate the distribution of U.S. aid under the EUROPEAN RECOVERY PROGRAMME and to encourage intra-European trade by facilitating the settlement of intra-European BALANCE OF PAYMENTS deficits. Based on a set of intra-European bilateral trade forecasts, a country for which a surplus balance of payments was expected received U.S. aid above a certain minimum only on condition that it extended drawing rights to its European partners in its own CURRENCY. A deficit country, therefore, received aid both from the U.S. and from the European countries in surplus. The surplus country, on the other hand, to obtain similar levels of U.S. aid was required itself to extend aid to its partners. This system, based on what were known as 'compensation agreements', was very ungainly and the forecasts often proved hopelessly inaccurate. It was replaced by the EUROPEAN PAYMENTS UNION in 1950.

Inventories. Term for STOCKS of raw materials, work in progress and finished goods. Inventories represent CAPITAL tied up in unsold goods and require storage space, insurance and other incurred costs, but are an inevitable part of the process of production and distribution. This is because: (a) in most cases, customers are not willing to wait while goods are produced, but expect delivery off the shelf; (b) it is not possible to forecast sales accurately and sales might be lost if stocks were not held, while it may be uneconomic to interrupt production to match short-term fluctuations in sales because of loss of ECONOMIES OF SCALE; (c) while production may be continuous, deliveries of components and raw materials arrive in batches (the Japanese Just in Time system attempts to minimize the need for stocks by matching deliveries more closely to production requirements); (d) transport arrangements may be such that finished goods also need to be dispatched in batches, for example by the lorry-load. *Inventory investment* may be intentional, for example where stocks are built up to meet an anticipated seasonal peak in demand, or unintentional, when demand falls sharply. Since increasing the level of stocks is an INVESTMENT, running them down is DISINVESTMENT. Market prices of goods or materials in stock may change while they are in stock, for example through INFLATION, and this will present accounting problems (for example in valuing inventories (◊ FIRST IN,

FIRST OUT) and distorting PROFITS ($\Diamond$ CORPORATION TAX; INFLA-
TION ACCOUNTING)).

The value of the physical change in stocks and work in progress is typically quite significant in relation to changes in the components of AGGREGATE DEMAND. In 1985 the physical change in inventories was equivalent to 1·7 per cent of U.K. NOMINAL GROSS DOMESTIC PRO-DUCT, compared with an increase in nominal G.D.P. of 9·8 per cent over the previous year. In 1984, inventories fell to the extent of 1·3 per cent of G.D.P. Changes in inventory investment may have significant MACROECONOMIC consequences. $\Diamond$ INVENTORY INVESTMENT CYCLE.

Investors in Industry. $\Diamond$ FINANCE FOR INDUSTRY.

Inventory investment. $\Diamond$ INVENTORIES.

Inventory investment cycle. Fluctuations in economic activity caused by changes in INVENTORIES. Although firms may increase or run down stocks to maintain a steady rate of production, there will be upper and lower limits to inventory accumulation determined by the need to hold a minimum stock and the cost of excessive stocks. For these reasons, many firms will try to keep stocks at so many days' sales or output. Since production will increase faster than sales when inventories are increasing (and vice versa) changes in inventories tend to accelerate the effect upon production of changes in sales, thus contributing to TRADE CYCLES. $\Diamond$ ACCELERATION PRINCIPLE.

Investment. 1. Real CAPITAL formation, such as the production or main-tenance of machinery or the construction of dwellings, that will produce a stream of goods and services for future consumption. Investment involves the sacrifice of current CONSUMPTION and the production of investment goods which are used to produce COMMODITIES ($\Diamond$ PRO-DUCER GOODS) and includes the accumulation of INVENTORIES. In the national accounts ($\Diamond$ SOCIAL ACCOUNTING) investment is the sum of gross fixed CAPITAL FORMATION and the physical change in stocks and work in progress. Students are often given the example of Robinson Crusoe, who diverts his time from eating wild berries so as to make a net to catch fish. It follows that investment (at least when the economy is producing at full capacity) is essential for growth. Investment may be stimulated by changes in DEMAND or TECHNOLOGY, by high PROFITS or by low interest rates (since much *investment expenditure* is financed by borrowing). The theory of INCOME DETERMINATION shows how SAVINGS and investment are brought into equilibrium. $\Diamond$ CAPITAL; DEPLETION THEORY; GROSS INVESTMENT; NET INVESTMENT. **2.** In common usage, expenditure on the acquisition of financial or real ASSETS. To the economist this is not investment, but simply a shift of savings from one form (cash) to another.

Investment, inward. $\Diamond$ FOREIGN INVESTMENT.

Investment, negative. ⟡ DISINVESTMENT.

Investment allowances. ⟡ CAPITAL ALLOWANCES.

Investment appraisal. The evaluation of the prospective costs and revenues generated by an investment in a capital project over its expected life. Such appraisal includes the assessment of the risks of, and the sensitivity of the project's viability to, forecasting errors. The appraisal enables a judgement to be made whether to commit resources to the project. ⟡ DISCOUNTED CASH FLOW; INTERNAL RATE OF RETURN; PRESENT VALUE.

Investment bank (U.S.). A financial intermediary which purchases new issues and places them in smaller parcels among investors. In Britain, a MERCHANT BANK or ISSUING HOUSE.

Investment expenditure. ⟡ INVESTMENT.

Investment function. ⟡ ACCELERATION PRINCIPLE.

Investment goods. ⟡ INVESTMENT.

Investment grants. ⟡ INVESTMENT INCENTIVES.

Investment incentives. Government assistance designed to encourage firms to invest in physical ASSETS in total, in particular industries or in particular locations. In the U.K. those incentives take the form of CAPITAL ALLOWANCES for tax relief and special incentives in the DEVELOPMENT AREAS. ⟡ ENTERPRISE ZONES; FREE-TRADE ZONES.

Investment trust. A company whose sole object is to invest its CAPITAL in a wide range of other companies. An investment trust issues SHARES and uses its capital to buy shares in other companies. A UNIT TRUST, on the other hand, issues units that represent holdings of shares. Unit holders thus do not share in the PROFITS of the company managing the trust. Although sharing the advantages of widespread investment with unit trusts, investment trusts pay their management expenses out of taxed INCOME and not out of shareholders' incomes. The total funds managed by investment trusts are twice as great as those of unit trusts. Investment trusts can also raise part of their capital by fixed-interest SECURITIES, and the YIELD on ORDINARY SHARES can thus benefit from GEARING. There are some 250 investment-trust companies in Britain, and like most INSTITUTIONAL INVESTORS they have been investing an increasing proportion of their funds in EQUITIES. Some investment trusts underwrite new issues (⟡ NEW-ISSUE MARKET).

Investors in Industry. ⟡ FINANCE FOR INDUSTRY.

Investor's yield. ⟡ INTERNAL RATE OF RETURN.

Invisible. Those 'invisible' items, such as financial services, included in the current BALANCE OF PAYMENTS accounts, as distinct from physically visible IMPORTS and EXPORTS of goods. Invisibles account for about 25 per cent of total INTERNATIONAL TRADE and are increasing at a faster rate than visible merchandise. Invisible trade is, however, generally less free from PROTECTIONISM than visible trade. Examples of protective policies are (a) the exclusion of foreign INSURANCE companies from some domestic markets, (b) restrictions on foreign-owned banks (◊ BANKING) setting up branches, (c) that some countries allow only a limited percentage of their visible trade to be carried on foreign-flag ships, and (d) EXCHANGE CONTROLS. In the U.K. balance-of-payments accounts invisibles include government grants to overseas countries and subscriptions to international organizations, net payments for shipping services, travel, royalties, commissions for banking and other services, transfers to or from overseas residents, INTEREST, PROFITS and DIVIDENDS received by or from overseas residents. The surplus earned on invisibles increased from £0·3 billion in 1967 to £1·8 billion in 1975, to £3·0 billion in 1981 and to £5·7 billion in 1985. This growth is mainly due to a rapid increase in the surpluses earned by the private sector from SERVICES such as insurance and banking, and from interest, profits and dividends earned by the private sector overseas.

Invisible balance. ◊ BALANCE OF PAYMENTS.

'Invisible hand.' ADAM SMITH believed that society was such that, although individuals pursued their own advantage, the greatest benefit to society as a whole was achieved by their being free to do so. Each individual was 'led by an invisible hand to promote an end which was no part of his intention'. ◊ MANDEVILLE, B. DE; PRICE SYSTEM; RESOURCES.

Involuntary saving. ◊ FORCED SAVING.

Inward investment. ◊ FOREIGN INVESTMENT.

Irredeemable security. A SECURITY which does not bear a date at which the CAPITAL sum will be paid off or redeemed, e.g. $2\frac{1}{2}$ per cent CONSOLS or certain DEBENTURES. Sometimes called UNDATED SECURITIES. Possession of an irredeemable security entitles the owner to INTEREST payments but not to repayment of face-value capital. This affects the price at which the security is marketable. For example, $2\frac{1}{2}$ per cent consols which are irredeemable £100 stock bearing $2\frac{1}{2}$ per cent interest, might, depending on prevailing interest rates, fetch only about £50, i.e. the price at which they will give a 5 per cent yield. If this stock were redeemable in one year's time, their price would obviously be very much higher.

IS–LM model. A model developed by J. R. HICKS shortly after the publication of J. M. KEYNES's *General Theory*, providing a framework for analysing the factors determining the level of demand in an economy. It has become the standard framework for studying MACRO-ECONOMICS, primarily because it has appeared to be able to encompass widely differing views of how the economy works. The strength of the model is that it combines events in the financial market with events in the market for goods and services to establish an equilibrium level of overall demand. Two variables – aggregate expenditure and the INTEREST RATE – adjust to ensure that the demand for INVESTMENT goods matches the supply of SAVINGS, and the demand for cash (or liquid assets) matches the supply. On a graph with the interest rate on the vertical axis and the level of spending on the horizontal axis, two curves can be plotted. The I–S (investment–savings) curve slopes down from left to right depicting the set of combinations of interest rate and spending which ensure equilibrium in the investment and savings market. For each level of the interest rate, there is a unique level of spending which ensures that planned investment equals planned saving. The second curve, L–M (liquidity–money supply), plots combinations of interest rates and income levels which ensure the demand for money (◊ LIQUIDITY PREFERENCE) is equal to the supply. A high interest rate suppresses the demand for cash and thus may be combined with a high level of national income (which stimulates the demand for cash) if equilibrium is to be maintained. This curve usually thus slopes upwards. Where the two curves intersect there is an equilibrium level of both AGGREGATE DEMAND and the interest rate.

Much of the dispute between *monetarists* and *Keynesians* can be interpreted as arguments over the relative slopes of the I–S and L–M curves (◊ MONETARISM). However, the IS–LM model says nothing of the factors determining the AGGREGATE SUPPLY of goods and services, and in recent years more attention has been paid to this area of analysis rather than the level of demand. (◊ SUPPLY-SIDE ECONOMICS. ◊ ECONOMIC DOCTRINES; TRANSMISSION MECHANISM.)

Isocost line. A graphical representation of combinations of inputs each of which may be purchased for a given cost. It may be that by spending £1,000 per week a firm could hire ten men or ten robots or any combination between. In this case, the isocost line could be plotted on a graph with a quantity of robots on one axis and a quantity of men on the other. It would be a straight, downward-sloping line passing from the point of ten robots and no men to ten men and no robots. Every point on such a graph would represent a combination of inputs costing a certain level and each point would be on one and only one isocost line.

The isocost line, which is analogous to the BUDGET LINE in consumer theory, is useful for analysing the optimal combination of inputs firms should employ. ◊ ISOQUANT.

Isoproduct curve. ◊ ISOQUANT.

Isoquant. A graphical representation of combinations of inputs each of which produces the same output. A farmer, for example, might be able to produce fifty tons of grain either with five men and five combine harvesters, or with ten men and four combine harvesters. If so, an isoquant could be plotted on a graph on one axis of which was the number of combine harvesters and, on the other, the number of men employed. Each point on such a graph would represent a combination of inputs and each would thus produce some level of output. Each would be on one, but only one, isoquant. Normally, economists allow for two inputs – capital and labour – but the analysis can be extended. Isoquants have the following properties: first, they are downward-sloping because, as one factor is removed (and we move down one axis), more of another factor must be added to maintain the old level of output (moving up the other axis). Second, they are convex to (i.e. bulge towards) the origin, because increasing amounts of a second factor are required to compensate for unit decreases in the first (◊ DIMINISH-ING MARGINAL PRODUCT). The isoquant is analogous to the INDIFFERENCE CURVE in the theory of consumer demand. (◊◊ ISO-COST LINE; RATE OF TECHNICAL SUBSTITUTION.)

Issued capital. That part of a company's CAPITAL that has been sub-scribed to by shareholders. It may or may not be paid up (◊ PAID-UP CAPITAL).

Issuing broker. A BROKER acting as an agent for a new issue of SECUR-ITIES.

Issuing house. An institution, usually a MERCHANT BANK, that organizes the raising of CAPITAL by new issues of SECURITIES on behalf of clients. The issuing house will advise the client on the timing and form of the issue in conjunction with the ISSUING BROKER, and in return for a commission will underwrite all or part of the issue. The sponsorship of an issue by an established issuing house greatly affects the confidence of the investor and success of the issue. Increasingly, and especially in UNLISTED SECURITIES MARKETS, other securities dealers are sponsoring new issues while other financial institutions will underwrite issues. ◊◊ NEW-ISSUE MARKET; UNDERWRITING.

Issuing Houses Association (I.H.A.). An association of institutions acting as ISSUING HOUSES, set up in 1945 to represent the interests of its members to maintain standards and to liaise with the council of the STOCK EXCHANGE, the CAPITAL ISSUES COMMITTEE, the BANK OF ENGLAND and other official bodies. It has fifty-five members.

Issuing Houses Committee. ◊ ISSUING HOUSES ASSOCIATION.

J

J-curve. A depreciation or devaluation of the EXCHANGE RATE has the immediate effect of raising import prices and reducing export prices. In the short run, therefore, the BALANCE OF PAYMENTS could worsen before the effects of the change in the relative price of exports, as compared with imports, induce the longer-term expansion of exports and a cut in imports which would improve the balance of payments. The J-curve traces the initial worsening in the balance of payments followed by a recovery. ♢ INTERNATIONAL TRADE; 'LEADS AND LAGS'.

Jamaica Agreement. ♢ INTERNATIONAL MONETARY FUND.

Jevons, William Stanley (1835–82). Jevons studied natural science and worked as an assayer to the Australian Mint from 1853 to 1859. He became Professor of Logic at Owens College, Manchester, in 1866 and in 1876 at University College, London. His main theoretical economic work is *Theory of Political Economy* (1871). Other aspects of his work are collected together in *Investigations in Currency and Finance* (1884). He was one of the three economists to put forward a MARGINAL UTILITY theory in the 1870s. He argued that one COMMODITY will exchange for another such that the ratio of the PRICES of the two commodities traded equals the ratio of their marginal utilities. EDGE-WORTH criticized the way Jevons developed these ideas, and in so doing invented the INDIFFERENCE CURVE. Jevons also made an important contribution to the theory of CAPITAL, many aspects of which were, in fact, taken over by the AUSTRIAN SCHOOL. He super-imposed on the CLASSICAL ECONOMIC theory the idea that capital should be measured in terms of time as well as quantity. An increase in the amount invested is the same as an increase in the time period in which it is being employed. Output can be increased by extending the period in which the investment is available by, for instance, reinvesting the output instead of consuming it at the end of the production period. With given levels of LABOUR and capital, output becomes a function of time only. He derived from this a definition of the RATE OF INTEREST as the ratio of the output gained, by an increase in the time capital remains invested divided by the amount invested (♢ BÖHM-BAWERK, E. VON; MARGINAL PRODUCTIVITY OF CAPITAL). Jevons was also one of the founders of ECONOMETRICS: he invented MOVING AVERAGES. He also propounded a theory of the TRADE CYCLE based on sun-spots, but this is of little importance except for the stimulus it gave to the study of statistics for economic empirical work. ⟡ GOSSEN, H. H.; MENGER, C.; WALRAS, M. E. L.

Jobber. A dealer in securities who will buy and sell specific SECURITIES at all times and who thus makes a market in these securities. A *market maker*. Prior to the BIG BANG jobbers were one of two distinct classes of members on the STOCK EXCHANGE who were permitted to deal only with BROKERS and not with the general public. All members of the stock exchange are now broker/dealers who are free to deal with each other or with the public, though some specialize in making markets for institutional investors and other brokers, while others (STOCK-BROKERS) continue to buy and sell shares mainly on behalf of private investors. Not all market makers are members of the stock exchange. Like any other dealer, a jobber or market maker makes his PROFIT out of the difference between the price at which he buys and the price at which he sells, and he must keep a 'book' or stock of the securities in which he deals so as to be able to meet demand. If demand for a share rises rapidly, he must mark up his price or run out of stock that will have to be replenished at a higher price.

Joint costs. COSTS arising simultaneously in the production of two or more COMMODITIES that cannot be precisely allocated to each product. ⟡ ECONOMIES OF SCOPE.

Joint demand. DEMAND for two or more COMMODITIES or FACTORS OF PRODUCTION which are used together so that a change in demand for one will sooner or later be reflected in a change in demand for the other; for example, cloth and thread. Another term for COMPLE-MENTARY DEMAND.

Joint products. COMMODITIES which are produced in such a way that a change in the output of one of them necessarily involves a change in the output of the other. For example, in refining crude oil into petrol, fuel oil and other heavier oils, limits are set to the relative propor-tions of each product that can be achieved. Leather and beef are joint products. Under conditions of joint production, the allocation of costs between the products will be arbitrary. ⟡ ECONOMIES OF SCOPE.

Joint-stock banks. ⟡ COMMERCIAL BANKS.

Joint-stock company. A now virtually obsolete term for a business enterprise in which the CAPITAL is divided into small units permitting a number of investors to contribute varying amounts to the total, PROFITS being divided between stockholders in proportion to the number of SHARES they own. The joint-stock company developed, from the seventeenth century onwards, out of the need for increasingly large amounts of capital by certain types of enterprise, such as overseas trading companies. By 1720, abuse of the joint-stock system (cul-minating in the South Sea Bubble crisis) made it necessary to control business more closely, and the statutory company has its origins in the Act of that date. ⟡ COMPANY LAW.

Joint supply. ⟡ JOINT PRODUCTS.

K

Kaldor, Nicholas (1908–86). Born in Budapest, Kaldor graduated at the London School of Economics in 1930 and lectured there until 1947. Between 1943 and 1945 he was a Research Associate at the National Institute of Economic and Social Research, and in 1947 was appointed Director of the Research and Planning Division of the Economic Commission for Europe, a post he held for two years. He was a member of the U.K. Royal Commission on Taxation of Profits and Incomes from 1951 to 1955. In 1952 he moved to Cambridge University as Reader, and in 1966 was appointed Professor of Economics. From 1964 to 1968, and from 1974 to 1976, he was special adviser to the Chancellor of the EXCHEQUER on economic and social aspects of TAXATION policy. His published works include 'The Quantitative Aspects of the Full Employment Problem in Britain', Appendix to *Full Employment in a Free Society by* W. H. BEVERIDGE (1944), reprinted in *Essays in Economic Policy* (1964), *An Expenditure Tax* (1955), *Essays on Economic Stability and Growth, Essays on Value and Distribution* (1960), *Capital Accumulation and Economic Growth* (1961), *Causes of the Slow Rate of Growth of the U.K.* (1966), *Conflicts in Policy Objectives* (1971) and *Collected Economic Essays* (1978). In his capacity as government adviser, Professor Kaldor was an advocate of the long-term CAPITAL GAINS tax and the SELECTIVE EMPLOYMENT TAX and he put forward the idea of the COMPENSATION PRINCIPLE in WELFARE ECONOMICS. ⟨⟩ CAMBRIDGE SCHOOL; DISTRIBUTION, THEORIES OF.

Kennedy Round of Trade Negotiations. There has been a series of rounds of negotiations between the signatories of the GENERAL AGREEMENT ON TARIFFS AND TRADE designed to reduce TRADE BARRIERS on a multilateral basis. The first round took place in 1947, and the Kennedy Round was the sixth. It commenced in 1964 and was concluded in July 1967. This round was distinguished from its predecessors by the fact that its aim was straight percentage tariff reductions right across the board rather than item-by-item agreements. This approach was made possible by the fact that in 1962 President Kennedy obtained the authority of the U.S. Congress to negotiate reductions in tariffs of up to 50 per cent under the Trade Expansion Act. Forty-nine countries took part in the Kennedy Round, including all the principal industrial and trading nations of the world except the U.S.S.R. and China. In the event, agreements for the reduction of industrial tariffs by up to 50 per cent, with an overall average of 30 per cent, were achieved. Two timetables were agreed. The first, being followed by the U.S., provided for reductions in five annual stages and commenced in January 1968. The second, being followed by the EUROPEAN ECONOMIC COMMUNITY, the EUROPEAN FREE TRADE ASSOCIATION and Japan, laid down that two-fifths of the reduction should be made in July 1968, so coinciding with the final tariff adjustments of the E.E.C. Subsequent reduction took place in January 1970, 1971 and 1972. In 1973 ministers agreed in Tokyo to a seventh round of negotiations, which began in 1974. ⬦ DUMPING; TOKYO ROUND OF TRADE NEGOTIATIONS; URUGUAY ROUND OF TRADE NEGOTIATIONS.

Keynes, John Maynard (1883–1946). Educated at Eton, Keynes won prizes there in mathematics as well as in English and Classics before going up to King's College, Cambridge. At university he graduated with a first in mathematics. During his stay at Cambridge he studied philosophy under Alfred Whitehead and economics under ALFRED MARSHALL and A. C. PIGOU. After a period in the Civil Service, he accepted a lectureship in economics at King's College, Cambridge. In 1911 he became editor of the *Economic Journal*. During the First World War he held a post in the TREASURY, but resigned because he believed that the figure for German war reparations was set too high (*The Economic Consequences of the Peace* (1919)). He was also a severe critic of the decision of the government to return to the GOLD STANDARD and at the pre-war EXCHANGE RATE (*The Economic Consequences of Mr Churchill*). In 1930 he published *A Treatise on Money*, and in the same year was appointed a member of the MACMILLAN COMMITTEE on Finance and Industry. His major work, *The General Theory of Employment, Interest and Money*, appeared in 1936. He served a second spell in the Treasury during the Second World War, and was responsible for negotiating with the U.S. on Lend-Lease. He took a leading part in the discussions at BRETTON WOODS in 1944 which established the INTERNATIONAL MONETARY FUND.

UNEMPLOYMENT during the inter-war period persisted in the U.K. at very high levels, never falling below 5 per cent, and at its worst reaching as much as 20 per cent of the total LABOUR force. The failure of the economy to recover from such a long depression was unprecedented in the economic history of industrial society. Fluctuations in activity were well known, and had received much attention from theorists on the TRADE CYCLE in the past. The classical economists (⬦ CLASSICAL ECONOMICS) held that in the downturn of the trade cycle both wage rates (⬦ EARNINGS) and the RATE OF INTEREST fell. Eventually, they reached levels low enough for businessmen to see a significant improvement in the profitability of new INVESTMENTS. The investment so induced generated employment and new INCOMES and the economy expanded again until rising prices in the boom brought the next phase in the cycle. The classical economists therefore concluded that the failure of the economy to expand was because wages were inflexible. Their policy recommendations were that the unions should be persuaded to accept a wage cut. Keynes argued that, although this policy might make sense for a particular industry, a general cut would lower CON-SUMPTION, income and AGGREGATE DEMAND, and this would offset the encouragement to employment by the lowering of the 'PRICE' of labour relative to the price of CAPITAL, e.g. plant and machinery. A. C. PIGOU countered Keynes's argument by pointing out that, by lowering wages, the general price level would be lowered; therefore, liquid balances which people owned would have a higher spending value (◊ PIGOU EFFECT). The upturn, it was agreed, was stimulated by businessmen responding to lower wages with increased investment expenditure. Why, said Keynes, should not the government take over the businessman's function and spend money on public works? Current opinion upheld the belief that government budget deficit financing would bring more hardship than already existed. The BALANCED BUDGET was regarded as equally correct an accounting practice for the government as it was for a private household. Most economists of the period accepted that public-works expenditure would reduce unemployment, even given the need to keep the budget in balance. A. C. Pigou showed the mechanism by which this could be brought about. However, the Treasury view was that public works would merely divert SAVINGS and labour from the private sector, and as the former was less productive, the net effect would be a worsening of the situation (◊ CROWDING OUT). It was not until after Keynes had written his *General Theory* and crystallized his arguments into a coherent theoretical framework that his views were accepted.

Keynes did not deny the classical theory. He agreed that a reduction in wage rates could, in theory, be beneficial, but it would operate only through the LIQUIDITY PREFERENCE schedule. A fall in prices would increase the value of the stock of money in people's hands in real terms. This would make available an increase in the amount that people were willing to lend, with a consequent drop in the rate of interest to the benefit of investment. However, if this were so, why not operate directly on the rate of interest or the quantity of money in the economy? Moreover, Keynes argued that there exists a level of interest rate below which further increases in MONEY SUPPLY are simply added to idle balances (◊ INACTIVE MONEY) rather than being used to finance investment. Wage cuts or not, the economy would stick at this point with chronic unemployment. In the classical system, the national product (◊ NATIONAL INCOME) was determined by the level of employment and the latter by the level of REAL WAGES. The quantity of money determined the level of prices.

Savings and investment were brought into balance by means of the rate of interest. In Keynes's system, the equality of savings and investment was achieved by adjustments in the level of national income or output working through the MULTIPLIER. The rate of interest was determined by the quantity of money people desired to hold in relation to the money supply. The level of output at which savings equals investment does not necessarily correspond to full employment. The innovation in the Keynesian system was that the rate of interest was determined by the quantity of money and not the level of output, as in the classical system. In the Keynesian model if you increased the propensity to invest or consume, you did not simply raise the rate of interest, you raised output and employment (▷ CONSUMPTION FUNCTION). Keynes's study of monetary aggregates of investment, savings, etc., led to the development of national accounts. Keynes's general theory of employment is now criticized for its reliance on special cases (wage rigidity, the insensitivity of investment to the rate of interest, and the idea of a minimum rate of interest at which the demand for money became infinitely elastic), its preoccupation with EQUILIBRIUM and the fact that, despite its presentation as a radical new departure, it nevertheless embodies many of the analytical limitations of the 'CLASSI-CAL SCHOOL' of economics. However, the transformation which Keynes brought about, in both theory and policy, was considerable. In effect, he laid the foundations for what is now MACROECONOMICS. (▷ KEYNESIAN ECONOMICS; KEYNESIAN UNEMPLOYMENT.)

Keynes Plan. The U.K. TREASURY submitted proposals for the establishment of an International Clearing Union for discussion at the BRETTON WOODS Conference in 1944. These proposals were primarily the work of J. M. KEYNES, and became known as the Keynes Plan. The International Clearing Union would have basically the same functions as a domestic BANK and CLEARING-HOUSE. International DEBTS would be cleared on a multilateral basis between its members. It would give OVERDRAFT facilities to a member running a temporary BALANCE OF PAYMENTS deficit and would create its own unit of CURRENCY, called BANCOR, in which the overdraft facility would be made available. Bancor would have a gold EXCHANGE RATE in the initial phases of the scheme, though it was expected that it would eventually break the gold connection and replace gold in international finance. Each member would have a quota which determined the limits of its credit facilities with the International Clearing Union. There was a set of suggested safeguards and penalties to encourage the elimination not only of deficits but also of persistent surpluses. The plan did not win approval at Bretton Woods and the less radical INTER-NATIONAL MONETARY FUND was established, which was more in line with the ideas put forward by the U.S.A.

Keynesian economics. The branch of economic theory, and the doctrines, associated with J. M. KEYNES. In general, Keynesian economics tends to support the following propositions:

(a) AGGREGATE DEMAND plays a decisive role in determining the level of real output.

(b) Economies can settle at positions with high unemployment and exhibit no natural tendency for unemployment to fall.

(c) Governments, primarily through fiscal policy, can influence aggregate demand to cut unemployment.

It would be wrong, however, to consider Keynesian economists to be a single, united body of theorists. Since 1945, two predominant Keynesian schools have emerged. First the *Neo-Keynesians* reached a consensus view with more classically oriented economists. Under what is known as the *neo-classical synthesis* (◊ NEO-CLASSICAL ECONOMICS), it was largely accepted that the practical conclusions of Keynes were correct, but that, at least in theory, the market *did* have a natural tendency towards full employment. It was on account of price rigidities and institutional inflexibility that unemployment could persist. This neo-Keynesian view used the IS–LM MODEL to describe the determination of aggregate demand and the PHILLIPS CURVE acted as a description of the behaviour of AGGREGATE SUPPLY.

The synthesis dominated MACROECONOMICS until it was challenged by M. FRIEDMAN and MONETARISM. At the same time, a second strand of Keynesian thought emerged. This held that economists were mistaken in considering the behaviour of an economy only in EQUILIBRIUM. It was possible that because of interactions between different sectors of the economy, a state of DISEQUILIBRIUM could persist. When the economy left an equilibrium state, no amount of price flexibility could guarantee its return to full employment. This branch of disequilibrium economics is associated with Robert Clower, Axel Leijonhufvud and E. Malinvaud. (◊ KEYNESIAN UNEMPLOYMENT; QUANTITY RATIONING.)

Keynesian unemployment. A situation in which the number of people able and willing to work at prevailing wages exceeds the number of jobs available, and, at the same time, firms are unable to sell all the goods they would like. EXCESS SUPPLY thus exists in both the labour and goods markets. Keynesian unemployment is one of four possible regimes in an economy in which QUANTITY RATIONING exists, i.e. that markets are not in equilibrium. Its important distinguishing feature is in its possible cures. For CLASSICAL UNEMPLOYMENT, a cut in wages should make it profitable for employers to take on new workers. In the Keynesian case, however, firms are already unable to sell all their output. This induces them to cut their prices at the same time that workers will be trying to price themselves into jobs by accepting lower wages. When both prices and wages fall REAL WAGES remain constant, and it is real wages which determine the level of employment. Thus, when both the labour market and goods market are in excess supply, even if prices and wages are flexible, there will be no natural tendency for the economy to lift itself out of recession. In this case, the most obvious solution is for the government to inject some demand through higher borrowing. ⟡ KEYNESIAN ECONOMICS; UNEMPLOYMENT.

Klein, Lawrence R. (b. 1920). Professor Klein studied at Berkeley, the University of California, and obtained his Ph.D. at the Massachusetts Institute of Technology. After working for the Cowles Commission, he was at Michigan University from 1949 to 1954 and at Oxford University until 1958. Professor Klein was then appointed Professor of Economics and Finance at the Wharton School of Finance, University of Pennsylvania. He was awarded the NOBEL PRIZE in Economics in 1980. His major publications include *The Keynesian Revolution* (1947), *Economic Fluctuations, 1921–1941* (1950), *Econometric Model of the United States, 1929–1952* (1955), *An Essay in the Theory of Economic Prediction* (1971) and *The Economics of Supply and Demand* (1983).

Professor Klein pioneered the design, construction and application of large-scale ECONOMETRIC MODELS for forecasting G.N.P. and its components in the 1950s and the 1960s, capitalizing on the emergent computer technology of the time. Professor Klein's work has contributed to the development of applied econometrics and stimulated the development of statistical information about MACROECONOMIC fluctuations.

Knight, Frank Hyneman (1885–1973). Appointed Associate Professor of Economics at the University of Iowa in 1919 and Professor in 1922; after studying at Cornell and Chicago Universities, Knight returned to Chicago as Professor of Economics in 1928. His major published works include *The Economic Organization* (1933), *The Ethics of Competition and Other Essays* (1935), *The Economic Order and Religion* (1945), *Freedom and Reform* (1947), *Essays on the History and Method of Economics* (1956) and *Intelligence and Democratic Action* (1960). His most influential work has been *Risk, Uncertainty and Profit*, published in 1921. In this work, he made a clear distinction between insurable RISK and uninsurable uncertainty. It was the latter which gave rise to PROFIT. A businessman must guess future demand and selling prices and pay in advance his FACTORS OF PRODUCTION amounts based on his guesses. The accuracy of his guesses is reflected in the profit he makes. It follows that profits are related to uncertainty, the speed of economic change and business ability.

Kondratieff cycle. A TRADE CYCLE of very long duration – J. A. SCHUMPETER applied the term to a cycle of fifty-six years in duration. Named after the Russian economist N. D. Kondratieff, who made important contributions in the 1920s to the study of long-term fluctuations. Kondratieff studied U.S., U.K. and French wholesale prices and interest rates from the eighteenth century through the 1920s and found peaks and troughs at regular intervals. Similar work has been carried out at Harvard, confirming a fifty-four-year cycle in U.K. wheat prices since the thirteenth century. ◊ KUZNETS, S. S.

Koopmans, Tjalling C. (b. 1910). Professor Koopmans was born in the Netherlands and studied physics and mathematics at the Universities of Utrecht and Leiden. After four years with the League of Nations in Geneva, he went to the U.S.A. in 1940 to take up a post as Statistician with the Allied Combined Shipping Adjustment Board. Professor Koopmans moved to the Cowles Commission at Chicago in 1944, where he was appointed Director in 1961. He was a Professor of Economics at Yale University from 1955 until his retirement in 1981. Professor Koopmans was awarded, in 1975, the NOBEL PRIZE in Economics (jointly with L. V. Kantorovich). His publications include *Linear Regression and Activity Analysis of Economic Time Series* (1937), *Statistical Inference in Dynamic Economic Models* (1950), *Analysis of Production as an Efficient Combination of Activities* (1951), *Three Essays on the State of Economic Science* (1957) and *The Scientific Papers of Tjalling C. Koopmans* (1970). Professor Koopmans introduced the mathematical procedures of LINEAR PROGRAMMING (or *activity analysis*) to economics. He demonstrated the application of linear programming to the solution of transportation problems, to general EQUILIBRIUM analysis and to problems in INVESTMENT APPRAISAL. Professor Koopmans has made important contributions to the theory of ECONOMETRICS.

Kuznets, Simon S. (b. 1901). Professor Kuznets, who was born in Russia, went to the U.S.A. in 1922 where he studied economics at Columbia University, receiving his Ph.D. in 1926. After a number of years at the National Bureau of Economic Research, he went in 1930 to the University of Pennsylvania where he was later to be appointed Professor of Economics, a post he held until 1954. There followed a period as Professor of Economics at Johns Hopkins University until 1960 when he accepted a Chair in Economics at Harvard, where he remained until his retirement in 1971. Professor Kuznets was awarded the NOBEL PRIZE in Economics in 1971. His publications include *Secular Movements in Production and Prices* (1930), *National Income, 1929–1932* (1934), *National Income and Its Composition, 1919–1938* (1941), *National Product since 1869* (1946), *Six Lectures on Economic Growth* (1959), *Economic Growth and Structure* (1965), *Modern Economic Growth: Rate, Structure and Spread* (1965), *Economic Growth of Nations* (1971), and *Population, Capital, and Growth* (1979). Professor Kuznets has made important contributions to the development of applied ECONOMETRICS through the compilation of macroeconomic statistics. His analysis and statistical identification of fifteen-to-twenty-year fluctuations in time series of production and prices initiated a continuing debate in the analysis of TRADE CYCLES. Professor Kuznets has completed major studies in income distribution, exploring the relationship between growth in income per head and the distribution of income.

L

Labour. Labour is a FACTOR OF PRODUCTION. The term not only includes the numbers of people available for or engaged in the production of goods or services but also their physical and intellectual skills and effort.

Labour, demand for. The amount of labour that firms will employ at different wage levels. In a simple model of the structure of the LABOUR market, firms employ labour as long as it is profitable for them to do so. It will be profitable as long as the selling price of the output of the marginal worker is greater than the cost of that worker. To maximize profits, therefore, firms employ additional workers until the MARGINAL REVENUE PRODUCT (that is, the marginal revenue of the firm's output times the number of extra units produced by taking on one more worker) is equal to the wage costs. In this situation: (a) when the price of the firm's output rises, its demand for labour rises; (b) when the physical output of workers rises (from more developed skills or harder work), the demand for labour rises; (c) when the wage rate falls, the demand for labour rises; (d) when the amount of capital employed increases, the demand for labour will either increase, as the capital enhances the productivity of each worker, or it will fall, if the capital displaces workers.

This account, in which all workers are assumed to be identical, has been developed in many directions. First, complications can be added – for example, trade unions and industries where there is only one employer (◊ MONOPOLY). Secondly, alternative models have been developed to account for the stickiness of wages and to describe alternatives to fixed wage contracts (◊ PROFIT-SHARING). Finally, the whole subject can be viewed in a MACROECONOMIC perspective, in which the demand for labour is viewed as a function of AGGREGATE DEMAND only. In this case high wages can be portrayed as stimulating employment through their effect on maintaining high aggregate demand. (◊◊ MARGINAL PRODUCTIVITY THEORY OF WAGES; PHILLIPS CURVE.)

Labour, division of. ◊◊ DIVISION OF LABOUR.

Labour, mobility of. The degree to which workers are able and willing to move between jobs in different occupations and areas. A lack of LABOUR mobility may manifest itself in high FRICTIONAL UNEMPLOYMENT or high STRUCTURAL UNEMPLOYMENT and it has been an object of policy to encourage workers to move to areas where jobs are available and to take on jobs in new occupations requiring skills different from those in which they were first trained. Policies to this end could include a faster rate of house-building, making it easier for people to find homes in different areas; the removal of taxes like STAMP DUTY on house transfer; the provision of full information on what jobs are available and where; the provision of training courses for the unemployed; and the abolition of restrictions on entry to different jobs. In practice, it has been found that, for a multitude of social and economic reasons, labour has been geographically and occupationally immobile. Moreover, it is recognized that high social costs are incurred by an itinerant population, not least the problem of regional overcrowding or depopulation. It is inefficient to bear these costs if a shortage of vacancies is expected to be only temporary and these factors have been used to justify SUBSIDIES to jobs in regions of high unemployment.

Labour, specialization of. ◊ DIVISION OF LABOUR.

Labour force. The total number of people in an economy in work or available for work (i.e. the total number of people in employment plus the number unemployed). The size of the labour force and its percentage of the total POPULATION depends on the age distribution of the population and PARTICIPATION RATES. In the U.K., the labour force rose from 45·6 per cent of the total population in 1974 to 47·6 per cent in 1980, from which it fell to 47·1 per cent in 1983, rising to 47·8 per cent in 1984.

Labour force participation rate. ◊ PARTICIPATION RATE.

Labour-intensive. A production technology is labour-intensive if relatively more labour value is required as input per unit of output than other FACTORS OF PRODUCTION. ◊ CAPITAL-INTENSIVE; PRODUCTION FUNCTION; PRODUCTIVITY.)

Labour market. The MARKET in which wages, salaries and conditions of employment are determined in the context of the supply of labour (◊ LABOUR FORCE) and the demand for LABOUR. (◊ LABOUR, DEMAND FOR.)

Labour theory of value. ◊ VALUE, THEORIES OF.

Labour turnover. The number of employees who leave a firm in a year as a percentage of the firm's total employment.

Laffer curve. A graphical illustration of the argument that there exists an optimum rate of tax at which government tax revenue is maximized. If tax rates are low, revenues will be increased if tax rates are increased. However, if rates are raised beyond the optimum point, the loss of incentive caused by the resultant low net incomes discourages production and tax revenues fall. The curve is named after the American economist Professor Arthur Laffer who argued that the economy could be expanded without government budget deficits. Lower taxes lead to lower prices, higher output and, therefore, higher government revenues. This argument has yet to find full empirical justification. (◊ SUPPLY-SIDE ECONOMICS.)

'**Laissez-faire.**' *Laissez-faire, laissez-passer'* was the term originally taken up by the PHYSIOCRATS. They believed that only agriculture yielded wealth. Consequently they condemned any interference with industry by government agencies as being inappropriate and harmful, except in so far as it was necessary to break up private MONOPOLY. The principle of the non-intervention of government in economic affairs was given full support by the classical economists (◊ CLASSICAL ECONOMICS), who took up the theme from ADAM SMITH: 'The Statesman, who should attempt to direct private people in what manner they ought to employ their capitals, would not only load himself with a most unnecessary attention, but assume an authority which could safely be trusted, not only to no single person, but to no council or senate whatever, and which would nowhere be so dangerous as in the hands of a man who had folly and presumption enough to fancy himself fit to exercise it' – *Wealth of Nations*, Book IV, Chapter 2. ◊ MANCHESTER SCHOOL; MANDEVILLE, B. DE; SISMONDI, J. C. L. S. DE.

Land. Taken to include, in economics, all NATURAL RESOURCES, including the sea and outer space. One of the FACTORS OF PRODUCTION, land is distinguished from the others in that its supply is more or less fixed. Since the productive power of land is conceptually distinct from that of CAPITAL, land is a factor of production only in its natural, unimproved state. ◊ DEPLETION THEORY.

Laspeyres index. An INDEX NUMBER whose weights (◊ WEIGHTED AVERAGE) are derived from values obtaining in a base-year. For instance, in 1986, the U.K. producer price index of home sales was calculated on weights reflecting the pattern of sales of the different industries making up the index in 1980. Because the weights are constant from one year to another, indices can be constructed to give a consistent time series. On the other hand, the weights do get significantly out of date eventually and have to be revised. The above index was previously based on 1975 weights. A base-weighted index/formula was first published in 1864, by Étienne Laspeyres. (◊ INDEX-NUMBER PROBLEM; PAASCHE INDEX.)

Last in, first out (L.I.F.O.). ◊ FIRST IN, FIRST OUT.

Lateral integration. ◊ MERGER.

Latin American Free Trade Association (L.A.F.T.A.). The treaty setting up the Latin American Free Trade Association was agreed at Montevideo in 1960 under which the seven participating countries – namely Argentina, Brazil, Chile, Mexico, Paraguay, Peru and Uruguay – agreed to establish a FREE-TRADE AREA. Ecuador and Colombia joined in 1961 and Venezuela in 1966. Significant reductions in internal import tariffs (◊ TARIFFS, IMPORT) were achieved, though little progress was made in the harmonization of a common external tariff. However, in 1969 Chile and Peru joined Bolivia, Colombia and Ecuador in forming a new economic group ($\diamond$ ANDEAN PACT). The members of the L.A.F.T.A. finally agreed to wind up the association in 1981 and to replace it with the Latin American Integration Association (A.L.A.D.I.). The latter has three groups of members: (a) Argentina, Brazil and Mexico, (b) Colombia, Chile and Peru, and (c) Bolivia, Ecuador and Paraguay. The intention to reduce tariffs between members has been retained but only on a pragmatic, industry-by-industry basis, compared to the across-the-board, fixed-timetable approach attempted by L.A.F.T.A.

Latin American Integration Association. $\diamond$ LATIN AMERICAN FREE TRADE ASSOCIATION.

Lausanne school. The Chair of Economics in the Faculty of Law at Lausanne was founded in 1870 with LÉON WALRAS as the first incumbent. He retired in 1892 and was succeeded by V. PARETO. The school was noted for the emphasis given to mathematics and the development of a GENERAL EQUILIBRIUM theory.

Law, John (1671–1729). A Scottish financier who put his monetary theories into practice in France through such institutions as the Banque Royale and the Compagnie des Indes. His most significant publication appeared in 1705 under the title *Money and Trade Considered, with a Proposal for Supplying the Nation with Money*. He was in favour of the replacement of specie coin by paper money ($\diamond$ BANKNOTE). Not only would this save expensive precious metals, but it would enable the state to manage the CURRENCY more effectively by making it independent of the MARKET for precious metals. Moreover, it would facilitate increasing the quantity of money in circulation and therefore the stimulation of economic activity. $\diamond\!\!\diamond$ HUME, D.; QUANTITY THEORY OF MONEY.

'Law of demand.' $\diamond$ DEMAND CURVE.

Law of diminishing returns. $\diamond$ DIMINISHING RETURNS, LAW OF.

Law of large numbers. $\diamond$ PROBABILITY.

Layfield Committee. The Committee of Inquiry into local government finance was set up in 1974 under the chairmanship of Sir (then Mr) Frank Layfield, Q.C., and made its report in 1976. Its terms of reference were 'to review the wide system of local government finance in England, Wales and Scotland and to make recommendations'. The committee concluded that there was a lack of financial accountability in local government partly because of the confusion of responsibilities between the central government and local authorities. The expenditure of local authorities had increased to over 18 per cent of the GROSS NATIONAL PRODUCT compared with 10 per cent in the late 1950s, and local rates contributed only 10 per cent of this expenditure because of the growth in the central government's grant payments. The committee argued that either control by the central government should be much tighter, with the government responsible directly for more local services, or alternatively that there should be local autonomy over a wider range of activities. There was no middle-of-the-road solution. Given more local autonomy, there would be a need for local INCOME TAX to supplement revenue from the rates. This, the committee found, was administratively feasible but expensive. It would cost £100 million to collect and the Inland Revenue would require additional staff of 13,000. ⟡ RATES.

'Leads and lags.' The differences in timing in the settlement of DEBTS in INTERNATIONAL TRADE. These differences could cause a deficit or surplus for a short period in the BALANCE OF PAYMENTS, even though the underlying trade was in balance. The effect may be particularly acute when there is an expectation of a change in the EXCHANGE RATE. Importing countries will delay payment to their supplying country if it is expected that the latter's rate of exchange will fall. ⟡ DEVALUATION; ⫣-CURVE.

Lease. An agreement between the owner of property (lessor) to grant use of it to another party (lessee) for a specified period at a specified RENT payable annually, quarterly or monthly. The rental may be subject to review, say, every five years. It is possible to lease cars, office equipment, machinery, etc., as well as buildings or LAND, and a recent development has been the rapid growth of leasing arrangements for business requirements. In most cases these include servicing and maintenance. In some cases the title of the property passes to the lessee at the end of the lease for a nominal charge. In effect, this is a form of HIRE PURCHASE without a down payment, and is subject to differences in tax treatment which may be advantageous.

Leaseback. An agreement in which the owner of property sells that property to a person or institution and then leases it back again for an agreed period and rental. Leaseback is often used by companies that want to free for other uses CAPITAL tied up in buildings.

Least-developed country. In 1971 the General Assembly of U.N.C.T.A.D. (⟡ UNITED NATIONS CONFERENCE ON TRADE AND DEVELOPMENT) approved a list of least-developed countries, made up of countries with a per capita GROSS DOMESTIC PRODUCT of $100 or less, a share of manufactures of 10 per cent or less of its G.D.P. and a literacy rate of 20 per cent or less. In 1980 thirty-one countries were classified as least-developed, twenty in Africa and nine in Asia, plus Samoa and Haiti. The average per capita income of these countries is only about a quarter of that of all DEVELOPING COUNTRIES.

Least-squares regression. A statistical technique for estimating the relationship between a DEPENDENT VARIABLE and INDEPENDENT VARIABLES. The method derives estimates for the PARAMETERS and constants in the equation postulated as representing the nature of the relationship between the variables (⟡ MODEL). For example, a DEMAND FUNCTION may take the form, $D = a + bP$, in which D is the quantity demanded of a good and P its price. The observed values of D and P, that is, how much was actually demanded at each of a number of price levels, may be plotted on a graph, with D on the x-axis (horizontal) and P on the y-axis (perpendicular) (called a 'scatter' diagram). We would expect in this case that the points on the graph would be grouped such as generally to slope downwards from left to right (the lower the price, the higher the demand). The least-squares regression finds that line such that the difference between the actual observations and those traced by the line along its length is at a minimum. The slope and position of the line yields the estimates for b and a respectively.

Legal tender. That which must be accepted in legal settlement of a money DEBT. Although in Britain BANK OF ENGLAND notes and £1 coins are legal tender up to any amount, 5p and 10p silver (actually cupronickel) coins are only legal tender up to the value of £5, 50p and 20p coins up to £10 and bronze coins up to 20p. Cheques and postal orders are not legal tender.

Lemon problem. ◊ ADVERSE SELECTION.

Lender of last resort. An essential function of a CENTRAL BANK is to be willing to lend to the BANKING system at all times, although it does so on its own terms. In practice, this permits the bank to influence the level of RATES OF INTEREST and the MONEY SUPPLY as well as providing a basis of confidence for the banking system (◊ BANK RATE). In Britain, the BANK OF ENGLAND acts as a lender of last resort only to the DISCOUNT HOUSES, and will not lend to the COMMERCIAL BANKS. When the discount houses (strictly speaking, members of the Discount Houses Association only) have insufficient CASH to balance their books, they can obtain cash from the discount office at the Bank of England. This assistance cannot be refused, although the bank can decide whether to grant a LOAN secured by BONDS or to rediscount SECURITIES (ELIGIBLE PAPER). The minimum rate at which it will do either of these things is deliberately set at a 'penal' level, i.e. somewhat above MONEY MARKET rates and at what used to be called the MINIMUM LENDING RATE prior to 1981. In other countries, the central bank lends directly to the commercial banks.

Leontief, Wassily W. (b. 1906). Born in Leningrad, Leontief obtained a post at the University of Kiel in Germany in 1927. In 1931 he moved to Harvard and was appointed Professor of Economics there in 1946. In 1973 he was awarded the Alfred Nobel Memorial Prize (◊ NOBEL PRIZE) in Economics. Apart from the works mentioned below, his publications include *Studies in the Structure of the American Economy* (1953), *Input–Output Economics, Collected Essays* (1966) and *The Future of the World Economy* (1977). The interdependence of the various sectors of a country's economy has long been appreciated by economists. The theme can be traced from CANTILLON and QUESNAY and the 'TABLEAU ÉCONOMIQUE' through MARX and WALRAS. The sheer complexity of the interactions and interrelationships between the different sectors of a modern economy was a Gordian knot which had to be cut before the theoretical structure could be translated into a practical reflection of an actual economy and serve as the basis for policy recommendations. Leontief's achievement was to see the solution of this problem in MATRIX algebra, and modern computers have made INPUT–OUTPUT ANALYSIS a practical proposition. His book *The Structure of the American Economy, 1919–1929* was first published in 1941, and a second edition, *1919–1939*, appeared in 1951. In these studies he attempted, with the limited statistical facts available to him, to establish a 'Tableau Économique' of the U.S.A. The economy was described as an integrated system of flows or transfers from each activity of production, CONSUMPTION or DISTRIBUTION to each other activity. Each sector absorbs the outputs from other sectors and itself produces COMMODITIES or SERVICES which are in turn used up by other sectors, either for further processing or for final consumption. All these flows or transfers were set out in a rectangular table – an input–output MATRIX. The way in which the outputs of any industry spread out through the rest of the economy could be seen from the elements making up the rows. Similarly, the origins of its INPUTS could be seen directly from the elements of the appropriate column. Given such a structure, the implications of a specific change in one part of the economy could be traced through to all the elements in the system. ⟡ SOCIAL ACCOUNTING.

Lerner, Abba Ptachya (1903–82). ⟡ MARSHALL–LERNER CRITERION.

Letter of credit. An order from a bank to a bank abroad authorizing payment to a person named in the letter of a particular sum of MONEY or up to a limit of a certain sum. Letters of CREDIT are often required by exporters who wish to have proof that they will be paid before they ship goods, or who wish to minimize delay in payment for the goods. Letters of credit, unlike BILLS OF EXCHANGE, are not negotiable, but being cashable at a known bank, are immediately acceptable to the seller in the exporting country. A confirmed letter of credit is one that has been recognized by the paying bank. Letters of credit may be irredeemable or revocable, depending on whether or not they can be cancelled at any time.

Leverage. ⟡ GEARING.

Lewis, Sir William Arthur (b. 1915). Professor Lewis was born in St Lucia in the Caribbean. He received his university education at the London School of Economics and the University of Manchester. Professor Lewis was appointed to a Chair of Economics at Manchester University in 1948 where he remained until he took up the post of Principal of the University College of the West Indies in 1959. He was subsequently appointed Professor of Public and International Affairs at Princeton University in 1963. Professor Lewis was awarded (jointly with T. W. SCHULTZ) the NOBEL PRIZE for Economics in 1979. His published works include *Overhead Costs* (1949), *Economic Survey, 1918–1939* (1949), *The Principles of Economic Planning* (1950), *The Theory of Economic Growth* (1955), *Development Planning* (1966), *Some Aspects of Economic Development* (1969), *Tropical Development, 1880–1913* (1971), *The Evolution of the International Economic Order* (1977) and *Growth and Fluctuations, 1870–1913* (1978). Professor Lewis has made fundamental contributions to the theory and application of economics in the context of the problems of growth of DEVELOPING COUNTRIES. Developing countries were characterized by dual economies of urban growth centres within large areas of traditional agriculture in which the latter was the source of a supply of labour that kept urban wages low. Wages remained low until urban industrialization had absorbed the surplus labour from the agricultural sector.

Liabilities. Sums of MONEY for which account has to be made. The liabilities of a company include its BANK LOANS and OVERDRAFT, short-term DEBTS for goods and SERVICES received (*current liabilities*) and its LOAN capital and the CAPITAL subscribed by shareholders. ⬦ BALANCE SHEET.

'Lifeboat operation.' ⬦ SECONDARY BANK.

Life-cycle hypothesis. A theory which suggests that consumers during their lifetime will save when their income is high and spend more than they earn when their income is low. In this way, they smooth their consumption flow, despite the fact that income varies over a lifetime. The theory, attributable to F. MODIGLIANI, complements the PERMANENT-INCOME HYPOTHESIS. (⬦ CONSUMPTION FUNCTION.)

Limited liability. The restriction of an owner's loss in a business to the amount of CAPITAL that he has invested in it. If a limited public company is put into LIQUIDATION because it is unable to pay its DEBTS, for example, the individual shareholders are liable only for the nominal VALUE of the SHARES they hold. Before the principle of limited liability was recognized, investors could be made liable for the whole of their personal possessions in the event of INSOLVENCY. The extension of limited liability to private as well as public companies that wished to register for it in the second half of the nineteenth century greatly increased the flow of capital, and today the limited-liability company is the predominant form of business organization. ⬦ COMPANY LAW; JOINT-STOCK COMPANY.

Linear programming. A mathematical technique for the solution of problems in which a maximum or minimum of a function is to be determined, subject to a set of constraints. Examples of such problems are:

(a) Stocks of a commodity are located at a number of ports and need to be shipped to meet a demand for specific quantities at a number of other ports. The cost per tonne for shipping differs between the various ports of loading and discharge. The problem is to find the minimum cost of shipment, subject to the constraints that no more than the stock available can be loaded at a port and the total amount discharged at a port should equal the demand at that port.

(b) A firm able to produce a range of commodities, each of which would require a different mix of inputs ($\Diamond$ FACTORS OF PRODUCTION). Given the selling prices of the commodities and the costs per unit of the various inputs, the firm chooses the mix of output which maximizes profits: subject to the technical constraints of its PRODUCTION FUNCTION and restrictions on the availability of the different inputs.

As its name implies, the technique is applicable only to problems in which all the relationships are linear ($\Diamond$ LINEAR RELATIONSHIP). In problems of resource allocation of the firm and the economy as a whole ($\Diamond$INPUT–OUTPUT ANALYSIS), linear programming is also synonomous with *activity analysis*.

Linear relationship. A mathematical FUNCTION which traces a straight line on a graph. The INDEPENDENT VARIABLES, of which there may be one or more, are additive. The simplest example is $y = ax + b$, in which x is the independent variable, a and b are constants. These functions are such that any given absolute increase in an independent variable (e.g. x), will give an absolute increase in the DEPENDENT VARIABLE (e.g. y), which will always be the same whatever the size of x on which it is based.

Liquid. 1. In economics, an ASSET is liquid if it is CASH or can be quickly converted into cash at little loss. Assets are said to possess degrees of LIQUIDITY which are their nearness to cash. Highly liquid assets other than cash and bank deposits are Post Office SAVINGS, TREASURY BILLS, MONEY at call, etc. $\Diamond$ LIQUIDITY PREFERENCE. **2.** INTERNATIONAL LIQUIDITY consists of the total of GOLD AND FOREIGN EXCHANGE RESERVES and SPECIAL DRAWING RIGHTS of all countries.

Liquidation. The termination, dissolution or winding up of a limited company ($\Diamond$ LIMITED LIABILITY). Liquidation of a company may be initiated by the shareholders, the directors (voluntary liquidation) or by its creditors, or by a court order if the company is insolvent ($\Diamond$ INSOLVENCY). Where initiated by the creditors, a liquidator is appointed to realize the company's ASSETS and to pay the creditors. In case of insolvency, these functions are performed, initially at least, by the Official Receiver. If the company is solvent, the ordinary shareholders will receive any surplus after the company's liabilities have been met. $\Diamond$ BANKRUPTCY.

245

Liquidity. The degree to which an ASSET can be quickly and cheaply turned into MONEY which, by definition, is completely liquid. A CURRENT ACCOUNT bank deposit is a liquid asset because it can be withdrawn immediately at little cost; an office building by contrast will take a considerable time to dispose of and estate agent's fees and other costs will be incurred. A company or individual is said to be liquid if a high proportion of its or his assets are held in the form of cash or readily marketable securities.

Liquidity preference. The desire to hold MONEY rather than other forms of WEALTH, e.g. STOCKS and BONDS. It can be thought of as stemming from the TRANSACTIONS MOTIVE, SPECULATIVE MOTIVE and PRECAUTIONARY MOTIVE for holding money, and so will be influenced by the levels of INCOME and wealth, RATES OF INTEREST, EXPECTATIONS and the institutional features of the economy which determine the INCOME VELOCITY OF CIRCULATION. ♢ KEYNES, J.M.

Liquidity ratio. 1. The proportion of the total ASSETS of a bank which are held in the form of CASH and LIQUID assets. These assets consist, in general, of money lent out to the MONEY MARKET at call and short notice, short-term BONDS issued by the government and other borrowers and balances at the BANK OF ENGLAND. Between 1951 and 1971, the London CLEARING BANKS were required to maintain a minimum liquidity ratio of about 30 per cent of gross deposits, reduced to 28 per cent in 1963 of which 8 per cent was the CASH RATIO. In 1971, the liquid assets ratio and the cash ratio were abolished (COMPETITION AND CREDIT CONTROL) and banks were expected instead to maintain a ratio of 12·5 per cent of certain eligible assets. There were several subsequent changes in the requirements and in August 1981 the reserve ratio was abolished. There is no longer a mandatory liquidity ratio, although all larger banks are required to deposit 0·5 per cent of eligible liabilities (♢ CREDIT CONTROL) with the Bank of England. Eligible liabilities now comprise the total sterling resources for each bank, including short-term deposits (except those by other banks), net inter-bank borrowing, net CERTIFICATES OF DEPOSIT at issue and net non-sterling liabilities. This *cash-ratio deposit* earns no interest and is effectively a tax to provide income for the bank; it has no significance for credit control or MONETARY POLICY. The Bank of England now monitors the adequacy of liquidity and its composition for each individual bank, but does not make public what it regards as satisfactory liquidity ratios. **2.** The ratio of liquid assets to the current LIABILITIES of a business. Also called the CASH RATIO, it is a very crude test of SOLVENCY.

Liquidity trap. A situation in which the RATE OF INTEREST is so low that no one wants to hold bonds, and people only want to hold cash. The interest rate can fall far enough for everybody to expect it to rise. If it rises, bond prices fall, and because no one wants to hold an asset whose price will fall, everyone will hold cash rather than bonds. In this situation, the interest rate can fall no further – LIQUIDITY PREFERENCE is absolute. If the government expands the money supply, instead of the usual fall in interest rates occurring, there is no effect at all. There is no need for the interest rate to drop to entice people to hold the extra cash available.

Although best described in terms of the simplifying assumptions of the IS–LM MODEL, the liquidity trap can also be applied to a world where wealth is stored in forms other than merely cash or bonds. It was first described by J. M. KEYNES as an example of a case where, at least theoretically, changes in the money supply did not affect AGGREGATE DEMAND. (⟡ TRANSMISSION MECHANISM.)

Listed company. A company the shares of which are listed on the main market of the STOCK EXCHANGE. ⟡ LISTED SECURITY.

Listed security. A security listed and tradable on the STOCK EXCHANGE. Companies wishing to have their EQUITY shares listed must comply with a number of requirements concerned with the disclosure of information, must be registered as U.K. public limited companies and a minimum of 25 per cent of the shares must be held by external investors. The market CAPITALIZATION of the company must also exceed £500,000. Companies which cannot fulful the stringent requirements for a full listing on the main market are traded on the UNLISTED SECURITIES MARKETS.

Lloyd's. An incorporated society of private insurers established by Act of Parliament in 1871. Some 22,000 members or 'names' are organized into over 400 syndicates, each led by a full-time underwriter (⟡ UNDERWRITING) who writes policies on behalf of the members, each of whom bears unlimited liability. Clients are dealt with through BROKERS. The Lloyd's insurance market deals with almost any kind of insurance but has traditionally specialized in the marine market and provides a comprehensive system of shipping intelligence.

Loan. The borrowing of a sum of MONEY by one person, company, government or other organization from another. Loans may be secured or unsecured (⟡ SECURITIES), INTEREST bearing or interest free, long term or short term, redeemable or irredeemable. Loans may be made by individuals and companies, banks, INSURANCE and HIRE PURCHASE companies, BUILDING SOCIETIES and other FINANCIAL INTERMEDIARIES, PAWNBROKERS, or by the issue of SECURITIES. ⟡ FINANCE; TERM LOANS.

Loan capital. Fixed-interest borrowed funds. Alternative term for DEBENTURES.

Loan guarantee scheme. ⟡ CREDIT GUARANTEE.

Loan stock. Synonym for DEBENTURE.

Loanable funds. Money available for lending in financial markets. It consists of current SAVING, DISHOARDING and any increase in the MONEY SUPPLY, for example credit creation by the banks. The *loanable funds theory* holds that the rate of interest (like any other PRICE) is determined by the supply and demand for loanable funds in the capital market. This theory has its origins in classical theory (◊ INTEREST, CLASSICAL THEORY OF) but was developed by KNUT WICKSELL.

Location theory. The area of economics concerned with the factors that determine where producers choose to locate and the effects of the location of a piece of land on the use made of it. The starting-point of this area of theory was developed by J. H. VON THÜNEN in 1826. Von Thünen held that farmers near a market would tend to grow things that would be relatively expensive to transport, while those further away from towns would produce lighter items that were cheap to carry. Thus, the location of land would have a significant effect on the ECONOMIC RENT it could derive. A second important theory, of industrial location, attributable to A. Weber, established that firms producing goods less bulky than the raw materials used in their production would settle near to the raw-material source. Firms producing heavier goods would settle near their market. The firm minimizes the weight it has to transport and, thus, its transport costs. These two theories primarily treated transport costs as the main factor in influencing location. However, many other factors have been identified as having an important role:

(a) Being able to capture monopoly power in the local market.
(b) The possibility of gaining external ECONOMIES OF SCALE, by settling in an area where firms requiring similar inputs have settled.
(c) The influence of non-profit-maximizing behaviour – notably the BEHAVIOURAL THEORY OF THE FIRM – suggests that location could be dependent on where a firm's management considers it pleasant to live.
(d) The possibility of attracting public assistance in the form of grants or subsidies paid out as part of a country's regional policy.
(e) The influence of local taxation and provision of PUBLIC GOODS. An area which has good roads, efficient refuse collection or low business taxation will be more attractive than a high-tax or low-service area. Firms will choose the combination of service provision and taxation that most suits their needs. Those producing a lot of refuse will perhaps value refuse-collection services more highly than low taxes, while the reverse might be true for a firm requiring no refuse collection at all.
(f) The location and cost of labour. Because workers are geographically quite immobile, especially across international borders on account of immigration controls, wages are not equal across countries. This makes it attractive for some labour-intensive firms to settle in areas

where wages are low. This has particularly manifested itself in the high investment that has occurred in South-East Asia. (◊ LABOUR MOBILITY.)

(g) Other international influences. Political and social factors have a particularly strong effect on the expectations multinational firms have as to the profits they can make. Local tariff regimes can also induce firms to produce domestically where otherwise they would be unable to sell in the local market at all. (◊ MULTINATIONAL CORPORATION.)

Logistic curve. A curve traced on a graph by the function, $y = a/(1 + be^{-cx})$, in which a, b and c are constants (◊ PARAMETERS), x is the INDEPENDENT VARIABLE, e = approximately 2·71828, which is a constant with many applications in the analysis of growth (e can be defined as follows: if £1 was invested at 100 per cent per annum, its worth at the end of the year would get closer and closer to £e, the more frequently interest was added and compounded ◊ COMPOUND INTEREST) for shorter and shorter periods during the year). The logistic function takes the following values: if $x = 0$, $y = a/(1 + b)$; if $x \to + \infty$, $y \to a$; and if $x \to - \infty$, $y \to 0$; as can be seen by substituting these values in the above equation. The curve is illustrated below. It is often used to describe the sales growth of a new product – an initial learning period when sales are low, rising rapidly as sales spread through the population and then slowing down as new demand for the product reaches SATURATION POINT.

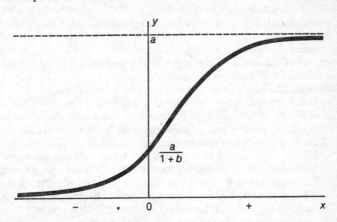

Lombard Street. A term sometimes used as a synonym for MONEY MARKET as many of the institutions of this market are located in or near this street in the City of London.

Lomé Convention. A convention signed in 1975 at Lomé, the capital of Togo, by the members of the EUROPEAN ECONOMIC COMMUNITY and forty-six DEVELOPING COUNTRIES in Africa, the Caribbean and the Pacific (A.C.P. states). It replaced previous association agreements made by the original six members of the E.E.C. with former colonies (Yaoundé Convention) and the East African Community (Arusha Agreement). (The East African Community was a common market of Uganda, Kenya and Tanzania.) Under the Lomé Convention all A.C.P. industrial exports, and most agricultural exports, to the E.E.C. are free of duty. Financial and technical aid – including an export income stabilization scheme, called Stabex, for agricultural exports – was also agreed upon, and the European Development Fund was set up by the E.E.C. to administer and channel aid funds to the Lomé countries.

In 1979 a second agreement was signed at Lomé between the E.E.C. and the developing countries in Africa, the Caribbean and the Pacific (A.C.P.), of which there are now sixty members. It continued duty-free access to the E.E.C. for most exports of A.C.P. The finance available for Stabex was increased, and the conditions of the loans were eased. In 1984, a third agreement was signed at Lomé renewing the convention along similar principles but with more emphasis on aid. Lomé III will be effective from 1986 to 1990. Aid through the European Development Fund was set at E.C.U. 7·5 billion ($7·8 billion).

London Inter-Bank Offered Rate (L.I.B.O.R.). ◊ INTER-BANK MARKET.

London International Financial Futures Exchange (L.I.F.F.E.). A MARKET to trade in financial FUTURES. Set up on 30 September 1982. Futures traded include an equity index contract based on the F.T/S.E. 100 SHARE INDEX.

Long-dated securities. ◊ DATED SECURITIES.

Long-end of the market. That part of the market for BONDS which is concerned with dealings in long-term issues.

Long rate. The RATE OF INTEREST on long-term BONDS.

Long run. A period of time in which all variables are able to settle at their equilibrium or final disequilibrium levels and all economic processes have time to work in full. Its most common application is in the theory of the firm (◊ FIRM, THEORY OF), in which it is the period of time in which the quantities of all FACTORS OF PRODUCTION employed are allowed to vary and all entry and exit that can occur into or from an industry has occurred. The duration of the 'long term' will clearly vary with the context in which the term is applied, depending on the speed with which the variables spoken of change. ◊ SHORT RUN.

Long-term capital. ◊ BUSINESS FINANCE.

Longfield, Samuel Mountifort (1802–84). An Irish lawyer who became the first incumbent of the Chair of Political Economy at Trinity College, Dublin. His most important work in economics was *Lectures on Political*

Economy, which was published in 1834. He argued convincingly against the labour theory of value (◊ VALUE, THEORIES OF) and developed a marginal revenue productivity theory (◊ MARGINAL REVENUE PRODUCT) of LABOUR and CAPITAL. Some of his ideas on capital and INTEREST foreshadowed the work of the AUSTRIAN SCHOOL.

Lorenz curve. A graphical representation showing the degree of inequality of a FREQUENCY DISTRIBUTION in which the cumulative percentages of a population (e.g. taxpayers, firms) are plotted against the cumulative percentage of the variable under study (e.g. incomes, employment). A straight line, rising at an angle of 45 deg. from the start on the graph will indicate perfect equality; for instance, if 10 per cent of firms employ 10 per cent of the total labour force, 20 per cent of firms employ 20 per cent of the total labour force and so on (◊ LINEAR RELATIONSHIP). However, if there are a large number of small firms which employ few people and a small number of large firms employing many people, the distribution will be unequal. When such a distribution is plotted, a curve will be traced below the 45 deg. line (see diagram) and the degree of curvature will be greater, the greater the inequality (◊◊ GINI COEFFICIENT).

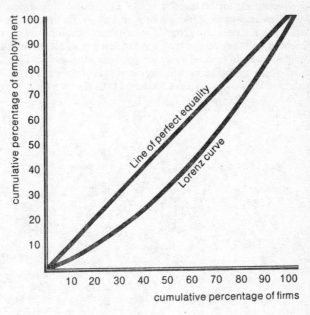

Lucas critique. An argument made by Robert Lucas in the 1970s that economists were mistakenly assuming that relationships they observed to hold would continue to hold even when conditions changed. The critique was an important component of the move towards accepting RATIONAL EXPECTATIONS as a significant development in MACROECONOMICS. In essence, Lucas argued that although economic agents may act in a certain way, you should not assume that they would continue to act in that way if you changed economic policy. For example, if consumers believed that inflation was to be 5 per cent next year, they might only demand 5 per cent wage increases. Suppose, knowing this, the government expands the money supply, causing inflation to be 10 per cent. The REAL INCOME of consumers would fall, and firms would find it cheaper to employ new staff to make high-priced goods. This would increase output by effectively exploiting people's expectation that inflation is 5 per cent and cutting their real wage. Lucas claimed that such policies may work for a while, but that, in the long run, if a government tried it enough, people would come to expect higher inflation and the policy would not work at all. (⟡ NEW CLASSICAL ECONOMICS.)

Lump-sum tax. A tax that must be paid irrespective of the behaviour of an economic agent; for instance, a tax of £100 on blue-eyed people that bore no relation to their income or spending. While usually considered impractical on political grounds, economists see lump-sum taxes as efficient in that they do not have any tendency to affect the incentives of individuals to work, save, purchase goods or services etc. These are all things which other taxes will necessarily distort. (⟡ FISCAL NEUTRALITY; MARGINAL TAX RATE; POLL TAX.)

M

Macmillan Committee. The Committee on Finance and Industry, set up in 1929, which published its report in 1931. It was under the chairmanship of Lord Macmillan, and J. M. KEYNES was a member. The committee carried out its task against an economic background in which the GROSS DOMESTIC PRODUCT had reached, after sixteen years, a level only 5 per cent above pre-war. Unemployment was 10 per cent in 1929, and was to rise to over 20 per cent by the time the committee published its report. The committee took the evidence from many leading economists of the day, such as A.C. PIGOU, D. H. Robertson and L. ROBBINS on the subject of UNEMPLOYMENT policy (◊ CLASSICAL SCHOOL). It decided in favour of the so-called TREASURY view that expenditure on public works was not the answer, in spite of the signing of Addendum I by some of its leading members. This addendum, which was signed by J. M. Keynes, A. A. G. Tullock, J. Frater Taylor, Sir T. Allen, Ernest Bevin and R. McKenna, advocated a programme of public works and IMPORT restrictions. However, the committee insisted that monetary policy should be concerned with 'the maintenance of the parity of the foreign exchanges before the avoidance of the credit cycle and the stability of the price level'. The maintenance of the EXCHANGE RATE was agreed to be the first priority by all, including the signatories of Addendum I. (Two months after the report was published, the U.K. came off the GOLD STANDARD and the exchange rate depreciated immediately by 2 per cent and continued downwards for twelve months.) The committee expressed concern that small companies found it difficult to raise long-term capital (◊ BUSINESS FINANCE) by the usual means of placing issues through the ISSUING HOUSES; this has become known as the 'MACMILLAN GAP'. It recommended the setting up of an institution which would 'provide adequate machinery for raising long-dated capital in amounts not sufficiently large for a public issue, i.e. amounts ranging from small sums up to say £200,000 or more'. This recommendation was eventually met by the creation of the Industrial and Commercial Finance Corporation (◊ FINANCE FOR INDUSTRY) in 1946. In 1945, the CLEARING BANKS and Scottish banks with the support of the BANK OF ENGLAND combined to finance the creation of the I.C.F.C. with initial resources of £45 million and a remit to make long-term loans and to subscribe to private placings of share capital between £5,000 and £200,000. ◊◊ BOLTON COMMITTEE; FINANCE FOR INDUSTRY; RADCLIFFE REPORT.

Macmillan Gap. The report of the Committee on Finance and Industry in 1931 (MACMILLAN COMMITTEE) highlighted the difficulties which small and medium-sized firms experienced in raising long-term capital (◊ BUSINESS FINANCE). The report made proposals for dealing with this 'gap' arising from the lack of facilities for public issues in small amounts. Facilities for coping with small issues were later developed, especially through ISSUING HOUSES, placing small amounts privately with INSTITUTIONAL INVESTORS, such as INSURANCE companies. In addition, new institutions have been set up, such as the INDUSTRIAL AND COMMERCIAL FINANCE CORPORATION. ◊ BOLTON COMMITTEE.

Macroeconomics. The study of whole economic systems aggregating over the functioning of individual economic units. It is primarily concerned with VARIABLES which follow systematic and predictable paths of behaviour and can be analysed independently of the decisions of the many agents who determine their level. More specifically, it is a study of national economies and the determination of NATIONAL INCOME. It focuses on sectors of the economy but not those that function as separate units, like the 'car production sector'; instead, those which run across the entire economy: the industrial sector; the personal sector; the financial sector; the government and the overseas sector. In classical macroeconomics (◊ CLASSICAL ECONOMICS) lay a presumption of the efficiency and effectiveness of free markets, and all macroeconomic variables were seen as the sum of the variables as they applied to individual firms or consumers. Macroeconomic mechanisms were largely embedded in the theory of MICROECONOMICS. Since J. M. KEYNES, however, economists have allowed for DISEQUILIBRIUM in macroeconomic variables as such, and, therefore, behaviour distinct from that of microeconomic theory.

The main topics covered by macroeconomics are: the determination of national income (◊ INCOME DETERMINATION, THEORY OF), prices (◊ INFLATION) and EMPLOYMENT; the role of FISCAL and MONETARY POLICY, analysed through different MODELS, each containing its own assumptions and emphasis; the determination of CONSUMPTION and INVESTMENT; the BALANCE OF PAYMENTS; and ECONOMIC GROWTH. (◊ CIRCULAR FLOW OF INCOME; ECONOMIC DOCTRINES.)

Mainstream corporation tax. ◊ CORPORATION TAX.

Maintaining capital intact. Making good the stock of CAPITAL consumed in production. This is a concept used in economic theory and national accounting in which 'true' DEPRECIATION is used to restore the INCOME-producing capacity of capital, so that, e.g., a measure of NET DOMESTIC PRODUCT or NET INVESTMENT can be made, i.e. the GROSS DOMESTIC PRODUCT or GROSS INVESTMENT less an estimate of CAPITAL CONSUMPTION. Net domestic product would thus measure total output while maintaining the nation's capital intact, while net investment would measure the net addition to the nation's stock of capital over the period.

Malthus, Thomas Robert (1766–1834). He was educated at St John's College, Cambridge, and became a Fellow there after studying mathematics and philosophy. He entered the Church of England and became a country parson. He was subsequently Professor of History and Political Economy at the East India Company's Haileybury College. His *Essay on the Principle of Population as It Affects the Future Improvement of Society* was published in 1798, with a revised edition in 1803. His other works include *An Inquiry into the Nature and Progress of Rent* (1815), *The Poor Law* (1817), *Principles of Political Economy* (1820), and *Definitions of Political Economy* (1827). Malthus is remembered for his essays on POPULATION. Population had a natural growth rate described by a GEOMETRIC PROGRESSION, whereas the natural resources necessary to support the population grew at a rate similar to an ARITHMETIC PROGRESSION. Without restraints, therefore, there would be a continued pressure on living standards, both in terms of room and of output. He advocated moral restraint on the size of families. Malthus also carried on a long argument with RICARDO against Say's law (◊ SAY, J.-B.). Briefly, Say's law stated that there could be no general overproduction or underproduction of COMMODITIES on the grounds that whatever was bought by somebody must have been sold by somebody else. (J. M. KEYNES found some affinity between Malthus's conclusions and his own in his *General Theory*.) Malthus, however, was arguing strictly within the basic assumption of the equality of planned SAVINGS and INVESTMENT in CLASSICAL ECONOMICS, and was a long way away from Keynes's revolutionary assumption that they are made equal only by movements in total INCOME. Saving to Malthus was investment. His argument for under-consumption was simply that an increase in savings necessarily diminished consumption on the one hand, and on the other increased the output of consumer's goods through increased investment. At the same time, because the LABOUR supply was inelastic (◊ ELASTICITY), wages rose and therefore so did costs. ◊ SISMONDI, J. C. L. S. DE.

Malynes, Gerald (1586–1641). An English merchant and government official and a leading exponent of MERCANTILISM. His publications include *A Treatise of the Canker of England's Commonwealth* (1601), *Saint George for England, Allegorically Described* (1601), *England's View in the Unmasking of Two Paradoxes* (1603), *The Maintenance of Free Trade* (1622), and *The Centre of the Circle of Commerce* (1623). He showed how an outflow of precious metals could lead to a fall in PRICES at home and a rise in prices abroad. This was an important clarification of the economic thought of the time. He suggested that higher import TARIFFS should be levied and EXPORTS of BULLION prohibited, because he believed that a country's growth was related to the accumulation of precious metals. He thought that exchange control should be used to improve the U.K. TERMS OF TRADE, supporting his policy on the belief that the U.K.'s exports were price inelastic ($ ELASTICITY). $ QUANTITY THEORY OF MONEY.

Managed bond. $ BOND.

Managed currency. A CURRENCY is said to be managed if the EXCHANGE RATE is not fixed by FREE MARKET forces, i.e. if the government influences the rate by buying and selling its own MONEY or other means. Most currencies are managed in some sense today, even when they are allowed to float. $ EXCHANGE CONTROL; INTERNATIONAL MONETARY FUND.

Management accountancy. Business accounting practice concerned with the provision of information to management for policy-making purposes as opposed to that required for the preparation of BALANCE SHEETS and other information required by law. In so far as the two sets of information overlap, the phrase is imprecise, but it usefully emphasizes the recent aspects of the development of accounting, notably in cost control ($ COST ACCOUNTING) and INVESTMENT APPRAISAL.

Manchester school. 'Manchesterism' was an epithet applied in Germany to those who subscribed to a political-economic philosophy of 'LAISSEZ-FAIRE'. It was applied, in particular, to the movement in England from 1820 to 1850 which was inspired by the propaganda of the Anti-Corn Law League. This was headed by Cobden and Bright, and supported by the economics of DAVID RICARDO. The 'school' believed in FREE TRADE and political and economic freedom with the minimum of government restraint.

Mandeville, Bernard de (1670–1733). Born at Dort in Holland, Mandeville obtained an M.D. at Leyden and established himself in London as a general practitioner. In 1705 he published a poem called *The Grumbling Hive*, which was reissued in 1714 and 1729 under the title of *The Fable of the Bees or Private Vices, Public Benefits*. In this pamphlet he showed how although individuals indulge in unholy vices in their private behaviour nevertheless in the aggregate they contributed to the public good and therefore could be excused. ADAM SMITH was severely critical of the satirical nature of the work ($ 'INVISIBLE HAND').

Marginal analysis. The study of VARIABLES in terms of the effects that would occur if they were changed by a small amount. For example, rather than analyse whether or not it is in the interest of an individual to spend money on food at all, attention can sensibly be focused on whether or not welfare could be enhanced by spending slightly more or less on food. Nothing better demonstrates the concept than the *paradox of* *value*: although water is more necessary to man than diamonds, it has a much lower price. This is because man usually has so much of it that extra water is worthless. This is not true of diamonds. ($\diamondsuit$ MARGINAL UTILITY.) The marginal value of a variable is equivalent to its rate of change: or mathematically, its first derivative. ($\diamondsuit$ CALCULUS). For example, a firm's sales revenue rises as sales increase and this can be plotted on a graph as total revenue. By taking the gradient of the total revenue curve, MARGINAL REVENUE can be derived, depicting how much extra revenue is gained, from an extra sale, at each different level of total sales. If the marginal revenue is plotted on a graph, total revenue can be derived by finding the area under the marginal-revenue curve up to a given level of sales. The marginal value of a variable lies below the average value of that variable if the average is falling. The marginal value lies above it if the average is rising.

The margin is important in economics as it is the impact of small changes in variables rather than their level *per se* that determines whether rational economic agents change them. It is the average level of utility, costs or revenues that tends to determine whether things are consumed or produced at all, but the marginal utility, costs or revenues that determine how much is consumed or produced once a decision to do so at all has been taken. ($\diamondsuit$ GOSSEN, H. H.; JEVONS, W. S.; MARGINAL COST; MARGINAL-COST PRICING; MARGINAL PRODUCT; MENGER, C.; THÜNEN, J. H. VON; WALRAS, M. E. L..)

Marginal cost. The increase in the total costs of a firm caused by increasing its output by one extra unit. If all costs are fixed, the marginal cost of the first unit of output will be very high, but all subsequent units can be made for nothing. Economists normally assume firms to be producing at a point at which marginal costs are positive and rising ($\diamondsuit$ FIRM, THEORY OF THE).

Marginal-cost pricing. The setting of the price of an item equal to the cost of producing one extra unit of the item. MARGINAL COST represents the OPPORTUNITY COST, or the total sacrifice to society from producing an item. The price represents the cost to consumers of buying it, and they will ensure therefore that they will buy it if and only if they value it more than or as much as the money it sells for. If price is below marginal cost consumers will be happy to buy an item even if they perhaps value it less than the goods that could have been made if it had not been produced. If, on the other hand, price is greater than marginal cost, some consumers who value the item more than it costs to make will still be deterred from buying it. For an efficient allocation of RESOURCES ($\diamondsuit$ ECONOMIC EFFICIENCY), therefore, marginal-cost pricing is considered essential.

There are, however, factors which undermine the case for marginal-cost pricing. Primarily, any company enjoying ECONOMIES OF SCALE will have average costs in excess of marginal costs ($\diamond$ MARGINAL ANALYSIS), and with marginal-cost pricing, average costs will exceed price. A company in such a position will therefore make a loss. Only if production is at a point at which marginal and average costs are equal will marginal-cost pricing be sustainable.

Marginal-cost pricing provides a major advantage of PERFECT COMPETITION over MONOPOLY or MONOPOLISTIC COMPETITION, and attempts to impose it on firms outside competitive markets – especially NATIONALIZED INDUSTRIES – have been made, with limited success. $\diamond$ HOTELLING, H.; PEAK PRICING.

Marginal efficiency of capital. $\diamond$ INTERNAL RATE OF RETURN.

Marginal efficiency of investment. $\diamond$ INTERNAL RATE OF RETURN.

Marginal product. The output created by the employment of one additional unit of a FACTOR OF PRODUCTION. In general, it is believed that the marginal product of a factor rises when the factor is employed in small quantities, but eventually falls as the amount of the factor employed increases. Marginal product is measured in the physical units of the output produced and it is thus sometimes called *marginal physical product*. ($\diamond$ DIMINISHING RETURNS, LAW OF.)

Marginal product of labour. The output created by the employment of one extra worker with all other FACTORS OF PRODUCTION held constant. It is a measure of the physical increase in output that occurs in a firm or in the economy as a whole when one extra person starts work. It is generally assumed that the marginal product of LABOUR rises initially, and then diminishes. In a hypothetical factory manned by a single worker, at first adding helpers would allow for specialization and the DIVISION OF LABOUR. Eventually, however, all such gains would be realized and the gains from employing additional staff would diminish. ($\diamond$ DIMINISHING RETURNS, LAW OF.)

Marginal productivity of capital. $\diamond$ INTERNAL RATE OF RETURN.

Marginal productivity theory of wages. The doctrine that the demand for labour is determined by the value of the output created by the employment of an extra worker. In this account of the determination of wages, firms employ workers as long as the revenue generated by the output of the marginal worker exceeds the cost of that worker; that is, until the worker's MARGINAL REVENUE PRODUCT is equal to the market wage rate. From this account of firm's behaviour, a curve depicting the demand for labour at different wage levels can be derived, and the wage rate is determined by the interaction of this curve with that of the supply of labour at different wage levels. As more workers are employed at a given level of capital stock the MARGINAL PRODUCT OF LABOUR will decline and the wage of all workers will fall ($\diamond$ DIMINISHING RETURNS, LAW OF). This fall in wages occurs because any new workers entering the labour market cannot profitably be employed at the going wage rate as the value of their output would be less than that of the workers already employed. If they are keen for work, therefore, they will offer themselves to employers at lower rates of pay than the current employees, and all wages will be bid down. At the new lower wage level, all workers can profitably be employed.

The theory is part of the *neo-classical theory of distribution* (◊ DIS-TRIBUTION, THEORY OF) which attempted to explain the share of total output accruing to labour, investors and landowners (◊ BAR-GAINING THEORY OF WAGES; NEO-CLASSICAL ECONOMICS).

Marginal propensity to consume (M.P.C.). The most important variable determining expenditure on consumption is income (◊◊ CONSUMP-TION FUNCTION). The *average propensity to consume* is the propor-tion of total income which is spent, rather than saved. The *marginal propensity to consume* is the proportion of a small increase in income which is spent rather than saved. It is generally held that as incomes increase the marginal propensity to consume will fall: the richer people (or countries) are, the more they save. (◊◊ KEYNES, J. M.; MULTI-PLIER; PERMANENT-INCOME HYPOTHESIS.)

Marginal propensity to save (M.P.S.). The proportion of a small increase in income which is saved. It is equal to 1 − M.P.C. (MARGINAL PRO-PENSITY TO CONSUME).

Marginal rate of substitution (M.R.S.). The rate at which a consumer needs to substitute one commodity for another in order to maintain constant total UTILITY from the commodities taken together. If a consumer values two boxes of Daz equally to one of Persil, the marginal rate of substitution between them is two, because if one box of Persil were taken away from the consumer two boxes of Daz would have to be provided to compensate. The marginal rate of substitution between commodity A and B usually diminishes as consumption of commodity A increases. If at consumption of twenty apples and twenty bananas the consumer is indifferent between one of either, at consumption of thirty apples and ten bananas the consumer is likely to start demanding more than a mere one apple before giving up a scarce banana. Graphically, the M.R.S. is the slope of an INDIFFERENCE CURVE and it is in INDIFFERENCE-CURVE ANALYSIS that the concept is important. Mathematically, it is the ratio of the MARGINAL UTILITIES of two items. As long as the M.R.S. declines with increased consumption of an item, the indifference curves are convex to the origin of an indifference map. (◊ TECHNICAL SUBSTITUTION, RATE OF.)

Marginal revenue. The increase in the total revenue received by a firm from the sale of one extra unit of its output. For a small firm which cannot influence market price (◊◊ PERFECT COMPETITION), the extra revenue gained is equal to the price of the sale. For a firm with a large share of the total market (◊ MONOPOLY), however, putting an extra item on sale drives down the market price slightly, so that the revenue gain equals the cash gained on the new sale *minus* the loss that occurs on all the sales that would otherwise have been made at the previously higher price.

Marginal revenue product. The revenue gained by a firm when it sells the output generated by the employment of one additional unit of a FACTOR OF PRODUCTION. It is influenced by three factors: (a) the physical output of the extra factor; (b) the sale price of the product made; (c) the rate at which that price falls when the extra supply of the new factor is put on to the market. To calculate it, MARGINAL PRODUCT must be multiplied by MARGINAL REVENUE (◊ MARGINAL VALUE PRODUCT).

Marginal social product. The effect on SOCIAL WELFARE of employing one additional unit of a FACTOR OF PRODUCTION. When new workers are taken on, for example, the physical output which they build has a private value to their employer, measured as the MARGINAL VALUE PRODUCT, or the price at which the output is sold. However, to measure the value of their output to society, two other factors must be taken into account. The first is CONSUMER SURPLUS: the amount by which consumers value something in excess of what they pay for it. The second factor is any EXTERNALITY which is present: a benefit (or cost) which accrues to those other than the purchaser of the item.

Marginal tax rate. The rate of tax paid on extra units of income. An individual may pay no tax on the first £1,000 of income, and 50 per cent tax on all pounds earned thereafter. Those individuals earning more than £1,000 will thus face a marginal tax rate of 50 per cent even though their overall tax rate will be less than 50 per cent. Someone earning £1,001, for example, will only pay 50p of tax – a tiny proportion of his total income. The marginal tax rates facing economic agents are often considered important in determining how far taxation impinges on incentives to work, save or spend money. They are not important in determining whether a tax is progressive or not (◊ PROGRESSIVE TAX). The fact that poor people may lose 80 per cent of any marginal earnings (◊◊ POVERTY TRAP) and the rich only 60 per cent is irrelevant in assessing whether the tax system is borne more heavily by either group – an assessment which depends not on the tax paid on incremental pounds of earnings, but on tax paid on all actual earnings. (◊◊ LUMP-SUM TAXES; TAXATION.)

Marginal utility. The extra satisfaction gained by a consumer from a small increment in the consumption of a commodity. More formally, it is the partial derivative of the UTILITY function with respect to the quantity of some commodity consumed (◊ CALCULUS). It is a concept of central importance to demand theory (◊ DEMAND, THEORY OF), one approach to which holds that marginal utility diminishes as consumption of an item increases ($\diamond$ MARGINAL UTILITY, DIMINISHING). Rational consumers will equalize the marginal utility gained from a unit of spending on all the different things they consume, because not to do so would imply that costless extra utility could be derived by switching spending from items yielding low marginal utility to those where it is higher. Such a theory can explain why a price rise causes consumers to cut demand of an item. As consumers, however, do not possess an objective scale of utility measurement ($\diamond$ ORDINAL UTILITY), in more modern theory ($\diamond$ INDIFFERENCE-CURVE ANALYSIS) no meaning is attached to the numerical magnitude of the marginal utilities themselves, but only to their ratios and signs. ($\diamond$ DEMAND THEORY.)

Marginal utility, diminishing. As extra units of a commodity are consumed by an individual, the satisfaction gained from each unit falls. For example, although for every extra Mars bar someone eats they derive extra pleasure, the more Mars that are eaten, the less the pleasure gained from each additional one. Eventually, as sickness strikes, subsequently consumed Mars bars will yield disutility.

The approach to consumer theory which uses the notion of diminishing marginal utility is flawed, as there is no common unit or scale by which the utility derived from a range of items can be measured ($\diamond$ ORDINAL UTILITY). Nevertheless, the concept remains relevant to many issues, especially when applied to consumption in general. For example, it provides a case against a POLL TAX which, it shows, cuts the utility of the poor (who treasure their every possession) more than the rich (who hardly notice relatively small losses). It also explains why people may like to avoid risk: the utility lost from a £100 cut in income is greater than the utility gained by a £100 increase in income and, consequently, most consumers would reject a fair bet in which they were faced with a 50 per cent chance of either, despite the fact that on average they would lose nothing in cash terms. ($\diamond$ BERNOULLI'S HYPOTHESIS; MARGINAL UTILITY; RISK AVERSION.)

Marginal utility of money. The pleasure or satisfaction gained by a consumer from an extra unit of money. The rational consumer should ensure that the marginal UTILITY of money with respect to the different things he consumes is the same: if someone would get more utility from spending an extra pound on clothes than they would get from spending it on books, by transferring some of their budget from books to clothes they would costlessly increase their utility. They should go on transferring until they have so many clothes that they no longer value them, pound for pound, more than books. The marginal utility of money diminishes the greater the quantity of money availiable to a consumer. ($\diamond$ DEMAND, THEORY OF; MARGINAL UTILITY; MARSHALL, A.; ORDINAL UTILITY.)

Marginal value product. The market value of the output generated by the employment of one additional unit of a FACTOR OF PRODUCTION. It is equal to the MARGINAL PRODUCT of a factor multiplied by the unit selling price of the output produced. It is thus comparable to the MARGINAL REVENUE PRODUCT, which is marginal product multiplied by MARGINAL REVENUE; in PERFECT COMPETITION, where price is equal to marginal revenue, the two are identical.

Market. A market is created whenever potential sellers of a good or service are brought into contact with potential buyers and a means of exchange is available. The medium of exchange may be MONEY or BARTER. Exchange agreements are reached through the operation of the laws of SUPPLY and DEMAND (♢ PRICE SYSTEM.)

Market capitalization. ♢ CAPITALIZATION.

Market economy. ♢ FREE-MARKET ECONOMY.

Market failure. A situation in which economic efficiency has not been achieved through imperfections in the market mechanism. Market failure may manifest itself either in the inability of the system to produce goods which are wanted or by a maldistribution of resources which could be improved in such a way that some consumers would be better off and none worse off, i.e. resource allocation is not Pareto-optimum (♢ ECONOMIC EFFICIENCY). Markets will fail where important costs, such as pollution, are not reflected in PRICES (♢ EXTERNALITIES) or where there is MONOPOLY or OLIGOPOLY or where government actions, for example the imposition of TAXATION, distort markets. Economic theory predicts that markets will usually fail in some sense except under conditions of PERFECT COMPETITION, so the term is reserved for cases where it is believed that a serious maldistribution of resources has occurred. In these cases it is often argued that government intervention is justified. (♢ ADVERSE SELECTION; IMPERFECT MARKET; PUBLIC GOODS.)

Market forces. The impact of SUPPLY and DEMAND which, in a FREE-MARKET ECONOMY, determine PRICE and the allocation of resources.

Market maker. A BROKER-dealer who is prepared to buy and sell specified SECURITIES at all times and is thus 'making a market' in them. Prior to the BIG BANG this function was carried out by the JOBBERS, who were not allowed to deal with the public. Post Big Bang all members of the STOCK EXCHANGE may deal with the public as broker-dealers some of whom specialize as market makers and others as STOCKBROKERS.

Market share. This can refer to (a) the sales of the product or products of a firm as a proportion of the sales of the product or products of the industry as a whole, e.g. sales of Ford motor-cars compared with total U.K. motor-car sales. Or to (b) the sales of a particular COMMODITY compared with the total sales for the class of commodity of which the particular commodity is a member, e.g. sales of twin-tub washing-machines compared with sales of all washing-machines. The presumption is that the firm's product in (a) and the particular commodity in (b) are faced with competitive SUBSTITUTES in their respective MARKETS.

Market shares may also be calculated in terms of the proportion of the product in the total existing stock of that class of products, as opposed to its share of the flow of new sales. ⟐ SATURATION POINT.

Market structure. The organizational and other characteristics of a MARKET and in particular those which affect the nature of competition and pricing. Traditionally, the most important features of market structure are the number and size distribution of buyers and sellers, which reflect the extent of MONOPOLY or MONOPSONY; this, in turn, will be affected by the existence or absence of BARRIERS TO ENTRY. ⟐ CONCENTRATION.

Marketable securities. SECURITIES dealt in on the STOCK EXCHANGE.

Marketing. Broadly, the functions of sales, distribution, ADVERTISING and sales promotion, product planning and market research. That is, those functions in a business that directly involve contact with the consumer and assessment of his needs, and the translation of this information into outputs for sale consistent with the firm's objectives.

Marshall Aid. At the end of the Second World War, only the U.S.A. had the necessary productive capacity to make good the losses experienced by other countries. European countries had heavy BALANCE OF PAYMENTS deficits vis-à-vis the U.S.A. In 1946, in order to alleviate the resultant shortage of dollars, the U.S.A. and Canada made substantial LOANS, including £1,000 million to the U.K. It was expected that these loans would be sufficient to cover requirements over the short period which was all that was expected to be necessary for the world economies to recover. However, in 1948 a general LIQUIDITY crisis was only avoided by further loans made under the EUROPEAN RECOVERY PROGRAMME, through which the U.K. received loans amounting to £1,500 million between 1948 and 1950. This programme was called Marshall Aid, after the then U.S. Secretary of State, General G. C. Marshall. The loans were allocated under the direction of the ORGANIZATION FOR EUROPEAN ECONOMIC COOPERATION set up for this purpose.

Marshall, Alfred (1842–1924). He was educated at Merchant Taylor's School and graduated in mathematics at St John's College, Cambridge. In 1868 he was appointed to a lectureship in moral science at Cambridge, and it was during this period that he began to study economics. In 1882 he moved to the Chair of Political Economy at Bristol. In 1885 he returned to Cambridge as Professor of Political Economy, a post he retained until his retirement in 1908. His most important works include *The Pure Theory of Foreign Trade* (1879), *The Principles of Economics* (1890), *Industry and Trade* (1919) and *Money, Credit and Commerce*

(1923). Marshall was in the long tradition of the English CLASSICAL SCHOOL, which was founded by ADAM SMITH and DAVID RICARDO, and his influence on succeeding generations of economists has been very great. His achievement was to refine and develop MICROECONOMIC theory to such a degree that much of what he wrote is still familiar to readers of the elementary economic textbooks today. His theory of VALUE brought together the diverse elements of previous theories. On the one hand, he showed how the demand for a COMMODITY is dependent on a consumer's UTILITY or welfare. The more of a commodity a consumer has the less extra utility or benefit accrues to him from an additional purchase (◊ GOSSEN, H. H.). He will not go on buying a commodity until this extra benefit falls to zero. Rather, he will stop buying extra when he finds that the MONEY he has to pay for it is worth more to him than the gain from having an extra unit of the commodity. At this point of EQUILIBRIUM a fall in the PRICE, therefore, will mean that it becomes worth while to him to exchange his money for more of the commodity. In general, therefore, a fall in price will increase the quantity of the commodity demanded, and in theory a schedule could be drawn up which shows how much would be demanded at each price. The resultant graph would show a downward-sloping DEMAND CURVE. Marshall invented the expression ELASTICITY to describe his measure of the response of demand to small changes in price. Similarly, on the supply side, higher prices are necessary to bring forward increased outputs and a supply schedule with its corresponding supply curve can be drawn up. The price of the commodity is determined at the point where the two curves intersect. These worked like a pair of scissors, neither blade of which cuts without the presence of the other. Marshall recognized that his consumer utility theory was in some ways an oversimplification. It does not take account of complementary or competitive goods (◊ COMPLEMENTARY DEMAND), and assumes that the MARGINAL UTILITY of money is constant. However, he argued that his analysis applied to small price changes and to goods upon which only an insignificant proportion of income was spent. It was within this framework that Marshall discussed the idea of CONSUMER SURPLUS (◊ DUPUIT, A. J. E. J.). For a given quantity of a commodity purchased on a competitive market, the price will be the same for each unit of the commodity sold. However, for any individual purchaser the price is equal to the utility to him of the last unit of the total quantity purchased; the last but one being worth more, the last but two worth more again, and so on. These utilities can be added up and the extra, over the price and quantity paid out, is the consumer's surplus. He was aware of the shortcomings of the 'stationary state' of the typical classical analysis and emphasized the importance of the production period. He recognized the element of time as the chief difficulty of almost every economic problem. He considered (a) a market period in which supplies are all fixed, (b) a short period in which supplies can be increased, but only to the extent possible by better use of current capacity, and (c) a long period in which capacity itself can be increased. The classical economists had shown how RENT is received by landowners as a surplus. As land was a FACTOR OF PRODUCTION in fixed supply, it differed from other factors of production in that its returns were not related to work done. Marshall extended the concept by pointing out that, in the short run, man-made CAPITAL was in fixed supply also, and during the period which it took to manufacture, it earned a QUASI-RENT. ⟡ COURNOT, A. A.; MARSHALL-LERNER CRITERION; MILL, J. S.

Marshall–Lerner criterion. A rule which states the ELASTICITY conditions under which a change in a country's EXCHANGE RATE would improve its BALANCE OF TRADE. A. P. Lerner set out the appropriate formulae in his book *Economics of Control* on the basis of the elasticity concepts developed by A. MARSHALL. In its simplest form, the rule states that the price elasticities of demand for IMPORTS and EXPORTS must sum to greater than unity for an improvement to be effected. The volume of exports increases and the volume of imports decreases in response to a fall in the PRICE of the former and rise in the price of the latter when a CURRENCY is devalued (assuming, for the sake of the argument, that there are no other factors influencing the MARKET, such as SUPPLY restrictions). There would, therefore, be an improvement in the balance of trade in volume terms, i.e. in terms of the prices ruling prior to DEVALUATION. However, what is important for the BALANCE OF PAYMENTS is the impact of devaluation on the value of trade. If the price elasticity of exports plus the price elasticity of imports is less than unity, it means that the increased cost of imports in terms of the domestic CURRENCY outweighs the value of the growth in exports. Putting it another way, the improvement in the volume of the balance of trade is not sufficient to offset the fall in the value of the balance of trade occasioned by the devaluation. ⟡ TERMS OF TRADE.

Marx, Karl (1818–1883). Born in Trier, Marx studied philosophy at Bonn University and at the Hegelian Centre at Berlin University, and took a doctorate at Jena. For a time, he was editor of *Rheinische Zeitung*, but the paper was suppressed, and in 1843 he fled to Paris. There he began his friendship and close association with Friedrich Engels, who encouraged in him an interest in political economy. After a brief return to Germany he was banished, and in 1849 he settled in London where he remained until his death in 1883. *The Communist Manifesto*, written jointly by Marx and Engels, was published in 1848. In 1859 the first fruits of his long, painstaking research at the British Museum appeared: the *Critique of Political Economy*. The first volume of *Das Kapital*

265

appeared in 1867. The remaining volumes, edited by Engels, were published posthumously in 1885 and 1894.

Marx's economics was essentially that of the CLASSICAL SCHOOL, especially of DAVID RICARDO, to whom he owed a great debt. However, he lifted economics out of its preoccupation with agriculture and stationary states. For Marx, CAPITALISM was a stage in the process of evolution, removed from the primitive agricultural economy and moving towards the inevitable elimination of private property and the class structure. Marx attempted a synoptic view of the development of the whole structure of human society. His economics was only a part, though a fundamental part, of his all-embracing sociological and political theories. Marx postulated that the class structures of societies, their political systems and, indeed, their culture were determined by the way in which societies produced their goods and SERVICES. Moreover, the whole structure was evolutionary. The class structure of a capitalist state was a reflection of the split between owners and non-owners of CAPITAL, which division characterized the manner in which production was carried out, and which already had within it the necessary ingredients of change.

Marx developed from ADAM SMITH and David Ricardo their labour theory of value ($\Diamond$ VALUE, THEORIES OF), which held the central place in his economic theory. For Ricardo, the amount of LABOUR used in the production of COMMODITIES was a rough determinant of relative prices in the long run. For Marx, however, the quantity of labour used up in the manufacture of a product determined value, and this value was fundamental and immutable. He did not satisfactorily explain any connection with relative prices. Labour consumption determined exchange value, which differed from use value. The distinction between the two in the case of labour, regarded in itself as a commodity, was a vital one in Marx's analysis. The capitalist pays wages which are determined by the exchange value of workers. This exchange value is, in turn, determined by the socially necessary labour time required to 'produce' the worker, that is, the labour inputs required to rear, feed, clothe and educate him. However, in return the capitalist receives the labourer's use value. The value of the labourer to the capitalist who uses him is greater than the value the capitalist paid in exchange for his services. This difference Marx called 'surplus value'(s). Only labour yields surplus value. Other FACTORS OF PRODUCTION, such as plant and machinery and raw materials, only reproduce themselves in the productive process. (These ideas have some affinity with the PHYSIOCRATS' *produit net*, although in their case it was LAND which was the only factor which produced a surplus.) The amount of capital required to pay wages Marx called variable (v) ($\Diamond$ WAGE-FUND THEORY), and the remainder he called constant (c). GROSS

NATIONAL PRODUCT in the Marxian system therefore is given by $c + v + s$. The ratio of constant capital in total capital $c/(c + v)$ he called the organic composition of capital. The 'exploitation rate' was s/v. The rate of profit was $s/(c + v)$. The desire for further wealth, coupled with competition and technical change, induced capitalists to invest from the surplus (which they expropriated from the workers) and in labour-saving machinery. The organic composition of capital therefore rose over time as more was spent on plant and machinery (c) compared with wages (v), with the result that, as only variable capital produced a surplus (and assuming that the exploitation rate remained constant), the rate of profit tended downwards ($\Diamond$ PROFIT, FALLING RATE OF). On the one hand, diminishing profits and stronger competition would lead to MONOPOLY and the concentration of WEALTH in a few hands, and on the other hand there would be an increasing squeeze on the REAL INCOMES of workers by the capitalists in their attempt to maintain PROFITS and the emergence of a large 'reserve army of unemployed' arising from mechanization ($\Diamond$ RICARDO, D.). The class conflict would become increasingly acute until the environment was such that the change inherent in the economic structure would be made manifest by the overthrow of capitalism.

Matrix. An array of numbers displayed in rows and columns. For instance:

$$\begin{bmatrix} 2 & 1 \\ 7 & 3 \end{bmatrix}$$

The numbers are called the *elements* of the matrix and are generally denoted by a_{ij} in which i refers to the row and j to the column. In the above example $a_{21} = 7$. The order of a matrix is given by the product of the number of rows times the number of columns. The above matrix is of order 4. An algebra exists for the manipulation of matrices, with rules for addition, subtraction, multiplication and division. Matrix algebra has found many useful applications in ECONOMETRICS, in particular in INPUT–OUTPUT ANALYSIS and LINEAR PROGRAMMING.

Maturity. The date upon which the principal of a redeemable security becomes repayable. $\Diamond$ REDEEMABLE SECURITIES; SECURITIES.

Maturity transformation. $\Diamond$ FINANCIAL INTERMEDIARIES.

Maximin strategy. A decision rule in the theory of games ($\Diamond$ GAME THEORY). The rule states that a 'player' with a number of optional strategies to choose considers first the minimum pay-offs that could be gained from each depending on the reaction of his 'opponent'. The 'player' should then chose that strategy which corresponds to the maximum of all the minimum pay-offs to him that are possible. For instance, consider a decision-maker faced with two optional strategies, each of which could have two pay-offs. They can be summarized in a MATRIX:

| | (1) | 2 | 5 |
| | (2) | 4 | 3 |

Strategy (1) could have a pay-off of 2 or 5, strategy (2) a pay-off of 4 or 3. The minimum pay-off of strategy (1) is 2 and that of strategy (2) is 3. The maximum minimum pay-off is therefore 3 and strategy (2) would be chosen under the rule. ⟡ PRISONER'S DILEMMA.

Meade, Sir James Edward (b. 1907). Educated at both Oxford and Cambridge Universities, Professor Meade was appointed Professor of Commerce at the London School of Economics in 1947. He was appointed to the Chair of Political Economy at Cambridge University in 1957, a post he held until 1969. Professor Meade was awarded the NOBEL PRIZE in Economics (jointly with B. OHLIN) in 1977. His published works include *The Theory of International Economic Policy* (1951), *A Geometry of International Trade* (1953), *The Theory of Customs Unions* (1955); *A Neo-Classical Theory of Economic Growth* (1961); *Efficiency, Equality and the Ownership of Property* (1964), *Principles of Political Economy* (1965/76), *The Inheritance of Inequalities* (1974), *The Intelligent Radical's Guide to Economic Policy* (1975) and *Stagflation* (1981/3). Professor Meade has made important advances in the theory of international trade, in the study of equilibrium conditions in domestic and external economies. In his work on the welfare effects (⟡ WELFARE ECONOMICS) of tariffs and customs unions (◊ CUSTOMS UNION), he introduced the concepts of the theory of the SECOND BEST. Professor Meade has contributed much to the analysis of income distribution and in the field of GROWTH THEORY, being an advocate of a PRICES AND INCOMES POLICY. ⟡ NOMINAL G.D.P.

Mean. ◊ AVERAGE.

Means test. The assessment of wealth or income as, for example, when determining the eligibility of a claimant for welfare benefits. Means-tested benefits contrast with those such as child benefit which are *universal* – given to all families irrespective of income. ◊ MARGINAL TAX RATE; POVERTY TRAP.

Median. ◊ AVERAGE.

Medium of exchange. ◊ MONEY.

Member banks (U.S.). ◊ COMMERCIAL BANKS.

Memorandum of Association. The document which forms the basis of registration of a company. As required by the Companies Acts, the Memorandum of Association must list the subscribers to the CAPITAL of the company and the number of SHARES they have agreed to take, the name and address of the company, and where appropriate, the powers and objects of the company, and that the LIABILITY of its members is limited (◊ COMPANY LAW). The *Articles of Association* set out the rules by which the company will be administered, e.g. the voting of directors, the calling of meetings.

Menger, Carl (1840–1921). Professor of Economics in the Faculty of Law at Vienna University from 1873 to 1903. His major work, in which he develops his marginal-utility theory, *Grundsätze der Volkswirtschaftslehre*, was published in 1871. He was one of the three economists in the 1870s who independently put forward the theory of VALUE based on MARGINAL UTILITY and whose work had a profound influence on the subsequent evolution of economic thought (◊ GOSSEN, H. H.; JEVONS, W. S.; WALRAS, M. E. L.). Exchange takes place, he argued, because individuals have different subjective valuations of the same COMMODITY. Menger saw commodities in terms of their reverse order in the productive process, i.e. bread is prior to flour and flour prior to wheat. The PRICE of the first-order commodities, which is determined by their exchange for CONSUMPTION, is imputed back through to the higher-ordered commodities. The theory of diminishing UTILITY was the catalyst which eventually unified the theories of production and consumption. Menger himself, however, overemphasized consumption demand in the theory of value, just as the CLASSICAL ECONOMISTS had overemphasized production supply (◊ MARSHALL, A.)

Mercantilism. The growth of INTERNATIONAL TRADE and the establishment of the power of the merchant after the medieval era led to the emergence of a body of thought, between the mid sixteenth and late seventeenth centuries, which was primarily concerned with the relationship between a nation's wealth and its balance of foreign trade. The mercantilists recognized the growing power of the national economy and were in favour of the intervention of the state in economic activity to maximize national WEALTH. Partly because the monetary system was very primitive in relation to the growing needs of economic expansion, mercantilist writing was often overburdened with the identification of national wealth with precious metals. However, its leading writers did make important progress in developing economic thought and made significant contributions to the analysis of international trade problems. ◊ MALYNES, G.; MISSELDEN, E,; MUN, T., SERRA, A.

Merchant banks. Institutions that carry out a variety of financial services, including the acceptance of BILLS OF EXCHANGE, the issue and placing of LOANS and SECURITIES, PORTFOLIO and UNIT TRUST management and some BANKING services. Several houses, often through subsidiaries, also provide RISK CAPITAL for small firms, deal in gold BULLION, insurance, HIRE PURCHASE and are active in the market for EUROCURRENCY. Historically, the merchant bankers were merchants dealing in overseas trade who used their knowledge of traders to accept bills of exchange and who developed other banking services connected with foreign trade, e.g. dealing in gold and foreign

CURRENCY and assisting foreign borrowers to raise money in London. In the 1960s and again more recently their most prominent function has been that of advising firms on MERGERS and TAKE-OVERS and other financial matters, and many merchant banks are well known, e.g. Rothschilds, Barings, Hambros, Lazards and Schroders. Merchant banks are also referred to as ISSUING HOUSES, ACCEPTING HOUSES or INVESTMENT TRUSTS in exercising particular functions. The merchant banks' deposits amount to less than 5 per cent of those of the banking system and they are in fact relatively small institutions which pride themselves on their personal, flexible management. There has been a recent trend, especially following the BIG BANG, for merchant banks to join financial CONGLOMERATES, so as to be able to offer a full range of financial services, including retail services.

Merger. The fusion of two or more separate companies into one. In current usage merger is a special case of combination, where both the merging companies wish to join together and do so on roughly equal terms, as distinct from a TAKE-OVER, which occurs against the wishes of one company. However, merger, take-over, amalgamation, absorption and fusion are sometimes all used as synonyms. Where two firms in the same business, i.e. competitors, merge, this is known as horizontal or lateral integration. Where two firms that are suppliers or customers of one another merge, this is known as VERTICAL INTEGRATION. Acquisitions and mergers have been an important cause of increasing CONCENTRATION and some economists have argued that major mergers should be more closely controlled by the authorities, even where they do not threaten to reduce competition directly. This is because pressures to maintain high short-term earnings and hence share prices to avoid the risk of a take-over bid may inhibit investment in research and development. Against this it is argued that mergers are the only way of transferring assets to more capable hands when existing management has proved deficient. In 1986, expenditure on acquisitions of 695 companies totalled £13·5 billion, a record level of recorded merger activity. These acquisitions were financed by: cash, 17·9 per cent of total expenditure; issue of ORDINARY SHARES, 63·8 per cent; and issues of fixed-interest securities, 18·3 per cent. ⟡ CONGLOMERATE; HOLDING COMPANY; REVERSE TAKE-OVER.

Merit goods. A COMMODITY the consumption of which is regarded as socially desirable irrespective of CONSUMERS' PREFERENCE. Governments are readily prepared to suspend CONSUMERS' SOVEREIGNTY by subsidizing the provision of certain goods and services, for example education.

Microeconomics. The study of economics at the level of individual consumers, groups of consumers or firms. No very sharp boundary can be drawn between microeconomics and the other main area of the subject,

MACROECONOMICS, but its broad distinguishing feature is the disaggregated level at which it is developed. The general concern of microeconomics is the efficient allocation of scarce resources between alternative uses (◊ RESOURCE ALLOCATION) but more specifically it involves the determination of PRICE through the optimizing behaviour of economic agents, with consumers maximizing UTILITY and firms maximizing PROFIT. It covers both the behaviour of individual sectors and the way the sectors interact in EQUILIBRIUM and disequilibrium in individual markets. The main areas of microeconomics are: demand theory (◊ DEMAND, THEORY OF); the theory of the firm (◊ FIRM, THEORY OF THE); the demand for labour (◊ LABOUR, DEMAND FOR), and other FACTORS OF PRODUCTION; WELFARE ECONOMICS; and the study of the interactions between markets in GENERAL EQUILIBRIUM THEORY.

Mill, John Stuart (1806–73). John Stuart Mill's childhood was subjected to a regime of severe educational discipline by his father, James Mill. He was acquainted with the major works of economics of the day by the age of twelve, and was correcting the proofs of his father's book, *Elements of Political Economy*, when he was thirteen. He learnt Ricardian economics and Benthamite UTILITARIANISM from his father. In 1823 he joined the East India Company, where he remained for thirty-five years. For three years, before moving to France to spend his retirement, he was a Member of Parliament. He was an extraordinarily prolific writer, especially when it is remembered that he had a full-time job to hold down. His reputation was made by his *A System of Logic, Ratiocinative and Inductive, Being a Connected View of the Principles of Evidence and the Methods of Scientific Investigation*, which was published in 1843. His essay *On Liberty* appeared in 1859, and his *Examination of Sir William Hamiliton's Philosophy in* 1865. His two most important works on economics are *Essays on Some Unsettled Questions of Political Economy* (which came out in 1844, though he actually wrote it in 1829 when he was only twenty-three) and *Principles of Political Economy with Some of Their Applications to Social Philosophy* (1848). The latter was intended to be a comprehensive review of the field of economic theory at the time, and was, in fact, an up-to-date version of ADAM SMITH's *Wealth of Nations*. It succeeded so well that it remained the basic textbook for students of economics until the end of the century. The work is regarded as the apogee of the CLASSICAL SCHOOL of Adam Smith, DAVID RICARDO, T. R. MALTHUS and J.-B. SAY. Mill himself said the book had nothing in it that was original, and indeed it is basically an eclectic work, intended simply to bring together the works of others. However, it is not true to say that Mill lacked originality altogether. He analysed the forces which lead to increasing RETURNS TO SCALE, arguing that as a result there will be a tendency for industries to become more and more concentrated in a few firms. The advantages this gave should be set against the disadvantages that will accrue in the form of higher prices from the loss of competition. Recognition of this tendency led him to support strike action by trade unions. Trade unions were a necessary counterweight to the powerful employer ($\diamond$ GALBRAITH, J. K.). In his exposition of the theory of VALUE, Mill showed how PRICE is determined by the equality of DEMAND and SUPPLY, although he did not demonstrate the relationship by means of graphs or schedules. Mill recognized as a distinct problem the case of COMMODITIES with JOINT COSTS. He showed also how reciprocal demand for each other's products affected countries' TERMS OF TRADE. Mill brought in the idea of ELASTICITY of demand (though the actual expression was invented later by A. MARSHALL) to analyse various alternative trading possibilities. His father had suggested that RENT, being a surplus according to Ricardian theory, was ideally suited to TAXATION. John Stuart took this idea up, and it became quite popular. Mill proposed that all future increases in unearned rents should be taxed ($\diamond$ GEORGE, H.).

Minimum lending rate (M.L.R.). The RATE OF INTEREST at which the CENTRAL BANK lends to the banking system, a term which has the same meaning as BANK RATE. M.L.R. replaced bank rate in 1971 under the new system of COMPETITION AND CREDIT CONTROL. At first M.L.R. was linked to the average discount rate on TREASURY BILLS but since 1978 it has like the bank rate been fixed by administrative decision. Since August 1981 the BANK OF ENGLAND no longer posts a minimum lending rate continuously, although it reserves the right to announce the rate at which it will lend to the DISCOUNT HOUSES should it consider it desirable to do so.

Minimum-wage laws. Legislation prohibiting the paying of wages below some specified level. The aim of such a prohibition is to boost the incomes of the low-paid. Economists, however, frequently doubt the efficacy of this method of income support because it amounts to a form of price control ($\diamond$ PRICES AND INCOMES POLICY). If the minimum wage is set too high, employers may simply decide that they cannot afford to employ as many staff ($\diamond$ LABOUR, DEMAND FOR). If, on the other hand, the minimum wage is set too low, it will not succeed in alleviating POVERTY. In defence of such laws, it has been argued that the demand for labour is in practice very inelastic ($\diamond$ ELASTICITY) and that minimum-wage laws do not give rise to the problem of the POVERTY TRAP.

Minorities, Minority interest. Elements shown in the consolidated accounts of groups of companies where one or more of the SUBSIDIARIES is not wholly owned by the parent. Where a company owns 95 per cent of the ordinary CAPITAL of a subsidiary, for example, and its accounts are consolidated, then the whole of the assets and income of the subsidiary will be included in the consolidated accounts. In showing net assets attributable to shareholders of the parent company, 5 per cent in this case belongs to the minority shareholders and must be deducted. Similarly, in calculating NET INCOME attributable to the same shareholders, earnings will be shown after minority interest.

Mintage. ◊ BRASSAGE.

Mises, Ludwig Edler von (1881–1973). Professor at Vienna University from 1913 until he joined the Graduate Institute of International Studies at Geneva in 1934. In 1940 he left Europe for the U.S.A. and was appointed five years later to a professorial chair at New York University, where he stayed until 1969. His published works include *The Theory of Money and Credit* (1912), *The Free and Prosperous Commonwealth* (1927), *Geldwertstabilisierung und Konjunkturpolitik* (1928), *Bureauracy* (1944), *Omnipotent Government* (1944), *Human Action* (1949), *Theory and History: An Interpretation of Social and Economic Evaluation* (1957) and *The Ultimate Foundation of Economic Science* (1962). Von Mises argued in favour of the PRICE SYSTEM as the most efficient basis of RESOURCE ALLOCATION. A PLANNED ECONOMY must be wasteful, because it lacks a price system and cannot institute such a system without destroying its political principle. He applied the MARGINAL UTILITY theory of the AUSTRIAN SCHOOL to develop a new theory of MONEY, and pointed out that UTILITY could be measured ordinally only and not cardinally (◊ HICKS, J. R.). He also outlined a PURCHASING-POWER PARITY THEORY comparable to that of Gustav Cassel. His TRADE CYCLE theory explained fluctuations in terms of an expansion of bank credit in the upturn which caused a fall in the RATE OF INTEREST and surplus INVESTMENT with a consequent reversal when the MONEY SUPPLY was reduced. ◊ HAWTREY, R. G.; HAYEK, F. A. VON.

Misselden, Edward (1608–54). A leading member of the merchant adventurers and a member of the group of writers referred to as MERCANTILISTS. He argued that international movements of specie and fluctuations in the EXCHANGE RATE depended on international trade flows and not the manipulations of bankers, which was the popular view. He suggested that trading returns should be established for purposes of statistical analysis, so that the state could regulate trade with a view to obtaining EXPORT surpluses.

Mitchell, Wesley Clair (1874–1948). ◊ INSTITUTIONAL ECONOMICS.

Mixed economy. A market economy in which both private and PUBLIC ENTERPRISE participate in economic activity, though not necessarily in all sectors, some of which may be reserved for public MONOPOLY. Mixed ownership of the means of production is, in fact, characteristic of all contemporary economic systems, although private enterprise is heavily circumscribed in communist countries.

Mobility of labour. ⇨ LABOUR, MOBILITY OF.

Mode. ⇨ AVERAGE.

Model. A representation of an economic system, relationship or state, that takes any of a variety of forms. At its most informal, a model can be said to consist of a *verbal description* or *analogy* of some real-world phenomenon. It may take the form of a *diagram* (for example, the graph of the COBWEB theorem), or *a set of equations* setting out the relationship between VARIABLES (CONSUMPTION as a FUNCTION of income, for example). In applied economics, a model is likely to be expressed in a computer PROGRAM or *spread-sheet* in which data (the 'input') are processed and manipulated to produce results (the 'output'). Model-building usually consists of two main stages. The first, inspired by economic reasoning, is to develop the structure of the model – setting out what factors affect which variables. Often, this is as far as construction goes. The second, using ECONOMETRICS, is to estimate the actual strength (⇨ PARAMETERS) of the relationship postulated.

Models have a variety of uses. First, they can illuminate and describe systems clearly by stripping them of all unnecessary complications. Second, computer models in particular are useful for SIMULATION. A variable, such as UNEMPLOYMENT, is defined in terms of the values of a set of other variables, and by simulating a change in these, the effect of different policies on unemployment can be estimated. Third, forecasts of the behaviour of variables can be made, based on past observations. Finally, the specification of models is a prerequisite to the testing of different theories. (⇨ EMPIRICAL TESTING; HYPOTHESIS.)

Modigliani, Franco (b. 1918). Born in Rome, Professor Modigliani studied at the University of Rome. Moving to the U.S.A., he obtained his Ph.D. at the School of Social Research in New York in 1944. He was appointed to a Chair of Economics at the University of Illinois in 1949 and in 1952 to the Chair of Industrial Administration at the Carnegie Institute. Since 1962, he has held the post of Professor of Economics and Finance at the Massachusetts Institute of Technology. Professor Modigliani was awarded the NOBEL PRIZE for Economics in 1985. His many published articles in the professional journals have been assembled in *Collected Papers of Franco Modigliani* (1980). Professor Modigliani has put forward an explanation of the constancy of the aggregate AVERAGE PROPENSITY TO SAVE, in the face of rising incomes in the economy, in terms of the balance between the high savings of the employed work-force and the dissavings of the retired population (⇨ LIFE-CYCLE HYPOTHESIS). He has also contributed to financial economics (⇨ MODIGLIANI–MILLER THEOREM).

Modigliani—Miller theorem. The proposition that the market value of a firm is independent of the way it chooses to finance its investment. If a firm wants to expand, it can choose between three methods of

financing its investment: borrowing, issuing shares and spending profits rather than giving them to shareholders in the form of dividends.
F. MODIGLIANI and M. H. Miller showed that in a perfectly functioning capital market the method of financing which a firm chooses
will ultimately not affect the cost of capital (◊ CAPITAL, COST OF). It
is the risk and expected rate of return of the expanded firm that will
determine how attractive investors find it, not the way the firm raises
the money. (◊ INVESTMENT APPRAISAL; RICARDIAN EQUIV-
ALENCE.)

Monetarism. The name applied to a theory of MACROECONOMICS which
holds that increases in the MONEY SUPPLY are a necessary and sufficient condition for INFLATION. Several strands of thought underlie
this doctrine and distinguish it from its main theoretical antagonist,
KEYNESIAN ECONOMICS (◊ KEYNES, J. M.). Two main beliefs
dominate the monetarist doctrine:

(a) The first is that changes in the money supply have a substantial
    effect on AGGREGATE DEMAND. Two separate reasons are given
    for this. The first is that the demand for money is stable and in-
    sensitive to the RATE OF INTEREST. The second is that the demand
    for goods in the economy, particularly INVESTMENT, is sensitive to
    the interest rate. Together, these determine the monetarists'
    TRANSMISSION MECHANISM, the way in which increases in the
    money stock affect spending in the economy. Under the monetarist
    account, if the authorities printed some crisp ten-pound notes and
    dropped them over the country from a helicopter, people would find
    they had more cash in this liquid form (◊ LIQUIDITY; LIQUIDITY
    PREFERENCE) than they wanted. They would therefore spend
    much of the cash on goods and services, increasing aggregate
    demand. To raise the demand for money to match the remaining
    excess supply, the interest rate would fall a little (because the money
    invested in interest-yielding assets would drive up their price and
    drive down their rate of return). Even the smallest cut in interest
    rates, they argue, would cause a large increase in investment, again
    boosting aggregate demand. If the monetarist is wrong, the heli-
    copter money would not be spent at all, but invested in financial
    assets. The interest rate would fall a great deal, but if investment is
    insensitive to interest rates, this would have no effect on the demand
    for goods. In effect, all that happens from expanding the money
    supply is that interest rates drop, and people hold more cash, without
    spending it, implying that the speed with which cash circulates has
    slowed down to offset the extra cash (◊ VELOCITY OF CIRCU-
    LATION).

(b) The second tenet of monetarism is that any change in aggregate
    demand the government succeeds in bringing about will manifest

itself in the long run in higher prices and not higher output ($\Diamond$ FISCAL POLICY; MONETARY POLICY). The economy will tend to an equilibrium position with all markets clearing: all that money can do is raise all prices equally, leaving all relative prices constant ($\Diamond$ NEUTRALITY OF MONEY). Increases in the stock of money can, however, have a short-term effect on the economy but only as long as people fail to anticipate price rises ($\Diamond$ HUME, D.). Once inflation is built into people's expectations, increases in the money supply only result in increases in the level of prices. This process could even be extremely fast if people have RATIONAL EXPECTATIONS.

In terms of the QUANTITY THEORY OF MONEY, of which monetarism can be seen as a revival, the above propositions are equivalent to holding that the velocity of circulation of money and the level of output are EXOGENOUS, and fixed independently of the money stock. Monetarism advocates SUPPLY-SIDE ECONOMICS; and denies a role for STABIL-IZATION POLICY. Instead, greatest stability can be achieved by adhering to a rule for money-supply growth in line with the growth of real output ($\Diamond$ REAL TERMS). The emergence of monetarism in the 1960s and among policy-makers in the 1970s can mainly be attributed to M. FRIEDMAN. $\Diamond$ ECONOMIC DOCTRINES.

Monetary base. The stock of an economy's most liquid financial assets ($\Diamond$ LIQUIDITY). The monetary base is usually taken as the stock of notes and coins. It has often been suggested that the MONEY SUPPLY as a whole could be controlled by strict rationing of the monetary base. However, the volume of notes and coins has been considered too small a proportion of the total volume of money to be a solid enough target.

Monetary compensatory amounts. $\Diamond$ GREEN CURRENCY.

Monetary policy. Central government policy with respect to the quantity of money ($\Diamond$ QUANTITY THEORY OF MONEY) in the economy, the RATE OF INTEREST and the EXCHANGE RATE. The importance of monetary policy is much disputed – MONETARISM as a doctrine holds that it is the determinant of aggregate demand, in the short run. J. M. KEYNES on the other hand held that FISCAL POLICY is important, and that monetary policy matters only in as far as it affects fiscal variables, like the PUBLIC-SECTOR BORROWING REQUIREMENT.

In deciding on how to conduct monetary policy, the authori-ties must make a number of decisions. The first is whether to target any VARIABLE or not: MONEY SUPPLY, interest rate, or the exchange rate. If no target is chosen, monetary policy becomes a matter of daily judgement about the manipulation of several variables. Monetarists have supported the targeting of variables, believing that by adhering to rules as opposed to using discretion, the authorities en-gender stability. The second issue is which variable to target: it is not possible to set up targets individually for the money supply, the exchange rate and interest rates because the three are simultaneously determined. If the money supply is increased, for example, the exchange rate tends to fall unless interest rates are raised. To target or stabilize one variable implies one other must be an instrument by which the first can be controlled.

Exchange-rate targets, such as those existing for members of the EUROPEAN MONETARY SYSTEM, encourage trade by reducing the risk of exchange-rate fluctuations. Interest-rate targets can encourage INVESTMENT by stabilizing the cost of borrowing, while targeting money supply, it is argued, can have an impact on inflationary expectations, and hence on wage demands (⋄ INFLATION). ⋄ CREDIT CONTROL.

Monetary sector (U.K.). Defined by the BANK OF ENGLAND to include its own banking department, the RETAIL BANKS, ACCEPTING HOUSES, other British and foreign banks and the DISCOUNT HOUSES. Other FINANCIAL INTERMEDIARIES such as the BUILDING SOCIETIES, insurance companies and PENSION FUNDS are not counted as part of the monetary sector.

Money. Something which is widely accepted in payment for goods and services and in settling DEBTS. In primitive economies, goods and services were exchanged wholly through BARTER. Exchanging goods for one another or using property (cows, sheep) as money was cumbersome and inconvenient and inhibited the DIVISION OF LABOUR. Later, coins made of valuable metals came into use as intermediate commodities, but in the modern economy BANKNOTES and coins have little or no intrinsic value, while BANK DEPOSITS are simply book entries (⋄ BANKING): their use as money depends upon confidence that they can be exchanged for things of value. In addition to its use as a medium of exchange, money acts as a store of value, making SAVING convenient, a measure of value (or unit of account) and as a standard of deferred payments which facilitates the granting of CREDIT, though all these functions can be threatened by INFLATION, ⋄ MONEY SUPPLY; TRANSACTIONS MOTIVE.

Money, demand for. ⋄ LIQUIDITY PREFERENCE.

Money, inactive. ⋄ INACTIVE MONEY.

Money, neutrality of. ⋄ NEUTRALITY OF MONEY.

Money, superneutrality of. ⋄ SUPERNEUTRALITY OF MONEY.

Money at call and short notice. In Britain, MONEY loaned to the DISCOUNT HOUSES, i.e. to the MONEY MARKET, on a short-term basis by the COMMERCIAL BANKS. These LOANS are regarded as part of the LIQUID assets of the banks because they can be withdrawn immediately or at periods of notice of up to fourteen days. They also include overnight loans. The terms of the loans vary, and in practice the money may not be called in for long periods. The discount houses use the money to purchase TREASURY BILLS and other short-term paper, so that the call-money rate is normally always below the treasury bills rate. If the banks do call in their loans, then the discount houses may be forced to borrow from the BANK OF ENGLAND. The commercial banks are willing to loan their liquid funds to the money market in this way, because they know that the Bank of England will act as a LENDER OF LAST RESORT. In most other countries the major commercial banks invest directly in short-term paper and have direct access to the CENTRAL BANK for loans (e.g. ⟡ FEDERAL RESERVE SYSTEM).

Money illusion. If someone's salary is increased by 10 per cent over a period when consumer prices have risen by 20 per cent, he is suffering from money illusion if he thinks he is better off in REAL TERMS. Money illusion is the confusion of changes in money values and changes in real values.

Money in circulation. MONEY in use to finance current transactions as distinct from idle money (⟡ INACTIVE MONEY).

Money market. The financial institutions that deal in short-term SECURITIES and LOANS, gold and FOREIGN EXCHANGE. MONEY has a 'time value', and therefore the use of it is bought and sold against payment of INTEREST. Short-term money is bought and sold on the MONEY MARKET, and long-term money on the CAPITAL MARKET. Neither the money market nor the capital market exists in one physical location. In the money market most transactions are, in fact, made by telephone or telex. In Britain the money market sometimes refers only to the DISCOUNT HOUSES and the COMMERCIAL BANKS dealing in TREASURY BILLS, BILLS OF EXCHANGE and MONEY AT CALL, with the BANK OF ENGLAND acting as LENDER OF LAST RESORT (⟡ DISCOUNT MARKET). In a wider context, the money market also includes PARALLEL MONEY MARKETS, the FOREIGN-EXCHANGE MARKET and the BULLION market.

Money supply. The stock of liquid assets in an economy which can freely be exchanged for goods or services. Money supply is a phrase that can describe anything from notes and coins, alone, to the sum of all cash plus bank deposits, because by writing cheques, individuals exchange bank deposits for goods or services. There is a spectrum of assets of different LIQUIDITY in the economy, and any degree of liquidity may be chosen to define an asset as money. A set of very liquid assets is known as narrow money. A set includes also less liquid assets, known as *broad money*. In general, the wider the definition, the harder it is for the authorities to control the money supply, but the more direct the relationship between money supply and other economic variables. For example, the quantity of notes and coins in the economy, a narrow definition, is easy to control, but is of little importance in influencing the spending of individuals.

In the U.K., several definitions of money supply are used. 'M0' is the stock of notes and coins in circulation. 'M1' is M0 plus the value of bank (⟡ BANKING) current accounts. 'M2' is M1 plus some deposit or interest-bearing bank accounts. 'Sterling M3' is M2 plus the remaining, mostly very large, deposit accounts. Finally, another well-used measure is 'PSL2' which adds most building-society deposits to Sterling M3. At times of rapid financial innovation or change, particular definitions can exhibit rather erratic behaviour, compounding the problems of control and interpretation of the money supply. (⟡ CREDIT CONTROL; DOMESTIC CREDIT EXPANSION; MONETARY POLICY.)

Money terms. ⟡ REAL TERMS.

Monopolies Commission. A U.K. commission set up by the Monopolies and Restrictive Practices (Inquiry and Control) Act of 1948. Under this Act, the commission was given the necessary powers to obtain any information it needed to investigate monopolies referred to it by the Board of Trade. MONOPOLY was defined in a broad way to include any firm which controlled more than one-third of the MARKET, and the commission was required to judge them in the light of the public interest. The commission's report in 1955, *Collective Discrimination – A Report on Exclusive Dealing, Aggregated Rebates and Other Discriminatory Trade Practices,* was the basis for the RESTRICTIVE TRADE PRACTICES ACT of 1956, which set up a register for collective agreements and a Restrictive Practices Court. The commission's powers were widened by the Monopolies and Mergers Act of 1965. MERGERS between firms in a monopoly situation or over a certain size could be referred to the commission by the Board of Trade (later the Department of Trade and Industry) and also firms in the service industries which had previously been exempt. The Acts of 1948 and 1965 were repealed by the FAIR TRADING ACT of 1973. Under the latter, the commission became the 'Monopolies and Mergers Commission' and the Director-General of Fair Trading was empowered to make references, in addition to the minister. The powers of the Office of Fair Trading were widened by the COMPETITION ACT (1980). As a consequence, any activity considered by the O.F.T. to be anti-competitive could be referred to the commission (⟡ MONOPOLISTIC (IMPERFECT) COMPETITION.)

Monopolistic (imperfect) competition. An industry in which there are many competing firms each producing products that are close SUBSTITUTES. Three features characterize such an industry. First, the firms make products between which consumers slightly differentiate (they may have different-coloured packets, for example) and consequently, the demand for any individual firm's product is not perfectly elastic (⟡ ELASTICITY). Some consumers will prefer it to those of its competitors, sufficiently to exhibit a limited amount of loyalty to that brand when its price rises. This means that each firm has a small amount of monopoly power

279

($\diamond$ MONOPOLY) and is thus not a price-taker in the market for its own product ($\diamond\!\!\!\diamond$ PERFECT COMPETITION). In this regard it is similar to a monopoly, but not a perfect competitor. The second feature is that firms are able to enter the industry if the level of PROFITS is attractive. This is a feature shared with the perfectly competitive industry, but not the monopoly. Thirdly, like both perfectly competitive and monopolistic firms, producers in monopolistic competition are assumed to maximize profits.

In monopolistic competition, firms set output to equate MARGINAL COST and MARGINAL REVENUE. Price at the specified output is determined by the firm's demand. Profits are zero in the long term, on account of entry occurring whenever they are positive, driving up SUPPLY in the industry and cutting the DEMAND for each company's product. While it shares this with perfect competition, its output will be rather lower than it would be under perfect competition, and its price above marginal cost and thus rather higher. Moreover, production will not take place at the lowest cost point as it does under perfect competition. Each firm operates with some EXCESS CAPACITY. The theory of such markets, which lie between monopoly and perfect competition, was simultaneously developed by E. H. CHAMBERLIN in the U.S.A. and J. V. ROBINSON in Britain.

Monopoly. A market in which there is only one supplier. Three features characterize the market. First, the firm in it is motivated by PROFITS. Secondly, it stands alone and barriers prevent new firms from entering the industry ($\diamond$ BARRIERS TO ENTRY); and thirdly, the actions of the monopolist itself affect the market price of its output ($\diamond$ MARGINAL REVENUE) – it is not a price-taker ($\diamond$ BILATERAL MONOPOLY). The *output* of the monopolist will be set at the point at which MARGINAL REVENUE is equated with MARGINAL COST. If marginal revenue were any higher it would pay the monopolist to increase production because the additional costs generated would be lower than the revenue, and profits would rise. The reverse would be true if marginal revenue were any lower than marginal cost. ($\diamond\!\!\!\diamond$ MARGINAL-COST PRICING.) The price of the monopolist is determined by DEMAND as the firm cannot set both output and price. For its chosen output, the monopolist can read price off a market DEMAND CURVE, which will lie above the marginal revenue curve.

The monopoly will make profits in excess of those merely necessary to keep in business, and no pressure exists for price to fall and reduce these. Theory suggests that under monopoly, prices are higher and output lower than they would be under PERFECT COMPETITION. The power of the monopolist derives from the fact that demand for his product is not perfectly elastic ($\diamond\!\!\!\diamond$ ELASTICITY), so that when price rises, sales largely hold up. This is not so for a perfect competitor, who will sell nothing if he raises his price even a fraction above the going rate. The degree of *monopoly power* a firm enjoys can be measured by how inelastic demand for its product is. The more inelastic demand is, the more the monopoly can raise its prices without losing sales.

Monopoly is inefficient because, under it, price will be higher than marginal cost, so that even if some consumers value an item more than it costs to make, they may not choose to buy it (◊ CONSUMER SURPLUS). Moreover, in the long term there is no tendency for costs to be at their lowest possible level, because the pressure of more efficient, incoming competitors does not exist. It is not surprising given these results that most nations choose to control monopolies, which are usually defined as any firm dominant in a particular industry (for example, with a market share in excess of 25 per cent). However, in some industries, efficient production requires a single dominant supplier (◊ ECONOMIES OF SCALE; NATURAL MONOPOLY).

Monopoly, discriminating. A MONOPOLY that charges different prices for the same product to different consumers. (◊ PRICE DISCRIMINATION.)

Monopsony. A market in which there is only one buyer of the item sold. Unlike individual consumers in most markets, a monopsonist will have an impact on the market price. When he purchases an extra unit of the item, market demand perceptibly increases and the market price rises. This means that to buy one extra item costs the monopsonist not only the price of that item, but also the extra price that has to be paid for all the items that were previously being bought at the lower price.

Monte Carlo method. A technique for estimating PROBABILITIES. The method involves the construction of a MODEL and the SIMULATION of the outcome of an activity a large number of times. Probabilities are then estimated from an analysis of the range of outcomes from the model.

Mortgage. A legal agreement conveying conditional ownership of ASSETS as SECURITY for a LOAN and becoming void when the DEBT is repaid. BUILDING SOCIETIES and INSURANCE companies (*mortgagees*) loan a proportion of the purchase PRICE of houses to individuals or companies (*mortgagors*), the property being mortgaged to the lender until the loan is repaid.

Mortgage debenture. ◊ DEBENTURE.

Most-favoured nation clause. The clause in an international trade treaty under which the signatories promise to extend to each other any favourable trading terms offered in subsequent agreements to third parties. ◊ GENERAL AGREEMENT ON TARIFFS AND TRADE.

Moving average. A TIME SERIES derived from another by the calculation of a sequence of AVERAGES. The averages are calculated in sequence from a consecutive group in the series; for each average, the next value in the series is added and the earliest value in the group is dropped. The number of values in the group to be averaged may be two or more, depending on the time series from which they are to be derived. Moving averages are calculated to eliminate seasonal variations from a series and to highlight the longer-term trends in the series.

Multicollinearity. CORRELATION between the INDEPENDENT VARIABLES in a regression ($\diamondsuit$ REGRESSION ANALYSIS) equation. If such correlation exists, the application of LEAST-SQUARES REGRESSION for estimation of the parameters in an equation is inadmissible because it contradicts the assumptions upon which the technique is based.

Multilateralism. INTERNATIONAL TRADE and exchange between more than two countries without discrimination between those involved. In contrast to BILATERALISM. $\diamondsuit$ GENERAL AGREEMENT ON TARIFFS AND TRADE; MOST-FAVOURED NATION CLAUSE.

Multinational corporation (M.N.C., M.N.E.). A company, or more correctly an ENTERPRISE, operating in a number of countries and having production or service facilities outside the country of its origin. A commonly accepted definition of an M.N.E. is an enterprise producing at least 25 per cent of its world output outside its country of origin. There are over 10,000 corporations with direct investments outside their headquarters country, with over 80,000 affiliates over which they have effective control, but fewer than 500 M.N.E.s account for three-quarters of foreign affiliates and only 200 of these derive 25 per cent or more of their sales from foreign activities. The multinational corporation takes its principal decisions in a global context and thus often outside the countries in which it has particular operations. The rapid growth of these corporations since the Second World War and the possibility that conflicts might arise between their interests and those of the individual countries in which they operate has provoked much discussion among economists in recent years. M.N.E.s possibly account for one-quarter of world trade, but earlier fears that they would come to dominate the world economy now seem misplaced. Also called *international companies* and *transnational corporations*.

Multi-plant operations. Firms which produce at more than one plant or location. Most small firms operate from a single establishment. Large firms serving a national market, for example in the brewing industry, may find that lower transport costs to the final consumer from multiple plants outweigh the ECONOMIES OF SCALE in a single large plant. $\diamondsuit$ ENTERPRISE.)

Multiple correlation coefficient. A statistical measure of the accuracy by which a known VARIABLE is estimated by an equation, or MODEL, containing two or more INDEPENDENT VARIABLES ($\diamondsuit$ CORRELATION). It can take values between zero and unity. At zero, there is no correspondence at all between the predicted and actual variable, and at unity the coefficient indicates a perfect correspondence.

Also called the *coefficient of determination* (◊ PARTIAL CORRELATION; REGRESSION).

Multiple exchange rates. ◊ EXCHANGE RATE.

Multiplier. The multiplier is defined as the increase in NATIONAL INCOME divided by the increase in expenditure generating that increase in income. In simple models, the size of the multiplier depends on the MARGINAL PROPENSITY TO CONSUME. For example, if the government increased its investment expenditure by £100, this sum would be paid out in wages, salaries and profits of the suppliers. The households and firms receiving these incomes and profits will, in turn, save a proportion and spend the remainder. These expenditures will in turn again generate further incomes and profits and so on. At each round, therefore, a proportion of receipts will be paid and a proportion spent, the latter being the *marginal propensity to consume*, denoted, say, by c. We have, therefore:

	Expenditure	Saving
Round 1	£100	
2	£100c	£100$(1 - c)$
3	£100c^2	£100$(1 - c)^2$
$\vdots$	$\vdots$	$\vdots$
n	£100c^n	£100$(1 - c)^n$

and, therefore, the total increase in national income generated by the £100 is the sum of the infinite number of expenditures:

$$£100 + £100c + £100c^2 + £100c^3 + \cdots £100c^n$$
$$= £100(1 + c + c^2 + c^3 + \cdots c^n)$$

This series is the sum of a GEOMETRIC PROGRESSION whose sum can be shown to be equal to £100$[(1 - c^n)(1 - c)]$. The marginal propensity to consume is less than unity, so that as n gets larger, c^n becomes smaller. Therefore, the series converges to £100$/(1 - c)$ and the multiplier is, therefore, equal to $1/(1 - c)$ or $1/s$, where s is the marginal propensity to save. ◊ ACCELERATOR–MULTIPLIER MODEL; KEYNES, J. M.

Multi-product firm. A business producing two or more different COMMODITIES or products. Most large firms produce more than one product and are often engaged in more than one industry (◊ DIVERSIFICATION), although for simplicity the basic theory of the firm (◊ FIRM, THEORY OF THE) is couched in terms of a single-product firm.

Mun, Sir Thomas (1571–1641). An English mercantilist (◊ MERCANTILISM) and a director of the East India Company. His publications include *Discourse of Trade from England unto the East Indies* (1621) and

England's Treasure of Forraign Trade (1664). He attacked the idea that
EXPORTS OF BULLION should be completely prohibited and other
restrictions put on trade, pointing out that restrictions on trade invited
retaliation in foreign MARKETS and raised domestic PRICES. He did
emphasize, however, that an export surplus should be sought in the
BALANCE OF TRADE for the country as a whole, although it was unnecessary to seek to achieve this with each trading partner.

Mutual company. A company without ISSUED CAPITAL owned by
those members that do business with it. The PROFITS of a mutual
company, after deductions for reserves, are shared out among members. Some SAVINGS BANKS and INSURANCE companies, e.g. Standard
Life, are mutual companies. In the U.S.A. the term 'mutual' is also used
to refer to open-ended TRUSTS or *mutual funds*, which correspond to
UNIT TRUSTS in the U.K.

Mutual funds. ◊ MUTUAL COMPANY.

Mutual Security Agency. ◊ ECONOMIC COOPERATION ADMINISTRA-
TION.

Myrdal, Gunnar Karl (1898–1987). Born in Sweden, Professor Myrdal
graduated in law at Stockholm University in 1923. After a period in
private practice he obtained a degree in economics in 1927 and took a
post as lecturer in political economy at Stockholm University, eventually
succeeding GUSTAV CASSEL to the Chair of Political Economy and
Financial Science in 1933. From 1936 to 1938 he was a Member of
Parliament as a Social Democrat. After a period as Economic Adviser
to the Swedish legation in the U.S.A., he was appointed Minister of
Commerce in the Swedish government, a post he held from 1945 to
1947. He resigned from this post to become Secretary-General of the
U.N. Economic Commission for Europe at Geneva, where he stayed
until 1957. In 1957 he was appointed Professor at the Institute for
International Economic Studies of Stockholm University and in 1974
was awarded the Alfred Nobel Memorial Prize (◊ NOBEL PRIZE) in
Economics jointly with F. A. VON HAYEK. His published work includes
Price Formation under Changeability (1927), *Vetenskap och Politik i
Nationalekonomin* (1929), *Om Penningteoretisk Jamvikt* (1931), *An
American Dilemma* (1944), *Economic Theory and Underdeveloped Re-
gions* (1957), *Value in Social Theory* (1958), *Beyond the Welfare State*
(1960), *Challenge to Affluence* (1963), *Asian Drama: An Inquiry into the
Poverty of Nations* (1968), *Objectivity in Social Research* (1969), *The
Challenge of World Poverty* (1970) and *Against the Stream – Critical
Essays in Economics* (1973).

Professor Myrdal invented the terms and formulated the distinction
between EX ANTE and EX POST, in particular in relation to the equality
of aggregate savings and investment in equilibrium. He emphasized the
need to study the dynamics of MACROECONOMIC processes. His book

Monetary Equilibrium, published in 1931, which developed the economics of K. WICKSELL, foreshadowed many aspects of J. M. KEYNES's *General Theory*. In recent years, he argued that economists should accept the need to make explicit value judgements, without which their theoretical structures are unrealistic. He became an advocate of INSTITUTIONAL ECONOMICS. Professor Myrdal believed that such a framework was necessary in any economic studies of the DEVELOPING COUNTRIES.

N

Nash equilibrium. A concept central to GAME THEORY. It applies to the situation when all the participants in a game are each pursuing their best possible strategy in the knowledge of the strategies of all other participants. A game is any situation in which there are participants, rules of conduct and pay-offs. One might imagine a simple game in a two-person country where both the people have to decide the side of the road on which to drive. The pay-offs are either 'no crash' (when both drive on the left or right) or 'crash' (when one drives on the left and the other on the right). In this situation, two possible Nash equilibria exist: either both driving on the left, or both driving on the right. If one drives on the left and the other on the right, it is not a Nash equilibrium because, given the choice of the other, each would change their own policy. Popular examples of Nash equilibria arise in HOTELLING'S LAW and the PRISONER'S DILEMMA. ⟡ EQUILIBRIUM.

National accounts. ⟡ SOCIAL ACCOUNTING.

National Association of Securities Dealers Automated Quotations system (N.A.S.D.A.Q.) (U.S.). ⟡ OVER-THE-COUNTER MARKET.

National debt. The total outstanding borrowings of the central government EXCHEQUER. Some definitions may include the debt of the whole public sector, including the NATIONALIZED INDUSTRIES, local authorities, etc. Until 1968 the debt was transacted through the CONSOLIDATED FUND but it now appears in the NATIONAL LOANS FUND. The National Debt Commissioners and the National Investment and Loans Office (⟡ PUBLIC WORKS LOAN BOARD) have certain responsibilities towards the debt. The size of the national debt grew as a result of expenditure incurred in various wars ('deadweight debt') and more recently in nationalization and other forms of government expenditure, including overseas borrowing to influence the BALANCE OF PAYMENTS and to support the EXCHANGE RATE. The national debt as a proportion of the GROSS DOMESTIC PRODUCT declined almost continuously from 1945 until 1975 and has since stabilized at around 40–45 per cent, though it was larger than the G.D.P. until the early 1960s. 78 per cent of sterling market holdings of the national debt consists of government and government-guaranteed stock, 15 per cent consists of national savings (⟡ NATIONAL SAVINGS, DEPARTMENT FOR). The table shows the amount of the national debt and the holders. Much of the debt is held by government agencies, so that the net national debt, which excludes debt held by government, is much lower than the gross debt.

Market and official holdings of national debt.
Amounts outstanding at 31 March 1986

	£m.
Public corporations and local authorities	1·1
MONETARY SECTOR	9·0
Other financial institutions	79·2
Overseas residents	16·0
Individuals and private trusts	36·1
Other	13·2
Total market holdings	154·6
Official holdings	13·1
Total sterling debt	167·7
Foreign currency debt	3·9
Total	171·6

Source: *Bank of England Quarterly Bulletin.*

The national debt can be divided into three categories:

(a) FUNDED DEBT, that is, UNREDEEMABLE SECURITIES. This is now only a very small part of the total.

(b) FLOATING DEBT, which in this context refers to short-term borrowings such as TREASURY BILLS and WAYS AND MEANS ADVANCES.

(c) Other unfunded debt. This is the largest item of all, accounting for about three-quarters of the total. It includes principally DATED SECURITIES, some of which are repayable in external currencies such as dollar liabilities, but also non-marketable securities such as National Savings Certificates, DEFENCE BONDS and PREMIUM SAVINGS BONDS.

The national debt is of great importance in the financial system of the private sector and plays quite an important role in the interdepartmental accounting of government. Government securities provide convenient investments for INSURANCE companies, for example, and these securities form an important part of the reserve assets of banks and other financial institutions. Although it is spoken of as a burden, the interest paid on the national debt held by U.K. residents is not a burden on the nation as a whole since the interest payments are actually transfers between those residents who pay taxation and those who also receive the interest. The national debt is a 'stock' variable, in contrast to the PUBLIC-SECTOR BORROWING REQUIREMENT, which represents a 'flow' of borrowing each year. ◊ BALANCED BUDGET.

National Economic Development Council (N.E.D.C.). A council set up by the U.K. government in 1962 and known colloquially as 'Neddy'. The Chancellor of the EXCHEQUER is the chairman and the other members of the council are made up of representatives from industry and the trade unions. The council is supported by a secretariat (National Economic Development Office) (N.E.D.O.). In 1964 the first Economic Development Committee ('little Neddy') was set up. These committees investigate the economic problems of specific industries or services.

National Economic Development Office (N.E.D.O.). ◊ NATIONAL ECONOMIC DEVELOPMENT COUNCIL.

National Enterprise Board (N.E.B.). A statutory corporation set up under the 1975 Industry Act. The principal task of the board is to promote industrial efficiency, international competitiveness and employment in the U.K. by assisting existing enterprises, establishing new ones and stimulating reorganization. The N.E.B. has a number of wider responsibilities, including the promotion of INDUSTRIAL DEMOCRACY, in the undertakings which it controls. The board acts as a commercial undertaking and is subject to fair-trading legislation (◊ FAIR TRADING ACT). It is expected to earn an adequate return on capital employed. It can buy, hold and dispose of securities, form enterprises, borrow, make loans and give guarantees. The N.E.B. has no powers of compulsory acquisition. It is required to inform the Secretary of State for Industry before acquiring more than 10 per cent of the voting share capital of a company without the agreement of the directors of that company, or where the cost of acquiring share capital exceeds a specified minimum, or where the acquisition would give the board 30 per cent or more of the voting rights. Since 1981 it has operated with the NATIONAL RESEARCH DEVELOPMENT CORPORATION, within the British Technology Group. (◊ INDUSTRY ACTS.)

National Girobank. A bank established within the Post Office in 1968. The Girobank provides a CREDIT TRANSFER service, current accounts, deposit accounts and personal loan facilities. It has almost two million accounts, though much of its business depends upon the Department of Health and Social Security for whom it makes large numbers of social-security payments.

National income. The total incomes of residents of an economy in a given period after providing for CAPITAL CONSUMPTION. Also referred to as *net national product at factor cost* (◊ FACTOR COST). Incomes in this calculation will include all payments for the use of the FACTORS OF PRODUCTION, i.e. wages, salaries, PROFITS (i.e. DIVIDENDS and retained profits), RENTS and net income from abroad but excluding TRANSFER PAYMENTS. The national income may be calculated in this way, or as the sum of VALUE ADDED in all sectors of the economy at factor cost, or as the sum of expenditure on final consumption and

INVESTMENT GOODS, plus EXPORTS and minus IMPORTS. These three methods should, in theory, yield the same figure since all incomes should equal total expenditure plus net SAVING or INVESTMENT, which in turn should also equal the value of output. (Provided output is defined as value added, i.e. intermediate expenditure is excluded.) In practice, each of the three methods involves estimation and the totals never agree exactly, so an averaging procedure is often used. Comparisons of output and expenditure will be affected, among other things, by the extent of evasion (◊ BLACK ECONOMY).

National income before capital consumption is equal to the GROSS NATIONAL PRODUCT and if net income from abroad is also excluded it is equal to the GROSS DOMESTIC PRODUCT.

National income or other aggregates from the national accounts are regarded as an indicator of welfare in the market economy but they are not unambiguous in this respect. (◊ INCOME DISTRIBUTION). One reason is that some activities which contribute to welfare are not included because they are not valued in markets, for example the services of housewives, and EXTERNALITIES may not be taken into account. Comparisons between the national incomes of various countries are subject to many qualifications: the distribution of income will differ and so too may methods of estimation; moreover, the exchange rates used may not reflect purchasing-power parities (◊ PURCHASING-POWER PARITY THEORY).

National Insurance. A social-security scheme in the U.K. which provides UNEMPLOYMENT benefit, sickness benefit, flat-rate pensions, maternity benefits, children's allowances and other grants or benefits on widowhood, incapacity or death in return for regular contributions paid by employees, employers and others. The National Insurance Scheme in force from 1948 to 1975 differed in a number of ways from that introduced in the Social Security Act 1975. The 1975 Act also discontinued the Graduated Pension Scheme, which provided an earnings-related supplement to the flat-rate pension. This was replaced by a new earnings-related pension scheme from April 1978 (State Earnings Related Pension Scheme (S.E.R.P.S.). Under the previous National Insurance Scheme contributions were paid at a flat rate by affixing stamps to an insurance card. Under the new scheme both employers' and employees' contributions are earnings-related (so-called Class 1 contributions) within a fixed band of earnings and are collected through the PAY-AS-YOU-EARN system. Self-employed persons pay a flat-rate contribution but, in addition, pay contributions based upon earnings (Class 4 contributions). National insurance contributions accounted for almost 18 per cent of total tax receipts in 1985 and in that year the government announced plans for a major reform of the system, including the abolition of the earnings-related scheme and the introduction of 'portable pensions'. ◊ PERSONAL PENSION.

National Insurance Fund. ◊ CONSOLIDATED FUND.

National Investment and Loans Office. ◊ PUBLIC WORKS LOAN BOARD.

National Loans Fund. A government account opened in 1968 for the domestic lending of government and all the transactions relating to the NATIONAL DEBT. The *payments* of the Fund include interest, management and expenses of the national debt, deficit on the CONSOLIDATED FUND and loans to the nationalized industries and public corporations, local authorities and the private sector. *Receipts* include interest on loans, profits of the Issue Department of the BANK OF ENGLAND, interest transfer from the Consolidated Fund and borrowings.

National product. ◊ NATIONAL INCOME.

National Research Development Corporation (N.R.D.C.). A body set up in the U.K. by the Development of Inventions Act 1948 to stimulate innovation, provide funds for private inventors and to hold or dispose of the rights of inventions resulting from public research. Part of the British Technology Group which also includes the NATIONAL ENTERPRISE BOARD.

National Savings, Department for (D.N.S.). Government department responsible to Treasury ministers for the administration of government savings schemes. Its responsibilities include the NATIONAL SAVINGS BANK, SAVINGS CERTIFICATES. PREMIUM SAVINGS BONDS, SAVE-AS-YOU-EARN and a selection of GILT-EDGED SECURITIES held on the National Savings Stock Register and available for purchase through post offices.

National Savings Bank (N.S.B.). A SAVINGS BANK administered by the D.N.S. (◊ NATIONAL SAVINGS, DEPARTMENT FOR) and operating through the post-office network. The N.S.B. provides a deposit-taking and withdrawal service through two types of account: ordinary accounts, on which interest is paid and from which withdrawals may be made on demand (up to £50), and investment accounts, which offer a higher rate of interest, though withdrawals require one month's notice. Interest on deposits in ordinary accounts is tax-free up to a limit of £70 a year. The N.S.B. has some 15 million active accounts. It was formerly called the Post Office Savings Bank (P.O.S.B.).

National Savings Certificates. A BOND issued by the government (NATIONAL SAVINGS, DEPARTMENT FOR). There have been some thirty-one different issues of these certificates on which interest, an index-linked increase (◊ INDEXATION) or a bonus are payable on MATURITY or earlier. The certificates can be encashed at any time and interest is tax-free.

Nationalized industries. State-owned enterprises in the market economy, such as the provision of postal services, as distinct from state activity in PUBLIC GOODS such as health services. In Britain, most of nationalized industry is literally private industry that was taken into public ownership, i.e. nationalized; for example, British Steel, British Leyland (now the Rover Group) and Rolls-Royce. In the U.K. as in other European countries most of the public utilities, electricity, water, coal, transport and communications undertakings are, or were, in state ownership, although several countries, led by Britain, have recently begun a programme of denationalization (⧠ PRIVATIZATION). Public ownership of industry is less usual in the United States.

The growth of nationalization largely began after the Second World War. The general requirement then was that nationalized industries should break even taking one year with another. In 1967 rate-of-return criteria with specific reference to appropriate techniques for INVESTMENT APPRAISAL and the desirability of MARGINAL COST PRICING were laid down with an intended policy of providing SUBSIDIES for 'non-economic' but socially desirable services, such as railway lines or postal services in remote areas. The efficiency of nationalized industries attracted increasing attention in the 1950s and 1960s. In 1965 they became subject to the scrutiny of the National Board for Prices and Incomes and subsequently by the Office of Fair Trading (⧠ FAIR TRADING ACT) and the MONOPOLIES COMMISSION. Nationalized industries have always been a subject of controversy in Britain: the steel industry was nationalized in 1951, denationalized in 1953 and renationalized in 1967. The heads of these industries have often complained of political interference, for example in the interests of broader MACROECONOMIC objectives. Whatever the relative merits of state versus private enterprise, some form of REGULATION in many nationalized industries is inevitable given their economic importance and MONOPOLY powers.

Natural monopoly. An industry in which technical factors preclude the efficient existence of more than one producer (⧠ MONOPOLY). Examples are the public utilities such as water, gas and electricity, where there is a requirement for a network of pipes or cables. In order to derive the efficient (⧠ ECONOMIC EFFICIENCY) results of PERFECT COMPETITION from a market which is necessarily monopolistic various suggestions of control have been made: notably, government regulation if the firm is in private ownership, PUBLIC OWNERSHIP and FRANCHISING. Under any of these, control is enhanced if the monopoly can be regionally divided, allowing performance comparison between different regions. Alternatively, licensing arrangements can be set up so that a dominant supplier runs a network (e.g. pipes or cables), but is obliged to lease the use of it to competing suppliers. (⧠ PRIVATIZATION.)

Natural rate of growth. ⧠ GROWTH THEORY; HARROD–DOMAR MODEL.

Natural resources. Commodities or assets with some economic VALUE which do not exist as a result of any effort of mankind. The value they have is usually only realized, however, when they are exploited by man's labour, that is, dug out of the ground, processed or refined. Natural resources are a necessary ingredient of all economic activity. Natural resources can be of three types. The first are *non-renewable*, like oil and coal, stocks of which will eventually run out ($\diamond$ DEPLETION THEORY). The second are *renewable*, like water and fish, which are reproduceable. The third are *non-expendable*: they are not used up in the consumption process. An example is a landscape of outstanding beauty, which yields UTILITY for those that see it, and tourist income for the owner.

Near money. An ASSET which like MONEY acts as a store of value but which is not immediately acceptable as a medium of exchange, for example a BUILDING SOCIETY deposit. What constitutes money and what does not, however, is controversial and important for defining the MONEY SUPPLY.

'Neddy.' $\diamond$ NATIONAL ECONOMIC DEVELOPMENT COUNCIL.

Neo-classical economics. A school of economic thought in the tradition of CLASSICAL ECONOMICS, which has developed since the Second World War and which contrasts with that of the CAMBRIDGE SCHOOL. Neo-classical economics is characterized by MICROECONOMIC theoretical systems constructed to explore conditions of STATIC EQUILIBRIUM ($\diamond$ COMPARATIVE STATIC EQUILIBRIUM ANALYSIS). The analysis often takes the form of the comparative study of equilibrium states which are timeless, in the sense that they do not explore the dynamics of the economic system. Statements about macro-events are often derived from the aggregation of micro-relationships, and this has led to criticism, particularly from the Cambridge school. In contrast to J. M. KEYNES, the neo-classical economists consider that savings determine investment (rather than the other way around). Equilibrium is achieved at full employment by changes in FACTOR prices. Essentially, the neo-classical school has been concerned with the problems of equilibrium and growth at full employment, again in contrast to Keynes, who was primarily concerned with the underemployment of resources. $\diamond$ SAMUELSON, P.A.

Neo-classical synthesis. $\diamond$ KEYNESIAN ECONOMICS.

Neo-Keynesianism. $\diamond$ KEYNESIAN ECONOMICS.

Net assets. The CAPITAL employed in a business. It is calculated from the BALANCE SHEET by taking fixed ASSETS plus current assets less current LIABILITIES. Often used as a basis for calculating RATE OF RETURN on CAPITAL.

Net Book Agreement. The Net Book Agreement between publishers and booksellers came into force in 1900. The agreement laid down that books designated by publishers as net books should be subject to the terms of the agreement. Under this agreement, net books are not supplied to a bookseller unless he agrees to sell them at not less than their published price. Any default by a bookseller could lead to him being stop-listed collectively by the publishers, and his source of supply of books on trade terms cut off. In 1933 an amendment allowed booksellers to grant a 10 per cent discount to recognized public libraries. In a judgement delivered in 1962 under the RESTRICTIVE TRADE PRACTICES ACT of 1956, it was deemed to be in the public interest that RESALE PRICE MAINTENANCE should be continued on books.

Net capital employed. ◊ CAPITAL EMPLOYED.

Net capital formation. ◊ CAPITAL FORMATION.

Net cash flow. ◊ CASH FLOW.

Net domestic product. GROSS DOMESTIC PRODUCT less capital consumption.

Net income. Net PROFIT on earnings after tax and, where appropriate, after MINORITY INTEREST.

Net investment. The addition to the CAPITAL STOCK after gross expenditure on CAPITAL FORMATION and CAPITAL CONSUMPTION has been deducted. Corresponds to capital expenditure minus DEPRECIATION in accounting terms.

Net national product. ◊ NATIONAL INCOME.

Net output. ◊ VALUE ADDED.

Net present value. ◊ PRESENT VALUE.

Net profit. ◊ PROFIT.

Net tangible asset ratio. ◊ FINANCIAL RATIOS.

Net tangible assets (N.T.A.). Fixed ASSETS plus current assets minus intangible assets such as goodwill and minus current LIABILITIES.

Net worth. ◊ BALANCE SHEET.

Net worth ratio. ◊ FINANCIAL RATIOS.

Neutrality of money. The inability of changes in the stock of MONEY in an economy to affect anything except the general level of prices. If money is neutral, an increase in the MONEY SUPPLY causes INFLATION, but stimulates no growth in the real level of output. The issue of whether money is neutral or not is central to debates in MACROECONOMICS. In CLASSICAL ECONOMICS and under MONETARISM, money *is* held to be neutral. J. M. KEYNES and his followers, however, have had a more complicated attitude to monetary neutrality. On the one hand, they have downgraded the importance of money in influencing AGGREGATE DEMAND; on the other hand, they have argued that aggregate demand has an important role in influencing real VARIABLES; because of this latter belief, modern Keynesian economics is associated with asserting that money is *not* neutral. It would be more accurate, however, to say that they believe aggregate demand is not neutral.

The degree to which money can have some real impact on the economy depends on the degree to which certain prices or wages are fixed in nominal terms. For example, suppose Harrods decide never to raise their prices. If the money supply authorities drop freshly printed £10 notes over the countryside (an increase in money supply), people will have high money balances which they may attempt to spend at Harrods. Under classical economics, this increase in demand for their goods should induce Harrods to raise its prices to the point at which the same number of items sell as would have sold before the money supply increased. However, if Harrods cannot raise their prices, they will sell more of their products than otherwise and will have to ask their suppliers to produce more, causing a real increase in output. The view that money is neutral stems from a belief that market forces function reasonably effectively (i.e. that Harrods doesn't fix its prices) and that economic agents are rational. (⟡ ECONOMIC DOCTRINES; MONETARISM; SUPPLY-SIDE ECONOMICS.)

New classical economics. A development of CLASSICAL ECONOMICS and associated with MONETARISM, a theory of MACROECONOMICS which emphasizes the role of RATIONAL EXPECTATIONS in decision-making and the natural rate of unemployment (⟡ UNEMPLOYMENT, NATURAL RATE OF) in EQUILIBRIUM growth. Unlike the monetarists, the proponents of this theory argue that no government demand-management intervention is effective even in the short run. Growth can only be enhanced by influencing SUPPLY. (⟡ LUCAS CRITIQUE; SUPPLY-SIDE ECONOMICS.)

New Deal. The U.S. Federal government under President Roosevelt began, in 1933, a number of projects designed to give financial assistance and work to the large number of people thrown out of employment by the great DEPRESSION, which followed the stock-market collapse on Wall Street in 1929. This change of policy was called the New Deal. It met with a certain amount of opposition, because it led to budget deficits (⟡ BALANCED BUDGET). ⟡ KEYNES. J. M.

New-issue market. That part of the CAPITAL MARKET serving as the market for new long-term CAPITAL. Those institutions needing capital (industrial, commercial and financial companies and public authorities) offer SHARES and SECURITIES which are then purchased by each other and the general public. Internally generated funds provide about 70 per cent of the capital required by business and the new-issue market is not large, accounting on average for about 5 per cent, although it is of some importance. The new-issue market does not include certain other sources of new long-term external finance, such as MORTGAGES and other LOANS from financial institutions. Borrowers in the new-issue market may be raising capital for new INVESTMENT, or they may be converting private capital into public capital; this is known as 'going public' (⟡ PUBLIC COMPANY).

In the U.K. new issues of ordinary shares by industrial and commercial companies amounted to a record £3,406 million in 1985, inflated by the process of PRIVATIZATION. Net new issues of DEBENTURES and PREFERENCE SHARES were £860 million. Net new purchases of government and government-guaranteed marketable securities were some £9,232 million.

The largest concerns are able to issue stocks and shares direct to the public. These stocks and shares will normally be quoted on the STOCK EXCHANGE. Other concerns will raise their new capital through an ISSUING HOUSE that will either underwrite the issue or first purchase the securities and then offer them for sale to the public. (◊ UNLISTED SECURITIES MARKETS). In all cases the issues will actually be handled by an ISSUING BROKER. A full prospectus describing the company and its prospects as well as public advertising are necessary, and, for smaller issues, costs can be reduced by private placing, that is by selling the shares to INSURANCE companies or other investors. Quoted companies may issue unquoted shares in this way, although the volume of business is relatively small (less than 5 per cent of new issues by quoted companies in recent years). Rather larger amounts are raised by private placing by other PUBLIC COMPANIES which have no quoted securities, but PRIVATE COMPANIES have no access to the new-issue markets, since they cannot achieve quotations while retaining their private status. Well-established companies can greatly reduce the cost of raising new capital by offering shares to their existing shareholders by what are known as 'RIGHTS ISSUES'. Rights issues save the cost of advertising, issuing brokers and underwriting commissions, although the shares will normally have to be offered at well below market price to ensure the issue is fully taken up. The difficulty that smaller quoted and unquoted companies experience in raising new long-term capital was noted in the 1931 Macmillan Report (◊ MACMILLAN COMMITTEE), although a number of new institutions have since emerged to meet this need outside the new-issue market. ◊ BOLTON COMMITTEE.

The new-issue market, sometimes called *primary market* (◊ SECONDARY MARKET), like the rest of the capital market, is increasingly becoming an international one and public companies and the public sector raise money in overseas capital markets.

Newly industrialized country (N.I.C.). A country which is not a DEVELOPING COUNTRY but has not yet achieved the status of the ADVANCED COUNTRIES. Singapore, Greece and Mexico, for example, are usually counted as N.I.C.s.

New York Stock Exchange (N.Y.S.E.). The leading New York stock exchange and the largest in the world in terms of share volume and market capitalization. The second U.S. exchange, also in New York, is the American Stock Exchange (Amex). The N.Y.S.E. is also referred to as the *Big Board* and as *Wall Street*.

Nobel Prize. The sixth Nobel Prize, for Economics, in memory of Alfred Nobel (1833–96), the Swedish chemist, was introduced in 1969 and is financed by the Swedish National Bank. The following economists have been awarded this prize in each year: 1969, J. Tinbergen and R. FRISCH; 1970, PAUL ANTHONY SAMUELSON; 1971, SIMON KUZNETS; 1972, SIR JOHN RICHARD HICKS and KENNETH J. ARROW; 1973, WASSILY W. LEONTIEF; 1974, FRIEDRICH AUGUST VON HAYEK and GUNNAR KARL MYRDAL; 1975, L. V. Kantorovich and TJALLING C. KOOPMANS; 1976, MILTON FRIEDMAN; 1977, J. E. MEADE and BERTIL OHLIN; 1978, HERBERT A. SIMON; 1979, THEODORE W. SCHULTZ and SIR A. LEWIS; 1980, LAURENCE KLEIN; 1981, JAMES TOBIN; 1982, GEORGE J. STIGLER; 1983, GÉRARD DEBREU; 1984, Sir Richard Stone; 1985, FRANCO MODIGLIANI; 1986, JAMES MCGILL BUCHANAN.

Nominal gross domestic product. The value of the GROSS DOMESTIC PRODUCT at CURRENT PRICES. Many economists, notably JAMES MEADE, have suggested that the government should set a target for nominal G.D.P.; if workers take low pay rises, this target will be reached by real output increases; if workers take high pay rises, then the nominal G.D.P. rise will almost entirely consist of INFLATION.

Nominal value. The FACE VALUE of a SHARE or BOND, which may be more or less than its market price. ⟡ PAR VALUE.

Nominal yield. The return or YIELD on a SECURITY in which DIVIDEND or INTEREST is expressed as a percentage of the NOMINAL VALUE of the security as opposed to its market price.

Non-accelerating inflation rate of unemployment (N.A.I.R.U.). ⟡ UNEMPLOYMENT, NATURAL RATE OF.

Non-price competition. Attracting or attempting to attract business from rivals by means other than selling at lower prices, for example by the use of ADVERTISING or product differentiation (⟡ DIFFERENTIATION, PRODUCT). Non-price competition is commonly found under conditions of OLIGOPOLY, where price-cutting could lead to a damaging price war, thus the use of free gifts, coupons and special offers.

Non-tariff barriers (N.T.B.s). Obstacles to imports other than QUOTAS or TARIFFS. Examples include safety or construction and use regulations which favour domestic over imported products; legal requirements that providers of insurance services should be domiciled within national boundaries; and deliberate delay or obstruction at customs facilities.

Normal profit. ⟡ PROFIT.

Normative economics. Concerned with judgements about 'what ought to be' in contrast to POSITIVE ECONOMICS which is concerned with 'what is'. A normative statement would be that 'industry should be more concentrated'. Such a statement should rest upon a positive assertion about the existing level of CONCENTRATION and a VALUE JUDGE-MENT that fewer firms would lead to greater efficiency or some other benefit.

O

Obsolescence. A reduction in the useful life of a CAPITAL good or consumer DURABLE GOOD through economic or technological change or any other external changes, as distinct from physical deterioration in use (DEPRECIATION). For example, a new process or machine may be developed which renders existing equipment uneconomic, because a firm could significantly reduce its costs by scrapping its existing machinery even though it might still have many years of physical life. Then the old equipment has become obsolescent. 'Planned obsolescence' is a term used to describe the way certain consumer durables, e.g. motor-cars, are altered in appearance or performance so that users will wish to buy new ones earlier than they would otherwise have done. In this instance, a consumer's UTILITY or satisfaction is said to be reduced subjectively by the knowledge that his car is not the latest model, even though its performance has not deteriorated in any way.

Occupational pension schemes. ◊ PERSONAL PENSION.

Office of Fair Trading. ◊ FAIR TRADING ACT.

Ohlin, Bertil (1899–1979). Born in Sweden, Professor Ohlin studied at the University of Lund and the Stockholm School of Economics. He was appointed to a Chair of Economics at Copenhagen University in 1925. In 1930, Professor Ohlin moved to the Stockholm School of Economics where he remained until his retirement in 1965. He was a Member of Parliament from 1938 until 1970 and Chairman of the Swedish Liberal Party for many years. Professor Ohlin was awarded the NOBEL PRIZE in Economics in 1977 (jointly with Professor J. E. MEADE). His major contribution, to INTERNATIONAL TRADE theory, was published in *Interregional and International Trade* (1933). Professor Ohlin refined the theory of comparative advantage by building upon the work of Eli Heckscher (◊ HECKSCHER–OHLIN PRINCIPLE). He made also important contributions to MACROECONOMIC theory, in many ways anticipating in the 1930s the work of J. M. KEYNES.

Okun, Arthur M. (1928–80). Professor Okun graduated from Columbia University in 1956 and became Professor of Economics at Yale in 1963. From 1969 until his death, he was Senior Fellow at the Brookings Institute. His major publications include *The Political Economy of Prosperity* (1970) and *Prices and Quantities: A Macro Economic Analysis* (1981). Professor Okun argued that SUPPLY and DEMAND are not necessarily brought into EQUILIBRIUM by lowering prices but they are by adjusting output. Excess capacity may not lead to lower prices in an economy. In *Potential GNP, Its Measurement and Significance* (1968), he analysed U.S. gross national product through the 1950s and 1960s. He discovered that a 1 per cent increase in unemployment was associated with a 3 per cent drop in the ratio of actual G.N.P. to full-capacity G.N.P. This relationship has become known as Okun's law.

Okun's law. ◊ OKUN, ARTHUR M.

Oligopoly. A market which is dominated by a few large suppliers (◊ CONCENTRATION). Oligopolistic markets are characterized by heavy PRODUCT DIFFERENTIATION through advertising and other marketing ploys, with long periods of price stability intermittently disrupted by keen price competition. Petrol sales and soap powder are notable oligopoly industries in the U.K. in which free offers, competitions and advertising are more heavily used than price competition for attracting custom.

There is no single theory of oligopoly equivalent to that of PERFECT COMPETITION or MONOPOLY because the behaviour of oligopolistic firms is determined by the reaction and behaviour of their rivals, and the assumptions they make about those reactions. Instead, there are a number of alternative theories. The first was developed by A. A. COURNOT and assumed that each firm sets its price and output on the assumption that its rival does not react at all. In such a situation, each firm will leap-frog past the other, lowering price and increasing output to gain a higher market share. The result is nevertheless a market in which prices are higher and output lower than they would be if the firms behaved as perfect competitors. The second theory is that firms recognize their interdependence, and one among them leads in price setting with others following. In this case, the leader enjoys higher profits than any followers, but all firms benefit from the stability and predictability of the industry. A third case is that in which all firms attempt to act as leader; then they all earn lower profits than they would under Cournot's solution (◊ PRISONER'S DILEMMA). A fourth case is that firms assume their rivals will follow their prices down but not follow their price if it rises; in this situation, firms will be very reluctant to change their price. It could account for the fact that prices are often stable in oligopolistic industries despite large changes in costs. A fifth case is that in which firms collude and between them achieve the outcome that would occur if a MONOPOLY existed in the industry. However, if one firm colludes, it always pays another to cheat and sell more than agreed, so that maintaining collusive agreements may be difficult in situations where firms cannot monitor each other's behaviour. Otherwise, hefty state penalties for collusion can deter oligopolists from making agreements that have negative effects on consumers.

Other approaches to oligopoly exist; notably GAME THEORY has been used to simulate the reactions of firms to each other's behaviour.

◊ ANTI-TRUST; NASH EQUILIBRIUM; ORGANIZATION OF PETROLEUM EXPORTING COUNTRIES.

On cost. The contribution of the COST of OVERHEADS added to the direct costs of production.

Open economy. A situation in which foreign trade (exports and imports) and payments and movements of labour and capital into and out of a country are unrestricted. The term is also used to refer to countries for which foreign trade is a large percentage of the GROSS DOMESTIC PRODUCT. The degree of openness of an economy may act as a constraint on the freedom of governments to pursue particular types of economic policy, for example the reduction of interest rates to stimulate expansion may in an open economy lead to a flight of capital to other countries, depressing the EXCHANGE RATE with adverse consequences for exports and the price level.

Open-market operation. The purchase or sale of SECURITIES by the CENTRAL BANK to influence the supply of funds in the CAPITAL MARKET, and so interest rates and the volume of credit. The BANK OF ENGLAND often buys or sells GILT-EDGED SECURITIES to reinforce movements in the rate at which it will DISCOUNT securities (◊ MINIMUM LENDING RATE). When the bank buys securities, this tends to push the price of securities up and interest rates down; sales of securities have the opposite effect. Since certain securities form part of the reserve assets of the banking system, open-market operations influence the volume of bank credit and hence the MONEY SUPPLY. ◊ CREDIT CONTROL.

Opening prices. The PRICES at which dealings start at the commencement of business in a MARKET. In the STOCK EXCHANGE, for example, at the time of official opening dealers must begin by quoting prices before they have a full appreciation of the relative strength of SUPPLY and DEMAND. If they have reason to think that demand will be heavy where favourable news has been released overnight, then they will mark up their opening prices, compared with the closing prices of the previous day.

Operating cost (U.S.). A term for prime or VARIABLE COSTS.

Operating profit. 1. Profit on current activities. **2.** The difference between total revenue and total operating costs (or VARIABLE COSTS) and before deduction of FIXED COSTS. ◊ PROFIT; INFLATION ACCOUNTING.

Operating ratios. Various measures of the efficiency of a business, e.g. the operating rate or CAPACITY UTILIZATION RATE, the stock–sales ratio. LABOUR turnover ratio, the creditor–debtor ratio and other FINANCIAL RATIOS.

Operations research (O.R.). A multidisciplinary approach to the solution of quantifiable business or administrative problems, for example the determination of OPTIMUM levels of INVENTORIES, quality control and vehicle routeing. O.R. usually involves the use of computer models to test alternative solutions and the basic discipline of O.R. personnel may be mathematics, engineering or economics. A number of techniques used in economics are of this type, for example CRITICAL-PATH ANALYSIS, DISCOUNTED CASH FLOW and LINEAR PROGRAMMING.

Opportunity cost. ◊ COST.

Optimal-growth theory. The area of economics concerned with analysing the level of economic growth which maximizes social welfare. The starting-point is known as the *golden rule of capital accumulation* which, under a large number of assumptions, suggests that the optimal-growth path will be the one which maximizes consumption per worker over time. To vary consumption per worker, society can vary its stock of capital per worker: if there is too much capital, maintaining the capital–labour ratio will require such high levels of investment that workers would have to save a lot and refrain from consumption. If there is too little capital, however, while it is easy to maintain the stock, the product of workers is low because they are poorly equipped. The rule suggests that the optimal position is one in which the rate of growth of population equals the marginal productivity of capital, or which, in a perfectly competitive economy, equals the rate of profit. An alternative way of expressing the same rule is to say that the rate of saving should equal the rate of profit. The golden rule is limited in its application to a society where BALANCED GROWTH is achieved from an ideal starting-point. It does not suggest how growth should proceed in the absence of an optimal starting-point nor whether balanced growth is itself desirable.

Alternative rules and principles have been developed, notably that of F. P. Ramsey in 1928 that the marginal productivity of capital should equal the proportionate decline in the marginal utility of consumption. Other theoreticians have attempted to show that it is sometimes optimal to adopt the maximum or near maximum possible balanced-growth path; this allows an economy to move from an unsatisfactory state to a more satisfactory one very quickly even if consumption is lower in the interim than it is at either the starting- or finishing-point. Known as *turnpike theorems* (turnpike being the American term for motorway), such theorems imply that the quickest route between two states of the economy may not be the shortest in distance terms, as is the case with many motorway journeys. Optimal-growth theory is an area of economics grounded in complicated mathematics, in contrast to the more popular debate which has raged about whether growth is desirable at all. (◊ ECONOMIC GROWTH.)

Optimum. A position in which the aim of any economic unit is being served as effectively as it possibly can be, within the constraints applying. Where a situation is not optimal, gains in welfare (⟡ WELFARE ECONOMICS) can be made for some without any sacrifice by others. Essential to the meaningful application of the concept of an optimum is the existence of some *objective* (such as the maximization of UTILITY) and some *constraint* on the pursuit of that objective (such as a specified set of prices and a given income). While it is possible to have two conflicting objectives (for example, money and leisure), an optimum can only be attained with respect to both of them if some desired trade-off between them can be expressed; this is roughly equivalent to finding a single criterion by which both can be judged and optimizing with respect to that criterion. Individuals, trade unions, firms and countries are generally assumed to be rational in economic theory and thus exhibit optimizing behaviour. (⟡ ECONOMIC EFFICIENCY; LINEAR PROGRAMMING.)

Option. An agreement with a seller or buyer permitting the holder to buy or sell, if he chooses to do so, at a given PRICE within a given period. In the STOCK EXCHANGE, an option may be purchased from a dealer, giving the right to purchase a certain number of SHARES at a certain price within a certain time, e.g. a three-month option. If, in the meantime, the price falls by more than the cost of the option, then the dealer will lose and the purchaser gain, and vice versa. An option to buy is a 'CALL OPTION', an option to sell is a *put option*, and one to buy or sell is a *double option*.

Ordinal utility. A measure of consumer satisfaction expressed in terms of rankings of preferred combinations of commodities rather than through the assignment of values of some absolute UTILITY measure to them. (⟡ MARSHALL, A.) Until the turn of the last century, economists assumed that individuals possessed a cardinal measure of utility, with the consumer able to give a mark to each basket of products to reflect the pleasure it generates, rather as an examiner does to a multiple-choice paper. It came to be realized, however, that no sensible meaning could be given to statements of the form, 'This apple provides me with twice as much utility as it provides you.' Fortunately, no such scale was necessary for a consumer theory to be derived. All that is required is that consumers list bundles of commodities in order of preference and group bundles between which they have no preference. The difference between the two approaches can be highlighted by contrasting the way in which they show that a rise in the price of a product leads consumers to DEMAND less of it. The cardinal approach holds that rational consumers will equalize the utility derived from the marginal unit of cash spent on each item. A rise in the price of eggs thus requires that consumers raise the marginal utility they derive from eggs. Given the assumption of DIMINISHING MARGINAL UTILITY, the only way to effect such an increase is to cut consumption to a point at which eggs are more appreciated than they were and their marginal utility rises. The ordinal approach is only concerned with the *relative* attractiveness of items. It is the ratio of marginal utilities that is important and neither the consumer nor the economist needs to rely on a concept of utilities of some absolute value. In this approach, consumers will ensure that the ratio of prices of items equals the ratio at which the consumer would choose to swap the items with indifference. (⟡ INDIFFERENCE-CURVE ANALYSIS; MARGINAL RATE OF SUB-STITUTION; PARETO, V. F. D.; PIGOU, A. C.; SLUTSKY, E.; SOCIAL-WELFARE FUNCTION.)

Ordinary share. Shares in the EQUITY capital of a business entitling the holders to all distributed PROFITS after the holders of DEBENTURES and PREFERENCE SHARES have been paid.

Organization for Economic Cooperation and Development (O.E.C.D.). The O.E.C.D. came into being in September 1961, renaming and extending the ORGANIZATION FOR EUROPEAN ECONOMIC COOPERATION. It was based on the convention signed in Paris in December 1960 by the original member countries of the O.E.E.C., plus Spain, the U.S.A. and Canada. Later Finland, Japan, New Zealand and Australia also became members. Yugoslavia has observer status. The aims of the O.E.C.D. are (a) to encourage economic growth and high employment with financial stability among member countries, and (b) to contribute to the economic development of the less advanced member and non-member countries and the expansion of world multilateral trade (⟡ MULTILATERALISM). The organization carries out its functions through a number of committees – namely, the Economic Policy Committee, the Committee for Scientific Research, the Trade Committee and the Development Assistance Committee – serviced by a large secretariat. It publishes regular statistical bulletins covering the main economic statistics of member countries and regular reviews of the economic prospects of individual members. It also publishes *ad hoc* reports of special studies covering a wide range of subjects, e.g. world POPULATION growth, agricultural surpluses, etc. The O.E.C.D. has been particularly important as a forum for the industrial countries to discuss international monetary problems and in promoting aid and technical assistance for DEVELOPING COUNTRIES. ⟡ INTERNATIONAL MONETARY FUND.

Organization for European Economic Cooperation (O.E.E.C.). A conference was held in Paris in 1947 which established a Committee of European Economic Cooperation for the coordination of the economic recovery programme of Western Europe. In 1948, a convention was signed in Paris by the ministers of sixteen European countries and Allied representatives for Germany. The sixteen countries were Austria, Belgium, Denmark, France, Greece, Iceland, the Republic of Ireland,

Italy, Luxembourg, the Netherlands, Norway, Portugal, Sweden, Switzerland, Turkey and the U.K. Under the agreement, multilateral trading (◊ MULTILATERALISM) was to be re-established with a multilateral payments system, and trade adjustments or restrictions were to be reduced. Its immediate function was to propose a recovery programme and to carry it out. The EUROPEAN PAYMENTS UNION, which was established in July 1950, was the agency through which the O.E.E.C. fulfilled its obligation to institute a multilateral payments system. In subsequent years considerable progress was made in freeing LABOUR and CAPITAL movements and payments among member countries. The O.E.E.C. opened negotiations for the setting up of a EUROPEAN FREE TRADE AREA linking the EUROPEAN ECONOMIC COMMUNITY with the other member countries, but they proved abortive. In 1961, to mark its widening and changing functions, the O.E.E.C. was replaced by the ORGANIZATION FOR ECONOMIC COOPERATION AND DEVELOPMENT, which included Canada and the U.S.A. as full members.

Organization of Petroleum Exporting Countries (O.P.E.C.). A group of thirteen countries which are major producers and exporters of crude petroleum. The organization, set up in 1960, acts as a forum for discussion of and agreement on the level at which the member countries should fix the price of their crude petroleum EXPORTS by production quotas. The organization also acts as a coordinator for determining the level of aid to DEVELOPING COUNTRIES granted by the members. The thirteen member countries are: Algeria, Ecuador, Gabon, Indonesia, Iran, Iraq, Kuwait, Libya, Nigeria, Qatar, Saudi Arabia, the United Arab Emirates and Venezuela. These countries accounted for about 60 per cent of total world crude-oil production and about 90 per cent of total world exports in the early 1970s. However, their high oil prices led to substitution by other fuels, and by the expansion of supplies from non-O.P.E.C. producers. As a result, O.P.E.C. share of world exports fell to about 40 per cent by 1986. ◊ INTERNATIONAL ENERGY AGENCY.

Origin. ◊ CERTIFICATE OF ORIGIN; EUROPEAN FREE TRADE ASSOCIATION.

Outlay. ◊ COST.

Output budgeting. ◊ PROGRAMME, PLANNING, BUDGETING SYSTEM.

Overdraft. A LOAN facility on a customer's CURRENT ACCOUNT at a bank permitting him to overdraw up to a certain agreed limit for an agreed period. INTEREST is payable on the amount of the loan facility actually taken up, and it may, therefore, be a relatively inexpensive way of financing a fluctuating requirement. The terms of the loan are normally that it is repayable on demand, or at the expiration of the agreement, and it is thus distinct from a TERM LOAN.

Overfull employment. A situation in which there are more job vacancies than workers willing to fill them. In short, a state of EXCESS DEMAND in the labour market. If market forces are able to operate, the existence of spare jobs should increase the bargaining power of workers until wages rise enough to choke off the excess demand. If there is simultaneously excess demand for goods in the shops, a state of REPRESSED INFLA-TION exists. (⟡ LABOUR, DEMAND FOR.)

Overheads. ⟡ FIXED COSTS.

Overseas banks. 1. Banks operating in the U.K. but which are foreign-controlled. There are about 490 overseas banks and their subsidiaries in London. **2.** U.K.-owned banks which conduct their business mainly abroad and especially in the present or former countries of the Commonwealth. Many of these banks are subsidiaries of the COMMERCIAL BANKS.

Overseas Development Administration. ⟡ FOREIGN AID.

Overseas investment. ⟡ FOREIGN INVESTMENT.

Over-subscription. Where a new issue of SHARES is made and the demand for the shares exceeds the number on offer, the issue is said to be over-subscribed. It is, of course, extremely difficult for the ISSUING HOUSE to estimate precisely the price at which a share issue will be fully taken up, and new issues are usually either over- or under-subscribed. It is very common for an attractive issue to be ten times or more over-subscribed, especially because of purchases by *stags* – speculators who subscribe to new issues in the expectation that they will be over-subscribed and that dealings will begin at a PREMIUM. Very often new issues that start at a premium fall back to below the issue price as a result of PROFIT-TAKING by stags.

Over-the-counter (O.T.C.) market. A group of licensed dealers who provide two-way trading facilities in company SECURITIES outside the STOCK EXCHANGE. The term originated in the United States in the 1870s when stocks were first purchased across bank counters. Today the O.T.C. in the United States is an elaborate electronic dealing system, with MARKET MAKERS across the country, called N.A.S.D.A.Q.: the National Association of Securities Dealers Automated Quotations system, which trades in 40,000 EQUITIES through 5,000 broker-dealers. ⟡ UNLISTED SECURITIES MARKETS.

Overtime. The hours worked in excess of the standard number of hours of work laid down in the conditions of employment. Hourly paid employees are normally paid at a higher rate per hour for overtime than for standard hours, and it is therefore in their interests to get the number of standard hours reduced. Despite higher hourly rates, it may well be cheaper to pay overtime to existing employees than to recruit new employees, especially when demand fluctuates. A substantial proportion of operatives work overtime in U.K. manufacturing industries and their average overtime hours were 9 per week in 1985–6.

Overtrading. A firm is said to be overtrading when it has insufficient WORKING CAPITAL to meet the needs of its present level of business. For example, a firm which doubled its production, and then found that it could not meet all its current expenditure because too much CAPITAL was tied up in stocks and work in progress, would be overtrading, even though it had correctly forecast the demands for its products. In such circumstances, the firm's CURRENT RATIO would probably be less than unity.

Overvalued currency. ⟡ UNDERVALUED CURRENCY.

Own rate of interest. The percentage change in the price of a good between one time period and another.

Ownership. ⟡ SEPARATION OF OWNERSHIP FROM CONTROL.

P

Paasche index. An INDEX NUMBER which employs weights (◊ WEIGHTED AVERAGE) derived from current statistics rather than from those of some past period (◊ LASPEYRES INDEX). As an example, an annual Paasche price index would calculate the price change (the *price relative*) of each commodity or service included in the index, between the current year and a base year, and then derive the weighted average of these *price relatives*; each weight being the amount spent on each commodity in the current year.

Page Committee. A committee of inquiry under the chairmanship of Sir Harry Page appointed in 1971 to review national savings (◊ NATIONAL SAVINGS, DEPARTMENT FOR). The committee's report in 1973 recommended the introduction of index-linked government securities (INDEXATION) and the restructuring of the TRUSTEE SAVINGS BANKS, which led to their PRIVATIZATION.

Paid-up capital. That part of the ISSUED CAPITAL of a company that has been paid up by the shareholders. It is extremely rare among SHARES dealt with on the London STOCK EXCHANGE for the issued capital not to be paid up, and the phrase is sometimes used loosely as a synonym for issued capital to distinguish it from AUTHORIZED CAPITAL.

Paper profit. An unrealized MONEY increase in the VALUE of an ASSET or assets. An individual, for example, will have made a paper profit on his house if it is worth more now than it was when he bought it.

Par value. The PRICE at which a SHARE or other SECURITY is issued, i.e. the FACE VALUE of the INVESTMENT. A share is said to be standing above par if its quoted price on the STOCK EXCHANGE is greater than that at which the share was issued. The term was also used to describe the official fixed EXCHANGE RATE of currencies in terms of gold and U.S. dollars, as declared to the INTERNATIONAL MONETARY FUND.

Paradox of voting. The paradox (also referred to as 'Condorcet's paradox', after the eighteenth-century French philosopher) that a majority voting system can produce a set of inconsistent social preferences from a set of individually consistent preferences. Suppose electors Anne, Bill and Caroline rank three options, defence, education and social security, as follows:

	Anne	*Bill*	*Caroline*
Defence	1	2	3
Education	2	3	1
Social security	3	1	2

When the options, taken in pairs, are voted on, defence beats education; education beats social security but social security beats defence. In each case two of the voters rank the winning option higher than its opponent, thus ensuring its victory. As a result, the electors could either never determine which of the three options to put first, or their choice will merely depend on the order in which voting takes place – the social ranking does not possess TRANSITIVITY. As transitive preferences are a precondition for the meaningful derivation of INDIFFERENCE CURVES, the paradox is one indication that the theory of optimal behaviour for individuals cannot easily be extended to 'democratic' societies. (⟡ IMPOSSIBILITY THEOREM, SOCIAL-WELFARE FUNCTION.)

Parallel money markets. Markets in short-term securities other than TREASURY BILLS, BILLS OF EXCHANGE and BONDS dealt with on the DISCOUNT MARKET. Until the mid-1950s the discount market alone provided the main market for short-term money. Since 1955, when local authorities were no longer allowed to borrow at will from the PUBLIC WORKS LOAN BOARD, a large market in short-term loans to local authorities has developed. Other markets have developed in EUROCURRENCY, CERTIFICATES OF DEPOSIT, finance-house deposits and inter-company and inter-bank loans. ⟡ INTER-BANK MARKET; INTER-COMPANY LOANS MARKET.

Parameter. The values in a mathematical function which remain constant against movements in the *variables* of the function. For instance, in the demand equation, $d = aY + bp + c$, d (quantity demanded), Y (disposable income) and p (price) are all *variables*, a, b, c are *parameters* (constants).

Pareto, Vilfredo Federico Damaso (1848–1923). An Italian born in Paris, Pareto was trained as, and practised as, an engineer. He succeeded his father to a post in the Italian Railways, and in 1874 was appointed Superintendent of Mines for the Banca Nazionale, Florence. He succeeded M. E. L. WALRAS to the Chair of Economics in the Faculty of Law at Lausanne University in 1892. His publications include *Cours d'économie politique* (1896–7) and *Manuale di economica politica* (1906). He retired in 1907. He developed analytical economics from the foundation laid by Walras. He pointed out the shortcomings of any theory of VALUE in so far as it rested upon assumptions of measurable or 'cardinal' rather than ORDINAL UTILITY. He demonstrated that an effective theory of consumer behaviour and exchange could be constructed on assumptions of ordinal utility alone. Exchange would take place in a competitive MARKET between individuals such that the ratios of the MARGINAL UTILITIES of the goods traded equalled the ratio of their prices. An optimum point of exchange could be defined without the need to compare one individual's total UTILITY with another's. He defined an increase in total welfare as occurring in those conditions in which some people are better off as a result of the change, without at the same time anybody being worse off (◊ COMPENSATION PRINCIPLE). Pareto's work in this field, coupled with the development of INDIFFERENCE CURVE analysis, invented by F. Y. EDGEWORTH, was the foundation upon which modern WELFARE ECONOMICS is based. A study of the distribution of personal incomes in an economy led him to postulate what became known as *Pareto's law*, that whatever the political or TAXATION conditions, INCOME will be distributed in the same way in all countries. He noted that the distribution of the number of incomes is heavily concentrated among the lower income groups, and asserted that the number of incomes fell proportionately with the size of income. Pareto's law has not, in fact, proved valid in its strict sense. ◊ ECONOMIC EFFICIENCY; INCOME DISTRIBUTION; SLUTSKY, E.

Pareto-optimal. ◊ ECONOMIC EFFICIENCY.

Pareto's law. ◊ PARETO, V. F. D.

Paris Club. ◊ INTERNATIONAL MONETARY FUND

Partial correlation. The CORRELATION between two variables, after having adjusted for any correlation either variable or both the variables may have with a third variable. For instance, observations of the quantity of a commodity sold over a number of years may be highly correlated with consumers' disposable income over the period. A simple correlation between the two would be misleading if, during the same period, there was a substantial fall in price; so that there was also a strong simple correlation between quantity and price. The correlation between income and quantity is calculated, after having deducted the correlation between quantity and price, to obtain the *partial correlation*.

Partial-equilibrium analysis. The study of the behaviour of VARIABLES which ignores the indirect effects that changes in the variables have on themselves through the impact they have on the rest of the economy. When we study, for example, the market for pet dogs, we do not consider the impact that a change in the number of dogs sold has on the economy, through the profits of pet-food manufacturers and increased corporation taxes. These and other effects will have an impact on employment, income and taxation and, through these, have a feedback effect on the demand for dogs. The usual partial-equilibrium approach is considered adequate for the study of most markets because such feedback effects are swamped by the direct effects of events in any individual market and are considered negligible. This approach contrasts with GENERAL EQUILIBRIUM ANALYSIS. (◊ MARSHALL, A.)

Participation rate. The proportion of the population of working age who are in work or unemployed (i.e. seeking work). In the U.K. the *labour force participation rate* in 1985 was 73·8, i.e. 73·8 per cent of the population aged 15–64 were in the LABOUR FORCE. The corresponding figure for men was 87·7 and for women 59·8. The participation rate for women has risen compared with that for men, which has the result that the labour force has grown faster than the POPULATION.

Partnership. An unincorporated business formed by the association of from two to twenty persons who share RISKS and PROFITS. The legal basis of partnerships is determined by the Partnership Act of 1890. Except in a limited partnership, which, although a legal institution since 1907, is still relatively unusual in Britain, each partner is liable for the DEBTS and the business actions of the others, to the full extent of his own RESOURCES (although he is taxed as an individual). Partnerships are a common form of organization in the professions, and in businesses where CAPITAL requirements are relatively small, e.g. retail shops and other service trades. Partnerships, with sole traders (◊ SOLE PRO-PRIETORSHIP), i.e. self-employed persons working on their own, account for about 85 per cent of the total number of businesses. For the tax treatment of partnerships ◊ CORPORATION TAX.

Pawnbroker. A person who lends MONEY against a pledged article which he is free to sell if the LOAN is not repaid with INTEREST within a stated period. The article, which is a form of COLLATERAL SECURITY, might be clothing, jewellery or the tools of a man's trade. Pawn-brokers today are principally traders in used goods, and, as a CREDIT institution, pawnbroking is of very small and declining significance.

Pay-as-you-earn (P.A.Y.E.). System of collecting INCOME TAX through regular deduction by the employer from weekly or monthly earnings. Confidentiality of the taxpayer's private circumstances is preserved through the use of code numbers, which, in conjunction with tax tables, enable the employer to calculate the amount of tax he has to deduct. The system was introduced in 1944 and had been recommended by J. M. KEYNES. It is thought to be a stabilizing factor in the economy, since the tax yield automatically varies directly and rapidly with INCOME and employment, whereby the government tends to spend proportionately more tax yield in recession (◊ DEPRESSION) and less in time of high demand and employment. ◊ BUILT-IN STABILIZERS.

Pay-back. The period over which the cumulative net revenue from an INVESTMENT project equals the original investment. It is a commonly used but crude method for analysing CAPITAL projects. Its main defects are that it takes no account of the PROFITS over the whole life of the investment, nor of the time profile of the CASH FLOW. ◊ INVESTMENT APPRAISAL.

Pay pause. ◊ PRICES AND INCOMES POLICY.

Payment in kind. Payment in goods or services instead of money WAGES; made illegal by the Truck Acts. ◊ FRINGE BENEFITS.

Payments, balance of. ◊ BALANCE OF PAYMENTS.

Payroll tax. A TAX levied on employers' WAGE bills. It is favoured by many economists in developed economies as a means of encouraging both capital intensiveness (◊ CAPITAL-INTENSIVE) and the more efficient use of LABOUR, and of discouraging labour hoarding. This type of tax is not used in the U.K., although authority to do so was obtained in the 1961 BUDGET as one of two 'regulators'. A flat-rate employment tax (SELECTIVE EMPLOYMENT TAX) was introduced in 1966.

Peak pricing. The setting of higher prices than average when supplying services during a period of peak demand. For instance, enough electricity capacity must be installed to satisfy demand at peak times, because electricity cannot be stored. At off-peak times the cost of electricity is lower at the margin than at the peak, at which less-efficient power stations have to be switched in to meet the demand. ($\lozenge$ MARGINAL-COST PRICING.)

Peg. $\lozenge$ EXCHANGE RATE.

Pension funds. Sums of money laid aside and normally invested to provide a regular INCOME on retirement, or in compensation for disablement, for the remainder of a person's life. Nearly all developed countries have state pension schemes, e.g. the British NATIONAL INSURANCE Scheme, but unlike these schemes, private pension schemes for which contributions receive favourable tax treatment are usually *funded*, i.e. placed in managed invested funds. Many private pension schemes are based upon ASSURANCE. Occupational pension schemes may be contributory or non-contributory by the employee; the benefits of private schemes are normally related to the length of service of the employee and the level of his salary or contributions. Pension schemes began with the Civil Service in 1832, and later spread to salaried persons in other occupations and, more recently, to wage earners. Today pension funds have considerable economic significance and provide an important flow of funds to the CAPITAL MARKET ($\lozenge$ INSTITUTIONAL INVESTORS). The pension funds of the largest corporations are often significant shareholders in other companies. Higher rates of inflation following 1973 raised acute problems for pension funds since it did not prove possible to invest these funds at rates that would maintain their value in REAL TERMS. However, with the more recent decline in the inflation rate, surpluses have emerged in pension funds. Civil Service pensions are indexed ($\lozenge$ INDEXATION). $\lozenge$ PERSONAL PENSION.

Per capita income. Income per head, normally defined as the NATIONAL INCOME divided by the total population.

Percentile. The xth percentile is that value of a distribution of numbers below which are x per cent of the number of observations. For instance, the 50th percentile is the value below which there are 50 per cent of the observations (this is called the *median*) ($\lozenge$ AVERAGE). The *quartiles* are at 25 per cent and 75 per cent. Similarly, *deciles* subdivide the distribution into 10ths.

Perfect competition. A model of industrial structure in which many small firms compete in the supply of a single product. Three primary features characterize a perfectly competitive industry: (i) There is a multitude of firms (buyers as well as sellers) all too small to have any individual impact on market price, Therefore, MARGINAL REVENUE and PRICE are equal. (ii) All firms aim to maximize PROFIT. (iii) Firms can costlessly enter and exit the industry. (iv) Outputs traded are homogeneous.

Perfect competition is economically efficient in three ways (⋄ ECONOMIC EFFICIENCY):

(a) In the SHORT RUN, profit maximization ensures that each firm will set its output so that its MARGINAL COST is equal to its MARGINAL REVENUE (⋄ FIRM, THEORY OF THE). To produce when marginal cost exceeds marginal revenue implies that cutting back production would save more than the revenue lost; and to produce when marginal revenue exceeds marginal cost implies that expanding production would increase revenue more than costs. Thus, marginal revenue will equal marginal cost. Moreover, under the price-taking assumption, the effect is that marginal cost equals price. This is efficient for the allocation of resources, because it ensures that no consumer will be deterred from buying something which he values more than it cost to make.

(b) In the long run, freer entry and exit ensures new entrants will be attracted into any industry where high profits are made. The effect of these new entrants is to increase supply and bid down price until no profit is made (apart from a normal entrepreneurial return), that is, when average revenue equals average cost. The zero profit result means that no entrepreneur or factor of production earns more than it just needs to be persuaded into an industry.

(c) Again, in the long run, as average revenue equals marginal cost (from the profit maximization assumption) and average revenue equals average cost (from the free entry and exit assumption), we can deduce that average cost equals marginal cost. The only point on the average cost curve for which this is true is at the bottom of it: that is, at the lowest cost point. Finally, therefore, perfect competition ensures minimum-cost production.

Although the features of perfect competition make it look a poor description of modern industry, it is a realistic description of world commodity markets where many traders deal in a homogeneous product. Moreover, its very powerful results indicate that the achievement of even a partially competitive market can be advantageous. Thus, the simple perfect competition model provides a good starting-point for illuminating the forces underlying the real behaviour of firms. (⋄ CONTESTABILITY; IMPERFECT MARKET; MARGINAL-COST PRICING; MONOPOLY.)

Peril point. A term used by the U.S. Tariff Commission to describe the point beyond which tariff reductions would threaten the existence of domestic industry (⋄ TRIGGER PRICE).

Permanent-income hypothesis. The theory proposed by M. FRIEDMAN which suggests that, however variable their income, consumers will attempt to smooth out the pattern of their consumption (◊ CONSUMPTION FUNCTION). If, for example, someone's income varies between zero and £20,000 p.a., averaging £10,000, he will spend at a rate equivalent to a constant £10,000 p.a. Given that the MARGINAL UTILITY OF MONEY declines with the increasing amounts of spending, it is sensible to transfer spending from bountiful times to times when one is poor. By saving in some periods and 'dissaving' in others, this can be achieved. The theory has several implications: first, the MARGINAL PROPENSITY TO CONSUME will equal the AVERAGE PROPENSITY TO CONSUME: any extra pound a consumer gets will be treated not as a cause for a quick spending spree, but as a temporary bonus that should raise lifetime consumption by the value of the pound spread over a lifetime. Secondly, a large increase in short-run INCOMES will not lead to corresponding increases in consumption.

Personal annuity schemes. ◊ PERSONAL PENSION.

Personal disposable income. ◊ DISPOSABLE INCOME.

Personal equity plan (P.E.P.). A scheme introduced in the Finance Act 1986 to provide tax relief on the proceeds of personal investments in the ORDINARY SHARES of companies listed on the STOCK EXCHANGE. A maximum of £2,400 per annum may be invested and gains from selling the shares are free of CAPITAL GAINS tax and DIVIDENDS are free of INCOME TAX if reinvested. To qualify for these benefits, the shares must be held from the start of the plan until 31 December of the following year. The plan must be administered by a financial institution. Several countries have schemes to encourage investment in stock-exchange SECURITIES, for example the loi Monory in France, introduced in 1978.

Personal loan. A BANK LOAN made without COLLATERAL SECURITY to a private customer for specific purposes. Personal loans are granted for a fixed period, normally up to two years, and are repaid by equal monthly instalments. Introduced first by the Midland Bank in 1958, the personal-loan system was principally designed to secure for the banks a share of the expanding CREDIT business for consumer durables.

Personal pension. A regular income after a certain age and usually after retirement from work provided by a state or private scheme. The flat-rate state *retirement pension* is paid to men over 65 and women over 60 who have paid appropriate NATIONAL INSURANCE contributions and amounts (in 1986/7) to £38·70 per week for a single person. There is also the State Earnings Related Pension Scheme (S.E.R.P.S.) (◊ NATIONAL INSURANCE) and an Old Age Pension, the latter for those who have not participated in the National Insurance scheme. There are two broad types of private pension schemes:

(a) *occupational pension schemes*, provided by employers, which usually involve 'contracting out' of S.E.R.P.S. and provide a guaranteed minimum pension (G.M.P.). These schemes are either contributory or non-contributory; in the latter the employee pays no pension contributions.

(b) *personal annuity schemes*, for the SELF-EMPLOYED or others who are not members of an occupational scheme. Under these schemes, individuals pay contributions into a fund managed by an IN-SURANCE company or other INSTITUTIONAL INVESTOR which provides a cash lump sum at retirement age, part of which, if it is to qualify for tax relief on the premiums, must be used to purchase an ANNUITY. The 1986 Social Security Act, which initiated a run-down of S.E.R.P.S., also introduced *portable pensions*. After 6 April 1988, employers will no longer be able to make membership of a contributory occupational pension scheme a condition of employment. All employees will have the option of paying premiums into a personal private-sector scheme of their own choice in much the same way as for the personal-annuity schemes for the self-employed. This means that the employee will be able to take his pension scheme with him if he changes employment. Up to stated limits, pension contributions by individuals and employers qualify for INCOME TAX and COR-PORATION TAX relief. PENSION FUNDS also receive favourable tax treatment. Pension schemes may be *funded* (a capital-reserve system), in which contributions are paid into a fund that is invested in SECURITIES and other ASSETS and from which pensions are ultimately paid, or *unfunded*, as in the National Insurance scheme, where pensions for retirees are paid out of the contributions of those in work (pay-as-you-go system).

Personal sector. Households and individuals. In the national accounts the personal sector includes unincorporated businesses. (⟡ PRIVATE SECTOR.)

Petty, Sir William (1623–87). The pioneer of numerical economics. His main interest lay in public finance, and he made important contributions to monetary theory and FISCAL POLICY. His approach to these subjects contributed to the development of CLASSICAL ECONOMICS, and his work in the field of comparative statistics is in direct line of descent to the work of modern economists in the field of economic statistics. His best-known work is *Political Arithmetic*, published in 1691. The so-called *Petty's law* was a remarkably far-sighted statement of the tendency for the proportion of the working population engaged in SERVICES to increase as an economy develops.

Petty's law. ⟡ PETTY, SIR WILLIAM.

Phillips, Alban William Housego (1914–75). After a number of jobs in electrical engineering, and after serving in the R.A.F. during the Second

World War, Phillips began lecturing in economics at the London School of Economics in 1950. From 1958 until 1967 he was Tooke Professor of Economics, Science and Statistics in the University of London. In 1968 he accepted the Chair of Economics at the Australian National University. Professor Phillips published many articles exploring the relationships between the MULTIPLIER and accelerator in mathematical MODELS ($\Diamond$ ACCELERATOR–MULTIPLIER MODEL) with various time lags, and applied the engineering technique of closed-loop control systems to the analysis of MACROECONOMIC relationships.

In an article in *Economica* in 1958 Professor Phillips set out empirical evidence to support the view that there was a significant relation between the percentage change of money wages and the level of UNEMPLOYMENT – the lower unemployment, the higher the rate of change of wages. This relationship, which became known as the *Phillips curve*, has attracted considerable theoretical and empirical analysis. Its main implication is that, since a particular level of unemployment in the economy will imply a particular rate of wage increase, the aims of low unemployment and a low rate of INFLATION may be inconsistent. The government must then choose between the feasible combinations of unemployment and inflation, as shown by the estimated Phillips curve, e.g. 3 per cent unemployment and no inflation, or $1\frac{1}{2}$ per cent unemployment and 8 per cent inflation, etc. Alternatively, it may attempt to bring about basic changes in the workings of the economy, e.g. a PRICES AND INCOMES POLICY, in order to reduce the rate of inflation consistent with low unemployment. However, the relation between unemployment and inflation has not been sufficiently stable in practice to permit exact judgements to be made.

Phillips curve. $\Diamond$ PHILLIPS, A. W. H.

Physical controls. Direct controls on production and CONSUMPTION, licensing of buildings or IMPORTS, and the rationing of goods are examples of physical controls. These controls are alternatives to the use of monetary or fiscal measures ($\Diamond$ FISCAL POLICY), which control production and consumption through the price mechanism ($\Diamond$ PRICE SYSTEM). $\Diamond$ QUOTAS.

Physiocrats. A group of eighteenth-century French economists, led by F. QUESNAY, who later became known as the Physiocrats or '*les Économistes*'. They believed in the existence of a natural order and regarded the state's role as simply that of preserving property and upholding the natural order. They held that agriculture was the only source of WEALTH and therefore this sector should be taxed by *l'impôt unique*. In this, and in their advocacy of free trade, their views were directly opposed to those of the mercantilists ($\Diamond$ MERCANTILISM). In their belief in LAISSEZ-FAIRE, they had much in common with, and certainly influenced, British CLASSICAL ECONOMICS, and especially

ADAM SMITH. Quesnay's *Tableau économique*, published in 1758, has in it the origins of modern ideas on the circulation of wealth and the nature of interrelationships in the economy. ⟡ CANTILLON, R.; GEORGE, H.; MILL, J. S.

Pigou, Arthur Cecil (1877–1959). A pupil of ALFRED MARSHALL, whom he succeeded to the Chair of Political Economy at Cambridge in 1908, Pigou continued in this chair until he retired in 1944. His major publications include *Principles and Methods of Industrial Peace* (1905), *Wealth and Welfare* (1912), *Unemployment* (1914), *Economics of Welfare* (1919), *Essays in Applied Economics* (1923), *Industrial Fluctuations* (1927), *The Theory of Unemployment* (1933) and *Employment and Equilibrium* (1941). His work on monetary theory, employment and the NATIONAL INCOME, which was in the tradition of the CLASSICAL SCHOOL, led him into controversy with J. M. KEYNES. He was the first to enunciate clearly the concept of the real balance effect, which as a consequence became known as the *Pigou effect*. The Pigou effect is a stimulation of employment brought about by the rise in the real value of LIQUID balances as a consequence of a decline in prices – as the real VALUE OF WEALTH increases, so CONSUMPTION will increase, thus increasing income and employment. This was one of the processes by which the classical MODEL envisaged that full-employment EQUILIBRIUM could be obtained as a result of a reduction in real wages. Although his work on MACROECONOMICS was partly superseded by Keynes, he made a lasting contribution with his original work in WELFARE ECONOMICS. He strongly resisted the belief that practical policies based on propositions from welfare economics were impossible, because interpersonal comparisons of UTILITY cannot be made. He argued that, though this may be true for individuals, it was possible to make meaningful comparisons between groups. His distinction between private and social product now plays an important role in the formation of government economic policy in the field of PUBLIC EXPENDITURE.

Pigou effect. ⟡ PIGOU, A. C.

Pink Book. Informal name for the annual publication, *United Kingdom Balance of Payments*. The Pink Book appears in the late summer each year, and gives estimates of the BALANCE OF PAYMENTS in detail over the previous ten years and in summary for the previous twenty-one years. Quarterly and more recent estimates of the balance of payments appear in the *Monthly Digest of Statistics* and elsewhere.

Placing. The sale of a new issue of SHARES or STOCK. (⟡ NEW-ISSUE MARKET), usually to INSTITUTIONAL INVESTORS, by a financial intermediary, such as a firm of stockbrokers, acting on behalf of the company issuing the shares. This method of 'private placing' of shares minimizes the cost of a new issue for small firms, since it does not involve the advertising and other costs associated with an offer for sale or subscription. For shares which are to be quoted on the STOCK EXCHANGE there are limitations on the total market CAPITALIZATION of shares which can be issued by this method and at least 25 per cent of the shares must be offered to MARKET MAKERS so that they may be purchased by clients other than those of the sponsoring broker-dealer.

Planned economy. An economy where state authorities rather than market forces directly determine prices, output and production. Although planned economies can take a variety of forms, their most important features usually include: (a) production targets for different sectors of the economy, that determine the SUPPLY of different commodities; (b) rationing of certain commodities, to determine DEMAND for them; (c) price- and wage-fixing by state bodies; (d) (sometimes), a conscripted LABOUR MARKET in which workers take jobs assigned to them.

When all or nearly all economic activity is governed by the state, two advantages can prevail. First, the external costs and benefits of all activities which are not reflected in prices and are ignored by the market economy can be taken into account by the authorities (◇ EXTERNALITIES). Secondly, a distribution of income (◇ INCOME DISTRIBUTION) nearer to many people's view of that which is just can be achieved. There are, however, disadvantages of planning. The first is the practical problem of setting optimal prices in all markets (◇ PRICE SYSTEM). Too often, the authorities set excessively low prices causing goods to be rationed by queues. The second is the lack of worker and management motivation that attends a system in which earnings are not performance-related and PROFITS not retained by the companies making them. The third is the fact that when wages and prices differ from their market levels, substantial control of individual activities is required. For these reasons, many planned economies do allow flexibility in pay and the operation of the price mechanism in inessential goods markets and performance-related wage bonuses. (◇ FREE-MARKET ECONOMY; STATE PLANNING.)

Planning agreements. ◇ INDUSTRY ACTS.

Ploughing back. ◇ SELF-FINANCING.

Political economy. ◇ ECONOMICS.

Poll tax. A TAX levied equally on each person in the community. ◇ LUMP-SUM TAX; MARGINAL UTILITY, DIMINISHING.

Population. 1. The number of people living in any defined area, such as London or the U.S.S.R. **2.** In statistics, a term applied to any class of data of which counts are made or samples taken, e.g. car population.

The statistical study of the characteristics of human populations is called *demography*. While total population statistics derived from the registration of births and deaths and from CENSUSES of population are reasonably accurate in advanced countries, the population of many

DEVELOPING COUNTRIES can only be estimated within wide margins of error because the necessary administrative machinery is not available. Projections of population, even for advanced countries, can also be wide of the mark. In 1959 the U.K. population for the year 2000 was officially forecast at 58 million and the 1966 forecast for the year 2000 was 75 million, while in 1971 it was for 66 million and in 1976 the estimate was back to 58 million again. The forecast for the year 2000 published in 1986 was 57·6 million. The difficulty arises principally from instability in BIRTH RATES. In the U.K., the overall population has increased at 0·3 per cent per annum in the past twenty years and was estimated at 56·5 million in 1984. ⟨⟩ MALTHUS, T. R.; POPULATION, CENSUS OF.

Population, census of. In the U.K. a count of the number of inhabitants has been taken every ten years since 1801 (except in 1941). Enumerators visit every house in areas assigned to them, leave census forms, which they later collect, and check on the accuracy of the answers. Information is collected on place of residence, age, sex, marital condition, occupation and certain supplementary information on living conditions, education and occasionally other matters. All advanced countries have regular censuses, but many DEVELOPING COUNTRIES are now in the process of organizing them for the first time. It is not possible to obtain information accurately by other means. Calculations based on births, deaths and migrations have not proved, in the past, to be very precise means of estimating, except as a means of interpolation between censuses. Annual estimates of the present and future population of the U.K. are prepared and published by the government actuary in consultation with the registrar-general. The next decennial census of the U.K. will be in 1991. ⟨⟩ POPULATION.

Portable pensions. ⟨⟩ PERSONAL PENSION.

Portfolio. The collection of SECURITIES held by an investor.

Portfolio theory. A branch of financial economics which analyses the most efficient amounts of different assets an investor should hold. Underlying portfolio theory is the assumption that investors like high returns and dislike risk (⟨⟩ RISK AVERSION). Risk represents a likelihood of the actual return on an asset deviating from the expected return. In general, therefore, investors will have to expect a higher return from a risky asset than a safe one in order to be persuaded to hold it, although, of course, a risky asset may actually deliver a return either higher or lower than it was expected to yield in advance.

An *efficient* PORTFOLIO is one which delivers the highest expected possible return for a given amount of risk, or the smallest possible risk for a given expected return. In general, by holding a variety of assets, the risk of a portfolio can be reduced, because when one asset happens to perform badly, it may be that others will be doing well. Thus,

DIVERSIFICATION does pay, and this explains the popularity of UNIT TRUSTS. However, diversification can only succeed in reducing risk if the performances of the assets in a portfolio do not coincide: in as far as the assets' returns move together (because, for example, they are all affected by the state of the British economy) there will always be some systematic risk remaining that cannot be diversified away. It is the development of these basic principles which is the concern of portfolio theory. ⟡ CAPITAL ASSET PRICING MODEL.

Positive economics. The study of economic propositions which can, at least in principle, be verified by observation of events or states of the real world; that is, without reference to VALUE JUDGEMENTS. Broadly, positive economics is descriptive and can either consist of statements like 'unemployment is very high' or conditional statements like 'if the economy is reflated, unemployment will fall'. Prescriptive statements, in contrast, like 'unemployment *ought* to be cut', fall into the sphere of NORMATIVE ECONOMICS. In practice, the distinction between the two is not a sharp one, because those who make what sound like prescriptive statements may reasonably claim that in fact they are implicitly making conditional statements, like 'unemployment ought to be cut if overall welfare is to be enhanced'. This has the form of a descriptive statement but is no more devoid of opinion than the first clause taken alone.

Post Office Savings Bank (P.O.S.B.). ⟡ NATIONAL SAVINGS BANK.

Post-war credits. During the Second World War, the British government reduced certain personal allowances against INCOME TAX and credited the additional tax for repayment to the taxpayer when the war was over. Post-war credits were all finally repaid in 1973.

Poundage. ⟡ RATES.

Poverty. The situation facing those in society whose material needs are least satisfied. Poverty can be defined by some *absolute* measure (the number of those who cannot afford more than two pairs of shoes, say) or in *relative* terms (the number of the poorest 10 per cent of households, for example). In either case it is necessarily an arbitrarily defined concept.

Poverty exists not merely because incomes are low, but also because the needs of certain low-income households are high. A single person earning £100 a week may not be in poverty, though a family of four on the same income would be. Consequently the *poverty line* – the chosen level of income below which people are defined as impoverished – will differ for different types of household. In the U.K., the poverty line is usually set at the level of the minimum entitlement to state income support.

Measures of the problem of poverty usually concentrate on either the number of people whose income is below the accepted poverty line or on the gap between the total incomes of these people and the poverty line. The former measures the extent of the problem, the latter the extent and intensity of it. ($\diamondsuit$ MINIMUM-WAGE LAWS; SOCIAL SECURITY.)

Poverty trap. The combination of losing state benefit entitlement and paying tax that can ensure that poor families keep very little of any extra money they earn. Under any social-security system using MEANS TESTS, as the poor earn more, they lose state benefits. For example, a poor family may lose 60p of benefit for every extra £1 it earns, and it may also pay 25p in tax on that pound. In this case the family benefits by only 15p of the extra pound. Apart from the inefficiency of suppressing the incentive for people in the poverty trap to work, concern exists over the debilitating human effects of removing from people the power to alter their own living standards. ($\diamondsuit$ MARGINAL TAX RATE; POVERTY; SOCIAL SECURITY; UNEMPLOYMENT TRAP.)

Prebisch, Raúl D. (1901–86). Professor of Economics at the University of Buenos Aires. Economic adviser to Argentina and the U.N Economic Commission for Latin America and the first Director-General of the UNITED NATIONS CONFERENCE ON TRADE AND DEVELOPMENT at Geneva from 1964 to 1969. At this conference he argued that there is a permanent tendency for the TERMS OF TRADE to shift against agricultural products, and that it was in the interests of the DEVELOPING COUNTRIES to industrialize behind protective TARIFFS. He also made proposals for improving the export incomes of primary producers, for increased aid and for an expansion in trade in EXPORTS of manufactured goods from the developing countries.

Precautionary motive. The factor which causes people or firms to hold a stock of MONEY to finance unforeseen expenditures. It is one of the three motives for holding money outlined by J. M. KEYNES. A firm may know what its average pay-outs are each month, but if these payments fluctuate, given that there are costs to being short of the cash necessary to finance them, firms will keep money in excess of what they need for the average month. The amount they keep will first depend upon the INTEREST RATE. This represents the cost of keeping money which would earn a return if it was invested. Secondly, it will depend upon the probability of overshooting the foreseeable expenditures – the higher the probability the more money firms will hold. Thirdly, it will depend upon the size of the firm's average spending – a big firm will keep more than a small firm. Finally, it will depend on the cost of not having cash to meet unforeseen pay-outs – the higher the cost, the more precautions a firm will take. ($\diamondsuit$ MONEY, DEMAND FOR; SPECULATIVE MOTIVE; TRANSACTIONS DEMAND FOR MONEY).

Predatory pricing. Setting PRICES at very low levels with the objective of weakening or eliminating competitors or to keep out new entrants to a MARKET. Since prices will be raised again once these objectives have been achieved, there is no permanent benefit to the consumer. Predatory pricing is a means of establishing or maintaining MONOPOLY power.

Preference shares. Holders of preference shares precede the holders of ORDINARY SHARES, but follow DEBENTURE holders, in the payment of DIVIDENDS and in the return of CAPITAL if the issuing company is liquidated (◊ LIQUIDATION). Preference shares normally entitle the holder only to a fixed rate of dividend, but participating preference shares also entitle the holder to a share of residual PROFITS. Preference shares carry limited voting rights and they may be redeemable or not (◊ REDEEMABLE SECURITIES). *Cumulative preference shares* carry forward the right to preferential dividends, if unpaid, from one year to the next. From the investor's point of view, preference shares lie between debentures and ordinary shares in terms of RISK and INCOME, while to the issuing company they permit some flexibility in distribution policy at a lower cost than debentures. Preference shares now account for a very small proportion of issues. ◊ NEW-ISSUE MARKET.

Preferential duty. ◊ TARIFFS, IMPORT.

Preferential Trade Area for East and Southern Africa. A treaty was signed in Lusaka in 1982 for the establishment of a FREE-TRADE AREA between nine African countries: Zambia, Malawi, Kenya, Somalia, Ethiopia, Uganda, Mauritius, the Comoros Islands and Djibouti. The treaty required the ratification of seven states before coming into effect. ◊ EAST AFRICAN COMMUNITY; ECONOMIC COMMUNITY OF WEST AFRICAN STATES.

Premium. 1. The difference, where positive, between the current PRICE or VALUE of a SECURITY, or CURRENCY, and its issue price or PAR VALUE. **2.** A regular payment made in return for an INSURANCE policy.

Premium Savings Bonds. A BOND first introduced by the U.K. government in 1956. Instead of being distributed directly to bondholders, the INTEREST payable is put up as prize money which is won in a draw of the serial numbers of the bonds outstanding.

Prepayments. Payments for services such as rent and rates made in one accounting period for consumption wholly or partly in a following period and written into the balance sheet as a current ASSET.

Present value. The discounted value of a financial sum arising at some future period. For instance, if the *discount rate* is 10 per cent per annum, the present value this year of £110 earned next year is £100. £100 this year is equivalent to £110 next year because £100 invested at the going RATE OF INTEREST of 10 per cent yields £110 in one year. If there are financial flows over a number of years, the discounted sums are additive. For instance, if £110 were earned in each of two years, the present value would be: £110 earned in year two, discounted to year one, = £110/1·10; this sum is then to be discounted, again, to the base year = (£110/1·10) × 1·10 = £110/(1·10²). Finally to this sum must be added the discounted value of the sum earned in year one, that is £110/1·10. The present value, therefore, is £110/(1·10²) + £110/1·10. In general:

$$\text{Present value (PV)} = \frac{X_1}{(1 + r)} + \frac{X_2}{(1 + r)^2} + \frac{X_3}{(1 + r)^3} + \cdots \frac{X_n}{(1 + r)^n},$$

where X_n is the financial flow in year n, and r is the rate of interest (discount rate). The *net* present value is the difference between the present value of a future flow of profits arising from a project and the capital cost of the project. ($\Diamond$ DISCOUNTED CASH FLOW; INVESTMENT APPRAISAL.)

Price. What must be given in exchange for something. Prices are usually expressed in terms of a quantity of MONEY per unit of a COMMODITY (a good or service) but in BARTER the price of a good is what other good or goods it can be exchanged for. Price changes are the means by which the competitive process determines the allocation of resources in the FREE-MARKET ECONOMY. $\Diamond$ PRICE SYSTEM; PRICE THEORY; SHADOW PRICE.

Price Commission. An independent body set up by the British government in 1973 to administer PRICE CONTROL. In addition to administering the Price Code ($\Diamond$ PRICES AND INCOMES POLICY) the commission reported on matters referred to it by the government for investigation and reported regularly on its activities. The commission, which reported both to the Secretary of State for Prices and Consumer Protection and the Minister of Agriculture, had eighteen regional offices and a staff of about 250. The regional offices provided information and advice, investigated complaints about price increases and checked up on the observance of the code. The commission was abolished by the COMPETITION ACT (1980).

Price control. Government measures to prevent price rises. The U.K. government imposed price control during the Second World War together with a system of rationing. Direct fixing of prices is a temporary measure applicable to special conditions; it does not in itself cure INFLATION. However, other methods of controls on margins between costs and prices have been used in the U.K. ($\Diamond$ PRICE COMMISSION; PRICES AND INCOMES POLICY.) In 1982 France (for three months) and New Zealand (for one year) imposed a freeze on prices and incomes. In Sweden an Act enabling the government to regulate prices has been in operation since 1956. However, in 1981 a committee of inquiry considered that such controls did little to restrict inflation, and accordingly the Swedish government decided to abandon price controls in 1982 and limit the powers of the Swedish Price and Cartel Board.

Price discrimination. The selling of the same commodity to different buyers at different prices. Several conditions must prevail for it to be profitable. First, there must be a separation between markets that does not allow buyers in one to resell the item in another (no ARBITRAGE must be possible). Secondly, the seller must possess some degree of monopoly power (◊ MONOPOLY) in at least one market, for under competitive conditions, prices will be driven down to the level of costs in all markets. Thirdly, buyers in different markets must have a different level and elasticity of demand for the good. The monopolist who discriminates will set output for each market where MARGINAL COST is equal to the MARGINAL REVENUE in that market. Sales will be at a higher price in markets where elasticity is generally low than where it is high. The monopolist, in effect, takes advantage of the fact that in one market consumers are prepared to pay more for his item than in the other, without losing sales in the other market. In *perfect price discrimination* the monopolist charges a different price to every individual consumer and effectively has a sales revenue equivalent to the area under the DEMAND CURVE for his product.

Price–earnings (P/E) ratio. The quoted price of an ORDINARY SHARE divided by the most recent year's EARNINGS per share. The P/E ratio is thus the reciprocal of the earnings YIELD and a measure of the price that has to be paid for a given income from an EQUITY share. A company whose 25p ordinary shares were quoted at £1.00 on the STOCK EXCHANGE and which, in the previous year, had earnings of 10p per share, would have a P/E ratio of 10 to 1, i.e. the price of every one new penny in earnings would be ten new pennies, or the earnings yield would be 10 per cent. The price of earnings will vary with the stock market's assessment of the risks involved. Thus a reasonably large company with a good earnings record might have a P/E of 15/1 or more, but a company with a poor record might have a P/E ratio of considerably less than that.

Price elasticity of demand. ◊ ELASTICITY.

Price elasticity of supply. ◊ ELASTICITY.

Price index. INDEX NUMBER.

Price level, average. A term used in MACROECONOMICS to refer to a base from which changes in the exchange value of MONEY can be measured (◊ INDEX NUMBER). It is a useful concept, but not literally calculable: an AVERAGE of the unit PRICES of all goods and services on offer in the economy would, in itself, be a meaningless number.

Price maintenance. ◊ RESALE PRICE MAINTENANCE.

Price schedule. ◊ COST SCHEDULE.

Price support (U.S.). A system of agricultural support by which MARKET prices are fixed at above FREE MARKET levels and the U.S. government purchases unsold surpluses, thus supporting the PRICE and raising farmers' INCOMES. ◊ COMMON AGRICULTURAL POLICY.

Price system. The mechanism which sends prices up when DEMAND is in excess and prices down when SUPPLY is in excess (◇ RESOURCE ALLOCATION). The mechanism referred to is not some coordinated control from a central authority, but relies on the disparate decisions made by independent agents; it is the mechanism which makes a butcher reduce the price of a leg of lamb he is unable to sell, or an ice-cream salesman raise the price of cornets on a hot day. It is usually assumed that one price eventually settles in each market until some disturbance in costs or demand occurs (◇ EQUILIBRIUM). The importance of the price system is (a) that it serves as a means of rationing limited supplies among consumers, and (b) that it signals to producers where money is to be made and thus what they ought to be producing (◇◇ COMPARATIVE STATIC EQUILIBRIUM ANALYSIS; ECONOMIC EFFICIENCY.)

Price theory. The area of economics concerned with the determination of prices in individual markets. It is an area of MICROECONOMICS and is not directly connected to the study of INFLATION. The two components of price theory are the DEMAND side and the SUPPLY side; it is the interaction of the two that determines EQUILIBRIUM output and price in any market. On the demand side, the theory of demand (◇◇ DEMAND, THEORY OF) explains consumer behaviour in terms of rational agents maximizing UTILITY. On the supply side, various alternative market structures are investigated: PERFECT COMPETITION; MONOPOLISTIC COMPETITION; OLIGOPOLY; and MONOPOLY. There are also alternative theories of the behaviour of firms which do not assume that profit maximization is the sole goal of producers (BEHAVIOURAL THEORY OF THE FIRM) (◇◇ FIRM, THEORY OF THE; RESOURCE ALLOCATION; MARSHALL, A.).

Prices and incomes policy. Generally, a policy for restraining both PRICES and INCOMES in the interests of price stability. The persistent upward trend in prices during the post-war period in Europe led the ORGANIZATION FOR ECONOMIC COOPERATION AND DEVELOPMENT to recommend an incomes policy as a useful and desirable means of controlling rising prices in 1962. At that time and earlier, most, though not all, countries had preferred to rely mainly upon monetary and fiscal measures (◇ FISCAL POLICY) to regulate AGGREGATE DEMAND, but it had become increasingly difficult to achieve price stability without endangering full EMPLOYMENT and ECONOMIC GROWTH, particularly so because of the problems involved in determining the appropriate timing and strength of any new measure. In the U.K. a policy of relating incomes to productivity and controlling prices was in operation between 1965 and 1971, being given statutory force in the Prices and Incomes Act, 1966. Until 1973 the principal reason for concern over rising prices in Britain had been their effect upon the BALANCE OF PAYMENTS equilibrium rather than the social or economic dangers of

INFLATION. The increase in oil prices that took place in that year reinforced an earlier acceleration in the rate of increase in costs and prices which was to lead to the largest annual rises in the U.K. retail price index in the twentieth century. After a 'standstill' from the end of 1972 to the spring of 1973 (Stage I of the policy) a new prices and incomes policy was introduced under the Counter Inflation Act of 1973. This, and subsequent Orders, established a Price Code setting out the detailed rules in determining prices, and set up a PRICE COMMISSION to which certain companies in certain specified 'categories' were obliged both to give advance notice of intentions to raise prices and to report periodically on profit margins (Stage II of the prices policy). The commission had powers to reject or modify price increases. All firms were required to follow the Price Code in determining their prices, but the code was eased under Stage II of the policy in the hope of encouraging investment. From 1974 various other measures, including subsidies, were taken to keep down the prices of certain goods, including bread. Increases in incomes were also restricted under the new policy, first by a 'freeze', then by specific target maxima (Phases II and III). From the autumn of 1974, under the *Social Contract*, there was an understanding that the unions would voluntarily adhere to a specific maximum increase in return for the rapid implementation of certain industrial and social policies by the Labour government. Between July 1975 and July 1976 increases in incomes were limited to £6 per week, plus any step due on an incremental scale, with no increase for those earning over £8,500 per annum. The legislation expired in 1977 and the Price Commission was abolished by the COMPETITION ACT (1980). ⟡ HARROD. R.F.; PRICE CONTROL; STAGFLATION.

Pricing policy. The method used by firms for determining their prices. In this area, there appears to be a discrepancy between the suggestions of theory and the observed practice of firms.

(a) In theory, firms in PERFECT COMPETITION take the market price as given – which will equal the marginal cost of production – without being able to influence that price. A MONOPOLY or any firm in MONOPOLISTIC COMPETITION first determines its output and only then sets a price at the level that just sells the output chosen.

(b) In practice, firms appear to use 'rules of thumb' rather than accurate assessments of MARGINAL REVENUE and costs. COST-PLUS pricing, for example, involves charging the average cost of producing an item, plus a profit margin, the size of which is loosely determined by market conditions.

Much debate on pricing policy has surrounded the appropriate policy for NATIONALIZED INDUSTRIES; in particular whether they should attempt to emulate the MARGINAL-COST PRICING of perfect competition (⟡ HOTELLING, H,; PEAK PRICING).

Primary market. ⇨ NEW-ISSUE MARKET.

Prime costs. Strictly, VARIABLE COSTS plus administrative and other FIXED COSTS that can be avoided in the short or long term if there is no output, even while the firm remains in business. Often used loosely as a synonym for variable costs. ⇨ SUPPLEMENTARY COSTS.

Prime rate (U.S.). The RATE OF INTEREST charged by COMMERCIAL BANKS to first-class-risk corporate borrowers for short-term LOANS. The prime rate is the basis of the whole structure of commercial interest rates in the U.S.A. The rate applies only to, perhaps, the top fifty U.S. corporations; other corporations pay higher rates.

Prior charges. DEBENTURE and PREFERENCE shareholders have a prior claim over ORDINARY shareholders to PROFITS or CAPITAL repayments. The amount of these claims is known as prior charges on the company.

Prisoner's dilemma. A situation in which it pays each of several economic agents individually to behave in a particular way, even though it would pay them as a group to behave in some other way. The prisoner's dilemma is a classic and fundamental concept in GAME THEORY. It is best exemplified by the story from which it derives its name: A sheriff picks up two suspected criminals and puts them in separate cells. He gives each the chance to confess to having committed the crime with the other, and tells them their fate as follows:

(a) If you don't confess and your partner doesn't confess, you will get three years in gaol.

(b) If you confess and your partner confesses, you will four years in gaol.

(c) If your partner confesses and you don't, you will get twelve years in gaol.

(d) If your partner doesn't confess and you do, you'll get two years in gaol.

		Criminal 2	
		Confess	*Don't confess*
Criminal	*Confess*	4, 4	2, 12
1	*Don't confess*	12, 2	3, 3

These results are summarized in the table, where the left-hand number in each pair is criminal 1's sentence, and the right-hand number is criminal 2's. Given these four choices, the optimal one is for them not to confess and get three years each. However, if they each believed the other was to behave in this way, it would pay them to confess in the hope of getting two years. Indeed, scrutiny of the choices shows that if one believes his partner is going to confess, he ought to confess also (avoiding the twelve years); and if one believes his partner is not going to confess, he still ought to confess in order to get two years instead of three. This compelling logic will drive both criminals to confess unless they genuinely have as much concern for each other as they do for themselves.

Although it recurs in many contexts, the prisoner's dilemma is usually seen as a way of characterizing OLIGOPOLY. Here it may pay firms to collude and jointly act as a monopolist, but it will pay individual firms to cheat on the colluding deal and produce more than they agreed to. ⟡ NASH EQUILIBRIUM.

Private company. A type of business organization that permits a limited number of shareholders to enjoy LIMITED LIABILITY and to be taxed as a company. Unlike the PUBLIC COMPANY, the only other incorporated form of business in the U.K., a private company may not offer SHARES for public subscription, but unlike a PARTNERSHIP, and if it requires the protection of limited liability, it is obliged to file accounts. Smaller private companies are exempted from certain of the so-called *disclosure requirements* (⟡ COMPANY LAW). Prior to 1967, *exempt private companies* (companies with not more than fifty shareholders) were not required to publish accounts at all. The vast majority of all companies in Britain are private companies, and about 80 per cent of these were classed as exempt until that category was abolished in the 1967 Companies Act. At the end of 1985 the number of private companies registered in Britain was 862,000, though probably about 50 per cent of these were virtually inactive. ⟡ CLOSE COMPANY; COMPANY LAW.

Private enterprise. Economic activity in the private as distinct from the public sector (⟡ PUBLIC ENTERPRISE). ⟡ CAPITALISM; MIXED ECONOMY.

Private net product. A term first used by A.C. PIGOU for the net NATIONAL INCOME or product to distinguish it from the SOCIAL NET PRODUCT.

Private sector. That part of the economy in which economic activity is carried on by PRIVATE ENTERPRISE as distinct from the PUBLIC SECTOR. The private sector includes the PERSONAL SECTOR and the corporate sector.

Privatization. Principally, the sale of government-owned EQUITY in NATIONALIZED INDUSTRIES or other commercial enterprises to private investors, with or without the loss of government control in these organizations. Since 1981, shares in the following enterprises have been sold by the U.K. government: British Aerospace (100 per cent), Amersham International (100 per cent), Cable & Wireless (80 per cent), National Freight Corporation (100 per cent), Britoil (51 per cent), Associated British Ports (49 per cent), Jaguar Cars (100 per cent), Sealink, British Gas, British Telecom, British Airways, British Shipbuilders and British Airports Authority (100 per cent). Further privatization sales were planned or outstanding in 1987, such as the electricity boards and the regional water authorities. U.K. government revenue from sales of equity in state-owned enterprises rose from £377 million in 1979/80 to £2,600 million in 1985/6 and was planned to rise to £4,750 million per annum (⏵ PUBLIC-SECTOR FINANCIAL DEFICIT). The French government passed similar legislation in 1986 for authority to privatize sixty-five state-owned banks, insurance companies and industrial corporations. Similar policies were being pursued in many other countries world-wide. Other forms of privatization may take the form of deregulation of a state-supported CARTEL or the subcontracting to the private sector of work previously carried out by state employees. ⏵ CONTRACTING OUT; NATURAL MONOPOLY.

Probability. If a dice is thrown, any number from 1 to 6 may result, each of which is just as likely (assuming that the dice is not loaded). Three out of the six possible results are even numbers. The probability of throwing an even number is defined as $3/6 = 1/2$. In general, if an event results in n out-turns and, of these out-turns, r of them have a particular characteristic, the probability of that characteristic occurring is defined as r/n. It has a value of between zero (impossible) and unity (certain).

Producer goods. A COMMODITY used in the production of other goods and services as distinct from final or consumer goods. Whether or not a good is a producer or consumer good will depend not upon the good but upon the use to which it is put. For example, a pencil bought for use in a drawing-office is a producer good but one bought for a child is a consumer good. Producer goods are also known as intermediate goods.

Producer's surplus. The excess of the revenue received by a supplier of a COMMODITY over the minimum amount he would be willing to accept to maintain the same level of supply. It is a similar concept to CONSUMER SURPLUS. (*See chart opposite.*) ⏵ ECONOMIC RENT; QUASI-RENT.

Product differentiation. ⏵ DIFFERENTIATION, PRODUCT.

Product-moment correlation coefficient. ⏵ CORRELATION.

Production, census of. In the U.K., a census of production has been carried out annually since 1970; prior to that year, it was taken at five-year intervals. The census covers all firms in manufacturing, construction, utilities and extraction industries employing twenty people or more. Although still referred to as a census, sampling techniques (⏵ RANDOM SAMPLE) are used for firms employing fewer than 100 people. The results of the census are used in compiling national accounts (⏵ SOCIAL ACCOUNTING), input–output tabulations (⏵ INPUT–OUTPUT ANALYSIS) and the weights used in calculating the index of production and producer price index numbers. (⏵ INDEX NUMBER.)

Production, factors of. ⏵ FACTORS OF PRODUCTION.

Production, theory of. The economic analysis of the transformation

Producer's surplus

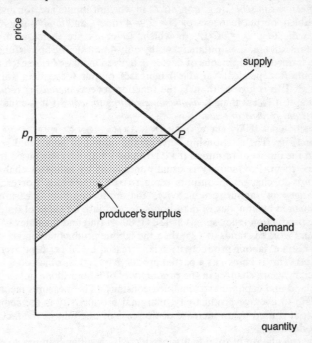

through a PRODUCTION FUNCTION of INPUTS such as LABOUR and CAPITAL into outputs. Production possibilities (◊ ISOQUANTS; TRANSFORMATION CURVE) will depend on technology, the mix and level of factor inputs on factor prices and marginal productivities, and the level and price of output demanded (◊ ECONOMIES OF SCALE; FIRM, THEORY OF THE).

Production function. The mathematical relationship between output of a firm or economy and the inputs (◊ FACTORS OF PRODUCTION) used to produce that output. In mathematical notation it is written $q = f(L, C, t \ldots)$ where q is the dependent VARIABLE (output) and L, C, $t \ldots$ etc. are independent variables (inputs). The amount of inputs, e.g. labour, capital, raw materials, etc., required to produce a given output depends on technology and this will be reflected in the form of the function. For instance, it may be linear (◊ LINEAR RELATIONSHIP) or non-linear. An example of the latter is the COBB–DOUGLAS FUNCTION. A production function of the form $q = aL^b \cdot C^{1-b}$ describes a technology with *constant returns to scale*: that is, if inputs are increased by x, output is increased by x. Similarly, a function may exhibit *increasing returns to scale*, (e.g. $q = aC \cdot L$, in which if inputs are, for instance, doubled, output increases by $2 \times 2 = 4$ times), and *diminishing returns to scale* (e.g. $q = aC^{\frac{1}{2}}L^{\frac{1}{2}}$, in which, if inputs are increased by, for instance, 8 times, output increases by only 4 times). The above functions are termed homogeneous of degree n; a given increase (x) in each of the inputs (independent variables) increases output (dependent variable) by x^n. If n is greater than 1, the function reflects *increasing returns to scale*; if it is less than 1, *diminishing returns to scale*; if it is equal to 1, *constant returns to scale*.

Production possibility curve. ◊ TRANSFORMATION CURVE.

Productivity. The relationship between the output of goods and services and the inputs of resources (FACTORS OF PRODUCTION) used to produce them. Productivity is usually measured by ratios of changes in inputs to changes in outputs using INDEX NUMBERS. For example, changes in labour productivity, the most common measure, are measured by an index of man-hours divided into an index of output. If the production index stands at 150 (1980 = 100) and the index of man-hours worked stands at 125, then the labour productivity index stands at 120, i.e. labour productivity has increased by 20 per cent over 1980 levels. This is known as a partial productivity index, which does not, in fact, measure changes in the productivity of labour alone unless inputs of land and capital have remained constant. (The measures mentioned relate to average productivity; marginal productivity is the change in output caused by an increase or decrease of one unit of the factors of production.)

The calculation of total factor productivity is difficult in practice since the proportions of the different factor inputs do not remain constant over time and their individual contribution to output change is difficult to disentangle. Comparisons between labour productivity in different sectors of the economy, for example between CAPITAL-INTENSIVE manufacturing and LABOUR-INTENSIVE services, need to be interpreted with care for the same reason. Another problem in productivity calculations is that the quality of unit inputs may vary; for example, the use of more highly trained labour may lead to higher output without any increase in the number of man-hours. Since changes in productivity are affected by the level of capacity utilization, the underlying trend of productivity growth may be very different from that indicated by short-term movements in productivity indexes. In the long run productivity advance is the main cause of increases in real PER CAPITA INCOME.

Products, final. ◊ FINAL GOODS.

Products, joint. ◊ JOINT PRODUCTS.

Profit. 1. The residual return to the ENTREPRENEUR. In economic theory, profit does not include any of the return to LAND, LABOUR or CAPITAL (the FACTORS OF PRODUCTION), but is the surplus remaining after the full OPPORTUNITY COSTS of these factors have been met, formally total sales revenue minus total COSTS. Two types of profit are distinguished in economics. *Normal profit* is the opportunity cost of the entrepreneur, i.e. the minimum amount necessary to attract him to an activity or to induce him to remain in it. *Super-normal profit* or *excess profit* is any profit over and above normal profit. Super-normal profit will be earned only in the SHORT RUN and is a return to MONOPOLY power, which, unless there are BARRIERS TO ENTRY, will be eroded by new entrants. (◊ ECONOMIC RENT.)

2. In the accounting sense of the term, *net profit* (before tax) is the residual after deduction of all MONEY costs, i.e. sales revenue minus wages, salaries, rent, fuel and raw materials etc., INTEREST on LOANS and DEPRECIATION. Net profit after tax is after deduction of CORPORATION TAX or, in the case of a SOLE PROPRIETORSHIP or PARTNERSHIP, INCOME TAX. (However, ◊ ASSESSABLE PROFITS.) *Gross profit* is net profit before depreciation and interest.

Accounting profit and economic profit will only be the same where all the factors of production have been credited with their full opportunity costs. The reported profits of quoted companies (◊ PUBLIC COMPANY) consist mainly of the return on capital for the shareholders which is not profit in the economic sense of the term. If a company is receiving a subsidized loan from the government, for example, or is paying RENT below the market rate because it has a long leasehold interest, it would also be necessary for the economist to deduct full IMPUTED COSTS for these returns to factors of production, rather than simply the actual money outlays from revenue in arriving at profit. A firm may, therefore, be making an accounting profit while operating at an economic loss.

Profit, falling rate of. The early classical economists (◊ CLASSICAL ECONOMICS) believed that it was a feature of the economic system for the general rate of PROFIT to decline. ADAM SMITH argued that CAPITAL accumulation took place at a faster rate than the growth of total output. Although the absolute level of profits rose, competition lowered the RATE OF RETURN on capital. For RICARDO, the decline of the general rate of profit was induced by the decline in the marginal productivity of LAND, to which all profits were linked. MARX took up ideas similar to Smith's, and predicted a fall in the rate of profit because of an intensification of competition between capitalists (◊ CAPITALISM). There would follow, he concluded, a strong pressure to reduce REAL WAGES.

Profit-and-loss account. ◊ DOUBLE-ENTRY BOOKKEEPING.

Profit-sharing. The name given to describe any scheme under which workers in a firm receive a remuneration which is explicitly conditional upon the future PROFITS of the firm. Typical profit-sharing schemes would give workers a profit-related bonus at the end of the year, or would pay workers an amount based on a formula in which profit was a component. Two primary motivations underlie arguments for profit-sharing. First is the desire for workers' wages to be flexible and reflect the performance of their company. If remuneration automatically falls when profits fall, the need for redundancies will be minimized. The second motivation is the desire for workers to identify their interests with those of their employer – to feel that they have a personal stake in the success of the company. Against profit-sharing, it can be argued that workers desire stable INCOME and that any risk of company failure should be borne by the shareholders. Secondly, that in a properly functioning free LABOUR market, wages would be flexible anyway.

Profit-taking. The sale of SHARES on the STOCK EXCHANGE in order to realize CAPITAL appreciation. When share prices rise and then fall back again as sellers appear, including those who bought the shares in the expectation that the price would rise, the fall off in prices is said to be the result of profit-taking. ⟡ STAG.

Program. A list of instructions coded for, and executed by, a computer. A program typically reads some set of data (for example, levels of consumption and income over time), manipulates the data (removes the outlying or implausible values) and analyses them (finding the relationship between income and consumption for example (⟡ ECONOMETRICS)). A program can be written in one of many computer languages; however, it is increasingly unusual for economists to write programs themselves. Instead, it is possible to buy flexible programs, written by experts, that can execute most of the activities economists need, and that can be applied to different sets of data.

Programme, planning, budgeting system (P.P.B.S.). An approach to the activities of government and other non-profit-making operations which attempts to take into account the objectives they are expected to achieve, the RESOURCES available and the way these interrelate so as to use limited resources in the most effective way. It proceeds by (a) breaking down broad programmes (health, defence, education, etc.) into detailed sub-programmes, (b) devising methods of measuring the level of output of the sub-programmes and of evaluating the resources required to provide this output, (c) clarifying the objectives laid down by the policy-makers in respect of the broad programmes, and possibly the sub-programmes, (d) finding the least-cost ways of meeting these objectives, and (e) clarifying the 'opportunity costs' (⟡ COST) of these objectives – e.g. one extra university implies fifty fewer secondary schools – and thus in turn helping to formulate future policy objectives. It is an attempt to introduce rational methods of management into an area where considerable difficulties of measurement and evaluation exist.

Progressive tax. A TAX which takes an increasing proportion of INCOME as income rises.

Promissory note. A legal document between a lender and a borrower whereby the latter agrees to certain conditions for the repayment of the sum of money borrowed. When one borrows from a COMMERCIAL BANK, one signs a promissory note. Particular forms of promissory notes, known as commercial paper, can be bought and sold. They are usually issued by large corporations, especially when MONETARY POLICY is restrictive, making it difficult to obtain CREDIT.

Propensity to import. A relationship between INCOME and IMPORT levels. We would expect the DEMAND of a HOUSEHOLD for foreign goods to depend on its income as does its demand for domestically produced goods. Similarly, we would expect firms' demands for foreign goods – raw materials, machine tools, components, etc. – to depend on their output. The whole economy's demand for imports thus depends on NATIONAL INCOME.

(a) *The average propensity to import:* the ratio of the total value of imports to national income. It is the proportion of national income spent on imports.

(b) *The marginal propensity to import:* the proportion of an increase in national income which is spent on imports. For instance, if national income increased by £100, and imports increased by £20, then the marginal propensity to import would be £20/£100 = 1/5. The marginal propensity to import is a useful concept in two ways. First, if it can be accurately measured and it is relatively constant over time, then it can be used to predict the increase in imports which will result from an increase in income. To continue the above example, if the marginal propensity to import is estimated as 1/5 and national income is expected to increase by £10 billion, then we can predict that imports will increase by £2 billion, and this may be very useful from the point of view of control of the economy and the BALANCE OF PAYMENTS. Secondly, the marginal propensity to import determines, among other things, the value of the MULTIPLIER, and an estimate of it will therefore be required if we are to be able to predict the effects on national income of a change in INVESTMENT, government expenditure (♢ BUDGET), exports or TAXATION.

Though, in the short run, the average and marginal propensities to import may be taken as relatively constant, it must be remembered that they reflect demands for foreign goods from firms and households, and are therefore influenced by (a) relative prices of foreign and domestic goods, (b) tastes and (c) technology and other factors, any or all of which may change over time.

333

Propensity to save. ⟡ AVERAGE PROPENSITY TO SAVE.

Property bond. ⟡ BOND.

Proportional tax. A TAX which is levied at the same rate at all INCOME levels. Hence it is intermediate between a PROGRESSIVE TAX and a REGRESSIVE TAX.

Proprietorship. ⟡ SOLE PROPRIETORSHIP.

Protection. The imposition of TARIFFS or QUOTAS to restrict the inflow of IMPORTS. Arguments in favour of protectionism (⟡ PROTECTION) and against FREE TRADE have their origin in the earliest periods of economic discussion (⟡ MERCANTILISM). The arguments take many forms. Domestic industries, especially agriculture, must be maintained at a high level in case foreign sources are cut off during a war. Similarly, key industries which have a significant defence role should be protected to avoid reliance on a foreign supplier. In conditions of EXCESS CAPACITY, protection increases employment by switching demand away from foreign to domestic production, and, through an increase in the surplus on the BALANCE OF PAYMENTS, enables aggregate INCOME to be raised through the MULTIPLIER effect. Protection also enables new industries to develop to an optimum size – the INFANT-INDUSTRY ARGUMENT. Protection can be used as a counter to DUMPING and as a retaliatory measure against other countries' restrictions. The case for protection for the DEVELOPING COUNTRIES was put forward by Professor PREBISCH. The developing countries have experienced a long-run decline in their TERMS OF TRADE. Their demand for imported manufactures grows much more rapidly as their REAL INCOMES rise than does the advanced countries' demand for their exports, with a consequent pressure on their balance of payments. Protection can improve their terms of trade by causing a reduction in the price of their imported manufactures arising from their reduced demand, and it can also be used as a means for allocating the limited supply of FOREIGN EXCHANGE. ⟡ CUSTOMS UNION; GENERAL AGREEMENT ON TARIFFS AND TRADE; TARIFFS, IMPORT.

Public company. An incorporated business enterprise with limited liability which is not a PRIVATE COMPANY. A public company may be quoted or unquoted (⟡ QUOTATION). Under the 1985 Companies Act, the MEMORANDUM OF ASSOCIATION of a public company must state that it is a 'public limited company' or use the abbreviation plc, there must be at least two subscribers and the nominal share capital must be at least £50,000. At the end of 1985, 6,000 public companies were registered in Great Britain. ⟡ COMPANY LAW.

Public debt. ⟡ NATIONAL DEBT.

Public enterprise. Economic activity in the market carried on by state-owned or controlled ENTERPRISES. ⟡ NATIONALIZED INDUSTRIES.

Public expenditure. Spending by general government ($\Diamond$ PUBLIC SECTOR). Final consumption of goods and services by the public sector accounted for 21 per cent of the U.K. GROSS DOMESTIC PRODUCT at market prices in 1985, but if all expenditure, including debt interest, TRANSFER PAYMENTS, and capital grants (but not capital formation by public corporations), is included, public expenditure accounted for almost 45 per cent of G.D.P. The control of public expenditure involves the publication of forward plans, including those for the next four years, in the Public Expenditure White Paper, preceded by intensive activity by departments and the *Public Expenditure Survey Committee* (*P.E.S.C.*), an interdepartmental committee that reviews expenditure plans. The formal request to Parliament for funds is in the SUPPLY SERVICES estimates presented at the time of the BUDGET. At the end of the financial year, *Appropriation Accounts* are prepared by the Comptroller and Auditor-General which show actual expenditure. During the preparation of the appropriation accounts the Public Accounts Committee and the National Audit Office attempt to verify that the funds have been used honestly and effectively.

Public Expenditure Survey Committee (P.E.S.C.). $\Diamond$ PUBLIC EXPENDITURE.

Public finance. A branch of economics concerned with the identification and appraisal of the means and effects of government financial policies. It attempts to analyse the effects of government TAXATION and expenditure on the economic situations of individuals and institutions, and to examine their impact on the economy as a whole. It is also concerned with examining the effectiveness of policy measures directed at certain objectives, and with developing techniques and procedures by which that effectiveness can be increased. $\Diamond$ BUDGET; COST–BENEFIT ANALYSIS; FISCAL POLICY; PROGRAMME, PLANNING, BUDGETING SYSTEM.

Public goods. Public goods have three characteristics. The first is that they yield *non-rivalrous* consumption: one person's use of them does not deprive others from using them. The second is that they are *non-excludable* – if one person consumes them it is impossible to restrict others from consuming them: public television is non-excludable, although if devices are made for scrambling television pictures, except to those who own picture-decoding cards, television becomes an excludable service. Thirdly, public goods are often *non-rejectable* – individuals cannot abstain from their consumption even if they want to. National defence is a public good of this sort, although television is not. Non-excludability and non-rejectability mean that no *market* can exist and provision must be made by government, financed by TAXATION.

Many items are partly public and partly private goods. A developed patent system, for example, has public-good properties, benefiting not only the community as a whole, but especially inventors who take out patents.

Public ownership. ◊ NATIONALIZED INDUSTRIES.

Public sector. Comprises central government and local authorities (*general government*), together with the nationalized industries or public corporations. *Central government* includes all those departments and other bodies for whose activities a minister of the Crown or other responsible person is accountable to Parliament. ◊ PRIVATIZATION.

Public-sector borrowing requirement (P.S.B.R.). The excess of public-sector spending over its receipts. The P.S.B.R. was adopted as a specific target of U.K. government policy in 1980. It was seen as important as a measure of the government's fiscal stance (◊ FISCAL POLICY), influencing AGGREGATE DEMAND, and as a measure of the burden created for future generations – it is future generations that will have to pay back the debt created, or at least service the interest payments on it. However, it became apparent in 1983 that the P.S.B.R. was meaningless as a target in both of these roles, because by financing current spending through the sales of assets (◊ PRIVATIZATION), the government was implicitly relaxing the fiscal stance and worsening its future financial position (through the loss of nationalized-industry profits) without increasing the P.S.B.R.

The P.S.B.R. can be financed in two ways: by the printing of MONEY (or, more formally, the sale of liquid assets (◊ LIQUIDITY) to the banking private sector), or by borrowing. If it is financed by the *printing of money*, it causes an increase in MONEY G.D.P. – this will lead to either a real increase or a purely inflationary (◊ INFLATION) increase, depending on the state of the economy at the time. If it is financed by *borrowing*, a high P.S.B.R. is likely to drive INTEREST RATES up or, in an OPEN ECONOMY, drive the EXCHANGE RATE up (as CAPITAL from abroad is lent to the government) (◊ CROWDING OUT).

Confusion surrounds the P.S.B.R. because the way it is financed determines its economic effects: an increase in the money supply causes, at least in the short term, low interest rates, and probably a drop in the exchange rate. This is the opposite of the expected results of an increase in borrowing. The P.S.B.R. is a *flow* concept, in contrast to the NATIONAL DEBT, which is the cumulated STOCK of all past P.S.B.R.s. (◊ PUBLIC-SECTOR FINANCIAL DEFICIT.)

Public-sector financial deficit (P.S.F.D.). The excess of PUBLIC SECTOR spending over TAXATION revenues and other receipts. It differs from the PUBLIC-SECTOR BORROWING REQUIREMENT in that it includes the proceeds of capital transactions like the sale of assets (◊ PRIVATIZATION).

Public utility. An industry supplying basic public services to the market and enjoying MONOPOLY power, which necessitates ownership or

REGULATION by the state. Usually, electricity, gas, telephones, postal services, water supply and rail and often other forms of transport are regarded as public utilities. These services all require specialized capital equipment and elaborate organization and it would be uneconomic to have two sets of gas pipes or telephone lines serving the same street, for example, so that some form of spatial monopoly is usual. ⟡ NATURAL MONOPOLIES.

Public Works Loan Board. A board responsible for administering the provision of long-term government LOANS in the U.K., mainly to local authorities who find it difficult to raise money on the market or to finance their CAPITAL requirements from the RATES. In 1980 the amount of local authority debt outstanding with the P.W.L.B. was £14 million, 38 per cent of the total. Since 1980 the P.W.L.B. has been part of the National Investment and Loans Office, which also includes the National Debt Office (⟡ NATIONAL DEBT).

'Pump priming.' ⟡ DEFICIT FINANCING.

Purchase tax. An indirect tax (⟡ DIRECT TAXATION) levied at different percentage rates for different COMMODITIES on their wholesale prices. This tax was abolished in the U.K. on the introduction of a VALUE-ADDED TAX in 1973.

Purchasing-power parity theory. A theory which states that the EXCHANGE RATE between one CURRENCY and another is in EQUILIBRIUM when their domestic purchasing powers at that rate of exchange are equivalent. For example, the rate of exchange of £1 = $1·40 would be in equilibrium if £1 will buy the same goods in the U.K. as $1·40 will buy in the U.S.A. If this holds true, purchasing-power parity exists. The theory has its source in the mercantilist (⟡ MERCANTILISM) writings of the seventeenth century, but it came into prominence in 1916 through the writings of the Swedish economist, Gustav Cassel (1866–1945). The basic mechanism implied by the theory is that, given complete freedom of action, if $1·40 buys more in the U.S.A. than £1 does in the U.K., it would pay to convert pounds into dollars and buy from the U.S.A. rather than in the U.K. The switch in demand would raise prices in the U.S.A. and lower them in the U.K., and at the same time lower the U.K. exchange rate until equilibrium and parity were re-established. Cassel interpreted the theory in terms of changes in, rather than absolute levels of, prices and exchange rates. He argued that the falls in the FOREIGN-EXCHANGE MARKETS in the post-war period were a result of INFLATION due to unbalanced BUDGETS increasing the quantity of MONEY. In practice, the theory has little validity because exchange rates, which are determined by the DEMAND and SUPPLY of currency in the foreign-exchange markets, are related to such forces as BALANCE OF PAYMENTS disequilibria, CAPITAL transactions, SPECULATION and government policy. Many goods and SERVICES do not enter into international trade, and so their relative prices are not taken into account in the determination of the exchange rate. Moreover, it is impossible to measure satisfactorily what purchasing power a currency in one country has relative to that in another because of the difficulty of determining the appropriate mix of commodities, and also of measuring their average price level. This means that international comparisons of standards of living, etc. based on current exchange rates have to be interpreted with great care. ⬦ MISES, L. E. VON; INDEX-NUMBER PROBLEM.

Put option. ⬦ OPTION.

Pyramiding. ⬦ HOLDING COMPANY.

***q* theory.** A theory of INVESTMENT behaviour which suggests that firms invest as long as the value of their SHARES exceeds the replacement cost of the physical assets of the firm. Developed by J. TOBIN, *q* theory is attractive because it encompasses other theories of investment in a simple framework. The *q* referred to is the ratio of two numbers. The first is the value of a firm to its shareholders; this is equivalent to the expected future profits of the firm. The second number is the replacement cost of the assets of the firm: the machines, buildings etc. If the first number exceeds the second (i.e. *q* is greater than one) the firm should want to expand, as the profits it expects to make from its assets are greater than the cost of the assets. If *q* is less than one, the shares of the firm are worth less than the assets and it will pay the firm to engage in DIVESTMENT: to sell the assets rather than try to use them. What should happen is that firms invest or divest until *q* is approximately equal to one.

Quantitative restrictions. ◊ QUOTAS.

Quantity rationing. The name given to one of four states of an economy that can exist when EXCESS DEMAND or EXCESS SUPPLY persists in the MARKET for LABOUR or in the market for goods and services. Quantity rationing is an area of MACROECONOMICS in the tradition of J. M. KEYNES (◊ KEYNESIAN ECONOMICS). It focuses on the study of DISEQUILIBRIUM, in contrast to NEW CLASSICAL ECONOMICS, which is predominantly concerned with the behaviour of economies in which all markets clear.

In quantity-rationing theory, in both the labour market (where firms buy and households sell) and the goods market (where households buy and firms sell) prices are not flexible. The wage level should adjust to clear the labour market, and the price level to clear the goods market. If wages or prices are sticky in the short run, disequilibrium arises because prices or wages fail to adjust to clear markets. This leaves either buyers or sellers 'rationed' in how much they can trade. Once quantity constraints apply in markets, the effectiveness of price signals can be undermined. Four different regimes arise in the following situations:

(a) REPRESSED INFLATION: Excess demand exists in both the labour and the goods market (buyers are rationed in both markets).

(b) KEYNESIAN UNEMPLOYMENT: Excess supply exists in both the labour and the goods markets (sellers are 'rationed' in both markets – they don't sell everything they would like to sell).

(c) CLASSICAL UNEMPLOYMENT: Excess supply exists in the labour market and excess demand in the goods market.

(d) Underconsumption: Excess demand exists in the labour market and excess supply in the goods market.

Despite the assumption that prices and wages are sticky in the short run, the most important implication of quantity rationing is that, even if prices are flexible in the long run, under Keynesian unemployment, there will be little or no tendency for the economy to move towards an equilibrium. This contrasts with other ECONOMIC DOCTRINES which hold that, as long as prices and wages are flexible, all markets clear eventually.

Quantity theory of money. The theory that changes in the MONEY SUPPLY have a direct influence on prices and nothing else. The theory is derived from the identity $MV = PT$ (called the FISHER equation), where M is the money stock; V the velocity with which the money circulates ($\diamondsuit$ VELOCITY OF CIRCULATION), P the average PRICE LEVEL, and T the number of transactions. All this equation says is that the amount of money spent equals the amount of money that is used; it is not a theory, it is a truism. The theory has two key elements: (a) that the velocity with which money circulates is stable, at least in the short term; and (b) that the number of transactions (which is closely related to the level of physical output) is fixed by the tastes of individuals and the real behaviour of firms in equilibrium. In this case, increases in M can only lead to increases in P; that is, money-supply increases cause INFLATION.

The theory provided the basis of MACROECONOMICS prior to J. M. KEYNES's *General Theory*, and had a plausibility about it in the eyes of the NEO-CLASSICAL ECONOMISTS, who strongly believed in the power of markets to settle at equilibria. It was largely superseded by Keynesian thinking when both elements of the theory came under attack. Increases in M were held to lead to falls in V, and, in some circumstances, increases in REAL INCOME ($\diamondsuit$ RADCLIFFE REPORT). However, in the 1960s the quantity theory re-emerged in a more sophisticated form through the work of M. FRIEDMAN. Friedman accepted the Keynesian view that V could alter when M altered, but said that it did so only in stable and predictable ways. On the second postulate, whereas Keynes said that unemployment could exist at an equilibrium of the national economy and therefore an increase in the money supply could increase real output, Friedman, although admitting that unemployment could persist, held that this was caused by structural factors in the economy ($\diamondsuit$ UNEMPLOYMENT, NATURAL RATE OF) and could not be influenced by AGGREGATE DEMAND measures, at least not for very long. ($\diamondsuit$ ECONOMIC DOCTRINES; MONETARISM).

Quartile. $\diamondsuit$ PERCENTILE.

Quasi-money. ◊ NEAR MONEY.

Quasi-rent. A term applied by A. MARSHALL to the earnings of CAPITAL, the supply of which is fixed in the short run. It is the excess made in the short run by a firm from the difference between the selling price and the AVOIDABLE COST of the product. For example, suppose a firm can make pens at a cost of 10 pence in labour and raw materials, and can sell them at 40 pence. A quasi-rent of 30 pence is earned; this is not, however, the profit of the firm, because there are costs of other fixed inputs which have to be covered by sales, even though they don't add to the cost of making extra pens. A loss-making firm can earn a quasi-rent.

Quasi-rent is analogous to ECONOMIC RENTS, because it represents a return in excess of that necessary to keep the firm in production – whenever price exceeds avoidable costs. It differs from economic rent, however, in that it is a temporary phenomenon. It can exist because, in the short run, price may differ from marginal cost, because firms take time to enter an industry and reduce excess profits.

Quesnay, François (1694–1774). A surgeon by profession, Quesnay held the post of secretary of the French Academy of Surgery and edited its official journal. He became physician to Madame de Pompadour. His major economic works appeared in various articles in the *Encyclopédie* in 1756 and 1757, and in the *Journal de l'agriculture, du commerce et des finances* in 1765 and 1767. The *Tableau économique* and *Maximes*, a commentary on the *Tableau*, were both published in 1758. The *Tableau* set out three classes of society, and showed how transactions flowed between them. The three classes were (a) landowners, (b) the farmers and farm-labourers and (c) others, called the 'sterile class'. Only the agricultural sector produced any surplus value, the rest only reproducing what it consumed (◊ MARX, K.). He anticipated MALTHUS's fear of underconsumption arising from excessive SAVINGS. Net INCOME would be reduced if the flows in the *Tableau* were interrupted by delays in spending. This was the first attempt to construct a MACROECONOMIC input–output MODEL of the economy (◊ INPUT–OUTPUT ANALYSIS). In fact, progress in this field had to await the application of MATRIX ALGEBRA and computerization (◊ LEONTIEF, W. W.). Quesnay suggested a single tax, '*l'impôt unique*', on the net income from land, arguing that the nation would thereby save tax-collecting costs. Only agriculture yielded a surplus, and therefore ultimately it bears all taxes anyway (◊ GEORGE, H.; MILL, J. S.). He was the central figure in the group of economists called the PHYSIOCRATS, who flourished in France between 1769 and 1770.

Queue, The. ◊ CAPITAL ISSUES COMMITTEE.

Quota sample. A method of sampling (◊◊ RANDOM SAMPLE) in which interviewers are given a quota of interviews to carry out with people or households with specified characteristics. For instance, in a travel survey an interviewer may be instructed to interview ten Americans, five Europeans and four Japanese. In this case, the sample is stratified (◊ STRATIFIED SAMPLE) by country of origin. The interviewer is free to chose, within the constraint of the quota, the person to be interviewed and, because of this freedom, bias can easily be introduced, so that the sample is not truly random. For example, the interviewer may select people who are both willing and able to speak English. Quota sampling is cheap but can lead to misleading results, because of conscious or unconscious bias.

Quotas. In INTERNATIONAL TRADE, the quantitative limits placed on the importation of specified COMMODITIES. The PROTECTION afforded by quotas is more certain than can be obtained by raising import TARIFFS as the effect of the latter will depend on the price ELASTICITIES of the imported commodities. Quotas, like tariffs, can also be used to favour preferred sources of supply. ◊ GENERAL AGREEMENT ON TARIFFS AND TRADE; IMPORTS. The term also applies to quantitative restrictions on production which may be set by CARTELS or colluding oligopolists. ◊ COLLUSION; OLIGOPOLY.

Quotation. The privilege granted to the issuer of a SECURITY by the STOCK EXCHANGE Council of placing the price of that security on the official list. A quoted security is for this reason referred to as a LISTED SECURITY. Only public companies fulfilling certain requirements designed to safeguard the investing public are granted quotations; lesser standards apply in the UNLISTED SECURITIES MARKETS, but companies for which MARKET MAKERS post prices in these markets are not properly described as *quoted companies*; this term is reserved for those on the official list of a recognized STOCK EXCHANGE. At the end of September 1986, 2,702 companies were on the official list of the London Stock Exchange; 2,123 were U.K.-registered companies, 506 were registered overseas and 73 in the Republic of Ireland.

Quoted company. ◊ QUOTATION.

R

Radcliffe Report. The Committee on the Working of the Monetary System was set up in May 1957, under the chairmanship of Lord Radcliffe, with wide terms of reference. It published its report in August 1959. Its members were Professor A. K. Cairncross, Sir Oliver Franks, Lord Harcourt, W. E. Jones, Professor R. S. Sayers, Sir Reginald Verdon Smith, George Woodcock and Sir John Woods. The report received considerable critical acclaim for the high standard of its description of the U.K. financial system and its institutions. At the same time, however, it gave rise to some criticism that the report had not given sufficient weight to the importance of regulating the quantity of money (▷ MONEY SUPPLY) as part of economic and financial policy. In the late 1960s the U.K. government became increasingly criticized (especially by economists in the U.S.A. and other advisers to the INTERNATIONAL MONETARY FUND who were particularly influenced by the work of M. FRIEDMAN) for following too closely the recommendations of the Radcliffe Report, which were embedded in the U.K. TREASURY's and BANK OF ENGLAND's philosophy. The Radcliffe Report had concluded that monetary policy should give priority to controlling the LIQUIDITY of the monetary system, and not the quantity of money in the system: 'Rejecting from among such measures [i.e. monetary measures to control INFLATION] any restriction of the supply of money, we advocate measures to strike more directly and rapidly at the liquidity of spenders. We regard a combination of controls of CAPITAL issues, bank advances and CONSUMER CREDIT as being most likely to serve this purpose.' Reasons for taking this view were the 'theoretical difficulties' of identifying 'the supply of money' and the 'Haziness that lies in the impossibility of limiting' the INCOME VELOCITY OF CIRCULATION. Nevertheless, the report did not dismiss the quantity of money as unimportant, but rather believed that given proper control of liquidity it would look after itself. 'Although we do not regard the supply of money as an unimportant quantity, we view it as only part of the wider structure of liquidity in the economy.' In external policy, the report was in favour of fixed EXCHANGE RATES. 'It would be more difficult, if there were no fixed rate to be defended, to keep domestic costs in line with costs abroad, and the need to devalue might result from the very ease with which the external value of the currency could be adjusted.' The report gave support to the need to strengthen the INTERNATIONAL LIQUIDITY position, and saw much

merit in strengthening the I.M.F. along the lines of the KEYNES PLAN.
▷ MACMILLAN COMMITTEE; SPECIAL DRAWING RIGHTS.

Random sample. A SAMPLE in which every member of the POPULATION
(*simple random sample*) or some subset of the population (STRATIFIED
SAMPLE) being tested has an equal chance of being included in
the sample. The purpose of sampling is to be able to infer, from the
sample taken, the attributes of the population as a whole. Only if the
sample is random can the PROBABILITY be calculated that a sampled
attribute applies to the population as a whole. ▷ QUOTA SAMPLE.

Rate of interest. The proportion of a sum of money that is paid over a
specified period of time in payment for its loan. It is the price a borrower
has to pay to enjoy the use of cash which he does not own, and the
return a lender enjoys for deferring his consumption or parting with
liquidity. The rate of interest is a price that can be analysed in the
normal framework of DEMAND and SUPPLY analysis. It may be seen
as a price in two different markets:

(a) The market for INVESTMENT funds. It equalizes the *demand* for
such funds, which is for investment, and the *supply*, which is
SAVING. If investors believe that they can earn a return of 10 per
cent on borrowed money by building a factory, and the rate of
interest is 5 per cent, they will demand all the funds that are available, indeed will eventually offer more than 5 per cent to obtain
cash which will earn them a profit at any rate up to 10 per cent.
Savers, on the other hand, have a rate of TIME PREFERENCE reflecting the compensation they require for putting money aside for
the future and not spending it in the present. If they need only 4 per
cent to be induced to save, and the rate of interest is 8 per cent,
there will be so much money put into savings that the rate will be
driven down. The rate of interest thus adjusts to ensure that investment equals saving, with saving reflecting the weight people attach
to current consumption over future consumption, and investment
the amount of extra future production that can be expected to result
from building new plant and machinery.

(b) The market for liquid assets (▷ LIQUIDITY). Firms and consumers
may prefer their assets to be in a readily available form – they
would prefer money worth £1 million to a factory worth the same;
however, most borrowers will need cash for long-term use, and will
need the certainty that they won't have to pay it back at short
notice. Thus, to compensate people for giving up ready access to the
money they lend (their loss of liquidity), interest is paid. This means
that the interest rate has an important influence on the demand for
money, and on very liquid assets.

The interest rate is thus affected by LIQUIDITY PREFERENCE and TIME
PREFERENCE; J. M. KEYNES introduced the idea of its impor-

tance in the demand for money and emphasized it in this role. Classical economists ignored liquidity preference, believing it to be in the market for investment that the rate of interest was determined. The problem of bringing the money market and the investment market to equilibrium with one price was at the heart of Keynesian economics. It would be surprising if a satisfactory equilibrium was achieved in both markets simultaneously. In simple theory, only one interest rate should prevail in the economy – if, for example, one building society offers a lower return than another, investors should move their cash from the first until it has so little money that it is forced to raise its rate ($\diamond$ A R B I T R A G E). However, for two main reasons, many rates prevail at any one time. The first is that F I N A N C I A L I N T E R M E D I A R I E S charge for their services by adding to the interest rate they charge borrowers or subtracting from the rate they pay lenders. This means there is an interest-rate differential: lenders get less than borrowers pay if a financial intermediary arranges the loan. The second is that interest rates also carry a risk premium: those lending money will want a higher-than-market rate of return if their investment has an uncertain return ($\diamond$ R I S K). ($\diamond$ C A P I T A L A S S E T PRICING MODEL; INTEREST, ABSTINENCE THEORY OF; INTEREST, CLASSICAL THEORY OF; INTEREST, NATURAL RATE OF; INTEREST, PRODUCTIVITY THEORIES OF; INTEREST, TIME PREFERENCE OF; LIQUIDITY TRAP.)

Rate of return. Usually, net P R O F I T after D E P R E C I A T I O N as a percentage of average CAPITAL EMPLOYED in a business. One of a number of FINANCIAL RATIOS used to measure the efficiency of a business as a whole, or of particular INVESTMENT projects. The rate of return may be calculated using profit before or after T A X, and there are a number of other variations of the concept. Profit may be defined as net of tax but not of depreciation and interest, i.e. profits available for EQUITY shareholders, or as operating profit, i.e. to exclude investment income and CAPITAL GAINS. Capital employed may be defined to exclude LOAN CAPITAL, in which case the return measured is that on equity capital; sometimes WORKING CAPITAL is excluded. The use of simple rates of return in the analysis of alternative investment projects is open to the serious criticism that it does not take account of the timing of capital outlays and earnings, and hence does not allow for the time value of money ($\diamond$ INVESTMENT APPRAISAL). Strictly speaking, the rate of return on capital employed in a business does not measure the return to capital alone or the efficiency of the use of R E S O U R C E S by that business, since the returns to each of the FACTORS OF PRODUCTION cannot be separated out. However, in normal circumstances a firm which is earning a long-term rate of return lower than its cost of capital ($\diamond$ CAPITAL, COST OF) could be said to be using resources inefficiently.

Rate of technical substitution (R.T.S.). The increase in production of one commodity an economy can achieve by cutting the production of another commodity by one unit. If a country could transfer resources from making one spoon to make two forks, the rate of technical substitution between spoons and forks is two. The rate of technical substitution between commodity A and B usually diminishes as production of A increases. If, at production of twenty aircraft and twenty million loaves of bread, society can produce a million loaves with equal ease to one aircraft, at production of thirty aircraft and ten million loaves, the production of one aircraft will require a much larger sacrifice in terms of loaves. Graphically, the R.T.S. is the slope of the TRANSFORM-ATION CURVE. Mathematically, it is the ratio of the MARGINAL PRODUCTS of producing two items. ($\diamondsuit$ ECONOMIC EFFICIENCY; MARGINAL RATE OF SUBSTITUTION.)

Rates. A DIRECT TAX paid by firms or individuals to local government authorities in the U.K. proportional to the rateable value of their premises. The rateable value is determined in relation to the annual rent the premises would attract if let on the open market, though the *poundage*, or rate per pound of rateable value, differs between local authorities and between business and domestic premises. A green paper published in the summer of 1986 proposes the abolition of the present form of domestic rates in the U.K. and their replacement by a 'community charge', a flat-rate charge on each member of a household, effectively a POLL TAX. Business rates would remain in their present form but levied at a common-rate poundage across the country. In other countries local government is also financed by taxation on incomes, profits, ASSETS and sales. ($\diamondsuit$ ALLEN REPORT; LAYFIELD COMMITTEE; SALES TAX.)

Rational expectations. A hypothesis of behaviour of individuals by which their predictions contain no systematic errors. Nobody can predict the future with perfect foresight because unforseen, random happenings are bound to occur. However, someone with rational expectations will construct their expectations so that on average they are correct; that is, they will be wrong only because of random, non-systematic errors. The disadvantage of other ways in which individuals may be assumed to predict the future is that they allow them to make systematic errors. ADAPTIVE EXPECTATIONS, for example, postulate that individuals predict next year's price inflation on the basis of last year's, and the rate of change up to last year. At a time of increasing inflation, their expectation will perpetually lag behind the actual inflation rate – but despite this, under the hypothesis of adaptive expectations, everybody carries on using this predictive method although it produces biased forecasts. The theory of rational expectations has stimulated debate in economics because it has controversial implications. The first is that it appears to demolish any case for government policy aimed at stimulating demand in the economy: if the government expands the money supply by 5 per cent, everybody will believe that prices will rise as a consequence. This will make them add 5 per cent to their wage demands or prices and a 5 per cent price inflation occurs without there being any positive effect on output or employment. The second is that markets behave efficiently (◊ EFFICIENT MARKETS HYPOTHESIS). The price of the shares of a company reflects the profits the company is expected to make. If expectations are rational, the price at any point in time is based on expectations which have taken into consideration all possible information about the company. This has two consequences. The first consequence is that if some 'news' arrives that indicates the company's fortunes are likely to change, that information will cause the price to change immediately. Secondly, however, as the 'news' that arrives can only reflect random, not systematic, events, the price of the company's shares must follow a random path.

The interesting implications of rational expectations should not necessarily make them appear a plausible description of men's behaviour. Nevertheless, like PERFECT COMPETITION in MICROECONOMICS, rational expectations provide a model of an extreme form of human behaviour that provides a benchmark against which the behaviour of people in the real world can be judged. In the very long term, the hypothesis that systematic forecasting errors are not made appears by no means implausible. (◊ EXPECTATIONS; LUCAS CRITIQUE; NEW CLASSICAL ECONOMICS.)

Real balance effect. ◊ PIGOU, A. C.

Real income. ◊ REAL TERMS.

Real terms. A MONEY value adjusted for changes in PRICES. The nominal value of the NATIONAL INCOME may rise by 10 per cent over a year with a similar increase in personal expenditure, but if consumer prices have risen by 8 per cent the quantity of goods and services that are purchased by the consumer will have increased only by about 2 per cent. Thus to convert money values to *constant prices* or real terms it is necessary to deflate (◊ DEFLATION) data at current prices by an appropriate INDEX NUMBER. In the same way money wages or other forms of income can be adjusted to *real wages* or *real income* to allow for changes in the purchasing power of earnings. ◊ MONEY ILLUSION.

Real wages. ◊ REAL TERMS.

Receiver. ◊ BANKRUPTCY.

Recession. An imprecise term given to a sharp slow-down in the rate of economic growth or a modest decline in economic activity, as distinct from a slump or DEPRESSION which is a more severe and prolonged downturn. Recessions are a feature of the TRADE CYCLE. Two successive declines in seasonally adjusted (◊ SEASONAL ADJUSTMENT) real GROSS DOMESTIC PRODUCT would constitute a recession.

Reciprocal demand. ◊ EQUATION OF INTERNATIONAL DEMAND.

Reciprocity. The practice, sometimes called a 'fair trade' or 'beggar-my-neighbour' policy, by which governments extend to each other similar concessions or restrictions in trade. It is reflected in U.S. trade policy in the Reciprocal Trade Agreements Acts of 1934, the Trade Expansion Act of 1962, which made possible the KENNEDY ROUND OF TRADE NEGOTIATIONS under the GENERAL AGREEMENT ON TARIFFS AND TRADE, and the Trade Act of 1974.

Recognized investment exchanges (R.I.E.s). ◊ SECURITIES AND INVESTMENTS BOARD.

Redeemable securities. STOCK or BONDS that are repayable at their PAR VALUE at a certain date, dates or specified eventuality. Most fixed-interest SECURITIES are redeemable, though CONSOLS bear no redemption date. ORDINARY SHARES and some PREFERENCE SHARES are irredeemable. ◊ REDEMPTION DATE.

Redemption date. The date at which a LOAN will be repaid or release given from other obligations. ◊ REDEEMABLE SECURITIES.

Redemption yield. ◊ YIELD.

Reducing balance. A means of recording DEPRECIATION expenses in which the original COST of an ASSET is 'written down' by a fixed fraction each year. In this way, the amount of depreciation allowed falls each year: e.g. a machine costing £500 could be written down by 20 per cent per annum, i.e. £100 in the first year and then 20 per cent on its written-down value of £400, i.e. £80 in the following year, and so on. A rate can be chosen to write down an asset to an expected residual value in a chosen period of years, e.g. five years and £50, which in our example would require an annual depreciation rate of about 53 per cent. Although the reducing-balance system gives a lighter depreciation charge in later years when maintenance and repair costs as well as risk of OBSOLESCENCE may be higher (as opposed to the straight-line method, where equal depreciation is charged every year), it is unlikely to accord very closely with actual depreciation. However, the taxation authorities in Britain and other countries base TAX allowances for certain CAPITAL investment on a reducing balance. ◊ CAPITAL ALLOWANCES.

Reflation. A MACROECONOMIC policy of increasing aggregate demand in the economy in order to reduce unemployment. The argument for reflation can most clearly be seen in terms of KEYNESIAN interpretations of the economy. When a *deflationary gap* exists, unemployment exists, indicating that there is spare capacity in the economy, and additional demand leads to a rise in spending, itself boosted by the MULTIPLIER, with a consequential rise in the number employed. Criticisms have been made of reflation as a policy prescription however, often associated with the doctrine of MONETARISM. The argument is as follows: the reflation is generated by either printing money or by increased borrowing. ($\lozenge$ PUBLIC-SECTOR BORROWING REQUIRE-MENT). If it is through printing money, no non-monetary variables can change. The level of aggregate demand rises; prices rise; more labour is sought to produce the extra demand, so wages rise; at the end of the process *real wages* ($\lozenge$ REAL TERMS) are constant, as are all relative prices. Nothing changes except the absolute price level. If, on the other hand, the reflation is financed by borrowing, every pound the government borrows the private sector lends, and thus for every extra pound of government spending there is a pound less of private spending: this is called CROWDING OUT, and it occurs because, when the government borrowing increases, INTEREST RATES rise, squeezing private investment ($\lozenge$ CLASSICAL ECONOMICS). These criticisms rely on a belief that market forces work effectively and that unemployment is at its natural rate ($\lozenge$ UNEMPLOYMENT, NATURAL RATE OF). suggesting that a deflationary gap could never exist. They also imply that private investment is highly responsive to interest-rate changes and that interest rates themselves are highly sensitive to changes in the supply of government bonds. ($\lozenge$ KEYNESIAN UNEMPLOYMENT.)

Regional employment premium. An addition to the SELECTIVE EMPLOY-MENT TAX refund payable to manufacturing firms in the assisted areas ($\lozenge$ DEVELOPMENT AREAS). It came into operation in September 1967 at a rate of £1·50 per week per man, and was subsequently raised to £3·00. It was abolished in 1977.

Registrar of Restrictive Practices. $\lozenge$ RESTRICTIVE TRADE PRACTICES ACTS.

Regression analysis. A mathematical technique for estimating the PAR-AMETERS of an equation from sets of data of the independent and dependent VARIABLES. For instance, in the demand equation $q = aY + bP + c$, in which q = quantity bought of a good, Y = income and P = price, the parameters a, b and c can be estimated, provided there is a sufficient number of actual observations of the variables, q, Y and P. Regression analysis finds the values of a, b and c, which when substituted in the expression $aY + bP + c$ yields the least error in estimating q. Regression analysis is widely used in ECONO-METRICS. $\lozenge$ AUTO-CORRELATION; LEAST-SQUARES REGRESSION; MULTICOLLINEARITY.

Regression model. $\lozenge$ REGRESSION ANALYSIS.

Regressive tax. A TAX which takes a decreasing proportion of INCOME as income rises.($\lozenge$ ALLEN REPORT.)

Regulation. The supervision and control of the economic activities of PRIVATE ENTERPRISE by government in the interest of economic efficiency, fairness, health and safety. Regulation has a long history, pre-dating the industrial revolution, and takes many different forms. The regulation of private NATURAL MONOPOLIES and other instances of MONOPOLY power ($\Diamond$ RESTRICTIVE TRADE PRACTICES ACTS) can be seen as an alternative (and in the United States is preferred) to public ownership ($\Diamond$ NATIONALIZED INDUSTRIES). When British Telecom was privatized ($\Diamond$ PRIVATIZATION), for example, it became necessary to create a regulatory agency, the Office of Telecommunications (Oftel). EXTERNALITIES such as noise and pollution have made it necessary (among other reasons) to regulate road and air transport, while fears that government economic policy might be frustrated by the flight of capital and, originally, the need to conserve foreign currency for war purposes, led to the imposition of EXCHANGE CONTROL. These types of regulation have all received extensive analysis by economists. More recently interest has extended to the justification for and consequences of a broader range of regulatory instruments. These other forms of regulation include: measures to safeguard the rights of employees (for example the Employment Protection Acts); to regulate the trade unions; the financial system ($\Diamond$ SECURITIES AND INVESTMENTS BOARD); personal privacy (the Data Protection Act); the Health and Safety at Work Act; fishing rights; the CONSUMER CREDIT ACT; town and country planning; food and drugs; industrial training; the licensing of street traders and taxicabs.

Regulation may be imposed simply by enacting laws and leaving their supervision to the normal processes of the law, by setting up special regulatory agencies or by encouraging self-regulation by recognizing, and in some cases delegating powers to, voluntary bodies. Except where regulation is necessary to prevent the abuse of monopoly power, in the interests of preserving health and safety or to correct EXTERNALITIES or other instances of MARKET FAILURE, and even then, there is a risk that the COMPLIANCE COSTS and other costs of regulation may exceed the SOCIAL BENEFITS. The rapid growth of regulation since the Second World War has led to increasing concern about the costs of regulation and a call for the reform and even abolition of regulatory requirements, i.e. *deregulation*.

Relative-income hypothesis. A theory of CONSUMPTION and SAVING that suggests individuals are more concerned with their consumption relative to other people's than they are with their absolute living standard. If everybody wants to 'keep up with the Joneses' in their consumption, the poor will spend a higher proportion of their income than the rich. This is observed to be the case. However, as society as a whole gets richer, no one will feel able to consume less, because everybody will also be getting richer. This too is observed. The relative-income hypothesis, developed by James Duesenberry, is an alternative theory to the PERMANENT-INCOME HYPOTHESIS and the LIFE-CYCLE HYPOTHESIS. ($\Diamond$ CONSUMPTION FUNCTION.)

Rent. The income accruing to the owner for the services of a DURABLE

GOOD such as a piece of land, property or a computer. ⇨ ECONOMIC RENT; QUASI-RENT; RICARDO, D.

Rentier. Someone who receives his income in the form of INTEREST and DIVIDENDS rather than in wages or salary and who does not otherwise participate in the process of production. A provider of CAPITAL and person of independent means.

Replacement-cost accounting. ⇨ INFLATION ACCOUNTING.

Replacement rate. ⇨ UNEMPLOYMENT TRAP.

Repressed inflation. The state of a set of markets or an economy in which there is persistent EXCESS DEMAND for goods and services. If prices are below their market clearing levels, demand will outweigh the available supply; this should drive prices up, causing INFLATION. If, however, prices are prevented from rising, for example, because of price controls (⇨ PRICES AND INCOMES POLICY), the inflation can be prevented but consumers will not be able to obtain as much of things as they want. Features of markets suffering repressed inflation will thus be queues, explicit state rationing, constant shortages or black markets.

While the term repressed inflation can be used to refer to a state of any set of markets in which excess demand is not removed by price increases, more specifically it is one of four forms of QUANTITY RATIONING in the macroeconomy; the others are KEYNESIAN UNEMPLOYMENT, CLASSICAL UNEMPLOYMENT and UNDERCONSUMPTION. In terms of these models of the economy, repressed inflation is one in which buyers in both the labour and goods markets are rationed: households cannot get the goods they want and firms the labour they want. It can be cured by freeing prices and wages and letting them rise, so that they meet equilibrium prices, or by cutting aggregate demand so that the equilibrium price in each market moves down to the level of the actual price.

Resale price maintenance (R.P.M.). The practice whereby a manufacturer requires the distributors of his product to resell at certain PRICES, or at not less than minimum prices, which he has set for his products. There have been a number of U.K. governmental inquiries into the practice to determine whether or not it was in the public interest. The inquiries of 1920 and 1931 were in favour of continuing to allow manufacturers to follow the practice. The arguments in favour were that price-fixing set PROFIT margins which ensured fair returns, both to the manufacturer and to the distributors for their services, and that no government had the right without very good reason to interfere with the freedom of private citizens to make contracts. In 1955 the MONOPOLIES COMMISSION's report *Collective Discrimination – A Report on Exclusive Dealing, Aggregated Rebates and Other Discriminatory Trade Practices* recommended that R.P.M., collectively enforced by manufacturers, should be made illegal, although individual manufacturers should be permitted to continue the practice. The report served as the basis for the

RESTRICTIVE TRADE PRACTICES ACT of 1956. This Act specifically prohibited the collective enforcement of R.P.M. and set up the Restrictive Practices Court to decide each individual case on its merits. Restrictive agreements had to be registered. The manufacturer could, under the Act, take a price-cutting retailer to court, even if there was no explicit contract between them, and the court could issue an injunction restraining the retailer. In 1964 the Resale Prices Act was passed under which all resale price agreements were assumed to be against the public interest unless it could be proved otherwise to the court ($\Diamond$ COMPETITION ACT; FAIR TRADING ACT; NET BOOK AGREEMENT).

Research and development (R. & D.). Includes: (a) basic or pure research intended to increase knowledge without any particular application in view, such as research into the properties of materials; (b) applied research directed at a particular objective, for example searching for a new material for a product; (c) experimental or development work on new inventions or the improvement of existing products and processes. All three types of R. & D. are carried out by government research laboratories, universities, research institutes and company research establishments. About 2 per cent of the employed LABOUR FORCE are engaged in R. & D. work in the United States and about half that percentage in Europe. However, these figures relate to professional, recorded R. & D. workers only; a substantial amount of research and development is carried on by amateurs and in small firms which goes unrecorded. Expenditure on R. & D. by U.K. industry in 1985 was £4·8 billion, somewhat lower than in 1981. Total U.K. employment on R. & D. in 1985 was 157,000. R. & D. activity is important because of its role in defence policy and in commercial INNOVATION.

Reserve asset ratio. $\Diamond$ CREDIT CONTROL.

Reserve currency. A CURRENCY which governments and international institutions are willing to hold in their GOLD AND FOREIGN EXCHANGE RESERVES and which finances a significant proportion of INTERNATIONAL TRADE. These two conditions normally require that (a) the value of the currency must be stable in relation to other currencies, (b) the currency is that of a country which holds an important share of world trade, (c) there exists an efficient FOREIGN-EXCHANGE MARKET in which the currency may be exchanged for other currencies, and (d) the currency is convertible ($\Diamond$ CONVERTIBILITY). The dollar and the pound sterling were the dominant reserve currencies in the period between 1945 and the early 1970s. Since the upheaval in international finance in 1973–4 caused by the increase in oil prices, governments have diversified their foreign-exchange holdings into other currencies such as the West German Deutschmark and the Japanese yen. In addition the EUROPEAN CURRENCY UNIT (E.C.U.) has become prominent recently. In 1985, about 57 per cent of official reserves were held in U.S. dollars, 11 per cent in Deutschmarks, 11 per cent in E.C.U.s, 5 per cent in yen and 3 per cent in Sterling. ⟡ INTER-NATIONAL LIQUIDITY; STERLING AREA.

Resource allocation. The assignment of a role to scarce resources (⟡ FAC-TORS OF PRODUCTION) in the economy to the production of outputs. The fact of SCARCITY leads to the need for allocation. As this allocation of scarce inputs determines the composition and size of an economy's output, each possible bundle of goods and services produced by an economy constitutes an allocation of resources. Each allocation there-fore can be defined in two ways: either by the use made of inputs *or* by the mix of total output. In a world consisting of only two goods, say milk and honey, each allocation may be represented by a point on a graph with output of one of the commodities on each axis. In such an economy if no more milk can be produced without a fall in the output of honey, the allocation is efficient and lies on the TRANSFORMATION CURVE of the economy. If the combination lies within that curve, resources are used inefficiently because by, say, swapping some of the beekeepers assigned to tending dairy cows with some of the farmers assigned to beekeeping, production of both milk and honey can be increased. Economics may be said to be about the allocation of scarce resources. It is concerned with the optimum allocation of those resources to the production of goods and services required by society and deter-mined through the PRICE SYSTEM. (⟡ ECONOMIC EFFICIENCY; MARKET FORCES.)

Resources. Scarce inputs that can yield UTILITY through production or provision of goods and services (⟡ FACTORS OF PRODUCTION; NATURAL RESOURCES; PRODUCTION FUNCTION; RESOURCE ALLOCATION).

Restriction, exchange. ⟡ EXCHANGE CONTROLS.

Restrictive Practices Court. ⟡ RESTRICTIVE TRADE PRACTICES ACTS.

Restrictive Trade Practices Acts. The Restrictive Trade Practices Act of 1956 was based on the recommendations of the MONOPOLIES COM-MISSION's 1955 report on *Collective Discrimination – A Report on Ex-clusive Dealing, Aggregated Rebates and Other Discriminatory Trade Practices.* This Act required the registration of all agreements between two or more firms, whether buyers or sellers, which contain restrictions on PRICES, quantities or quality of goods traded or on channels of distribution. It set up a Restrictive Practices Court, serviced by five judges and up to ten laymen and a Registrar of Restrictive Trading Agreements. The court was required by the Act to assume that each agreement is against the public interest unless it could be shown to have advantages on reference to seven explicit factors: (a) that the restriction is necessary for public safety; (b) that it confers specific and substantial benefits or advantages on consumers; (c) that it neutralizes monopolistic or restrictive activities of others; (d) that it is necessary in order to be able to negotiate fair terms with strong buyers or sellers; (e) that removal of the agreement would lead to significant regional UNEMPLOYMENT; (f) that removal would reduce EXPORT earnings; and (g) that it is necessary to support other restrictive practices which are in the public interest. Under the 1956 Act, only agreements of 'No substantial economic significance' could be exempted from appearing before the court, and even this could be achieved only by their removal from the register. In 1968, a second Restrictive Trade Practices Act was passed by which agreements could be exempted from court proceedings as a result of a Board of Trade directive. The Act also gave the Board of Trade (now the Department of Trade and Industry) powers to call certain information agreements for registration which were excluded from the previous Act. The functions of the Register of Restrictive Trading Agreements were taken over by the Director-General of Fair Trading under the FAIR TRADING ACT, 1973, which also extended the scope of the legislation to include commercial services. The Restrictive Trade Practices Act of 1976 consolidated previous legislation. ⇔ COMPETITION ACT; RESALE PRICE MAINTENANCE.

Retail banking. ⇔ WHOLESALE BANKING.

Retail-price index. ⇔ INDEX NUMBER.

Retail trade. The final link in the chain of distribution from the manufacturer to the final consumer. The economic functions of the retailer are to hold stocks at a location convenient to the consumer so as to provide him with choice, guidance and after-sales service and, where appropriate, credit facilities (⇔ CONSUMER CREDIT). In providing these services, the retailer adds value to the goods he purchases from the wholesaler or direct from the manufacturer (⇔ VALUE ADDED). There were 264,000 retail businesses registered for VALUE-ADDED TAX at the end of 1984 in the U.K. (not all retailers need to register for V.A.T.) but the number has fallen substantially since 1950 mainly as a result of competition from the large multiple retailers which enjoy ECONOMIES OF SCALE in operation and in purchasing from their suppliers (⇔ COUNTERVAILING POWER).

Retained earnings. Undistributed PROFITS. ⇔ SELF-FINANCING.

Retentions. Undistributed PROFITS. ⇔ SELF-FINANCING.

Return on capital employed. ⇔ RATE OF RETURN.

Return on investment (R.O.I.). ⇔ RATE OF RETURN.

Returns to scale. The proportionate increase in output resulting from proportionate increases in all inputs. If the number of workers, raw materials and machines used by a firm are all doubled, three situations can result: *decreasing returns to scale* would hold if output less than doubled; *constant returns to scale* would exist if output exactly doubled; and *increasing returns to scale* would hold if output more than doubled.

Decreasing returns to scale should not be confused with the LAW OF DIMINISHING RETURNS which traces the response of output to an increase in one individual input with all others held constant. (◊ ECONOMIES OF SCALE; PRODUCTION FUNCTION.)

Revaluation. ◊ DEVALUATION; EXCHANGE RATE.

Revealed preference. An approach to demand theory which derives the traditional laws of demand using only information on the choices the consumer makes in different price and income situations coupled with the assumption that such choices are made rationally. It can be seen as a third approach to consumer behaviour, in contrast to the cardinal approach (◊ MARGINAL UTILITY), which requires there to be an absolute, single, measure of utility, and the ORDINAL UTILITY approach (based on INDIFFERENCE-CURVE ANALYSIS), which requires there to be some measure of relative utility, albeit one that does not require actual magnitudes of utility to be ascribed to bundles of commodities. The revealed-preference approach holds that only two types of information are theoretically necessary to predict the behaviour of consumers and derive the laws of demand. The first is the observed spending of a consumer in different price–income situations – this reveals which bundles of commodities are preferred to others. The second is the assumption that the consumer's behaviour accords to certain axioms of 'rationality' – to predict how someone will spend their money, we must know that they will not behave erratically (◊ TRANSITIVITY). It can be shown that, if such information were available in full, an indifference map could be constructed for the consumer. Implicitly, therefore, the approach does construct at least a partial indifference map of the form used in indifference-curve theory and should best be seen as an alternative expression of this theory rather than a replacement for it. (◊ DEMAND, THEORY OF; SAMUELSON, P. A.)

Revenue reserves. ◊ COMPANY RESERVES.

Reverse take-over. The acquisition or 'TAKE-OVER' of a public company by a private company. Often also used to refer to the acquisition of a company by another, smaller, one.

Reverse yield gap. ◊ YIELD GAP.

Ricardian equivalence. The idea originally expounded by D. RICARDO, and more recently by Robert Barro, that government deficits do not matter because private citizens anticipate the fact that any borrowing now has to be repaid later, and thus increase their saving with that in mind. The essence of the proposition is that individuals can unravel the effect of government policy. If the government consumes more and borrows the money to do so, and if the private sector did not want overall consumption to rise, the private sector would save more now so that when the debts had to be repaid, the money was available. The government might as well have taxed people rather than borrow the money. Ricardian equivalence can be seen as part of a thread of economic thinking which holds that only decisions about real variables – like consumption and production – matter; and that decisions about financing will, in perfectly functioning markets, never have an effect. ◊〉 MODIGLIANI–MILLER THEOREM.

Ricardo, David (1772–1823). The son of Jewish parents who were connected with the MONEY MARKET, first in the Netherlands, and later in London, Ricardo had little formal education. At the early age of fourteen, however, he was already working in the money market himself. It was James Mill (the father of J. S. MILL) who persuaded Ricardo, himself diffident about his own abilities, to write. Nevertheless, Ricardo succeeded in making a fortune on the STOCK EXCHANGE, sufficient for him to be able to retire at forty-two. Not surprisingly, many of his earlier publications were concerned with money and banking. In 1810 he published a pamphlet on *The High Price of Bullion, a Proof of the Depreciation of Bank Notes*; in 1811 appeared the *Reply to Mr Bosanquet's Practical Observations on the Report of the Bullion Committee*; and in 1816 *Proposals for an Economical and Secure Currency*. However, his work on monetary economics did not have the originality or exert the influence comparable to his studies in other branches of economics. In 1815 he published his *Essay on the Influence of the Low Price of Corn on the Profits of Stock*, which was the prototype for his most important work. This first appeared in 1817 under the title of *The Principles of Political Economy and Taxation*, a work which was to dominate English CLASSICAL ECONOMICS for the following half-century. In his *Principles* Ricardo was basically concerned 'to determine the laws which regulate the distribution (between the different classes of landowners, capitalists and labour) of the produce of industry'. His approach was to construct a theoretical MODEL which abstracted from the complexities of an actual economy so as to attempt to reveal the major important influences at work within it. His economy was predominantly agricultural. With DEMAND rising as a result of increasing POPULATION, and a level of subsistence which tended, by custom, to rise also over time, more and more less-fertile LAND had to be brought into cultivation. The return (in terms of the output of corn) of each further addition of CAPITAL and LABOUR to more land fell (◊ DIMINISHING RETURNS, LAW OF). This process continued until it was no longer considered sufficiently profitable to bring any additional plots of land under cultivation. However, COSTS and PROFITS must be the same on all land, whether or not it was marginal. Labour cost the same wherever it was applied. If profits were higher at one place than at another, it would encourage capital to be invested at the place of high return, until by the process of diminishing returns, profit fell into line with profits elsewhere. Therefore, as costs and profits were the same throughout, a surplus was

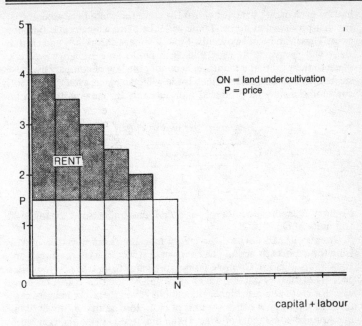

ON = land under cultivation
P = price

RENT

capital + labour

earned on the non-marginal land, and this was RENT (*shaded in the diagram*).

The consequence of this was that, as the population expanded and more less-fertile land was brought into cultivation, profits became squeezed between the increasing proportion of total output which went in rent and the basic minimum level of subsistence allocated to the wages of labour. Ricardo assumed that prices were determined principally by the quantity of labour used during production (◇ VALUE, THEORIES OF). However, he recognized that capital costs did nevertheless also have an influence on prices and that the effect of a rise in wages on relative prices depended on the proportion of these two FACTORS OF PRODUCTION in the various COMMODITIES. With a rise in wages, CAPITAL-INTENSIVE goods became cheaper relative to LABOUR-INTENSIVE goods, with a consequent shift in the demand and output in favour of the former (◇ RICARDO EFFECT). In the theory of INTERNATIONAL TRADE Ricardo stated explicitly for the first time the law of comparative costs. This law can best be illustrated by means of the example of two countries (*A* and *B*) producing two commodities (say cloth and wine). If the relative cost of cloth to wine is the same in both countries, then no trade will take place because there is no gain to be

357

had by exchanging wine (or cloth) for cloth (or wine) produced abroad for that produced at home. Trade will take place where cost differences exist. These can be of two kinds. First, if wine is cheap in *A* and cloth in *B*, *A* will specialize in wine and *B* in cloth, and exchange will take place to their mutual advantage. Secondly the law of comparative costs states the condition under which trade will take place, even though both commodities may be produced more cheaply in one country than another.

Man-hours per unit of output

Country	Wine	Cloth
A	120	100
B	80	90

Country *B* exports one unit of wine to *A*, and imports in exchange 120/100 units of cloth.

If Country *B* had devoted the eighty man-hours employed in making wine for exports to making cloth instead, it would have produced only 80/90 units of cloth. Country *B* therefore gains from trade by the difference $[(120/100) - (80/90)]$ units of cloth. As long as *B* can exchange wine for cloth at a rate higher than 80/90, it will therefore gain from the trade. If Country *A* exports a unit of cloth to Country *B*, it will obtain in exchange 90/80 units of wine. If the hundred man-hours required by *A* to produce a unit of cloth had been devoted to the home production of wine, only 100/120 units of wine would be obtained. The gain from trade therefore is $[(90/80) - (100/120)]$ units of wine. Provided therefore *A* can exchange cloth for wine at a rate higher than 100/120, it will gain from the trade. Within the range of exchange of wine for cloth of 120/100 and 80/90 both countries therefore benefit.

The law of comparative costs survives as an important part of the theory of international trade today. Otherwise Ricardo's main contribution is the analytical approach of theoretical model building which has contributed substantially to economists' methodological tool-kits.
▷ EQUATION OF INTERNATIONAL DEMAND; HECKSCHER–OHLIN PRINCIPLE; RICARDIAN EQUIVALENCE.

Ricardo effect. F. A. VON HAYEK argued that, if the PRICES which firms received for their outputs increased more than the COSTS of their raw materials and wages, the average rate of PROFIT on CAPITAL employed per year increased more for those firms with a short than for those with a long turnover period. This can best be illustrated by a simple arithmetical example. If the rate of profit per year is 5 per cent, £100 of capital will yield £105 in one year and £110 in two years (approximately, ignoring COMPOUND INTEREST). If output prices rise by, say, 1 per cent, the YIELD rises to £6 for one year and to £11 in two years. The rate of profit, therefore, rises to 6 per cent per annum for the capital which can be turned over in one year, but only to 5½ per cent per annum for capital with a two-year turnover period. Consequently, in a boom, when COMMODITY prices rise faster than wages, firms are discouraged from investing in capital goods industries because of the long production time required. This reaction is called the Ricardo effect because of its affinity to Ricardo's argument that, if REAL WAGES fall, firms tend to substitute LABOUR for machinery. This conclusion contrasted sharply with J. M. KEYNES's views based on the principle of the accelerator (◊ ACCELERATION PRINCIPLE).

Rights issue. An offer of new SHARES to existing shareholders. A company will offer the 'rights' in a certain proportion to existing holdings, depending upon the amount of new EQUITY capital it wishes to raise. Thus, in a 'one for one rights issue', each shareholder would be offered a number of new shares equal to the number he already holds. To ensure that the issue is taken up, the new shares are offered at well below the market price of the existing shares. The choice of the discount below the ruling price is not as critical in normal circumstances as is often supposed, because when the rights issue is announced the market price of the shares will adjust to the market's view of the value of the rights price. Rights issues are a relatively cheap way of raising CAPITAL for a quoted company since the costs of preparing a brochure, UNDERWRITING commission or press advertising involved in a new issue are avoided. ◊ NEW-ISSUE MARKET.

Risk. A state in which the number of possible future events exceeds the number of events that will actually occur, and some measure of PROBABILITY can be attached to them. This definition distinguishes risk from UNCERTAINTY in which the probabilities are unknown. A gambler, for example, faces risk because he could either be very much richer tomorrow than he is today or (more likely) slightly poorer, depending on whether a roulette wheel spins the ball into the right hole – and he knows the odds of the roulette wheel. (◊ BERNOULLI'S HYPOTHESIS; PROBABILITY.)

It is normally assumed that economic agents dislike risk (◊ RISK AVERSION) and in the market for financial assets the riskier an asset, the higher the expected return investors will require of it (◊ PORTFOLIO THEORY).

Risk aversion. The placing of a higher value on a prospect arriving with certainty than on an uncertain prospect which has the same expected outcome, but with some RISK or UNCERTAINTY attached. If you would prefer to be given £10 with certainty than to have a 50 per cent chance of £15 and a 50 per cent chance of £5 (which gives an average of £10) then you are risk-averse. Economists normally assume that consumers are risk-averse on account of DIMINISHING MARGINAL UTILITY. The displeasure of losing £5 outweighs the pleasure of winning an extra £5 because the richer we are, the less we probably value £5 (◊ BERNOULLI'S HYPOTHESIS). Risk aversion explains why people normally insure against disaster. Gambling, on the other hand, is *risk-loving* behaviour; people at casinos on average pay out more than they win back. (◊ EXPECTED UTILITY.)

Risk capital. Long-term funds invested in enterprises particularly subject to RISK, as in new ventures. Sometimes used as a synonym for EQUITY capital, it is also used instead of the term *venture capital*, a somewhat more precise term meaning CAPITAL provided for a new business undertaking by persons other than the proprietors. Neither term is unambiguous, since all capital except that secured by fixed assets is at risk, and even extensions to existing business may be described accurately as a new venture. Venture capital is provided by private investors and by institutions such as the MERCHANT BANKS. There are also a number of specialized venture capital institutions, such as the Industrial and Commercial Finance Corporations. ◊ FINANCE FOR INDUSTRY.

Robbins, Lionel, Baron Robbins of Clare Market (1898–1984). Lord Robbins became a lecturer at the London School of Economics after graduating there. After a brief period as a lecturer at New College, Oxford, in 1924, and again from 1927 to 1929, he was appointed in 1929 to the Chair of Economics at the London School of Economics, a position he held until 1961. During the Second World War he was, from 1941 to 1945, director of the economics section of the Cabinet Office. In 1961 he became chairman of the *Financial Times* newspaper. He chaired the Committee on Higher Education. An economist in the tradition of the English CLASSICAL SCHOOL, in *An Essay on the Nature and Significance of Economic Science*, which appeared in 1932, he defined economics as 'a science which studies human behaviour as a relation between ends and scarce means which have alternative uses'. Economic analysis should beware of including propositions based on value judgements; that is, it should be a scientific logical process without ethical or moral overtones. His other publications include *The Great Depression* (1934), *Economic Planning and International Order* (1937), *The Economic Problem in Peace and War* (1947), *The Economist in the Twentieth Century* (1956), *Robert Torrens and the Evolution of Classical Economics* (1958), *Politics and Economics* (1963), *The Evolution of Modern Economic Theory* (1970) and *Autobiography of an Economist* (1971).

Robinson, Joan Violet (1903–83). Educated at Girton College, Professor Robinson took up a post as assistant lecturer at Cambridge University in 1931, becoming reader in 1949. She was elected to the Chair of Economics in 1965 on the retirement of her husband, Professor Sir E.

A. G. Robinson, and remained in this post until 1971. Economic theorists in the 1920s were much concerned with the problem of the meaning of a theory of VALUE based on PERFECT COMPETITION. In particular, it was felt of doubtful validity to assume a situation in which there were so many firms supplying a COMMODITY that none of them individually could affect the PRICE – in face of the existence of the economies of large-scale output, Professor Robinson broke out of the analytical framework of perfect competition and built up her analysis on the basis of firms in 'imperfect competition' (◊ MONOPOLISTIC COMPETITION). Each firm had a MONOPOLY in its products which was based on the preferences of consumers (◊ CONSUMER PREFERENCE), in spite of the existence of very close substitutes produced by other firms. (◊◊ E. H. CHAMBERLIN, who developed similar ideas simultaneously and independently.) These ideas were set out in her book *Economics of Imperfect Competition*, published in 1933. Her other published works include *An Essay on Marxian Economics* (1942), *Accumulation of Capital* (1956), *Essays on the Theory of Economic Growth* (1963), *Collected Economic Papers* (3 vols., 1951, 1960 and 1965), *Economics: An Awkward Corner* (1966: the 'awkward corner' being the present-day confusion of 'partial LAISSEZ-FAIRE'), *Freedom and Necessity* (1970), *Economic Heresies* (1971), *Contributions to Modern Economics* (1978) and *Aspects of Development and Underdevelopment* (1979). Government economic controls are confined to the regulation of aggregate effective DEMAND, and the allocation of the country's economic RESOURCES is left to FREE MARKET competition. There is, however, no more reason to suppose that competition efficiently allocates available resources, given the political and social aims of society, better than it can regulate AGGREGATE DEMAND. Professor Robinson played a dominant role in the CAMBRIDGE SCHOOL of economic thought, with the development of post-Keynesian MACROECONOMICS linked to the early classical period of RICARDO and MARX (◊ CAPITAL RE-SWITCHING).

Robinson–Patman Act. ◊ ANTI-TRUST.

Roll-over. ◊ CORPORATION TAX.

Rostow, Walt Whitman (b. 1916). Educated at Yale, and at Oxford as a Rhodes Scholar, Rostow served during the Second World War in the Office of Strategic Services, and was the assistant chief of the Division of German–Austrian Economic affairs of the U.S. Department of State from 1945 to 1946. He was Pitt Professor of American History at Cambridge University for 1949–50, and Professor of Economic History of Massachusetts Institute of Technology from 1950 to 1965. Since 1969 he has been Professor of Economics and History at the University of Texas. He was appointed special assistant to the President in 1966. His major publications include *Essays on the British Economy of the Nineteenth Century* (1948), *The Processes of Economic Growth* (1952), *The*

Growth and Fluctuations of the British Economy 1790–1850 (1953), *Stages of Economic Growth* (1960), *Politics and the Stages of Growth* (1971), *How It All Began – Origins of the Modern Economy* (1975), *Why the Poor Get Richer and the Rich Slow Down* (1980) and *British Trade Fluctuations 1868–1896* (1981). He postulated that societies passed through five stages of economic development: (a) the traditional society; (b) the preconditions for take-off; (c) the take-off, when growth becomes a normal feature of the economy; (d) the drive to maturity; and, some sixty years after take-off begins, (e) maturity, reached in the age of high mass CONSUMPTION. ◊ ECONOMIC GROWTH, STAGES OF; GROWTH, THEORY OF.

'Roundabout methods of production'. ◊ BÖHM-BAWERK, E. VON; CAPITAL.

Rounding error. Discrepancy sometimes arising where numbers are shown to fewer digits than those in which they were calculated. When suppressing a decimal place it is usual to round down where a number is below 0·5 and to round up where it is above 0·5. The same principle applies to the rounding of whole numbers. For example, the following numbers total 6·68 to two decimal places or 6·7 to one decimal place. If each is rounded to the nearest whole number the total of 7 is still retained, although the rounded numbers add to 8.

1·64	2
1·66	2
1·69	2
1·69	2
6·68	8

S

Sales promotion. ♢ ADVERTISING.

Sales tax. A tax levied as a proportion of the retail PRICE of a COMMODITY at the point of sale. An indirect tax (♢ DIRECT TAXATION), the term is sometimes used to refer to all taxes on expenditure, i.e. to include VALUE-ADDED TAX, which is levied at all levels of production and distribution. There are no single-stage sales taxes as such in the U.K., though they are levied in the United States and some other countries. Sales taxes may be general, i.e. levied on all sales, or targeted, i.e. levied on a selective basis. ♢♢ FISCAL NEUTRALITY; TAXATION.

Sample. The study of a few members of a POPULATION for the purpose of identifying attributes applicable to the population as a whole. The advantage of sampling is that it is cheaper than a study covering the entire population, Moreover, testing the entire population may be impractical; for example, when the test procedures are destructive (e.g. food-tasting). Provided that the sampling procedures are properly designed, the margin of error in the estimates may be calculated and the degree to which the error may be reduced by increasing the sample size. ♢ QUOTA SAMPLE; RANDOM SAMPLE; STRATIFIED SAMPLE.

Samuelson, Paul Anthony (b. 1915). Professor Samuelson was appointed to the Chair of Economics at Massachusetts Institute of Technology in 1947. He served in the U.S. Treasury for seven years after the end of the Second World War. In 1970, he received the Alfred Nobel Memorial Prize in Economics (♢ NOBEL PRIZE). His publications include *Foundations of Economic Analysis* (1947), *Economics* (1948) and *Linear Programming and Economic Analysis* (with R. Dorfman and R. SOLOW) (1958). Samuelson developed the HECKSCHER—OHLIN PRINCIPLE by showing how an increase in the PRICE of a COMMODITY can raise the INCOME of the FACTOR OF PRODUCTION which is used most intensively in producing it (♢ CAPITAL-INTENSIVE). This led to his formulating the *factor price equalization theorem*, which states the conditions under which, as FREE TRADE in commodities narrows differences in commodity prices between countries, in so doing the prices (incomes) of factors of production are also brought into line. In other words, free trade is a substitute for the free mobility of factors of production. Professor Samuelson has made important contributions to the development of mathematical economics, general EQUILIBRIUM theory and the theory of CONSUMER BEHAVIOUR. To free the latter from what he considered to be the constraint of the traditional concept of

UTILITY, he invented REVEALED PREFERENCE. In macroeconomic theory (◊ MACROECONOMICS), he was, in an article in 1939, the first to formulate the interaction between the accelerator and the multiplier. He was a leading figure on the side of NEO-CLASSICAL ECONOMICS in the debate with the CAMBRIDGE SCHOOL regarding the integration of classical (◊ CLASSICAL ECONOMICS) microeconomics and modern macroeconomics in growth theory (◊ ACCELERATOR–MULTIPLIER MODEL; SOCIAL-WELFARE FUNCTION; TURNPIKE THEOREM).

Sandilands Committee. The INFLATION ACCOUNTING Committee under the chairmanship of Sir Francis Sandilands, which was appointed in January 1974 and reported in September 1975. The committee concluded that existing accounting conventions did not adequately allow for changes in costs and prices and recommended a new system of current-cost accounting.

Satisficing. Behaviour which attempts to achieve some minimum level of a particular VARIABLE, but which does not strive to achieve its maximum possible value. The most common application of the concept in economics is in the BEHAVIOURAL THEORY OF THE FIRM, which, unlike traditional accounts, postulates that producers do not treat PROFIT as a goal to be maximized, but as a constraint. Under these theories, although at least a critical level of profit must be achieved by firms, thereafter priority is attached to the attainment of other goals. (◊ OPTIMUM; SIMON, H.A.)

Saturation point. A level beyond which the *relative* absorption of a product or service is not expected to increase. It is defined in terms of a ratio, e.g. ownership of videos per household or per hundred persons. Once the saturation point is reached, the growth of demand slows down to levels determined by population growth and replacement, although in some cases predictions of saturation points have been falsified by the emergence of multiple ownership, e.g. of cars and television sets. ◊ LOGISTIC CURVE; MARKET SHARE.

Save-as-you-earn (S.A.Y.E.). Schemes, now largely discontinued, for regular monthly savings in deposits with the Department for National Savings (◊ NATIONAL SAVINGS, DEPARTMENT FOR), BUILDING SOCIETIES or TRUSTEE SAVINGS BANK. These savings and the interest they earn are free of tax. Monthly contributions to the S.A.Y.E. third issue are indexed to the retail price index (◊ INDEXATION) and are to that extent protected from inflation. The only S.A.Y.E. scheme available now (1987) is the share-option issue for those entitled to purchase shares under a share-option scheme approved by the Inland Revenue.

Saving. INCOME not spent. At the end of any period, saving is equal to income in that period minus CONSUMPTION, and could be negative if expenditure exceeds income (◊ DISSAVING). In economics, saving is a purely passive concept and does not imply any decision about the form saving may take, such as putting it into a BUILDING SOCIETY. Saving can occur in the PUBLIC SECTOR when tax revenues exceed final consumption by government plus TRANSFER PAYMENTS and SUB-SIDIES and in the company sector where PROFITS are not distributed (◊ SELF-FINANCING) as well as in the HOUSEHOLD, though typically the public sector is a net borrower (◊ PUBLIC-SECTOR BORROWING REQUIREMENT) while the personal sector and industrial and commercial companies are net lenders.

For the economy as a whole, if total saving is equal to total INVEST-MENT, then expenditure by firms and individuals will be in EQUILI-BRIUM (for simplicity we ignore the public sector and foreign trade); if saving exceeds investment then expenditure from wages, salaries and dividends will not return to firms in the form of payments for goods and services (including investment goods) and output would have to fall, thus reducing incomes and bringing saving and investment into balance (◊ INCOME, CIRCULAR FLOW OF). What determines the level of saving is, therefore, important in MACROECONOMICS. There are several interpretations of this problem: one is that saving will be a function of the level of income (◊ CONSUMPTION FUNCTION) (this assumption underlies the mechanism of INCOME DETERMINATION just outlined), another is that changes in savings will be used to maintain a steady rate of consumption (◊ PERMANENT-INCOME HYPOTHE-SIS). ◊◊ SAVINGS RATIO.

Savings and loan (S. & L.) associations. (U.S.) ◊ SAVINGS BANK.

Savings bank. A bank which accepts INTEREST-bearing DEPOSITS of small amounts. The earliest savings banks were established in the private sector but later were set up or supported by governments, to encourage individual SAVINGS. In the U.K., the two main forms of savings bank are the NATIONAL SAVINGS BANK and the TRUSTEE SAVINGS BANK, although the BUILDING SOCIETIES share the basic objectives of the savings banks. In the United States savings banks are also called thrift institutions or *savings and loan* (*S. & L.*) *associations*, many of which are MUTUAL COMPANIES.

Savings certificates. ◊ NATIONAL SAVINGS CERTIFICATES.

Savings function. ◊ SAVINGS RATIO.

Savings ratio. The proportion of income which is saved, usually expressed for personal savings as a percentage of personal DISPOSABLE INCOME. The savings ratio in the U.K. increased from an average of about 2 per cent in the late 1940s and early 1950s to around 8–10 per cent in the 1960s. It peaked at 15 per cent in 1980 and has since fallen to 11 per cent. Since wealthy people save more than the poor, the increase in the ratio has been partly the result of increased real incomes, but apparently also from a desire to maintain the real value of savings under inflation. The *savings function* gives the relationship between aggregate savings, which include non-personal savings, and INCOME and is the inverse of the CONSUMPTION FUNCTION.

Say, Jean-Baptiste (1767–1832). A practical businessman, Say developed an interest in economics and began lecturing in the subject in 1816. In 1819 he was appointed to the Chair of Industrial Economy at the Conservatoire National des Arts et Métiers. In 1831 he was appointed Professor of Political Economy at the Collège de France. His most important published works are *Traité d'économie politique*, which appeared in 1803, and *Cours complet d'économie politique pratique*, which was published in 1829. Although he can claim some credit for the introduction of the concept of an ENTREPRENEUR into economic theory, and also the division of the fundamental FACTORS OF PRODUCTION into three – LAND, LABOUR and CAPITAL – his fame and notoriety spring from his '*loi des débouchés*', or 'law of markets'. It is probable that his 'law' would not figure so prominently in economics today had not J. M. KEYNES accused the CLASSICAL SCHOOL of being gravely misled by accepting it as the pivot of their macroeconomic theory (◇ MACROECONOMICS). According to Keynes, the law said that the sum of the values of all COMMODITIES produced was equivalent (always) to the sum of the values of all commodities bought. By definition, therefore, there could be no underutilization of RESOURCES; 'supply created its own demand'. However, there is some considerable doubt about what Say actually meant. Several versions have been put forward; some are incontrovertible platitudes, such as in barter a seller must also be a buyer, and if a good is sold somebody must have bought it. Probably the most meaningful interpretation is that of Keynes, but only as a condition which must be satisfied for EQUILIBRIUM to exist.
◇ WALRAS, M. E. L.

Say's law of markets. ◇ SAY, J.-B.

Scarce currency. ◇ HARD CURRENCY.

Scarcity. A situation in which the needs and wants of an individual or group of individuals exceed the resources available to satisfy them. In the presence of scarcity, choices have to be made between those wants which can be satisfied and those which cannot be; the available resources must in some way be rationed, either through price or some central distribution system. In the absence of scarcity, no difficult choices would need to be made, no prices would need to be attached to anything, and the study of economics would be rendered entirely unnecessary. As the economist uses the term, scarcity is present in any society in which there is anyone whose desires are not all completely satisfied; it is not a concept of any more relevance to a poor society where want and deprivation are rife than a rich one, where even a scarcity of Rolls-Royces is considered a shortcoming worthy of attention. (◊ PRICE SYSTEM; RESOURCE ALLOCATION; RESOURCES.)

Schedule D. ◊ INCOME TAX.

Schedule E. ◊ INCOME TAX.

Schultz, Theodore W. (b. 1902). After graduation in economics at the South Dakota State College, Professor Schultz obtained a Ph.D. at the University of Wisconsin. In 1943, he accepted a Chair in Economics at the University of Chicago where he remained until his retirement in 1974. He was awarded the NOBEL PRIZE in Economics in 1979 (jointly with Professor W. A. LEWIS). His major publications include *Agriculture in an Unstable Economy* (1945), *The Economic Organization of Agriculture* (1953), *The Economic Value of Education* (1963), *Transforming Traditional Agriculture* (1964), *Economic Crises in World Agriculture* (1965), *Economic Growth and Agriculture* (1968) and *Investment in Human Capital: The Role of Education and Research* (1971). Professor Schultz developed the ideas of human-capital theory in his work on the economics of education and made major contributions to the analysis of agriculture in DEVELOPING COUNTRIES. He highlighted the distortion of policy in taxation and trade which biases development against agriculture, condemning the sector to subsistence farming.

Schuman Plan. ◊ EUROPEAN COAL AND STEEL COMMUNITY.

Schumpeter, Joseph Alois (1883–1950). In 1919 Schumpeter was appointed Professor of Economics at Czernowitz, subsequently moving to Graz. He was appointed Minister of Finance in the Austrian Republic for a short period after the First World War. From 1925 until 1932 he held the Chair of Public Finance at Bonn. From 1932 until his death he was at Harvard University. His major publications include *Theory of Economic Development* (1912), *Business Cycles* (1939), *Capitalism, Socialism and Democracy* (1942) and *History of Economic Analysis*, which appeared posthumously and unfinished in 1954. He built up a theory of the TRADE CYCLE which was based on three time periods, (a) short, (b) medium and (c) long, to each of which he attributed different causes. He tested his theory against actual fluctuations from the eighteenth to the twentieth century. Although it was reasonably successful, he was doubtful of the predictive efficiency of his theory for future periods. He attempted to work out a theory of economic growth and fluctuation around an explicit recognition of the contribution of technical INNOVATION. He tried to argue that, without the latter, an economy would reach a static EQUILIBRIUM position of a 'circular flow' of goods with no net growth. He emphasized the evolutionary nature of the capitalist system (◊ CAPITALISM). He argued that under MONOPOLY capitalism, firms would place less emphasis on PRICE competition, but would increasingly compete in technical and organizational innovation, thus sending 'gales of creative destruction' through the economic system.

He predicted that capitalism would evolve gradually into socialism. ⟡ KON-DRATIEFF CYCLE.

Scitovsky, Tibor (b. 1910). ⟡ COMPENSATION PRINCIPLE.

Scrip issue. An issue of new SHARES to shareholders in proportion to their existing holdings made, as distinct from a RIGHTS ISSUE, without charge. A scrip or bonus issue does not raise new CAPITAL. It is merely an adjustment to the capital structure which capitalizes reserves, usually consisting of past PROFITS. The word 'scrip' is an abbreviation of 'subscription certificate'. ⟡ CAPITALIZATION.

Seasonal adjustment. The elimination from a TIME SERIES of fluctuations that exhibit a regular pattern at a particular time during the course of a year which are similar from one year to another. For instance, unemployment rises in the winter months because of the interruption of work by winter weather conditions. From a study of a series of winter periods, the percentage effect this has on the numbers unemployed may be estimated and the time series of unemployment statistics may be offset by this percentage. The resultant, adjusted, series gives a clearer picture of the underlying trend in unemployment.

Seasonal unemployment. UNEMPLOYMENT which varies with the season as in the construction, tourist and agricultural sectors. ⟡ SEASONAL ADJUSTMENT.

Second best, theory of. A theory formulated by R. G. Lipsey and K. Lancaster in *The General Theory of Second Best*, 1956, which says that in the absence of being able to attain all the conditions necessary for the existence of the most desirable possible economic situation, the second-best position is not one in which the remaining conditions will necessarily hold. In an efficient economy, for example, price will equal MARGINAL COST in all industries. This will ensure that no consumer who values a commodity more than it costs society to produce will be deterred from buying it (⟡ MARGINAL-COST PRICING). If in one industry, however, price is higher than marginal cost, the theory of the second best suggests that it is not efficient for price to be equal to marginal cost in all the other industries for this would encourage too much consumption of those items relative to the more highly priced one. In the second-best world, all other items would be taxed so that everything was priced in excess of marginal cost, and consumers would allocate their budgets almost identically to the way they would in a world of full marginal-cost pricing. (⟡ WELFARE ECONOMICS.)

Secondary bank. A financial institution which accepts deposits and makes loans but which has relatively few branches (in the U.K.) and therefore does not play a major role in the payments system as far as the general public is concerned. Included in the term are the MERCHANT BANKS, and other money-market banks, the British OVERSEAS BANKS, consortium banks, and some FINANCE HOUSES. There was a secondary banking crisis in 1973 when a number of minor banks (mainly deposit-taking FINANCE HOUSES and other institutions heavily lent to the property sector) got into difficulties when MONETARY POLICY was tightened following the oil crisis. Problems were intensified in the ensuing collapse of property values and the BANK OF ENGLAND mounted a *lifeboat operation* to rescue some of the banks. ⟆ BANKING.

Secondary market. A MARKET in which ASSETS are resold and purchased, as distinct from a primary market in which assets are sold for the first time. The STOCK EXCHANGE is a secondary market in which financial SECURITIES are traded, although it is also a primary market where these securities are issued for the first time (⟆ NEW-ISSUE MARKET). Another example is the secondary MORTGAGE market in the U.S.A. where holders of mortgages who need funds can dispose of their holding before maturity. Secondary markets are typically larger than primary markets and perform an important function, since purchasers of new issues of securities would be reluctant to purchase and would offer a lower price for them (a bigger DISCOUNT) unless they were confident that they could, if necessary, dispose of them in the secondary market.

Secular trend. A long-term directional movement in the trend of an economic TIME SERIES, as distinct from effects generated by the fluctuations of the TRADE CYCLE or seasonality (⟆ SEASONAL ADJUSTMENT). Such movements could, for instance, be due to changes in tastes or technology, or the contraction of an industry due to the growth of overseas competitors.

Securities. 1. In the widest sense, documents giving title to property or claims on INCOME which may be lodged, e.g. as SECURITY for a BANK LOAN. **2.** Income-yielding and other paper traded on the STOCK EXCHANGE or in SECONDARY MARKETS. Usually a synonym for STOCKS and SHARES. An essential characteristic of a security is that it is saleable. The main types of security are: (a) *fixed interest:* DEBENTURES, PREFERENCE SHARES, stocks and BONDS (including all GOVERNMENT SECURITIES and local authority securities); (b) *variable interest:* ORDINARY SHARES; (c) *other:* BILLS OF EXCHANGE, ASSURANCE policies, WARRANTS. Securities may be REDEEMABLE or IRREDEEMABLE, quoted or unquoted (⟆ QUOTATION). ⟆⟩ BOND; EQUITIES; GILT-EDGED SECURITIES.

Securities and Investments Board (S.I.B.). A private-sector body with statutory backing set up to oversee the conduct of investment businesses in the post-BIG BANG period. The S.I.B. has delegated powers under the *Financial Services Act 1986* and is, in turn, delegating some of its responsibilities to a second tier of *self-regulatory organizations (S.R.O.s).* At the time of writing (January 1987) seven S.R.O.s are planned, including the STOCK EXCHANGE and other bodies for INSURANCE, investment managers and securities dealers. *Recognized investment* exchanges (*R.I.E.s*), of which the stock exchange is one, are distinct from S.R.O.s and will safeguard trading standards.

Select Committee on Estimates. A select committee of the British House of Commons, whose purpose is to investigate whichever of the ESTIMATES of projected government expenditure it thinks should be examined. Its purpose is essentially to find if any economies may be achieved consistent with the policies implied in the estimates.

Selective employment tax (S.E.T.). A per capita PAYROLL TAX introduced in the U.K. in September 1966. S.E.T. was paid by all employers, but refunded with a premium in manufacturing, refunded without a premium in the primary sector and transport and borne in full by the construction, distribution and service sectors. The ideas behind the tax were: that it would improve the 'fiscal balance', since PURCHASE TAX applied not to services but only to physical COMMODITIES; that it would encourage economy in the use of labour (which was a concern at a time of high employment); and finally that it would assist manufacturing industry and exports. S.E.T. was cheap to administer since it was collected via the NATIONAL INSURANCE system and it raised substantial revenue, but it was a controversial and unpopular tax. S.E.T. was abolished in 1973 on the introduction of VALUE-ADDED TAX.

Self-employed. Someone who works on his or her own account. The number of self-employed persons in the U.K. is estimated to have risen by over 700,000 since 1979 and more than doubled as a percentage of the LABOUR FORCE. A self-employed person may be a proprietor of an unincorporated business either with or without employees.

Self-financing. CAPITAL generated from INCOME. A firm which is self-financing is generating its INVESTMENT funds from internal sources, i.e. the ploughing back of retained PROFITS (or retentions), and DEPRECIATION, as opposed to external borrowing, A quoted company has the choice of financing fixed-capital formation or increasing its stocks and work in progress or acquiring other companies or SHARES in them, either by borrowing on the STOCK EXCHANGE (or from other sources, including banks) or by using undistributed income. If it borrows, it will have to pay INTEREST or DIVIDENDS and issuing costs on new issues. If it uses undistributed income, it is choosing to pay its ordinary shareholders a lower dividend, i.e. to distribute less of its income. Unquoted companies do not have the alternative of new issues of shares, although they may take further EQUITY from private sources and borrow from other sources. In fact, the bulk of capital expenditure is financed from internal sources. Of total sources of funds of U.K. industrial and commercial companies over 70 per cent in recent years have been provided from internal sources. The remainder comes from NEW ISSUES, BANK LOANS, MORTGAGES, inward investment (⟡ FOREIGN INVESTMENT) and capital transfers.

Self-financing ratio. INVESTMENT funds derived from undistributed INCOME as a proportion of total investment funds in any accounting period. ⇔ SELF-FINANCING.

Self-liquidating. A low-RISK financial transaction or LOAN which incorporates a procedure for simultaneous termination and clearing indebtedness. A HIRE PURCHASE transaction is self-liquidating in that regular payments culminate in a final instalment which clears the DEBT. More generally, the term is applied to any form of finance to fill a temporary shortfall of funds, e.g. BILLS OF EXCHANGE, or a bridging loan by a bank to a customer in the process of selling one house and buying another.

Selling costs. COSTS incurred in MARKETING and distributing a product, including the costs of advertising, sales promotion, packaging and sales staff.

Senior, Nassau William (1790–1864). Educated at Oxford University, Senior was called to the Bar in 1819 and became a Master in Chancery in 1836. In 1825 he was appointed the first Drummond Professor of Political Economy at Oxford. He held this position twice, the first time until 1830 and the second from 1847 to 1852. He served on many Royal Commissions. His major work on economics was an *Outline of the Science of Political Economy*, which appeared in 1836. He is remembered mainly for his abstinence theory of INTEREST. Interest was a reward for abstaining from the unproductive use of SAVINGS. The creation of new capital involved a sacrifice. A positive return must therefore be expected to make the sacrifice worth while. Senior can be regarded as one of the first pure theorists in economics. He attempted to elaborate economic theory on the basis of deductions from elementary propositions.

Separation of ownership from control. The situation where the owners of a corporation do not actively participate in its management. In its earliest form, business was owned and managed by the same people. Economic and technological development led to the advent of the JOINT-STOCK COMPANY in the seventeenth century to meet the need for larger amounts of CAPITAL. This began the process of the separation of ownership from control that continued with the introduction of LIMITED LIABILITY for both PUBLIC COMPANIES and PRIVATE COMPANIES, and the gradual emergence of the modern giant corporation in which none of the directors or managers have more than a minority financial interest. This process has given rise to the possibility that the interests of those who control business and those who own it may conflict, a subject of continuing controversy among economists since the publication of *The Modern Corporation and Private Property* by A. A. Berle and G. C. Means in 1932. ⇔ FIRM, THEORY OF THE; GALBRAITH, J. K.

Serial correlation. ⇔ AUTO-CORRELATION.

Serra, Antonio (15?–16?). A Neapolitan writer in the mercantilist tradition (◊ MERCANTILISM), who was the first to analyse and fully use the concept of the balance of trade, both visible and invisible. He explained how the shortage of precious metals in the Neapolitan kingdom was a result of a deficit on the BALANCE OF PAYMENTS. In so doing, he rejected the idea, current at the time, that the SCARCITY of money was due to the unfavourable EXCHANGE RATE. The solution was to be found in the encouragement of EXPORTS.

Services. Intangible, non-transferable economic goods as distinct from physical COMMODITIES. Services are difficult to define unambiguously. The output of some services from, for example, a bank may take a physical form (a cheque or bank statement), while although many services are consumed at the point of sale and are not, therefore, transferable (for example a concert or a haircut), a service in which knowledge is imparted (for example a medical consultation or tax advice) may be freely transferable from one consumer to another. The intangible nature of much of the output of the service sector creates difficulties in the calculation of unit PRODUCTIVITY. Generally speaking, the service sector of the economy is more LABOUR-INTENSIVE than the manufacturing sector, but even this generalization is misleading because with computerization and the development of telecommunications, automated warehouses, special-purpose buildings and other plant and equipment, much of the service sector now employs more CAPITAL per worker than manufacturing industry. The service sector also contributes proportionately less to exports than manufacturing, but INVISIBLE exports are of growing importance and world trade in services is growing slightly faster than world trade in physical commodities. Some parts of the service sector and that sector as a whole, on average, have lower levels of CONCENTRATION than the manufacturing or extractive industries, but some parts of the service sector (for example BANKING) are highly concentrated in the U.K. Some parts of the service sector, notably distribution, banking, business services, and communications have been growing very rapidly in the past decade. The relative decline of agriculture and manufacturing has given rise to fears of DE-INDU-STRIALIZATION, though these fears are probably misplaced, since the growth of services has been characteristic of all the ADVANCED COUNTRIES and the exceptional relative (and absolute) decline of the manufacturing sector in Britain to some extent, at least, reflects the growth of the North Sea oil industry. ◊ PETTY'S LAW.

Servicing debt. ◊ DEBT.

Shadow price. The OPPORTUNITY COST to a society of engaging in some economic activity. It is a concept applied to situations where actual prices cannot be charged, or where actual prices charged do not reflect the real sacrifice made when some activity is pursued. In a perfectly functioning economy, market prices will be equal to MARGINAL COST (◊ PERFECT COMPETITION), which itself represents the true cost to society of producing one extra unit of a commodity; it is equivalent to the value of the items that could have been made as alternatives to the last unit of the commodity produced, with the same resources. In the competitive economy, therefore, the market price of an item is equal to the opportunity cost of producing that item. In an economy which does not function perfectly, however, this is not so. Suppose there is unemployed labour in the economy: the cost of using that labour to society is virtually zero – by employing it no sacrifice is made in terms of other goods produced. The shadow price of labour is zero, even though the workers, if employed, would have to be paid a wage. Alternatively suppose that there is an EXCESS DEMAND for labour; at the going wage rate, labour is in short supply. In this case, employing a worker may only cost a firm the going wage, but the cost to society of that firm employing that worker is the production the worker could have produced in an alternative occupation: this will be worth more than the wage rate if labour is in excess demand. The shadow price of labour in this case is higher than the wage rate. In effect, it reflects the benefit that would result from relaxing the constrained supply of workers by one unit.

More generally, shadow prices are used in valuing any item which is implicitly rationed or constrained in some way. Shadow prices can be derived using LINEAR PROGRAMMING techniques, and can be used in social COST–BENEFIT ANALYSIS, which attempts to achieve an optimal RESOURCE ALLOCATION in the absence of an effective PRICE SYSTEM.

Share. One of a number of equal portions in the nominal CAPITAL of a company entitling the owner to a proportion of distributed PROFITS and of residual VALUE if the company goes into LIQUIDATION; a form of SECURITY. Shares may be fully PAID-UP or partly paid, VOTING or non-voting (sometimes called 'A' shares). ◊ ORDINARY SHARES; PREFERENCE SHARES; STOCKS.

Share certificate. A document showing ownership of SHARES in a company. ◊ TRANSFER DEED.

Share indices. INDEX NUMBERS indicating changes in the average prices of SHARES on the STOCK EXCHANGE. The indices are constructed by taking a selection of shares and 'weighting' (◊ WEIGHTED AVERAGE) the percentage changes in prices together as an indication of aggregate movements in share prices. Roughly speaking, a share index shows percentage changes in the MARKET value of a PORTFOLIO compared with its VALUE in the base year of the index. Index numbers are published by several daily papers and weekly journals. ◊ FINANCIAL TIMES ACTUARIES SHARE INDICES; FINANCIAL TIMES STOCK INDICES; F.T./S.E. 100 SHARE INDEX.

Share options. ◊ OPTION.

Shareholders' interest. ◊ BALANCE SHEET.

Sherman Act. ◊ ANTI-TRUST.

Short-dated securities. ◊ DATED SECURITIES.

Shortfall assessment. ◊ CORPORATION TAX.

Short run. A period of time in which only some VARIABLES change or economic processes work. It is a concept which can only strictly be defined in the particular context in which it is applied, because its meaning depends on which variables or processes the user of the term has in mind as flexible. Its most common use is in the theory of the firm (◊ FIRM, THEORY OF THE), where it is defined as the period in which the quantity of certain FACTORS OF PRODUCTION employed, (for example, plant and machinery) is fixed and only, say, the number of workers hired can be changed. The specific period of time being referrred to as the 'short run' also varies with every application of the term, because, for example, it takes different amounts of time to build the plant and machinery for different industries. (◊ IMPACT EFFECT; LONG RUN; MARSHALL, A.)

Short-run cost curves. A graphical representation of the relationship between the output of a firm and the cost of producing that output with the firm's given level of fixed assets. For example, a record company may have one plant capable of producing anything between no records and one million. The short-run cost curve shows how much it would cost to make any number of records with that plant, taking into account the extra labour and raw materials that would be required to produce a given quantity (◊ FIRM, THEORY OF THE). In contrast, the *long-run cost curve* would depict how much each number of records would cost if the number and size of the plants of the record company were allowed to alter. There is, therefore, one short-run cost curve for every number of plants and level of plant size. The long-run cost curve joins the average short-run curves tangentially at their minimum points.

Any short-run cost curve can be broken down into two elements. First, short-run *fixed costs*: the payments incurred independently of the level of production. Second, short-run *variable costs*: like raw materials and labour costs which vary with the level of output. The sum of these produces short-run total *costs*. This cost function may be depicted as an average cost curve (in which case it is generally assumed that as production rises it falls to a minimum, and then rises). (◊ MARGINAL ANALYSIS.)

Short-term capital. ◊ BUSINESS FINANCE.

Short-term gains. ◊ CAPITAL GAINS.

Simon, Herbert A. (b. 1916). A graduate of the University of Chicago, Professor Simon held the post of Director of Administrative Measurement Studies at the Bureau of Public Administration of the University of California from 1939 to 1942, in which year he moved to the Illinois Institute of Technology, becoming a Professor of Political Science there in 1947. In 1949, Professor Simon was appointed Professor of Administration and Psychology at the Carnegie Mellon University, becoming Professor of Computer Science and Psychology in 1955. He was awarded the NOBEL PRIZE in Economics in 1978. His major publications include *Administrative Behaviour* (1947), *Public Administration* (1950), *Organizations* (1958), *The New Science of Management Decisions* (1960), *The Shape of Automation for Men and Management* (1965), *Models of Discovery* (1977) and *Models of Bounded Rationality and Other Topics in Economics* (1982). Simon argued that the central assumption in economic theory of a rational 'economic man', who maximizes benefits and minimizes costs, is unrealistic. Any decision faced by an individual, in a household or in a firm, is bounded by uncertainties and ignorance. Individuals 'satisfice' (⟡ SATISFICING). They adjust their behaviour and ambitions continually in the light of experience.

Simple interest. ⟡ COMPOUND INTEREST.

Simple random sample. ⟡ RANDOM SAMPLE.

Simulation. The construction of a MODEL which describes mathematically the structure and processes of a real-world situation to be studied and the inputting of values of VARIABLES in the model in order to generate appropriate out-turns. The model enables the results of a process to be simulated without the need to test the process in an actual situation. (⟡ MONTE CARLO METHOD; OPERATIONS RESEARCH.)

'Single tax' party. ⟡ GEORGE, H.

Sinking fund. ⟡ AMORTIZATION.

Sismondi, Jean Charles Léonard Simonde de (1773–1842). A Swiss historian and economist, who after a period in exile in England began lecturing at Geneva Academy in 1809 on history and economics. His economic works include *Richesse commerciale* (1803), *Nouveaux principes d'économie politique* (1819) and *Études sur l'économie politique* (1837). Sismondi argued against the doctrine of LAISSEZ-FAIRE in favour of state intervention. He recommended UNEMPLOYMENT and sickness benefits, and pension schemes for workers. With T. R. MALTHUS, he attacked D. RICARDO for not recognizing the possibility of economic crisis developing from underconsumption. He tried to emphasize the dynamic nature of the economic process, compared with the comparative statics of Ricardo (⟡ COMPARATIVE STATIC EQUILIBRIUM ANALYSIS), and was the first to use sequence analysis as an analytical device. Increased output in one period, he argued, is faced with a level of INCOME generated by a lower level of output in the previous period. Total demand falls short of the available supply. Lags in the economic system, therefore, could give rise to underconsumption.

Size distribution of firms. ◊ CONCENTRATION RATIO.

Slutsky, Eugen (1880–1948). He was appointed a professor at Kiev University in 1918, where he remained until 1926. In 1934 he accepted a post at the Mathematics Institute of the Academy of Sciences of the U.S.S.R., where he remained until his death. He published an article in the Italian journal *Giornale degli economisti* in 1915 on consumer behaviour in which he showed how the concept of ORDINAL UTILITY could be used to build a theory of consumer behaviour of the same scope as that of A. MARSHALL, but without the underlying assumption of the measurability of UTILITY. However, the article lay unnoticed until J. R. HICKS and R. G. ALLEN rediscovered it in 1934. In his book *Value and Capital*, Hicks applied Slutsky's name to the mathematical formulae which illustrate how a consumer would react to PRICE and INCOME changes (◊ CONSUMER BEHAVIOUR, THEORY OF; PARETO, V. F. D.). Slutsky did little further work in economic theory, but made important contributions to statistics and PROBABILITY theory which are of relevance to economics. He emphasized the danger of assuming causes for observed fluctuations in TIME SERIES by showing how regular cycles could be generated in the derivation of MOVING AVERAGES from a series, even though the latter was made up of random numbers. He also made important advances in the study of AUTO-CORRELATION.

Small business. A firm, managed in a personalized way by its owners or part-owners, which has only a small share of its market and is not sufficiently large to have access to the STOCK EXCHANGE in raising CAPITAL. Given that small firms typically have little recourse to institutional sources of finance other than the COMMERCIAL BANKS and rely heavily upon the personal savings of the proprietors, their families and friends, the long-term growth in TAXATION on income and wealth is believed by some economists to have inhibited the growth of the small-firm sector. A number of other inhibiting factors were also identified by the BOLTON COMMITTEE and this committee and the subsequent WILSON COMMITTEE recommended a number of measures to promote small business many of which, including tax reliefs and a CREDIT GUARANTEE scheme, have been implemented. The onset of slower economic growth from the early 1970s has been associated with a reversal of the secular decline in the share of small firms in output and employment. Various estimates put the number of small firms in the U.K. at between 1,500,000 and well over 2 million. Most small businesses are SOLE PROPRIETORSHIPS and PARTNERSHIPS, but the vast majority of Britain's active 400,000 or so PRIVATE COMPANIES are small firms. ◊ ENTERPRISE; ESTABLISHMENT; SELF-EMPLOYED.

Smith, Adam (1723–90). A Scotsman brought up by his mother at Kirkcaldy, he became a student under Francis Hutcheson at Glasgow University at the age of fourteen and won a scholarship to Oxford, where he spent six years until 1746. He lectured at Edinburgh University from 1748 to 1751. From 1751 until 1763 he was at Glasgow, first in the Chair of Logic and a year later the Chair of Moral Philosophy, which he took over from Hutcheson. From 1764 to 1766 he toured France as the tutor to the Duke of Buccleuch. His major work on economics, *An Inquiry into the Nature and Causes of the Wealth of Nations*, appeared in 1776. This work of Adam Smith's became the foundation upon which was constructed the whole subsequent tradition of English CLASSICAL ECONOMICS, which can be traced from D. RICARDO through A. MARSHALL to A. C. PIGOU. Smith was primarily concerned with the factors which led to increased WEALTH in a community and he rejected the PHYSIOCRATS' view of the pre-eminent position of agriculture, recognizing the parallel contribution of manufacturing industry. He began his analysis by means of a sketch of a primitive society of hunters. If it cost twice the labour to kill a beaver as it does a deer, one beaver would exchange for two deer. LABOUR was the fundamental measure of VALUE, though actual PRICES of COMMODITIES were determined by SUPPLY and DEMAND on the MARKET (◊ RICARDO and MARX). There were two elements in the problem of increasing wealth: (a) the skill of the LABOUR FORCE and (b) the proportion of productive to unproductive labour. (According to Smith, the SERVICE industries did not contribute to real wealth.) The key to (a) was the DIVISION OF LABOUR. To illustrate his point, he quoted the example of the manufacture of pins. If one man were set the task of carrying out all the operations of pin manufacture – drawing the wire, cutting, head-fitting and sharpening – his output would be minimal. If, however, each man specialized in a single operation only, output would be increased a hundredfold. The size of the output need only be limited by the size of its market. The key to (b) was the accumulation of CAPITAL. Not only did this enable plant and machinery to be created to assist labour, but it also enabled labour to be employed. Capital for the latter was the wages fund (◊ WAGE-FUND THEORY). The workers must be fed and clothed during the period of production in advance of the INCOME earned from their own efforts. Smith believed that the economic system was harmonious and required the minimum of government interference (◊ LAISSEZ-FAIRE). Although each individual was motivated by self-interest, they each acted for the good of the whole, guided by a 'hidden hand' (◊ INVISIBLE HAND) made possible by the free play of competition (◊ MANDEVILLE, B. DE). Free competition was the essential ingredient of the efficient economy. However, from his *Wealth of Nations* it is clear that not only did his scholarship range widely over the fields of history and contemporary business, but that, at the same time, he was a very practical man. He was quite aware, for instance, of the forces which were at work to limit competition: 'People of the same trade seldom meet together even for merriment and diversion, but the conversation ends in a conspiracy against the public, or on some contrivance to raise prices' (Book One, Chapter X, Part 2). In his discussions of PUBLIC FINANCE, he laid down four principles of TAXATION: (a) equality (taxes proportionate to ability to pay), (b) certainty, (c) convenience and (d) economy. ⟡ HUME, D.

Smithsonian Agreement. An agreement concluded in December 1971 between the 'Group of Ten' of the INTERNATIONAL MONETARY FUND at the Smithsonian Institute, Washington. Under the agreement, the major currencies were restored to fixed parities but with a wider margin, $\pm 2\cdot 25$ per cent of permitted fluctuation around their par values. The dollar was effectively devalued by about 8 per cent and the dollar price of gold increased to \$38 per oz. Sterling was set at \$2·6057 (⟡ EXCHANGE RATE).

Smithsonian parities. ⟡ SMITHSONIAN AGREEMENT.

Social accounting. The presentation of the NATIONAL INCOME and expenditure accounts in a form showing the transactions during a given period between the different sectors of the economy. The tabulations are set out in the form of a MATRIX showing the source of INPUTS of each sector or part of sector and the distribution of their outputs. The production sector, for instance, shows for an industry how much of its inputs were bought from other home industries, how much it imported and how much it spent on wages, salaries and DIVIDENDS. At the same time, it shows how much of its output it sold to other industries, how much it exported and how much was consumed by private individuals or the government sector. These transactions of the producers' sector are counterbalanced by corresponding transactions of the other sectors. For instance, the personal sector shows the value and sources of INCOMES earned from the producers' sector and others, as well as the way these incomes are saved or spent on the outputs of the various industries or on IMPORTS. ⟡ INPUT–OUTPUT ANALYSIS; LEONTIEF, W.

Social benefits. The total increase in the welfare of society from an economic action. In effect, it is the sum of two benefits: (a) the benefit to the agent performing the action, for example the PROFIT made; (b) the benefit accruing to society as a result of the action, for example an increase in tax revenues (⟡ EXTERNALITIES). The phrase is sometimes used to describe the second of these on its own. (⟡ SOCIAL WELFARE.)

Social capital. The total stock of a society's productive assets, including those that allow the manufacture of the marketable outputs that create private-sector profits, *and* those that create non-marketed outputs, such as defence and education (⟡ CAPITAL).

Social cost. The total cost to society of an economic activity. It is the sum of the opportunity COSTS of the RESOURCES used by the agent carrying out the activity plus any additional costs imposed on society from the activity. For example, when people drive their cars they incur the private cost of petrol and wear and tear on the vehicle, but the social cost of them driving also adds wear and tear on the roads, and the congestion and pollution they cause, which they do not pay for directly. By taxation, social costs can be incorporated into private costs so that market prices properly represent the true costs to the community. (⟡ EXTERNALITIES; PIGOU, A. C.; SHADOW PRICE.)

Social net product. The difference between the SOCIAL BENEFITS and the SOCIAL COST arising from the use of some FACTOR OF PRODUCTION or from some form of economic activity.

Social overhead capital. ⟡ INFRASTRUCTURE.

Social security. A system of government-financed income transfers designed to effect a distribution of income considered desirable. The main component of most social-security systems is welfare benefits, given to those in POVERTY. This can be done in two ways: (a) by identifying groups that are likely to be poor, and giving benefits to them (e.g. the unemployed, the elderly and the disabled) irrespective of their actual income; (b) by identifying, through MEANS TESTS, people who are poor. The second of these approaches is a less expensive method of eradicating poverty, but leads to the problem of the POVERTY TRAP. ⟡ NATIONAL INSURANCE. ⟡ LIFE-CYCLE HYPOTHESIS; MINIMUM-WAGE LAWS.

Social welfare. The total well-being of a community. It is not measurable because it is not possible to sum the benefits or UTILITIES enjoyed by the individuals composing the community. It is possible, however, for the community to judge whether it prefers one situation to another. (⟡ COMPENSATION PRINCIPLE; INDIFFERENCE-CURVE ANALYSIS; PIGOU, A. C.; SOCIAL-WELFARE FUNCTION; WELFARE ECONOMICS.)

Social-welfare function. An expression of society's taste for different economic states. The analysis of society's optimal behaviour is analogous to INDIFFERENCE-CURVE ANALYSIS for individuals. Just as the individual's taste can be defined by his or her ranking of different combinations of commodities, social priorities can be defined by a list of preferences of alternative national combinations of commodities. (Just as for the individual, such a list would never in practice approach a complete ordering of every possible allocation, but in theory there is no reason for this limitation to be imposed.) The comparison between individual and social-welfare functions can be taken no further however, for whereas any bundle of commodities is assumed uniquely to define a level of UTILITY for an individual, it does not do so for society, because each bundle can be distributed between individuals in different ways. Each alternative distribution will produce a different level of total welfare unless all individuals are identical and their interests are all considered of equal importance. In short, the individual only has to decide how much of each commodity to consume. Society has to choose how much of each commodity should be produced, *and* how it should be distributed. For this reason, unlike the individual's utility function, which is expressed in terms of commodity quantities, the social-welfare function is usually expressed in terms of the utility of the members of society. The function may, for example, be the simple sum of all individual preferences or it might attach a high weighting to the preferences of a particular group of citizens and a low weight to the rest. VALUE JUDGEMENTS must be made; but the procedure can be applied to derive the consequences of such judgements.

The importance of the social-welfare function is that it provides a criterion for choosing between different economically efficient (⟡ ECONOMIC EFFIENCY) states. Suppose moving from an efficient allocation, A, to another efficient allocation, B, makes one person better off and another worse off; the social-welfare function can be used to determine which of A and B is to be preferred. There are two approaches to the derivation of the welfare function. The first is that it can be imposed on society. Each individual has a social-welfare function representing their own ranking of different allocations of resources, and the charge of producing one for society as a whole could be assigned to government. The second approach is to devise a constitution or voting system which can turn the rankings of each individual into a single social ranking. To find such a constitution which can guarantee to provide consistent and decisive results is, however, not possible, as Kenneth Arrow shows in the IMPOSSIBILITY THEOREM. It is this issue which has dominated discussion of social-welfare functions in economic literature. (⟡ WELFARE ECONOMICS.)

Socialism. A social and economic system in which the means of production are collectively owned and equality is given a high priority. There are various forms of socialism from MARXISM to the social-democrat systems in Western Europe, but all share a belief in the necessity for collective intervention in economic affairs. ⟡ PLANNED ECONOMY; STATE PLANNING.

Soft currency. A CURRENCY whose EXCHANGE RATE is tending to fall because of persistent BALANCE OF PAYMENTS deficits or because of the building up of speculative selling of the currency in expectation of a change in its exchange rate. Governments are unwilling to hold a soft currency in their FOREIGN-EXCHANGE RESERVES.

Soft loan. A LOAN bearing either no RATE OF INTEREST, or an interest rate which is below the true cost of the CAPITAL lent. It is the policy of the INTERNATIONAL BANK FOR RECONSTRUCTION AND DEVELOPMENT working through its affiliate, the INTERNATIONAL

DEVELOPMENT ASSOCIATION, to give 'soft' loans to DEVELOPING COUNTRIES for long-term capital projects.

Sole proprietorship, sole trader. An unincorporated business owned by one person which may or may not have employees. The majority of small firms are sole traders or PARTNERSHIPS. ◊ BOLTON COMMITTEE; COMPANY LAW; SELF-EMPLOYED.

Solow, R. ◊ CAPITAL RE-SWITCHING.

Sources and uses of funds. An accounting statement describing the CAPITAL flows of a business. Sources of funds are PROFITS from trading operations, DEPRECIATION provisions, sales of ASSETS and borrowing, including capital issues. Uses of funds are purchase of fixed or financial assets (including CASH), and distribution of INCOME. ◊ SELF-FINANCING.

Special deposits. Cash deposited at the BANK OF ENGLAND by the CLEARING BANKS in response to a special directive. The scheme, which was introduced in 1958 although it did not become effective until 1960, was designed to provide a mechanism for reducing banks' lending by reducing their LIQUIDITY RATIO. The banks were instructed to increase their gross deposits at the Bank of England (part of their LIQUIDITY base) by a certain percentage. The banks received interest on the special deposits at approximately the current TREASURY BILL rate. Besides the clearing banks, the scheme also then applied, on somewhat different terms, to the Scottish banks. Theoretically, the requirement for special deposits appears to be a powerful method for reducing bank lending, since it operates directly on the CASH RATIO of the banks and quite small percentage increases in deposits should have a significant effect on bank advances. However, the banks could offset the increase in deposits by reducing their holdings of government BONDS and, in practice, the importance of an announcement of a requirement for special deposits is that it is a signal of the intention of the monetary authorities to squeeze CREDIT. Until 1971 these authorities continued to rely on a direct limitation on bank advances, as they did in 1957 before special deposits were introduced, and on the other means of controlling credit. From 1971 a new system of CREDIT CONTROL was introduced. Special deposits continued in force and were extended to a wider range of banks, but did not form part of the reserve assets of the new system. Under the new scheme the Bank of England was able to call for special deposits in proportion to the sterling and overseas eligible liabilities (that is, deposits) of the commercial banks (◊ CREDIT CONTROL). In December 1973 a further supplementary-deposit scheme was introduced. These supplementary deposits (S.S.D.) were not interest-bearing and were called for in proportion to the excess of growth of the banks' liabilities over a target set by the Bank of England. The S.S.D. was called for in 1973, 1976 and again in 1978. The effectiveness of *the* corset, as the S.S.D. was called, was seriously affected by what is known as *disintermediation*, i.e. lending through new credit instruments in PARALLEL MARKETS. For example, banks would meet a corporate borrower's requirements not by an advance but by guaranteeing a bank bill (◊ BILL OF EXCHANGE) instead. This bank would in this way be incurring a contingent liability only and its liabilities for the purposes of the S.S.D. scheme would not be affected. The S.S.D. scheme was discontinued in 1980. Similar schemes are operated by the FEDERAL RESERVE SYSTEM in the U.S.A. ◊ CREDIT SQUEEZE.

Special Development Areas. ◊ DEVELOPMENT AREA.

Special drawing rights (S.D.R.s). The instruments for financing international trade after the Second World War were predominantly the RESERVE CURRENCIES, such as dollars and sterling, and gold. Dependence on the latter, as J. M. KEYNES pointed out, is an anachronism which had been successfully terminated as far as domestic economies were concerned. The problem of depending on the former was that the supply of these currencies was regulated by their countries' BALANCE OF PAYMENTS deficits or surpluses. The deficit on the U.S. balance of payments had been an important source of the flow of LIQUIDITY into CENTRAL BANK reserves. The difficulty was that persistent deficits led to doubts about the maintenance of the currency's EXCHANGE RATE and made central banks less willing to hold dollars. This problem came to a head in August 1971, when the U.S. government imposed various measures to correct its balance-of-payments deficit. In December 1971 the dollar was devalued by about 10 per cent.

J. M. Keynes had put forward the idea of an international currency, to be called BANCOR, regulated by a central institution (◊ KEYNES PLAN). This idea was turned down then for fear that the creation of liquidity would generate INFLATION. In 1969, the 'Group of Ten' (◊ INTERNATIONAL MONETARY FUND) agreed to establish S.D.R.s, which are similar in principle to Keynes's original idea, and their agreement was ratified by the I.M.F. The S.D.R. was linked to gold and equivalent to $1 U.S. at the gold rate of exchange of $35 per oz. Until December 1971, an S.D.R. was equivalent to $1, but with the effective devaluation of the dollar following the SMITHSONIAN AGREEMENT, the rate became I.S.D.R. = $1·08571. With the subsequent breakdown of the fixed-parity system, the I.M.F. valued the S.D.R. in terms of a 'basket' of sixteen currencies, so that, as from July 1974, the rate in relation to the dollar 'floated'. At the beginning of 1976 the rate was 1 S.D.R. = $1·17183. By 1986, S.D.R. 21·4 billion had been created. These sums are distributed to each member country in proportion to its I.M.F. quota. In 1981 the S.D.R. was simplified to a weighted AVERAGE of U.S. dollars (42 per cent), German Deutschmarks (19 per cent), French francs, Japanese yen and U.K. sterling (13 per cent each). The

S.D.R. has slowly become more acceptable, and now commercial BANKS accept S.D.R.-denominated deposits.

Specialization. ◊ DIVISION OF LABOUR.

Specie points. The limits between which the EXCHANGE RATE between two CURRENCIES on the GOLD STANDARD fluctuated. For instance, before the First World War the same amount of gold could be bought in London for £1 and in New York for $4·87, and therefore the par rate of exchange was £1 for $4·87. If the pound fetched less than $4·87 in London, it would pay a merchant to ship gold to the U.S.A. to settle his debts provided the cost of freight and insurance were less than the difference between the par rate and the London rate. Therefore in practice the rate never fell by an amount more than the cost of shipment. Similar forces applied in reverse to prevent the rate rising by an amount in excess of the cost of shipment.

Specific tax. ◊ TAX, SPECIFIC.

Speculation. Buying and selling with a view to buying and selling at a PROFIT later when PRICES have changed. ◊◊ ARBITRAGE; BEAR; BULL; STAG.

Speculative motive. The reason which causes people or firms to hold a stock of MONEY in the belief that a capital gain or the avoidance of a loss can be achieved by so doing. It is one of three motives for holding money outlined by J. M. KEYNES. When the price of bonds falls, the attraction of holding them increases; this is because people will expect their price to rise again, and anyone owning them when this happens will make a capital gain. People will tend to buy bonds when their price is low, and will thus hold little money. When the price of bonds is high, on the other hand, they will believe their price could fall and hold more money. The amount of money held under this motive thus varies with the price of bonds; as the INTEREST RATE varies inversely with the bond price, the speculative motive for money varies inversely with interest rates. (◊◊ LIQUIDITY PREFERENCE; LIQUIDITY TRAP; PORTFOLIO THEORY; PRECAUTIONARY MOTIVE; TRANSACTIONS MOTIVE.)

Spillover effect. ◊ EXTERNALITIES.

Spot market. A MARKET in which goods or SECURITIES are traded for immediate delivery, as distinct from a FORWARD MARKET. 'Spot' in this context means 'immediately effective', so that *spot price* is the price for immediate delivery.

Spot price. ◊ SPOT MARKET.

Spot sterling. ◊ FORWARD EXCHANGE MARKET.

Stability analysis. The study of the behaviour of VARIABLES in DIS-EQUILIBRIUM to see whether they have a tendency to converge on an EQUILIBRIUM level (◊ DYNAMICS). Most equilibria considered in economics are stable, but models have been developed which are unstable. (◊◊ COBWEB MODEL; HARROD–DOMAR MODEL.)

Stabilization policy. 1. Government action aimed at reducing fluctuations in NATIONAL INCOME. Such policy – to expand demand when UN-EMPLOYMENT exists and reduce demand when INFLATION threatens – became the norm after the Second World War in all Western economies, and the low rates of unemployment prevailing during the 1950s coupled with high rates of economic growth were seen as a testimony to its success. In the 1960s, however, the U.K. faced difficulties sustaining a stabilization policy, with a STOP–GO cycle by which REFLATION occurred, the economy would 'overheat' and then a rapid DEFLATION would be necessary. In the 1970s STAGFLATION developed, and the traditional-style stabilization policy became obsolete. In the 1980s, it was replaced in the U.K. by an explicit non-stabilizing policy in the form of the *Medium-Term Financial Strategy*.

Stabilization policy fell out of favour for two main reasons. First, there are immense practical difficulties in implementing it primarily because of a lack of sufficient information. All that is known about the economy is how it was behaving several months ago, but actions have to be taken several months in advance. The problem has been likened to attempts at controlling the temperature of water coming out of a shower when any twist of the hot or cold tap takes half a minute to affect the temperature of that coming out of the nozzle. Secondly it is argued that the temptation to attempt to keep unemployment below its market level (◊ UNEMPLOYMENT, NATURAL RATE OF) inevitably causes ever-accelerating inflation. Instead, it is suggested, if the equilibrium level of unemployment is too high, measures affecting the supply of labour, rather than demand, are necessary (◊ SUPPLY-SIDE ECONOMICS). Despite the criticisms, stabilization to some extent exists in all economies: built-in stabilizing factors (◊ BUILT-IN STABILIZERS) (for example, in recession, unemployment benefits paid out rise, causing an increase in government spending) will never be removed. Moreover, most economists allow that moderate REFLATION at times of recession can be justified. What is rarely attempted is the fine tuning of the economy that occurred in earlier decades. (◊ FISCAL POLICY; MONE-TARY POLICY.)

2. The action of government or trade associations to stabilize the price of certain commodities. By holding stocks of the item in question, the authorities can, at least temporarily, affect demand and supply in the market and maintain a constant price. (◊ COMMODITY AGREE-MENTS.)

Stag. A speculator (◊ SPECULATION) who subscribes to new issues in the expectation of selling his allotment of SECURITIES at a profit when dealings in them begin. ◊ NEW-ISSUE MARKET.

Stagflation. INFLATION associated with static or declining output and employment.

Stamp duty. A form of indirect taxation ($\diamond$ DIRECT TAXATION) which involves the fixing of pre-paid stamps to legal and commercial documents. The tax may be *ad valorem* ($\diamond$ TAX, AD VALOREM), as on the conveyancing of property, or specific ($\diamond$ TAX, SPECIFIC), as on declarations of trust. Other stamp duties include those on share transactions ($\frac{1}{2}$ per cent), the capital of limited companies, insurance policies and leases. Compliance is enhanced by the fact that specified documents are invalid in law unless stamped. Stamp duty is a very ancient form of taxation and raised £911 million in revenue in 1984/5.

Standard deviation. A measure of the spread of a series of values of a VARIABLE around its mean ($\diamond$ AVERAGE). It is defined as the square root of the VARIANCE. The formula for the standard deviation is:

$$\sigma = \sqrt{\frac{1}{n} \sum_{i=1}^{n} (x_i - \bar{x})^2}.$$

where x_i is the ith value, $\bar{x}$ is the mean and n is the number of observations.

Standard Industrial Classification (S.I.C.). A categorization of economic activity used in compiling and presenting official statistics. It consists of *Minimum List Headings* grouped into *Order Numbers*. First introduced in 1948 and revised in 1958, 1968 and 1980, the British S.I.C. system follows the same principles as the International Standard Industrial Classification (I.S.I.C.) issued by the United Nations.

Standard rate. $\diamond$ INCOME TAX.

State Earnings Related Pensions Scheme (S.E.R.P.S.). $\diamond$ NATIONAL IN-SURANCE.

State planning. The regulation of any sector or sphere of an economy by public administrators rather than the PRICE SYSTEM. If state planning is comprehensive, a PLANNED ECONOMY is said to exist. In many countries, however, there is partial planning, that can take one of two broad forms. The first is very detailed planning in certain key sectors of an economy. For example, the U.K. National Health Service is controlled by administrators rather than prices: queues ration the supply of certain operations, and the wages and activity of health workers are determined by the administrators, albeit after consideration of where demand is greatest and what supply of labour is available. The second common type of state planning covers virtually all sectors of the economy, but only in a very limited way, with production targets, performance monitoring and some state subsidies, and in the form of a national plan. $\diamond$ INPUT–OUTPUT ANALYSIS; NATIONALIZED INDUSTRIES.

Static equilibrium. EQUILIBRIUM in which the relevant VARIABLES do not change over time (in contrast to dynamic equilibrium in which the variables change over time). ($\diamond\!\diamond$ BALANCED GROWTH.)

Statistical inference. The method of discovering information about a statistical population by sampling procedures (◊ SAMPLE).

Steady-state growth. A feature of an economy in which all variables grow (or contract) at a constant rate: for example, population may rise at 3 per cent a year, national income at 4 per cent and the capital stock at 5 per cent. If these rates are maintained indefinitely, steady-state growth exists. It is distinct from BALANCED GROWTH in which all variables grow at the *same* constant rate. Steady-state growth is an EQUILIBRIUM concept, and much of GROWTH THEORY has been concerned with whether it is likely to be achieved. (◊ ECONOMIC GROWTH; HARROD–DOMAR MODEL.)

Sterling area. The sterling area had its origins in the supremacy of the U.K. in the INTERNATIONAL TRADE and finance of the nineteenth century. The pound sterling became the most convenient CURRENCY in which to settle international BALANCES OF PAYMENTS, and London the leading centre for raising the finance required to open up the new colonies. The sterling area, however, remained only a loose association of countries until the U.K. went off the GOLD STANDARD in 1931. At that time, these countries had to choose between linking their currencies to gold or to sterling. With the outbreak of the Second World War in 1939, the area became more formalized by the acceptance of EXCHANGE CONTROL in respect of transactions with non-sterling-area members. The Exchange Control Act of 1947 defined the sterling area as a list of 'scheduled territories', and the area discriminated against trade with 'HARD CURRENCY' areas, particularly the U.S.A., against the background of the inconvertibility of sterling. The 'scheduled territories' were reduced to the U.K., including the Channel Islands and the Isle of Man, Gibraltar and the Republic of Ireland by 1978, in which year Ireland left. Exchange controls were abolished by the U.K. in 1979.

Stigler, George Joseph (b. 1911). Professor Stigler graduated from the University of Washington in 1931 and, after a year at the Northwestern University, obtained his Ph.D. at the University of Chicago. In 1936, he was appointed Assistant Professor in Economics at Iowa State University and in 1938 moved to the University of Minnesota. In 1947, he was appointed to the Chair of Economics at Columbia University, where he stayed until 1959, in which year he returned to the University of Chicago as Professor of American Institutions. Professor Stigler was awarded the NOBEL PRIZE in Economics in 1982. His publications include *Production and Distribution Theories* (1941), *The Theory of Prices* (1942), *Five Lectures on Economic Problems* (1948), *Capital and Rates of Return in Manufacturing Industries* (1963), *Essays in the History of Economics* (1965), *The Organization of Industry* (1968), *Domestic Servants in the U.S.A.* (1974), *The Citizen and the State: Essays on Regulation* (1975),

Demand and Supply of Scientific Personnel (1975) and *The Economist as Preacher* (1982). Professor Stigler analysed the cost of obtaining economic information by firms faced with a range of prices offered by competitive suppliers. He contributed to the analysis of UNEMPLOYMENT, pointing up the need for workers to devote time to look for the highest available pay rates for the work and conditions they require. Professor Stigler has advocated a more empirical approach to the study of government REGULATION and has demonstrated that often regulations set for the benefit of consumers will rather turn out in practice to benefit producers.

Stochastic process. A process subject to random influences (◊ PROBABILITY; RANDOM SAMPLE). For instance, a dependent VARIABLE may be determined by an independent variable x plus a random element, so that the process generating y is not fully determined by x and predictable by x. The process is stochastic because the value of y depends partially on chance.

Stock. 1. A particular type of SECURITY, usually quoted in units of £100 value rather than in units of proportion of total CAPITAL, as in SHARES. Stock, or stocks and shares, have now become synonymous with securities, and the original distinction between shares and stock has become blurred. The term stock, however, is now coming to mean exclusively a fixed-interest security, i.e. loan stock in a company or local or central government stock. **2.** An accumulation of a COMMODITY. ◊ INVENTORY. **3.** (U.S.) A share in the ownership of a company, i.e. EQUITY.

Stock appreciation. Increase in the value of stock resulting from an increase in market prices. Stock appreciation is treated as a taxable profit in the U.K., although between 1974–5 and 1983–4 the increase in stock values on which corporation tax would be payable was limited. The introduction of *stock relief* became necessary following the increase in the general rate of inflation after 1973. ◊ CORPORATION TAX. It was important as a partial recognition of the need for INFLATION ACCOUNTING.

Stock exchange. A MARKET in which SECURITIES are bought and sold. There are stock exchanges in most capital cities, as well as in the larger provincial cities, in many countries. The largest in terms of EQUITY turnover is the NEW YORK STOCK EXCHANGE, followed by Tokyo, N.A.S.D.A.Q. (◊ OVER-THE-COUNTER MARKET), London and the Association of Exchanges of the Federal Republic of Germany. Continental European exchanges are often referred to as *bourses* (Fr.). The economic importance of stock exchanges is that they facilitate SAVING and INVESTMENT, first by making it possible for investors to dispose of securities quickly if they wish to do so, and secondly in channelling savings into productive investment. However, they are declining in importance as a source of new capital for industrial and commercial companies. Ready marketability requires that new issues ($\Diamond$ NEW-ISSUE MARKET) should be made or backed by reputable borrowers or institutions, that information should be available on existing securities, and that there should be both a legal framework and market rules to prevent fraud and sharp practice ($\Diamond$ SECURITIES AND INVESTMENTS BOARD). Stock exchanges have their own rules and conventions, but their functioning depends also on the existence of company and other law and FINANCIAL INTERMEDIARIES, such as the ISSUING HOUSES.

The British Stock Exchange, founded in 1773, developed from informal exchanges in coffee houses in the City of London, It is managed by a council of members. There are over 4,000 broker-dealer members who alone may transact business on the exchange. Members are formed into a declining number of firms now including major MERCHANT BANKS, the CLEARING BANKS and other financial intermediaries, some of which are foreign-owned. Business is still conducted by word of mouth, but the traditional trading floor where broker-dealers gathered to buy and sell is declining in importance following the BIG BANG. The bulk of business is conducted between members by telephone and soon, for small transactions, dealing will be carried out automatically by electronic means. The STOCK EXCHANGE AUTOMATED QUOTATION (S.E.A.Q.) service allows MARKET MAKERS and others to see competing quotations on their screens and STOCKBROKERS to select the best bid/offer for their clients. Prior to October 1986 the rules of the exchange did not permit JOBBERS to deal directly with the public, but only through stockbrokers, but now any member may make a market in shares and deal either with other members or the public as they wish. Following the agreement in 1986 to merge the *International Securities Regulatory Organization* (*I.S.R.O.*) (the members of which dealt in Eurobonds ($\Diamond$ BOND) and international equities in both registered and AMERICAN DEPOSITORY RECEIPT form) and the Stock Exchange, the full title of that body is the International Stock Exchange of the United Kingdom and the Republic of Ireland.

On 31 December 1986, 6,744 securities were listed on the main market of the stock exchange (i.e. not including shares traded on the Unlisted Securities Market or the Third Market – $\Diamond$ UNLISTED SECURITIES MARKETS). Of these, 4,921 were company securities and the remainder were public-sector and Eurobond securities; 2,101 U.K.-registered companies and 584 Irish and overseas companies are listed. The aggregate value (turnover) of purchases and sales of all securities on the Stock Exchange was £570,310·4 million in 1986, over 60 per cent of which was accounted for by British government stocks (*British Funds*).

The dismantling of EXCHANGE CONTROL, the DEREGULATION of stock markets and developments in telecommunications and electronic information systems have led in recent years to a major expansion in international trading of stocks and shares and in the links between stock markets in the ADVANCED COUNTRIES.

Stock Exchange Automated Quotation (S.E.A.Q.). A screen-based SECURITIES dealing system which allows MARKET MAKERS on the London STOCK EXCHANGE to report their price quotes and trading volumes to users of the system. S.E.A.Q. was introduced in preparation for the BIG BANG and it enables the bulk of transactions on the exchange to be carried out by telephone rather than on the trading floor.

Stock jobber. ◊ JOBBER.

Stock relief. ◊ CORPORATION TAX.

Stock–sales ratio. ◊ INVENTORIES; TURNOVER.

Stock split. An issue of new SHARES to shareholders without increasing total CAPITAL. The object of a stock split is to reduce the average quoted price of shares to promote their marketability.

Stock turnover. ◊ INVENTORIES; TURNOVER.

Stockbroker. A member of the STOCK EXCHANGE, who buys and sells SECURITIES for clients, in return for a COMMISSION on the PRICE of the shares. ◊ BROKER; MARKET MAKER.

Stockholm Convention. ◊ EUROPEAN FREE TRADE ASSOCIATION.

Stop–go. A phrase used to describe the attempted management of AGGREGATE DEMAND in the U.K. during the post-war period and particularly in the 1960s as the period of fixed EXCHANGE RATES drew to a close. The exchange rate came under pressure during periods of rising economic activity, but as FISCAL POLICY and MONETARY POLICY were applied to reduce aggregate demand and improve the BALANCE OF PAYMENTS it soon became necessary to stimulate the economy again to counteract RECESSION. The stop–go cycle tended to amplify movements in the TRADE CYCLE.

Stratified sample. A method of sampling (◊ RANDOM SAMPLE) which is used when the population to be sampled is not homogeneous and the nature of the population's heterogeneity is pertinent to the characteristic of the population about which information is sought. Suppose we wish to find out the percentage of households (the population) which owns dishwashers. Households are not homogeneous; they may be classified into subgroups or strata by, for instance, social group, or income level and, moreover, these subgroups are likely to differ in their ownership of consumer durables, such as dishwashers. Rather than take a random sample of the whole population of households, the latter is first subdivided into the appropriate categories or strata and random samples taken from each. If the population is heterogeneous a stratified sample will give more accurate results than a simple random sample of the same size.

Structural unemployment. UNEMPLOYMENT arising from changes in DEMAND or TECHNOLOGY which lead to an over-supply of labour with particular skills or in particular locations. Structural unemployment does not result from an overall deficiency of demand and therefore cannot be cured by REFLATION, but only by retraining or relocation of the affected work-force, some of which may find work at low wages in unskilled occupations (◊ CLASSICAL UNEMPLOYMENT). Structural unemployment is distinct from FRICTIONAL UNEMPLOYMENT, which is essentially a short-term phenomenon.

Subsidiaries. Companies legally controlled by other companies. Although a shareholding of less than 50 per cent may be sufficient to control a company effectively, it is not correctly described as a subsidiary unless between 50 and 100 per cent of the SHARES are owned by another. Companies may choose to retain subsidiaries rather than to integrate them fully into their own organizations for a variety of reasons e.g. the desire to allow local participation, a wish to conceal a business connection or to avoid the cost and complication of integrating an acquired company.

Subsidy. Government grants to suppliers of goods and services. A subsidy may be intended to keep prices down (i.e. to raise REAL INCOMES of buyers), to maintain incomes of producers (for example farmers) or to maintain a service or employment (for example subsidies to British Rail or the Rover group). An essential characteristic of a subsidy, as distinct from a TRANSFER PAYMENT, is that it has the object of keeping prices below the FACTOR cost of production. Subsidies, by distorting market PRICES and COSTS, may lead to a misallocation of resources although they may be justified in certain circumstances (for example to correct for EXTERNALITIES) and may be used instead of TARIFFS to protect new industry (◊ INFANT-INDUSTRY ARGUMENT) where not banned by international agreements. It may be possible to achieve the objectives of subsidies by alternative means which have less distorting effects, for example by direct income support through the TAXATION system.

Subsistence theory of wages. ◊ WAGES-FUND THEORY.

Substitutes. Products which at least partly satisfy the same needs of consumers. Products are defined as substitutes in terms of cross-price effects between them. If, when the price of records goes up, sales of compact discs rise, compact discs are said to be a substitute for records, because consumers can to some extent satisfy the need served by records with compact discs. This account is complicated by the fact that, when the price of an item changes, it affects both the REAL INCOME of consumers and the relative prices of different commodities. Strictly, one product is a substitute for another if it enjoys increased demand when the other's price rises *and* the consumer's income is raised just enough to compensate for the drop in living standards caused. One product is a *gross substitute* for another if it enjoys an increase in demand when the price of the other rises and no compensation is made.

Substitution is not a relationship that only holds between individual commodities – groups of commodities can also be substitutes for each other. Benson & Hedges cigarettes may be a substitute for Marlboro; while cigarettes in general may be a substitute for alcoholic drink. Both together may be a weak substitute for restaurant meals. Substitution (but not gross substitution) is a symmetric relationship: if apples are a substitute for bananas, bananas are a substitute for apples. ($\Leftrightarrow$ COM-PLEMENTARY DEMAND; CROSS-PRICE ELASTICITY OF DEMAND.)

Substitution effect. The rate at which consumers switch spending to or from a commodity when its relative price changes but the total UTILITY of consumers is left constant ($\Leftrightarrow$ CROSS-PRICE ELASTICITY OF DEMAND). The substitution effect measures how much consumers would switch their spending away from or towards an item whose price had changed, if the resultant change in purchasing power were offset by a compensating transfer of income that would allow them to maintain their total utility (enough to keep them on their INDIFFERENCE CURVE). It thus isolates the impact of a change in relative prices from the INCOME EFFECT. In terms of INDIFFERENCE-CURVE ANALYSIS, the substitution effect represents a swivel of the budget line around a single indifference curve while the income effect represents a parallel shift of the budget line on to a new indifference curve.

The substitution effect is always negative: consumers always switch spending away from items whose prices rise as they attempt to shield their living standards from the impact. If the price of butter rises by 10 per cent, no great loss is incurred by the consumer who can switch to margarine. The substitution effect is not a concept unique to consumer theory. It arises in many areas of economic analysis including, for example, the demand for LABOUR and CAPITAL by firms. $\Leftrightarrow$ GIFFEN GOOD; INFERIOR GOOD; SUBSTITUTES.

'Sun-spot' theory. $\Leftrightarrow$ JEVONS, W. S.

Sunk costs. COSTS incurred in the past which are irretrievable and there-fore not relevant to current decisions; in W. S. JEVONS's famous phrase 'bygones are for ever bygones'. For example, a small bakery might buy an oven at a fixed cost, but which it could sell at some future date should it want to. It also might pay out a large amount in advertising its services. However, this latter cost could not be recovered later on – once paid for, the advertising has gone, whether or not the promotion is successful. Sunk costs represent a BARRIER TO ENTRY in an industry because they scare potential entrants from entering – should they fail, they would have wasted all the sunk costs.

Superneutrality of money. The inability of changes in the growth rate of the MONEY stock in an economy to affect any VARIABLE except the rate of INFLATION. Money is *neutral* (◊ NEUTRALITY OF MONEY) if the *level* of the money supply only affects inflation. It is *superneutral* if the rate at which that level changes only affects inflation.

Super-normal profit. ◊ PROFIT.

Supplementary costs. A now little-used synonym for FIXED COSTS or OVERHEADS.

Supplementary special deposits. ◊ SPECIAL DEPOSITS.

Supply. The quantity of a good (or service) available for sale at any specified PRICE. Supply is determined by a number of influences. The first is price itself: the higher the price, the more profitable it is, other things being equal, for producers to sell a good and the more they will attempt to sell. The second is the cost of inputs: the lower are costs, the more profitable it is to sell a good at a given price and more will be offered for sale. The third is the price of other goods: when the price of other goods rises, the supplier of a good may find it advantageous to switch his production to the supply of the newly high-priced goods rather than stay in the relatively less profitable industry, where supply will fall. It should be noted that supply is *planned* supply, not necessarily what is actually sold. The latter depends on EQUILIBRIUM in the market. The conditions of supply constitute but one aspect of the determination of the quantities sold and market price, the other being the conditions of DEMAND (◊ FIRM, THEORY OF THE; MARSHALL, A.).

Supply curve. A graphical representation of the quantity of a good or service supplied at different price levels.. With PRICE on the vertical axis and quantity supplied on the horizontal axis, supply curves normally slope upwards for two reasons: (a) higher prices allow profits to be made at higher levels of production for firms already in the market; (b) if profits are made, new entrants are attracted into a market.
SUPPLY curves can be drawn for the SHORT RUN and the LONG RUN. In the short term, new firms do not have time to enter a market and higher output results only from an increase in production by market incumbents. In the long term, however, new entry occurs. The long-run supply curve links demand–supply equilibrium points on these short-run curves, which (*as shown in the diagram on page 393*) will be steeper than the long-run curve. (◊ FIRM, THEORY OF THE.)

Supply services. An item in the British BUDGET and government accounts consisting of expenditures which are estimated annually and voted in Parliament. It includes expenditure by government departments, such as defence, agriculture, including SUBSIDIES, the National Health Service, etc.

Supply-side economics. The study of the factors affecting and the policies appropriate for influencing the *real* economy, that is, the physical be-

Supply curve

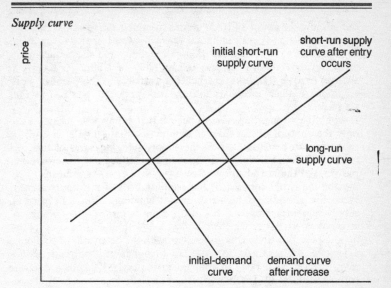

price

initial short-run
supply curve

short-run supply
curve after entry
occurs

long-run
supply curve

initial-demand
curve

demand curve
after increase

quantity

haviour of economic agents, and its response to changes in the structure of relative PRICES rather than nominal prices.

SUPPLY-side economics is roughly based on a positive and negative thesis. On the *negative* side, supply-side economists tend to deny a role to a STABILIZATION POLICY. Because, they believe, economic agents are only concerned with their real income and because markets have a tendency to clear at their EQUILIBRIUM levels, an artificial increase in AGGREGATE DEMAND cannot achieve anything. When demand is boosted, the price of all goods rises, and out of a desire to feed the extra demand, more labour will be sought, requiring an increase in wages. Out of all this, nothing changes in real terms: REAL WAGES are the same as they were, as are relative prices; all economic agents behave in the same way as they did before, even though the absolute price level might have changed, and possibly some temporary aberration from market equilibria occurred. The *positive* views of such economists relate to the policies that they believe can be effective in influencing the performance of an economy. Anything that attempts to influence the supply of LABOUR or the supply of goods can be called a supply-side measure. Such policies could include: (a) cutting taxes to improve incentives (affecting people's personal trade-off between going out to work and staying at home); (b) heavily legislating against MONOPOLY in order to encourage free competition, low prices and incentives to be efficient; (c)

393

diminishing the ability of trade unions to inhibit the workings of a free labour market; (d) restricting the growth of the MONEY supply to control INFLATION, improve economic stability and encourage investment; (e) measures to increase the mobility of labour ($\lozenge$ LABOUR, MOBILITY OF); (f) cutting the benefits available to those out of work to improve their incentive to take on work ($\lozenge$ REPLACEMENT RATIO).

It would be wrong, however, to believe that supply-side measures are only the concern of free-market economists. State interference in the economy can be classed as on the supply side: measures of this sort might include: (g) increases in spending on education to retrain employees; (h) the introduction of PROFIT-SHARING as a means of removing industrial conflict; (i) the establishment of a state investment bank for subsidizing high-risk, new-technology firms. In general, supply-side measures can be justified in terms of the findings of MICROECONOMICS, which is concerned with the behaviour of individual workers and firms rather than with the behaviour of economic aggregates ($\lozenge$ MACROECONOMICS). Free-market supply-side economics emerged as a body of thought in the early 1980s as a doctrine complementary to MONETARISM, which first provided a macroeconomic case against demand-management; it was strengthened by the theoretical revolution that arrived in the form of RATIONAL EXPECTATIONS. $\lozenge$ LAFFER CURVE.

Surplus value. $\lozenge$ MARX, K.

Surtax. An additional tax on higher incomes levied on net income after certain deductions, such as earned-income relief or approved-pension-scheme contributions. Surtax, which was abolished in 1973, was charged according to a sliding scale and was payable on 1 January following the year of assessment. $\lozenge$ INCOME TAX.

T

'Tableau économique.' The table with which QUESNAY analysed the circulation of WEALTH in the economy by setting out the different classes of society. The table showed how the '*produit net*' produced by the agricultural sector circulated between the owners of the LAND, the tenant farmers and other classes such as artisans and merchants. Only agriculture produced any net additions to wealth; all other activities were 'sterile'. The table showed, too, how output is annually reproduced. The sterile classes were essential in that they created the necessary demand for the agricultural sector. ⟡ CANTILLON, R.; LEONTIEF, W.; PHYSIOCRATS.

Take-off in economic development. ⟡ ECONOMIC GROWTH, STAGES OF.

Take-over. The acquisition of one company by another. Take-overs are sometimes financed by paying CASH at an offer PRICE in excess of the MARKET price of the SHARES, but, more frequently for large acquisitions, by the exchange of shares or loan STOCK, possibly with some cash adjustment, issued by the acquiring company for the shares of the acquired company. The term 'take-over' is normally used to imply that the acquisition is made on the initiative of the acquirer and without the full agreement of the acquired company; as distinct from a MERGER. ⟡ REVERSE TAKE-OVER.

Tap issue. An issue of TREASURY BILLS to government departments and others at a fixed PRICE and without going through the MARKET; as distinct from a tender issue (⟡ TENDERS).

Tariffs, import. Taxes imposed on commodity IMPORTS. They may be levied on an *ad valorem* basis, i.e. as a certain percentage of VALUE, or on a specific basis, i.e. as an amount per unit. Their purpose may be solely for raising revenue, in which case the home-produced product corresponding to the import would bear an equivalent compensatory tax. However, import duties are generally applied for the purpose of carrying out a particular economic policy, and in this context may be used to serve many functions:

(a) To reduce the overall level of imports by making them more expensive relative to their home-produced SUBSTITUTES, with the aim of eliminating a BALANCE OF PAYMENTS deficit. ⟡ DE-VALUATION.

(b) To counter the practice of DUMPING by raising the import price of the dumped commodity to its economic level.

(c) To retaliate against restrictive measures imposed by other countries (⟡ RECIPROCITY).

(d) To protect a new industry until it is sufficiently well established to compete with the more developed industries of other countries (◊ INFANT-INDUSTRY ARGUMENT).

(e) To protect 'key' industries, such as agriculture, without which the economy would be vulnerable in time of war.

For instance, in respect of members compared with non-members of the EUROPEAN FREE TRADE ASSOCIATION and the EUROPEAN ECONOMIC COMMUNITY tariffs are preferential. However, it was an accepted principle under the MOST-FAVOURED NATION CLAUSE of the GENERAL AGREEMENT ON TARIFFS AND TRADE that tariffs should be non-discriminating and any concessions agreed between two or more countries should automatically be extended to all. It has, however, been accepted that this principle may be waived in the interests of the DEVELOPING COUNTRIES. Since the end of the Second World War, significant progress has been made through the G.A.T.T. in the reduction of tariff levels by means of a series of negotiations, of which the TOKYO ROUND OF TRADE NEGOTIATIONS was the latest to be completed.

Tatonnement process. The 'tatonnement' (or 'groping') process was suggested by M. E. L. WALRAS to illustrate that equilibrium in perfect markets (◊ PERFECT COMPETITION) can be attained at a particular set of prices no matter what the original disequilibrium position of the markets and the route by which prices move before reaching equilibrium. Buyers and sellers make known their prices in the first round. In the second round, buyers and sellers increase their published prices, where there is excess demand, reduce them where there is a shortfall in demand and keep them the same where demand and supply are in balance. The process continues until there is a balance of demand and supply in all markets. At this stage, actual transactions take place; no trade is done until equilibrium is reached.

Taussig, Frank William (1859–1940). Apart from a period from 1917 to 1919 when he was chairman of the U.S. Tariffs Commission, Taussig spent his whole career at Harvard University. His works on economics include *Tariff History of the United States* (1888), *Wages and Capital* (1896), a textbook, *Principles of Economics* (1911) and *International Trade* (1927). An economist in the tradition of RICARDO and MARSHALL, Taussig attempted to relate his theory to established statistical data.

Tautology. ◊ HYPOTHESIS.

Tax. ◊ TAXATION.

Tax, ad valorem. An indirect tax (◊ TAXATION) which is expressed as a proportion of the PRICE of a COMMODITY – hence it is 'by value'. VALUE-ADDED TAX is an *ad valorem* tax. ◊◊ SALES TAX.

Tax, 'cascade'. ◊ TURNOVER TAX.

Tax, progressive. ⟡ PROGRESSIVE TAX.

Tax, proportional. ⟡ PROPORTIONAL TAX.

Tax, regressive. ⟡ REGRESSIVE TAX.

Tax, specific. A tax (⟡ TAXATION) of an absolute amount levied per unit of a COMMODITY sold or produced. Examples are STAMP DUTY and EXCISE DUTIES. An indirect tax (⟡ DIRECT TAXATION) not to be confused with a TAX, AD VALOREM.

Tax, turnover. ⟡ TURNOVER TAX.

Tax and price index. An INDEX NUMBER which measures the percentage change in gross income required by taxpaying individuals to maintain their real disposable income (⟡ REAL TERMS). The index takes into account the movement in the retail price index and changes in DIRECT TAXATION and employee National Insurance contributions.

Tax avoidance. Arranging one's financial affairs within the law so as to minimize taxation LIABILITIES, as opposed to *tax evasion*, which is failing to meet actual tax liabilities through, e.g., not declaring INCOME or PROFIT.

Tax base. The quality or coverage of what is taxed. The tax base for INCOME TAX is the assessed incomes of the whole population. The tax base for VALUE-ADDED TAX does not include sales of most foods, books and financial services.

Tax burden. The amount of MONEY which an individual, institution or group must pay in TAX. It should include all costs to the taxpayer which he incurs in paying the tax, e.g. the net-of-tax cost of employing an accountant to complete a tax form, as well as the tax itself. ⟡ COMPLIANCE COST.

Tax equalization account. ⟡ COMPANY RESERVES.

Tax evasion. ⟡ TAX AVOIDANCE. ⟠ BLACK ECONOMY.

Tax expenditures. The costs of tax allowances and reliefs. It has been argued that tax allowances are similar to SUBSIDIES and may be seen as a form of PUBLIC EXPENDITURE. However, tax expenditures can never be more than estimates since it cannot be assumed that the TAX BASE would remain unaltered if the allowances were abolished. The range of tax expenditures is very great; the Inland Revenue alone publishes estimates for almost 100 types of allowances and reliefs, most of which probably lead to the loss of some revenue and all of which complicate the administration of the tax system and raise COMPLIANCE COSTS. Tax expenditure estimates for 1984/5 include the following: married man's allowance, £11,700 million; capital allowances against CORPORATION TAX and INCOME TAX, £10,160 million; MORTGAGE interest relief, £3,500 million and CAPITAL GAINS taxation, £3,018 million. Tax allowances and reliefs necessitate higher rates of tax than would otherwise be necessary and lead to distortions in factor markets (⟡ FACTORS OF PRODUCTION) and probably also to higher TAX AVOIDANCE, and there is increasing interest in reducing them.

Tax impact. ◊ TAXATION, INCIDENCE OF.

Tax yield. The amount of MONEY which results when the rate of TAX is applied to the MONEY value of the TAX BASE, minus the costs of collecting the tax.

Taxation. A compulsory transfer of MONEY (or occasionally of goods and SERVICES) from private individuals, institutions or groups to the government. It may be levied upon WEALTH or INCOME, or in the form of a surcharge on PRICES. In the first case, it would then be called a DIRECT TAX; in the latter, an *indirect tax*. Taxation is one of the principle means by which a government finances its expenditure. ◊◊ CAPITAL GAINS; CAPITAL TRANSFER TAX; CORPORATION TAX; INCOME TAX; PUBLIC GOODS; SALES TAX; STAMP DUTY; TAX, SPECIFIC; TAX EXPENDITURES; UNIT TAX; VALUE-ADDED TAX.

Taxation, incidence of. The ultimate distribution of the burden of a tax. The initial *tax impact*, or formal incidence of an EXCISE DUTY on tobacco, for example, may be on the importer or wholesaler who has to pay over the tax to the authorities, but he is likely to pass on some or all of the tax in the form of higher prices to the retailer and the consumer. Whether or not a tax is wholly shifted forward will depend upon the price ELASTICITY of demand and supply for tobacco. If the consumer does not reduce his purchases following the increase in price then he will bear the whole of the tax. If he does reduce his purchases then the wholesaler and the retailer will also be worse off and will be bearing part of the tax. In general, a tax on any company must be paid by its shareholders, its employees or its customers.

Technical analysis. ◊ CHARTIST.

Technical Development Capital Ltd (T.D.C.). A subsidiary institution formed in 1962 by the Industrial and Commercial Finance Corporation (◊ FINANCE FOR INDUSTRY; MACMILLAN COMMITTEE), with a number of banks and INSURANCE companies, to invest in technical developments and INNOVATIONS.

Technical substitution, rate of. The rate at which one FACTOR OF PRODUCTION can be substituted for another in a production process (◊◊ PRODUCTION FUNCTION) and maintain a constant output. Its value is equal to the ratio of the MARGINAL PRODUCTS of the factors of production. It is represented by the slope of the TRANSFORMATION CURVE (◊ ECONOMIC EFFICIENCY; MARGINAL RATE OF SUBSTITUTION).

Technology. The sum of knowledge of the means and methods of producing goods and services. Technology is not merely applied science, because it often runs ahead of science – things are often done without precise knowledge of how or why they are done except that they are effective. Early technology – craft skill – was almost entirely of this sort. Modern technology is increasingly science-based, however, and, rather than relying on acquired skill, is easily communicable by demonstration and printed material to those qualified to receive it. It also includes methods of organization as well as physical technique. Technological change and the diffusion of technology are important in economics because new methods, including those embodied in INVESTMENT, play an important part in theories of ECONOMIC GROWTH. There is, however, some controversy about the extent to which technological development is an autonomous factor in economic growth. Because it is so difficult to measure there is also room for doubt about whether or not technological change is, or has recently been, accelerating.

Telex Output of Price Information by Computer (T.O.P.I.C.). A view-data system set up by the London STOCK EXCHANGE to disseminate share prices, exchange rates and other information. Share prices are fed into T.O.P.I.C. by the STOCK EXCHANGE AUTOMATED QUOTATION service.

Tenders. Offers to supply at a fixed PRICE. A DISCOUNT HOUSE tendering for an issue of TREASURY BILLS, for example, will offer to take up so many bills at a certain price.

Term loan. A bank advance for a specific period (normally three to ten years) repaid, with INTEREST, usually by regular periodical payments. Term loans are common practice in the U.S. commercial banking system for business finance, and for larger borrowings the LOAN may be syndicated, i.e. the provision of funds and the interest earned are shared between several banks. Similar facilities are increasingly available in Britain, mainly from the COMMERCIAL BANKS or other institutions such as FINANCE FOR INDUSTRY (▷ MACMILLAN COMMITTEE), but OVERDRAFTS are still the most common form of BANK LOAN, and are a cheaper form of finance. Unlike an overdraft, the interest of a term loan is fixed and the loan cannot be recalled in advance of its maturity date.

Term structure of interest rates. The relationship between the interest rate paid on a bond and the number of years there are until the bond is repaid. Suppose, for simplicity, bonds are held for either one year or two years. People wanting to invest for two years can do so either by buying a two-year bond or by buying a one-year bond now and then buying a new one when that one expires. The term structure compares the annual yield on each type of bond. It is affected by a number of factors. Most important, if interest rates are expected to rise next year, the two-year bond will have to offer a higher annual return than the one-year bond. Otherwise everyone would sell two-year bonds and hold a one-year bond this year and a higher-yielding one-year bond next year. ▷ YIELD CURVE.

Terms of trade. The ratio of the index of EXPORT prices to the index of IMPORT prices. An improvement in the terms of trade follows if export prices rise more quickly than import prices (or fall more slowly than import prices). In the decade from 1974 to 1984 the terms of trade of the U.K. improved by 20 per cent.

Theories of value. ◊ VALUE, THEORIES OF.

Theory of distribution. ◊ DISTRIBUTION, THEORY OF.

Theory of games. ◊ GAME THEORY.

Theory of income determination. ◊ INCOME DETERMINATION, THEORY OF.

Theory of production. ◊ PRODUCTION, THEORY OF.

Theory of second best. ◊ SECOND BEST, THEORY OF.

Theory of the firm. ◊ FIRM, THEORY OF THE.

Third Market. An OVER-THE-COUNTER MARKET set up by the London STOCK EXCHANGE to trade in the securities of unlisted companies and with less stringent entry requirements than either the UNLISTED SECURITIES MARKET or the Official List or main market. The Third Market opened on 26 January 1987.

Third World. A synonym for DEVELOPING COUNTRIES.

Thornton, William Thomas (1813–80). ◊ WAGE-FUND THEORY.

Thünen, Johann Heinrich von (1783–1850). A member of the landowning Prussian class of *Junkers*, after completing his education at agricultural college he attended the University of Göttingen. For the remainder of his life he farmed his estate at Mecklenburg. The first volume of his work *Der isolierte Staat in Beziehung auf Landwirtschaft und National-ökonomie* was published in 1826, and part one of volume two in 1850. The rest of volume two and volume three appeared in 1863. He used his farm as a source of facts for his theoretical work in agricultural economics. He built a theoretical MODEL which he used to find the important factors that determined the most profitable location of various branches of agriculture in relation to their sources of DEMAND. In so doing, he devised a theory of RENT similar to that of RICARDO. He set out a theory of DISTRIBUTION based on marginal productivity, using CALCULUS, which was considerably ahead of his own time, and he could be considered one of the founders of MARGINAL ANALYSIS. ◊ LOCATION THEORY.

Tied loan. A LOAN made on condition that certain purchases are made from the lender. In the brewing industry tied loans are made to pubs and clubs for fitting out bars and restaurants on the understanding that beer is supplied by the brewer making the loan. In foreign aid loans are made on favourable terms on condition that capital equipment or services are purchased from the lending country.

Tight money. ◊ DEAR MONEY.

Time deposit (U.S.). Money in a bank account for which the bank may require notice of withdrawal, usually of up to three months. ⟡ DEPOSIT ACCOUNT.

Time preference. The amount by which consumers value immediate CONSUMPTION in preference to deferred or postponed consumption. Suppose an individual has £1; he can either spend it now, or put it aside and spend it next year. The rate of time preference of that consumer is the amount of money necessary to just persuade him to save the pound. If he thinks he will be doing very well next year and has no need to save, or out of fear of nuclear war believes the world will no longer exist next year, he will require a large amount of compensation to persuade him not to spend the pound. If on the other hand he believes he is perfectly well off at the moment and conditions are unlikely to change much, he may think a rather small amount of compensation makes saving worth while.

Several factors affect the time preference of consumers. The first is the level of consumption they enjoy in the present. Other things being equal, the more consumption there is now, the lower the compensation needed for SAVING. As saving implies a fall in current consumption, the more that is saved, the higher the required level of compensation. As a corollary of this, the second factor is the level of consumption expected to be enjoyed in the future. If great wealth is expected tomorrow, a lot of reward will be needed to induce saving today. Again, as saving today implies higher consumption in the future, the more that is saved, the higher the required level of compensation. The third factor is the risk the consumer attaches to the arrival of the future: if tomorrow is unlikely to come, huge compensation is needed to cause saving. Finally, consumer taste will influence the time-preference rate – some people may believe that they can only enjoy spending money when they are young: others might believe the reverse.

The market RATE OF INTEREST expresses the amount a consumer will actually be compensated for saving, and rational consumers will save enough for their time-preference rate to equal the interest rate. If the interest rate exceeds their time-preference rate, they should save more, raising their time-preference rate until it is equal to the market interest rate. The reverse would be true if their time-preference rate exceeded the interest rate. If the interest rate is lower than their time-preference rate even when they are saving nothing, it is rational for them to borrow money and pay interest on it; this raises current consumption and lowers future consumption and thus lowers their time-preference rate. Optimal consumption through time can be analysed with the help of INDIFFERENCE CURVES, depicting the bundles of consumption today and in the future between which the consumer is indifferent. (⟡ FISHER, I.)

Time series. The values of a particular VARIABLE at consecutive periods of time.

Time-series analysis. The application of statistical methods to find explanations of movements of VARIABLES over time. ($\Diamond$ CROSS-SECTION ANALYSIS.)

Times covered. $\Diamond$ DIVIDEND COVER.

Tobin, James (b. 1918). Professor Tobin studied at Harvard University, obtaining his Ph.D. in 1947. He moved to Yale in 1950 and was appointed Sterling Professor of Economics. He was awarded the NOBEL PRIZE in Economics in 1981. Professor Tobin's major published works include *Liquidity Preference as Behaviour towards Risk* (1958), *National Economic Policy* (1966), *Financial Markets and Economic Activity* (1967), *Essays in Economics, Macroeconomics* (1971), *Economics, One Decade Older* (1974), *Essays in Economics: Consumption and Econometrics* (1975), *Asset Accumulation and Economic Activity* (1980) and *Essays in Economics: Theory and Policy* (1982). Professor Tobin has made important contributions to the theory of finance through his analysis of the demand for financial assets ($\Diamond\!\!\!\Diamond$ LIQUIDITY PREFERENCE). He criticized MONETARISM for its narrow emphasis on money. There is a range of financial assets which investors may be willing to hold in their portfolios, not only money but bonds and equities. Moreover, their preferences are determined by their weighing up the rates of return and capital-gains prospects, against the risks ($\Diamond$ PORTFOLIO THEORY). Professor Tobin explored the links between the mix of financial portfolios and the real assets of firms to show how government and central bank policy impinge on real G.N.P and employment. Professor Tobin has also contributed to the theory of ECONOMETRICS: Tobit, a statistical analytical technique for the estimation of variables subject to PROBABILITY, was named after him. ($\Diamond\!\!\!\Diamond$ Q THEORY.)

Tokyo round of trade negotiations. Agreement was reached in Tokyo in 1973 to initiate a seventh round of trade negotiations under the auspices of the GENERAL AGREEMENT ON TARIFFS AND TRADE. These negotiations began in 1974, after the passing in the United States of the TRADE ACT, which gave the President powers to negotiate. The negotiations were concluded at the end of 1979. Agreement was reached on the following matters:

(a) The major developed countries agreed to reduce their tariffs ($\Diamond$ TARIFFS, IMPORT) by, on the average, one-third over a period ending on 1 January 1987.

(b) A new code of conduct was drawn up covering customs-valuation procedures, barriers caused by technical specifications, import licences and government procurement policies. For instance, the American Selling Price system was abolished. Under this system the United States revalued imports of chemicals to the higher level of that charged by U.S. domestic producers and then calculated the import duty on this higher figure.

(c) A new code was also agreed concerning the application of COUNTERVAILING DUTIES. These duties may only be applied when it can be demonstrated that material injury is being caused to the domestic producers of a commodity because of the importation of that commodity from a subsidized overseas source. (⟡ URUGUAY ROUND OF TRADE NEGOTIATIONS.)

Trade barrier. A general term covering any government limitation on the free international exchange of merchandise. These barriers may take the form of TARIFFS, QUOTAS, IMPORT DEPOSITS, restrictions on the issue of IMPORT LICENCES or stringent regulations relating to health or safety standards. ⟡ PROTECTION.

Trade bill. ⟡ BILL OF EXCHANGE.

Trade credit. The CREDIT extended by business firms to other business firms. It may occur explicitly through the issue of a BILL OF EXCHANGE, or may arise from the delay of receipts and payments for services performed. It can have an important influence on economic policy, because it is in total an important source of finance, comparable, for instance, with bank credit and, at the same time, it does not come under the direct control of the authorities as does the latter. ⟡ FACTORING.

Trade cycle. Regular fluctuations in the level of NATIONAL INCOME. The trade cycle is a well-observed economic phenomenon, though it often occurs on a generally upward growth path and has a variable time span, typically of the order of three years. It has been a matter of government policy in Western economies to dampen the amplitude, that is, the height of the peaks and depths of the troughs, of the cycle so that the trend path of output is followed without much fluctuation (⟡ STABILIZATION POLICY).

Several suggestions have been put forward as to the cause of cycles. The most well known, developed by SAMUELSON, HICKS, Goodwin, PHILLIPS and Kalecki in the 1940s and 1950s, combines the MULTIPLIER with the accelerator theory of investment (⟡ ACCELERATOR–MULTIPLIER MODEL). In certain cases, investment can be positively related to output one period back, and negatively related to output two periods back. This can cause an oscillating path for income. M. FRIEDMAN, in his analysis of U.S. monetary history, notes the correlation between money supply and economic activity and suggests that the business cycle is a monetary phenomenon. More recently, attention has been paid to the effects of shocks to the economy from technology and taste changes. These 'real' phenomena can, it is suggested, account for many economic fluctuations. (⟡ FRISCH, R. A. K.; INCOME DETERMINATION, THEORY OF.)

Trade discount. The percentage below the published retail PRICE at which a manufacturer sells to his distributors (wholesale or retail) or at which a wholesaler sells his goods to a retailer. In addition, further discounts are sometimes given on a scale related to the quantities of the goods taken. A '*concealed*' *discount* is one granted by a manufacturer or wholesaler to favoured customers and not made publicly known to prevent accusations of unfair trading. ⟡ RESALE PRICE MAINTENANCE.

Trade diversion and trade creation. ⟡ CUSTOMS UNION.

Trade investments. SHARES held by one company in another; normally minority holdings in customers or suppliers.

Trading currency. Currency in which INTERNATIONAL TRADE is invoiced. ⟡ RESERVE CURRENCY.

Trading stamps. Coupons given by a retailer to a customer according to the VALUE of goods purchased. The trading-stamp firm sells the stamps to the retailer and redeems them by exchanging them for goods or CASH when presented by the retailer's customer. The trading-stamp firm makes a PROFIT from selling the stamps to the retailer at a price greater than their value and from the fact that not all of their stamps are redeemed. The retailer benefits in so far as he would lose business if his rival gives stamps. The customer benefits only in so far as he likes collecting stamps, the financial benefit being generally small, and in any case being a cumbersome method of getting a TRADE DISCOUNT. The Trading Stamps Act of 1964 made it illegal to sell stamps without a cash value.

Transactions demand for money. The holding of cash by people or firms to finance foreseeable expenditures. When people are paid, they probably put their salary into a bank account, from which they can spend it very easily, using cheques or cash taken from a machine. If they wanted to, however, instead of putting it in the bank, they could invest it in, say, government bonds, which would pay interest. People, however, keep much of their money in easy-access, low-return accounts. This is the transactions demand for money.

The transactions demand depends on three factors. First, the volume and pattern of transactions to be financed. A rich man requires more ready cash than a poor man, because he spends more. The pattern of transactions matters too: if spending and income were £20 a day, virtually no money would be kept for transactions, but if spending were £20 a day and income £140 a week, for the first six days of the week a positive balance would be kept. Secondly, the rate of interest has an effect, because it represents the sacrifice made from not investing money. The third factor is the cost of making transactions in interest-bearing assets: the brokerage fees, costs of acquiring information, etc.

The foregoing applies equally to the corporate demand for money. It is generally believed that the transactions demand relates to the function of money as a medium of exchange (⟡ MONEY), and, of the various possible definitions of money supply, the most relevant to this demand is a 'narrow' one, of very liquid assets (⟡ MONEY SUPPLY). Although it was seen as the only possible reason for holding money by classical economists, it was J. M. KEYNES who introduced the idea that the interest rate might be important in determining the demand for money, and outlined other motives for holding cash too. (⟡ PRECAUTIONARY MOTIVE; SPECULATIVE MOTIVE; TOBIN, J.)

Transactions motive. The factor which causes people or firms to hold a stock of money to finance their foreseeable expenditures. It is one of three motives for holding money outlined by Keynes. (⟡ PRECAUTIONARY MOTIVE; SPECULATIVE MOTIVE; TRANSACTIONS DEMAND FOR MONEY.)

Transfer costs. The total COSTS of moving goods or materials from one place to another including loading/unloading costs and administrative costs as well as transport costs.

Transfer deed. A legal document by which ownership of SECURITIES is transferred from the seller to the buyer. In Britain, it is no longer necessary for both parties to sign such a document when disposing of a share. The seller gives his authority to the issuer of the security to remove his name from the records while the buyer's BROKER simply informs the issuer of the purchaser's name.

Transfer earnings. The minimum payment necessary to keep a FACTOR OF PRODUCTION in its existing use and deter movement to other employment. Earnings in excess of transfer earnings are ECONOMIC RENT.

Transfer payments. Grants or other payments not made in return for a productive service, for example pensions, UNEMPLOYMENT benefits and other forms of income support, including charitable donations by companies. Transfer payments are a form of income redistribution, not a return to the FACTORS OF PRODUCTION. Current grants to the personal sector represented 31 per cent of the total revenue of general government (⟡ PUBLIC SECTOR) in 1985. SUBSIDIES which are paid by government to producers are not counted as transfer payments.

Transfer pricing. Internal (as distinct from MARKET) prices used in large organizations for transactions between semi-autonomous divisions. A MULTINATIONAL CORPORATION, for example, will have to set transfer prices for the supply of components from one subsidiary to another. Transfer prices between subsidiaries acting as profit centres may approximate to market prices or they may be set above or below them so as to minimize the payment of TARIFFS or to shift PROFIT from a high-TAXATION country to a low-taxation country.

Transformation curve (production possibility curve). A graphical representation of the maximum amount of one good or service that an economy can produce by reducing production of a second good or service and transferring the resources saved to the production of the first good. For example, an economy might be capable of producing fifty battleships if it produces no food, or no battleships if it produces a million tons of food. Either of these combinations would be a point on the transformation curve, which can be plotted on a graph with the number of battleships produced on one axis and the amount of food on the other. It traces the number of tons of food that can be made using the resources required for any given level of battleship production.

A transformation curve is normally assumed to be concave to (i.e. bulge away from) the origin. This is because the RATE OF TECHNICAL SUBSTITUTION declines the more of a commodity that is produced: a large amount of food can be made for the sacrifice of one battleship if no food is being made to start with, because the best fields can be used and the people good at farming but poor at battleship building can be transferred to farming productively. However, suppose that only one battleship is being built and the rest of the economy is geared to food production; transferring resources from the battleship to food will have hardly any effect on food output. Thus, the rate at which battleships can be transformed into food declines as food production rises. ⟡ ECONOMIC EFFICIENCY.

Transitivity. A characteristic of rational preferences which holds that if a combination of goods, *A*, is preferred to another combination, *B*, and *B* is preferred to a third combination, *C*, then *A* must be preferred to *C*. Transitivity is also assumed to hold for the indifference relation between combinations of goods. (⟡ INDIFFERENCE-CURVE ANALYSIS; PARADOX OF VOTING.)

Transmission mechanism. The process by which changes in the money supply affect the level of AGGREGATE DEMAND. There are different ways in which the mechanism can operate. First, with extra cash people may choose to buy new goods. Second, and more indirectly, with extra cash, people may buy more BONDS, as a means of storing their new wealth. This increase in the demand for bonds will push their prices up and interest rates down and this will stimulate new INVESTMENT. MONETARISM concentrates on the more direct process, while KEYNESIAN ECONOMICS has tended to play down the power of money, believing that its effects work only through the second, indirect mechanism.

Treasury. Managed on a day-to-day basis by the Chancellor of the EX-CHEQUER though the First Lord of the Treasury is the Prime Minister, this British government department coordinates national economic policy (including MONETARY POLICY), and controls PUBLIC EX-PENDITURE. Some of the Treasury's functions passed to the Department of Economic Affairs when it was set up in 1964, but returned to it in 1969 when the D.E.A. was closed. Also, prior to the establishment of the Civil Service Department in 1970, the Treasury was responsible for the management of the Civil Service, but this role is now performed by the Management and Personnel Office in the Cabinet office.

Treasury bills. Instruments for short-term borrowing by the government. The bills are promissory notes to pay to the bearer £5,000 upwards ninety-one days from the date of issue. The bills are issued by tender to the MONEY MARKET and to government departments through TAP ISSUES. TENDERS are invited every week from bankers, DISCOUNT HOUSES and BROKERS. On the one hand, treasury bills provide the government with a highly flexible and relatively cheap means of borrowing MONEY to meet its fluctuating needs for CASH. On the other hand, the bills provide a sound SECURITY for dealings in the money market, and the BANK OF ENGLAND, in particular, can operate on that market by dealing in treasury bills. Commercial bills (◊ BILL OF EXCHANGE) have declined in importance, but treasury bills, which date from 1877, now account for the bulk of the national FLOATING DEBT.

Treasury deposit receipt (T.D.R.). An instrument of compulsory government borrowing from the COMMERCIAL BANKS during the Second World War. The T.D.R.s were, in effect, unmarketable TREASURY BILLS bearing a RATE OF INTEREST of $1\frac{1}{8}$ per cent. First issued in 1940, they reached a total of £1,800 million by 1945, after which they were gradually replaced with treasury bills.

Treasury notes. In denominations of £1 and 10s. (50p), these, also known as *currency notes*, were issued to replace the gold coins withdrawn in Britain in 1914. At that time the lowest denomination of BANK OF ENGLAND notes (◊ BANKNOTE) was £5, and the two kinds of CURRENCY complemented one another until 1928, when treasury notes were amalgamated with the Bank of England issue. ◊ FIDUCIARY ISSUE.

Treaty of Rome. ◊ EUROPEAN ECONOMIC COMMUNITY.

Treaty of Stockholm. ◊ EUROPEAN FREE TRADE ASSOCIATION.

Trigger price. A minimum price level applied to IMPORTS of steel into the United States. If import prices were below this minimum, there was a presumption of DUMPING, and a countervailing duty (◊ TARIFFS, IMPORT) could be imposed or a QUOTA set. This price was based on Japanese delivered prices to certain areas of the United States.

Truck system. ◊ FRINGE BENEFITS.

Trust. 1. MONEY or property vested with an individual or group of individuals to administer in the interest of others. Trusts of this kind are usually set up to continue interests in accordance with the general instructions of the initiator and to protect them from outside interference and for tax reasons. Thus people set up trusts or appoint trustees to administer their estates after their death. Certain newspapers are administered by trusts. Banks act as trustees for a fee, and a similar service is provided by the Public Trustee, established in 1908. The term is a legal one. **2.** Financial trusts are also established for commercial purposes where particular protection is required against fraud, e.g. UNIT TRUSTS or INVESTMENT TRUSTS. **3.** (U.S.) A very large amalgamation of firms. ⟡ ANTI-TRUST.

Trustee Savings Bank (T.S.B.). A SAVINGS BANK originally established in Scotland in 1810 to encourage saving by people with low INCOMES. There were several hundred T.S.B.s ten years later but the number had fallen to seventy-three by the time the PAGE COMMITTEE recommended in 1973 that they should be restructured and set free to become a new force in BANKING. At that time the T.S.B.s were allowed only to invest in government securities, having only in 1965 been authorized to issue CHEQUES. Since then they have developed a fuller range of financial services and the T.S.B. was floated on the STOCK EXCHANGE in 1986.

Turgot, Anne Robert Jacques, Baron de l'Aulne (1727–81). Educated for the Church, he became an abbé at the Sorbonne in Paris, but then took up a career in the civil service, where he remained for the rest of his life. He was the Administrator of the District of Limoges from 1761 to 1774, when he became Secretary of State for the Navy. For a short time, he held the post of Controller of Finance. His economic work appeared in *Réflexions sur la formation et la distribution des richesses*, published in 1766. In this work he gave a clear analysis of the law of DIMINISHING RETURNS. He demonstrated how more and more applications of a FACTOR OF PRODUCTION (CAPITAL) to a constant factor (LAND) will first increase then decrease the return at the margin. He was the first to equate capital accumulation with SAVING, a view which became a central feature of CLASSICAL ECONOMICS.

Turnover. The total sales revenue of a business.

Turnover tax. A TAX levied as a proportion of the PRICE of a COMMODITY on each sale in the production and distribution chain; also called a *cascade tax*. Such a tax encourages VERTICAL INTEGRATION. Turnover taxes were widespread in Europe, for example in Germany, before the introduction of the VALUE-ADDED TAX now standard throughout the EUROPEAN ECONOMIC COMMUNITY.

Turnpike theorem. ⟡ OPTIMAL-GROWTH THEORY.

U

Unavoidable costs. COSTS which have to be borne even if no output is produced. ◊ FIXED COSTS.

Uncalled capital. AUTHORIZED CAPITAL issued to the public, but not called (◊ CALL) and not PAID-UP CAPITAL.

Uncertainty. The state in which the number of possible outcomes exceeds the number of actual outcomes and when no probabilities can be attached to each possible outcome. It differs from risk, which is defined as having measurable probabilities. Where probabilities are measurable, insurance can be taken out to cover the worst contingencies: the risk of them occurring is spread among many people or taken on by someone who can reasonably certainly bear them. In the case of uncertainty, however, no insurance company could properly assess what premium to charge to cover bad outcomes: it is simply a possibility that has to be faced. It is the role of the entrepreneur in facing each uncertainty when setting up a new company that justifies PROFIT as a reward. (◊ RISK.)

Undated securities. SECURITIES not bearing a REDEMPTION DATE or OPTION, hence IRREDEEMABLE SECURITIES.

Underconsumption. ◊ QUANTITY RATIONING.

Underdeveloped country. ◊ DEVELOPING COUNTRIES.

Undervalued currency. A CURRENCY whose EXCHANGE RATE is below either its FREE MARKET level or the EQUILIBRIUM level which it is expected to reach in the LONG RUN. Conversely, an overvalued currency may develop as a consequence of balance-of-payments deficits. ◊ DE-VALUATION; REVALUATION. ◊ INTERNATIONAL MONETARY FUND.

Underwriting. The business of insuring against RISK. An underwriter in return for a COMMISSION or PREMIUM agrees to bear a risk or a proportion of a risk. Specifically, an underwriter is a member of LLOYD'S, who joins with others to underwrite the risk of damage or loss to a ship or cargo – if the ship sinks and is not recoverable he will pay a porportion of the cost of the loss to be insured – but the term is generally used to describe the basic activity of INSURANCE. An ISSUING HOUSE also underwrites directly or indirectly a new issue of SHARES – if the public do not take up the whole issue, the balance will be taken up by the underwriters. ◊ NEW-ISSUE MARKET.

Unearned income. ◊ EARNED INCOME.

Unemployment. The existence of a section of the labour force able and willing to work, but unable to find gainful employment. Unemployment is measured as the percentage of the total labour force out of work. Historically, it was very high in the 1930s; it fell to its lowest level in the 1950s and re-emerged as a worsening phenomenon in Western economies after the oil crisis of 1973, for the first time simultaneously appearing with high inflation. Four distinct causes of unemployment can be distinguished:

(a) FRICTIONAL UNEMPLOYMENT is caused by people taking time out of work being between jobs or looking for a job.

(b) CLASSICAL UNEMPLOYMENT is caused by excessively high wages.

(c) STRUCTURAL UNEMPLOYMENT refers to a mismatch of job vacancies with the supply of labour available, caused by shifts in the structure of the economy.

(d) KEYNESIAN UNEMPLOYMENT results from the existence of a deficiency of AGGREGATE DEMAND which is simply not great enough to support full employment. A fall in wages – which should cause an increase in the DEMAND FOR LABOUR – merely reduces aggregate demand further because it reduces the spending power of the employed, and thus fails to clear the excess supply of workers. Much economic debate has centred on whether, in the long term, cuts in wages cannot in fact increase demand (◊ REAL BALANCE EFFECT), and thus whether Keynesian unemployment is not just a special case of CLASSICAL UNEMPLOYMENT in which workers are simply pricing themselves out of jobs.

Monetarist and neo-classical economists have tended to argue that all unemployment is either classical or voluntary (◊ UNEMPLOYMENT, NATURAL RATE OF).Either, they assert, the market fails to clear because wages are artificially held too high; or, if the market does clear, the unemployed have chosen not to take a job at the going rate. However, in particular circumstances it has been shown to be possible for the economy to stick at a less than true employment EQUILIBRIUM, the only way out of which is to boost aggregate demand. The labour market is widely recognized as being slower to adjust than any other; excess supply in this market persists in a way that it could not elsewhere, despite the high social and human costs of unemployment. ◊ EMPLOYMENT, FULL.

Unemployment, natural rate of. The level of UNEMPLOYMENT that prevails when all markets in the economy are in equilibrium, (◊ GENERAL EQUILIBRIUM). The natural rate is equivalent to the voluntary unemployment rate, because if there is neither excess demand nor excess supply on the labour market, anybody not working must have chosen not to take a job at the prevailing wage. This is also roughly equivalent to the FRICTIONAL UNEMPLOYMENT rate because it is those who are between jobs who are making a rational choice as to whether it pays them to work or not. The level of natural unemployment reflects the structural characteristics of an economy: this includes such factors as the level of benefits for the out-of-work, the ease with which workers can change jobs and the stigma attached to being out of work.

M. FRIEDMAN argued that it is beyond the influence of policies designed to affect AGGREGATE DEMAND. It is only possible to cause a temporary deviation from the natural rate by increasing demand in the economy; this is because it leads to both higher wages and higher prices, but as long as price increases outstrip workers' expectations of them, they will think REAL WAGES are higher than they are and be fooled into taking jobs they actually believe not to be worth the money. This would only be as long as expectations lagged behind actual inflation (◊ RATIONAL EXPECTATIONS). Three policies can thus be pursued towards the natural rate: first, accelerating rates of inflation to hold price increases ahead of expectations and keep people working who would otherwise choose to stay at home; secondly, supply-side policies can be pursued (◊ SUPPLY-SIDE ECONOMICS), such as cutting benefits for the out-of-work, making jobs relatively more attractive (◊ REPLACE-MENT RATIO); or thirdly, the natural rate itself must be endured. (◊ MONETARISM.)

Because unemployment cannot be held below the natural rate without accelerating inflation, it is often called the non-accelerating inflation rate of unemployment (N.A.I.R.U.).

Unemployment trap. The existence of SOCIAL SECURITY benefits for the out-of-work that erode any incentive for the unemployed to take a job. The incentive for the unemployed to find a job can depend on (a) the generosity of state benefits, (b) the level of pay offered, (c) the tax paid on that pay. ◊ POVERTY TRAP.

Unfunded. ◊ PERSONAL PENSION.

Unit banking. ◊ BRANCH BANKING.

Unit cost. ◊ AVERAGE COSTS.

Unit tax. An indirect tax (◊ DIRECT TAXATION) levied as a cash amount per unit of the product produced or sold, e.g. 30p per gallon or £1·50 per lb. Synonym for TAX, SPECIFIC.

Unit trust. An organization which invests funds subscribed by the public in SECURITIES, and in return issues units which it will repurchase at any time. The units, which represent equal shares in the trust's investment PORTFOLIO, produce INCOME and fluctuate in value according to the INTEREST and DIVIDENDS paid and the STOCK EXCHANGE prices of the underlying INVESTMENTS. The trustees which actually hold the securities are usually banks or INSURANCE COMPANIES, and are distinct from the management company. The subscriber to a unit trust does not, unlike a shareholder in an INVESTMENT TRUST, receive any of the PROFITS of the organization managing the trust. Management derives its income from a regular service charge as a percentage of

411

the income of the trust's investments and the difference between the (bid) price at which it buys in units and the (offer) price at which it sells them, which includes an initial charge. Unit trusts are strictly controlled by the Department of Trade, which must give its approval to a trust before units can be offered to the public, and which sets maximum management charges and generally supervises the operation of the trusts. Unit trusts were introduced in Britain as long ago as 1930, but they have grown particularly rapidly since the late 1950s. The number of unit holdings doubled between 1981 and 1986. Total funds under management were over £31,000 million in November 1986 and net sales of units (sales minus repurchases) were running at over £400 million per month. In March 1987 there were 1,000 unit trusts in existence in Britain. Unit trusts are directed particularly at the investor with small sums at his disposal. Units are easily purchased and resold, and risks are widely spread, it being usual for holdings of any one security to be kept below 5 per cent of the total. The investor also benefits from expert management, although the performance of the trusts varies enormously. Trusts may be fixed or flexible, i.e. their PORTFOLIO may remain the same or be altered as market conditions dictate. Some unit trusts specialize in small companies or BLUE CHIP shares, others in COMMODITIES or foreign companies or countries. Some are designed to maximize income, others CAPITAL growth. The latter offer the option of distributed or reinvested income, and there are also trusts incorporating life assurance which can be subscribed to by regular payments. ◊ ASSURANCE.

United Nations Conference on Trade and Development (U.N.C.T.A.D.). A conference convened in 1964 in response to growing anxiety among the DEVELOPING COUNTRIES over the difficulties they were facing in their attempts to bridge the standard-of-living gap between them and the developed nations. Full meetings have been held in 1968, 1972, 1976 1979 and 1983. The first Director-General of U.N.C.T.A.D., Professor R. D. PREBISCH, summarized the problem in his report *Towards a New Trade Policy for Development*. The growth rate of 5 per cent per annum which was required for the developing countries to make progress in terms of REAL INCOME per head implied a required IMPORT growth of 6 per cent. However, the trend rate of growth of their EXPORTS had been only about 4 per cent in value, and this had been reduced to the low figure of 2 per cent because of the deterioration in their TERMS OF TRADE. If this relationship continued, they would suffer chronic BALANCE OF PAYMENTS deficits which would lead to a worsening in their economic welfare. The problem could be tackled on two fronts: through measures (a) to offset the deterioration in the terms of trade and (b) to promote their exports. The terms-of-trade approach could be through INTERNATIONAL COMMODITY AGREEMENTS, which would be designed to prevent primary prices from falling, and through compensatory finance arrangements. Professor Prebisch suggested that the developed countries which benefited from the terms-of-trade shift should contribute to a fund which would be used to reimburse the losers. He had suggested that the developing countries should be free to combine to discriminate against imports of manufactures from the developed countries, and at the same time the latter should give preferences (▷ INFANT-INDUSTRY ARGUMENT). The distaste felt by the developing countries for the MOST-FAVOURED NATION CLAUSE of the GENERAL AGREEMENT ON TARIFFS AND TRADE was recognized by that institution.

A new chapter to the G.A.T.T. was added in 1965 on trade and development, which called for the reduction of TARIFFS and QUOTAS on developing countries' exports. It became possible for preferential duties to be given to imports from developing countries without having to extend these preferences to all the contracting parties of the G.A.T.T. In 1970 agreement was reached by which the developed nations in the EUROPEAN FREE TRADE ASSOCIATION and the EUROPEAN ECONOMIC COMMUNITY, as well as the U.S.A., gave preferences in specified manufactured goods to the developing countries. The fourth conference in 1976 agreed to negotiate a *common fund* to finance an integrated commodity price-support scheme. Agreement in principle to set up a common fund of $750 million was reached in 1980. This sum would be used to finance stabilization stocks of specified commodities and to support export promotion. Such a common fund was, however, still not operational by 1986. U.N.C.T.A.D. has a permanent secretariat and publishes regular papers and studies on development problems and an annual report.

Unlisted Securities Market(s) (U.S.M.). 1. Generally, the markets for shares of PUBLIC COMPANIES not included in the Official List for the main market (or first tier) of the STOCK EXCHANGE. Most of the larger ADVANCED COUNTRIES have organized and regulated lower-tier markets as well as informal 'placing markets' in which unlisted shares are traded. These markets are less stringently regulated and perform an important function in providing a stepping-stone to the main markets. ▷ OVER-THE-COUNTER MARKET; THIRD MARKET. **2.** Specifically, a market set up in 1980 by the London Stock Exchange to trade in designated unlisted securities. In December 1986 the shares of 368 companies were dealt with by MARKET MAKERS on the U.S.M. with a combined market CAPITALIZATION of almost £5,000 million. Over 500 companies had been floated on the U.S.M. and some 76 of these had moved up to the main market.

Unredeemable securities. ▷ IRREDEEMABLE SECURITY.

Unrequited exports. EXPORTS for which there is no reverse flow of goods or finance in payment. They take place in the settlement of past DEBTS.

Uruguay round of trade negotiations. ◊ GENERAL AGREEMENT ON TARIFFS AND TRADE.

Utilitarianism. The philosophy by which the purpose of government was the maximization of the sum of UTILITY, defined in terms of pleasure and pain, in the community as a whole. It was not hedonistic (◊ HEDONISM) in so far as pleasure could include, for instance, the satisfaction of helping others. The purpose of government was to ensure the 'greatest happiness of the greatest number'. It implied that utility could be measured and interpersonal comparisons made. Its chief advocate was JEREMY BENTHAM.

Utility. The pleasure or satisfaction derived by an individual from being in a particular situation or from consuming goods or services. Utility is defined as the ultimate goal of all economic activity, but it is not a label for any particular set of pursuits such as sensual pleasure or the acquisition and use of material goods. Jeremy Bentham described it as that which appears 'to augment or diminish the happiness of the party whose interest is in question', but this barely illuminates the issue, given that the notion of happiness used is a complex one. Some things which appear to make people unhappy, like sad films, can generate utility while other things appear to make people happy but do not. As no single measure of utility exists (◊ ORDINAL UTILITY), it is by their choices of combinations of available commodities that consumers reveal what it is that generates utility for them. Economists ignore possible circularities in the concept and rarely argue about what consumers enjoy, taking it as a matter of psychological fact. (◊◊ ALLEN, R. G. D.; HICKS, J. R.; INDIFFERENCE-CURVE ANALYSIS; MARGINAL UTILITY, DIMINISHING; PARETO, V. F. D.; SLUTSKY, E.)

V

Value. The worth of something to its owner. Two concepts of value have been distinguished in economics. The first is value in use – the pleasure a commodity actually generates for its owner; the second is value in exchange – the quantity of other commodities (or, more usually, money) a commodity can be swapped for. Water, for example, has high value in use, but low value in exchange. (⟡ VALUE, THEORIES OF.)

Value, theories of. Explanations of what determines the VALUE of different commodities. The different approaches have tended to distinguish two notions of value: that determined by the UTILITY it gives a consumer and reflected in the DEMAND for it (high utility, high value, ⟡ GALIANI, F.); or the cost of producing the commodity reflected by the SUPPLY of it (high cost, high value).

The CLASSICAL ECONOMISTS held that in the long term price, and hence the exchange value of an item, is determined by its costs of production (supply), but that it is the fact that a demand exists for it that determines whether an item has any value at all. D. RICARDO developed a LABOUR THEORY OF VALUE, asserting that value derives from the effort of production, again, based on supply. The novelty of his approach was in showing that all costs of production reduce to labour costs, either paid directly or stored in the form of capital. However, there is a need to reward those who store labour, and thus defer consumption, and this undermined his theory. Late-nineteenth-century economists like A. MARSHALL subverted theories of value to theories of price, determined by demand and supply; with each determined by MARGINAL UTILITY or MARGINAL COST. Since then, the theories of price and value have not been separated except by followers of K. MARX. (⟡ GOSSEN, H. H.; JEVONS, W. S.; WALRAS, M. E. L.)

Value accounting. ⟡ INFLATION ACCOUNTING.

Value added, or net output. The difference between total revenue of a firm, and the cost of bought-in raw materials, services and components. It thus measures the VALUE which the firm has 'added' to these bought-in materials and components by its processes of production. Since the total revenue of the firm will be divided among CAPITAL CHARGES (including DEPRECIATION), RENT, DIVIDEND payments, WAGES and the costs of materials, services and components, value added can also be calculated by summing the relevant types of cost and subtracting that total from total revenue. Although 'value added' and 'net output' are often used synonymously, net output in the census of production

($\diamondsuit$ PRODUCTION, CENSUS OF) is calculated by subtracting the value of materials purchased (allowing for stock changes) from the value of each industry's sales. Payments for *services* rendered by other firms, e.g. R. & D. (RESEARCH AND DEVELOPMENT) work, hire of machinery, are not deducted, so that in this technical sense, 'net output' is distinguished from 'value added', a term sometimes used to describe the contribution of an industry to the GROSS DOMESTIC PRODUCT. $\diamondsuit$ VALUE-ADDED TAX.

Value-added tax (V.A.T.). A general tax ($\diamondsuit$ TAXATION) applied at each point of EXCHANGE of goods or SERVICES from primary production to final consumption. It is levied on the difference between the sale price of the goods or services (outputs) to which the tax is applied and the cost of goods and services (INPUTS) bought in for use in its production. The cost of these inputs is taken to include all charges, including all taxes except V.A.T. itself. The method of payment and collection is as follows. Each registered trader sells his outputs at a price increased by the appropriate percentage of V.A.T. He is then liable to Customs and Excise for the payment of the tax so obtained from his customers, but can claim a refund of any V.A.T. included in the invoices for the inputs which he himself purchased from his suppliers. His customers do likewise, and so on down to the final consumer. At each point of exchange the tax is passed on in the form of higher prices. Being at the last point in the chain of exchange, the final consumer bears the whole tax. The traders within the chain do not bear any tax but act as collecting agencies. Traders with a turnover of taxable supplies of less than £20,500 need not register.

V.A.T. was introduced in the U.K. in 1973 because it is the form of INDIRECT TAXATION applied in the EUROPEAN ECONOMIC COMMUNITY and is the basis of contribution to the community budget. It replaced existing indirect taxes such as PURCHASE TAX and SELECTIVE EMPLOYMENT TAX. Basic foodstuffs, housing, books, most financial services, education, health and EXPORTS are excluded from the tax. V.A.T. may be applied to different goods or services or in different industries at different rates, including zero and exempt. The difference between the latter two is that only with the former can refunds be claimed. In the U.K. the standard rate of tax is 15 per cent; some other countries have several rates including a low rate for basic necessities and a higher rate for 'luxury' goods. $\diamondsuit$ TURNOVER TAX.

Value judgement. A proposition which cannot be reduced to an arguable statement of fact but which effectively asserts that something is good or that something ought to happen. Economists usually attempt to draw a distinction between facts and value judgements, but the two often merge. For example, the statement, 'We can control inflation by cutting the money supply', is clearly arguable but not a value judgement. However, the statement 'Therefore, we ought to cut the money supply', may be a value judgement (based on the belief that inflation is an evil *per se*), or alternatively could be an economic judgement made on the basis of a belief that the control of inflation stimulates long-term economic growth. In practice, all statements of economists can be of two types: descriptive statements (e.g. unemployment is falling); or prescriptive (e.g. unemployment should be cut). The former should be devoid of any value judgements. The latter will always be a combination of value and economic judgement. Usually, but not always, the value judgements contained in prescriptive statements are either uncontroversial or explicit enough for the reader to make a clear assessment of them. (◊ NORMATIVE ECONOMICS; POSITIVE ECONOMICS; ROBBINS, L. C.)

Variable. A number that may take different values in different situations For instance, quantity of a good demanded will vary according to its price.

Variable costs. Costs which vary directly with the rate of output, e.g. LABOUR costs, raw-material costs, fuel and power. Also known as *operating costs, prime costs, on costs* or *direct costs*.

Variance. A measure of the degree of dispersion of a series of numbers around their mean (◊ AVERAGE). The larger the variance the greater the spread of the series around its mean. The formula is as follows:

$$\text{Variance} = \sigma^2 = \frac{1}{N} \sum_{i=1}^{N} (x_i - \bar{x})^2$$

where $\bar{x}$ is the mean, x_i is the value of the ith item and N is the number of items in the series. For example, consider the two series (a) 8, 10, 12 and (b) 2, 10, 18. The mean of both (a) and (b) is 10. Variance of (a) is $[(-2)^2 + (2)^2]/3 = 2.67$. The variance of (b) is $[(-8)^2 + (8)^2]/3 = 42.67$. The variance of (b) is greater than (a), reflecting the wider spread of the (b) series. (◊ STANDARD DEVIATION.)

Veblen, Thorstein Bunde (1857–1929). ◊ CONSPICUOUS CONSUMPTION; INSTITUTIONAL ECONOMICS.

Vector. A set of numbers (elements) arranged as a row or a column. For instance, [1, 5, 8] is a row vector, and $\begin{bmatrix} 1 \\ 5 \\ 8 \end{bmatrix}$ is a column vector. A vector of n elements is referred to as n-dimensional. The above vectors, therefore, are three-dimensional. The *null vector* has all its elements equal to zero. A *unit vector* is a vector with one element equal to unity and the rest all equal to zero. There are therefore, n unit vectors possible for an n-dimensional vector. There is an algebra for vectors, with appropriate rules for addition and multiplication. (◊ MATRIX).

Velocity of circulation. The speed with which the money in an economy circulates. Each £10 note that exists is used many times, and each time it is used a transaction of value £10 occurs. It is possible to imagine two economies, one with twice as much money in it as the other, but where on average the money is used half the number of times. The total value of all transactions in each economy would be the same, because it equals the value of the stock of money multiplied by the velocity with which it circulates. The income velocity equals the money value of NATIONAL INCOME divided by the stock of money in the economy. The velocity of circulation is related to the demand for money (◊ MONEY, DEMAND FOR): if people hold cash, it circulates slowly. If, on the other hand, they do not wish to hold cash, they dispose of money holdings and the circulation of money increases. The velocity of money is central to the debate between MONETARISM and KEYNESIAN ECONOMICS. Monetarists hold that INTEREST RATES do not much affect the demand for money or its velocity. They claim that institutional factors, such as the frequency with which people are paid or the number of people who have bank accounts, affect it and these factors are unlikely to change in the short term. Keynesians on the other hand believe that the velocity of money varies substantially with the interest rate. Under both doctrines, however, a higher than expected INFLATION rate would increase the velocity. This is seen in an extreme form in an economy enduring HYPERINFLATION, in which anyone holding money is holding a depreciating asset; everybody attempts to rid themselves of cash and acquire goods whose value is stable. (◊ NEUTRALITY OF MONEY.)

Venture capital. ◊ RISK CAPITAL.

Vertical integration. The extent to which successive stages in production and distribution are placed under the control of a single ENTERPRISE. In Britain most brewing companies are vertically integrated, because they own breweries (some have integrated backwards into hop-growing), distribution depots and public houses. Oil companies which own oilfields, tankers, refineries and filling-stations also exhibit a high degree of vertical integration. Firms move to integrate, either forwards towards retailing or backwards towards sources of raw materials, in order to eliminate the profit margins of intermediaries or to secure sources of supply or markets.

Viner, Jacob (1892–1970). ◊ CUSTOMS UNION.

Visible balance. The BALANCE OF PAYMENTS in VISIBLE TRADE (IMPORTS and EXPORTS of merchandise).

Visible trade. INTERNATIONAL TRADE in merchandise, IMPORTS and EXPORTS. ◊ INVISIBLE.

Voting shares. EQUITY shares entitling holders to vote in the election of directors of a company. Normally all ORDINARY SHARES are voting shares, but sometimes a company may create a class of non-voting ordinary shares if the holders of the equity wish to raise more equity capital but exclude the possibility of losing control of the business. PREFERENCE SHARES are rarely, and DEBENTURE shares never, voting shares.

W

Wage drift. The difference between wage rates set by national agreements and the total earnings received by workers, which includes overtime pay, special bonuses and commissions. If wage negotiations take place between union leaders and management bodies at a national level, whatever the outcome of those negotiations in certain areas of the country, the wage agreed may not be high enough to attract all the workers demanded. In this case, local employers will attempt to entice workers with side payments that do not directly infringe national agreements. Such payments are difficult to monitor and control, and thus undermine attempts to run an INCOMES POLICY, but they are defended as necessary if the labour market is to work freely. If wage drift could lead to cuts in pay as well as increases, it would be a more economically efficient means of introducing pay flexibility. As it happens, though, wage drift has the consequence of making a nationally agreed pay rate the bare minimum anyone receives, with 'top ups' the norm.

Wage-fund theory. ADAM SMITH took over from the PHYSIOCRATS the idea that wages are advanced to workers in anticipation of the sale of their output. Wages could not be increased unless the CAPITAL destined to pay them was increased. Capital, in turn, was determined by SAVINGS. The CLASSICAL SCHOOL developed its theory of wages around these ideas. In the short run, there was a given number of workers and a given amount of savings to pay their wages. The two together determined the average wage. In the long run, the supply of LABOUR was related to the minimum of subsistence needed to sustain the LABOUR FORCE. (This subsistence level was not simply physiological; it was related to a standard of living accepted by custom.) If the wage rate rose above this, the POPULATION increased; if it fell below, it contracted. In the long run, the level of the demand for labour was determined by the size of the wage fund, and this, in turn, by the level of savings. This meant that, as J. S. MILL put it, 'the demand for COMMODITIES is not the demand for labour'. If you increased CONSUMPTION you reduced savings and therefore the wage fund. PRODUCTIVITY did not influence REAL WAGES, what mattered was the level of PROFITS, for savings depended on profits. The argument assumed that savings flowed into fixed capital and variable (wage) capital in equal proportions so that what MARX called the organic composition of capital remained constant. RICARDO worried about this point in his analysis of the effect of machinery on employment. Investment by-passed the wage fund and the demand for labour was reduced. W. T. Thornton criticized the wage-fund doctrine on the grounds that wages were determined by SUPPLY and DEMAND in the market. J. S. Mill accepted some of Thornton's points and admitted that the wage-fund idea might be more appropriate in the context of a discontinuous production process (akin to seed-time to harvest) rather than a continuous flow of output, which was the true state of affairs. There was some popular confusion at the time, because it was thought the economists meant there existed a definite fund available for wages so that there was no hope of workers obtaining higher average earnings.

Wage rates. ⟡ EARNINGS.

Wall Street (U.S.). ⟡ NEW YORK STOCK EXCHANGE.

Walras, Marie Esprit Léon (1834–1910). A mining engineer by training, Walras accepted the offer of a newly created Chair of Economics in the Faculty of Law at Lausanne in 1870. He held this post until he was succeeded by PARETO upon his retirement in 1892. His publications include *Éléments d'économie politique pure* (1874–7), *Études d'économie sociale* (1896) and *Études d'économie politique appliquée* (1898). One of the three economists to propound a MARGINAL UTILITY theory in the 1870s, he set out the theory of diminishing marginal utility and showed how PRICES at which COMMODITIES exchanged are determined by the relative marginal utilities of the people taking part in the transaction (⟡ GOSSEN, H. H.; JEVONS W. S.; MENGER, C.). He also constructed a mathematical MODEL OF GENERAL EQUILIBRIUM as a system of simultaneous equations in which he tried to show that all prices and quantities are uniquely determined. This is regarded as one of the foremost achievements in mathematical economics, of which Walras is considered the founder. ⟡ ARROW, K. J.

Warranted rate of growth. ⟡ GROWTH THEORY; HARROD–DOMAR MODEL.

Warrants. SECURITIES giving the holder a right to subscribe to a SHARE or a BOND at a given price and from a certain date. Warrants, which are commonly issued 'free' alongside the shares of new INVESTMENT TRUSTS when launched, and carry no income or other rights to EQUITY, immediately trade separately on the STOCK EXCHANGE, but at a price lower than the associated share or bond. This provides the investor in warrants with an element of GEARING since, if the associated share or bond price ultimately rises above the subscription price it will have a value corresponding to the difference between the subscription price at which the warrant rights may be exercised and the market price of the share or bond. Similar to an OPTION.

Washington Agreement. An agreement concluded with the U.S.A. in December 1945, under which $25,000 million of Lend-Lease aid to the Commonwealth was written off and the U.K. was granted a long-term loan of $3,750 million. The sterling value of this drawing in 1945 was £931 million. By the end of 1975, with two sterling DEVALUATIONS in the meantime and the floating of the exchange rate, the amount outstanding had risen to £1,264 million. ⟡ EUROPEAN RECOVERY PROGRAMME.

Wasting assets. ASSETS with strictly limited, though not necessarily determinate, lives, e.g. a mine, timber lands or a property on lease. Wasting assets have many of the characteristics of CURRENT ASSETS, but they are normally included under fixed assets.

Watering, stock. The issue of the nominal capital of a company in return for less than its money value, thus overstating the capital of the company and reducing its apparent return on capital (⟡ RATE OF RETURN).

Ways and Means Advances. Advances to the CONSOLIDATED FUND made by the BANK OF ENGLAND (⟡ NATIONAL DEBT).

Wealth. A stock of assets held by any economic unit that yields, or has the potential for yielding, income. Wealth can take a multitude of forms: cash, bank deposits, loans or shares are all financial assets. Diamonds, factories and houses are examples of physical assets. To these should be added human wealth, which consists of the earnings potential of individuals. These forms of wealth can be divided into those that constitute a liability to another economic agent, like loans; and those that do not, like physical assets. For the community as a whole, it is only really the latter which constitute net wealth, just as in a family, if a brother owes his sister £100, it comprises part of the sister's wealth but not that of the family as a whole.

In perfect markets, assets should be priced at the PRESENT VALUE of the future income they are expected to earn. However, the notion of income is general and would include, for example, the pleasure the owners of a picture would derive from its display (⟡ INCOME). The bulk of most individuals' wealth is held in the form of a house or accumulated assets invested in a pension fund.

'Wear and tear' allowances. ⟡ CAPITAL ALLOWANCES.

Weighted average. An arithmetic mean (⟡ AVERAGE) in which each item in the series being averaged is multiplied by a 'weight' relevant to its importance, the result summed and the total divided by the sum of the weights. For instance, suppose the price of meat has risen by 10 per cent and of vegetables by 20 per cent, the average rise is 15 per cent, being the arithmetic mean of 10 and 20. This could be misleading if we were considering the effect of the price increases on a particular household. The above mean assumes that the household regards meat and vegetables as equally important. If, however, the household spends £1 on vegetables for every £10 on meat, a more accurate representation of the average price change would be a weighted average, i.e. $[(10\% \times 10) + (20\% \times 1)]/10 + 1 = 120/11 = 10 \cdot 9\%$. In the example the weights are 10 (for meat) and 1 (for vegetables), so that the result is more in keeping with the importance the household attaches to meat in its budget. At the extreme, if no vegetables were bought at all, the 'vegetable' weight would be zero. (◊ INDEX NUMBER.)

Weights. ◊ WEIGHTED AVERAGE.

Welfare economics. The study of the social desirability of alternative arrangements of economic activities and allocations of RESOURCES. It is, in effect, the analysis of the optimal behaviour of individual consumers at the level of society as a whole. Just as, at the level of the individual, there is a need for a subjective ranking of bundles of goods dependent on the consumer's taste (◊ INDIFFERENCE-CURVE ANALYSIS), at the level of a society there is a need for a ranking of economic states, and this will usually rely on subjective or NORMATIVE criteria: judgements of taste about how society should look. Carrying the methods of indifference analysis from individuals to groups of individuals is not straightforward, however (◊ SOCIAL-WELFARE FUNCTION) and thus welfare economics is a broader subject than the theory of demand (◊ DEMAND, THEORY OF).

The study of welfare economics consists of the following: first, the determination of efficient states in which no individual can be made better off without an offsetting loss to another individual (◊ ECONOMIC EFFICIENCY); secondly, the choice between the many efficient states that can exist, either through a decision imposed by a dictator, or through democratically determined decisions (◊ IMPOSSIBILITY THEOREM; SOCIAL WELFARE; SOCIAL-WELFARE FUNCTION); thirdly, coverage of a number of other smaller topics like the optimal provision of PUBLIC GOODS, EXTERNALITIES, and the theory of the second best (◊ SECOND BEST, THEORY OF). All these topics share the common aim of helping to show when it is desirable to move from one economic state to another. (◊ COMPENSATION PRINCIPLE; COST–BENEFIT ANALYSIS; PIGOU, A. C.)

Wholesale banking. The making of loans or acceptance of deposits on a large scale between banks and other financial institutions, especially in the INTER-BANK MARKET. As distinct from *retail banking*, a term for the business of the COMMERCIAL BANKS carried out with customers of their branches.

Wicksell effect, price. In discussing the derivation of FACTOR prices from the value of MARGINAL PRODUCTS, K. WICKSELL pointed out that in equilibrium the rate of interest would be greater than the value of the marginal product of capital. This is because the whole of the existing stock of capital is revalued when rates of interest change (◊ CAPITAL RE-SWITCHING).

Wicksell, Knut (1851–1926). Educated at Uppsala University in Sweden, where he studied mathematics and philosophy, Wicksell was appointed to the Chair of Economics at Lund in 1904, a post he held until 1916. His major publications include *Über Wert, Kapital und Rente* (1893) and *Geldzins und Güterpreise* (1898). A synthesis of his work was published in 1901 and 1906 with the English title of *Lectures on Political Economy*. He assimilated the GENERAL EQUILIBRIUM analysis of WALRAS with the work of BÖHM-BAWERK and worked out a theory of DISTRIBUTION based on the new MARGINAL ANALYSIS of JEVONS, WALRAS and MENGER. In addition, he had a significant influence on monetary theory. He pointed out that high RATES OF INTEREST often coincided with high prices, which was contrary to what current theory predicted. He drew attention to the significance of the relative level of interest rates rather than their absolute level. Prices were related to the difference between changes in the real or natural rate of INTEREST (which was determined by the expected rate of PROFITS) and the money rate. The CENTRAL BANK had an important influence over the price level through its operations on the discount rate (◊ BANK RATE). These theories were incorporated into his theory of the TRADE CYCLE (◊ INTEREST, NATURAL RATE OF; WICKSELL EFFECT, PRICE).

Wieser, Friedrich von (1851–1926). Wieser succeeded MENGER to the Chair of Economics at Vienna University in 1903 after a period at Prague University. His most important works include *Über den Ursprung und die Hauptgesetze des Wirtschaftlichen Wertes* (1884), *Der natürliche Wert* (1889) and *Theorie der gesellschaftlichen Wirtschaft* (1914). He developed a law of costs which became known later as the principle of OPPORTUNITY COST. FACTORS OF PRODUCTION will be distributed by competition such that, in EQUILIBRIUM, the value of their marginal outputs will be equal. The costs of production of any COMMODITY reflect the competing claims in other uses for the services of the factors needed to produce it. The law became an important element in the theory of RESOURCE ALLOCATION (◊ ECONOMIC EFFICIENCY).

Williamson, Oliver. ◊ FIRM, THEORY OF THE.

Wilson Committee. The committee to review the functioning of financial institutions set up under the chairmanship of Sir Harold (now Lord) Wilson in January 1977. The committee issued an interim report, *The Financing of Small Firms*, in March 1979 and its final report in June 1980. The committee's terms of reference required it to 'review in particular the provision of funds for industry and trade; to consider what changes are required in the existing arrangements for the supervision of these institutions, including the possible extension of the public sector . . .' The report and its appendices contain a detailed description of the structure of the U.K. financial system and a review of recent trends. Attention was drawn to the growing importance of the financial institutions, particularly PENSION FUNDS and INSURANCE companies in the capital market; the growth of BUILDING SOCIETIES; the influence of taxation upon the operation of financial institutions and competition between them, especially in favouring savings in home purchase; pensions and life ASSURANCE; and the broadening role of the BANK OF ENGLAND following the greater emphasis given to MONETARY POLICY in economic management and other changes such as the extension of the bank's responsibility to include the supervision of fringe banks.

The report concluded that real INVESTMENT in the U.K. had not been unnecessarily constrained by shortages in the supply of external finance and that the price of finance in relation to expected profitability was the main financial constraint on investment. However, INFLATION had led to the drying up of the market for long-term industrial BONDS and there were difficulties in the provision of finance for small firms. The committee recommended against any extension of the public sector by the nationalization of banks or insurance companies. The two principal earlier inquiries into the financial system were the MACMILLAN COMMITTEE and the Radcliffe Committee (◊ RADCLIFFE REPORT).

Winding up. ◊ LIQUIDATION.

Window dressing. 1. The rearrangement of a company's financial affairs at year end to make the BALANCE SHEET look different from usual. **2.** Specifically, a practice of the British CLEARING BANKS prior to 1946, in which, in their half-yearly balance sheets, their CASH RATIO was shown to be substantially higher than it was at other times of the year. At the time, the banks wished to show that their cash ratio was about 11 per cent although they normally operated at nearer to 8 per cent. To achieve the desired figure for the purposes of the accounts, the banks temporarily called in MONEY AT CALL AND SHORT NOTICE from the MONEY MARKET. In fact, an 8 per cent operating cash ratio was quite adequate, and since 1946 the published figures have reflected this.

Withholding tax. TAXATION deducted from payments to non-residents. Withholding taxes are usually in the form of a standard rate of INCOME TAX applied to DIVIDENDS or other payments by companies and are often reclaimable against tax liabilities in the country of residence of the recipient under a double-taxation agreement.

Workers' participation. ◊ INDUSTRIAL DEMOCRACY.

Working capital. That part of current ASSETS financed from long-term funds. ◊◊ CURRENT RATIO.

World Bank. ◊ INTERNATIONAL BANK FOR RECONSTRUCTION AND DEVELOPMENT.

Writing-down allowance. ◊ CAPITAL ALLOWANCES.

X

X-efficiency. The effectiveness of a firm's management in minimizing the cost of producing a given output or maximizing the output produced by a given set of inputs. There is often a discrepancy between the efficient behaviour of firms as implied by economic theory and their observed behaviour in practice. This is frequently a result of a lack of the competitive pressures assumed. It was called *X*-efficiency by H. Liebenstein in 1966. (⟡ FIRM, THEORY OF THE.)

Y

Yaoundé Convention. ⟡ LOMÉ CONVENTION.

Yield. The INCOME from a SECURITY as a proportion of its current market price. Thus, the *dividend yield* is the current DIVIDEND as a percentage of the market price of a security. The *earnings yield* is a theoretical figure, based on the last dividend paid as a percentage of the current market price. The *redemption yield* is normally applied only to fixed-interest securities, and is the interest payment over the remaining life of the security, plus or minus the difference between the purchase price and the redemption value, i.e. it is the earnings yield adjusted to take account of any CAPITAL GAIN or loss to redemption. With fixed-interest securities, the nominal interest, or COUPON, is unlikely to be the same as the actual yield. An IRREDEEMABLE SECURITY in the form of a government bond having a flat yield of 3 per cent with a PAR VALUE of £100, but a market price of £50, provides an earnings yield of 6 per cent. The earnings yield will fluctuate with the price of the security, rising as security prices fall, and vice versa. ⟡ GILT-EDGED SECURITIES.

Yield curve. A graphical representation of the relationship between the annual return on an asset and the number of years the asset has before expiring. Longer-term assets usually offer some premium over short-term ones and yield curves thus slope upwards. This effect is more pronounced if short-term interest rates are expected to rise. ⟡ TERM STRUCTURE OF INTEREST RATES.

Yield gap. The difference between the YIELD on ORDINARY SHARES and the yield on GILT-EDGED SECURITIES, e.g. 2½ per cent irredeemable CONSOLS. If the latter exceeds the former, it is called the *reverse yield gap*.

Z

Zero-sum game. A game ($\diamond$ GAME THEORY) in which one player's gain is equal to other players' losses, whatever strategy is chosen. The players can only compete for slices of a fixed cake; there are no opportunities of overall gain through collusion. The sum of gains will always equal the sum of losses, the whole summing to zero. ($\diamond$ MAXIMIN.)

FOR THE BEST IN PAPERBACKS, LOOK FOR THE 🐧

In every corner of the world, on every subject under the sun, Penguin represents quality and variety – the very best in publishing today.

For complete information about books available from Penguin – including Puffins, Penguin Classics and Arkana – and how to order them, write to us at the appropriate address below. Please note that for copyright reasons the selection of books varies from country to country.

In the United Kingdom: Please write to *Dept E.P., Penguin Books Ltd, Harmondsworth, Middlesex, UB7 0DA.*

If you have any difficulty in obtaining a title, please send your order with the correct money, plus ten per cent for postage and packaging, to *PO Box No 11, West Drayton, Middlesex*

In the United States: Please write to *Dept BA, Penguin, 299 Murray Hill Parkway, East Rutherford, New Jersey 07073*

In Canada: Please write to *Penguin Books Canada Ltd, 2801 John Street, Markham, Ontario L3R 1B4*

In Australia: Please write to the *Marketing Department, Penguin Books Australia Ltd, P.O. Box 257, Ringwood, Victoria 3134*

In New Zealand: Please write to the *Marketing Department, Penguin Books (NZ) Ltd, Private Bag, Takapuna, Auckland 9*

In India: Please write to *Penguin Overseas Ltd, 706 Eros Apartments, 56 Nehru Place, New Delhi, 110019*

In the Netherlands: Please write to *Penguin Books Netherlands B.V., Postbus 195, NL–1380AD Weesp*

In West Germany: Please write to *Penguin Books Ltd, Friedrichstrasse 10–12, D–6000 Frankfurt/Main 1*

In Spain: Please write to *Longman Penguin España, Calle San Nicolas 15, E–28013 Madrid*

In Italy: Please write to *Penguin Italia s.r.l., Via Como 4, I-20096 Pioltello (Milano)*

In France: Please write to *Penguin Books Ltd, 39 Rue de Montmorency, F-75003 Paris*

In Japan: Please write to *Longman Penguin Japan Co Ltd, Yamaguchi Building, 2–12–9 Kanda Jimbocho, Chiyoda-Ku, Tokyo 101*

FOR THE BEST IN PAPERBACKS, LOOK FOR THE

PENGUIN REFERENCE BOOKS

The Penguin Guide to the Law

This acclaimed reference book is designed for everyday use and forms the most comprehensive handbook ever published on the law as it affects the individual.

The Penguin Medical Encyclopedia

Covers the body and mind in sickness and in health, including drugs, surgery, medical history, medical vocabulary and many other aspects. 'Highly commendable' – *Journal of the Institute of Health Education*

The Slang Thesaurus

Do you make the public bar sound like a gentleman's club? Do you need help in understanding *Minder*? The miraculous *Slang Thesaurus* will liven up your language in no time. You won't Adam and Eve it! A mine of funny, witty, acid and vulgar synonyms for the words you use every day.

The Penguin Dictionary of Troublesome Words Bill Bryson

Why should you avoid discussing the *weather conditions*? Can a married woman be *celibate*? Why is it eccentric to talk about the *aroma* of a cowshed? A straightforward guide to the pitfalls and hotly disputed issues in standard written English.

A Dictionary of Literary Terms

Defines over 2,000 literary terms (including lesser known, foreign language and technical terms), explained with illustrations from literature past and present.

The Concise Cambridge Italian Dictionary

Compiled by Barbara Reynolds, this work is notable for the range of examples provided to illustrate the exact meaning of Italian words and phrases. It also contains a pronunciation guide and a reference grammar.

FOR THE BEST IN PAPERBACKS, LOOK FOR THE 🐧

PENGUIN DICTIONARIES

Abbreviations
Archaeology
Architecture
Art and Artists
Biology
Botany
Building
Business
Chemistry
Civil Engineering
Computers
Curious and Interesting
   Words
Curious and Interesting
   Numbers
Design and Designers
Economics
Electronics
English and European
   History
English Idioms
French
Geography
German

Historical Slang
Human Geography
Literary Terms
Mathematics
Modern History 1789–1945
Modern Quotations
Music
Physical Geography
Physics
Politics
Proverbs
Psychology
Quotations
Religions
Rhyming Dictionary
Saints
Science
Sociology
Spanish
Surnames
Telecommunications
Troublesome Words
Twentieth-Century History

Lateral Thinking for Management   Edward de Bono

Creativity and lateral thinking can work together for managers in developing new products or ideas; Edward de Bono shows how.

Understanding the British Economy   Peter Donaldson and John Farquhar

A comprehensive and well signposted tour of the British economy today; a sound introduction to elements of economic theory; and a balanced account of recent policies are provided by this bestselling text.

A Question of Economics   Peter Donaldson

Twenty key issues – the City, trade unions, 'free market forces' and many others – are presented clearly and fully in this major book based on a television series.

The Economics of the Common Market   Dennis Swann

From the CAP to the EMS, this internationally recognized book on the Common Market – now substantially revised – is essential reading in the run-up to 1992.

The Money Machine   How the City Works   Philip Coggan

How are the big deals made? Which are the institutions that really matter? What causes the pound to rise or interest rates to fall? This book provides clear and concise answers to these and many other money-related questions.

Parkinson's Law   C. Northcote Parkinson

'Work expands so as to fill the time available for its completion': that law underlies this 'extraordinarily funny and witty book' (Stephen Potter in the *Sunday Times*) which also makes some painfully serious points about those in business or the Civil Service.